XML

Black Book

Natanya Pitts-Moultis
Cheryl Kirk

Publisher
Keith Weiskamp

Acquisitions Editor
Stephanie Wall

Marketing Specialist
Gary Hull

Project Editor
Melissa D. Olson

Technical Reviewer
Mark Watson

Production Coordinator
Meg E. Turecek

Layout Design
April Nielsen

Cover Design
Anthony Stock

CD-ROM Developer
Robert Clarfield

XML Black Book

The Coriolis Group, Inc.
An International Thomson Publishing Company
14455 N. Hayden Road, Suite 220
Scottsdale, Arizona 85260

602/483-0192
FAX 602/483-0193
http://www.coriolis.com

Library of Congress Cataloging-in-Publication Data
Pitts-Moultis, Natanya
    XML black book / by Natanya Pitts-Moultis and Cheryl Kirk
        p. cm.
    Includes index.
    ISBN 1-57610-284-X
    1. XML (Documentation markup language) I. Kirk, Cheryl. II. Title.
QA76.76.H94K45   1999
005.7'2–dc21   98-25738
                                                                                CIP

Printed in the United States of America
10 9 8 7 6 5 4 3 2 1

an International Thomson Publishing company

Albany, NY • Belmont, CA • Bonn • Boston • Cincinnati • Detroit • Johannesburg • London • Madrid
Melbourne • Mexico City • New York • Paris • Singapore • Tokyo • Toronto • Washington

CORIOLIS

14455 North Hayden, Suite 220 • Scottsdale, Arizona 8526

Dear Reader:

Coriolis Technology Press was founded to create a very elite group of books: The ones you keep closest to your machine. Sure, everyone would like to have the Library of Congress at arm's reach, but in the real world, you have to choose the books you rely on every day *very* carefully.

To win a place for our books on that coveted shelf beside your PC, we guarantee several important qualities in every book we publish. These qualities are:

- *Technical accuracy:* It's no good if it doesn't work. Every Coriolis Technology Press book is reviewed by technical experts in the topic field, and is sent through several editing and proofreading passes in order to create the piece of work you now hold in your hands.

- *Innovative editorial design:* We've put years of research and refinement into the ways we present information in our books. Our books' editorial approach is uniquely designed to reflect the way people learn new technologies and search for solutions to technology problems.

- *Practical focus:* We put only pertinent information into our books and avoid any fluff. Every fact included between these two covers must serve the mission of the book as a whole.

- *Accessibility:* The information in a book is worthless unless you can find it quickly when you need it. We put a lot of effort into our indexes, and heavily cross-reference our chapters, to make it easy for you to move right to the information you need.

Here at The Coriolis Group we have been publishing and packaging books, technical journals, and training materials since 1989. We're programmers and authors ourselves, and we take an ongoing active role in defining what we publish and how we publish it. We have put a lot of thought into our books. Please write us at **ctp@coriolis.com** and let us know what you think. We hope that you're happy with the book in your hands, and that in the future, when you reach for software development and networking information, you'll turn to one of our books first.

Keith Weiskamp
President and Publisher

Jeff Duntemann
VP and Editorial Director

Look For These Other Books From The Coriolis Group:

Windows 98 Registry Little Black Book

Windows 98 Optimizing and Troubleshooting Little Black Book

Windows 98 Black Book

Active Server Pages Black Book

Java Studio Blue Book

To Jim, for fine wine, gumbo on Sundays, Ninja rides, Tweety, and a friendship that always has been and will always be—even when nothing else remains.
—Natanya Pitts-Moultis

This book is dedicated to two hard-working editors who made this book a reality—Stephanie Wall and Melissa Olson. I don't envy them in the least!
—Cheryl Kirk

ৰ৶

About The Authors

Natanya Pitts-Moultis is an accomplished Webmaster and corporate trainer, as well as a published author. Natanya is the principal author of the *HTML Style Sheets Design Guide*, released in December 1997, and the *Dynamic HTML Black Book*, released in February 1998, both from The Coriolis Group. In addition to the *XML Black Book*, her publishing credits include two other Extensible Markup Language (XML) books. Also, she was a coauthor for *The Hip Pocket Guide to HTML 4.0* (1998) and *The Official BBEdit Book* (1997).

Natanya teaches beginning, intermediate, and advanced HTML and Web design classes at Austin (Texas) Community College. She will continue to teach in the physical and virtual classrooms during the spring and summer of 1999.

Natanya graduated from the University of Texas in 1993 with a bachelor's degree in Latin. She is currently employed at InCircuit Development, Inc., a software development company based in Austin. Prior to joining InCircuit in 1998, Natanya was the Webmaster for LANWrights, Inc., a network-oriented consulting firm, where she got her start as a technical writer and corporate trainer. Natanya can be contacted at **xmlbb@lanw.com**.

Cheryl Kirk is an independent consultant who works with Fortune 500 oil companies. She is also a SkillPath/CompuMaster trainer, who teaches people throughout the United States about the finer points of Windows 95, 98, and NT. Cheryl has written four other Internet-related books and is coauthor for six more computer books. In her spare time, she writes the computer column for the *Anchorage Daily News*, a Pulitzer Prize-winning newspaper. In addition, she cohosts an award-winning radio talk show that focuses on computers. Her show can be heard in Anchorage and on the Internet. Cheryl can be contacted at **ckirk@alaska.net**.

Acknowledgments

This book would not have been possible without the hard work and support of a great number of people. First, thanks to my husband, Colin, and my parents, Charles and Swanya. Your love and encouragement are what help me continue forward even on the worst of days. Special thanks to DJ, without whom so much in my life would not be possible. As a friend or manager, you're the best. An extra-special thank you goes to Mary Burmeister, whose editing and glossary skills helped make this book the quality reference tool that it is. And to the other folks at LANWrights—Ed, Michael, Dawn, and Bill—who provided me with knowledge and support throughout the course of this book. Thanks to my coauthor, Cheryl Kirk, who came in at a late hour and used her considerable knowledge and insight to get the job done quickly and well. A very large thank you to Melissa Olson at Coriolis who labored behind the scenes for months and was the driving force that made everything come together. Also, thank you to Meg, Stephanie, April, Tony, and Robert at Coriolis. Finally, thanks, as always, to my feline coterie—Gandalf, Nada, and the newest addition, Junior—for providing purring accompaniment to the beat of the clicking of the keyboard keys.

—Natanya Pitts-Moultis

I would like to thank the following people for doing such an outstanding job on the mush I turned in. They eventually turned my words into something you could understand. They include Melissa Olson for keeping things flowing, Judy Flynn for doing an outstanding job of copyediting, and Mark Watson for his keen technical eye and insightful comments. I would also like to thank Stephanie Wall for keeping the project going through what must have seemed like some pretty bleak times. Also, I would like to acknowledge Meg Turecek, April Nielsen, and Anthony Stock for their work in making this book look so good, as well as Robert Clarfield for his work on the CD-ROM. And last but not least, I would like to thank Natanya Pitts-Moultis, the lead author, who provided me with some great insights into XML.

—Cheryl Kirk

Contents At A Glance

Table Of Contents

Part I Introduction To XML

Part II   XML Pieces And Parts

Chapter 7
Working With XML Elements 191

Chapter 8
Working With XML Attributes 215

Chapter 20

Part V   The XML Users Guide

Part I

Introduction To XML

Chapter 1

Markup Languages

By Cheryl Kirk

In Depth

Most likely, you've picked up this book to learn what Extensible Markup Language (XML) is and how to implement it. You'll definitely learn all that and more, but before we jump right into the subject at hand, you should know a little bit about the theory behind markup languages and the differences between XML, Standard Generalized Markup Language (SGML), and Hypertext Markup Language (HTML). In this chapter, we explain what a markup language is, the various components of markup languages you should familiarize yourself with, and what today's current markup languages offer.

A solid understanding of markup languages is a prerequisite to learning how to develop XML documents. Without such knowledge, you won't be able to apply the concepts and practices to your own document development. In the example at the end of this chapter, you'll create your own simple XML document and use the various components markup languages use.

Markup Theory

Take a good look at this book. Thumb through it and you'll quickly see that there is a consistency in the design and layout. Chapter titles appear a certain way; text is displayed in a consistent font. Section headings are a specific height, and sidebars and tips are easily recognizable. In order to get this consistent look, and in order to make the publication process faster, specific styles—or rules—were created to accommodate the different types of information presented. When the designers got together and created the styles, they outlined the styles and detailed their attributes, assigning names to particular styles of text and formatting that could be easily identified.

Take, for example, a style named Code. The designers created this style to specify how text that is used to code XML documents should appear in this book. In order to separate the code you need to type from the text you should read, the designers made sure the code looks a certain way. That is, they used a font similar to what you might see on a computer screen. But the designers didn't stop there. They went through the entire book and "marked-up" which text should appear in which fashion.

Once the specifics for these styles were hammered out, electronic versions of the styles were created. For this particular book, the styles were created in Microsoft

Word, a common application used throughout the book-publishing industry. Special binary instructions built into the word processing program allow the editors to specify certain formatting instructions and then assign names to them. The collection of formatting rules, with specific user-defined names, are called *style sheets*. When the authors need a specific style, it is selected from a list of styles and applied to the text. Regardless of who writes what, the look and feel of the book is consistent throughout, and the styles are carried with the document, providing designers, editors, and authors with quick-and-easy access to a consistent format.

When chapters are exchanged electronically, Microsoft Word reads the list of styles and then displays the text in the format based on the style applied. The authors don't see any of the specialized instructions that turn the simple text into bold, 24-point, Times New Roman text, nor do they type any specialized commands to invoke a particular format. Instead, they simply indicate what text they want formatted a certain way, and that text is displayed with the proper formatting both on the screen and on the printed page.

Of course, the world of word processing wasn't always this simple. If you have ever used older versions of word processors, such as WordPerfect, or have been involved in the publishing industry for any length of time, you know exactly what we mean. Formatting text used to involve typing a long list of formatting codes before the text that needed formatting. The results weren't shown on the screen; they were only displayed after the file was printed. To type formatting commands, the user needed to know what commands were needed, exactly how they were to be typed, and where they had to be placed. In addition, the user had to be able to imagine just how the text would look based on the formats he or she applied.

That all changed with the introduction of software products that offered What-You-See-Is-What-You-Get (WYSIWYG) functionality. Programs such as PageMaker, QuarkXPress, FrameMaker, and even Microsoft Word display text and accompanying styles just as they would appear if they were printed. But unlike word processors of old, where the formatting commands were simply a string of text before and after the information that required formatting, today's software programs store the formatting instructions in binary format. However, if you try to open a Microsoft Word file with another application that doesn't understand Word's formatting commands, you'll see mostly gibberish at the top of the file, and then maybe you'll see the actual text below all that gibberish.

With some standardized types of markup formats, however, such as Rich Text Format (RTF), you can actually see the instructions used to mark up the text, in much the same way you could see formatting information in older word processors. RTF uses a set of commands to format text, and if other programs understand and can interpret RTF files, they can be shared between different word processors or even different applications. If you look at an RTF file, you can get a feel for how such formatting markup languages are interpreted, both on screen and through printers, and how they come to display text in a particular way. With RTF, ASCII codes represent the formatting or markup of the text. Here's an example of how RTF formats a simple paragraph:

```
\keepn\par\sb240\b0
Now is the time for all good men to come to the aid of their country.
```

Let's take a look at how the RTF markup language formats this simple paragraph. As you can see, each markup command starts with a backslash (\), and in this particular markup language, these commands can be strung along a single line, telling either the display software or the printer how to format the paragraph that follows. Specifically, the commands perform the following functions:

- **\keepn**—Instructs the display software or the printer to keep this paragraph with the next paragraph
- **\par**—Instructs the display software or the printer to start a new paragraph
- **\sb240**—Places a 12-point space before the paragraph
- **\b0**—Turns off bold formatting

Because this paragraph is formatted using RTF, which follows a particular set of rules and contains a certain number of commands, any word processor or other application that has an RTF interpreter can view and properly display it. It wouldn't matter if this paragraph was created on a Macintosh, a mainframe, or a Windows PC. The file is saved as an ASCII file, so the paragraph will display as intended as long as the application used to view the file (be it a word processor, browser, or even spreadsheet) includes an RTF interpreter.

The Concept Of Markup

RTF handles the on-screen and printed display of text. It does so with commands placed inside the actual file. To change the appearance of the file, you must open the entire file and make changes. You can't just apply a different set of rules to, for example, make all the text bold, 24-point font without opening the file. You can't have different processors process the data found in the file in different fashions. And, although you can create various styles, those styles aren't tied to specific sections of the content. For example, you can change the style of all paragraphs that have the Code style applied to them, but all of those "coded" paragraphs may not appear the same. Why? Because some of those paragraphs may have additional formatting applied. For example, the author of the document may decide to add bold formatting to a style already defined with italics.

RTF would allow that, because it does not require all the text to adhere to strict style rules.

Therefore, although RTF serves to describe how text can be formatted, it wouldn't work well with more complex formatting. It offers too many exceptions, and it fails to provide a true structure to define the entire document. RTF and other such formatting languages simply help to present the information rather than provide a more detailed structure for the document. As you saw in the previous code snippet, the only tag that actually described the structure of the document is the **\par** (paragraph) tag that serves to indicate that the following text will create a new paragraph.

True markup languages are much more structured than formatting languages like RTF. True markup languages, such as Standard Generalized Markup Language (SGML) and Extensible Markup Language (XML), go beyond the simple formatting languages to create specific, detailed structures for documents. Unlike formatting languages, true markup languages have the following characteristics:

- Content is separate from formatting. Formatting is usually handled through the use of style sheets, which are separate instructions that describe how various sections of the document should be formatted. With style sheets, you can change formatting without changing content.

- Markup languages describe the structure of the text within the document. Explicit rules determine where specific document structures begin and end. These explicit rules create a well-defined, almost tree- or outline-type structure from which the styles sheets work to display the information.

- Once a specific element is tagged, formatting changes affect all occurrences of that element.

Like formatting languages, markup languages require applications that can take the information and parse or display it accordingly.

When you apply a procedural markup language to the same document, it can be processed by many different types of software, and each can apply different processing instructions to the marked-up text. For example, a Web-based financial-analysis processor might only pull out the relevant numerical data and display that on the screen. A page-layout processor might include all the header and footer information in addition to the text-formatting information and gather all the data for printing and inserting page numbers and footnote references at the appropriate places. With procedural markup languages, like SGML, different processing instructions can be associated with the same file. Descriptive languages like RTF, however, concentrate on formatting and displaying the entire file. Procedural generalized markup languages basically map the document structures, identifying (essentially mapping) each specific document structure by its function and leaving the formatting to separate style sheets.

With structured markup languages like XML, you also have more searching flexibility. Not only can you search for any word like you can in a standard Web page, you can also search within the various elements of a document. For example, you may want to search for just header information, or you may want to search in specific headings, such as the chapter headings in a book. You wouldn't be able to do that if the book was created as an HTML document. If the whole book was one document, you would have to search through the entire file; if each chapter was an individual file, you would need the help of a separate Web server application to search them all at the same time.

Generalized Markup Languages

By now, you should be grasping the concept of how procedural markup languages work. Their main purpose is to provide a detailed description of how the document is to be structured, regardless of what processor might be processing the data, and the formatting is left to style sheets the developer creates. But there are more than just style sheets and structures included in generalized markup languages. Let's examine the specific components of generalized markup languages, such as SGML. These languages use specific tools to provide structure to documents:

• Document structures

• Tags or elements and their accompanying attributes

• Entities

• Comments

Understanding what each tool offers helps you to understand how the pieces of XML (and for that matter, just about any markup language) fit together. The easiest way to understand how generalized markup languages work is to break down a generalized markup language document into its most basic parts. Starting from the largest component and working down to the smallest piece, documents that incorporate a generalized markup language will have a specific document structure that defines how the document is formed. Within the various sections of the document, tags describe how certain formats or sections should or should not be displayed. And within those sections, entities describe how to handle data outside the document. In the following sections, we'll examine the individual components you'll find in any document that incorporates a generalized markup language, such as SGML or XML.

Document Structures

The first quality that separates documents formatted with a generalized markup language from the rest is that those using generalized markup languages are usually logical in order and highly structured. They include specific rules that state where various document structures should and must be placed. In fact, SGML and XML documents have a treelike structure, which you'll see if you display an XML document with any of today's XML parsers (such as Jumbo). It's around this tree structure that all other components, such as content and formatting, are built. Figure 1.1 shows how Jumbo takes an XML document and displays its structure, providing quick access to whatever section the reader might want to view.

This highly structured format makes describing the document's content easier, and in turn, it makes it easier to format sections within the document. It is easier to separate the content from the presentation and to apply specific formats for specific purposes from the same group of data. Reformatting can easily be done because the designer no longer has to wade through each line of code and change specific formats for specific items, as is required in HTML documents.

The treelike structure also makes it easier to redesign generalized markup documents or to pluck out the data for different audiences. Microsoft's Channels is an excellent example of how an XML application can be used to deliver the same data to a variety of applications, such as screen savers, HTML-formatted email, or the channels themselves on the user's desktop. This well-formed document structure starts with a foundation, and from that point, you can work with more

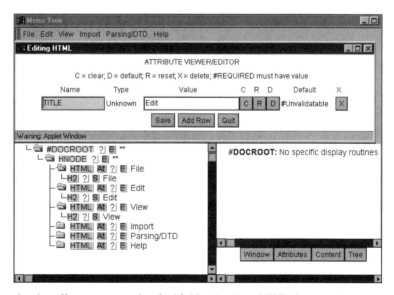

Figure 1.1   Jumbo offers an example of a highly structured XML document.

specific options, such as tags. It doesn't matter whether you are viewing the data in your HTML email application or through a channel placed on your desktop. With a highly structured document and the use of style-sheet technology, the same information can be delivered to a variety of viewing applications.

TIP: *Microsoft's Channel Definition Format is fully explained in Chapter 20.*

Tags

If you've created a Web page, you may already be familiar with the term *tag*. Markup languages (like HTML) that are used to create Web pages use tags placed at the beginning and end of each document item. All tags, or instructions, are enclosed within angle brackets and are usually fairly descriptive. For example, when you want to indicate where bold text begins, you would use the bold tag, **<B>**. Simply place the **<B>** tag before the text you want to identify as being bold.

But you also need to indicate where you want to end the bold formatting, and this is done through the use of a closing tag, which is normally the opening tag with a forward slash placed directly after the first angle bracket (**</B>**). The closing tag specifies where the instructions end, whether they are formatting instructions like the bold tag or more specific processing instructions, such as where a script (**<SCRIPT>**) language should start and end processing.

These two tags, the opening tag and its accompanying closing tag, are collectively known as *elements*. Elements, usually specified by a descriptive term called an *element type*, are placed within the document to identify its structure. With structured markup languages, such as XML or SGML, the inclusion of the ending tag is important; it is needed to properly parse or interpret the information found in the document.

Although some elements are used individually, you can also nest elements within other elements. For example, within this book there are chapters, within each chapter are sections, and within each section are paragraphs. If we were to mark up this entire book, we could nest a paragraph element within a section element, which could then be nested within a chapter element. If chapters need to be moved around, all the accompanying sections and paragraphs follow the chapter because they are nested within the chapters.

A simple example shows how we nest the italic tag within the bold tag:

```
<B><I>This text is bold, and it's also italic.</I></B>
```

Structure is important in generalized markup languages, such as SGML or XML, so closing tags are necessary. With HTML, however, most browsers will display text formatted with just a single open tag. If you leave out a closing tag in an SGML or XML document, you'll find that your code doesn't work properly.

Attributes

As you can see, elements (the opening and closing tags) offer a way to structure a document or specific sections within the document. Tags can provide formatting or processing instructions, but elements alone usually aren't enough. For example, if you used HTML and placed the element **IMG**, and its opening tag **<IMG>** in a Web page to specify where an image should display, your Web page would display nothing at all. The opening tag **<IMG>** signifies that the HTML processor should display an image, but without the capability of specifying exactly what image should display and where that image is located, the **<IMG>** opening tag won't do much. That's where the element attribute comes into play. Most elements, even some of the simplest ones in HTML, have *attributes*. Attributes are additional items that are added to elements to provide clarity to the element. For example, the **FONT** element offers access to several different attributes, including the font size and font family. The opening tag, **<FONT>**, incorporates two of its attributes in the following code:

```
<FONT FACE="Bookman" SIZE="12">
This text is displayed in 12 point Bookman
</FONT>
```

As you can see, the **FONT** element's attributes, which are placed directly after the opening tag, are **FACE** and **SIZE**, and each value for the attribute is enclosed in quotes. Placing the attribute values in quotes helps the processor distinguish between an attribute and a value.

TIP: *When you start coding your own XML documents, make sure you pay attention to quotes when you are specifying attribute values. Quotes are much more important in XML than they are in HTML. If you open with one, make sure you add a closing quote. And if you're not sure whether to put quotes around attribute values, do it anyway.*

With structured markup languages, such as SGML, it's often up to you to create your own document elements, which means your elements will most likely require additional attributes to further explain the elements themselves. For example, if we were to create an XML document from this book, we would define several elements, including elements for highlighting sidebars, tips, words of caution, and indicators for special text you should pay close attention to. With SGML, we could declare a sidebar element and then specify the attributes, or types of sidebars you'll find throughout the book. The code might look like the following example of a sidebar element with a specific attribute defined:

```
<sidebar type="caution">Make sure you use quotes around your
attributes!</sidebar>
```

Our sidebar tag now includes an attribution specification for the attribute type. This is different than nesting elements within each other. Sidebars are all specialized text that should be formatted a certain way, but each one may include slightly different images or additional elements. However, elements can contain more than just simple attributes. As a matter of fact, generalized markup languages, such as SGML, allow attributes with up to 15 different types of values that can be associated with the attribute, including:

- References, commonly referred to as *entities*, to any resource outside the document
- An ID, which is a unique identifier for the element within the document
- ID Pointers, which are cross-references for those elements with the IDs quoted within the document
- Notations or element attributes that specify a notation in the content of an element
- Character data, or **CDATA**, which includes any valid characters that will not be interpreted as an attribute value

XML uses attributes to pass information to programs. Such information may be specific to how the information should be presented and, in some cases, whether the information should be presented at all.

Entities

As you may have begun to realize, generalized markup languages deal mainly with formatting and processing text, not binary files. Elements and attributes are responsible for formatting text and providing processing information to the browser or parser (that is, the software that interprets the generalized markup language), and then the parser or browser provides the final output. But elements and attributes don't provide a way to handle nontextual information saved in binary format or shortcuts to a collective group of text. Nontextual information saved in binary format includes illustrations, specialized characters that may not have the same representation on different platforms (such as the letter *e* with an accent character placed over it), and multimedia files such as a video or audio files.

TIP: *Detailed information on XML entities can be found in Chapter 12.*

Languages such as SGML and XML use *entities* to handle groups of data that are treated as a unit. An entity is any non-SGML data. Think of entities as any part of a marked-up document that doesn't concern itself with any particular structural considerations. An entity could be a whole file or simply a string of text. You can have as many entity entries in an SGML or XML file as you need.

TIP: *Have you ever used the glossary or macro option in your favorite word processor? In most word processors, you can type your name, address, and phone number and then create a glossary entry for this text and name it address, for example. Instead of typing your name, address, and phone number when you write or send a letter, you can simply type in the word "address," press a few keys, and all the information is automatically displayed. Entities are like glossary entries. They can be files, shortcuts, or aliases to other textual groups of information, as well.*

Entities can save you a lot of typing and also allow you to include any type of binary file or special character you choose. When you use entities with groups of text, you can create a consistency throughout the document by specifying entities that in turn specify a set type of data. The syntax for declaring an entity is **<!ENTITY Name "EntityDefinition">**. You declare entities in the marked-up document. Here's how an entity to specify non-SGML data looks:

```
<!ENTITY amp "&#38;">
```

Let's break the code down a bit. The **!ENTITY** element declares that what follows is an entity. The word **amp** is the name of the entity. The **"&"** is the definition used to describe what the entity should display.

The name of the entity can only include letters, digits, periods, dashes, underscores, or colons. An entity name must also start with a letter or underscore. The **EntityDefinition** can contain any valid markup, but that information must be enclosed in quotes.

When a parser encounters an entity reference, it will substitute the entity name with the declared entity value. Remember that entities can be files, or they can be any data available to the processor, such as entity references. For example, entity references can be multimedia files, results of database queries, results of calls to systems, results of search strings, or representations of certain characters.

XML provides for two kinds of entities: *general* and *parameter*. General entities are widely used in HTML for coding specific characters, such as the ampersand (&), accent marks, angle brackets (which are used to define tags), or any non-basic ASCII characters. The code

```
<!ENTITY amp "&#38;">
```

is an example of a general entity. Once you declare an entity, it can be referenced from anywhere within the document. And when you want to include an entity in a document, you use an entity reference. An entity reference is the entity name with an ampersand before it and a semicolon after it. Here's an example of an entity reference:

```
&amp;
```

When the SGML or XML parser runs across the ampersand followed by the entity name and the semicolon, the parser displays the entity definition. An entity reference can be placed anywhere in the document.

When you mark up a document, you need to use various characters to identify where the markup instructions begin. These characters are reserved to identify various markup symbols. For example, the left angle bracket (<) is used to identify the beginning of an element's start- or end-tag. When you place these characters into a document as content (when you want to use an angle bracket, for example), there must be some way to display them. In XML, entities are used to represent these special characters (in addition to representing binary files or collections of text).

Let's go back to our example of the ampersand. Suppose you just type "amp" in your document. The SGML or XML parser would pretty much ignore the word or just interpret it as text. It certainly would not perform any specialized processing on the word. But once you add an ampersand (&) and a semicolon (;), the parser recognizes this combination of letters and processes the text as an entity. It looks for the accompanying entity declaration and replaces the **&** with &. Regardless of which operating system or platform is used, the ampersand is displayed.

For example, when the generalized markup language parser runs across **&**, the parser will know that this combination of ampersand, semicolon, and the entity name **amp** is an entity and not just more marked-up text.

> **WARNING!**   *Remember that case is important with entity names, although it's not important with element names. So, figure 1 is not the same as FIGURE 1. A list of entity declarations at the beginning of your document is known as an* **entity set.**

Now, let's take entities one step further. Say you want to create an employee handbook and place the employees and their job descriptions throughout the book. You could declare the following entity references:

```
<!ENTITY EmpName "John Doe">
<!ENTITY Job "Webmaster">
```

Because the employee manual has already been written with the entity references EmpName and Job, when you print the manual, those references will be replaced with John Doe and Webmaster accordingly. Here's how this works:

```
Dear &EmpName;,

Welcome to XYZ Design firm.
We are definitely looking forward
to you taking over
the &Job; duties for our company.
```

Once the SGML or XML parser has done its processing, you'll get the following results:

```
Dear John Doe,

Welcome to XYZ Design firm.
We are definitely looking forward
to you taking over
the Webmaster duties for our company.
```

Instead of having to search and replace through the entire document each time you get a new employee, all you have to do is simply change the entity attribute values, and the markup language processor does the rest.

TIP: *Remember, if you used **&empname;** instead of **&EmpName;**, the markup language processor would not replace the name and job description with the declared values. Entity names are always case sensitive.*

You can also use entities to include binary files, such as images, in your document. When you want to embed an image file in a document, you would first declare the figure entity as shown here:

```
<!ENTITY fig1 SYSTEM "http://www.site.com/fig1.tif" NDATA TIF>
```

If we dissect this entity declaration, here's what we come up with. **!ENTITY** is the element used to tell the markup language processor (or parser) that what follows is information that should replace entity references. The entity name **fig1** is the name you would use throughout the document where you want to place this image. **SYSTEM** signifies that the document following the **SYSTEM** identifier is an external document. The **SYSTEM** identifier is followed by a URL location for the file. In the example, this is pointing to the file labeled **fig1.tif**, which is located at **http://www.site.com**.

The **NDATA** keyword signifies that the data in the file is binary, or nontextual, data. You are required to indicate the file type of the entity following the **NDATA** keyword. In this example, the file type is TIF. If the file was a PC Paint file, you would have used BMP instead of TIF; if the file was a GIF, the **NDATA** keyword would have been GIF.

After you've declared it, any time you want to reference the binary, nontextual entity in your document, you do so by adding the line of code shown here:

```
This is an example of a graphic &fig1; placed
in the middle of the text.
```

Basically, all you have to do is specify the name of the entity labeled **fig1** in the document. Again, as with all other entities, case is important. Specifying **Fig1** for the **Figure Entity** value is different than specifying **fig1**. Notice also that you are not declaring the location of a file as you would in an HTML document. Instead, you are specifying the name of the entity, which in turn signifies the location of the binary, nontextual file you want to include in the document.

Comments

Comments are used to add additional information that is not supposed to be seen once the document is processed. You should use lots of comments throughout your documents in case other developers must take over their management. Comments also help you remember exactly what you were thinking when you created the document.

Comments begin with **<!--** and are closed out by adding **-->** at the end. If you've used JavaScript with HTML pages, you'll be familiar with this comment declaration; it is widely used in JavaScript. Comments can contain any text except for **--** because this string is used in declaring the comment. You can place comments anywhere within your document, and you can have as many comments as you like. Comments don't directly affect a document's processing speed. Again, comments are not considered or processed as any part of the content of the XML document. They are simply included within the source.

Document Type Definitions

Although Chapter 5 delves deeper into Document Type Definitions (DTDs), we want to take a few minutes here to explain this important element that is used in many XML documents. DTDs are what really separate both XML and SGML from other markup languages—they provide developers with the necessary tools to create the types of documents they need. So, what exactly is a DTD? In the most basic terms, a *Document Type Definition* is a file that is separate from the main XML document and that provides a set of rules for the XML document to which it is attached. DTDs set the instructions for the structure of the XML document and define what elements are going to be used throughout the document. The declared entities for the document are also included in the DTD. Think of a DTD as a road map/rule book for the document. More specifically, DTDs outline the following features within the DTD:

- The element types that will be allowed within the XML document
- The various characteristics of each element type, along with the attributes used with each element and the content each element is capable of having
- Any notations that can be encountered within the document
- The entities that can be used within the document

Generalized Markup Languages: SGML, XML, HTML

We've been talking about generalized markup languages, but let's get a bit more specific about the various generalized markup languages that you are familiar with.

HTML: Its Place

We'll start by examining HTML. As you probably know, HTML is relatively simple to use and quick to implement, and although it is simplistic, it offers enough capabilities to deliver documents over the Internet in the form of Web pages or HTML-formatted email. It uses element tags to identify limited document structures, like the head and body. And in the same document, HTML tags also define the way in which the document is viewed.

Plug-ins used with HTML come close to accomplishing what XML currently accomplishes. They offer the ability to view different types of data within a Web page. Plug-ins are external programs that are brought into play by using the HTML element **EMBED**. **EMBED**'s attributes specify the name of the plug-in to be used, along with additional information about what to do if the browser does not have that particular plug-in installed. By using an external set of code, which has to be downloaded by the user, a plug-in allows the user to view different data types almost as if that capability is built in to the browser.

The problem with plug-ins is that they are developed with the sole intent of displaying different proprietary sets of data. That means a plug-in that displays Adobe Acrobat documents most likely won't display Excel spreadsheet data. This type of technology is akin to creating and using proprietary browser tags. And this means that not every user will be able to take advantage of the data.

Plug-ins handle how the data is viewed rather than its structure; therefore, they may not be aware of certain structural elements.

TIP: *For more information on plug-ins, check out* Supercharged Web Browsers: A Plug-Ins Field Guide, *by this book's coauthor, Cheryl Kirk (Charles River Media, 1998).*

SGML: The Granddaddy Of Them All

SGML is a markup language widely used in many high-end information-publishing arenas. You'll find SGML used in the technical-writing arena, where the need to handle complex, large documents across platforms is common. You'll also find SGML used in the automotive industry, the health-care field, many areas of the telecommunications industry, and just about any place where large volumes of text need to be structured in easily accessible formats.

SGML has been used extensively for many years, even before it became an International Organization for Standardization (ISO) standard in 1986. It has a broad range of support, because it has a tremendous amount of features suited specifically for text-based applications. That's also the reason users avoid SGML. The language is so complex; plowing through the more than 500 pages of specifications is a daunting task that many text-processing professionals simply don't have time for, especially when it means converting their documents from paper to the Web. SGML's complexity also makes it daunting for software programmers to incorporate into desktop software applications. That fact contributes to the small number of applications that implement SGML into their core subset of programming instructions. It also contributes to the high price tag on SGML-enabled applications, such as FrameMaker—although the user base is there, the cost for adding such features is expensive. Murray Maloney, coauthor of *SGML and The Web*, published by Prentice Hall, put it best, "HTML is the low-end Volkswagen of markup languages, and SGML is the high-end Rolls Royce."

XML: The Simpler Subset

When Web-site designers and developers started pushing the limits of HTML far beyond its capabilities, the need for a more extensive language became apparent. HTML only provides a limited set of tags for structuring a document, so using it is relatively easy. Sure, designers could try to use browser-specific tags that both Netscape and Microsoft offered, but with that came the possibility of shutting out a wide range of users. So, most designers realized that, if they wanted to do anything advanced, they couldn't do it with HTML. They had to use a separate scripting language, such as JavaScript, or some CGI scripting language, such as Perl.

But these options didn't really give designers full control over the real structure of the document, let alone the structure of the data. XML is a subset of SGML, not an application of SGML like HTML is. That means that XML offers many of the same complex features but in a much more manageable fashion. The best part of XML is that it only uses the specific features of SGML that are needed to deliver information over the Internet or an intranet. Unlike SGML documents, XML documents are relatively easy to create and use on the Web, particularly now that both

Netscape and Microsoft have added a great deal of support for XML in the latest versions of their browsers.

XML provides a wide range of features that aren't found in HTML, including:

- An extensible language that provides you with the ability to define your own tags and attributes. These elements and their start and end tags along with their attributes help you to define the structural elements of the document, much like SGML's elements do.

- The ability to nest documents structures within other document structures to create complex documents.

- The ability to check for valid document structures during processing.

The Differences Between XML And SGML

You should be aware of the differences between XML and SGML, even if you have never developed a document in SGML. Although XML is derived from SGML, there are many differences between XML and SGML. The easiest way to explain the differences between SGML and XML is to say that XML is a much smaller language, or a subset of SGML. SGML's specification is more than 500 pages long, whereas XML's specification is a mere 50 pages. This means that, although XML can handle a wide range of documents, it's not intended to handle all the complex data SGML can handle. It also means that it is easier to write a parser for XML than it is to write one for SGML.

Another difference between SGML and XML is the need to validate documents. SGML documents must first be validated and used with a DTD. SGML documents must also use style sheets to display the information within the document. A DTD is not required with XML documents, and validation is not always needed. Basically, all an XML document needs is a style sheet if it is to be displayed within any type of textual formatting. (Style sheets, by the way, are also required with an SGML document, which means you have to have a DTD and a style sheet in order for an SGML document to be valid.) This major difference makes XML documents more portable and more accessible over the Web than SGML documents. With XML, there is less "baggage" to carry with the document, and that means less document storage needs. XML gives documents flexibility, which is definitely needed on the Web.

Specifically, XML is different from SGML in these ways:

- XML is more simplistic and created specifically for use over the Internet.

- XML documents are quicker to create than SGML documents.

- It's much easier to write applications that interpret XML documents than it is to write applications that interpret SGML documents.

- In XML documents, empty elements are simply specified with a **/>** at the end of the element tag.

But there still are similarities between the two languages. The similarities make it easy to convert XML documents to SGML, although converting SGML documents to XML documents can be a little more time-consuming. Specifically, XML and SGML are alike in many ways:

- Both support a wide variety of applications.
- XML is fully compatible with SGML.
- Both use style sheets to format the content.
- Both XML and SGML documents should be relatively easy to read and understand.
- Both XML and SGML documents use concise structures.

The Differences Between HTML And XML

Since you are probably already familiar with HTML, let's spend a few minutes examining the major differences between HTML and XML. You could say that XML is a more advanced markup language than HTML. And if you were to take that simplistic statement one step further and say that HTML is used mainly for presentation of content and XML is used for structuring data, you wouldn't be wrong. But there's more to it than that.

XML is in no way a replacement for HTML. And it isn't just HTML with extra tags thrown in, although the XML specification is much larger than the HTML specification. Although HTML is an application of SGML, and XML is a subset of SGML, HTML and XML differ considerably. Specifically, XML allows you to define your own tags for particular purposes. Other than that, the differences are most notable in what problems XML serves to solve. You could say that XML is actually a fix to the particular problems that are encountered when using HTML. With XML, you have:

- Better control over layout
- Less strain on the Web server because of the capability of accessing information on the client side
- The use of multiple types of hyperlinks
- The ability to deliver any type of information over both the Internet and intranets
- Less problems displaying long pages

As you can tell, the differences between HTML and XML are more than just format versus content, although that is one major selling point for XML. Let's take a look at some of these particular HTML problems and how XML can solve them.

Better Control Over Layout

The current implementation of HTML is one that designers have wrestled with since its inception. HTML includes the format and content within the same document. This creates problems when a designer wants to change the overall look and feel of an entire site. To do that with HTML, a designer would have to manually change each individual page.

With XML, the layout is separate from the content, so when a designer wants to change the layout of a site, he simply changes the style sheet that is attached. The content stays intact. This is a major change to the HTML concept and also makes for a much more flexible format for delivering the same information through a variety of mechanisms. Style sheets can be used to format content to different applications.

Even though the latest implementation of HTML, version 4, allows you to work closely with style sheets, the difference is that XML lets you associate styles with structural elements. That means, you can quickly format styles for particular structural elements, such as entities that declare images, specific paragraph formats, and even styles for different types of linking mechanisms.

Getting Beyond The Server

One of the most important features of XML is that documents no longer have to be tied directly to servers. Using what is called the *Document Object Model* (DOM), you can create XML documents that show all or only some of the data. For example, suppose the XML document you create is a simple address book. With HTML, you might create a form that allows the user to find a name in the address book. Of course, this would require the form to send the search request back to the server each time the user wants to look up an individual's name.

With XML's DOM, the document could contain the entire list and, with the style sheet attached, display only the information requested. All other elements of the document could be hidden. When the user wants to display or find more detailed information, instead of sending the request to the server, the XML document would simply display the rest of the hidden information by using a browser-side script. This style sheet mechanism allows the address book to be used both on and off the Internet.

Better Control For Long Documents

Have you ever tried to bring up a long Web page with today's browsers? HTML doesn't allow you to pick and choose which sections you want to view. The problem is that HTML does not allow for multiple sections in a single document; it only allows the **<HEAD>** or **<BODY>** sections. So, if you, the designer, want to create a single long document with links to its various sections, you would need to either break the document into smaller Web pages or incorporate frames. But again, frames point to multiple documents, usually, not an entire document with separate sections.

To explain this problem with HTML in more detail, we'll use this book as an example once again. This chapter is more than 20 pages long and has many sections. If we were to place it on the Web, we would have to make it smaller so the reader wouldn't have to wait hours for the document to load. And at the same time, we would need to provide the reader with the ability to jump back and forth between sections, either in a logical format or randomly. There is also the possibility of making a mistake and accidentally placing the wrong heading tag at the wrong location, which would hinder the flow of the document.

If we tried using the **<FRAMESET>** tag to place the chapter into frames, we'd also run into problems with those readers who don't have frames-enabled browsers. And again, we could misidentify a heading and ruin the flow of the text. Also, if we were to divvy up the chapter and place the parts into different pages, we would lose the ability to allow full-text searching.

XML promises to fix this particular problem simply because all XML documents are highly structured and well-formed. XML won't let you cut as many corners as HTML does, and through the use of various section elements, XML gives you a way to break a single document into segments that are presented as a single document with various levels. This multilevel structure appears much like the way Windows Explorer presents folders and subfolders in a hierarchical fashion. This also means that XML gives you a way to search the entire document without having to create separate scripts.

TIP: *Chapter 3 delves further into how HTML is currently being stretched beyond its current limitations.*

The Use Of Multiple Hyperlinks

Is your browser's Back button a little worn out? It's no wonder, since the current implementation of HTML only allows for single-direction linking. There is no convention for multiple-linking formats, allowing for multidirectional linking based on what role the document plays. But backward and forward is not the only direction many Web users want to go. And where do current HTML sources take you? To other resources, whether they are other Web pages, search engines, chat rooms, and so on.

So, what does XML offer in the way of linking that HTML and SGML leave out? Specifically, XML provides a standard model for linking through its linking specification, *Extensible Linking Language* (XLink). With HTML, only character data types are used with a link location or URL. Entities are not incorporated either. URLs also don't include notations that segment different data types. And internal links, those that are used to connect to other locations within a single document, use the **NAME** attribute of an element type, such as **<A NAME="bottom">**. All of this is relatively simplistic linking.

Linking in XML, however, is more complex than it is in HTML. XML offers advanced linking through XLL by:

- Giving you control over the semantics of the link.

- Using Extended Links. Extended Links can involve more than two resources.

- Using pointers to external references through the use of Extended Pointers, or *XPointers.*

An easy way to explain all these different linking functions is to examine the current linking method used in HTML. A simple link provides a way to identify a certain single source. Extended Links allow you to express relationships between more than two resources. Chapter 10 examines the various linking options available in XML.

Briefly, in layman's terms, the advanced linking options provide XML documents with:

- Bidirectional links

- Externally managed links (links that can be managed outside of the document content itself)

- Links that provide access to a ring of sites or lets the user open multiple windows

- Links with multiple sources attached

- Attributes associated with links

What Does An XML Document Look Like?

XML documents closely resemble SGML or HTML documents. As you've seen, elements, attributes, and entities are included as well as comments and other standard text. But there are some features that separate XML documents from their smaller or larger generalized markup cousins. First, let's look at a simple XML document in Listing 1.1.

Listing 1.1   An example of an XML document.

```
<?XML version="1.0"?>
<!DOCTYPE MEMO SYSTEM "http://www.site.com/dtds/memo.dtd">
```

```
<MEMO>
<HEADER>
<TO>
To:
<NAME>
John Doe
</NAME>
<CC/>
</TO>
<FROM>
From:
</FROM>
<SENDER>
Betty North
</SENDER>
</HEADER>
<!--This is the start of the memo text-->
<MEMOTEXT>
Please take note our phone number has changed.
</MEMOTEXT>
</MEMO>
```

First, notice that the document starts with the processing instruction **<?XML version="1.0"?>**. This line of code is called the XML markup declaration and serves to explain to the processor that this is an XML document and this document is using XML version 1 to structure the document. Although this declaration is not required, you should always include it so the processor understands that this is an XML document. Otherwise, processors or browsers may consider the document to be just standard HTML and not interpret the information properly.

Next, notice that, unlike SGML, there is no required DTD, but in this instance, we've included one. The DTD is stored on the server located at **www.site.com/dtds** and saved with the file name memo.dtd. This DTD sets up any of the elements or entities used in this document.

TIP: *Again, like the XML markup declaration, the Document Type Definition is not required, but you should consider supplying one, especially if the XML document you create actually would benefit from one.*

Also, notice the elements and how they use both open and close tags. They look just like elements used in HTML. But XML requires you have both open and close tags. Theoretically, you could leave out a closing tag in HTML and browsers would still interpret the document properly. With XML, the document wouldn't process correctly.

Now, take a look at the element **<CC/>**. Unlike elements that offer open and close tags, empty elements like **<CC/>** are slightly modified in their use of syntax and don't necessarily have to enclose themselves around any type of content. Instead, empty elements could best be considered as markers where something should occur or where a default value is specified. Empty elements are always signified by the name of the element followed by a slash, such as **<LATESTTIME/>**, but they can also be delimited with a start- and end-tag with no values in between as in **<LATESTTIME><LATESTTIME/>**. As you can see, XML documents are composed of both content and markup.

Also, notice how each element can be nested within other elements, such as the **<MEMO></MEMO>**, **<HEAD></HEAD>**, and **<MEMOTEXT></MEMOTEXT>**, just as they can be nested in HTML. You can also include comments (as you can with HTML) like the one that appears before the actual text of the memo. But also notice that there are no formatting tags. Instead, all the formatting is handled in a separate style sheet specified in a separate document.

XML Document Types

As you can see, Listing 1.1 used several features described earlier in this chapter. Those features actually encompass six kinds of markup items that can occur in XML:

- elements
- entity references
- comments
- processing instructions
- marked sections
- document types

We used elements, comments, marked sections, and document types in Listing 1.1. In subsequent examples throughout this book, you'll learn how to use these and the other items (processing instructions and entity references) for your specific needs.

Although we included a DTD in Listing 1.1, we didn't have to. That's why XML is well-suited for the Web; it doesn't need to know the DTD, or the structural model, that was used to create an XML document. That doesn't mean that XML doesn't work with DTDs. It just means that if a document does not use a DTD, it must be distributed in its complete form. It is this ability to either have a DTD or include the document structure form that makes XML so well-suited for Internet and intranet applications.

Documents that have a Document Type Definition and adhere to it are called *valid* documents. Documents that don't have a DTD but still conform to the XML standard are called *well-formed*. Well-formed documents can be used without a DTD, but they must follow some simple rules so that style sheets and linking can be used with them. Let's take a brief look at each document type in the next sections.

Well-Formed Documents

What exactly is a well-formed document? A well-formed document is one that conforms to the XML syntax used within the document. For example, if you don't include end-tags when placing elements in the document, if you forget to include the XML document declaration at the top of the document, or if the document includes characters that can't be parsed or are invalid, you don't have a well-formed XML document. Some markup constructs are only allowed in specific places. Place these constructs in the wrong place and you don't have a well-formed document.

TIP: *If you have a well-formed XML document, you also have a well-formed SGML document.*

But well-formed documents are actually more than just documents that follow the XML syntax. In addition, documents that are considered well-formed must meet the following conditions:

- No attribute can appear more than once in a single start-tag.

- You can't include references to external entities in a string attribute.

- You must declare all entities except for those included as part of the XML language.

- You can't reference a binary entity in the bulk of the content. Binary entities can only be used within **ENTITY** attributes.

- You cannot create recursive parameter or text entities either directly or indirectly.

- Parameter entities must be declared before you can use them within the document.

- Any non-empty tags must be properly nested.

- The name in an element's end-tag must match the element type in the start-tag.

- You cannot include an angle bracket (<) in the replacement text of any entity.

Valid Documents

Okay, so you have a well-formed XML document. You've paid attention to all the markup constraints, dotted all the i's and crossed all the t's, and formed the document according to the XML syntax. But a well-formed document is not valid unless it contains a proper DTD. Also, the document must also obey the constraints of that declaration.

Every valid XML document should start with header information that should contain the following information:

- A description of the structural rules that the document should follow.

- A list of any external resources or external entities that create any specific part of the document.

- Any declarations of internal resources or internal entities.

- Any notations or non-XML resources that should be listed in the document. These notations or non-XML resources should also specify any helper applications required.

- Lists of any non-XML resources (such as binary entities) that might be found in the document.

In Closing, XML Should...

By now, you should understand the theory of markup languages, their features, and their applicable uses. You should also have a clear idea of how XML should be implemented. For that, the governing body overseeing the creation of XML has defined exactly what features XML should offer. This governing body, called the *World Wide Web Consortium*, or W3C for short, has outlined that XML should follow these guidelines:

- *XML should be straightforwardly usable over the Internet.* XML should be simple enough for current Web designers to pick up and quickly put to use. It's designed to be used with proven Web features, such as linking, elements, and attributes. Transformation from HTML to XML is supposed to be almost painless.

- *XML should support a variety of applications.* XML should support as many applications as HTML does. The types of applications should be as varied, as well.

- *XML should be compatible with SGML.* Any SGML processor should be able to interpret XML documents. This provides an extensible way to expand XML to more than just Web users. There should be no problem working with SGML or XML documents when you are using SGML-specific applications.

- *XML should be easy enough to write programs that process XML documents.* Developers won't or shouldn't shun XML because it is too difficult to write desktop or personal applications that process XML documents. The old theory, "If you build it, they will come," is supposed to apply to XML. The easier it is to develop XML applications, the more likely users and developers will embrace it.

- *XML should have little or no optional features.* XML is supposed to be kept as simple as possible. Optional features have stymied acceptance of SGML. The idea is to keep XML simple and efficient.

- *XML documents need to be human-legible and reasonably clear.* XML documents should be interpretable not just by a parser or browser, but by people, as well. XML documents should be so readable that anyone can interpret the content and intent.

- *XML design should be able to be prepared quickly.* The actual design of XML has been on the fast track since its first proposal in 1996. Acceptance and implementation should happen at an even faster pace than was the case with HTML.

- *XML design should be formal and concise.* The actual elements or markup should be pretty self-explanatory. Instead of something like **<P>** to specify a paragraph, the element would instead be named **<PARAGRAPH>**. Instead of **<VLINK>**, the element would be named **<VISISTEDLINK>**. This makes XML documents easier for people to read.

- *XML documents should be easy to create.* In order for XML to catch on like HTML has, XML documents should be as easy to create. By incorporating structure and well-formedness, XML documents should also be easier to understand.

- *Terseness in XML markup is of minimal importance.* Instead of using shortened markup like HTML does, XML uses full, spelled-out markup. For example, **<A>** in HTML would be **<ANCHOR>** in XML.

By now, you should have a firm grasp of what a markup language is and the differences between the different types of markup languages. In subsequent chapters, you'll learn how to put this theory to good use. Chapter 2 will bring you up to speed on XML, its history, how the specification was created, and the various XML vocabularies used.

Immediate Solutions

In this section, you'll create a simple XML document and include various elements. You'll take each markup item and create it in the order in which it should be listed.

Creating An XML Document

You can use any text-editing application to create an XML document (just as you would to create an HTML document). For this project, you'll need a text processor, such as Notepad or any Unix-based text editor. If you want to view the results of your efforts, you should also have an XML processor. You'll need to save the document with the .xml extension. This signifies to the XML processor (such as Jumbo) that the file should be processed as an XML file instead of a text or HTML file.

Step 1: Declaring A Document As An XML Document

To declare a document as an XML document, follow these steps:

1. Start your text editor.

2. On the first line of the document, type the following code:

```
<?XML version="1.0"?>
```

This specifies to the processor that this is an XML document. It also specifies what version of XML will be used. All valid XML documents should begin with this declaration. This is the standard syntax for SGML processing instructions, which always begins with **<?**. However, XML processing instructions, such as this declaration, are slightly different than SGML in that they use **?>** to close the declaration.

This processing instruction is actually a combination of several parts. It includes the XML version number, **"1.0"**, which is the default for all current XML documents. When XML is upgraded, you can provide for total compatibility by specifying the correct version information.

Step 2: Specifying The DTD To Be Used With The Document

To specify the DTD, follow these steps:

1. Press the Enter key after the document declaration in your current document to move down a line.

2. Type the following code (on the second line of the document):

```
<!DOCTYPE memo SYSTEM "http://www.site.com/dtds/memo.dtd">
```

If you plan to use a DTD, it should be listed directly after the document declaration and before you use any of the elements listed in the DTD. A DTD is usually located externally, and it's important to reference its location. The DTD could be located on a server that is separate from the actual content. By keeping the DTD separate from the rest of the document, you can quickly and easily change features within the DTD without having to open the XML document.

Document type declarations always begin with **<!DOCTYPE** and are followed by the name, including the full path name of the DTD or the link to the DTD's location. The DTD file name should be understandable enough to describe the concept of the DTD. The keyword **SYSTEM** is used to specify that the DTD is not a public DTD. If it was a public DTD that was used by a large number of users, the keyword **PUBLIC** would be used.

Step 3: Adding Comments To The Document

To add comments to your document, follow these steps:

1. Press the Enter key after the DTD declaration in your current document to move down a line.

2. Type the following code (on the third line of the document):

```
<!--This is the first XML document-->
```

Your document should now look like this:

```
<?XML version="1.0"?>
<!DOCTYPE memo SYSTEM "http://www.site.com/dtds/memo.dtd">
<!--This is the first XML document-->
```

You should fully comment your documents, so other developers and users are aware of any particular features, elements, or tricks you might have used. Comments also serve as reminders to yourself about where various sections of documents begin and end. All comments start with an open angle bracket (<) followed by an exclamation point (!) and two dashes (--). Any text that follows will not be processed.

Step 4: Adding Elements To The Document

To add elements to your document, insert the following code after the comment:

```
<?XML version="1.0"?>
<!DOCTYPE memo SYSTEM "http://www.site.com/dtds/memo.dtd">
<!--This is the first XML document-->
<SIMPLEDOC>
<HEADING>This is the heading of the document</HEADING>
<BODY><FIRSTPARAGRAPH>This is the first paragraph of the body section.
</FIRSTPARAGRAPH>
<SECONDPARAGRAPH>This is the second paragraph</SECONDPARAGRAPH>
</BODY>
<FOOTER>This information is in the footer.</FOOTER>
</SIMPLEDOC>
```

Notice how each element must begin with a start-tag and close with an end-tag; otherwise, this would not be a well-formed document. Also, notice how you can nest elements within other elements and how each element specifies the structure of the document.

Chapter 2

XML Refresher

By Cheryl Kirk

In Depth

In Chapter 1, you were introduced to the wonderful world of Extensible Markup Language (XML) and some of the differences between this markup language and all the rest. By now, you should have a good grasp of what a markup language is and some of the features XML offers. In this chapter, we'll cover a lot more ground, by detailing XML's history and the support XML has garnered in its short life. We'll examine the XML specification itself as well as the process XML had to go through in order to make it past the World Wide Web Consortium, the governing body, if you will, for Web-based markup. The XML specification changes and evolves yearly. It's important for you to understand how to read the specification and make sense of its changes, deletions, and additions. We'll also cover a bit of the XML vocabulary, giving you a glimpse of what's available now and how you can implement the vocabulary in your development process.

TIP: *See Chapter 20 for an in-depth look at the XML vocabularies.*

The Need For XML

The Web is an amazing place where millions of people communicate with one another every single day. It doesn't matter where people are geographically located—the Web knows no physical boundaries. Yet with all the wonders the Web has to offer, its widespread use would lead to chaos if there weren't certain standards, or rules, for communicating across this vast network. It is from this need for standardization that HTML, and then XML, has evolved.

HTML initially provided the standard by which Web pages could be easily created on one platform, placed on a server, and viewed on different platforms. HTML, the GIF image file format, and then the JPEG image file format allowed document and graphic interchange and interoperability between operating systems, browsers, and computers. But for all its glory and ease of use (both in the development world and the user-interface world), HTML, although necessary to display information, is relatively insufficient for representing actual data as it might be structured, and it provides almost no mechanism for managing data remotely. All HTML provides is a visual layer, giving the user the ability to access text and pictures and then navigate in a single direction to yet another text- and picture-based document.

HTML does not provide any standards beyond the visual representation portion of the Internet's communication layer. Suppose you want to search a site. Because there currently are no standards for intelligent searches, you are at the mercy of whatever technology the site developer employs, and in many cases, that may be none at all. There is also no standard for data exchange. You could use the file transfer protocol (FTP) to transmit data from one location to another, but in doing so, you not only step out of the realm of the Web, but you are also limited to a single direction in which the data is exchanged. True data exchange would be bidirectional and allow transfers to take place over the Web. Products such as NetMeeting or Microsoft's Virtual Private Network can use the Internet for data exchange, but they use their own proprietary protocols and data-exchange methods.

Another sad reality of HTML and the Web is that there is little capability for personalization. HTTP cookies provide some level of personalization when a visitor browses a site, but this type of personalization is limited. Sites such as Microsoft's Investor or Expedia do take Web-site personalization a step further by allowing data exchange between the user's personal computer and the site. For example, the Investor site exchanges data with the popular personal financial management program Quicken to record, track, and display portfolio information, but it doesn't accomplish this feat through standard methods. The browsing visitor must be using Internet Explorer on a Windows-based platform, which means that the protocols, programs, and scripting methods used are tied to a particular operating system and browser.

Although proprietary in nature, such systems do demonstrate the Internet's potential, specifically in how the Web can offer tremendous personalization and interchange between local and remote systems. Yet, for these capabilities to be embraced throughout the Internet development community, we must move beyond the simple information-access and display standard HTML currently offers. Instead, there must be "an information understanding standard: a standard way of representing data so that software can better search, move, display, and otherwise manipulate information currently hidden in contextual obscurity," according to Microsoft's Site Builders Network XML section.

If you have worked with HTML at all, you know that HTML cannot provide the kind of capabilities Microsoft describes. HTML is used primarily for describing how a Web page should look, not how the data should be represented. When you examine HTML's limitations, you realize it would literally be impossible for HTML alone to provide standard ways for the following types of data interchange:

- Insurance companies sharing data about subscribers

- Decoding and processing electronic payment information

- Exchanging information about legal issues among lawyers, courts, judges, and litigants

- Sharing patient prescription and drug interaction information among doctors and pharmacists

- Creating company catalogs and sharing them with clients and salespeople, allowing both to place and take orders, browse the catalog, and view data on orders

You've probably seen these types of things on the Web already, and you might be thinking, "What do you mean HTML can't handle such data exchange?" It's true; you have seen these types of data exchange, but it's not HTML that handles it. HTML displays the results of searches or displays a form that will be sent to a remote Common Gateway Interface (CGI) script or database. Some sites might use Cold Fusion; others might use Perl to interface with Access databases. The point is that there is no standardization, and HTML alone cannot accomplish any of these feats.

TIP: *For a more detailed discussion of the differences between HTML and XML, read Chapter 3.*

What the Web needs is a language like HTML that provides a standard way to exchange data. The language must be flexible enough to allow users to create their own document definitions, whether they're sending electronic-payment information or standard search queries. XML is the Web's latest markup language for exchanging data. This new markup language is based on specifications outlined by the World Wide Web Consortium (W3C)—the Web's standards organization—and both Microsoft and Netscape are implementing it. The XML standard was created from a compilation of proposals submitted by sources such as Microsoft, ArborText, Netscape, and others.

XML Today

XML has attracted tremendous interest and support since it was first formulated in 1996. It provides a standard way to encode content and, more specifically, provide a way to create data structures in a flexible manner. XML uses the standard metaphor of element tags to mark up content based on a set of rules the document's developer has created. This set of rules is called the *Document Type Definition (DTD)*, and it allows developers to use XML to mark up a variety of documents, such as:

- A standard document that can contain text and links to graphics and external resources.

- A more structured document or record, such as an HTML form with a true structure encoded within the document. This category could include a purchase order, a medical prescription, an address book, or other types of documents with specific fields.

• An object with data and methods, such as a Java object or an ActiveX control.

• Database records that can be presented through a Web page, based on requests that browsing visitors submit to the database query engine.

• Metacontent, such as the content of an Internet Explorer channel.

• Anything else that provides data exchange between computers and people or between computers and computers or other types of processing machines.

Today, you can create all these types of documents with XML and use HTML and Dynamic HTML (DHTML) to present the content. XML also allows you to repurpose, or redefine and display, the content from a single source to a variety of different display mechanisms. For example, you could store a single database on a server and parse out the data to a number of different displays.

Here's a real-world, though somewhat futuristic, example. Suppose you own a restaurant and have your menu stored in a database. You have menu-display devices, little Palm-Pilot-type hand-held devices you distribute to all your customers. The waitpersons use the same type of hand-held devices to take orders. Orders are transmitted to the kitchen's receiving unit, which displays the order. When the chef prepares the meal, she marks off the order with the stroke of a pen.

You also service customers who order both takeout and delivery. They get their information about the specials of the day and the rest of your menu via your Web site. Some of your customers like to subscribe to the Daily Specials channel you've set up using Internet Explorer's Channels feature, which means your menu database gets lots and lots of use. You use the same database to manage your stock quantities. When someone orders a meal and the chef marks the order off as prepared and delivered, the stock levels in your food database are adjusted accordingly. Using additional Web automation tools, an order is automatically placed with your suppliers when quantities get low.

All the information in your database is used and reused in a variety of ways by your customers, your waitpersons, and your chefs. The relationships between the individual order and the food database do not necessarily reside in the schema data described by either the database of orders or the database of food. Instead, they are extensions defined by the instance of an order.

It is XML that provides all the structural representations of the data. The following code helps explain this point further:

```
<MEAL><ENTREE>Chicken Cordon Bleu</ENTREE></MEAL>
```

In this example, we included the **<ENTREE>** tag not so much to separate the entree from the rest of the meal record but rather to indicate that, in addition to being a part of the meal, it's the entree the diner has ordered. If your manager wanted to look at all the meals that have been ordered, he could. Because some people may only order dessert for their meal, he could also pull up all the entrees instead of the meals. Diners could also conduct their own searches to find out, for example, how many people ordered the Cordon Bleu and, if they are provided, read comments about the meal.

This example may work for the food and beverage industry, but what if the user wants to use XML for defining and keeping track of medical data, such as prescriptions? Because XML allows you to develop elements to suit your own needs, you could define elements that represent such things as dosages, generic drug names, doctors' names, patient names, and so forth. XML allows you to develop documents that have terms and definitions specific to the needs of the user. The specifications you use to describe your documents can be placed in a Document Type Definition—a separate document that sets the structure for your XML data—and can be used by many others, or it can be placed within the XML document itself.

Because the data is separate from the presentation, the same XML data (whether it's a menu or a prescription) could be presented in multiple ways on the user's desktop or laptop. It could even be presented on a hand-held device. An XML document does not by itself specify whether or how its information should be displayed. The XML document merely contains the data itself. With the help of the style-sheet mechanism, HTML is used to display the data. Either the Web server serving up the document or the Web browser displaying the document handles the conversion from XML data to HTML presentation. In addition, XML data can be updated automatically without having to refresh the entire page. Through this process of granular updating, XML allows the content of HTML pages to be more efficient and more dynamic.

How XML Looks

XML looks a lot like HTML, and it should, because both are derived from the same source, Standard Generalized Markup Language (SGML). Like an HTML document, an XML source document is made up of XML elements, each with a start-tag and an end-tag. The information between the tags, if there is any, is called the *content*. However, unlike HTML, XML allows for an unlimited set of tags that indicate what the data means, not how it should look. For example, this HTML element tag

```
<B>Cordon Bleu</B>
```

specifies that the title of the entree should appear in bold in the menu. But this XML element tag

```
<ENTREE>Cordon Bleu</ENTREE>
```

specifies that the same information is actually an entree. It's entirely up to the developer of the XML document to determine what tags are used and what content is placed within those tags. With HTML, the developer had to choose from a predetermined list of tags in order to display the data.

How to order and display the data is left up to the style-sheet mechanism. This allows the same information to be displayed in a variety of formats based on what style sheet is specified for a particular display. Let's take a closer look at some of the components of XML, how they work, and why becoming familiar with them is so important.

XML Components

Although you've already been introduced to some of the components of XML, we thought we would refresh your memory about the various pieces that make up an XML document. When we started exploring XML, even we had a hard time grasping some of the concepts because we were so used to working with HTML, a language that allows you to break all sorts of rules and requires little knowledge other than what a few tags do. XML is different, because you aren't just painting a picture on a page, you are constructing a document. The following sections describe the pieces you will use to construct your next XML masterpiece.

Elements

We've been somewhat casual in defining the term *element* for you, but we figured if you just stuck with us, you would catch on. In XML, an element is something that describes a piece of data. An element is different than the tag used in HTML, because the tag actually describes markup, not content. For example the **<B>** tag in HTML describes how the text should be marked up. In this case, the text would be marked up as bold:

```
<B>This is bold</B>
```

An element, on the other hand, is a fully formed application. It specifies how to handle the data contained within the start- and end-tags. For example, the paragraph element **<P>** specifies that the text contained within the start-tag **<P>** and the end-tag **</P>** should be structured as a paragraph:

```
<P>Now is the time for all good men
to come to the aid of their country.</P>
```

In XML, elements are really just storage containers for data. In HTML, tags are just indicators of where something should change in terms of the display. Every XML document has one main element that contains or holds all the data for the entire document. The following example will help you visualize exactly what we mean:

```
<BOOK>
<TITLE>XML Black Book</TITLE>
<TABLEOFCONTENTS>
Introduction
Chapter
Index
</TABLEOFCONTENTS>
<INTRODUCTION>
Welcome to the XML Black Book
</INTRODUCTION>
<CHAPTER>
<HEADING>Introduction</HEADING>
In this book we hope to examine everything there is about XML...
    .

    .

    .
</CHAPTER>
<INDEX>
List of INDEX content
</INDEX>
</BOOK>
```

Notice that the **<BOOK></BOOK>** element holds all the contents of this document. All the other elements, such as ****, are *subelements* nested below the **<BOOK>** element. More specifically, the **<BOOK>** element is the parent, and the rest of the elements are the descendents. The **<HEADING>** element, then, is actually a child of the **<CHAPTER>** element, which in turn is a child of the **<BOOK>** element. All these elements create the structure of the book; none of them create the look of the book. That is left up to the HTML tags used in the style sheet we assign to this document.

TIP: *For more information on elements, check out Chapter 7.*

Elements can contain a number of different types of content, including:

- Character data, such as text you would place in a document
- Other elements, called subelements or children, as outlined in the preceding paragraph

- **CDATA** sections, which are sections of the DTD that include literal data that the XML processor will ignore, such as scripting code that might be used to specify a JavaScript

- Processing instructions

- Comments

- White space

- Entity references

You declare elements either within the XML document or in a separate document, the Document Type Definition (DTD), by specifying the following information:

```
<!ELEMENT elementName content>
```

Attributes

Attributes are elements' best friends. They explain exactly how elements work, whether data is required by the element, and what entities can be included within the element. Attributes are basically just sources of additional information about an element. You can specify attributes and their values within a DTD or in the start-tag of an element. You choose where to place them.

Think back to our diner example and the **<MEAL>** element we specified. In order for us to know whether the meal was prepared or not, we could create an additional element and call it **<PREPARED>**, but in doing so, we would be creating an additional element that really is simply describing the **<MEAL>** element. So instead, we'll create an element attribute and specify the status of the meal within the attribute itself, as shown in the following example:

```
<MEAL PREPARED="no">Chicken Cordon Bleu</MEAL>
```

If we searched the database of orders, we could quickly query all the meals that had not been prepared. Of course, as we did with the element, we would have to declare our attribute within either the XML document or the external DTD. To do that, we would include the following code:

```
<!ATTLIST ElementName
AttributeName Type Default
(AttributeName Type Default...)>
```

TIP: *For more information on attributes, how to create them, and how to use them in XML documents, check out Chapter 8.*

Entities

As mentioned in Chapter 1, there are two types of entities: general and parameter. Without getting into the major differences, we'll explain simply that an entity is any piece of character data you may want to reference in a document. The character data, which is a section of text, can be one of the following:

- A reserved character that cannot be placed within an XML document without the processor assuming it is used for an intended purpose
- A group of character data that you don't want to have to type again and again throughout the document

Suppose we need to specify the angle bracket in the content of an XML document. If we placed an angle bracket by itself, the XML processor would assume we were declaring either an element or an attribute and expect that whatever follows is some sort of declaration. So, the following sentence would cause grief for an XML processor and would return an error:

```
<SENTENCE>In Math class, I never really could grasp which to use
to specify greater than, the < or the >.</SENTENCE>
```

Instead, we would use a general entity that is built into XML and used to specify such reserved characters. Then, our code would look something like this:

```
<SENTENCE>In Math class, I never really could grasp which to use
to specify greater than, the &lt; or the &gt;.</SENTENCE>
```

It would end up displaying something like this:

```
In Math class, I never really could grasp which to use
to specify greater than, the < or the >.
```

You can also use general entities to specify more mundane character data that you simply don't want to type again and again. For example, if you're tired of typing your address again and again on your Web pages, you could define an entity that contains your address. Then, just as you specified a general entity to depict a reserved character (as shown in the previous example), you could specify the entity you created throughout your document. In this chapter's Immediate Solutions section, we'll show you how to do just that.

Document Type Definitions

The Document Type Definition (DTD) is the construct that provides all the tools used to create XML documents. In the most basic terms, a Document Type Definition is a file that is separate from the main XML document and provides a set of rules for the XML document to which it is attached. DTDs set the instructions for the structure of the XML document and define what elements are going to be used throughout the document. In our previous example, we could have declared our **<ENTREE>** element in the restaurant's DTD along with all the other elements we would use. Declared entities for the document are also included in the DTD. Think of a DTD as a road map and rule book for the document. More specifically, the following features of an XML document are outlined within the DTD:

- The element types that will be allowed within the XML document

- The characteristics of each element type, along with the attributes used with each element and the content each element is capable of having

- Any notations that can be encountered within the document

- The entities that can be used within the document

It may sound like there are no rules governing XML, but that's actually not true. Sure, XML lets you develop your own element tags and also allows you to create attributes, or specific rules, for those tags. You can also create entities (pieces of character data you find yourself using again and again). But XML *does* have rules, and they are outlined in a document called the XML specification. The specification outlines exactly how elements must be declared and how XML must be constructed in order for XML processors (which interpret XML code) to process the XML information properly and send it on to the Web browser for display. Later in this chapter, we'll examine what the XML specification says and how to understand its rules. But first, let's take a step backward and talk a bit about the relatively short history of this powerful new markup language.

The Short History Of XML

It really started back in the 1960s when IBM started working on the Generalized Markup Language (GML). The developers needed a way to easily describe and exchange documents with most of the formatting left in place. They decided a generalized markup language—something that could provide a universal set of instructions—would work best, so they embarked on the long and arduous task of creating something that was extensible enough to work across different platforms. But the process of creating and implementing such a language and gaining widespread support for it wasn't easy.

Work on GML continued for many years, although acceptance was not quick or universal. Then in 1986, the International Organization for Standards (ISO) decided to adopt IBM's version of this generalized markup language, which then became known as the Standard Generalized Markup Language (SGML). Almost 20 years since the concept first came about, SGML became the markup language for many sophisticated documentation systems, because it provided a standard way to create, present, and exchange documents with other users regardless of the system or platform used. SGML also gave large organizations the flexibility to create their own document formats, offering a high level of sophistication not previously available. But with this high level of sophistication came problems. Mainly, the language was *too* sophisticated and *too* complex for many to use, particularly when it came to publishing smaller documents.

The Web's Debut

When the Web came into worldwide focus in the early '90s, SGML was tapped as the perfect language to use to develop a subset markup language that could in turn create Web pages. The features of SGML allowed a certain functionality that was perfectly suited for the delivery of documents across disparate systems. Hypertext Markup Language (HTML), which was an SGML application, was created by the World Wide Web Consortium.

HTML caught on quickly because it lacks almost all of SGML's complexity but still provides a fair number of SGML features, within a relatively simple group of predefined tags. It was the document-sharing features of SGML and the limited number of tags you had to learn with HTML that made it and the Web so enormously popular in such a short span of time. Virtually anyone could easily develop a Web page using only a few tags. No specialized programming knowledge was required. No real structure needed to be followed. In some cases, you could even bend the rules a bit—leaving out a quote here, a closing tag there—and the document would still display. HTML demanded little of its developers and, in return, provided a way for millions of people to make millions of Web pages.

However, HTML's simplicity quickly became its downfall. With its relatively easy text-oriented features and linking options, it worked well in the early days of Web development. But as prices for computers dropped in the mid-90s and more systems were shipped with multimedia features, the strain on HTML began to show. Developers quickly demanded more out of HTML and out of Web browsers. They wanted to create, enhance, and tie in more and more sophisticated features and options to Web pages. They wanted to make the Web the portal into anything and everything, from databases to cameras and from videos to radio stations. Seeing this need, many browser manufacturers quickly began creating their own customized tag sets or features, such as plug-ins, that extended the capability of the browser.

Browser developers, such as Netscape and Microsoft, started adding their own groups of tags and hooks into operating systems. This created a hodgepodge of Web features, many of which could only be viewed on one browser or another. The rampant modification of the HTML standard put a strain on developers, who had to keep up with all these new enhancements and feature sets. Also, it proved difficult for users, who simply wanted to view information across global networks with whatever browser or whatever computer they saw fit. Many sites were no longer compatible with standard browsers. Users were befuddled by pages that didn't load quite right or crashed their computers entirely. Soon, the strain of all these incompatibilities had all but sucked the life out of HTML.

Why wasn't HTML, this subset of the hugely capable SGML, able to withstand the pressure? Basically because, unlike SGML, HTML wasn't extensible. It had no room to grow, which, in the computer world, was a signal of certain and almost impending death. Sure, browser manufacturers like Netscape and Microsoft could add their own tags. But you, as a developer, were stuck with several choices: using HTML; being forced to use limited browser-specific tags; creating scripts that attached to outside resources; or simply forgetting the whole thing, giving up, and turning on *Baywatch*.

Although it has worked for some time to display simplistic pages, HTML is far from a true page-layout language. It doesn't allow you to structure your documents as you see fit. There are hooks to allow connections to Java, JavaScript, or Active Server Pages, but once again, as a developer you are stuck using what others have dictated; you have no control over your own developmental destiny.

The problem soon became, not which browser manufacturer will win out in the war of the browsers, but rather, how can the developer and end user win? The world simply was not—and will never be—ready to give up full control of the development of the Web to a single software vendor. If it did, it would literally end innovation. Why research, develop, and create new things when there is no competition and no need to stay on top of advances? No, a better way is to come up with an extensible, expandable, flexible markup language that can use many of the best features of SGML while still utilizing all the great options HTML has to offer. The best of both worlds means creating something in between SGML and HTML. XML is the best of both worlds.

The Beginning Of XML

It was back in 1996 that XML really got started. Publishing gurus and Web nerds got together and came up with an idea to create a subset of SGML that would work specifically on the Web. The idea was to create this subset called the Extensible Markup Language—*extensible* meaning expandable—so that it used all the advanced structural markup features without the complexity of SGML.

The first working draft outlining the XML specification was published in November 1996. Not too much later, in January 1997, the first XML parser appeared, and in March 1997, the first XML applications, such as Lark, started to appear. Then, in the fall, support for XML was implemented in Microsoft's Internet browser. Finally, in February 1998, the XML 1 recommendation was published, and support for this new Web-based development language grew.

XML promises to give developers the tools needed to produce new kinds of applications—advanced applications that span not only simple Web pages, but also databases, electronic commerce systems, and virtually any display system possible. XML can do this, because, unlike HTML, XML is all about data. XML concentrates on forming the data that will be presented and leaves the presentation to HTML-oriented style sheets.

XML also brings great promise to intranets by giving developers the ability to link to databases regardless of the system used. More importantly, XML gives developers the ability to create customized data structures for particular industry-specific needs. These data structures and databases can be viewed with a variety of devices, without the need for custom-built interfaces to view the same data on each different display device. Eventually, no more warning signs will appear on sites saying "Best Viewed With Netscape" or "This Site Requires Internet Explorer." Instead, any XML-enabled browser will be able to interpret and display the data created with XML.

Vendor Support For XML In Browsers

You are probably thinking, "Why would vendors support something like XML, a markup language that serves to take away their competitive advantage?" True, XML does level the playing field greatly, but the features vendors have already placed in their browsers will still be developed. More importantly, however, instead of using their own specialized languages, they can use XML to develop their own XML applications. Such XML applications have already been developed and are continuing to be developed and placed within the latest versions of browsers. Microsoft's Internet Explorer Channel Definition Format (CDF) is one prime example of how XML only helps to augment a browser. Vendors will continue to create new XML applications and most likely will continue to add their own tags.

> *WARNING!   At the time this book was written, both Microsoft and Netscape were in the process of implementing XML in their browsers. Some of the more technical aspects may have changed since this book was printed. You should check the development sections of both companies' Web sites for any changes to these products.*

Currently, XML is supported in a variety of browsers, editors, parsers, and development products. Both Internet Explorer versions 4 and 5 offer XML support, although it is somewhat limited in version 4. Netscape has also added XML support in Navigator version 5. Both companies implement XML in varying ways and to varying degrees. Let's take a look at how each company implements XML in their browsers.

Microsoft Internet Explorer

Microsoft is actually one of the first developers to add XML support within its browser. Obviously, Microsoft saw how beneficial XML support could be for its product, and how, in conjunction with scripting languages, it extends the functionality of the browser. XML support appeared first in Internet Explorer 4 and continues to extend to Internet Explorer 5. Let's look at the type of support each version of Internet Explorer offers.

TIP: *In this chapter, we simply want to give you an idea of what you can expect so you'll realize the wide range of support XML already has. If you need detailed information about XML support within browsers, check out Chapter 23.*

Internet Explorer 4

Internet Explorer was the first browser to offer a relatively complete array of support for XML. The browser is bundled with a C++ parser, which is used to parse XML documents. The parser also supports the XML object model. What the object model offers the developer is the ability to interact with and manipulate individual XML elements as independent objects. With Internet Explorer, XML elements become objects, which in turn can be referred to and manipulated by programming and scripting languages to perform whatever function you want them to perform.

In terms of displaying XML, Microsoft has provided the XML Data Source Object (XML DSO) feature. This feature, which uses the data-binding facility in Dynamic HTML, displays XML as HTML. But XML support in Internet Explorer 4 doesn't stop there. Version 4 also includes a technology preview release of Microsoft's Extensible Style Sheet Language processor, called MSXSL. This processor lets developers turn XML data into HTML by using a style sheet to define the presentation rules for the XML data.

Internet Explorer 5

Never wanting to stay too far behind the curve, Microsoft once again upgraded its popular Internet Explorer browser and added quite a few new XML-related features. The folks at Redmond have extended the XML support in this version considerably, and undoubtedly Microsoft will continue to include as much XML-specific code in subsequent versions.

First, they've shored up the inconsistencies and instabilities that are somewhat apparent in Internet Explorer 4. This means that when you are viewing XML documents, your browser is less likely to crash. The code now matches the XML 1 specification, whereas version 4 still had some incompatibilities. Also, the browser now works as an optional validating processor. The Java parser is also slated to become part of the browser.

Version 5 now allows embedding of XML in HTML, and a new XML-based feature called *scriptlets* lets you store the JavaScript code outside of the page, which means you can more easily manage your scripts. Microsoft has also added behaviors to style sheets. If it is programmed properly, you can use Cascading Style Sheet (CSS) tags to make version 5 display XML elements.

TIP: *At the time this book was written, the Cascading Style Sheet feature still required the entire XML code to be placed in the HTML document. Microsoft was working on implementing the code into the top-level text/xml and application/xml media types.*

Netscape Navigator

Admittedly, Netscape has been much slower at jumping on the XML bandwagon. Microsoft included XML support in its browser as early as the fall of 1997, but it took Netscape much longer to display specific XML support in its Navigator browser. It wasn't until spring 1998 that Netscape announced that a future component of Netscape Communicator would provide true XML support. However, once Netscape realized the need for XML implementation in its browser, the amount of support the company outlined far outpaced Microsoft's first XML offering.

Netscape originally showed off its support of XML at an XML developer's conference in early 1998. The company presented its new browser, at that time code-named Aurora and now named Communicator 5, displaying XML documents. At the conference, Netscape vowed to fully support XML as a data and metadata syntax.

To support XML, Netscape placed an XML parser within the browser and added application support for the XLink, XML's linking specification. Also included is support for XML namespaces. In an effort to display all this XML code, Netscape, like Microsoft, takes advantage of Cascading Style Sheets (CSS), which format the text encoded within the XML tags. Netscape also supports *transclusions*. Transclusions are tags that mark an object to be included by reference.

Netscape does all this through the emerging standard framework for metadata called the *Resource Description Framework* (RDF). RDF, which was built on XML, provides a single mechanism for organizing, describing, and navigating information on Web sites. With RDF, a single interface—Communicator—manages and integrates information from Web sites, push channels, bookmarks, email, and legacy database systems. Undoubtedly, Netscape will add even more support in the future as their browser and server products continue to evolve.

TIP: *For more information on Netscape's XML implementation, see Netscape's Developer Network at **developer. netscape.com**.*

The XML Specification

The World Wide Web Consortium (W3C) can best be described as the Web's governing body. This organization sets the standards for the languages used to deliver information to Web users. The W3C was responsible for formulating HTML and is doing the same with XML. Having a single governing body decide how the language should evolve creates a standard that software developers can adhere to. Many companies and individuals have contributed to the creation of the XML specification. A short list of those individuals and companies include Jon Bosak of Sun, Tim Bray of Textuality and Netscape, Jean Paoli of Microsoft, Dave Hollander of Hewlett-Packard, Eve Maler of ArborText, and Joel Nava of Adobe. All the people and companies involved have offered or submitted ideas, information, and programming support to help write what is known as the XML specification, a relatively small (about 50 pages) document that outlines the semantics of XML. The entire list of editors and contributors is listed at the end of the specification.

The XML specification is the single most important document you'll need to study if you plan on learning XML inside and out. It is basically the official definition on how XML works and how you should use XML to design DTDs, elements, attributes, and entities. It's not the easiest thing to read and understand, however, which is why we've included a section here about the specification and, more importantly, about how to decipher some of the rather cryptic information contained within it. If you plan to create your own DTDs, you'll need to learn exactly how to read the specification and put the information to good use, because the document defines what is and isn't legal for XML.

> **WARNING!**   The specification may have changed since this book was written. For the most up-to-date information on the specification, check out www.w3.org/XML.

At the time this book was written, the XML specification was finalized and reviewed by the W3C members and endorsed by the W3C director as an official W3C recommendation.

How Specifications Are Created

When a markup language such as XML is created, it goes through a lengthy process. First, the need is realized, and the W3C forms a working group to address the issue and create a specification. Specifications must be formally approved by the W3C's membership, which is made up of many industry software and hardware leaders. A working draft is created, followed by a proposed recommendation and then a final recommendation.

The working group submits a working draft to the W3C director as a proposed recommendation. After the director approves the document, it becomes the official proposed recommendation that is forwarded to the W3C membership. The membership votes on whether the recommendation should become an official W3C recommendation, which signals widespread support for the proposed topic. The W3C advisory committee votes yes, yes with comments, or no. If a no vote is cast, the committee thinks the entire recommendation should be abandoned. If a yes vote is cast, or a yes with comments, the recommendation is adopted, press releases are sent out, testimonials are gathered, and champagne flows all around.

Overview Of The XML Specification

The XML specification, like almost all others, is broken down into a number of sections, each describing a certain part of the language. The specification itself is a simple document that can be read within your Web browser or viewed in a variety of other formats. Because we know how confusing the document seems at first glance and how we wish someone had explained it to us the first time we read it, we'll outline exactly how to read it. The entire specification is included in Appendix B of this book. You might want to flip back and forth between this chapter and the specification as you learn how to read and understand the document. Each W3C specification, by the way, is written in pretty much the same format, so learning how to read the specification will help you to understand XML and other W3C recommendations.

At the top is the header section (see Figure 2.1). It includes the version number, the various formats in which you can view the specification, and the names and

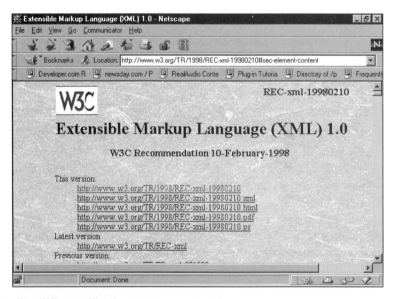

Figure 2.1   The XML specification header.

email addresses of the editors. This section also provides links to all versions of the specification. Make sure you look for the latest version; previous drafts of the document may not contain the most up-to-date information.

Following the header is a brief abstract that describes what the specification is and does. The abstract spells out exactly what XML is in a succinct fashion:

"The Extensible Markup Language (XML) is a subset of SGML that is completely described in this document. Its goal is to enable generic SGML to be served, received, and processed on the Web in the way that is now possible with HTML. XML has been designed for ease of implementation and for interoperability with both SGML and HTML."

The next section is called "Status Of this Document." It describes the current status of both the specification and the recommendation process. This section also outlines exactly who is responsible for the document and where you can gather more information about XML. Finally, it includes information about the terminology that appears in the document and the standards used throughout. The status section is followed by a hyperlinked table of contents and an introduction.

After the introduction, which includes a statement of the goals for XML, there is a list of terms (with definitions) used throughout the specification. The next section provides the complete syntax for creating and using XML documents and includes examples and syntax definitions for each component of XML, such as elements, entities, **CDATA** sections, and so on.

The next section includes some additional appendices that list references and information about character classes, XML and SGML, and character encodings. The document ends with more links and information about the people responsible for developing the specification.

Sections Of The XML Specification

Let's quickly examine each section of the specification, so you can find the information you need. The hypertext links that are highlighted throughout the specification will take you to explanations of the various terms and concepts and point you to additional information in other sites and other XML-related specifications.

Section 1: Introduction

The introduction gives you a brief overview of XML. Within a single paragraph, it introduces you to the basic concepts, such as entities, characters, character data, and markup. It also outlines the origins and goals of XML. To help you understand the rest of the specification, it's important to read and understand the terminology in this section.

Section 2: Documents

"Documents" describes what an XML document is and what makes up a well-formed and valid document. It lists the elements used in a document and defines how documents should be expressed. This section also outlines the character data and markup syntax used in documents. It shows you how to include comments in an XML document and what processing instructions look like and how they should be specified. It explains the DTD and its declaration, how to handle white space, and how to define different languages within the document.

Section 3: Logical Structures

"Logical Structures" explains what elements can appear in an XML document and how empty elements and end-tags are used. In this section, you'll learn how well-formed XML documents are created and what attribute values need to be declared. If you need to know how to specify any kind of element, attribute, or empty element, this is the section you'll need to read. You'll also learn what content is valid element content and how to properly nest elements and work with mixed-content data. Finally, this section explains how to declare attribute lists.

Section 4: Physical Structures

"Physical Structures" describes everything you would ever want to know about entities. In technical terms, entities are storage units that can appear in XML documents. Both character and entity references are defined and explained, as are parsed entities. You'll learn how XML deals with interpreting character and entity reference. Character encodings and how XML processors treat entities and references are discussed at some length. Predefined entities and notation declarations are also listed within this section.

Section 5: Conformance

"Conformance" explains how XML processors work. If you plan on developing XML processors, or if you simply want to know how processors take data and process it, you need to read this section. If you don't really care what goes on behind the scenes, you can skip this section. The section has plenty of links to information about XML processing.

Section 6: Notation

"Notation" is the actual formal grammar used in the XML specification. It's somewhat boring, but it helps to explain the various notations used throughout the specification. We suggest that you read this section first so you can familiarize yourself with the notations.

Appendices

The "Appendices" lists all the references that are used throughout the specification. This section will be useful if you need additional information or want to contact the people who actually helped write the specification.

How To Read And Understand The Specification

Knowing how to read the specification is paramount to really understanding how XML is structured. There are six major sections you need to understand; the first three are helpful for those who are simply building XML documents and not creating XML processors. You should pay close attention to the second section, "Documents," because it includes the definitions for such things as well-formed documents, elements, and other XML components. Although we'll cover most of what is included in the specification, you should still read through the entire document at least twice. The first reading will give you an overview. With the second reading, the information will start to sink in.

TIP: *One of the best ways to read the XML specification is to use Tim Bray's Annotated XML Specification. This site is both frame and Java enabled. The important parts of the specification are annotated and explained in plain English. You'll find the Annotated XML Specification at www.xml.com/axml/axml.html.*

A couple things you should pay special attention to are the boxes of text you'll see throughout the specification and the hypertext links. The boxed text defines what are called the *production rules*, which are necessary for creating well-formed or valid XML code (see Figure 2.2).

To understand the specification, you need to know how to read the production rules. The specification follows what is called the Extended Backus-Naur Form (EBNF) notation, which was developed by computer scientists in the 1960s as a

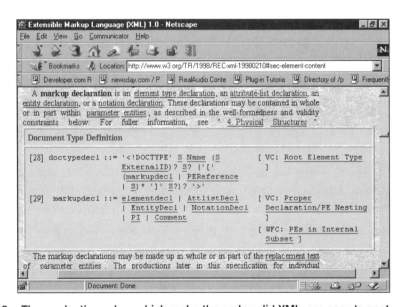

Figure 2.2   The production rules, which make the code valid XML, are easy to spot.

way to standardize syntax rules for computer languages. It's basically a standard notation for stating the syntax of any formal computer language, and it can be a bit difficult to read.

Production Rules

Reading a production rule is much like reading a mathematical equation. Basically, the statement on the right side of the equal sign is equivalent to the statement on the left. Here's what a standard production rule looks like:

```
[1] symbol ::=expression
```

The number within the bracket is the number of production rule. Production rules appear in boxes, as do the examples. The difference between a production rule and an example is that there is no number in an example. The word **symbol** refers to the rule's name. The **::=** symbol separates the symbol from the expression. The word **expression** refers to the definition of the symbol or what the symbol is supposed to do.

Before you can really understand production rules, you should know the following rules for production rules. (So many rules, so little time!) These rules are part of the EBNF syntax. First, let's take a look at the production rule for comments (remember that **[15]** specifies the production rule; the actual rule follows):

```
[15] Comment ::= '<!--' ((Char - '-') | ('-' (Char - '-')))*'- - >'
```

The rules for the production rules are as follows:

- The elements will appear within the production rule in the order in which they should appear.
- A vertical slash or pipe character between symbols—as shown between the first character and second character specification in the preceding code example—indicates that only one option can be chosen and included with the element. Those choices are placed within the parentheses, but they can also be specified in square brackets.
- Any information that is placed within parentheses is considered a regular expression. A regular expression is a sequence of elements that can be expressed in a single pattern.
- Comments within the production rule itself are specified by the /* text representation.
- An asterisk, when not used within comments, specifies that a symbol can appear zero or more times within the production rule.

- Characters or symbols that are enclosed in square brackets ([ ]) define a range of values or a list of values from which you can choose.

- If a left square bracket is followed by a caret symbol, such as **[^&]***, the characters or symbols that follow the **[** and **^** symbols must be excluded from the definition. Some exclusions are nested within already defined symbols. And some exclusions include an asterisk that isn't within comments. Remember that the asterisk is telling you that certain characters are being excluded.

- Any characters that are within single or double quotation marks are considered literals.

- A plus sign (**+**) means one or more symbols must occur.

- The S stands for white space within a literal character string.

- A rule followed by **[VC:...]** must apply if the resulting XML production is to be valid. **VC** stands for validity constraint.

- A rule that starts with **[WFC:...]** must apply if the XML production is to be well-formed. Pay particular attention to these types of rules because you need to follow these rules in order to create a well-formed document. **WFC** stands for well-formedness constraint.

An Overview Of XML Applications

By now, you know that XML gives developers the ability to create their own set of elements, their own attributes, and even their own entities. Because of this flexibility, all sorts of vocabularies (or sets of XML components) can be created as standards for various industries or types of Web functions. An XML vocabulary is a set of elements and rules for creating a particular structure and syntax to meet a particular need. For example, the Mathematical Markup Language is an XML vocabulary that is an XML DTD that allows the XML developer to create mathematical equations within a Web page. This information is defined in the XML DTD, which can be stored within the XML document or stored outside the document and specified in the XML document header. Think of XML as the grammar and the particular application—such as the Channel Definition Format—as the vocabulary.

Collections of different XML applications have already been created. These various XML applications fall within one of three categories:

- *Horizontal-industry applications/vocabularies*—Push-based delivery, software distribution, searching/filtering, e-commerce, and so on

- *Vertical-industry applications/vocabularies*—Pharmaceuticals, telecommunications, aerospace, and so on

- *Internal applications/corporate vocabularies*—Internal data processes

There are a handful of horizontal, vertical, and industry-specific internal XML applications either in the process of development or fully developed. Sometimes referred to as *frameworks*, some of the most popular applications include:

- *Channel Definition Format (CDF)*—The Channel Definition Format lets developers publish Web-based content automatically to subscribers through a variety of different methods, such as a Web browser, an Active Desktop component, HTML-formatted email, and Web crawlers. A channel is a set of HTML-formatted documents that can be sent to a client in a group or individually. The channel is defined through XML, and such information as the subelements contained within the channel, the update schedule, and the delivery mechanism are part of the definition. This is an example of a horizontal vocabulary.

- *Chemical Markup Language (CML)*—The Chemical Markup Language was invented by British chemists for the purpose of exchanging descriptions of formulas, molecules, and other chemical specifications between people and computers. You can use CML for accomplishing such tasks as rendering 2D and 3D molecules. This is an example of a vertical vocabulary.

- *Distribution and Replication Protocol (DRP)*—DRP is a new protocol that has been proposed by Marimba Corporation. DRP is intended to optimize and speed up delivery of information over the Internet. It does so by creating an index of data and keeping track of software versions when content, data, or applications are updated via the Internet. This is an example of a horizontal vocabulary.

- *Mathematical Markup Language (MathML)*—This vocabulary was created primarily for supporting the need to display and exchange mathematical formulas and symbols. You can use MathML in specialized applications to render mathematical content and notation over both the Internet and an intranet. This is an example of a vertical vocabulary.

- *Open Financial Exchange (OFE or OFX)*—The OFX vocabulary or format is used by both Intuit's Quicken and Microsoft's Money. This vocabulary framework sets the standard for communication among financial software applications and financial institutions. This is an example of a vertical and internal vocabulary.

- *Open Software Description (OSD)*—Microsoft and Marimba understood there was a need to create a standard for distributing software over the Internet. Their standard, called the Open Software Description, uses unique XML element tags to describe the delivery of software applications over the Internet. These elements describe such things as the version of the product, the platform on which the product should work, and the upgrade mechanism. Software packages can be delivered by using the Channel Definition Format, which means software can now be updated with a push method on a specific schedule. This is an example of a horizontal vocabulary.

- *Resource Description Framework (RDF)*—RDF is a framework for specifying general-purpose Web metadata, such as security information, content information, subject-heading information, copyright notices, and so on. RDF is a standard framework that can include many other vocabularies. This is an example of a internal vocabulary.

- *Synchronized Multimedia Integration Language (SMIL)*—The SMIL vocabulary assists developers in integrating multimedia into their sites. SMIL provides a standardized way to describe multimedia and the various components needed to use, display, and manipulate multimedia on the Internet. This is an example of a vertical vocabulary.

- *Web Interface Definition Language (WIDL)*—WIDL is an object-oriented XML application. WIDL is best described as an automation tool used to enable automation of all interactions with HTML and XML documents. WIDL-defined services map existing Web content into program variables, making Web resources available, without modification, in formats suited for integration with diverse business systems. This is an example of a horizontal and internal vocabulary.

XML has come a long way in a short period of time. It has gathered a great deal of support from those in the Web-development community who want more than just a simple display markup language, such as HTML. The XML specification includes the new features XML offers and gives you a detailed outline of how XML is structured. By now, you should be familiar with the specification and know how to access it.

Immediate Solutions

In this section, you'll create the parts of an XML document. You'll declare an element, an attribute, and an entity. You'll also learn how to read the XML specification and interpret production rules.

Specifying Parameters

Each XML document must first specify its parameters, either in the beginning of the document, after the XML declaration **<?XML version="1.0"?>** (but before the content of the document), or within the **!DOCTYPE** declaration that specifies the DTD. For example, if you want to specify a DTD called memo.dtd, which had already been created for memo-type documents and stored on a remote server with the URL **http://www.site.com/dtd**, you would supply the following line of code after the XML declaration:

```
<!DOCTYPE MEMO SYSTEM "http://www.site.com/dtd/memo.dtd">
```

After you've defined the parameters—where the element, attribute, and entity declarations will be stored—you can either define or refine them. In the next section, you'll learn how to declare elements, specify their attributes, declare entities, and use character entities that are already part of the XML standard.

Defining An Element

To define an element, decide what name you want to use. The name will be referenced throughout the XML document with start- and end-tags. You can declare the element in the DTD or at the beginning of the XML document itself. The element must be composed of letters, digits, periods, dashes, underscores, or colons, and it must always be enclosed in angle brackets. The keyword **!ELEMENT** is used to define it as an element. There are four types of element content:

- *A mixed-content declaration*—allows for both elements and character data

- *A list of elements*—specifies a single or multiple element tag listed within the content section of the element declaration

- *The keyword **EMPTY***—specifies that the element contains no content
- *The keyword **ANY***—allows the element to contain any type of data or markup

To create an element named paragraph with the content type specified as **ANY**, insert the following code:

```
<!ELEMENT paragraph ANY>
```

Using An Element To Tag Content

To tag content with the element you've just defined, place a start-tag and an end-tag around it. Before you do, however, you must ensure than the element's content type matches the type of content in the document. If the element type is a list of other elements, only those elements specified in the definition of the element can be included within the start- and end-tags. To use the paragraph element you've just defined to mark up content, place the following tags around the content you want to specify as a paragraph:

```
<PARAGRAPH>This is the paragraph element's content.</PARAGRAPH>
```

Defining An Attribute

When you define an attribute to further clarify the meaning of an element, you need to declare the attribute either at the beginning of your XML document or within the DTD specified in the **!DOCTYPE** declaration. Attribute specifications can appear only within start-tags and empty-element tags. The attribute's first value is the name of the element to which it applies. You can include the element attribute directly after the element declaration in the DTD or the document, although it is not required. Once you've specified the name of the element the attribute is associated with, specify the attribute definition list, consisting of the attribute name, the attribute type, and any declared value. All attribute names must follow the same naming conventions as elements must follow. To define an attribute for the paragraph element in the preceding section, use the following code:

```
<!ATTLIST PARAGRAPH
          TYPE     CDATA     #IMPLIED>
```

Placing A Character Entity In A Document

To use special reserved characters within a document, you need to use a character entity that has already been defined within the XML standard. For example, if you want to use the ampersand sign (&) in the name of a company, you need to specify the XML character entity that represents the ampersand, because the ampersand is used to specify built-in character entities.

Entities that represent reserved characters always start with an ampersand, are followed by the entity name, and are closed by adding a semicolon to the end of the entity name. No additional white space is permitted around or inside the entity. To specify a built-in entity, place the following code within the content of your XML document:

```
&amp;
```

This code can be used anywhere within the content of an XML document, for example:

```
Welcome to the Diggins &amp; Kirk Consulting Firm!
```

The content, once processed, would display as follows:

```
Welcome to the Diggins & Kirk Consulting Firm!
```

Creating Your Own Entity

To create your own entities to specify groups of character data, you must first declare them in your DTD or within the beginning of your XML document as you do with elements and attributes. The name of the entity can be made up of letters, digits, periods, dashes, underscores, or a colon and must begin with a letter or an underscore. The value of the entity, called the entity definition, must be enclosed in quotes and can contain any valid markup. The syntax of an entity declaration is the entity element **!ENTITY**, the name of the entity, and then the entity declaration. To define an entity that specifies the city and state, Anchorage, Alaska, include the following code in your XML document or within your DTD:

```
<!ENTITY AK "Anchorage, Alaska">
```

Using The Entity You Have Declared

Once you have declared an entity, you can place it anywhere within the content of the XML document. The entity reference must start with an ampersand (&), include the entity name, and end with a semicolon (;). Case is important, so if you've defined an entity in uppercase, you must also use uppercase when you place the entity notation in the document. To place the previously defined entity in your document, use the following code where you want the entity value to display within the content:

```
Kirk Consulting is located in beautiful downtown &AK.
```

This would be processed through the XML processor and displayed within the XML application accordingly:

```
Kirk Consulting is located in beautiful downtown Anchorage, Alaska.
```

Reading The XML Specification

The XML specification is a difficult document to digest in a single pass. However, you must read the specification and familiarize yourself with it. Although it isn't a tutorial, the XML specification is the definitive guide to the XML syntax and to the rules for creating XML documents and XML options, such as entities, elements, and attributes. In this section, you'll learn how to locate the latest version of the specification and how to read and interpret it.

Locating The Latest Version Of The XML Specification

The XML specification is located at the World Wide Web Consortium's Web site (**www.w3.org/XML**). To locate the most up-to-date version of the specification, follow these steps:

1. Start your browser, and type "http://www.w3.org/XML" in the address field (without the quotes).

2. Click on the Events/Specs link at the top of the page.

3. Locate and click on the XML 1.0 Recommendation link. All other links lead to either older versions or other XML-related specifications still in the works.

4. This link should take you to the most recent version of the specification. If it doesn't say *Latest Version*, scroll down until you see a Latest Version link, and click on it.

Reading And Understanding The XML Specification

This section is meant to give you some practice reading the XML specification. You'll learn how to navigate the specification and find the sections you need. Follow these steps:

1. Locate the latest version of the specification.

2. Scroll down to the table of contents.

3. Locate Section 6 (Notations) in the table of contents, and click on the link to move to the "Notations" section of the document.

4. Read through the brief list of notations so you will know when certain character strings specify various parameters in XML syntax. Once you've familiarized yourself with the notations, scroll back to the table of contents at the top of the specification.

5. Click the link entitled 3.3 Attribute-List Declarations. This section includes information about defining attributes.

6. Read the first section about what an attribute is and what can be included in an attribute list. Take a look at the production rules [52] and [53]. Note what needs to be included within the attribute list definition in the production rule box.

7. Read through the rest of the attribute information until you get to the section "Validity Constraint: Fixed Attribute Default." The blue box displays an example of how you can create an attribute list with a fixed value set as the default. This is a real-world example you can use or modify—it is not just the production rule syntax as is specified in most of the production rule boxes.

8. For a clearer understanding of the XML specification, make sure you also read through Tim Bray's Annotated XML Specification located at **www.xml.com/xml/pub/axml/axmlintro.html**. You must be using a frames-enabled or Java-enabled browser to read the Annotated XML Specification.

Chapter 3

XML Best Practices

By Cheryl Kirk

In Depth

Face it. The Web, for all its wonders, is pretty dead. HTML's limitations are becoming apparent and have all but stymied the creativity that visionary designers like yourself thrive on. Sure, tables let you do some nifty things, and there is hope on the horizon with Dynamic HTML (DHTML). But, be honest. Tables barely offer you the ability to handle the dynamic data you have tucked away in those company databases. Also, DHTML does little good if half your visitors are Netscape Navigator users who won't be able to take advantage of your sites. XML, when it's combined with the Extensible Style Language (XSL), provides the answer to all your nondynamic and dynamic dilemmas. It brings data to the Web—and at just the right time—in a much better way than HTML and in a more compatible fashion than browser-specific options.

In this chapter, you'll learn why HTML has reached its breaking point and what you can do about it. Specifically, you'll learn how you can use XML to move beyond the limitations of HTML. In addition, you'll learn how closely related the two markup languages really are. At this point, you should be ready to graduate from using the **<BLINK>** tag and are champing at the bit to test your XML wings. If so, then read on and you'll learn the right habits for creating good XML. You'll learn where HTML has lost its momentum and, more importantly, some of the pitfalls you might run into when you are designing your first XML document. Finally, you'll learn what is involved in converting your existing HTML documents to XML.

From HTML To XML

Almost all documents on the Web are stored in HTML format or are transmitted into HTML format from server-side scripting. The language is relatively small and compact, which allows documents to be transmitted quickly. Because only a small set of elements have been defined, there is no need to transmit any additional language specifications or document definitions with an HTML document. A page can be built quickly by using any of the defined elements. HTML dictates the rules and you follow them. Sure, you can mix and match elements to create whatever effect you want, but just like thousands of other HTML developers, you are restricted to using the defined tags to describe and create your documents. Although it's easy to create documents this way, it severely limits your development capabilities. Specifically, HTML doesn't allow the developer to extend, structure, or validate the design of the document.

HTML's Lack Of Extensibility

When you first learned about the various elements HTML offered, it may have seemed like a daunting task to master it all. Not only did you have to memorize all those tags and what they did, but you also had to remember their attributes, the key features each element tag offered. But after a while, with only some 40-odd major element tags to learn, using HTML tags probably became second nature. When you wanted something to appear bold within the browser, you used the **<B>** element. If you needed a different font size, you used the **<FONT>** element and specified the **SIZE** attribute. And if you wanted to place a link to another document on the page, the anchor element, **<A>**, worked just fine, provided you included the URL in the **HREF** attribute of the anchor tag.

But what if you wanted to define a special tag to specify that the text was actually a date? Or what if you wanted the ability to mark up your document and specify where certain chunks and types of data were located? You can mix and match HTML elements to get a variety of results on the screen, but you can't create your own element tags and give them specific attributes. There is no way to describe the data you are presenting in an HTML document. It's this lack of extensibility that has brought HTML to the breaking point. HTML serves a great purpose in displaying data, but it doesn't allow developers to extend beyond the limited parameters of the predefined tags. We'll examine this limitation in greater detail in the section "The Differences Between XML And HTML" later in this chapter and show you how limiting HTML can be when you start to consider the type of data you are presenting.

HTML's Lack Of A Clearly Defined Structure

HTML fails to provide any clearly defined structure for documents. There is no way, outside of scripting, that you can present a database full of data by using just HTML. No hierarchies exist within HTML. Instead, every document created in HTML is flat. There is no depth to the document, only links out of and away from the document. This creates a problem for you when you are designing the data within a document and a problem for users when they are discovering the data.

From the design perspective, you must think ahead, break apart the data manually, and then create a visual representation of it. This is time-consuming for not only you, the developer, but also for visitors to your site. It prevents visitors from really discovering the data you have to offer in their own unique ways. Visitors must take your word that the data is presented in the best way it can be. Just think how many times you've run across a site and thought, I can't find a thing here. Chances are you moved on to another site where the presentation of information was logical and allowed you to easily find what you needed. With XML, you can create structures for data—with HTML, you can't.

HTML's Lack Of Structure Validation

Because there is no structure to an HTML document, it can't be checked for structural validity. HTML lacks support for any kind of language specification that applications use to check for valid document structure. The browser simply views the data and displays it. The developer of the HTML document may have left out the **<HEAD>** element or accidentally placed the **<BODY>** element before the **<HEAD>** element. In such a case, the browser may leave out some content because of the odd structure, causing problems for those who came to the site for information.

The Differences Between XML And HTML

XML is an excellent vehicle for manipulating structured data on the Web. Because of HTML's ability to present data, the two markup languages actually complement each other. When you stop considering the presentation of data and start concentrating on the structure of documents, you start to see XML's usefulness. Unlike HTML, XML is an excellent markup language for building complex Web applications. But, don't worry. Your knowledge of HTML will actually help you learn XML. The transition from HTML to XML will be quicker, and the concepts outlined in the XML specification will be easier to understand.

XML is an excellent language to use when you've outgrown the simple presentation options HTML has to offer. Microsoft Internet Explorer supports XML with the data-binding capability of Dynamic HTML (DHTML) and the Channel Definition Format (CDF), and Netscape Navigator offers similar support. Because both of today's popular browsers support the Document Object Model (DOM), the elements you're accustomed to using can now be defined in XML as objects. This means you can program them through scripting languages, giving them the ability to come alive and not just blink. This extensibility makes XML the ideal language to use when you need to display dynamic data on different platforms.

To you, the developer, what all this means is that you can now supply your site with a plethora of dynamic content, and you don't have to worry about any of the limitations of HTML. XML not only lets you specify dynamically changing data in your documents, it also enables you to create data sources that can be used for a variety of purposes, which in turn makes interoperability between applications on a server or client machine and your site a reality.

In more basic terms, XML and HTML differ in three major aspects:

- With XML, you can define your own set of tags and attribute names whenever you need to.

- With XML, document structures can be nested to any level of complexity, assuming they following the XML rules of proper nesting.

- XML documents can contain an optional description of the document's grammar so other applications that need to perform validation on the document's structure can do so.

As you may have gathered by now, XML differs from HTML in some relatively fundamental ways. That doesn't mean learning XML requires you to tear down everything you've ever learned about using HTML—quite the contrary. As a matter of fact, there are numerous similarities between XML and HTML, and you'll soon see that the languages look very similar and work in much the same way. Because both XML and HTML originate from Standard Generalized Markup Language (SGML), the granddaddy of markup languages, features such as syntax, elements, rules, and design principles are similar.

Comparing HTML Code To XML Code

Both XML and HTML use or are made up of elements. You may not be familiar with the term *elements*, but you've used them again and again. Most likely, you're familiar with the term *tags*. In Chapter 1, you learned that tags are actually just parts of elements. Specifically, tags are the parts of elements that either start or end them. In technical terms, a tag is a singular entity that opens or closes an element. The **<P>** tag—which in HTML marks up the text that follows it as a paragraph element—is an example of an opening tag (or start-tag). If you have been minding your p's and q's, you may already be using good HTML by including the end-tag **</P>** to close the paragraph element. Both the start- and end-tags and the content enclosed between them represent the entire element.

HTML and XML use elements to itemize where text should be marked up, which in turn is used to describe the content of a document. But you'll notice a big difference between HTML and XML when you start examining XML more closely. Unlike HTML, XML does not describe how content should be displayed. Instead, XML describes what the content is. Never in your wildest dreams have you used HTML to describe content. You've used it for displaying content, not structuring it. With XML, the Web author can mark up the contents of a document by describing it in terms of its relevance as data.

The easiest way to explain the difference is by looking at a relatively simple example, which we'll expand upon as we go. HTML code, such as the following, should be familiar and easy to read:

```
<P>Gone With the Wind</P>
```

It's obvious this line of code is simply describing the content of a paragraph. When it is processed through the HTML browser, the text specified within the **<P>** element is displayed with whatever other content is included in the page. And that's the point. Specifically, HTML *displays* the content of this paragraph element.

This kind of markup language works fine if all we want to do is display the information with the paragraph element. But think about how we might want to use this content in the future. We might want to create a database of our favorite movies, a database that could easily be searched by anyone who visits our site. Instead of just *displaying* the content of the paragraph element, we may want to *access* it as data. In that case, we could do one of two things: We could use a scripting language that interfaces with a database, or we could use XML. How? First we would specify which elements would be used to mark up the titles of movies (in this case, *Gone With the Wind*). In XML, we could create an element to specify that the words in the title *mean* something (as shown in the following example) instead of creating an element that just displays text:

```
<FILM>Gone With the Wind</FILM>
```

We could use a style sheet to display the content of the **<FILM>** element in any way we choose. The element **<FILM>** creates a structure for our document, one that will follow a certain function and form, and the style sheet will be used to display the content of the XML document. For example, we may set up one style sheet to display this film information on a Web browser, specifying that if the user has a Palm Pilot, a specific style sheet will be used to display the same information on a smaller screen. HTML is the display language and XML is the structure language. But before we get into the style of our XML file, let's take this example one step further.

How XML And HTML Fit Into The Web

By now, you should have a relatively good concept of what XML offers and how limiting HTML is, when you start looking at your data as data and not just text that needs to be displayed. It's with data applications that can't be structured by simple HTML that XML will shine the most on the Web. Examples include the following:

- Applications that send the same data across the Web to users who have different display mechanisms

- Applications that require some sort of intelligent agent to customize and tailor the information discovery for individual user needs

- Applications that require perusal through or mediation between two or more similar databases

- Applications for which the processing is done on the client side rather than on the server side

There's no doubt you could meet all of these requirements by using the Common Gateway Interface (CGI), Java, or Visual Basic to create server- or client-side scripts or even by using browser plug-ins. But think about the constraints you impose on the user with these methods. For example, users must go through one extra step if they have to download a plug-in to see your data. They also must know *how* to download plug-ins and, if the plug-in is browser specific, have a computer that is capable of running it. This may severely limit the number of users who can view your data.

The philosophy of XML is that the data format used to deliver the information should not bind the user or even the developer to a particular delivery engine, set of content-creation tools, or even scripting language. XML is meant to offer a vendor-independent platform regardless of whether you're developing or displaying XML data.

HTML's Loss Of Standardization

Because XML doesn't limit you to a certain set of elements like HTML does, you can choose to create your own set of elements—a library, if you will— that construct the foundation of a document. You can name these elements whatever you want or create whatever attributes you need to be associated with certain elements. You can't do this with HTML, although as you've probably discovered, browser manufacturers have been creating elements that are specific to their own browsers. The problem is that the World Wide Web Consortium has not standardized these tags (such as the X tag). If you want to use browser-specific tags, your visitors must be using that particular browser and, in most cases, that particular version of the browser.

Disparity In HTML Tools

We haven't yet examined HTML or XML editing tools, but we'll say a few words about how HTML tools are not always your best friends. Many tools let you get away with code murder. Why is this? The problem is fourfold. First, browsers are relatively forgiving of bad HTML code, because they are dealing with the presentation of the document and not the structure. Second, different HTML editors may supply browser-specific tags that work only on one type (or even one version) of a browser. If you're using this type of editor, you're not creating consistent HTML code that can be used across the board by virtually any user.

Third, HTML editors are not always consistent with the tags they place within the content of your document. For example, Claris Home Page places the proper start- and end-tags (**<P></P>**) for specifying a paragraph element in your document. But Netscape Composer doesn't. Instead, it simply places a single **<P>** tag in the document or, in some cases, replaces what you thought was a carriage return with what really is a line break specified by the **
** tag.

Let's create two versions of a simple Web page, one using Netscape Composer and another using Claris Home Page. The page simply says, "Now is the time for all good men to come to the aid of their country." We've broken it down to three lines by pressing the Enter key at the end of each line. We've also added a simple GIF image to the end of our sentence. Now, let's compare the code we get from each Web-composing application. Here is the code Netscape Composer generated:

```
<HTML>
<HEAD>
<META NAME="Author" CONTENT="C.Kirk">
<META NAME="GENERATOR" CONTENT="Mozilla/4.05">
</HEAD>
<BODY>
<P>Now is the time for all good men to come
<BR>to the aid of their
<BR>country. <IMG SRC="picture.gif" HEIGHT=240 WIDTH=10>
</BODY>
</HTML>
```

Now, let's take a look at the same page generated by Claris Home Page. Notice that even simple things, like the paragraph element, are different. Claris Home Page uses the **<P></P>** element between lines instead of the **
** element, even though we pressed the same key on the keyboard. Also, notice that Claris Home Page specified white as the page background color but Composer didn't, although we used it in both page-layout programs. The code Claris Home Page generated looks like this:

```
<HTML>
<!--This file create at 7/17/99 at 12:00 AM by Claris Home
Page version 3.0-->
<HEAD>
<META NAME="GENERATOR" CONTENT="Claris Home Page 3.0">
<X-CLARIS-WINDOW TOP=42 BOTTOM=469 LEFT=4 RIGHT=534>
<X-CLARIS-TAGVIEW MODE=minimal>
</HEAD>
<BODY BGCOLOR="FFFFFF">
<P>Now is the time for all good men to come</P>
<P>to the aid of their</P>
<P>country. <IMG SRC="picture.gif" HEIGHT=240 WIDTH=10
ALIGN=bottom></P>
</BODY>
</HTML>
```

This code disparity even in simple documents is a big problem. Both pages display exactly the same way in both Netscape Navigator and Internet Explorer. But the code is different, which means that converting documents from HTML to XML can be a chore, especially if we are using a variety of HTML tools (almost all of which add their own little nuisances and quirks). Because of this lack of standardization, it's hard to catalog, view, and print documents throughout the Web. A standardized approach may sound boring, but in the end, it's less time-consuming and allows the developer to spend more time developing the content instead of cleaning up sloppy or inconsistent code.

Finally, until recently, new elements were being introduced almost hourly when new versions of browsers and new HTML specifications hit the street. To keep up with the new additions to HTML, Web page editors had to update their HTML page creation tools frequently or hand-code the new HTML elements.

How can XML help? XML requires a document to be well-formed. All elements must be a combination of start-tag and end-tag, and elements must be nested properly. The XML specification is all about structure. The minute you declare a document an XML document, you must follow the rules of the specification, or the foundation of your structure will fall flat. XML editors can't be as loose with XML code as HTML editors are with HTML code—there are just too many rules to follow.

XML To The Rescue

XML gives you the flexibility that browser manufacturers don't. For example, if the element title **<FILM>** doesn't explain the film well enough and doesn't help differentiate between certain kinds of films, we can create an element that does. First, let's say we create the element **<FILM>** but decide that we want to differentiate between the film titles that are black and white and those that are color. We would create another element with the name **<BW-FILM>** and use it this way:

```
<BW-FILM>Bringing Up Baby</BW-FILM>
```

This works great for this particular case. But if we want to offer the ability to access all films on our site regardless of whether they are color or black and white, and if we want to differentiate between such things as different versions, different dates, and so on, we could take our element one step further. We could create an attribute to describe more specific types of film attributes. HTML has a specific set of elements, and each element has a specific set of attributes that you can't add to or change, but with XML, you can create attributes for elements.

Not only can you can create names for your elements, you can also define names you want for element attributes. If we use an attribute with our **<FILM>** element, we can easily describe any film we want to describe. We can use a variety of attributes and allow all elements and their content to be viewed or searched. For example, we can specify whether a film is black and white, silent, or created in a particular year. We can also list the film's major actors. In the following line of code, our **<FILM>** element specifies a black-and-white film:

```
<film color="no">Bringing Up Baby</film>
```

Let's take this example a bit further, so you can see how expansive XML is. Suppose there is more than one version of a movie, such as the thriller *Godzilla*. The preceding example only has one attribute to describe the **<FILM>** element. With XML, we can create multiple attributes to describe the elements more specifically. The following code gives us another attribute to specify the year the film was made:

```
<film color="yes" year="1998">Godzilla</film>
```

Sure, this makes marking up a document a lot more work, and it's certainly more complex than just placing the paragraph element in front of the film title. But after we get specific with our markup, we are able to distinguish between when the word *Godzilla* is referring to a film and when it's referring to your last blind date. It also helps us differentiate between one version of *Godzilla* and another. By structuring the document and creating this kind of foundation, we make it much easier to catalog and find data in a document. It's not that XML works better than HTML in all circumstances, it just gives you more features and options for dealing with detailed data than HTML gives you.

Why HTML Isn't The Ticket Anymore

Although the previous example probably gave you a glimpse into how XML provides better structure to documents, to understand why HTML simply won't do it for you anymore, you need to know what HTML does well and what it does poorly. Both XML and HTML are called markup languages, and for a time, you could convince most people that HTML *was* being used for markup. After its popularity grew, however, people began to stretch HTML to the max, and the limitations started to show. For example, because HTML doesn't specify structure, on a site that lists films, their actors, and their directors, a user searching for a specific actor, for instance, "Robert Redford," would get all the films Redford was in as well as all the films he directed.

As you already know, the problem with HTML really lies in the fact that HTML handles the display of data relatively well but has no clue about how to handle the structure of the data. When you start to design a Web site, you'll quickly realize that, although displaying data is what HTML does best, it can't handle displaying data on a variety of platforms. HTML will still be useful for designing Web sites or intranets, but developers now need to decide which projects will work best with HTML and which will more easily fit within XML.

Let's look at a simple example that will illustrate the differences between HTML and XML. Suppose you have a chunk of data (some corporate manuals and some brochures) that you need to display on a variety of platforms. You've got on-the-road salespeople using hand-held Palm Pilot computers. You've also got corporate businesspeople sitting at their desks using Netscape Navigator. Add to that customers using a multitude of different computers—from Macs to Windows-based PCs. If you want to use HTML to deliver the data to everyone involved, you would most likely have to do what thousands of other Web-site designers have done in the past—create separate pages of the same data for each type of user. For example, you would have to set up pages specifically for the Navigator users. You would set up a site specifically for customers who can take advantage of the special features Internet Explorer offers, and you would have to condense more pages into a document the hand-held computer users can view quickly. Then, when the data changes, you would have to plow through all the pages and make the changes, which would be a laborious process and one that leaves a huge door open for mistakes. Let's take a closer look at why HTML doesn't work for everything you will do on the Web or within an intranet.

Why HTML Doesn't Work For Handling Data

HTML was created to provide a quick and simple solution for displaying documents on a variety of platforms. Initially, the documents consisted mainly of text and included a few graphics and maybe a link or two that pointed to a single document or particular section of a document. Because of a variety of factors—including bandwidth constraints, incompatibility between file formats, and lack of multimedia PCs—the idea of offering up video, sound, and access to databases wasn't even considered in the early days. HTML was really meant more for accessibility to relatively bland text-based documents than to a diverse amount of files, formats, and data. It could display text and simplistic formatting, but it couldn't do what page-description languages, such as PostScript, could do. As the Web started to become more popular around 1994, developers and designers quickly realized HTML's limitations. Specifically, they found that it couldn't or didn't offer the following features:

- The ability to publish one chunk of data in a variety of ways and to a variety of display devices

- Linking options that were more complex than simple one-way links

- Flexibility to structure and describe different types of data

- Control over how the data is displayed

Differences In Syntax

Let's examine the differences and similarities between XML's and HTML's language syntax. Although there are differences, you'll probably be surprised to learn that there are plenty of similarities between the two languages, especially if you've followed the rules of good HTML coding. If you have, it will be easier for you to convert existing HTML documents to XML. Let's start by examining what HTML lets you get away with, what XML requires, and whether those requirements also exist in HTML.

With HTML, you can get away with creating sloppy documents. How many times have you viewed the source of an HTML document and found a dizzying array of mistakes, missing elements, and just downright sloppy code? Some of the problems are due to people not knowing proper HTML syntax, while others are due to HTML editors that simply haven't kept up with HTML. Because most of today's browsers are relatively forgiving, a lot of these faux pas are glossed over and the data is displayed. With HTML, you can be sloppy without great fear of retribution. For example, if you leave out the **</A>** in the anchor element when you specify a link to another document, the rest of the text from that point forward will turn into one big hypertext link, but the information would still display. It may not display the way you intended, but it would display nonetheless.

With XML, you can't be sloppy. As a matter of fact, the first objective for designing any XML document is that it be well-formed. Tags must be nested properly. Start-tags must have end-tags. If you have one missing end-tag, your XML processor will return an error—there's no sliding by with sloppiness like there is with HTML. And this is a good thing. Really. It means that the end user won't be left wondering if the document is as it should be. Not only is the data and information displayed properly, but the structure of the data is clearly and accurately defined.

XML requires that you tell the parser the document is an XML document. With HTML, you can get away with not declaring which markup language will be used. You could be using HTML 2 or HTML 4 and the browser usually figures out how to display the data. With XML, you must declare that your document is an XML document and what version of the XML specification you plan to use. You do so with the XML declaration, a small piece of code that appears at the top of any XML document. The declaration allows the processor to understand that you intend this document to be an XML document:

```
<?XML version="1.0"?>
```

All XML elements have a start-tag and an end-tag. If you've created even a single Web page, you've used at least one element in your effort to create an HTML document. For example, you may have used the **<TITLE>** element to specify the title of the Web page. To tell the browser where the title begins and ends in an XML document, you need to use a start-tag and an end-tag, as shown in this example:

```
<TITLE>This is the title of my Web page</TITLE>
```

When you developed your HTML pages, you may have used the paragraph element, **<P>**, without its end-tag, **</P>**. You'll find that lots of HTML developers are guilty of this. With XML, every time you use a paragraph element with the start-tag specified as **<P>**, you must also use its accompanying end-tag, **</P>**. You might be surprised (as we were) to see how many start-tags and how few end-tags you've used throughout your HTML code. You'll need to make sure your HTML document has end-tags before you can convert it to XML.

Empty elements need to be formatted correctly in XML documents. Lots of developers have created thousands of HTML pages and probably never knew there was such a thing as an empty element. But they are used frequently, not only in HTML but also in XML. For example, HTML has the image element, specified as **<IMG>**. To specify a link to a particular image file in HTML, you would type the following code:

```
<IMG SRC="file.gif">
```

This is considered an empty element because it has no content associated with it; **"file.gif"** is the **SRC** or source-attribute value, and it's not considered the **<IMG>** element's content. But **<IMG SRC="file.gif">** is still a tag. Because it has no content, you probably wouldn't think of adding an end-tag to this element declaration. Remember, however, that in XML, every start-tag must have an end-tag. So, what do you do with elements that don't normally offer content and thus require you to specify an end-tag? You can do one of two things. You can specify the element as an empty element, sans content, by doing what comes naturally:

```
<IMG SRC="file.gif"></IMG>
```

Or you can do what comes naturally in XML—something you'll find you do a lot if you use the Channel Definition Format to develop Internet Explorer channels. You can specify the empty element in this fashion (the preferred way to specify empty elements in XML documents):

```
<IMG SRC="file.gif"/>
```

Go through your HTML documents and you'll start to realize how many empty elements exist in your code. By doing so, you'll get an indication of how much work you'll have to do to convert HTML documents to XML documents.

3: XML Best Practices

XML requires quotes around all attribute values. While we're on the subject of elements, and because we just looked at one empty element that included an attribute, let's talk about how XML requires quotes around attribute values. In HTML, only certain attribute values—such as text strings and URLs—need to be quoted. Take, for example, the following line of code:

```
<FONT SIZE=+1>This is one size larger</FONT>
```

Notice that there are no quotes around the value for the font size. The **<FONT>** element's **SIZE** attribute value of **+1** will work fine in HTML. But if this same line of code was placed in an XML document, the parser would return an error. With HTML, this code simply signals to the browser that the default font used to display the text should be one point larger for the enclosed content of the element and the browser will interpret the value regardless of whether quotes appear or not. HTML does not require you to place quotes around the **SIZE** attribute value, but if this were an XML document, quotes would be required. For our XML document to be well-formed, the preceding code example would need to be changed to the following:

```
<FONT SIZE="+1">This is one size larger</FONT>
```

It doesn't matter whether you use single or double quotes as long as you are consistent. Also, if an attribute has a single value—a default value, if you will—such as the following example illustrates, you need to include quotes around the value:

```
<ELEMENT ATTRIBUTE="default">
```

Tags need to be nested correctly in XML documents. If you're a careful developer, you may already nest your tags correctly in your HTML documents. If so, when it comes to being a top-notch XML developer, you're halfway there. With HTML, to nest tags properly, you close first what you opened last. For example, although this code listing would work just fine in HTML, it wouldn't work in XML:

```
<I><B>This is bold and italics</I></B>
```

This code wouldn't work in XML because we didn't close the **<B>** tag first as we should have; it was the last tag we opened. Nesting tags correctly is important in XML, because so much of the XML document depends on the parser knowing where things begin and end. The following line of code illustrates the proper way to nest bold and italic elements:

```
<I><B>This is bold and italics</B></I>
```

With HTML, white space is ignored. Go ahead. Press the spacebar a hundred times between text while you're writing your HTML code in your favorite text editor. What do you get? Most likely a sore thumb. White space in HTML is ignored. Only a single space is recognized. That's why developers were so happy when tables were invented. Tables allowed more control over the placement of text or graphics.

But with XML, the content of any element is treated as data, and that means if you've pressed the spacebar a hundred times within the content of an element, you'll end up with a large segment of white space. For example, the following code

```
<film>Gone With the      Wind</film>
```

is not the same as

```
<film>Gone With the Wind</film>
```

When you create an XML document, you must pay attention to extra spaces in your element content. You must also clean up any sloppy HTML code you want to convert so the content is represented as you had intended it to be.

In XML documents, you need to specify when characters are data. In XML, unlike HTML, you need to specify when characters are supposed to be data and when they are simply just characters. For example, suppose you want to specify some sample code in the contents of an XML element. Rather than replacing each reserved character with its decimal code equivalent, you can simply mark it as character data. You might also want to do the same thing when you are including the contents of a script within an XML data source. The following code demonstrates how this is done:

```
<![CDATA[Information]]>
```

The **!** in the line of code indicates this is an element. The **[CDATA]** section specifies that this is a section of the DTD that includes literal data the XML processor should ignore. The **[Information]** section is the script that the XML processor will ignore, but the HTML browser will process the scripting information.

Unlike HTML, XML is case sensitive. You'll read it here, and you'll read it again and again, because it's such an important concept for developers: XML is case sensitive. Why is this so important to remember? Because in HTML, case is not important, and if you're like most HTML developers, you may not have typed your element names in uppercase. In fact, you may have used both upper- and lowercase throughout your documents with no ill effects. When you specify elements and attributes in XML, you must use the same case. We suggest you use upper-case. This code

```
<director>Don Simpson</director>
```

is not the same as

```
<DIRECTOR>Don Simpson</DIRECTOR>
```

It wouldn't be interpreted the same through the XML processor, because the element name, **director**, is lowercase in one instance and uppercase in another. You should start looking through the code you plan to convert from HTML to XML to make sure you've been consistent.

XML uses the Document Object Model. The Document Object Model (DOM) is basically an interface that defines the mechanisms for accessing the data in a document. The DOM is a platform- and language-independent interface that lets programs and scripts interact and update the content, structure, and style of documents. Web page objects such as elements, links, and character data can be added to, changed, or deleted. You can therefore create scripts that directly access these objects. Basically, the DOM describes an object model. The DOM specifies the way to manipulate and change Cascading Style Sheets (CSS). HTML doesn't use DOM—only XML does. However, Navigator and Internet Explorer have their own proprietary DOMs that are not supported by the W3C. When the W3C standardizes on a DOM, both companies will most likely drop their DOMs and go with W3C's version.

By using the DOM, the developer can script dynamic content in a standardized way. You can make a specific piece of content in a browser's document tree behave in a certain way. For example, you can script text to turn a particular section of it a certain color when the mouse moves over it. This may sound familiar if you've used JavaScript. However, the difference is that the DOM will be standardized, meaning all browsers should handle the scripting of these objects exactly the same. Differences currently exist between browsers using DHTML, Cascading Styles Sheets, or JavaScript.

TIP: *For more information on the Document Object Model, see the W3C's DOM specification at **www.w3.org/DOM**.*

XML can define entities. Haven't you ever found yourself endlessly typing the same character data again and again on your Web pages? Unlike HTML, XML allows you to create your own entities to specify certain characters or groups of characters you use again and again in documents. With HTML, there are character entities that specify reserved characters, such as the open angle bracket (<), but there is no convention for creating your own entities to specify characters other than reserved characters. For more information about creating XML entities, check out Chapter 12.

XML can define new applications. Imagine having not only the flexibility to define a document's structure, but also the ability to create your own Web-based applications in a single markup language. Unlike HTML, XML can be used to define new applications. The Channel Definition Format (CDF) and the Resource Description Framework (RDF) are two prime examples of XML applications—applications that use XML to define their capabilities, elements, and syntax. With the CDF, you can create customized delivery channels for a variety of display types, such as HTML-formatted email, Active Desktop items, or even Windows 95 or 98 screen savers.

Because HTML doesn't allow you to define any of your own elements or tags, you are stuck with elements that cannot be combined or changed in any way to create your own application. The closest you can come to such a thing in HTML is scripting, either with Java, JavaScript, CGI scripting on the server site, or VBScript. And even then, you have to learn an entirely different language and its syntax. With XML applications, you already know the rules. You simply have to learn the individual elements and their attributes, but you still follow the same structural concepts that XML requires.

HTML uses a universal DTD. XML is primarily a system for defining your own language for your own Web documents. You can create your own set of rules for the elements you create. There are no preset rules. With HTML, however, there is a universal Document Type Definition (DTD) that defines the rules and syntax of all the elements you use. The DTD specifies where you can use various elements in a document, in what order you can use them, and what attributes you can use.

With XML, you can define or choose not to define a DTD. If you create one, or decide to use one that is already defined for your particular industry, you are in effect creating your own rules. Because you can't do that with HTML, your ability to extend your HTML documents is limited.

TIP: *Would you like to see a DTD in action? Check out the Wall Street Journal Interactive Edition, located at* **www.wsj.com**. *The Journal uses its own DTD to define information that appears regularly in each edition, such as bylines, summaries, charts, pages, and so on. They've called their DTD the Dow Jones Markup Language. This DTD started out as an SGML DTD but has since been converted to an XML DTD.*

A Quick HTML-To-XML Conversion

Although Chapter 21 covers the exact steps used to convert HTML and other documents to XML, let's take a quick look at how a simple HTML document can be converted. We'll build on the example used earlier in this chapter and convert an HTML movie-oriented page to an XML data document. This site describes the videotaped movies of someone we'll name Bobby Diggins. Here's the HTML code we'll start with:

```
<H1>Bobby Diggins Video Library</H1>
<TABLE>
<TBODY>
<TR>
<TD>Shag</TD>
<TD>Bringing Up Baby<TD/>
<TD>As Good As It Gets</TD>
<TD>The Graduate</TD>
<TD>Godzilla</TD>
<TD>Godzilla</TD>
<TD>Psycho</TD>
</TR>
</TBODY>
</TABLE>
```

Notice that we've used the **<TABLE>** element to give the HTML document a kind of hierarchical look and feel, although there really is no true structure. We just placed the movie titles within the table as we saw fit. If someone wanted to search this document for a particular title, the search feature of the browser would simply move through the document, stopping at each occurrence of the word the visitor is looking for. If the visitor is looking for *Gone With the Wind* and Bobby included a reference to another movie with the word *wind* in its title, the search feature would stop on that movie, too.

TIP: *For an interesting glimpse at how a Web page can be made over, check out Microsoft's Extreme XML column, "Web Page Makeover," located at **www.microsoft.com/xml/articles/xml041398.asp**. It's an interesting step-by-step look at using a variety of scripting options to convert from HTML to XML.*

If we look closer at the document, we really don't know what Bobby owns. Does he own two copies of *Godzilla*? Maybe. Perhaps he owns the original version. Then again, he could own the Japanese version or maybe the 1998 version. To answer such questions, we need to convert this document to XML, so we can use XML's flexibility to create our own elements for our own purpose.

First, let's consider what elements we need. We would need an element called **<FILM>** and maybe one called **<COLORFILM>**. No wait, that won't do. What if we want to access all the black-and-white *and* color films? We couldn't do that if we separated the types of films into two different elements. Instead, we need to make sure we create the appropriate attributes to specify the types of films we might want to search for. Then, we can incorporate more complex searches and not leave a single film out.

In that case, we would create several attributes for our **<FILM>** element. The attributes could specify whether the film is in color, what year the film came out, maybe whether it has sound, or possibly whether it is a foreign film. These attributes allow us to get specific with each film without putting the films into different predefined categories.

TIP: *If you want more information on how to create elements, see Chapter 7. For more information on creating attributes, check out Chapter 8.*

Now, let's convert our HTML document into an XML document. The following code uses our **<FILM>** element along with several attributes we've declared:

```
<library>
<owner>Bobby Diggins</owner>
<films>
<film color="yes" year="1984">Shag</film>
<film color="no" year="1945">Bringing Up Baby</film>
<film color="yes" year="1997">As Good As It Gets</film>
<film color="yes" year="1969">The Graduate</film>
<film color="no" year="1935">Godzilla</film>
<film color="yes" year="1998">Godzilla</film>
<film color="no" year="1954">Psycho</film>
</films>
</library>
```

Looking at the XML code, we are now able to tell more about the films Bobby has in his video library. Specifically, we now know he has two different versions of the film *Godzilla*: the original and the 1998 remake. We also know that he has a collection of both black-and-white films and color films. But what else can we gather from this XML document? In the next section, you'll learn how XML creates a document tree structure that can be referenced in a variety of ways. Knowing about how XML structures data, compared to how HTML does, will help you in the conversion process.

The XML Document's Tree Structure

When you create a document in XML, what you are really doing is creating a tree structure, unlike with HTML. Let's back up a bit. With HTML, when you create a document, you really aren't creating a structure from which the browser can parlay the information into various sections. Sure, there are the **<HEAD>** and **<BODY>** elements, which signal to the HTML browser that it should place the title information or meta-tag information in the proper places. These elements also specify where the body content should begin and end. But after that, there really is no structure to your document, even if you use head elements like **<H1>**, **<H2>**, or **<H3>**. Because of the nonstructured method in which HTML works, you could easily place an **<H2>** element before an **<H1>** element, and the structure of the document wouldn't be affected. Because HTML just displays—and doesn't really interpret—the elements as structures, the content within these elements would still display, regardless of whether we use them in the proper place.

But XML is different. When you create an XML document, what you are really doing is defining a hierarchy and specifying elements, subelements, and so on. If we were to create a diagram of Bobby's video library document, it would look something like Figure 3.1.

TIP: *Microsoft's Channel Definition Format is a prime example of how an XML application follows a structured format. Open a channel in Internet Explorer, and if the channel contains subelements and the subelements contain additional content or elements, you'll see a tree structure. For more information on the Channel Definition Format, read Chapter 20.*

Every XML document has a single root element, and from this root element, all of the other document elements branch off. This is different than HTML, where there really are only two separate sections of a document, the **<HEAD>** section and the **<BODY>** section. To illustrate this point, Figure 3.2 shows the Windows 95

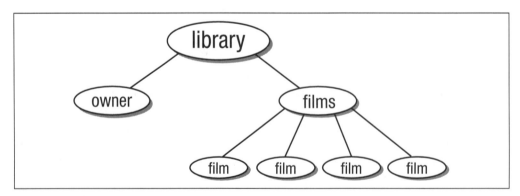

Figure 3.1   An example of how the video library is structured.

Figure 3.2   The directory structure in Windows 95 Explorer is much like XML's document structure.

Explorer window displaying its directory structure. The root element is My Computer and all the subelements are branches from the root.

In our previous XML example with Bobby's video library, the **<LIBRARY>** element is the root element in the XML document. From this root element, all other elements—often referred to as descendants—branch off. This is an important concept to grasp and one you probably didn't pay much attention to when you were creating HTML documents. In fact, you were probably more concerned about where the HTML elements appeared on the page than about which elements were descendants of other elements. To create effective XML documents, you should start thinking about the structure of the document and leave the look of the document to the style sheets. When you work with large documents or a lot of data, it's imperative that you start paying attention to structure, so the data falls into the right places.

TIP: *Make sure you read Chapter 24 to get a glimpse at how people have taken static data in HTML and turned it into more dynamic data with XML.*

Taking Markup A Bit Further

In our video library example, we created a relatively structured data document. The elements we used helped to create the structure and specify that certain data represents films. We can, however, take the markup a bit further and mark up specific text in the document. We can mark up the document much like we would do with HTML, but instead of describing how the data should look, we're actually designating certain pieces of text as important pieces of data. For example, if we were to take the following sentence

```
In the Graduate, a movie produced in 1969,
Dustin Hoffman made his first major film debut,
and the critics all agreed, he was an emerging
talent that would soon make it big.
```

and use XML to mark it up in an effort to make the text more explicit, we would come up with code that would look like this:

```
<review subject-type="film">
In
<film color="yes" year="1969">The Graduate,
a movie produced in
<year>1969</year>,
<actor>Dustin Hoffman</actor>
made his first major film debut, and the critics
all agreed, he was an emerging talent
that would soon make it big. </review>
```

If we mark up the text within the document as shown in the preceding code example, we make it possible for a program to search for films that feature Dustin Hoffman as an actor or films that were produced in 1969. It would be almost impossible to offer a search feature such as this if we used current HTML elements.

Good XML And HTML Design

Most of what you'll read about good HTML design focuses on using specific elements to achieve a certain effect in the *display* of data. But good design, regardless of whether you're using XML or HTML, depends on some basic rules for structuring the site and, more importantly, for planning for the site. It's important to remember the following guidelines:

• Specify a reason for your site.

• Define or know your intended audience.

• Know what hardware and software your users will need to view your site.

• Know your own limits and the limits of your site.

• Plan your site.

• Structure the flow of your site by creating a site map.

- Don't forget the importance of navigational controls.

- Test, test, test, and retest your site.

Notice that none of these design principles relates specifically to the capabilities of any language. Instead, they outline a larger concept of site design. Let's take a look at each one of these principles in more detail.

TIP: *For more tips on site design, check out the article "Building a Better Interface" in the Web Graphics section of CINet Central's Site Builder site at* ***www.builder.com/Graphics/UserInterface***.

Specify A Reason For Your Site

The first thing you need to do is specify a reason for your site. You don't have to declare it outright on the site itself, but as the developer, you need to know exactly why you are designing your site. Do you want to inform, promote, dazzle, or teach? (If you have a development team, make sure its members also know the purpose of the site.) If the purpose of your site is to share information about your favorite movies, for example, information about your dog would seem out of place to your visitors.

If the site is made up of simple, informative short bits of information, is XML really necessary? HTML may be all you need for those nifty, eye-catching brochures. But do they really need to be XML documents, especially if they are more for show than for data? If, however, you need to keep data and add to it over time, XML may be the solution. Suppose you want to set up a list of available homes for sale in a given market. You want to allow visitors to pick and choose their potential homes based on the criteria they supply in a form instead of having to wade through link after link. In this case, you would need to seriously consider XML. When you specify your site's purpose and keep it in clear focus, you'll start realizing what elements you'll need, how the information should be structured, and more importantly, which markup language you need to use.

Define Your Audience

The audience will dictate exactly how you structure your data. In some cases, the audience could dictate whether HTML will be better suited for your site than XML. Not everyone will be perfectly matched to your site. If you are creating a site that lists all the places you could travel to in Alaska, your audience will undoubtedly be vacationers, but it could also include travel agents, tour guides, hikers, adventure seekers, bed and breakfast guests, and lots of senior citizens. Make sure you cater to the largest segment of your intended audience. If only 10 percent are hikers, it would be counterproductive to fill the site with hiking information and lose the visitors who simply want a relaxing cruise.

Is your site the local alternative weekly newspaper that has several years worth of archived stories that you want to present to your visitors (both on the Web and in a way that it can be easily printed)? Then you need to consider XML. However, if all the visitors want to do is read the latest quick clips of news bytes, HTML may be a better alternative.

Determine Your Visitors' Requirements

It's amazing how many sites are designed in-house with high-speed connections but are never viewed with what most of the site's audience will use—low-speed connections to the Internet. Determining user requirements is more important than designing around your own system's capabilities. Ask your potential users what connections they have, what software they use, and how they want to view and manipulate data on your site. If your site is on an intranet, the design considerations are different than if you are designing for Internet users. This will help dictate exactly what types of information you can offer and in what format.

Find out what your audience will want to do once they make it to your site. It's useful to know what languages and browsers they will be using. If most of your visitors will be using only one browser and speak English, you can use HTML to create your site. But if you want to accommodate a wider range of users, XML would probably work better, because you can create different displays of the same data. And if your audience wants to search your site quickly and easily, you should use XML. Knowing your audience, and more specifically, knowing what they expect from your site will help you determine which features you need to create and implement.

Know Your Limits

To implement XML, you need to know whether your server can handle the site and whether you can handle the demands the site will place on you and your coworkers. Microsoft's Internet Information Server, with its Active Server Pages, offers a great deal of flexibility, not only with HTML-only sites but also with XML-enabled sites. If you plan on offering multimedia features, remember to consider the amount of bandwidth your site will need.

The most important thing is to know your server's capacity and what programs you can run on it. Consider what processing you can or should run on the server and what processing you can off-load to the client. And speaking of clients, make sure your system is capable of handling the maximum number of simultaneous requests you think it will get. Ensuring security features and knowing the security configuration is also an important component of planning correctly for your site.

Although it's not a technical consideration, it's important to understand what your own requirements are in terms of time, money, and stress. You need project-management capabilities as well as a good eye for graphic design. In addition, you'll need to know good grammar and have good editing skills if you plan to provide textual content. If a site requires a lot of updating and you work two full-time jobs, you may want to consider finding someone to help. Your role may best be played out as the builder of the site, leaving the Webmaster duties to another person.

The idea, of course, is that you keep the information dynamic. With HTML, you'll forever be adding new pages, changing old ones, keeping track of links, finding and deleting dead links, and updating graphics. With XML, creating dynamic sites is much easier.

Plan Your Site

This goes without saying, but you would be surprised at how many people really don't plan their sites properly. When you plan your site, you not only determine what its purpose will be and the tools you'll need, but also its structure. When you use XML, you need to spend more time planning the site's structure so you can determine what elements and attributes you'll need to create and what style sheets are needed for displaying the content. Also, proper planning gives you an opportunity to know exactly what links—and the kinds of links—are needed. This in turn will help you define exactly what markup language you should use. If you simply need to link from one document to another, HTML may work for you. But if you need to create more complex structures, only XML will do.

Create A Site Map

After you determine your site's purpose, its capabilities, and the type of documents and links it will include, the next thing to do is put it down on paper. Create a road map of your site. Where will the links take the visitor? What pages are descendants of other pages? What internal and what external documents, scripts, and applications will be used and how will they be invoked?

A visual road map will help you determine where things will go and will prevent your visitors from getting lost in "hyperspace." If you can't visualize the organizational structure of your site before you begin, you'll soon be lost in the myriad pages you've created.

TIP: *For more information on how to design your site with XML, read Chapter 17.*

Don't Forget Navigational Controls

Navigational controls are one of the most important design features used in creating a successful site. It doesn't matter whether your site is mainly HTML or XML—navigational controls are necessary. But without a good document structure or a clear road map, navigational controls can lead you to one dead end after another. You can use a template or index cards, or you can sketch your road map on a paper napkin. Remember to include navigational controls that will lead the visitor back to square one, or at least back to the preceding page. Although XML allows more complex linking structures, the principles of good navigation still apply. Every site will require some form of navigational controls. Navigational controls should be apparent to visitors so they can move freely within the site, and they should consistently take visitors where they ask to go.

TIP: *For an excellent example of how to design Web sites, mainly of the HTML variety, check out IBM's Web Guidelines at **www.ibm.com/IBM/HCI/guidelines/web/print.html**.*

Test The Site

Take the site for a spin, but make sure you bring along some friends to see how well it drives for them. Failure to test a site is the key design flaw many developers are guilty of. The site may work great at ISDN speeds, but how does it work with a 28.8Kbps modem? Maybe it's a masterpiece on your 24-inch screen, but how well does it display on a lowly 13 incher? You may have been able to easily pluck and pull data out within your intranet, but will all that plucking and pulling work from miles away over the Internet?

It doesn't matter whether you are developing HTML or XML documents. What matters is that you test the site and that you test it on a variety of platforms, on a variety of machines, and in a variety of locations.

XML has come a long way in a short period of time and has gathered a great deal of support by those in the Web-development community who want more than just the simple display markup capabilities HTML offers. The XML specification details the new markup language's features and structure. By now, you should be familiar with the specification, where it comes from, where you get it, and how you make heads or tails of it.

Immediate Solutions

In this chapter, you learned the differences between HTML and XML and how you can shore up your sloppy HTML skills into the best practices for using XML. You've learned exactly how to plan for a site and what points to consider when you design any site, regardless of whether you use HTML or XML. In this section, you'll learn how to put those practices to good use and how to recognize what specifications XML requires.

Determining Whether To Use XML Or HTML

Before you start converting all your HTML documents to XML, you should learn a few simple steps that will speed up the process. These steps reinforce what you just learned in terms of the differences and similarities between HTML and XML. First, you should determine whether the document is better suited for HTML or XML. Use Table 3.1 as a quick reference guide to help you determine exactly which markup language to use.

Table 3.1   Determining whether to use XML or HTML.

Problem	Solution
Does the data consist of a few simple pages and graphics, much like you would find in a brochure?	Use HTML
Does the data require advanced searching so users can get what they need out of the site?	Use XML
Is the data going to be viewed on a variety of different platforms or appliances?	Use XML
Does the content stay relatively static?	Use HTML
Do you need to interface the data between different machines or database engines?	Use XML
Are you having problems with your existing site in terms of users getting lost or not being able to find what they need?	Use XML
Will the site have primarily multimedia, such as sound clips or videos?	Use HTML, possibly with plug-ins

Fixing HTML Problems

When you convert from HTML to XML, you should do some initial spot-checking of your HTML documents to see exactly where your problems may lie and what you need to do to fix them. You may need to use a text editor with find-and-replace capabilities to handle some of the more mundane changes, or you might want to write a script, depending upon your development platform, to make some of the changes more automatic, especially if your code inconsistencies are recurrent. Here are the issues you need to address when you convert a document from HTML to XML:

- Did the same developer or HTML editor prepare all the HTML code? If not, find out what pages were developed by what editor or developer and group them together. This will help you spot patterns of inconsistency.

- Find all extra spaces within the documents and remove them. XML interprets white space as character data (unlike HTML, which ignores it). Unless you clean up any extra spaces in your HTML documents, they won't be fully compatible with XML.

- Place the XML declaration at the top of all the documents you want to convert. If you leave the **<HTML>** tag, browsers will still interpret the data within in the document as HTML. However, by placing the following code as the first line in your document, you'll prepare the document to be parsed as XML:

```
<?XML version="1.0"?>
```

- Make sure all your elements have both a start-tag and an end-tag, even elements you're used to specifying with no end-tag (which are called empty elements in XML), such as **
** or **<HR>**. In these cases, you can either use a closing tag such as **</BR>** or close the tag within the element, by using **
. Make sure you convert the empty element **<IMG> to **<IMG/>**.

- Make sure all tag attributes' values are quoted. For example, if you are specifying the height of a graphic, make sure you enclosed the size in quotes:

```
<IMG SRC="file.gif" HEIGHT="410" WIDTH="210"/>
```

- Make sure your HTML elements are nested correctly. Close first what you opened last.

- If you want to specify certain characters as data, make sure you use the **<CDATA>** element.

- Make sure you use the same case, uppercase normally, when you are specifying elements and attributes.

Moving From HTML To XML

After you've decided which documents should be converted and which should stay as HTML pages, and after you've cleaned up your HTML code and readied it for XML, the following checklist will help the transition go more smoothly:

- Define the structure of your document, specifying what the root and its various descendants will be.
- Identify the specific elements, attributes, and entities you will need.
- Create the XML DTD.
- Decide which style sheets will be required to display the data and the steps you need to take to create the style sheets.
- Set up a testing procedure that will help you identify early on what kinds of problems you will encounter in the conversion process. Take sample HTML pages from the various groups of HTML code you have collected, clean them up, and then convert the pages to XML documents. Run them through an XML processor to see how many errors you encounter. Then, identify the steps you need to take to fix the problems.
- Determine what server and additional programs and scripts you'll use to complement the data you'll be converting.

Designing Your Site

It doesn't matter whether you keep most of your HTML pages and add a few XML documents or whether you convert all your HTML pages to XML. Either way, you should design your site according to some specific design principles.

Planning Ahead

Planning ahead means understanding the direction you plan to go and who you will cater to once you get there. Poll your potential audience to find out the following information:

- What do they expect from your site?
- What specific data are they looking for and how do they want to access it— through a search engine or via simple links?
- What browsers and versions are they using?
- What appliances are they using to view your site. Are they using PCs, hand-held computers, Web TVs?
- What demands will they put on your site?

Sketching Out The Site

When you sketch out the site, you need to create not only a road map, but also a navigational structure:

- Create an element hierarchy. Specify what element will be your root element and what elements will branch off and be nested within other elements. Sketch out the hierarchy to show the relationships the elements will have with one another.

- Create a document or page hierarchy. Specify what pages will go where and what links will move the user in what direction. An easy way to do this is to use index cards or popular outlining programs. Determine where the user can or should go next and how the user gets back to where he or she wants to go within your site.

- Make sure you define the various sections of documents so you can refer to them in groups, either in your general document structure or within links. Consider building your site with depth, making the content on each page relatively short.

- When you sketch out your site, consider using identifiable elements to help users know where they are and where they can go next. Consider giving users the flexibility to jump to various sections in your site in a variety of ways, not just in a linear fashion.

- Make sure none of your documents are orphaned in any way. Always allow access to both the previous location and the home page or main menu.

- Make sure your site is organized in a way your users, and not just you, will recognize. The structure you use internally may not make sense to anyone outside your organization. Take time to view other sites' organizational structure to get ideas on how to create an understandable navigational flow.

Chapter 4

Implementing XML In A Corporate Environment

By Cheryl Kirk

In Depth

XML and the corporate network are well suited for each other. XML offers the extensibility that HTML doesn't have, and at the same time, XML offers the ability to interface with existing legacy systems. XML is perfect for any corporation looking for more structured capabilities from a markup language without the complexity of the Standard Generalized Markup Language (SGML). Many software vendors are incorporating XML features into their software. You'll find XML features in Web servers, XML editors, XML parsers, databases, and standard desktop document-creation and -management systems, such as those found in the latest version of Adobe FrameMaker.

In this chapter, we'll start by exploring how XML can benefit the corporation and how corporate environments can maximize the advantages of XML. This discussion is aimed at helping you understand where XML fits in the corporate world. (If you're a programmer trying to convince your boss that XML is the way to go, we suggest you pass along this book and ask your boss to skim through it.) We'll examine the various reasons why XML fits so well in the corporate world and why the switch to XML from HTML is a natural progression.

Many Reasons For Implementing XML

In this chapter, you'll be introduced to three Web sites and five companies that are utilizing XML in one form or another. Both the Web sites and the companies used a variety of XML-enabled software programs, database engines, editors, browsers, parsers, and glued-together code to make the complete connection between different systems, XML, and the Web. In some cases, sites use only a comprehensive Document Type Definition (DTD) with some additional lines of code and a few scripts. Other sites use extensive SQL databases, XML editors, DTDs, and Microsoft IIS servers.

We won't kid you; in most of these systems, it took more than just a few lines of code to create a cohesive system, but it's the XML that is used throughout that makes data transfer from one system to the next possible. In each scenario, we'll introduce you to the problem, outline the solutions, and then review how XML and other products (such as Insight's Enigma, Chrystal's Astoria, DataChannel's ChannelManager, and other XML-based software programs) help do the trick. As you read through each story, remember that without XML these systems would continue to work in a proprietary fashion, offering little if any connectivity and compatibility between systems.

We'll start by examining how XML fits within the corporate structure to help extend the data found in the corporation. Then, we'll move on to explain how various components of XML work well within corporations and why other markup languages, such as HTML, leave the corporations looking for a better alternative. Finally, we'll recap with an overview of how several companies are using XML to handle their data needs. These companies cover a broad spectrum of businesses, all with varying data needs. Each business deals with data that needs to flow from one location or one user to the next. Each has decided to standardize on intranet technology, meaning whatever they choose must eventually interface to the browser's desktop. These companies and their problems are:

- *Siemens*—This company needed an integrated timecard system that would allow employees to track their time and attendance and relay this information to their managers.

- *RivCom*—This company needed to offer clients the ability to monitor job requirements and pass along those requirements to prospective employees and the human resources department.

- *DataChannel*—This company offers an "extended" channel application that helps many companies, including magazines, push information to users and employees desktops.

There's no doubt that XML is primed for the corporate world. Not only does it offer many of the features SGML offers, it offers them without the complexities of SGML. It also offers the extensibility HTML simply can't offer. Yet, it's more than just extensibility and complexity. XML DTDs are relatively easy to create, especially if you've done any HTML development. XML documents are even easier to deploy, and all XML components make it easier to manage the various architectures of intranets and extranets. XML can revolutionize the corporation's document management, electronic data interchange, and information planning with relatively little investment and a small learning curve.

XML is amazingly flexible. It can perform many of the tasks HTML and server-side scripts currently perform, and it can interface with existing legacy systems and databases. That means corporations really don't have to choose between using disparate systems. XML can bring systems together and, in some cases, even replace them. Development staffs don't have to learn a wide array of programming languages, and they don't have to worry about developing intranet sites around a particular browser for which they must use specialized tags. Instead of spending so much time on developing the "look," developers can spend time on the content and structure.

With XML, corporations aren't tied into specific vendors or languages or even operating systems. If a corporation uses one operating-system platform and then decides to move to another, the XML data stored on the systems can move across platforms. If the corporation decides to move from one browser to another, there is no need for recoding. XML is probably one of the most flexible and versatile markup languages around, because it allows you to create the elements you need to build the document structure you want.

Although flexibility is a key selling point for XML, there are numerous other reasons for replacing many HTML and script-oriented documents as well as other types of documents:

- XML offers cross-platform compatibility between systems, browsers, and external applications.

- Standardized Document Type Definitions (DTDs) can be used across the company or across industries, and in some cases, there may even be a DTD for your corporation.

- XML documents can be used on more than just the Web and can be read within existing SGML environments.

- The same XML document can be repurposed, so it can be viewed on a variety of display devices without having to restructure the data. Extensible Style Language (XSL) or style sheets allow for better control over presentation and the ability to keep the content and display together for better management.

- XML documents off-load information to the client, thus reducing the load on servers.

- The creation of entities can reduce development time and allow for character and group standardization.

- Links can be used to create multiple actions in a simultaneous fashion, allowing linking to multiple sources.

- XML is based on strict syntax rules, forcing documents to be more readable and follow certain design standards. There are few shortcuts.

- When XML is used in conjunction with various XML applications, such as the Channel Definition Format (CDF), information can be pushed automatically to users on a network. Information such as updates to policy and procedure manuals can be delivered without the need to notify users that new information is available on a Web server and without the need to fill up email servers.

- When XML is used in conjunction with the Open Software Description (OSD), software applications and operating systems can be automatically updated on a timely basis without the need for human intervention.

Before we examine in more detail some of the important features XML offers, let's first discuss why the way XML handles documents is so much better than the way other popular document-management systems, such as Portable Document Format (PDF) and even HTML, handle them.

Comparing Basic Document Formats To XML

More and more companies are moving toward using intranets to help manage documents, document creation, and document distribution. Just think about how many documents you handle every day, including email messages, memos, and corporate manuals—you could work with hundreds of documents in a single day. XML lets you handle a wide variety of documents in a relatively simple, hierarchical fashion.

When you compare other document creation systems—such as HTML, Adobe's PDF file format, or even various word-processing systems, such as Microsoft Word—none offer the hierarchical option XML does. HTML, PDF, and Word all create documents, but they really have no document-management capabilities. Unless you create your own hierarchical structure, handling massive amounts of Word documents is difficult at best. Finding information stored within these types of documents is even more frustrating. By using XML's hierarchical document-handling capabilities, users can pick and choose the exact data they want without having to plow through all the rest. Unlike HTML and other technologies, such as PDF, XML allows you to store documents in parts, not in a hodge-podge mess.

TIP: *If you would rather not transform all the documents stored on your desktop PC, you might want to consider a third-party indexing product to help you search your computer files, inlcuding your email messages, from a single search interface. AltaVista, the search site, located at **www.altavista.digital.com**, offers a free PC indexing product called AltaVista Discovery that will index not only Web pages but also email messages, PDF files, Word files, and more on a single PC.*

Because XML separates the content from the presentation, it is much easier for search engines, scripting tools, and programming or scripting languages to work with the XML data. Presentation tags don't get in the way. Document structures can be matched within existing systems. Search queries can specify the exact level in the XML document where the user needs to search for information. And all the information can be parsed, processed, and then passed on to a standard Web browser.

Why HTML Doesn't Work

At this point, HTML is definitely the standard for delivering information over an intranet or through the company's extranet, partly because HTML is relatively easy to create, manipulate, and present. Yet with this ease comes a lot of problems for corporations. First, information technology departments must decide on standards: standards for creating files, standards for delivering information, and standards for storing, converting, and searching for information on the company's servers. HTML offers no standards. Instead, standards must be set by the developers themselves. HTML requires no conformity, whereas XML requires conformity for documents to be at the least well-formed and at the most valid. HTML browsers are notoriously forgiving, which means document structures usually correspond to what the designer wants, not what the corporation needs.

Spend a few minutes on your company's intranet viewing various documents' HTML source code, and you'll see that different designers sometimes use different tags and features to accomplish the same thing. Structure? What structure? That's usually the question. The only structure HTML designers have to deal with is simple **<HEAD>**, **<FRAME>**, or **<BODY>** sections. Everything else is left up to interpretation. There really is little or no document validation. The terms *well-formed* and *valid* almost have no meaning within the HTML world. Searching for documents across your network requires a lot more on the back end in terms of scripting and processing. And if a search facility isn't instituted, you must try to figure out the designer's plan on your own.

With HTML, you actually have to create chunks of data, parse them down into workable size, and then think ahead to create hyperlinks that will allow users to jump through the site to the information they need. XML, on the other hand, does all this automatically. Its tree structure, almost like a table of contents, not only makes it easier for humans to pick out the data they want, it also makes it easier for computers to snatch the data components they need. These strict structural requirements make XML a much more sophisticated document-management system than HTML.

Because an XML document does not by itself specify whether or how its information should be displayed, it still needs to work with HTML. The XML data merely contains the facts of the document. HTML is great for presentation but not for dealing with searching or indexing vast amounts of data. There are no facilities within HTML to organize data, describe the content, or specify the various elements that could be searchable. HTML, however, does offer the ability to reference scripting languages, which makes it an ideal system to work with XML data files. XML can provide a means for embedding arbitrary data and annotations within HTML, which extends the possibilities for Web-based applications based on HTML and scripts.

For example, suppose you have a bookstore database. You want your employees to be able to search the online database and your customers to be able to place orders. Both employees and customers would use a standard Web browser to find the information they need. It's not, however, the HTML that finds the information for them. Instead, the individual data records are expressed in XML on the back end, and the results are expressed to the users in HTML. To construct the results, the Web server or the Web browser needs to convert the XML data records into some form of HTML or use an ActiveX control or scripting language to fetch and display the data.

With such data binding mechanisms available to pull the data out of the XML file and arrange it correctly, you have the ability to interactively create pages on the fly. You also reduce the amount of static HTML pages that need to be created for each potential user of the system. And you cut down on server processing because technologies such as Dynamic HTML can quickly do most of the processing on the client side, not the server side.

With XSL, the language used to create style sheets, you can create a collection of programming rules for how to pull information out of an XML document and transform it into another format, such as HTML. Because XSL uses a declarative method to structure style sheets, more people can grasp XSL concepts quicker than if, for example, they were programming the display of the data in another language, such as C++.

TIP: *For more information on how you can convert HTML documents to XML, see Chapter 21. Even if you just skim the chapter, you'll see some of the problems regarding structure and standardization you'll encounter with HTML.*

Why PDF Doesn't Work

When you think about the amount of textual information exchanged in the corporate environment, from policy and procedure manuals to stock reports, the concept behind Adobe's Portable Document Format (PDF) seemed to make sense when it first hit the market several years ago. PDF provides a way to essentially print to a file the contents of any type of document (whether it's a word processing document or a spreadsheet) while still using the fonts inherent in the system that created the file. The electronic file, entirely platform independent, can then be passed around from computer to computer. If users have the Acrobat Reader software or the Acrobat Reader plug-in is installed in their browsers, they can read, search, and print the file in the format in which the original designer created it.

PDF has gained a substantial amount of support, and many Web sites, particularly Web sites for software companies and corporate intranets, use this technology. But PDF is not without problems, not so much in terms of usage but in document management. PDF is basically a display technology. It deals little with document format or structure. In essence, a PDF file is simply a snapshot of a file and has limited capabilities. Documents can be searched but only within the individual document itself.

XML, on the other hand, is much more capable of handling and managing documents, because it is able to provide structured information that a wide variety of applications can understand. You have full control over what applications are deployed on your corporate network to view and manipulate XML documents. Better still, with such structured documents, you can provide a more effective way to search for information—users can base a search on a document's structure instead of just searching for words on a page. Better still, XML lets you specify how the document is presented, whereas the layout and format of PDF documents is hard-coded in the page.

Standardization Is The Key

Although XML offers flexibility, your corporation may find that one of its best features is its need to conform and to be highly structured. The need for structure can mean using industry DTDs or simply creating a template for data input that everyone can use. Already, companies such as Chrysler and Ford have come up with a standard set of element tags for the automotive industry. These element tags are on their way to becoming finalized. And the Open Financial Exchange (OFX) format, which is an XML application created specifically for consumer financial transactions, was proposed by Microsoft and other companies and is up for review by the World Wide Web Consortium. It would provide a standard mechanism for transferring financial data from the consumer to the merchant and then on to the bank or bankcard company.

MasterCard International, along with AT&T, Hewlett-Packard, and Wells Fargo, is leading an initiative for an XML-based application for financial information interchange—the Open Trading Protocol (OTP). It will help financial companies transfer information about their clients through disparate financial systems without the need to replace their existing systems. XML could provide a conduit that passes information from one financial institution to the next.

All of these groups chose XML because of its ability to structure data and, at the same time, offer a tremendous amount of flexibility. Because XML is quickly becoming an industry standard, more and more industry-specific DTDs will be created. And XML is flexible enough that an entirely new programming language can be created for your particular industry. In addition, XML can be used in conjunction with binary systems or client-side scripting languages, such as JavaScript, to extend its functionality.

However, this doesn't mean that binary-based architectures should be tossed in favor of XML—they often work well together. In fact, many vendors that currently offer multi-tier applications that use binary messaging technologies are already looking to XML as a means of providing more efficient data exchange. Their goal is to eliminate data redundancy and foster data reuse. When you add XML to binary messaging transports, you can often leverage the strengths of each to create a more manageable distributed environment.

Standardizing A Simple Memo

Consider why standardization from the document-structure standpoint is important. Take a simple example, such as the corporate memo, and soon you'll see why XML is an excellent language to implement. In the worst-case scenario, although everyone may use the same word processor, employees could be creating their own templates for memos, with various fonts and all sorts of sections, headers, and conventions. There is no standardization; employees may even refer to the company name in a variety of ways.

Even in the best-case scenario, where everyone uses one memo template, various body text formats might be used. Some may put everything in one paragraph, others may use spaces instead of tabs to line up information in columns, and still others may simply use the table option to create columns. Certain advanced users may use style sheets, and others may use only the most basic formatting rules.

You can use XML to define the entire structure of the memo, leaving the content up to the author and the formatting up to the style sheet. The user simply fills in the information, and the XML document, with its accompanying DTD and style sheet, does the rest. The structure of all memos is the same, so when employees need to search for a table outlining last year's production schedule, they simply search the **<TABLE>** element. Because there is a structure and a defined element for tables, they don't have to view each document to find the information they need. Each memo that contains content for the **<TABLE>** element can be accessed quickly.

Entities can be created to further standardize the information included in a memo. For example, if the company name is XYZ Consulting Partners Limited, you could create an entity that everyone within the organization could use in their memos. This would ensure that the use of the company name is consistent and correct. The following line of code is an example of an entity declaration in a company's memo DTD:

```
<!ENTITY coname "XYZ Consulting Partners Limited">
```

When employees need to reference the company name in their documents, they simply insert the entity reference and let the XML parser do the rest. The parser takes the information defined for the entity, locates instances where that entity is referenced in the XML document, and replaces it throughout the document. When it finds the entity reference, it expands the entity and replaces the reference with the information defined for the reference. The code to include the entity reference in memos would look like this:

```
Here at &coname; we pride ourselves on quality consultations.
```

After the code is parsed, the results would look like this:

```
Here at XYZ Consulting Partners Limited we pride ourselves on
quality consultations.
```

But entity references don't have to be simplistic. They can also contain entire sections of documents. For example, specialized clauses for the contracts department could easily be inserted by referencing the intended entity. Groups of Web-page links could be combined in a single entity and referenced on a single Web page. If a link changes, you simply change the link in the entity. You don't have to worry about changing it in your XML document or throughout a collection of XML documents.

By using XML to create a standardized data structure for documents such as memos, the information systems department can integrate an existing XML application called the Channel Definition Format (CDF) to push memos to employees desktops with a few lines of code and an agreed-upon schedule for delivery. Without the ability to standardize the structure of documents, the IS department wouldn't be able to take the memo information and turn it into electronically deliverable documents.

XML Provides Programming Standards

XML provides both XML document developers and XML document authors an easy-to-use, easy-to-learn set of rules. Because of the XML design principles and the ability to create XML documents in standard text format, XML documents and DTDs are usually readable by both humans and computers. Yet, documents built on a set of nested elements can grow complex as layers and layers of additional detail are added.

Although documents can be complex, XML can still easily interface with other systems. It supports a number of standards for character encoding, allowing it to be used by a variety of different computing languages, including Java and C++. When XML is combined with a generic application programming interface

(API), programmers can build parsers relatively easily. One such example is the Simple API in XML (SAX), a free parser available for the PC platform. Parsers are also available in C++, C, JavaScript, Tcl, and Python, to name a few programming languages.

Standardization In Terms Of Data And Display

With XML, you can use the style-sheet features for formatting and displaying XML content or create scripts that turn the XML data into HTML-formatted information. This allows developers and designers to create centralized document formats that can easily be revised without fear of disturbing the actual content or additional programming functionality. Style sheets can be shared by many XML documents. And a single XML data file can be displayed on a variety of systems, including Web-based systems and even portable phone displays.

The way in which the information is displayed depends on how the style sheet has been constructed. The XML data itself knows no boundaries, which means documents no longer have to be created for particular browsers. No longer are companies required to settle on one browser platform or another. With XML, the display is left up to standardized style-sheet mechanisms set forth in XML's Extensible Style Language. Because all the information about style sheets can be stored in a centralized location and then passed along to the browser for processing on the client end, most XML files require less bandwidth to display than their HTML cousins require.

Information and data can be processed at the users' end, so users can extract the XML data from documents and keep it in their own systems if the XML content has been cached there. This would make it easy for users to manipulate and view the information. Price lists, catalog information, the latest news, and company bulletin board information could all be cached, with scheduled updates delivered as necessary. In addition, because the information is formatted in XML and stored locally, it could easily be searched and read offline, extending the capabilities of the content.

XML's modular document and design approach means that XML content editors can edit, programmers can program, and designers can get back to designing without having to worry about content. And because you can link XML files to various programming and scripting languages, many pages can be generated on the fly when a user makes a request for XML data.

All in all, XML requires a corporation to think ahead about how it structures its documents and how the delivery of documents will take place. XML also forces groups within corporations to come together to create DTDs and standard elements, attributes, and entities. Yet the language is flexible enough for designers to create their own style sheets to format information as they see fit.

A prime example of this language's flexibility was demonstrated at the 1997 Seybold conference, when XML was beginning to catch on in the developer community. One conference presentation highlighted the flexibility of XML by creating a complete data set for the *Wall Street Journal* newspaper. This data set information was loaded, processed, and displayed in a variety of views, each accommodating a particular type of reader. There was one page created for the desktop Web user, another for the hand-held computer user, and another for the actual print product. All information was culled from the same data source, but the display changed based upon the user's preference.

Cross-Platform Compatibility

XML files are actually just text files, so they are immediately compatible across platforms. They aren't written for a specific operating system, and they don't require anything more than a text editor and a sharp mind to create. Therefore, there is no need to scrap existing systems or buy new software or hardware just to implement XML. By far, XML is a much easier language to implement than binary-based messaging technologies, such as those implemented on the CORBA or Distributed Component Object Model platform.

XML gives corporations flexibility to store data in a text format without the fear that it will become obsolete or incompatible with future systems. Because the element tags are not specific to a particular browser, corporations won't be limited to one browser or another. Documents can reside on different servers and can easily be moved from one system to another. The only thing you need to do when you move XML data from one location to another (from a Unix server to a Windows NT server, for example) is double-check both relative and external references.

Namespaces In XML

You may be wondering how a DTD can be used across networks and how conformity can be maintained when everything in XML is so extensible. XML inherently provides a mechanism for developers to invent new element names and publish them so more than just the internal network can use them. This functionality is called *namespaces*.

Every element name is subordinated to a Universal Resource Identifier (URI). The URI ensures that even if two developers choose the same name for a particular element, the element name remains unambiguous. The namespace facility lets developers define their own dictionary of elements and XML terms to be used not only on an internal network but also on a public network, such as the Internet. The easiest way to explain how it works is to show you some code that contains namespaces, such as the following:

```
<?XML version="1.0"?>
<xml:schema>
    <namespaceDcl href="http://www.site.com"
     name="site"/>
        <namespaceDcl href="http://www.siteb.com"
        name="siteb"/>
    </xml:schema>

 <xml:data>
    <order>
        New Macintosh iMac
    </order>
    <purchasedby>John B.</purchasedby>
    <siteb:digital-signature>6787409
    </siteb:digital-signature>

    <order>
        Pentium II Computer
    </order>
    <purchasedby>Harry Smith</purchasedby>
    <site:digital-signature>x8931kx
    </site:digital-signature>

</xml:data>
```

What does this code mean? It means that a name that begins with this information is defined by whoever owns the namespace specified in the identifier, **http://www.siteb.com"name="siteb"**. When the site designator is used before the element name, such as in **<site:digital-signature>**, the element name comes from the site that owns it, in this case **http://www.site.com**. By using this kind of element-naming format, you ensure that element names do not conflict with elements defined elsewhere. In other words, when every element is defined in the XML document, the name of the site that owns that predefined element is specified. This indicates that the element is not defined locally, but rather elsewhere. Using this element-naming convention helps to clearly define where the namespaces are located. However, they do not specify processing instructions; they simply tell the person or machine viewing the document where the elements originated. Namespaces simply keep the element and attribute names straight, not only in your network but also across the Internet.

Standardized Character Set And Encoding

All information in XML uses standard character sets and encoding. In fact, all XML information, from the DTD to the actual content, uses Unicode text, which means the elements, attributes, notations, and entity declarations have a standard character set and method of encoding. XML supports the full representation of all international character sets, making it a truly universal markup language.

You can choose to use 16-bit or 8-bit Unicode characters when you create your documents. The default is the UTF-8, or 8-bit encoding. You must use the same encoding throughout the entire document. Parsers, processors, browsers, servers, and other applications, such as Java, must also use Unicode, and surprisingly, programming languages such as Java already do.

XML Integrates With Existing Systems

Because XML data is text only, the content can easily be integrated with existing systems. This can be done through tabular matching methods, by scripting languages, or by simply importing the data directly into the existing systems. XML has no proprietary control over the data, and whatever data is stored in the XML document can easily be extended. XML can be used to provide that bridge or that link between disparate systems. It can interface with Web browsers, databases, editors, and other applications to exchange data.

You can send the client the chunk of data it needs and the client can massage the data according to its specification. This means less server load and less bandwidth requirements because the server isn't being accessed for every single piece of information. Also, because XML documents conform to structural standards to be well-formed, there is no sloppy code. In addition, many standard relational database systems can be used as a means for deploying XML-based messaging systems. Since documents conform to structural standards, data in XML systems can easily be used not only as Web documents but also as other documents, such as email messages. Let's take a look at some of these database systems and how they work with XML to deploy the data users need.

XML And The Database

XML is well suited to work with databases, more so than any other markup language. You can create the structures found in your existing databases, match them to an XML data file, and by using scripting tools and Open Database Connectivity (ODBC), automatically extract the information from the database. From there, you can parse the results to a Web browser. XML is the glue that binds everything together, and as one Sun Microsystem's executive remarked, it "finally gives Java something to do." In this section, we'll examine how you can use XML and a variety of tools, such as Java and XML-specific server technology, to link to database systems.

TIP: *In his keynote address at Seybold '97, Sun's John Gage predicted that XML will end up being the glue that will integrate databases, electronic data interchange, and possibly even operating systems, in essence turning the computer into just another extensible linked document and database.*

Working With Data You Already Have

Database applications, such as Access, Oracle, and even Microsoft Excel, make it relatively easy to organize, store, and view data. With little effort, you can create simple databases to store and display anything from the corporate phone directory to the company's entire payroll records. Most of these applications let you create tabular reports from the data contained in the database. Some even let you create automated functions, such as buttons that, when pressed, print out reports of specific information from the database. This all works great because the data the user wants is formatted the way the user needs it, much like XML can format data in the way users need to view it. The problem with database applications, however, is that other people must have the same application you're using to access the data you've created and formatted. This is not a problem with XML.

To share data, you could export information into an HTML table so those with Web browsers can view it. By doing so, however, you end up with static data instead of dynamic data. When you add something to your database, you have to export and upload a new set of data. You could insist that your visitors use a plug-in, such as KeyView or FormulaOne/Net, for viewing certain file types online, but then the user must download additional software, which may or may not be cross-platform compatible. And other applications the user may have may or may not be able to display the data properly or even at all. This is not compatible with the theory of an intranet or the Internet, where information should be accessible regardless of what platform created the data.

If you use XML, these problems won't arise. Once converted into an XML data source, the data in your database can easily be accessed and manipulated by other XML-aware applications. More importantly, it can be viewed through a Web browser, either one that automatically parses and displays the data or one that works in conjunction with style sheets to display the data. When you turn your data into XML data, thereby turning it into a data source that can be accessed through a Data Source Object (DSO) or through a script, you can do virtually anything with it. And when the data changes, the structure remains the same, so the information is dynamically updated and made available.

You can also use Microsoft's Active Server Page technology to turn Access, Excel, or other tabular data into an XML data source. The data would then be transformed into an ASP file, which can be turned into an HTML Web page. You can accomplish several things by turning your data into an XML data source. First, you can populate, update, edit, delete, and manipulate your data through the use of scripting. You can create automatic scripts to update large chunks of data. For example, if you were working with a payroll database and wanted to give everyone in the accounting department a five percent raise, you could easily do that by scripting a mathematical equation used to grant a raise. Then, you could place that mathematical equation in the database application and apply the equation across the database file, for the specific group of employees who are up for the raise.

TIP: *For more information about connecting your Access databases to and turning them into XML files, read Chapter 13. There, you'll find an example of how Access data can be viewed with a standard Web browser by using XML as the conduit between the two systems.*

Because the XML data source is generated dynamically from the data within the database, as the database is updated, so too is the XML data source. You can use other database tools, such as Access or Excel, to create ad hoc reports, manage data, or simply work with a familiar interface and simultaneously maintain the XML data source with no additional effort.

XML Applications In The Corporate World

Many companies are using CDF to deliver companywide information at times when network usage is at a minimum. But the use of XML-based applications doesn't stop there. With the introduction of the Open Software Description (OSD), information systems departments are quickly and easily updating core software components without having to visit the client's desktop. All the information is specified with the OSD XML data file, including the links to the software cabinet files, and it is pushed to the user's desktop at a specified time. The updates are sent during slow network hours and do not affect the user's computer in any other way than to update the specified software.

TIP: *For more information on OSD and other XML applications, see Chapter 18. A full list of element tags is included, along with examples on how OSD can be put to good use.*

Software vendors are also incorporating XML into their server and processing software. One such company, DataChannel, has implemented XML in its ChannelManager software. You can think of ChannelManager as a kind of extended version of Microsoft's Channel Definition Format, because it takes the idea of push technology and maximizes the features to deliver documents to the user's desktop in one complete, easy-to-program package.

ChannelManager consists of three major components:

- A Web server to transmit the content of the channels and to process user logins

- A database that contains the channel content, presentation information, and list of users and groups who can access the information

- A dynamically generated Java applet, which is downloaded to users each time they log in to the Web server

This is how ChannelManager works. First, you create users and groups who are authorized to access certain content stored in the database. Any authorized user can create a new channel and publish information to the rest of the organization with a few clicks of the mouse button. Unlike Microsoft's CDF, users don't have to know anything about HTML or XML. They simply need to know what content they want to send out and the list of users who should receive the information.

Because the information is being transmitted through a Web server, it is viewable through any standard Web browser regardless of the computer the intended recipient uses. Mac, Windows, and even Unix users can easily view the channel information. There is no need for specialized browser software or specialized programming. Netscape Navigator 3 or Microsoft Internet Explorer 4 can be used. ChannelManager is not browser specific like Microsoft's CDF or Netscape's Netcaster XML-based push technology.

When new information becomes available or updates to existing information are required, ChannelManager uses scripting to locate the list of subscribed users, pushes (automatically sends) the information to the user, and dynamically generates a new Web page or pages on the user's desktop. The user doesn't have to go to a particular server or Web site or even log in to email to get the new information. No additional software or downloads are required.

Each ChannelManager database and server can be set up so that only certain people within the organization have permission to send or receive information. There are five levels of permissions available, and those who publish the content can specify who can and cannot see the information. For example, if the human resources department has recently completed the results of an employee benefit survey, it can share the information electronically with the managers of the company but lock out all other employees from seeing confidential data. Groups of users can be defined, and those groups can have certain restrictions placed on them for subscribing, viewing, and publishing content.

What's best about this type of XML-based application is that it requires no knowledge of HTML. Multiple data types can be used for the content, including Word,

PowerPoint, or even Excel documents. All these documents are considered part of the **<ITEM>** element within the ChannelManager software, which then extracts the metadata from the document specified as content and dynamically creates an XML file that can then be processed over the network.

Currently, several large organizations are using ChannelManager. One such company, an investment firm, uses it to send exchange investment information and commodity trading tips to its thousands of traders in 380 offices worldwide. Another organization, a large employment firm, uses it to send human resource information to its employees. The company also uses ChannelManager to send resumes of potential clients to its employees instead of clogging the email server with large files saved in Word document format.

A Glimpse At How Corporations Are Using XML

XML already has a jump-start in the corporate world in many respects. SGML has been used for years in the U.S. Government Printing Office, at IBM, and within the U.S. Department of Defense and the Internal Revenue Service. With everything moving toward the Web, the IRS will most likely begin to store tax form information in an XML-enabled database that can then be used to dynamically generate Web pages. These Web pages could be tax forms or they could be information about taxpayers and the amount of taxes they have already paid. Instead of offering information in PDF file format, the taxpayer would no longer need to download a separate application to view or print tax forms or taxpayer information.

But government agencies aren't the only entities using XML. Ericsson Incorporated, a division of the Swedish telecommunications equipment manufacturer, has licensed a software development product called the Web Automation Toolkit from a company called webMethods, located at **www.webmethods.com**. Ericsson plans to use this XML-based tool to create a link between the Web and their wireless telephones. Because XML can use style sheets to display information in almost any format the developer chooses, people can use wireless phones to search directory databases stored on a Web server the same way they do on their computers at home.

Some 30 designers are using webMethod's Automation Toolkit to create a search mechanism to help reduce the time it takes to find and retrieve images off CD-ROMs. The images, which are used in both print and television advertising, are sold by various stock photography agencies. Finding the right image for the job used to mean searching Web sites, books, and CD-ROMs for the perfect piece. Using the webMethod's Automation Toolkit, CD-ROM searches are cached and cataloged. Designers can use the search information again and again to quickly find the images they need without having to go back through each CD-ROM.

The healthcare industry is also jumping on the XML bandwagon in an effort to share patient data across various types of systems and networks. A group of healthcare-related vendors and service providers called the Health Level 7 (HL7) standards body is working on a plan called the Kona proposal that is aimed at enabling the exchange of medical information. This exchange would happen not with some vendor-based standard software package, but with XML and some SGML. The idea is to structure the patient data in such a way that the information could quickly move from one system to the next instead of tying it to a single vendor solution. This would allow patients to take their medical records with them and be assured that the same information will be valid at whatever healthcare facility they choose.

If a hospital needs to consult with the patient's insurance company, the hospital could theoretically use a standard Web browser to connect to the insurance company's system and then pull up the medical information and records it needs for the patient's care. XML would enable an open platform for this data. This is just one of many industry-specific proposals being introduced to the World Wide Web Consortium. Expect many more in the future.

TIP: *You can read more about the HL7 proposal on the World Wide Web Consortium's Web page at **www.w3.org/HL7**.*

4: Implementing XML In A Corporate Environment

Immediate Solutions

In this section, we'll take a look at how corporations are using XML within their intranets. Some use XML as an enhancement to existing technology, whereas others are creating whole new applications around XML. Many corporations are using XML in innovative ways to deliver data to the desktop.

XML At Work: The Siemens TimeCard System

With more than 7,000 employees to keep track of, Siemens needed to find a better way to manage employee time and save money at the same time. They needed a way to track, transfer, and analyze information about employee time cards and records. The Siemens TimeCard System, also called the Time and Attendance System, is entirely Web-based. A Microsoft Internet Information Server (IIS) handles the flow of data, distributing it to the various resources—employees, managers, and the accounting system. The system was developed by Open Minded Solutions, a company that creates specialized human resource applications that can be deployed over intranets. Open Minded Solutions first creates the data structure in XML and then provides a link to the data so employees can use the Internet Explorer browser to view it. When Microsoft releases its Office 2000 upgrade to the popular Microsoft Office suite of applications, the Seimens system will easily integrate with Microsoft Office, providing ways to view, exchange, and read XML data that is stored on the existing IIS server.

The system is relatively simplistic, but a great deal of planning went into setting it up. Various pieces of data needed to be reused throughout the employee Time and Attendance System. An employee can log into the time-card system and his or her time card data, including a work history where the employee has logged in and logged out, can be shared among supervisors, human resources, and accounting. Here is how the system works:

- The employee submits time cards electronically through a Web page form. The information about the employee—name, type of employee, shift, and employee identification number—is placed at the top of the time-card form after the employee has logged in. This employee information is stored in Siemens's Directory Database, and the application uses the Windows NT

Security Identifier (SID) to automatically identify the user. All of this is done on the fly; the page is dynamically generated. If there is a set schedule for the employee, the schedule is generated based on the current date and the employee's work schedule. Before the user can enter the hours worked, the application checks for system availability, authenticates the user, and checks for data incompatibility.

- This information is saved to the server, which stores it in the right location and, if necessary, forwards it to the appropriate manager.

- The manager approves the time card. The information stored within the electronic time card is tied to the company's HR records, so standard reusable information, such as name, Social Security number, and department, can be quickly displayed when the manager pulls up the employee time-card record.

- The time card is validated against payroll records based on a paycode specified in the employee record. Paycodes specify certain rules and pay-rate tables that provide information such as hourly rate, frequency of pay, and so forth.

- If a manager is not going to be available during the time-card processing period, he or she can temporarily delegate the approval authority to a subordinate because the managerial information, such as approval routing, is tied to the HR and organizational system.

- If the manager doesn't know the phone number of the person to which he or she wants to delegate authority, he or she can look it up in the corporation-wide Directory Database, which is also tied into HR and payroll records.

- The employees use only the information they need to access the various documents, and most of the data is processed locally on the client machine, thereby reducing the load on the server.

Constructing The System

XML provided Siemens with a way to develop such an elaborate system by simplifying the development process. Regardless of what the data was or how it was being accessed—whether it was an employee punching in electronically through a Web-based form or a manager viewing the results of a payroll through an email message—XML provided a standardized data structure. The Document Object Model was used to write additional data-intensive applets for the client.

First, the design team had to consider what information needed to be seen by both employee and manager. They were able to quickly create the data model by considering how a simple time card worked and what fields were contained in it.

The time card became the structural model for their time-card DTD, which is shown here:

```
<!-- Siemens Employee Timecard -->
<!element timecard - - (paycodes?,submitted?,approved?)>
<!attlist timecard
period cdata #implied -- WEEKEND_DATE --
serial cdata #implied -- SERIAL --
fullname cdata #implied -- FULLNAME --
email cdata #implied -- MAIL_STOP --
manager cdata #implied -- MANAGER --
department cdata #implied -- DEPT --
exempt cdata #implied -- EXEMPT --
status cdata #implied -- STATUS --
type cdata #implied -- TYPE --
shift cdata #implied -- SHIFT --
days cdata #implied -- SCHEDULED_DAYS --
hours cdata #implied -- SCHEDULED_HOURS --
effective cdata #implied -- EFFECT_DATE --
>
<!element paycodes - - (paycode*)>
<!element paycode - - empty>
<!attlist paycode
batch cdata #required -- BATCH_NUM --
period cdata #implied -- WEEKEND_DATE --
code cdata #required -- CODE --
mon cdata #required -- MON --
tue cdata #required -- TUE --
wed cdata #required -- WED --
thu cdata #required -- THU --
fri cdata #required -- FRI --
sat cdata #required -- SAT --
sun cdata #required -- SUN --
total cdata #required -- TOTAL_HOURS --
submitted cdata #implied -- SUBMITTED_DATE --
submitter cdata #implied -- SUBMITTED_SERIAL --
approved cdata #implied -- APPROVED_DATE --
approver cdata #implied -- APPROVED_SERIAL -->

<!element submitted - - rcdata>
<!attlist submitted
date cdata #implied
serial cdata #implied
fullname cdata #implied>
```

```
<!element approved - - rcdata>
<!attlist approved
date cdata #implied
serial cdata #implied
fullname cdata #implied>
```

Next, the design team created a DTD that models the existing Directory Database, the database that contains all the information about the employee—from name to serial number to pay rate. Then, they used XML's search ability to match up the fields in the two DTDs in an effort to populate the initial time-card Web-page entry form. When the employee logged on, information about the employee was generated on the fly to the Web page and displayed.

From that point, it was a matter of managing all the data that flowed in and out of the Web pages, IIS server, and various databases. The design team used a product called ObjectStore to manage the data. ObjectStore is an object database management system that provides native storage for structured data such as XML, C++ objects, or Java objects. The Object Minded Solutions developer team realized that using such an object-oriented database meant they did not have to write or maintain any mapping code to match up the structure of the XML document with other data systems.

One important element that had to be managed and that worked well in XML were the pay periods. The DTD to define the pay periods looked like this:

```
<!-- PayPeriods -->
<!entity #default system>
<!element payperiods - o (payperiod*)>
<!attlist payperiods
future cdata #required
history cdata #required
schema cdata #required
period cdata #implied
>
<!element payperiod - - empty>
<!attlist payperiod
week cdata #required -- WEEK_DATE --
cycle cdata #required -- PAY_PERIOD --
holiday cdata #required -- HOL_WEEK --
batch cdata #required -- LAST_BATCH_NUM --
current cdata #required -- CURR_PROCESS --
calculate cdata #required -- CALC_DATE --
>
```

If for some reason the pay period needed to be adjusted (such as for holidays), the XML developer simply needed to add a holiday attribute to the payperiod DTD. Because the software stores all the information in an object database, when a new branch from the overall element tree is added, the ObjectStore software simply adds a pointer to the new element attribute object.

After all the information is entered, the manager, who has his or her own DTD, processes the time card. Email messages are sent to employees notifying them that their time cards have been accepted. All the data is reused once again in the email message by simply picking it out of the XML Document Object Model. The manager DTD creates the data structure for the managerial information needed to process the time card:

```
<!-- Siemens Manager -->
<!element manager - - (departments,delegations,others)>
<!attlist manager
serial cdata #required -- SERIAL --
fullname cdata #required -- FULLNAME --
>
<!element departments - - (department*)>
<!element delegations - - (department*)>
<!element others - - (department*)>
<!element department - - empty>
<!attlist department
depart cdata #required -- DEPART --
>
```

The ObjectStore software supports cross-references between the DTDs because it stores the relationships between the objects in the XML DTDs in its database. Once that information is used, pointers are stored in memory so the information can again be easily accessed.

Continuing on, if the manager is to approve the time cards, the Time and Attendance System needs to surmise which department the manager has approval authority for. Because managers may delegate that authority, the system has to be able to check not only the current manager's authority, but any temporarily designated manager's authority as well. That means a separate DTD needed to be built to cross-reference any delegated managers and their authority:

```
<!-- Siemens Employee Timecards -->
<!entity % timecard.dtd system "timecard.dtd">
<!element department - - (payee*)>
<!attlist department
depart cdata #implied -- DEPART --
```

```
period cdata #implied -- WEEKEND_DATE --
>
<!element payee - - (timecard*)>
<!attlist payee
serial cdata #required -- SERIAL --
fullname cdata #required -- FULLNAME --
manager cdata #implied -- MANAGER --
department cdata #implied -- DEPT --
email cdata #implied -- MAIL_STOP --
>
%timecard.dtd;
```

After this information has traversed through the ObjectStore database and the signing authority has been verified, it can be passed along to the final payroll and accounting systems. ObjectStore can retain and forward the information on to the various systems as required, and the final paycheck can then be processed.

Using XML As A Conduit Between Systems

By using XML and combining it with an object-oriented database that understands XML, the developers reduced the overall amount of code that needed to be written for all this information to be processed. This is a prime example of how XML can act as a conduit between systems, carrying information back and forth from time card to Web page form to company directory database and finally on to the payroll system. Siemens anticipates saving $500,000 a year by reducing duplication, data entry errors, and redundancy. And the director of account services, Pat Nocero, has said that the company anticipates saving millions with the system that can easily grow without having to employ additional support costs.

Examining RivCom's Competence Gap Analysis Tool

RivCom, a consulting firm in England (**www.rivcom.com**), used XML to create a rather elaborate system for Shell Services International. Called the Competence Gap Analysis Tool, this system was designed to be an interactive tool to help people define what skill levels were needed for certain jobs within the organization and how those skills rated in the overall job requirements. It was also a tool that helped define exactly how individual employees ranked in terms of job skills. This was a massive data-driven application that required a database that lists jobs, skill levels, employees, and job requirements.

Because Shell operates worldwide and uses a variety of hardware and software platforms, the information has to be available across platforms. XML was chosen not only because it is cross-platform compatible, but also because it would allow different views of the same data. Also, the consulting company, RivCom, decided to go with XML, because it is relatively easy to use and combine with existing systems. For RivCom, XML could be used to quickly create a system that appears to meet the needs of all the users without spending a lot of time writing additional programs to work with XML.

The system RivCom developed is called RivComet. It uses XML to store the data and style sheets to display the results. The information users access can easily be downloaded and manipulated a variety of ways without strain or overload on existing servers. The cost to develop such an application was relatively low, and the anticipated update costs appear to be relatively minimal as well because most of the changes will be simple modifications to the style sheets.

RivCom decided to use an ActiveX control working in conjunction with the Internet Explorer browser and the XML data. The XML job data is a collection of nested elements. These nested elements enable the user to browse through the list of rules for job competency. From this list, the user can then add additional requirements for the job so that prospective employees and human resource people can know exactly what's required. The person setting up those additional requirements can assign what requirements are needed for the job by easily selecting those nested elements that are tied to the additional job requirements. The following is an example of a portion of the XML file used to accomplish this:

```
<comp ID="cpcf1" required="0" indiv="0">
<title>Delegation</title>
<desc>
Creates appropriate scope of work, authority,
and schedules for staff and is able to delegate work
in the confidence that at least the desired output
will be achieved.
</desc>
</comp>

<comp ID="cpcf2" required="0" indiv="0">
<title>Respect</title>
<desc>
Demonstrates a fundamental respect for,
and a genuine interest in, people at work,
understands individuals and provides caring support for
them at times of need.
</desc>
</comp>
```

In this example, the attributes of the **<COMP>** element are **required** and **indiv**. Both are set to zero, and this indicates that no competency levels for this particular job have been set yet. When competency levels have been set, the style sheets determine how the information will be displayed.

RivCom decided to use virtually no HTML to create the resulting files. All the information displayed is actually generated on the fly by the RivComet ActiveX control created for Shell. The process of generating the results is as follows:

1. The initial HTML page contains RivComet, the small piece of JavaScript. It also contains some HTML that consists of a single empty **DIV** element.

2. Internet Explorer 4 is used to create a Document Object Model.

3. From there, the JavaScript sends the RivComet ActiveX control the name of the file that should be retrieved and displayed.

4. The ActiveX control uses a Windows API to retrieve the specified file.

5. At this point, the file contains XML content, a set of style sheets, and RivCom's own declarative style language, which is used to further format the data.

6. The ActiveX control parses the XML document and attaches a style sheet and formatting rules to the file. It also applies the rules to the XML content. It does this in order to generate HTML, which it then creates dynamically and places within the empty **DIV** element created in the DOM.

7. Finally, the browser re-renders the page with the fully populated DOM, and the HTML page appears on the screen.

Comparing HTML To XML

Here, we'll examine how HTML and XML compare for creating and delivering some standard corporate-type data. This information needs to be delivered over the Web with a standard Web browser. The company in this example is a bookstore with an online catalog that needs to be accessed by customers and other vendors. The following elements need to be created, so these individuals can interact with the online bookstore:

- *ISBN*—The publishing industry's identifying number for each book

- *Title*—The title of the book

- *Author*—The author of the book

- *Publisher*—The publisher's name

- *Price*—The retail price of the book

- *Book club price*—Special discount price for book club members

Before XML, you may have considered creating a Web page for each book you have in inventory or stock on a regular basis. You might even place your list of books in your own database and add reviews and publicity information from a variety of sources to the final Web page for each book.

After you've switched to XML, created a bookstore DTD, and created style sheets to present the information in a variety of ways, you can do away with the Web pages. You can also do a lot more with a lot less, especially in terms of processing the information:

- *Automate*—Automate the process of ordering. If a publisher comes out with a new book and uses the same DTD you use to describe the book, you immediately have that book in your catalog. You can also automate the process of ordering books by providing key information for each order. It wouldn't matter what system you used, because you could easily pull the data out of your database, construct it in XML, and pass it along to the book reseller's systems.

- *Provide better searching*—Not only will you be able to provide better searching for your employees, but you can now provide better searching for those using your online system. All books are now cataloged by the same elements and can easily be searched across these elements.

- *Exchange data with publishers and other suppliers*—Because the data is structured in a standard format, you can exchange information with suppliers and publishers. Information may contain comments and reviews about the books, pricing information, sales history, and so on. This information could easily be sent to their systems to help track marketing and sales promotions.

- *No worry about the browser*—No longer do you have to worry that your online customers have the latest software. The store employees no longer have to answer calls about browsers or where to locate the right browser to view your site. If you want to create a page that uses specific features of a new browser, you can simply adjust the formatting of the style sheets, leaving all the data intact. Also, you can easily create a style sheet for Palm Pilot users and not have to worry about structuring or repurposing content just for them.

Part II

XML Pieces And Parts

Chapter 5

DTDs In XML

By Cheryl Kirk

In Depth

A *Document Type Definition* (DTD) is the foundation from which XML documents are created. You can create DTDs or use predefined DTDs from such industries as medicine and automobile manufacturing that describe standardized documents. Whether you create your own DTD or use a predefined DTD, you need to know what a DTD is, how it is constructed, and how it works.

In this chapter, we'll show you how to read, understand, and create DTDs. We'll show you how to determine when an external DTD is needed and when to use an internal DTD. We'll explore why you might want to use previously defined DTDs. Creating a DTD is the first step in structuring your XML documents properly. It's the DTD that provides the XML parser with the information necessary to do its job.

What Is A DTD?

A Document Type Definition (DTD) defines the parts of a document and outlines how they can and cannot be used, what can be placed in them, and whether they are required pieces of the document. Basically, a DTD is a set of rules that define the instructions that will be sent to the parser for the document that is going to be parsed. A DTD can include a set of element and attribute declarations and the entities, notations, and comments you want to use. The various component declarations determine how the document will be structured and then send that information (the instructions) to the parser. The parser in turn sends the results to the viewing application.

The easiest way to explain what a full DTD looks like and how it works is to take a quick look at one. The following DTD is for a relatively simple document and is meant to demonstrate how a DTD looks and operates. It is an example of an internal DTD, which is a DTD that is included within an XML document:

```
<?XML version="1.0" encoding="UTF-8" standalone="no"?>
<!DOCTYPE DOC [
<!ELEMENT DOC (SUBJECT, DATE, ADDRESS, MEMO)>
<!ELEMENT SUBJECT (#PCDATA)>
<!ELEMENT DATE (#PCDATA)>
<!ELEMENT ADDRESS (#PCDATA)>
<!ELEMENT MEMO (#PCDATA)>
<!ENTITY PUBLISHER "The Coriolis Group">
```

```
]>
<DOC>
<SUBJECT>Today's Memo</SUBJECT>
<DATE>August 1, 2000</DATE>
<ADDRESS>200 West 34th Suite 953, Anchorage, AK</ADDRESS>
<MEMO>This memo is to alert you to the new XML
Black Book has now been printed. Published by
&PUBLISHER;, this book outlines everything you
need to know about XML.</MEMO>
</DOC>
```

Notice that the definitions that set up the document are included in order (from the first to the last) within the document itself. These definitions, which are actually processing instructions, tell the XML parser exactly how to handle the various data that will be placed within the document and what information or text should replace any entities specified within the document itself. A DTD that is included within a document is called an *internal DTD subset* because all the processing instructions and the document data itself are included within a single document.

After the preceding example is parsed and displayed in a browser, the result would be as follows (assuming an applicable style sheet is attached):

```
Today's Memo
August 1, 2000

200 West 34th Suite 953, Anchorage, AK

This memo is to alert you to the new XML
Black Book has now been printed. Published by
The Coriolis Group, this book outlines everything you
need to know about XML.
```

The XML parser checks the marked-up document against the various element declarations. It also replaces the entity that is specified with the entity value declared in the entity declaration. In this example, it replaces the **&PUBLISHER;** entity reference with the declared entity value, **The Coriolis Group**. The style sheet specified later in a separate HTML file handles the display of the data.

TIP: *For more information on creating and incorporating style sheets into your XML documents, check out Chapter 14.*

Let's take a closer look our example to get a feeling for what each line of code is doing in terms of defining the document. Here's a quick rundown of the most important components of this document:

5: DTDs In XML

- **<?XML version="1.0" encoding="UTF-8" standalone="no"?>**—The XML declaration specifies that the document is an XML document. It is the first line of instructions that is sent to the parser. For more specific information about the XML declaration, see "The XML Declaration" section later in this chapter.

- **<!DOCTYPE DOC [**—The document type declaration specifies where the DTD is located. In this case, it's located within the document itself, but it could have been specified as being in another location, such as **<!DOCTYPE novel PUBLIC "-//Megginson//DTD Novel//EN" "novel.dtd>**.

- **<!ELEMENT DOC (SUBJECT, DATE, ADDRESS, MEMO)>**—Defines the list of elements for the root **DOC** element. This element declaration tells the parser that the root element **DOC** contains the child elements **SUBJECT**, **DATE**, **ADDRESS**, and **MEMO** and that they must appear in this order within the document. If they don't, the processor will return an error.

- **<!ELEMENT SUBJECT (#PCDATA)>**—Defines the element **SUBJECT** and specifies that the element will contain parsed character data.

- **<!ELEMENT DATE (#PCDATA)>**—Defines the element **DATE** and specifies that the element will contained parsed character data.

- **<!ELEMENT ADDRESS (#PCDATA)>**—Defines the element **ADDRESS** and specifies that the element will contain parsed character data.

- **<!ELEMENT MEMO (#PCDATA)>**— Defines the element **MEMO** and specifies that the element will contain parsed character data.

- **<!ENTITY PUBLISHER "The Coriolis Group">**—Defines a simple entity, **PUBLISHER**, and specifies that the value for this entity is **"The Coriolis Group"**.

- **]>**—Indicates the end of the DTD.

Declarations

A *declaration* is markup that gives the XML processor special instructions on how to process the document. You can have element declarations, attribute declarations, entity declarations, notation declarations, processor declarations, and document type declarations. Let's examine the two most important declarations, the processor declaration and the document type declaration. Unlike element, attribute, entity, and notation declarations, the processor declaration and the document type declaration don't construct the document. They don't explain the structural role of any particular element or attribute. Instead, they tell the processor what standards to use, what type of document is being processed, and where the DTD that actually constructs the document is stored.

Let's take a look once again at the two lines of code that define the processor declaration, or *XML declaration*, and the document type declaration:

```
<?XML version="1.0" encoding="UTF-8" standalone="no">
<!DOCTYPE DOC [
```

The XML Declaration

The first line in the preceding example is called the XML declaration, and it tells the processor to use version 1 of the XML specification to process the document as an XML document. Currently, there is only one version of the specification, but as new versions become available, you can indicate which processor applications can and cannot process the document based on the version of XML the processor recognizes. The second part of the XML declaration specifies what kind of encoding will be used for the document. In this example, we are using the 8-bit Unicode character-encoding scheme, but we could specify 16- or 32-bit as well. For an in-depth discussion of Unicode, see "Parts Of A DTD" later in this chapter.

The final piece of information that we've included in our XML declaration is called the *standalone document declaration*. It specifies whether or not an XML document relies on any external sources of information. For example, if the value is set to "**yes**", the document wouldn't use an external DTD or any external parameter entities. In other words, the document is completely self-sufficient and all the pertinent information is contained with the XML document itself.

A value of "**yes**" also tells the processor to ignore any markup declarations that point to external references. A value of "**no**" tells the processor that it can process any external markup declarations. When you set the standalone attribute to "**no**", you are simply telling the XML processor that the document can reference any external declarations, such as external DTDs. That doesn't mean you have to include external references, only that the processor should accept and process any if they are noted in the document.

When do you set the standalone declaration to "**no**" and when do you set it to "**yes**"? If your external DTD contains attribute declarations with any default values set and those values apply to elements appearing in your document, you need to set the value to "**no**". You also need to set the value to "**no**" if your document contains any white space at all. You can also consider setting the value to "**no**" when your document contains entities and the entity references appear within the actual content of the document. You can set the value to "**yes**" if you aren't using external entity references and if you're only using the general entities that are specified as part of the XML language, such as an ampersand, a greater than or less than symbol, an apostrophe, or quotation marks.

The Document Type Declaration

The second line of code is called the **DOCTYPE** declaration, or document type declaration, and it's used to associate the XML document with its corresponding DTD. Following **<!DOCTYPE** is the name of the DTD used. In the case of an internal DTD, the list of elements and attributes defined for the internal DTD follows the **<!DOCTYPE** declaration. The document type declaration is where the XML author specifies the DTD as public or private. Next, after the close bracket, either the actual DTD appears or a reference locator to where the DTD exists is specified. If you don't specify a DTD, you don't give the XML processor the information needed to construct the document.

You can specify that the DTD is part of the document by including brackets and outlining the DTD within the document, or you can specify an external DTD. For a discussion about when you should use internal DTDs or external DTDs, see "External Vs. Internal DTDs" later in this chapter.

Here is an example of a DTD that is included in a document:

```
<!DOCTYPE DOC [
<!ELEMENT DOC (SUBJECT, DATE, ADDRESS, MEMO)>
<!ELEMENT SUBJECT (#PCDATA)>
<!ELEMENT DATE (#PCDATA)>
<!ELEMENT ADDRESS (#PCDATA)>
<!ELEMENT MEMO (#PCDATA)>
<!ENTITY PUBLISHER "The Coriolis Group">
]>
```

Here is an example of an externally stored DTD:

```
<!DOCTYPE book PUBLIC "-//CompanyXYZ//DTD book//EN"
 "http://www.site.com/dtds/book.dtd">
```

Where DTDs Can Be Stored

A DTD can be stored internally or externally. In this example, we are storing the DTD internally:

```
<?XML version="1.0" encoding="UTF-8" standalone="no">
<!DOCTYPE DOC [
```

Internal DTDs combine all the elements, attributes, notations, and entities within the XML document. Internal DTDs are placed at the beginning of the document within the document type declaration. The document type declaration is responsible for pointing the processor to the DTD. It connects the DTD to the document.

Think of it as the glue that binds the document to the definition that explains the document. Internal DTDs are specified with the following code within the document type declaration:

```
<!DOCTYPE [ Beginning of the DTD....]>
```

External DTDs are also placed within the document type declaration, but instead of holding all the elements, attributes, and entities, the document type declaration specifies the external file that holds the DTD. The name of the external DTD doesn't have to correspond to the XML document, but it does have to have the three-letter extension of .dtd. For example, if your XML document is named BIZMEMO, you might want to name the DTD MEMO.DTD, instead of something like XYZ.DTD. Remember, DTDs can be used and reused. You can create multiple documents that use the same DTD. This is one of the most powerful features of XML. Having the ability to create a single DTD to encompass a variety of documents that are based on a common structure makes it possible for you to create standardized ways to present information.

Public And System DTDs

You may find yourself using publicly available DTDs that have already been defined for a particular need, or you may settle on using your own locally developed DTD. When you use a publicly available DTD, you need to use the keyword **PUBLIC** within the document type declaration when you specify the DTD. And when you use your own DTD, you need to use the keyword **SYSTEM**. Here's an example of the code for declaring a publicly available DTD:

```
<!DOCTYPE book PUBLIC "-//CompanyXYZ//DTD book//EN"
 "http://www.site.com/dtds/book.dtd">
```

The public identifier structure used by XML for publicly available DTDs is the same structure used for Standard Generalized Markup Language (SGML) public identifiers. If the specified entity or DTD is an ISO standard, you must start the DTD with ISO. If it's not an ISO standard but the standard is officially approved by a standards body, start the declaration with a plus sign; if it's not officially approved by a standards body, start the declaration with a minus sign. Following the identifier are two forward slashes (//) and then the owner of the DTD. If we dissect the document type declaration in the preceding example, we find that the DTD specified is not standard and that CompanyXYZ owns this DTD. We also find that the name of the DTD is **book** and it's located at **http://www.site.com/** in the dtds directory.

Now, let's take a look at an example of what a document type declaration looks like when we are specifying a DTD stored on a local system:

```
<!DOCTYPE book SYSTEM "http"//www.site.com/dtds/book.dtd">
```

This declaration includes just the keyword **SYSTEM** followed by the location and file name of the DTD. Because it's assumed that this DTD is owned internally, there are no double slashes, nor is there an owner name for the DTD.

TIP: *You can nest one DTD within another, which means, in essence, that the first DTD is calling another DTD.*

To DTD Or Not To DTD

As you know by now, one of the features of XML is that it doesn't require a DTD (unlike SGML, which always requires one). Because XML was fashioned to work within the constraints of the World Wide Web, there may be times when a DTD simply doesn't work because of bandwidth limitations. In that case, you can include the element and attribute definitions within the document itself.

So, how do you know exactly when you need a DTD and when you don't? And how do you know when you should make it internal and when you should make it external? There are several mitigating factors that will help you decide:

- *Large documents require external DTDs.* DTDs are essential for large documents. With an external DTD, you can create a certain amount of standardization, which makes the document more coherent because users of the DTD will have to follow certain rules.

- *Small documents don't require external DTDs.* Unless you want to standardize every single bit of data in your company, you should consider not creating a DTD for simple correspondence, like one-page memos or faxes.

- *Some Internet-oriented documents don't require DTDs.* Bandwidth constraints may mean that having an external DTD means more bandwidth overhead.

- *Nonvalidating XML processors don't require a DTD.* When you use a nonvalidating XML processor that only checks for well-formedness, you don't need an external DTD.

Although we've given you guidelines to help you determine when you must include a DTD and when it's not required, you really should consider creating a DTD for each document you create and keep it separate from the document or documents with which it works. By creating and keeping DTDs in a separate file, they're not only reusable, but also easier to manage, update, and change. You can also make it easier to prevent people from changing the DTDs.

External Vs. Internal DTDs

Once you've decided to create a DTD, you need to determine if it should be stored internally or externally. The size of the document is only one consideration. You also need to consider exactly what your document needs are and whether you need to be concerned about its validity.

Internal DTDs

When you create a document, the first thing you should ask yourself is whether the document needs to be self-contained. A self-contained document can be moved from system to system without losing components. You can use the document on your local system without the need to be connected to the Internet. You can also place a self-contained document on a disk or cartridge drive and carry it with you wherever you go. And any XML processor can process it without having to look for an accompanying DTD.

Another reason for placing the DTD information within a single file is to cut down on the amount of processing time and the amount of bandwidth required to load, parse, and display the file. It is sometimes more efficient to place the DTD within the document so the XML processor only has to read one file—not two, three, or more—to display the information.

Finally, using an internally placed DTD means you are creating a self-contained file, that is both valid and complete. Any XML processor can process it without having to look for an external DTD file.

External DTDs

Although they do add to a certain amount of overhead, processing time, and bandwidth requirements, it's better to use external DTDs. Why? They offer many benefits, especially in the area of document management, updating, and editing. Here are just a few reasons you would want to use an external DTD:

- *If you use an external DTD, you can use public DTDs.* A public DTD may have all the capabilities you need. Instead of reinventing the wheel, you can use a DTD that someone else has already built, and that means your document structure will be standard. Updates to a public DTD are automatically incorporated within your documents.

- *With small documents, you can focus on content.* Instead of worrying about the structure of a small document, you can focus on creating the content. You can use an externally stored DTD so you don't have to worry about putting all the information about the document structure within a small document. For quick documents that need to match a particular structure, an external DTD is preferable.

- *External DTDs provide for better document management.* With external DTDs, you can easily create a set of documents that define rules for specific needs. Then, you can edit and update the DTD as required without having to open the XML content document, much as you would when reformatting a style sheet. Also, instead of reentering the same information again and again, you enter the information once. You don't have to worry about whether you've entered the same element name in a variety of documents.

- *External DTDs make it easier to validate your document.* If you need to use validating XML processors to find errors in your XML data and don't want to confuse the content with the structure, you can use external DTDs to find inconsistencies within your document.

Parts Of A DTD

As with any great masterpiece, there are certain building blocks you need to use to construct your DTD. DTDs have elements and attributes just as the actual XML document does. However, the DTD is not just used to mark up content—it defines these elements and attributes. Everything about the document—from the entities to the elements that help construct the document—is defined in the DTD. There is no content in a DTD, only definitions.

TIP: *You must use the correct XML syntax when you create your DTDs. Otherwise, you'll find that your document won't parse, and you'll have nothing but errors. Learn the syntax for elements, attributes, and entities. If you need more information about how to read the XML specification and understand how elements, attributes, and entities are constructed, review Chapter 2.*

When you think about it, the entire document rests on the shoulders of the DTD. The DTD does a great many things. It not only defines the elements, attributes, and entities of the document, it also describes everything that can be contained within the document. Describing what each element and attribute does makes the DTD more humanly readable. The DTD actually accomplishes many things:

- Defines and provides the names of all the elements used in the document

- Defines and provides the names of all the attributes used in a document

- Defines and provides the names and the content of all the entities used in the document

- Specifies the order in which elements and attributes must appear in the document

- Defines all attributes (and their default values) for each element

- Outlines any comments that may help in clarifying the structural context of the document

- Declares the document type

The DTD makes it possible for the document content to be marked up and then displayed properly once it's parsed. To construct a well-defined DTD, you must first know exactly what individual parts are included. DTDs include the following parts:

- Character data, including normal character and special character data

- White space characters

- Entities

- Elements, including their start- and end-tags

- Attributes

- Comments

- Processing instructions

Each part is used to create DTDs that make up both well-formed and valid XML documents. Let's examine each part briefly.

TIP: *We will briefly discuss both well-formed and valid documents later in this chapter. For more information about well-formed and valid documents, see Chapter 14.*

Character Data

The smallest piece of a DTD is a single character. So, how does a single character help form a well-designed DTD? It's simple. Characters make up the content of the document and also the content of entities, elements, attributes, and even comments. Character data specifies a certain process, marks up data, or represents some type of information.

Character data can be a mixture of text and markup information. When that happens, you have what is called *mixed content*. Here's an example of what mixed content would look like:

```
<SUBJECT>Creating DTDs</SUBJECT>
<INFORMATION>This section will help you understand
how to create well designed DTDs.</INFORMATION>
```

All characters used in both the DTD and the document itself within XML are based on the ISO 10646 character encoding scheme, commonly referred to as Unicode.

You can use Unicode to represent the same characters across different platforms. It supports encoding schemes for 8-bit, 16-bit, and 32-bit character sets.

Some special characters, however, are reserved and are used within XML to signify certain functionality. For example the left angle bracket (<) is used to indicate element and attribute declarations as well as to indicate a start-tag for an element used within an XML document. With the help of Unicode, you can use these special reserved characters within the content of a document without worrying that the processor will indicate an error in processing. Unicode helps create what is called internal entities, which are reserved entities that are used to specify various reserved characters. Table 5.1 lists several reserved characters and their Unicode hexadecimal assignments along with the escape character strings used to denote them in an XML document.

TIP: For more information about Unicode, check out the official Web site at **www.unicode.org**.

White Space Characters

White space is simply empty space between characters. However, white space can be more than just space. It can also be one of the following characters:

- The space character (Unicode character #x20)
- The line feed (Unicode character #xD)
- The tab character (Unicode character #xA)
- The carriage return (Unicode character #x9)

You can combine any of these characters in a string of character data. XML processes white space by using what is called *white space handling*. XML processors read all white space along with all other characters in a document. But you need to describe to the XML processor when white space is significant by using the **xml:space** attribute within the attribute list. For example, if you want to signify that white space is important and needs to display in the document itself, you would define the following within the attribute list:

```
<!ATTLIST listing xml:space
        (default | preserve) "preserve">
```

Table 5.1   Reserved characters in XML.

Character	Unicode Assignment	Escape Character String
<	&#x3C;	&lt;
>	&#x3E;	&gt;
&	&#x26	&amp;

Entities

While we're on the subject of characters, we might as well discuss entities. Entities specify additional character data or files that might be included within the content of the document. For example, if you use copyright information again and again in a document, you could create an entity with the following code:

```
<!ENTITY COPYRIGHT "Copyrighted 1999">
```

Then, you would specify the entity within the document by using the entity reference, as follows:

```
All this information is &COPYRIGHT;.
```

The previous code would display as follows once the document is parsed:

```
All this information is Copyrighted 1999.
```

Elements

Because elements are fully explained in Chapter 7, we'll only discuss them briefly here. Elements construct the parts of a document. You have full control over what elements you create and use in your XML documents. You usually create elements and their content right after you specify the XML processing instruction and **DOCTYPE** declaration at the top of a DTD with external DTDs, or at the top of an XML document when creating internal DTDs. An element declaration looks like this:

```
<!ELEMENT name content>
```

For example, if you were creating an online parts ordering system, you would need to declare the part number element and specify that this content can be parsed character data. To do so, you would include the following code in your DTD:

```
<!ELEMENT partno (#PCDATA)>
```

You can declare as many elements as you need in the DTD. Yet, depending upon how you structure the elements in the DTD, you may or may not need to use all those elements in your XML document. Or, depending upon how you've specified the elements' content, you may need to use one element before you use another. You determine such element preferences in the DTD. For example, if you specify that the element name must contain two other elements, first and last, and that the first has to appear before the last, you would declare the elements in your DTD in this order:

```
<!ELEMENT first (#PCDATA)>
<!ELEMENT last (#PCDATA)>
<!ELEMENT name (first, last)>
```

Attributes

Attributes help describe exactly what elements are, the kind of information that must be placed in them, and the order in which the information should be placed. Attributes can be placed directly after an element has been declared, or you can place them in groups (attribute lists) after all elements have been declared within the DTD. It's best to declare the element and then declare its attribute because it makes it easier to read the DTD. You'll know exactly what element has been declared and what attributes are specified if you follow the element with its attribute list.

For example, suppose we declare an element called **last** and we want to create an attribute for it. We want to specify that this attribute must contain character data and not markup data. In addition, we want the content of the element to be required. This tells the processor to return an error if no content is specified for this element's attribute. In order for the document to parse correctly, content for this attribute must be specified. The code would look like this:

```
<!ELEMENT last (#PCDATA)>
<!ATTLIST last
     Format    CDATA    #REQUIRED>
```

TIP: *To learn more about the various attribute options you can declare in your DTD, see Chapter 8.*

Comments

Comments are important in any DTD. They not only help you remember what you placed in the DTD, they also help others know the purpose for certain elements or attributes you create. Remember, one of the XML design principles is that XML data be humanly legible and easily understood. With a few well-placed comments, you can ensure that this design principle is followed. Here is the syntax for a comment:

```
<! - - comment - - >
```

The first part, **<! - -**, signifies the start of the comment, and **- - >** signifies the end. With the exception of two hyphens (- -), anything can be placed within the comment itself. No part of the comment is displayed or processed. Comments can be on a single line or broken up and placed within multiple lines like the following code:

```
<! - - The information
specified in this document
outlines the document structure.- - >
```

You should use a lot of comments when you first start creating XML documents. Consider the following DTD, which was created by David Megginson. The author has fully commented the entire DTD. He has indicated what each element's purpose is and specified where the entities start. Read through Listing 5.1 and you understand what the author's intentions were when he created each element, attribute, and notation. Each element and each attribute are identified with a comment. Each section that describes a particular set of DTD components is commented. As you can see, it doesn't matter where you place the comments. Placing them frequently throughout the DTD makes it easier to read and understand. Even the end of the DTD is described in detail.

Listing 5.1   A novel DTD.

```
<?xml encoding="UTF-8"?>
<!--
*****************************************************
novel.dtd: A simple XML DTD for marking-up novels.
Copyright (c) 1997 by David Megginson.
*****************************************************
-->
<!-- Content model for phrasal content -->
<!ENTITY % phrasal "#PCDATA|emphasis">
<!-- ******** -->
<!-- Elements -->
<!-- ******** -->

<!-- The top-level novel -->
<!ELEMENT novel (front, body)>

<!-- The frontmatter for the novel -->
<!ELEMENT front (title, author, revision-list)>

<!-- The list of revisions to this text -->
<!ELEMENT revision-list (item+)>

<!-- An item in the list of revisions -->
<!ELEMENT item (%phrasal;)*>
<!-- The main body of a novel -->
```

```
<!ELEMENT body (chapter+)>
<!-- A chapter of a novel -->
<!ELEMENT chapter (title, paragraph+)>
<!ATTLIST chapter
  id ID #REQUIRED>

<!-- The title of a novel or chapter -->
<!ELEMENT title (%phrasal;)*>

<!-- The author(s) of a novel -->
<!ELEMENT author (%phrasal;)*>

<!-- A paragraph in a chapter -->
<!ELEMENT paragraph (%phrasal;)*>

<!-- An emphasised phrase -->
<!ELEMENT emphasis (%phrasal;)*>

<!-- **************** -->
<!-- General Entities -->
<!-- **************** -->

<!--
  These really should have their Unicode equivalents.
-->

<!-- em-dash -->
<!ENTITY mdash "--">

<!-- left double quotation mark -->
<!ENTITY ldquo "``">

<!-- right double quotation mark -->
<!ENTITY rdquo "''">

<!-- left single quotation mark -->
<!ENTITY lsquo "`">

<!-- right single quotation mark -->
<!ENTITY rsquo "'">

<!-- horizontal ellipse -->
<!ENTITY hellip "...">

<!-- end of DTD -->
```

Processing Instructions

Processing instructions tell the XML processor to do far more than just replace an entity reference with its value or hide a comment. For example, the one processing instruction you'll use time and time again when you develop your DTDs is **<?XML?>**, as in:

```
<?XML version="1.0"?>
```

Like comments, processing instructions are not displayed; instead, they are passed through the processor. The target of the processing instruction is the value specified after the word **version**. For example, **1.0** specifies that this document will conform to the XML specification version 1. Every processing instruction must start with **<?** and end with **?>**.

Valid And Well-Formed Documents

In addition to the parts that make up a DTD, you need to know the difference between valid and well-formed documents, because valid XML documents require a DTD and well-formed documents don't. Knowing what components you need to include if you want to create valid or well-formed XML documents is important in creating an XML document that will parse correctly and not return errors.

Well-Formed XML Documents

If you want an XML processor to process a document correctly, the document must be *well-formed*, which means that the document and the code markup conform to the rules of XML syntax. Well-formed XML documents don't require a DTD to be valid XML files. But there's a little bit more to it. There are certain rules that determine whether a document is well-formed:

- The document must be surrounded by a single outermost root element or document element.
- No attribute can appear more than once in the same start-tag.
- Tags must be properly nested and all tags must have matching pairs.
- Parameter entities must be declared before they can be used, and all entities except general parameter entities must be declared.
- You can only use binary entities if you have declared them as **ENTITY** or **ENTITIES**. They cannot be referenced in the content.
- All entities, elements, and attributes are case sensitive.
- String attribute values cannot contain references to external resources.

If your document doesn't follow these conventions, it is not well-formed and therefore not considered an XML document. You should check the XML specification for more information about well-formed XML documents. If you violate any of the specification's rules, your parser will give you a fatal error. The XML parser will report the error to the XML application and may not display the content correctly or continue to process the application.

Here is an example of a well-formed document:

```
<?XML version="1.0"?>
<BODY>This is the body of a well-formed document.
</BODY>
```

Valid XML Documents

A valid XML document is one in which the code and content are correct and the rules of both XML and the DTD are followed:

- Valid documents follow the XML specification rules, including proper nesting, the presence of required attributes, and correct values for the attributes.

- The document has a corresponding DTD, either internally, externally, or both.

- The document complies with the rules of the associated DTD.

Well-formed documents obey the XML specification rules, whereas valid XML documents require conformation to both the XML specification and the DTD that accompanies the document. All valid XML documents are well-formed, but not all well-formed documents are valid.

Here's an example of a valid document:

```
<?XML version="1.0"?>
<!DOCTYPE body [<!ELEMENT body (#PCDATA)>
]>
<body>This is a well-formed valid document.</body>
```

You need to know what makes documents valid and well-formed so you'll know why your processor is returning errors. The best thing to do is read through the XML specification, which is included in Appendix B of this book and is available online at **www.w3c.org/XML**.

The Road To Good DTD Design

To create a well-designed DTD, you must first know two things: the type of documents you'll be marking up and your intended audience.

The first thing you need to do is determine the types of documents you need to mark up. Because XML is all about structure, you must plan ahead before you start developing the DTD, so you'll know exactly which building blocks you'll need to structure your documents. It's just like building a house. If you were going to build a stucco house in Phoenix, you would need to gather all the right supplies. You wouldn't go down to the local hardware store and buy truckloads of siding; instead, you would buy stucco material. Building a DTD is somewhat the same. You need the right building materials before you can start the job, and that means determining what types of documents you'll be creating. Are they going to be technical manuals? Maybe you're considering an online book. Perhaps you're just creating an automated office system with structured elements for faxes, memos, and reports.

Next, you need to sketch out on paper exactly what elements, attributes, entities, and notations you'll need to construct the perfect DTD for the job. You should also consider whether other people will be involved. You may not realize what elements are needed because you may not be doing the actual content creation. During the planning stage, it's imperative that you include everyone who will be involved in the project.

You should examine the document flow as well as the document content. How you structure your DTD may very well be determined by what external organizations will use the information and what requirements they may have. It's important that you know how documents will relate to one another and what constraints outside forces may place on your documents. It doesn't really matter if the DTD you're building is for a small company or a major publishing house. The steps in document analysis and creation are all the same:

- Define the environment in which existing documents work.
- Define the external requirements for your internal documents.
- Define and outline the elements needed for both internal and external use.
- Define how the elements will relate to one another and to outside elements.
- Define the flow of information from one document to the next.
- Determine what other systems will utilize the data.
- Document how the flow of information works, along with the elements, attributes, entities, and notations defined in the DTD.
- Create the DTD model.
- Parse the DTD to check for errors.
- Test the DTD with test content.
- Resolve any outstanding issues.
- Supply the DTD to everyone involved in the project.

5: DTDs In XML

These steps work toward a logical progression, from analyzing the problem the DTD will solve to parsing the DTD to check for errors. Without proper planning, your DTD may not accommodate all the markup that is necessary for the people involved. Let's take a look at the major steps involved in creating a DTD.

Defining All The Parts

Now that you know what parts make up a DTD, let's discuss how they all fall into place to create a well-designed DTD that works for you and anyone else who may use it. If you break down an XML document, you'll find two types of information: the content and the markup. The content determines what the markup will be. Before you create the DTD, you must examine content you already have. Examine documents that will provide content or will interface with the content you will create. Make sure you evaluate any restrictions or policies that may be associated with these documents. For example, a document may require part numbers with orders, or there could be more technical requirements, such as storage constraints on servers. The attributes you develop for the elements you create may depend on the restrictions that exist.

Once you know what documents you already have and the restrictions they impose, the next step is to ask yourself what purpose your DTDs are going to serve for both the documents you have and those you'll create. If you're creating a site to take online orders, you'll need to structure your documents with the right elements and attributes listed in proper order in the DTD. You might also consider creating another set of documents to handle purchase orders, and those documents might use the same DTD. If you're working with a government agency, what are their requirements for invoicing? In other words, what kinds of information need to be maintained? Asking yourself these questions will help you determine what elements are required and what attributes will help to further define them. To visualize exactly how all the elements will work, create a project map that outlines all the information and the information flow.

Defining The Elements

Let's take a quick look at something almost everyone is familiar with—a newspaper. If we were creating an online newspaper, we would need to consider that the information will eventually be made available in an online search archive. We might also send the newspaper to subscribers via email. And the same information may be sent to other news agencies. In addition, there may be companies that would want to buy the photos or graphics. Figure 5.1 is an example of an entertainment section from the *Anchorage Daily News*.

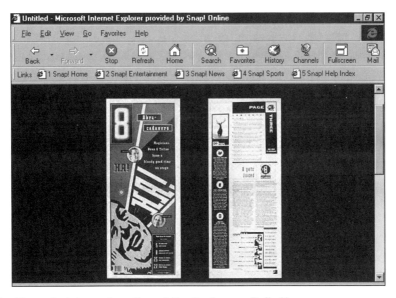

Figure 5.1   The entertainment section of the *Anchorage Daily News*.

In a section such as this, there are page numbers, articles, bylines, pictures of editors, editor email addresses, callouts, headlines, quotes, and more. Because this section is full of graphics, plenty of text, and lots of design, there are numerous elements we'll need to create. The elements we create will work across the printed version and the Web-site version as well as the email version. The elements will also be used to interface with a database system that will allow both reporters and readers to search for particular articles based upon keywords. That means the following elements could be defined for this particular newspaper:

- **<NEWSPAPER>**—This is the root element. Although we are considering just a single section of the newspaper, we should remember that it's just one part of a larger entity.

- **<SECTION>**—This is the secondary element. Each newspaper will have at least one section and each section will have multiple parts, such as articles and graphics. The section may have such attributes as the section name, section location, section page numbering scheme, and so on.

- **<HEADLINE>**—The headline will usually be a single sentence that defines the content of the article that follows. The **<HEADLINE>** element should always appear before the **<STORY>** element and may include other elements, such as subheads.

- **<SUBHEAD>**—The subhead is the secondary headline that may appear to further define the article that follows. This element will not be required, but it should always follow the **<HEADLINE>** element and be placed before the **<STORY>** element.

- **<BYLINE>**—The byline is the name of the article's author. It always appears before the **<STORY>** element but after the **<HEADLINE>** or **<SUBHEAD>** element.

- **<LEDE>**—The lead for the article is a separate element that is basically made up of the first paragraph of the **<STORY>** element. The lead is the teaser that brings the reader into the story. The **<LEDE>** element follows the **<BYLINE>** element but appears before the **<STORY>** element.

- **<STORY>**—The story is the content. The **<STORY>** element will contain several attributes that further explain the story. Those attributes may be the names of all the authors and editors of the story along with date and the edition in which the story appears.

- **<PULLQUOTES>**—These are quotes from stories that may be displayed beside the articles.

We won't discuss *all* the elements a newspaper would require, but these will give you an idea of some of the more important elements. Now that we have an idea of some of the elements we need to turn this newspaper section into an XML document, we're ready to sketch out the element relationships and hierarchies.

Element Relationships And Hierarchy

Sketching out the element relationships and hierarchy will help you define not only the elements but also the attributes each element needs. Here's what we need to define for each element:

- Sequence

- Relationship to other elements

- Hierarchy

- Occurrence

Before we move too far ahead, let's take a look at the DTD we showed you earlier in the chapter, the novel DTD, to see how sequence, hierarchy, occurrence, and relationships to other elements evolve within a DTD.

We'll strip out the comments and view just the elements, attributes, and entities to get an idea of how the DTD was created and how we can create our newspaper DTD. We recommend that you expose yourself to as many DTDs as you can find so you get an idea of how to write them and how others create them. We've also stripped out the general entities, so we can concentrate on the elements and attributes. You'll see one parameter entity in Listing 5.2 because it's referenced in some of the elements. However, we'll get to entities a bit later. Listing 5.2 contains the novel DTD.

Listing 5.2 A novel DTD without the comments and general entities.

```
<?xml encoding="UTF-8"?>
<!ENTITY % phrasal "#PCDATA|emphasis">
<!ELEMENT novel (front, body)>
<!ELEMENT front (title, author, revision-list)>
<!ELEMENT revision-list (item+)>
<!ELEMENT item (%phrasal;)*>
<!ELEMENT body (chapter+)>
<!ELEMENT chapter (title, paragraph+)>
<!ATTLIST chapter
  id ID #REQUIRED>

<!ELEMENT title (%phrasal;)*>
<!ELEMENT author (%phrasal;)*>

<!ELEMENT paragraph (%phrasal;)*>
<!ELEMENT emphasis (%phrasal;)*>
```

Now, let's examine the structure. The main element is called **<NOVEL>**. It contains two other elements, **front** and **body**. The **<NOVEL>** element is considered the root element and everything branches from it. The next big branches, so to speak, are **<FRONT>** and **<BODY>**, and from those, smaller branches sprout. The **<FRONT>** element must appear before the **<BODY>** element. We know this because the **front** element, with the comma and the **body** element, are listed in the content of the **<NOVEL>** element.

As we move through the code, we see that the **<FRONT>** element contains **title**, **author**, and **revision-list**. **<TITLE>** is a simple element; its content is what is specified in the entity outlined at the very beginning of the code. It is the same with **<AUTHOR>**, **<PARAGRAPH>**, and **<EMPHASIS>**. The **<FRONT>** element requires that the **title**, **author**, and **revision-list** are listed in that order.

The **<CHAPTER>** element contains the **title** and **paragraph** elements. **Title** must appear first, and there must be at least one **paragraph** within the **<CHAPTER>** element. We know this because of the plus sign after the **paragraph** element name.

So, here's the kind of structure this document offers:

```
NOVEL
  FRONT
    TITLE
      AUTHOR
        REVISION-LIST
          ITEM
```

```
BODY
  CHAPTER
    TITLE
     PARAGRAPH
```

By evaluating other DTDs, you can quickly get an idea of how your DTDs might also be structured. The easiest way to get a handle on your element relationships is to look at how others handle theirs. Once you do, you're ready to create your own relationships.

Constructing The Elements

Let's go back to creating a newspaper DTD. First, we should sketch out how the sequence and hierarchies of the elements will work. We'll start with the overall concept of the newspaper and drill down to more specific pieces. Because we already know what major elements we'll use, we need to start with the main root element, the newspaper element, and determine what other elements will branch off this root. The best way to determine what the other elements will be is to start small and work our way up. Every newspaper has sections, so this simple code structure would make sense:

```
<NEWSPAPER>
   <SECTION>
   </SECTION>
</NEWSPAPER>
```

Now, let's break down the **<SECTION>** element a bit more and define the next level down. Each section will have articles, which means the following code would be valid:

```
<NEWSPAPER>
   <SECTION>
      <ARTICLE>
      </ARTICLE>
   </SECTION>
</NEWSPAPER>
```

Considering newspapers have multiple sections and each section can have multiple articles, we would structure our elements so that they could be repeated throughout the newspaper. When we do that, each section would be on the same level as any other section, and all the subelements, such as **<ARTICLE>**, would be nested within the **<SECTION>** element. That means the following code would also be valid:

```
<NEWSPAPER>
    <SECTION>
        <ARTICLE>
        </ARTICLE>

        <ARTICLE>
        </ARTICLE>

    </SECTION>

    <SECTION>
        <ARTICLE>
        </ARTICLE>

        <ARTICLE>
        </ARTICLE>

        <ARTICLE>
        </ARTICLE>

    </SECTION>

</NEWSPAPER>
```

5: DTDs In XML

TIP: *As we build our structure, are you starting to see that an attribute for **<SECTION>** will be needed? Obviously, we will most likely need an attribute that specifies the **TITLE** of the section as well as other attributes for other elements. When you lay out the structure like this, you can start to visualize all the components you'll need.*

Now that we have the major elements in place, we can concentrate on refining the individual elements that will make up the rest of the structure. Let's further define the **<ARTICLE>** element. Each article will contain a headline, so we would create the following code in our DTD:

```
<ARTICLE>
    <HEADLINE>
        <SUBHEAD>
        </SUBHEAD>
    </HEADLINE>
<ARTICLE>
```

The **<HEADLINE>** element contains one subelement, which is called **<SUB-HEAD>**. The subhead will be the secondary headline, so to speak. It's not a child of the **<ARTICLE>** element, because although it's part of the **<ARTICLE>**

147

element, it actually relates directly to the **<HEADLINE>** element and not the **<ARTICLE>** element.

Next, the **<ARTICLE>** element would contain the **<BYLINE>**, **<LEDE>**, and **<STORY>** elements. We'll start by specifying the **<BYLINE>** element first and then move on to the rest:

```
<ARTICLE>
    <HEADLINE>
    </HEADLINE>
    <BYLINE>
    </BYLINE>
    <LEDE>
    </LEDE>
    <STORY>
        <PULLQUOTE>
        </PULLQUOTE>
    </STORY>
<ARTICLE>
```

Now, let's put it altogether and see what we come up with in terms of structure. Note that we are simply outlining our structure. Although we are indicating our structure by using standard start- and end-tag notations, we are not really creating the DTD just yet. Instead, we are outlining exactly how the elements will stack up in the DTD. The actual code we use to declare these elements and their relationships is much different. Here's the code for the structure of our DTD:

```
<NEWSPAPER>
<SECTION>
    <ARTICLE>
        <HEADLINE>
            <SUBHEAD>
            </SUBHEAD>
        </HEADLINE>
        <BYLINE>
        </BYLINE>
        <LEDE>
        </LEDE>
        <STORY>
            <PULLQUOTE>
            </PULLQUOTE>
        </STORY>
    <ARTICLE>
<SECTION>
<NEWSPAPER>
```

Take away all of the minor elements and the actual structure follows. We'll use this structure when we're creating the actual element declarations in our DTD. But for now, this is what we come up with:

```
<NEWSPAPER>
<SECTION>
    <ARTICLE>
        <HEADLINE>
        <BYLINE>
        <LEDE>
        <STORY>
```

This simple sketch gives us a lot of information about the elements we're structuring. First, the **<NEWSPAPER>** element is the root element. From it, all other elements are created. Each newspaper must have at least one section, and each section must have at least one article. Numerous sections can appear in the newspaper, but only one byline can appear within each article. Also, only one headline can appear within a single article. There is only one lead per article, but there could be multiple pull quotes.

The easiest way to keep track of all this is to refer to a table that lists all the elements and specifies their relationships. This will help us to specify some basic information and keep us on track in terms of what elements works where. Table 5.2 outlines some of the elements we need to specify before we start to declare them in a DTD.

Declaring The Elements

Now that we know what elements we're going to use, let's create the element declaration that we can then include in the DTD. This will simply be the list of elements, not yet the DTD, because we haven't determined or even specified what attributes need to be created. Although it may sound like we're jumping the gun, we need to define those elements and their structures before we define attributes or entities.

We declare elements by specifying the following information:

```
<!ELEMENT name content>
```

Because we know which elements contain other elements, let's start with the first root element, **<NEWSPAPER>**. It contains one element, **<SECTION>**. But remember, we can have multiple sections, so the following code would define our first element, **<NEWSPAPER>**:

```
<!ELEMENT NEWSPAPER (SECTION+)>
```

Table 5.2   Element listing.

Element Name	Parent Of	Child Of	Number Of Possible Occurrences	Needs To Appear
<NEWSPAPER>	All other elements	None	One per paper	At the beginning of each newspaper
<SECTION>	<ARTICLE>	<NEWS-PAPER>	Multiple	Before all elements that are placed before articles, but after the <NEWSPAPER> element
<ARTICLE>	<HEADLINE>, <BYLINE>, <SUBHEAD>, <LEDE>, <STORY>, <PULLQUOTES>	<SECTION>	Multiple	After the <SECTION> element, but before all child elements
<HEADLINE>	<SUBHEAD>, <STORY>	<ARTICLE>	One per <ARTICLE>	Before the <SUB-HEAD> element, and before the <STORY> element
<SUBHEAD>	None	<HEADLINE>	One per <HEADLINE>	After the <HEADLINE>
<BYLINE>	None	<ARTICLE>	One per <ARTICLE>	After the <SUBHEAD>, but before the <STORY>
<LEDE>	None	<ARTICLE>	One per <ARTICLE>	After the <BYLINE>, but before the <STORY>
<STORY>	None	<ARTICLE>	One per <ARTICLE>	After the <LEDE>
<PULLQUOTE>	None	<STORY>	Multiple	After the <STORY> element

This line of code defines an element named **<NEWSPAPER>**, which can contain an element named **<SECTION>**. We've added the plus sign after the **SECTION** name to signify to the XML processor that valid XML documents can contain more than one section.

Using what we know about declaring elements, we would continue creating the element list. If we keep the structure we created previously handy

```
<NEWSPAPER>
<SECTION>
  <ARTICLE>
     <HEADLINE>
     <BYLINE>
     <LEDE>
     <STORY>
```

we would come up with a list of elements that would look like this:

```
<!ELEMENT NEWSPAPER (SECTION+)>
<!ELEMENT SECTION (ARTICLE+)>

<!ELEMENT ARTICLE (HEADLINE, BYLINE, LEDE, STORY)>
<!ELEMENT HEADLINE (CONTENT, SUBHEAD?)>
<!ELEMENT STORY (STORYCONTENT, PULLQUOTES+)>

<!ELEMENT BYLINE (#PCDATA)>
<!ELEMENT LEDE (#PCDATA)>
<!ELEMENT CONTENT (#PCDATA)>
<!ELEMENT SUBHEAD (#PCDATA)>
<!ELEMENT STORYCONTENT (#PCDATA)>
<!ELEMENT PULLQUOTES (#PCDATA)>
```

Let's examine what some of this code means before we go on to create the attributes that further explain these elements. First, we already know that the **<NEWSPAPER>** element contains the **<SECTION>** element and that there can be more than one section. Second, the **<SECTION>** element contains the **<AR-TICLE>** element, and it can contain more than one article.

Next, the **<ARTICLE>** element must contain **<HEADLINE>** first, followed by **<BYLINE>**, **<LEDE>**, and finally, **<STORY>**. The **<HEADLINE>** element can contain parsable character data, as is defined in the **<CONTENT>** element. And it can contain a **<SUBHEAD>** element, which also contains parsable character data. However, the **<SUBHEAD>** element can be optional, as specified by the inclusion of the question mark.

TIP: *If you need more information about how to declare elements or what various element notations mean, see Chapter 7. It outlines all the special notations used to define certain structural elemental context.*

Defining The Attributes

Now that we have an idea of what elements we need, the number of times they can occur, and their relationship to other elements, the next step is to define what attributes those elements require. After we define elements for the document, we can provide additional information about those elements to the XML processor in the form of attributes. A list of attributes is defined for an element with the **ATTLIST** assignment to specify exactly what can and cannot be placed in an element and what information is required. Because a document's elements are completely configurable, we are free to create attributes as necessary.

Yet this is where the tough part begins. Although attributes help clarify what content the elements can contain, they require more information than elements because they help further clarify what an element does. Therefore, their construction is a bit more complex, and that means you really have to think about your elements and how to describe them, not just to humans, but to the parser. The parser that reads the XML DTD document uses the attributes to set certain flags, such as whether an order has been processed. The application in turn uses this flag to determine if data can be edited.

The basic format of an attribute is specified through the use of the **ATTLIST** assignment, as shown in the following code:

```
<!ATTLIST elementname attributename type default_usage>
```

If we break down this string of code from left to right starting with **elementname**, basically what it is saying is that the element to which the attribute is associated is specified first. Attributes can appear directly after elements or anywhere within the DTD, so we need to include this information because, in many cases, the attribute doesn't follow the actual element it describes.

Second, the **attributename** value specifies the name we want to give the attribute. You can pretty much give your attribute any name you want. Only when you need to reference it while using an application is the attribute name of any significance.

The **type** value specifies whether the attribute will be a string type, tokenized type, or enumerated type.

Finally, we can specify the default usage value of an attribute. The following list will give you an idea of some of the default values that can be used with attributes:

- **#IMPLIED**—A value is optional for this attribute. The processor should notify the system when no value is set, but the document can still be considered valid.

- **#FIXED**—The value is fixed and cannot be changed. The document is not valid if the attribute is used with a value different from the default.

- **#REQUIRED**—A value is mandatory for this attribute. If no value is set, the document is not valid.

Here's an example of an attribute for our **<ARTICLE>** element that helps further define exactly what the **<ARTICLE>** element can contain:

```
<!ELEMENT ARTICLE (HEADLINE, BYLINE, LEDE, STORY)>
<!ATTLIST ARTICLE AUTHORS CDATA #REQUIRED          EDITORS CDATA #IMPLIED
DATE CDATA #IMPLIED          EDITION CDATA #IMPLIED>
```

The first line of the preceding code declares the element. The second line declares the attribute, but actually, it's not just one attribute. The second line is declaring the following four attributes:

- **AUTHORS**—There might be several authors who contribute to the story. Although the reader may not care who the multiple authors are, the newspaper editor may, especially when handing out Pulitzer prizes.

- **EDITORS**—By including this piece of information as an attribute, you link the story to the actual editor or editors who helped create this particular masterpiece.

- **DATE**—This attribute will help further define the article and date-stamp it. We could create an element that defines the date of the newspaper, but in this particular instance, we want a **DATE** attribute for the **<ARTICLE>** element so we can more easily search on the date for a particular article.

- **EDITION**—This could be the attribute for either the **<NEWSPAPER>** or **<ARTICLE>** element, but in this example, we'll create this as an attribute for the **<ARTICLE>** element.

Notice in the following code that the only data required is the name of the authors. Everything else is implied (with the **#IMPLIED** attribute). All information is contained in character data, as shown here:

```
<!ATTLIST ARTICLE AUTHORS CDATA #REQUIRED
          EDITORS CDATA #IMPLIED
          DATE CDATA #IMPLIED
          EDITION CDATA #IMPLIED>
```

When To Use Attributes And When To Use Elements

Sometimes, it's hard to know when to use attributes and when to use elements. Although you know elements are used to define the structure of an object and attributes are used to define the aspect of that object, you could easily create an attribute when it should be an element and vice versa. The easiest way to determine whether you should use an attribute or whether you should use an element is to follow this guideline for attribute usage:

- Attributes that define a particular aspect about an element, such as size, height, weight, or color.
- Attributes that define formatting information. Such attributes further define the appearance of an element.
- Attributes that locate an object, such as a footnote, a graphics file, or a cross-reference.
- Attributes that locate external objects, such as links.

To determine whether an item should be an element or an attribute, think about whether the object needs further explanation or whether the item in question actually defines a new object. If it relates to another element you have defined, it is probably an attribute. If it's similar but actually describes an entirely new object, then it's probably an element. Determining which to declare can sometimes be tough, but if you sketch out your structure first and then determine the relationships, you'll quickly see when to create elements and when to create attributes.

Defining The Entities

Entities are those groups of markup that actually contain content within their definitions. It's our opinion that entities are by far the easiest portion of the DTD to create because, in their most basic form, entities provide a mechanism to specify content without much effort. Entities are also by far the most complex, because you can do so much with them. There are two types of entities: general entities and parameter entities. *General entities*, like those used in HTML, specify specialized reserved characters such as the ampersand character.

We've defined the necessary elements and their attributes, and with the exception of some additional data, such as the name of the newspaper and possibly the copyright information, we are almost finished defining all the parts of the DTD. We need to include this information on almost every page of the paper, but we don't want to type it in again and again. That's the glory of XML. XML provides a mechanism that makes it easier to create information that will be placed in the document again and again and to help maintain the document over time. This mechanism is called an *entity*.

An entity is a component, be it text or other data, that can be substituted into a document based on a declaration. The component can be a text string or any type of file; that's right, entities can also reference entire files. That means an entity could reference a masthead, a chapter in a book, or anything to which a reference can point. Because entities allow text and files to be substituted into a document, they can be used to replace values when a document is parsed and displayed.

Unlike HTML, XML allows you to define your own entities. So in our example, we'll define an entity for our newspaper's name along with some basic copyright information. Then, we'll add this information to the DTD in the form of entities. The code for such information would look like this:

```
<!ENTITY NEWSPAPER "Anchorage Daily News">
<!ENTITY PUBLISHER "Fuller Cowell">
<!ENTITY COPYRIGHT "Copyrighted 1999">
```

Once we've defined these entities in our DTD, we can reference them in our XML document like this:

```
All contents are &COPYRIGHT;, by the
&NEWSPAPER;, &PUBLISHER;, Publisher.
```

When the XML processor encounters the **&COPYRIGHT;** entity, it replaces the entity with its value, **Copyrighted 1999**. The previous line of code would look like this once it is parsed and displayed:

```
All contents are Copyrighted 1999 by the
Anchorage Daily News, Fuller Cowell, publisher.
```

One reason to use entities is that they make documents easier to maintain. For example, if the publisher decides to move up the corporate ladder and is replaced, we can simply replace the value of the entity reference instead of having to replace the publisher's name throughout the entire document.

Entities can also be used to insert symbols into a document. For example, we can use an entity to insert the Pulitzer prize icon in the newspaper's editorial page, or new column bugs can be easily replaced when columnists have their pictures retaken.

TIP: *Keep in mind that, by default, XML processors don't parse the replacement text. Therefore, entities defined within an entity would not be inserted correctly. You can, however, tell the processor to parse the contents of the replacement text. You do this by inserting the % character before the entity assignment.*

We can also define graphics files to be placed in the document. Fortunately, entities can be used to reference files to be inserted into the document. We'll use the **SYSTEM** keyword to identify the URL of the file. **SYSTEM** is a reserved keyword that tells the XML processor the referenced external entity is in a file. The following code would insert a file into an XML document:

```
<!ENTITY AddData SYSTEM "http://www.adn.com/docs/document.xml">
```

When the XML processor encounters the **AddData** entity, it processes the file and then replaces the entity with the processed contents of the file. We can also use this same type of code to include other types of files, such as the image file for the newspaper's logo. However, in some cases we may not want the entity to be parsed by the XML parser. We may want it processed by another application. In that case, we would specify that a different application or processor handle the file by using the keyword **NDATA**. **NDATA** is used as a pointer to a previously declared notation to specify what application will process the entity reference. The following code would allow you to insert a graphic in an XML document and have it processed as a GIF file, and not as any other type of file:

```
<!ENTITY adnlogo SYSTEM
"http://www.adn.com/images/logo.gif" NDATA gif >
```

When you use the **adnlogo** entity in a document, the processor uses the GIF notation to determine how to handle the entity.

TIP: *You can use the NOTATION assignment to declare the GIF notation. When you create a notation, identify the URL of the helper application by using the SYSTEM keyword and the following code (iviewer.exe is the application that can display the GIF file):*

```
<!NOTATION gif SYSTEM "http://site.come/iviewer.exe">
```

Creating The DTD

By now, we have just about all the components we need to create the DTD. We know about the structure of the document. We also know what elements we'll use, and we have a grasp on what attributes will be used to further explain those elements. We also know what entities will be included in the DTD. All that's left is to put all this information together along with some well-placed comments, and we have ourselves a DTD.

Let's go through the entire process from start to finish. We'll start by creating the elements, and along the way, we'll create the attributes for each element. We'll use as many comments as we can to make the DTD as humanly readable as possible. Because a newspaper DTD could actually encompass many, many elements, we won't be able to create the entire DTD here, but what we will create will be enough for you to get an idea of how a DTD is created.

After we decide what elements to use, we need to formally declare these components in the DTD. The DTD, as you'll recall, is actually a text file with the extension .dtd that can be stored locally or remotely. There are five separate parts to the structure of the DTD:

- Document types
- Elements
- Attributes
- Entities
- Comments

TIP: *You can start creating a DTD by building all the elements, but that may be counterproductive. It's best to start out with a few elements and attributes, parse them, and build up from there. It may be more difficult to troubleshoot your DTD with thousands of lines of code to pour through.*

When you create a DTD, you start by creating the document in text-only format. All DTDs, XML data, and display information are saved in standard text-only format. We can use the standard Windows Notepad application to create the file, or we could use a variety of different products, including XML Pro by Validate Software. Regardless of the editing software tool we use, we declare that the document is an XML document and specify what type of encoding the document provides by including the following line of code at the top of the document:

```
<?xml encoding="UTF-8"?>
```

Next, we'll add a comment that will identify the DTD and its purpose and include author information and a copyright notice:

```
<!--
**************************************************
newspaper.dtd: This is a sample DTD for marking up
newspapers. Copyright 1999 by Cheryl Kirk
**************************************************
-->
```

Now, we'll indicate what entities we plan to use. Actually, entities can be placed anywhere in the DTD, but because they can also be used within various elements, we'll define them at the beginning of our DTD. Here's the code we place in the DTD to specify our entities:

```
<?xml encoding="UTF-8"?>
<!--
```

```
*****************************************************
newspaper.dtd: This is a sample DTD for marking up
newspapers. Copyright 1999 by Cheryl Kirk
*****************************************************
-->
<!-- ******** -->
<!-- Entities -->
<!-- ******** -->
<!ENTITY NEWSPAPER "Anchorage Daily News"><!ENTITY PUBLISHER "Fuller
Cowell"><!ENTITY COPYRIGHT "Copyrighted 1999">
```

Next, we'll declare the elements we'll need to construct the document. Creating the elements in order helps us further concentrate on the order and hierarchy. We've already defined the elements, so we'll add them to the DTD. Because any newspaper would start with the **<NEWSPAPER>** element as the root, we need to define it first. Then, we'll create the rest of the elements that branch off of the main root element: **<SECTION>**, **<ARTICLE>**, **<HEADLINE>**, **<BYLINE>**, **<LEAD>**, and **<BODY>**, in that order. Here's a small sample of how our DTD would look as we progress through the list of elements:

```
<?xml encoding="UTF-8"?>
<!--
*****************************************************
newspaper.dtd: This is a sample DTD for marking up
newspapers. Copyright 1999 by Cheryl Kirk
*****************************************************
-->
<!-- ******** -->
<!-- Entities -->
<!-- ******** -->
<!ENTITY NEWSPAPER "Anchorage Daily News"><!ENTITY PUBLISHER "Fuller
Cowell"><!ENTITY COPYRIGHT "Copyrighted 1999">
<!-- ******** -->
<!-- Elements -->
<!-- ******** -->
<!ELEMENT NEWSPAPER (SECTION+)>
<!ELEMENT SECTION (ARTICLE+)>

<!ELEMENT ARTICLE (HEADLINE, BYLINE, LEDE, STORY)>
<!ELEMENT HEADLINE (CONTENT, SUBHEAD?)>
<!ELEMENT STORY (STORYCONTENT, PULLQUOTES+)>

<!ELEMENT BYLINE (#PCDATA)>
<!ELEMENT LEDE (#PCDATA)>
<!ELEMENT CONTENT (#PCDATA)>
```

```
<!ELEMENT SUBHEAD (#PCDATA)>
<!ELEMENT STORYCONTENT (#PCDATA)>
<!ELEMENT PULLQUOTES (#PCDATA)>
```

At this point, we need to include the attributes for the elements we've built. We'll place those attributes directly following the element declarations they describe. Our DTD now looks like this:

```
<?xml encoding="UTF-8"?>
<!--
*****************************************************
newspaper.dtd: This is a sample DTD for marking up
newspapers. Copyright 1999 by Cheryl Kirk
*****************************************************
-->
<!-- ******** -->
<!-- Elements -->
<!-- ******** -->
<!ENTITY NEWSPAPER "Anchorage Daily News"><!ENTITY PUBLISHER "Fuller
Cowell">
<!ENTITY COPYRIGHT "Copyrighted 1999">

<!-- ******** -->
<!-- Elements -->
<!-- ******** -->
<!ELEMENT NEWSPAPER (SECTION+)>
<!ELEMENT SECTION (ARTICLE+)>

<!ELEMENT ARTICLE (HEADLINE, BYLINE, LEDE, STORY)>
     <!ATTLIST ARTICLE AUTHOR CDATA #REQUIRED
        EDITOR CDATA #IMPLIED
            DATE CDATA #IMPLIED
            EDITION CDATA #IMPLIED >

<!ELEMENT HEADLINE (CONTENT, SUBHEAD?)>
<!ELEMENT STORY (STORYCONTENT, PULLQUOTES+)>

<!ELEMENT BYLINE (#PCDATA)>
<!ELEMENT LEDE (#PCDATA)>
<!ELEMENT CONTENT (#PCDATA)>
<!ELEMENT SUBHEAD (#PCDATA)>
<!ELEMENT STORYCONTENT (#PCDATA)>
<!ELEMENT PULLQUOTES (#PCDATA)>

<!-- end of the DTD -->
```

We've ended the DTD by adding a comment to specify to humans, not XML parsers, where the DTD ends. There are no conventions for signaling the end of the DTD to the XML processor. You might want it to parse this working DTD with a variety of different XML parsers. In Chapter 14, you'll find a discussion of some parsers that will help determine whether there are any problems with our DTD.

Using The DTD

Now that we have a working DTD, we need to specify it within our document. Because the DTD we created is an externally stored DTD, we'll include the following line of code in the actual content document:

```
<?xml version="1.0" encoding="UTF-8" standalone="no"?>
<!DOCTYPE paper PUBLIC "-//ADN//DTD Novel//EN" "newspaper.dtd">
```

From the document type declaration, we can then create the rest of the document and include the rest of the data. Now all we have to do is create the content.

Immediate Solutions

In this section, you'll specify external DTDs, then create the various components that make up your own DTD for a purchase order system. You'll place this DTD internally and reference it externally. This purchase order system will contain several elements that have attributes, along with several entities that offer predefined content.

Specifying An External DTD

To specify a DTD that is stored within a network, include the keyword **SYSTEM** and the location of the DTD in your **!DOCTYPE** declaration, as shown in the following code:

```
<!DOCTYPE book SYSTEM "http://www.site.com/dtds/book.dtd">
```

Specifying A Public DTD

To specify a public DTD that is stored in another location, include the keyword **PUBLIC** when you are describing the DTD. If the DTD is not an ISO standard, include an en dash (–) before the notation that specifies the DTD, as shown in the following **!DOCTYPE** declaration:

```
<!DOCTYPE book PUBLIC "-//CompanyXYZ//DTD book//EN"
 "http://www.site.com/dtds/book.dtd">
```

Specifying An Internal DTD

To specify an internal DTD (one that will be included within the XML document), include the entire DTD within the **!DOCTYPE** declaration. Add the name of the DTD and enclose the DTD itself within square brackets, as shown in the following **!DOCTYPE** declaration:

```
<?XML version="1.0?>
<!DOCTYPE purchases [
<!ELEMENT main (purchase)*>
<!ELEMENT purchase (date,account?,item+)>
<!ELEMENT date (#PCDATA)>
<!ELEMENT account (#PCDATA)>
<!ELEMENT item ((itemno,itemdescription,quantity)|#PCDATA)*>
<!ELEMENT itemnumber (#PCDATA)>
<!ELEMENT itemdescription (#PCDATA)>
<!ELEMENT quantity (#PCDATA)>
]>
```

Creating An Internal DTD

To create an internal DTD, you must specify all the elements and attributes within the XML document itself. The DTD components must be declared before the markup tags are used within the document. To create an internal DTD, follow these steps:

1. Specify the XML processing instruction by including the following code:

```
<?xml encoding="UTF-8"?>
```

2. Add the document type declaration by adding the following code, which specifies the name of the DTD along with all the components that make the DTD:

```
<!DOCTYPE purchases [
<!ELEMENT main (purchase)*>
<!ELEMENT purchase (date,account?,item+)>
<!ELEMENT date (#PCDATA)>
<!ELEMENT account (#PCDATA)>
<!ELEMENT item ((itemno,itemdescription,quantity)|#PCDATA)*>
<!ELEMENT itemnumber (#PCDATA)>
<!ELEMENT itemdescription (#PCDATA)>
<!ELEMENT quantity (#PCDATA)>
]>
```

3. Next, you need to use these elements within the document itself. You do this by marking up the document as you would any XML document, making sure you follow the rules specified in the internal DTD:

```
<item>
<itemnumber>3200
</itemnumber>
<itemdescription>External Outer Locking Value
</itemdescription>
<quantity>40
</quantity>
</item>
```

Creating An External DTD

For an external DTD, you must declare all the elements, attributes, and entities in a separate file. You should use comments to indicate each group of components you specify. In this example, you'll create a purchase order DTD with various elements and attributes. To create an external DTD, follow these steps:

1. Specify the XML processing instruction by including the following code:

```
<?xml encoding="UTF-8"?>
```

2. Next, document the file by adding comments to clearly describe what the DTD is and what elements will be declared next:

```
<!--
****************************************************
purchaseorder.dtd: This is a DTD for creating
a purchase order system.
****************************************************
-->
<!-- ******** -->
<!-- Entities -->
<!-- ******** -->
```

3. At this point, you'll declare the entities for the document so they can then be referenced within the element or attribute declarations if necessary. Define entity references by specifying the entity declaration followed by the entity name and the content of the entity. For example, the following code defines three different entities:

```
<!ENTITY Company "Purchase Orders R Us"><!ENTITY Address "200 West 34th,
Anchorage, Alaska">
<!ENTITY Email "ckirk@alaska.net">
```

4. To declare entities within the document type declaration that references external files, use the following type of code:

```
<!doctype book SYSTEM "book.dtd"
[
 <!entity toc SYSTEM "toc.xml"
 <!entity chap1 SYSTEM "chapters/chapter1.xml"
 <!entity chap2 SYSTEM "chapters/chapter2.xml"
]
<book<head&toc;</head
<body
&chap1;
&chap2;
</body></book
```

5. You are now ready to declare the various elements you'll use within the document. Specify the element declaration, the name of the element, and then the content of the element. The content can be data, other elements, or even entities. The following code declares several different elements for the purchase order system:

```
<!ELEMENT main (purchase)*>
<!ELEMENT purchase (date,account?,item+)>
<!ELEMENT date (#PCDATA)>
<!ELEMENT account (#PCDATA)>
<!ELEMENT item ((itemno,itemdescription,quantity)|#PCDATA)*>
<!ELEMENT itemnumber (#PCDATA)>
<!ELEMENT itemdescription (#PCDATA)>
<!ELEMENT quantity (#PCDATA)>
```

TIP: *The asterisk after an element indicates that the elements between the parentheses are optional and repeatable. The plus sign indicates that at least one of the subelements must appear within the main element, and the subelements can also be repeated. The comma indicates that the items must appear sequentially, meaning the customer element must precede the purchase element.*

---

6. Next, you'll create and include the attributes for each element that requires an attribute. To create an attribute, use the **!ATTLIST** declaration followed by the name of the element the attribute is describing, the content of the attribute, and any default value. The attribute is usually placed after the element declaration. The following code is an example of an attribute declaration:

```
<!ELEMENT account (#PCDATA)>
     <!ATTLIST ACCOUNT ACCOUNTNO CDATA #REQUIRED
        ACCOUNTADDRESS CDATA #IMPLIED
           ACCOUNTTYPE CDATA #IMPLIED>
```

7. After you've added all the elements, attributes, and entities, indicate the end of the DTD to humans by including a comment line, such as the following:

```
<!-- end of the DTD -->
```

8. Finally, save the file with the file extension .dtd. You can choose any name you like. Remember, however, XML is case sensitive, so if you use uppercase in the file name, you also need to use uppercase when you declare the DTD in your **!DOCTYPE** declaration. For example, if you saved a DTD with the file name purchaseo.dtd, this code in the XML document would be invalid:

```
<!DOCTYPE purchaseo PUBLIC "-//CompanyXYZ//DTD purchaseo//EN"
 "http://www.site.com/dtds/PURCHASEO.dtd">
```

5: DTDs In XML

Chapter 6

Inside XML Applications
And Documents

By Natanya Pitts-Moultis

In Depth

This chapter examines the relationship between XML applications and documents, explains methods for creating XML application road maps that make document creation easier, and demonstrates the development of XML documents for two specific XML applications.

It's been said that if you know HTML, you know XML. More accurately, it should be said that if you understand the basic precepts of one markup language, you understand the basic precepts of all markup languages. Chapters 1 through 6 have shown this to be true. But making the jump from creating an HTML-based Web page to creating an XML document for a specific application isn't as easy as the markup language gurus would like to make us think it is. Because the majority of us were introduced to markup languages via HTML, we're not used to making the connection between a document and its application. (A browser is not the kind of application we're talking about here.)

Instead, we're more concerned with how one or more software packages—that is, browsers—render our HTML page in the end. Therefore, when someone comments that HTML is an application of XML, it completely throws us off guard. The ties between an XML document and its related application can be both profound and multilayered. In most cases, you'll develop XML documents for specific applications, and you'll need to be fully cognizant of the intricacies of the application every step of the way. In this chapter, we give new meaning to some old terminology and show you how to make this important connection between XML documents and their related applications.

What Is An XML Application?

After reading the discussion of DTDs in Chapter 6, you might ask, "Isn't a DTD an XML application?" Basically, yes it is. However, to become an XML application, a DTD has to go a little beyond just being a DTD. In general, an XML application is a DTD or set of DTDs with a specific purpose. It is written and maintained in a standard way and with appropriate documentation. In addition, there is an unspoken agreement between parties that use the application that they will all follow the same rules. Software packages are then designed to work with the parsed data, according to the application's DTD.

As an example, let's look at two XML applications that are under development and have support from some pretty heavy hitters—including Microsoft—CDF and

OFX. The Channel Definition Format (CDF) is an XML application that was created to provide a better mechanism for push delivery of information through a channel across the Web. Open Financial Exchange (OFX) is an XML application that is a spinoff of the SGML applications that work behind the scenes in Microsoft's Money and Intuit's Quicken packages. The goal of OFX is to create a standard format for the exchange of information among financial institutions and software packages.

As you can see, these two applications of XML are very different in purpose and scope. However, both use XML as their metalanguage because it was designed to be so flexible. Documents created for CDF and OFX look similar because they are developed using a markup language, but that's where the similarities end. A generic XML parser is used to parse both CDF and OFX files, but specific software packages are developed to massage the parsed data from only one specific XML application. The developers of XML hope that the developers and implementers of these new XML applications will learn a few lessons from the history of HTML, which is fraught with browser wars, and agree to work with a single standard version of each application. Our fingers are crossed.

XML: The Application Jack-Of-All-Trades

One of the beauties of XML is that it is well suited as a base for a wide range of applications, as our CDF/OFX illustration shows. In general, XML applications fall into one of three expansive categories:

- Document delivery
- Database connectivity
- Data exchange

The document delivery category alone makes the possibilities for the development of XML applications seem almost endless. How exactly is XML used to develop applications for each of these three categories? The use of XML is open-ended, but we will give you some idea of the variety of applications that can be created using XML.

Document Delivery

The first and most obvious use for XML is the creation and delivery of customized documents. Whereas HTML is a step in the right direction, it's not flexible or extensible enough to meet a wide variety of needs. SGML lies on the other end of the spectrum by being too difficult and more complex than necessary. XML, the happy medium, allows for the creation of content-specific applications that give document authors the ability to make the markup fit the content, not the other way around. Now the creators of auto parts catalogs and academic publications won't be forced to use the same set of markup tags. In addition, XML markup is similar in form and function to HTML. Therefore, a large number of people already have the basic understanding and skill base necessary to create documents for XML applications.

The biggest hurdle to overcome in creating documents for XML applications isn't learning XML but rather unlearning the bad habits formed while trying to force HTML to do things it wasn't meant to do. HTML is treated as a page layout language, not a markup language. Therefore, document developers have to pay closer attention to those things that are vital to the creation of a well-formed and valid XML document. Tag pairs must contain both a start and end tag and be nested correctly. Empty tags take on a new format in XML, and the rules of content and required attributes must be followed strictly. This is a far cry from the world of HTML, in which browsers are forgiving and markup rules can be bent (or rather warped) to create the needed display. We're fairly confident that users will pick up on these rules quickly and that new tools will help them create documents that conform to the XML rule book. Ultimately, a user may have to create documents in many different XML applications, but so many lessons have been learned from the creation of HTML documents that documentation resources and quality editors will help users create XML documents to fit any XML application.

Database Connectivity

The use of databases in the Internet community is not a new solution. However, it is usually an expensive and proprietary one. The ability to create pages on the fly that pour data from templates into Web sites is powerful but costly. Large and useful Web sites almost always require some type of database connectivity to maintain up-to-date information. XML promises to change the way databases are connected to Web pages by using nonproprietary and open applications that allow Web pages to work with back-end software applications (the Web pages and the back-end software applications both speak XML). This removes the need for special CGI (Common Gateway Interface) programs to act as intermediaries between the HTML and database worlds. Expect to see XML solutions from all the major database companies, but also look for nonproprietary XML applications that work with any ODBC (Open Database Connectivity) compliant database system. The beauty of this is that one application is able to communicate with several different database packages. This makes solutions for publishing information stored online in heterogeneous databases easier than ever. What makes the most powerful data-base connectivity solution available? Quite simply, the ability for computers running various operating systems to communicate seamlessly with heterogeneous databases over the Internet without a plethora of scripts and interface applications.

Data Exchange

Do the words "MIME type," "plug-in," or "**<OBJECT>**" make your blood run cold? One of the biggest drawbacks of the current method of data exchange on the Internet is that only HTTP objects are supported by Web pages. Everything else must have an accompanying plug-in, browser add-in, or special helper application to work. In addition, if the MIME type isn't configured right, the file may not transfer correctly. Off the Internet, databases must speak the same language as software applications to exchange data. All in all, it's a cumbersome way to maintain data exchange in any environment. Because of the entity definition system and its ability to act as a nonproprietary database connectivity device, XML makes it possible for any type of data to be exchanged among any set of tools that support XML. Of course, specific applications support certain types of files as needed, but they have the ability to support every type of file.

In general, XML provides a structured but extensible environment that provides a nonproprietary way to create documents, connect databases, and exchange data between heterogeneous systems running a variety of operating systems. With XML as the common metalanguage, XML applications are able to work together without cumbersome translators or extra helpers, thus producing a true universal data language.

Of Applications, Vocabularies, And Dialects

In the introductory paragraph of this chapter, we promised to give some old terms new meaning. Far be it for us to not live up to our obligations. As defined earlier, an XML application is not a piece of software that works with XML, but rather a specific implementation of XML with a DTD or set of DTDs designed to serve a specific purpose. To make things even more complicated, XML applications are also known in the industry as XML vocabularies and dialects. All three terms are accurate, but we prefer XML application. What's important to remember is they all refer to a DTD that conforms to the XML rule book and can be parsed by an XML parser.

Any XML DTD—from an interoffice memo DTD to the OFX DTD—can technically be considered an XML application. However, we'd like to refine the definition so it applies to DTDs, such as the CDF and OFX, that have a more widespread implementation and are supported by groups of developers and implementers. We do this because chances are you'll be developing documents for other people's XML applications more than you'll be developing your own applications. We're sure Chapter 5 showed you that writing a DTD is not for the faint-hearted. To that end, the remainder of this chapter focuses on what an XML document is made of and how you go about creating one.

What Is An XML Document?

Whereas Chapter 5 discussed the basic structure of an XML document, we'd like to look at it from a slightly different perspective in this chapter. An XML-capable browser, or any other software package designed to work with XML documents, reads the XML application's DTD and displays the document based on its instructions. Because XML's entity definition structure is so robust, it is possible to include complex data (such as symbols and chemical equations) and a wide variety of media types (beyond GIF, JPG, and AVI files) in your XML documents as long as they are defined in the DTD. In addition, an XML document doesn't have to have an associated DTD for an XML-aware software package to read it. It can just be well-formed but not necessarily valid. If you're a little fuzzy on the differences between a well-formed document and a valid document, you may want to visit Chapter 13.

XML documents all follow the same structural guidelines. This makes them easy to create once you understand the requirements of their associated application (or just the basics of the XML rule book). Every XML document has the following components:

- Declarations

- Elements

- Comments

- Character references

- Processing instructions

In the next five sections, we'll take a closer look at each component.

Declarations

If a document is valid, it has an associated DTD that is declared as a set of *declarations* for the document. Therefore, in a real sense, the XML application itself is part of every document created for it. In addition, supplementary declarations that affect just the document may be made on the document level. This is a perfectly legal way to customize an application to fit your needs. It should only be done by an experienced XML developer who understands all the intricate ins and outs of creating DTDs. The supplementary declarations must fit within the structure of the already declared DTD and not violate any of its rules. If the DTDs conflict, there is no way for the document to be valid, and in the end, it might not be parsable. However, if used correctly, these "local" declarations take advantage of XML's extensibility to help users meet specific document creation and data exchange needs.

A sample set of declarations that specifies an external DTD, as well as a local declaration, looks like this:

```
<!DOCTYPE INVOICE SYSTEM "INVOICE.DTD" [
<!ELEMENT note (#PCDATA)>
]>
```

The main document DTD is invoice.dtd. But because it doesn't provide for a place to include notes, the developer of this invoice added a local declaration of the element **note**; this local declaration can contain any character data but no markup.

Entity Declarations

In addition to the elements and attributes, any entity that will be used in the XML document must also be listed in the DTD. Entities include figures, media files, included text and markup, or any other text or binary file referenced by the XML document.

The general rule is, if it's not declared, you cannot include it. To link to the image logo.gif in an XML document, it must first be declared as an entity by using the following declaration:

```
<!ENTITY logo SYSTEM "logo.gif" NDATA GIF>
```

If you want the entire contents of another file, footer.xml, to be included somewhere in the document, the following declaration is required:

```
<!ENTITY footer SYSTEM "footer.xml">
```

Just because an entity is declared doesn't mean it will automatically appear just anywhere in the text. Markup must be used to actually include the entity, as the following code shows:

```
<FIG SRC="logo" />
<STANDARD TYPE="footer" FILE="footer" />
```

Both the **<FIG>** and **<STANDARD>** tags are empty tags that are designed to insert something into the XML document. The entities **logo** and **footer** were declared at the beginning of the document. Therefore, they can be called by the markup using tag attributes.

Entity declarations and inclusions are complex, and this discussion doesn't even scratch the surface. It was only intended to show that entities must be part of every document's declaration. We discuss all of the details on declaring and implementing entities in Chapter 12.

The Required Markup Declaration

The one thing every XML document declaration set has in common is the Required Markup Declaration (RMD). Document authors should provide the RMD as a guide to the XML processor. The processor needs to know if it should treat the document as well-formed rather than valid, if it only needs to read the internal declaration subset, or if it should read and interpret both the external and internal DTDs associated with the document. Including the correct RMD assignment can save bandwidth and processing time. The RMD looks like this:

```
<?XML version="1.0" RMD="X"?>
```

X can be one of the following three values:

- *NONE*—The DTD does not have to be read for the document to be correctly parsed.
- *ALL*—Both external and internal DTDs must be read and interpreted for the document to be read correctly.
- *INTERNAL*—Only the internal declarations should be read and interpreted by the parser for the document to be read correctly.

A well-formed, but not valid, XML document that's being checked for structural integrity would carry this RMD:

```
<?XML version="1.0" RMD="NONE"?>
```

A fully functional, valid XML document that needs parsing based on both internal and external DTDs would contain this RMD:

```
<?XML version="1.0" RMD="ALL"?>
```

The default value of the RMD is **ALL**. If you don't include it, the XML parser will read and interpret all DTDs associated with the document.

Elements

Document *elements* consist of markup and the text contained by markup. The meat of an XML document is the combination of elements as defined by the document's related DTD. Elements can have attributes and nest within each other. Some elements are required, whereas others are optional. All of the rules that govern a document's elements are defined in the DTD. The following is an XML element:

```
<P>This is a paragraph</P>
```

If we were just shooting for a well-formed XML document, this single element could constitute an entire XML document. If the document needed to be valid, then this element would be only a part of the document and would have to be defined in the document's DTD. The technical definition of an XML element includes both markup and the text it contains. The preceding example is one single element, not three. We discuss XML elements in detail in Chapter 7.

Comments

As any HTML programmer knows, the ability to leave notes inside of a set of code is invaluable. XML *comments* are just that—notes in an XML document that are ignored by an XML processor. In this case, we can truly say that if you know HTML, you know XML because their comment mechanisms are identical. Here is an example:

```
<!-- This is an XML comment. All text and markup
between the open and close comment tags will be
ignored by an XML parser and associated software. -->
```

You can include as much text and markup in comment tags as you need. Be careful not to use any double hyphens (--) in your text other than the ones that are included in the start and end tags. If you do, you'll find portions of your comments hanging out for all the world (parsers and people alike) to see.

Character References

Did you know "character reference" is just a fancy name for text? Well, now you do. *Character references* refer to all the text used in the document to create declarations, markup, and text inside of XML elements. It seems we've discussed these aspects of a document before, so why make such a big deal out of characters? For one very good reason: Do you need to use non-ASCII characters in your XML document? If the answer is yes, then the character set you define for your XML document is key to how your character references are recognized and interpreted by the XML parser and associated software. XML uses the ISO 10646 character set, also known as Unicode, that uses 16-bit patterns to represent characters. Ultimately, this character set can represent 65,000 different characters, including Greek and special punctuation characters. If those 65,000 characters aren't enough, you can reference any other character set you like in your DTD—as long as you provide a source file for the parser to work from.

To include non-ASCII characters in your XML documents, you still need to use the entity naming system adopted by HTML. This means that you need to use either **©** or **©** to create a copyright (©) sign. The specifics of including and referencing character sets are covered in detail in Chapter 12.

Processing Instructions

It's entirely possible that XML documents can not only be created for specific XML applications, but also for specific software packages. Often, instructions need to be passed from the XML document through the parser to the software to tell the software how to process all or part of the document. These are called *processing instructions (PIs)*. A PI can be included anywhere inside an XML document. Usually, you'll want to place them in the prologue so they set up a global processing environment for the entire document. The RMD we discussed in an earlier section is actually a processing instruction:

```
<?XML version="1.0" RMD="X"?>
```

As this example shows, all processing instructions begin with **<?** and end with **?>**. Those instructions reserved for XML, such as the RMD, follow the **<?** in XML. With the exception of the XML string, you can assign any identifier to the PI as long as it's consistent with the requirements of the software that is going to use the PI. Other examples of PIs at work include creating links to XML style sheets and providing information about how multimedia files should be treated.

Immediate Solutions

Declarations, elements, comments, character references, and processing instructions are the logical structures behind an XML document. It's important to know how each works and how to implement each one correctly on an application-specific level. Knowing what an XML element is won't get you very far unless you know which ones work with your particular XML application. In the Immediate Solutions section, we'll look at sample XML documents created by an XML professional—a solid working example. Then, to make your document creation a bit easier, we'll discuss all you need to know about any XML application using the application created for the sample document as an example. Next, the chapter's project shows you how to create a road map for any XML application. The final tool in the chapter is a checklist of all you need to know about any XML application before you begin to create documents for it.

Evaluating An XML Document And Its DTD

It's been our experience that quality examples are often the best teachers, and re-minders, of how to do things correctly. The following XML document is no exception. In this section, we'll look at an XML version of *Heart of Darkness* and its DTDs. We'll show you a document from the DTD and then perform a quick analysis of the DTD. The point of this exercise is not to create a document for a novel DTD, but to show you how to learn all you need to know to create an XML document.

David Megginson has converted Joseph Conrad's short novel *Heart of Darkness* into an XML document to demonstrate a simple novel DTD. As our first step in analyzing the novel application, let's look at a document created for it (see Listing 6.1).

Listing 6.1   A document created for the novel application.

```
<?xml version="1.0" encoding="UTF-8" standalone="no"?>

<!DOCTYPE novel PUBLIC "-//Megginson//DTD Novel//EN" "novel.dtd"
[
  <!ENTITY chapter.01
    PUBLIC "-//Megginson//TEXT Heart of Darkness, Chapter 1//EN"
    "chap01.xml">
  <!ENTITY chapter.02
```

```
            PUBLIC "-//Megginson//TEXT Heart of Darkness, Chapter 2//EN"
            "chap02.xml">
        <!ENTITY chapter.03
            PUBLIC "-//Megginson//TEXT Heart of Darkness, Chapter 3//EN"
            "chap03.xml">
        <!ENTITY chapter.04
            PUBLIC "-//Megginson//TEXT Heart of Darkness, Chapter 4//EN"
            "chap04.xml">
    ]>

    <novel>

    <front>
    <title>The Heart of Darkness</title>
    <author>Joseph Conrad</author>

    <revision-list>

    <item>XML version 30 November 1997 by David Megginson,
    dmeggins@microstar.com (still needs to be proofread against the
    printed edition).</item>

    <item>TEI markup added April 1995 by David Megginson,
    dmeggins@aix1.uottawa.ca</item>

    <item>Corrections to typos made 6/22/94 by PDCChristy@aol.com</item>

    <item>Original text came from the Online Book Initiative (OBI)
    via the Internet Wiretap
    [obi/Joseph.Conrad/heart.of.darkness.txt]</item>

    </revision-list>
    </front>

    <body>

    &chapter.01;

    &chapter.02;

    &chapter.03;

    &chapter.04;

    </body>

    </novel>
```

This document tells us a great deal about the novel DTD without even looking at the DTD itself. Reading from the top down, we know that the document conforms to XML version 1, uses the UTF-8 character encoding system, and isn't a standalone document. We learned all that from the RMD one-liner.

TIP: *The RMD speaks volumes. It can tell you quite a bit, not only about the current document, but also about the XML application for which it was written. The XML version information is more important as time goes by and new versions of XML are released. In effect, the version number dates the document and gives you a good idea of which XML mechanisms are supported by the application. The character set information provides clues about how robust the document is linguistically. Those documents that are in a multilingual format, or that use advanced mathematical notation, require larger character sets—usually 16-bit or larger. Also, the smaller the character set, the faster the document parses. Finally, if a document is a standalone document, then it's only well-formed (not valid) or its entire DTD is stored inside the document itself rather than externally. Chances are, documents written for specific applications won't be standalone documents for purposes other than testing.*

The **<!DOCTYPE>** declaration fills us in on the basics of the DTD the document was written for and tells us what tag documents written for the DTD must start with. In this case, the DTD is called novel.dtd and its public identifier is "**-// Megginson//DTD Novel//EN**". All documents written for this DTD must be contained within the **<NOVEL>**...**</NOVEL>** tags.

TIP: **<!DOCTYPE>** *shows you where to start. The main document element for all XML documents written for the DTD declared by the* **<!DOCTYPE>** *tag must be listed as part of the tag. This is important to know because the DTDs don't have to specify the document element. The tag* **<!DOCTYPE MYDOC "MYDOC.DTD">** *specifies that the DTD for the document is mydoc.dtd and the document element is mydoc. The document must begin and end with* **<MYDOC>**...**<MYDOC>**. *Using any other tag pair as the document element causes the document to be both invalid and not well-formed.*

6: Inside XML Applications And Documents

Continuing on down the line, a series of entities specific to the document are listed. This doesn't tell us much about the XML application we'll be working with, only about what external entities we can link to the document. After the entities section, we get to the real meat of the XML document and—ignoring the specific content of the elements listed—we find the following markup tag structure:

```
<novel>
<front>
<title>
</title>
<author>
</author>
<revision-list>
<item>
</item>
<item>
</item>
```

```
<item>
</item>
<item>
</item>
</revision-list>
</front>
<body>
</body>
</novel>
```

If we rearrange these empty tags a bit and add some spaces to show nesting, as in the following code sample, we can learn quite a bit about the DTD:

```
<novel>
  <front>
    <title>...</title>
    <author>...</author>
    <revision-list>
      <item>...</item>
      <item>...</item>
      <item>...</item>
      <item>...</item>
    </revision-list>
  </front>
  <body>
  </body>
</novel>
```

What does this newly formatted markup skeleton teach us about the DTD? There are at least two elements that can be nested within the document element **<NOVEL>...</NOVEL>**, **<FRONT>...</FRONT>**, and **<BODY>...</BODY>**. The front element can contain at least three elements: title, author, and revision list. Finally, the revision list element can contain items. What this skeleton doesn't tell us is which tags are required and which are optional. We'll have to consult the DTD for that information.

Although the element names explain their roles fairly well, a look at the content within the tags tells us that the title and author tags should hold the title of the novel and its authorship information. The revision list provides information about changes to the XML document itself, not revisions to the novel. The body tags contain entity links to other XML documents. Therefore, it's probably safe to assume that the body tags should contain the actual novel text.

By examining an XML document, we know the following about the XML application it was created for:

- *XML version*—1
- *Character set(s) used*—UTF-8
- *External DTD required*—novel.dtd
- *DTD's public identifier*—"**-//Megginson//DTD Novel//EN**"
- *Document element*—**<NOVEL>**...**</NOVEL>**
- *Valid elements (some but not all)*—**<NOVEL>**, **<FRONT>**, **<TITLE>**, **<AUTHOR>**, **<REVISION-LIST>**, and **<BODY>**
- *Element nesting rules (some but not all)*—as previously discussed

That's quite a bit we didn't know before, and we haven't even looked at the DTD yet. This raises a valid question: Why not just read the DTD? It's quite simple really: The DTD language is not the easiest in the world to read. Even for experienced users of markup, DTDs can be difficult (at best) to slog through. It's often difficult to picture how the elements described in the DTD will work together in the end. If you can see how the DTD elements work before you read the DTD, it will make deciphering the DTD much easier. To prove our point, let's look at novel.dtd (see Listing 6.2).

Listing 6.2   The code behind novel.dtd.

```
<?xml encoding="UTF-8"?>
<!--
****************************************************************
novel.dtd: A simple XML DTD for marking-up novels.
Copyright (c) 1997 by David Megginson.
****************************************************************
-->

<!-- Content model for phrasal content -->
<!ENTITY % phrasal "#PCDATA|emphasis">

<!-- ******** -->
<!-- Elements -->
<!-- ******** -->

<!-- The top-level novel -->
<!ELEMENT novel (front, body)>

<!-- The frontmatter for the novel -->
<!ELEMENT front (title, author, revision-list)>

<!-- The list of revisions to this text -->
<!ELEMENT revision-list (item+)>
```

```
<!-- An item in the list of revisions -->
<!ELEMENT item (%phrasal;)*>

<!-- The main body of a novel -->
<!ELEMENT body (chapter+)>

<!-- A chapter of a novel -->
<!ELEMENT chapter (title, paragraph+)>
<!ATTLIST chapter
  id ID #REQUIRED>

<!-- The title of a novel or chapter -->
<!ELEMENT title (%phrasal;)*>

<!-- The author(s) of a novel -->
<!ELEMENT author (%phrasal;)*>

<!-- A paragraph in a chapter -->
<!ELEMENT paragraph (%phrasal;)*>

<!-- An emphasised phrase -->
<!ELEMENT emphasis (%phrasal;)*>

<!-- **************** -->
<!-- General Entities -->
<!-- **************** -->

<!--
  These really should have their Unicode equivalents.
-->

<!-- em-dash -->
<!ENTITY mdash "--">

<!-- left double quotation mark -->
<!ENTITY ldquo "''">

<!-- right double quotation mark -->
<!ENTITY rdquo "''">

<!-- left single quotation mark -->
<!ENTITY lsquo "'">

<!-- right single quotation mark -->
<!ENTITY rsquo "'">
```

```
<!-- horizontal ellipse -->
<!ENTITY hellip "…">

<!-- end of DTD -->
```

The author has been kind enough to provide us with a well-commented DTD, but this isn't always the case. Consider yourself pampered.

A read through the DTD shows that it contains the following elements: attributes, content, and status (required or optional), as illustrated by Table 6.1.

All of the elements, except for item and emphasis, are required. Any valid novel document must include the following structure:

```
<novel>
  <front>
    <title>…</title>
    <author>…</author>
    <revision-list>…</revision-list>
  </front>
  <body>
    <chapter ID=XX>
      <title>…</title>
      <paragraph>…</paragraph>
    </chapter>
  </body>
<novel>
```

Table 6.1   Elements found in the novel DTD.

Element	Attributes	Content	Status
novel	none	front, body	required
front	none	title, author, revision-list	required
revision-list	none	item	required
item	none	phrasal content	optional
body	none	chapter	required
chapter	ID	title, paragraph	required
title	none	phrasal content	required
author	none	phrasal content	required
paragraph	none	phrasal content	required
emphasis	none	phrasal content	optional

If this is the case, you're probably wondering why the first novel document we showed you is correct, because it didn't have the chapter and paragraph elements included. However, once the chapters are added into the document via the chapter entities defined in the internal DTD, it becomes valid.

In addition to these elements, the DTD also defines one parameter entity and six general entities. The parameter entity:

```
<!ENTITY % phrasal "#PCDATA|emphasis">
```

indicates that an element whose content is **%phrasal**, can contain either regular character data or character data nested within **<EMPHASIS>**...**</EMPHASIS>** tags. This being the case, both of these examples are valid:

```
<paragraph>this is regular character data</paragraph>
<paragraph>
  <emphasis>this is emphasized text inside a paragraph</emphasis>
</paragraph>
```

The DTD also specifies six non-ASCII character entities for general use throughout documents, as listed in Table 6.2. The DTD's author admits that the element probably should be listed using Unicode, but thanks to XML, they don't have to be.

There are a few things we learned from our initial reading of a document built for the novel DTD and from our analysis of the DTD. We have a clear understanding of what elements and entities are allowed in documents written for the application. We know which elements are required and which are optional. In addition, we have learned the content and nesting rules for novel documents. As we said earlier, you'll probably never write a document for this particular DTD, but all of the methods we've employed while analyzing this specific DTD can be applied to the examination of any DTD in preparation for writing documents for it. To see the entire text of *Heart of Darkness* as an XML document, visit David Megginson's sample document page at **http://home.sprynet.com/sprynet/dmeggins/texts/darkness/index.html**.

Table 6.2   Entities found in the novel DTD.

Name	Code	Final Display
Em dash	—	—
Left double quote	“	"
Right double quote	”	"
Left single quote	‘	'
Right single quote	’	'
Horizontal ellipsis	…	...

Creating A Road Map To An XML Application

Our examination of the XML novel application and accompanying XML version of *Heart of Darkness* showed that you need to understand many things about an XML application to create documents for it. You also know now that you don't just have to read the DTD to gather all of this information. In this project, we'll condense all that we learned in the previous section into a series of fully explained steps that apply to just about any XML application, with hints and tips on where to find the information you need about an XML application. When you've worked your way through the steps, you'll have a road map for an XML application that makes creating valid documents for the application easier.

We'll be guided by Microsoft in this particular endeavor because they've created an excellent road map to the Open Software Distribution (OSD) XML application. It provides a format similar to the one you'll want to use when you create your own road map. Check it out online at **www.microsoft.com/standards/osd/osdspec.htm**. You probably won't take the time to create a written document like Microsoft's OSD specification, but the information contained in the OSD specification is a perfect example of what you need to know about any XML application to work with it effectively. Because the majority of the specifications are in DTDese and not road map form, you'll often have to create the road map yourself—instead of having it created for you. The road-mapping process we outline may seem a bit primitive, but we guarantee that if you follow the steps from beginning to end, you'll have a clear idea of the goals, parameters, and mechanisms of any XML application you work with.

Step 1: Gathering Your Resources

To create your application road map, you need to have a few resources on hand, or at least bookmarked in your Web browser of choice. These include:

- A copy of the application's DTD

- Any online or offline documentation for the application

- Sample documents created for the DTD

Generally, you'll find all of this information on the Web somewhere, usually all in one place. However, as applications become more widely implemented, valuable resources will be strewn about the Web. Before you settle in to begin the creation of your road map, devote some time to constructive Web surfing. As you spend more time with XML, you'll discover which sites are the best repositories for information and which provide you with the best jumping-off points. Appendix A is devoted to a complete listing of the best XML sites found today—a hyperlinked listing is available in HTML on this book's companion CD-ROM.

Of that listing, the two most invaluable sites (ones that all XML users will want to have at the top of their bookmark list) are:

- The World Wide Web Consortium's XML page at **www.w3.org/XML**
- Robin Cover's XML repository at **www.sil.org/sgml/xml.html**

Step 2: Determining The Purpose Of The Application

We know this step seems a bit obvious. You're probably thinking that you've already done this and the purpose behind the application is what led you to choose it in the first place. Still, we'd like to encourage you to read as much about the intended purpose of the application as you can find. Taking a closer look at the OSD specification, we discover that it was created to work in conjunction with the CDF application. This doesn't mean OSD isn't useful on its own, but the added functionality of CDF might make the solution you're creating more robust and extensible. It's also important that you don't try to force an application to do things it wasn't meant to do. This has been a common fallacy of HTML page designers. The whole point behind creating XML applications is to define markup that doesn't have to be bent beyond recognition to achieve the desired results. In a nutshell, read everything about an application you can get your hands on before you begin dissecting it for specifics.

Step 3: Finding The XML Version

You need to know what version of XML the application—and by extension, the accompanying documents—is based on. Because only version 1 of XML is currently available, it's fairly obvious that all current applications and documents were developed under XML 1. As newer versions emerge, this will change. The XML version may not be listed in the DTD, but it should be part of any well-formed RMD. Look at a document created for an application to find this bit of information. If you can't immediately find a document specifically created for the application, dig around in the online documentation for the application and email the person responsible for maintaining the specification.

Step 4: Locating And Saving A Copy Of The DTD

It's been our experience with XML applications that DTDs aren't too hard to find. They're often part of the documentation and are available as text files. If for some reason the DTD isn't included in your documentation, simply look at a sample document's **<!DOCTYPE>** tag and it will tell you the name, public identifier, and location of the DTD. We recommend that you save a copy of the DTD locally, so you have quick access to it and can create documents for it without being connected to the Internet.

We don't recommend that you alter the DTD in any way—unless you created it and are responsible for its development. There are other developers and software out there using the same DTD, and you want your documents to integrate seamlessly with theirs. If you need to add additional declarations—beyond declaring external entities—think carefully before you do. Make them part of a document's internal declaration set rather than the "official" external DTD. We also suggest that you provide extensive comments about your additional declarations, and don't be surprised if these additions cause problems with the functionality of your document. Usually, it's best to adhere closely to the established DTD.

Step 5: Identifying The Document Element

Remember that the document element is the outside set of tags that every other tag within your document is nested within. If you don't use the correct document element, you won't be able to create a valid document. As we said earlier in Immediate Solutions, the DTD doesn't necessarily highlight any one document as the document element. After a bit of reading through the DTD, you can probably reason out the document element, and it's often listed first in the list of elements. But, it's easier to look at a **<!DOCTYPE>** declaration from a document written for the application. The document element is one of the required components of a valid **<!DOCTYPE>** declaration. It's there for the taking if you know where to look.

Step 6: Narrowing Down The Supported Character Sets

You need to know which character set or sets the application supports. Whereas XML, by default, supports 16-bit Unicode, the application you're working with may require a more extensive character set—32-bit instead of 16—or it may link to special character sets. This information can usually be found in the documentation about the application, but not necessarily in the DTD itself. You can also check the RMD of application documents to see what character sets are declared. When in doubt, assume the application uses the standard XML character set (but be sure to check it check first).

Step 7: Defining The Specifics Of Each Document Element

After you've gathered all the preliminary information about the purpose, XML version, character sets, and other assorted information of relevance, it's time to get down to the nitty-gritty—the application elements. There are five questions you need to ask about every application element:

- Is it required or optional?
- What are its attributes and their values?
- Which attributes are required?
- What are its content requirements?
- Which other elements can it nest within?

Earlier in the section, we showed you that you don't have to read the DTD from top to bottom to gather all this information. Instead, you should start by examining the skeleton of a document written for the application to see how the elements work together. This gives you a point of reference when you begin the somewhat painful process of deciphering the DTD. Eventually, you need to create an information box for each element that includes the answers to the five questions we just posed. Figure 6.1 demonstrates three complete element information boxes, as found in the OSD specification.

Element	ABSTRACT
Content	<string>
Child Of	SOFTPKG

Element	CODEBASE
Attributes	SIZE=<max-KB> The maximum allowable size for the software archive file. Kilobytes is the unit of measure. If SIZE is exceeded, the software will not be downloaded. HREF=<URL> Points to the archive to be downloaded. FILENAME=<string> Specifies a file contained within the same archive as the OSD. If the OSD is used as a standalone file, this attribute is ignored.
Child Of	IMPLEMENTATION

Element	DEPENDENCY
Attributes	ACTION= (Assert | Install) Assert means: Ignore this SOFTPKG entirely if the dependency is not already present on the client's machine. Install means: If the dependency is not already present on the client's machine, go get it, then install it, so that the SOFTPKG has all the pieces it needs.
Child Of	SOFTPKG, IMPLEMENTATION
Parent Of	SOFTPKG

Figure 6.1   Element information boxes as created for elements of the OSD specification.

Although you might not want to take the time to create a complex HTML table for each element, we do recommend that you devise a method for maintaining a record of each element's vital information—at least until you have more experience with the application. When we modify the element boxes from the OSD specification, we get the element record form shown in Figure 6.2.

The idea behind such detailed documentation is to get in the habit of storing away (on paper or in your head) all the pertinent information about each element in an XML application. As XML becomes more widely implemented and new tools and resource sites are developed, much of this work will be done for you. One way or the other, you're going to have to know the ins and outs of every element in an application's DTD.

Step 8: Evaluating Your Content

As you create your application road map, there is a good chance the specifics of the content you intend to include in the documents you develop for this application will be hovering on the fringes. You're now in a position to evaluate your content in the context of the XML application. You'll find that this process makes creating documents for the application from your content almost a breeze. You're now well versed in the intricacies and mechanisms of the application, you know all of the elements intimately, and you can follow the content and nesting rules without a problem. All that's left for you to do now is create a document, or set of documents, for the application. Armed with what you now know, you'll be done before you know it.

Element:	
Attributes:	
Content:	
Child Of:	
Parent Of:	

Figure 6.2   A generic element information record form.

6: Inside XML
Applications And
Documents

Application Checklist

To further condense the information presented in Immediate Solutions into a quick reference for application evaluation, we've created the following checklist of things you need to know about every XML application. If you've encountered a new application and are having a hard time getting a grip on it, run through this checklist in your mind. Take the time to make sure you have completely worked through each item on this list, and you'll soon find that the formerly elusive application is now firmly in your grasp:

❑   Resources

❑   Application purpose

❑   XML version

❑   Local copy of the DTD

❑   Document element

❑   Character sets

❑   Element information records

❑   Content evaluation

Chapter 7

Working With XML Elements

By Cheryl Kirk

In Depth

Elements and attributes are the building blocks of XML. Element declarations used in an XML document or within a Document Type Definition (DTD) specify the structure of the XML document and give you the flexibility to define the document for your specific needs. Although XML elements may look the same and in many ways act the same as HTML tags, they take on a whole new meaning because they give you the flexibility of designing your own document structure. Elements are more than just tags used to mark up text for formatting in a document. Instead, elements construct and hold together the document, providing markup to tell the document and the processor what you want the document to do. Every XML document forms a treelike structure, with each element creating a branch of the tree. Each of the elements can be nested, and all elements defined are nested below the root or main element of the XML document.

Knowing how to define elements, specify attributes for them, and provide inclusions or exclusions for specific element tags is a major stepping stone to learning XML. In this chapter, you'll learn what elements and attributes are, their syntax, how they work, and how to use them to create well-formed XML documents. In the Immediate Solutions section, you'll put that knowledge to good use by defining your own elements and specifying attributes to work with them.

Elements Revisited

If you've been diligently reading each chapter and following along with the Immediate Solutions examples, you should now know that elements are used to define XML documents. You should also know that elements look and work in much the way HTML tags work. You can create your own elements and specify the tag names to indicate a particular section, piece of text, or special processing instruction. Element and attribute names can be anything you want them to be as long as you conform to the XML standards and use descriptive element names. For example, **<PARAGRAPH>** is a more descriptive element name than just **<P>**, for defining where the XML processor should start a new paragraph.

TIP: *If you are already familiar with elements and attributes, you may want to move on to Chapter 9, which covers the concept of defining element content.*

Like tags in HTML, elements are delimited from the text used in the document by angle brackets. Both a start- and end-tag define or make up the element. Elements normally include some sort of textual information (or in some cases, a list of other elements) that follows the initial start-tag. The following example demonstrates how the paragraph element is used to define where you want a paragraph to begin (**<PARAGRAPH>**) and end (**</PARAGRAPH>**) and what text is provided within the start- and end-tags of the element:

```
<paragraph>
Now is the time for all good men to come to the aid of their country.
</paragraph>
```

All elements follow certain rules. Like entities, element names can only consist of letters, digits, periods, dashes, underscores, and colons. No spaces are allowed, and no reserved characters, such as the angle bracket, can be used in an element name. However, there are other special characters you can use to separate the type of content you want the element to display. For example, you can use the pipe character to separate nested content and attributes. For more information about element content specification delimiters, see this chapter's "Symbols For Specifying Element Rules" section.

As seen in the previous example, for every start-tag used to specify an element, there must be an end-tag. All tags must be properly nested, and all tags must match in order for a document to be considered well-formed. If you turned this book into an XML document, you would have section elements, chapter elements, heading elements, and paragraph elements. The following code is a brief example of how these elements might work and how certain elements could be nested within other elements:

```
<?XML version="1.0"?>
<book>
  <chapter>
    <chaptertitle>Elements in XML</chaptertitle>
      <section>Elements explained
        <paragraph>Elements are the building blocks of XML
        </paragraph>
      </section>
  </chapter>
</book>
```

Notice how the **<BOOK>** element defines the overall concept and context of the XML document and how certain elements such as **<PARAGRAPH>** and **<SECTION>** could easily be nested within **<CHAPTER>** elements, which in turn are nested in the entire **<BOOK>** element. Figure 7.1 shows how the

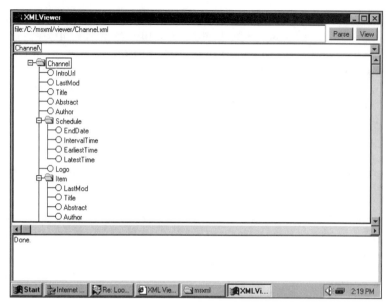

Figure 7.1   A document's tree structure is defined by its elements.

document's elements create a treelike structure. Notice that each element starts and ends—although not all on the same line, or possibly even on the same page—with start- and end-tags. The nesting of elements is an important concept, because you define not only the structure of the document, but also the rules for where the various elements can be placed. You would not, of course, place a paragraph element before the chapter title. And with the nesting features of XML elements, you can specify these rules.

Nesting Elements

As you can see, elements help define not only the start of paragraphs within a document, but also where an XML document begins and ends. In actuality, as you saw in our book example, the entire XML document is grouped within a single element that defines it. It is from that single element that the structure of the document is spelled out clearly, not only to the software, but also to anyone perusing the source of the document. And this is an important point. In order for a document to be well-formed, there must be a single element that constructs the document and in which all other elements are nested. To meet the XML standards, your element must be humanly legible; that means that the average human can understand the concepts and constraints of the document.

The easiest way to understand the nesting concept is by conceptualizing a simple XML document in the form of one big box. Open up that big box, and inside is a smaller box. Open that smaller box and you'll see an even smaller one. Open that box and another smaller box is inside. This concept of elements nested inside other elements that are nested inside other elements is technically referred to as parent/child nesting. The **<BOOK>** element is the parent and the **<CHAPTER**> element is the parent's child. However, the <**CHAPTER>** element has its own child relationship in the form of the **<SECTION>** element, which in turn is a parent to the **<PARAGRAPH>** element. Incestuous isn't it?

TIP: *In some XML documentation, you may also see all parent/child-nested elements commonly referred to as sub-elements.*

Regardless of what you call them, this concept of nesting and parent/child elements is important to learning how to properly structure your document and where you should and can place various elements. Once you understand the relationship of all your elements in the context of the entire document, you can structure your document accordingly.

Aside from understanding how the elements and your document relate to each other, it's from this parent/child nesting relationship that the document provides a root from which the markup tree structures grow and evolve. If you've experimented with any of the XML Java browsers, such as Jumbo, or even tried your hand at Channels (a fine example of an XML application), you've probably experienced this parent/child/tree structure without even knowing it. If you click on a channel in Internet Explorer, the channel will expand to show you all its children. Those children can have their own children, and so on. This structure is created through the use of elements.

It's from this tree structure that the outline of the document is created. The tree structure is also where various style sheets can be used on the various elements within the document to format the text. Because of the tree structure, it is much easier to search XML documents than it is to search even a simple HTML document. In an XML document, you can easily search through specific elements.

Document Elements

The main element of any XML document, the element that actually is the big box in which all other boxes are placed, is called the *document element*. The document element specifies the concept of the document. For example, if you were defining an XML document as a memo, after the XML declaration and the Document Type Definition, you would specify the document element as shown in the following code:

```
<?XML version="1.0"?>
  <memo>
    <to>John Smith</to>
```

```
<from>Betty Lou</from>
<subject>This memo</subject>
<content>
  <alert>Please read carefully</alert>
  <paragraph>Please make sure you read this memo.</paragraph>
  <closing>Thank you very much</closing>
</content>
</memo>
```

Notice that the element memo sets the structure of the file and makes this a well-formed XML document. Within the **<MEMO>** element are its children elements, such as **<TO>**, **<FROM>**, and **<SUBJECT>**. But **<CONTENT>**, although it is a child of **<MEMO>**, has children of its own. If you're a genealogy buff, you'll understand the concept of parents, children, and descendants. If we had placed the closing **</CONTENT>** tag before the closing **</ALERT>** tag, the document would not be considered well-formed. Now, take a look at the following code, and try to figure out why it *isn't* a well-formed XML document:

```
<?XML version="1.0"?>
<to>John Smith</to>
<from>Betty Lou</from>
<subject>This memo</subject>
<paragraph>Please make sure you read this memo,
<to>John Smith</to>.</paragraph>
<closing>Thank you very much</closing>
</memo>
```

Did you spot the problem? Notice that there are plenty of elements, but there is no *document element* defined at the beginning. Nothing tells the processor (or you, the reader of this XML file) exactly what type of document this is going to be. Instead, this document jumps right into the thick of things with the **<TO>** element, never once stopping to tell you what the XML document actually is or contains. The XML processor, then, would assume **<TO>** is the document element. But the processor would quickly error out because only one document element is allowed and the **<TO>** element shows up in two different places in this document. Also, because document elements cannot be nested, the **<TO>** element would cause this document to error when processed.

Remember, only one document element is allowed in any XML document. XML documents must have a document element defined, and that document element cannot be part of another element nor can it be nested with other elements. In essence, the document element is the glue that binds the entire document together and can be placed in an XML file or within a DTD.

A Closer Look At Elements

By now, you know what an element looks like, but we've been somewhat carefree in our examples of elements until now, using only the most simplistic examples. We kept it simple because we wanted to first introduce you to the concept of elements, how they control the document structure, and how nesting elements creates the overall structure within XML documents. Now, it's time to get down to the nitty-gritty and look closely at elements, how they are declared, and the attributes and content that make them work.

When you declare an element as a DTD (or within an XML document), you start by following the proper syntax for declaring elements. The following line of code shows the proper syntax for the element declaration:

```
<!ELEMENT name content>
```

When you declare an element, you are specifying the name of the element so it can be referenced throughout the document. You are also declaring the type of content that can be used, be it character data, other elements, or nothing at all. In this example

```
<!ELEMENT memo ANY>
```

the element name is memo and any type of content data can be defined for this element. When you want to use this element within the XML document, you do so just as you would an HTML tag, by specifying the element name and surrounding it with angle brackets. For example, once we've declared the memo element, as in the previous example, we can put it to use in our document by doing this:

```
<memo>This is the text of the memo.</memo>
```

Notice that, as with HTML, we add the start-tag and the end-tag. Since we've declared that this element can have any type of content, we can include text, other elements, or a combination of both. Notice also that we used memo, not MEMO, for the element name. The element name is case sensitive just like almost everything else in XML. So an element declaration of

```
<!ELEMENT book ANY>
```

is not the same as

```
<!ELEMENT BOOK ANY>
```

As mentioned previously, the name specified must be something that is descriptive and must not contain spaces or special reserved characters. Element names can only contain letters, digits, periods, dashes, underscores, and colons. You can use underscores or dashes when you want to create an element name that normally would have spaces between the words, such as **FIRST NAME**, which, if you follow proper syntax, can be **FIRST_NAME** or **FIRST-NAME**.

Element names should also not imply any particular formatting. Instead, they should imply structure or content. It is not a good idea to declare an element with the name 24-point, especially if what you really want to do is declare a heading element instead. The name heading is always preferred when you are specifying where the content should be marked up as a heading. You may not always be able to keep your element names specific to their intended process, but whatever you do, remember to leave the formatting tag names to the style sheets.

Element Content

In addition to declaring the name of the element, you need to define the content of the element. Element content specifies what content can appear within the element. That content may be characters, lists of elements, or specific keywords that signal to the processor certain information about the element. There are several types of element content you can use:

• Parsed character data

• Other elements

• Specific keywords

• A mixture of data and elements

Let's examine each content type individually. In the Immediate Solutions section, we'll put these types of content to work in some real-world examples. If you are already familiar with elements, you might want to skip to that section for ideas on how to work with elements and their content.

Parsed Character Data (#PCDATA)

Some elements can only contain character data—or text—and no other elements. This is the simplest content model an element can contain. No other elements can be nested. If you declare content as character data, the only thing you can include between the start- and end-tags is plain old text. In the following example, the **<TITLE>** element can contain only text, as indicated by the parsed character data notation (**#PCDATA**), which is listed in the element's content section:

```
<!ELEMENT TITLE (#PCDATA)>
```

Once declared, this element could then be placed in the document with the following content considered valid:

```
<TITLE>Welcome to the Wonderful World of XML</TITLE>
```

If you include any other elements within the tag, the XML processor will declare the document invalid and not well-formed. The following code would make the document invalid and not well-formed:

```
<TITLE>Welcome to the Wonderful World of <emphasis> XML</emphasis></TITLE>
```

The elements are nested properly, but because the element **<TITLE>** was defined to only contain parsed character data and not other elements, the document is invalid. Also, remember that you shouldn't include formatting elements within your document. Leave that to the style sheet. With character data, there is no limit to the amount of text that can be contained. You could go on and on and on and on and on!

Elements As Content

There may be times when you want to include other elements instead of content in the content model specification. If an element's content model specifies that it can only contain other elements and no text, it is said to have *element content*. Also referred to as the content specification or content model (as you've seen in the previous section where we defined the **<TITLE>** element content model as parsed data), the content notation outlines exactly what can and cannot be allowed as content. If we aren't specifying character data, but we're specifying elements, the element content specification or model describes how many elements can be specified and in what order they can be placed. There are four types of element content specifications you can define for each element:

- A list of other elements that can be specified as content
- A mixture of both data and elements
- The keyword **EMPTY**
- The keyword **ANY**

Let's examine each type, starting with the last first, the keyword **ANY**.

Specific Keywords

With XML elements, you can define element attributes in pretty much any fashion that you want. This gives you tremendous flexibility. Part of that flexibility is the ability to use specific reserved keywords to further define the element content. Two of those keywords are **ANY** and **EMPTY**. **ANY** allows any type of content to be defined for the element content model. The keyword **EMPTY** specifies the element will contain no content. Following is a discussion of both reserved keywords.

The ANY Content Declaration

We've used the keyword **ANY** in a previous example, but it needs some explanation. **ANY** specifies the type of content of an element just like **(#PCDATA)** does. Although **(#PCDATA)** content is relatively easy to understand and use, the **ANY** keyword is even more simplistic than the parsed character data content specification. The **ANY** declaration does what it says—it allows any type of content (data) or element markup information. That means that the element can use text, another element, or a mixture of both in the content of the element.

If we declare an element called **<BODYTEXT>** and use the **ANY** keyword to specify the content, we could use whatever we want in terms of content for the element. For example, we could place character data, elements, and even references to external information within this element's content structure. The element declaration statement would look like this:

```
<!ELEMENT BODYTEXT ANY>
```

When we put this element to good use in a document, it allows text and elemental markup information as long as the other elements have been defined previously. The following example first defines the elements:

```
<!ELEMENT BODYTEXT ANY>
<!ELEMENT PARAGRAPH ANY>
<!ELEMENT NOTE (#PCDATA)>
```

If we wanted to apply these elements to an XML document and still have the document be valid, this is how we could place them:

```
<BODYTEXT>
<PARAGRAPH>
Welcome to the wonderful world of XML. We certainly want
you to understand every important option available in XML.
<NOTE>
Make sure you read all the chapters thoroughly.
</NOTE>
There are plenty of things to learn.
</PARAGRAPH>
</BODYTEXT>
```

In this example, we can nest the paragraph element within the **<BODYTEXT>** element, and we can nest the note element within the **<BODYTEXT>** element as well. But we cannot nest the paragraph element within the note element because the note element allows for only parsed character data (**#PCDATA**). Table 7.1 shows what type of data can be used with the declared element.

TIP: *If you nest other elements, make sure they have been declared and specify the right content type to match. Otherwise, the first element would not be able to impose its rules on its content. Also, it wouldn't make for a very well-formed XML document if you didn't declare all the elements properly.*

As you can see, the **ANY** content declaration gives you tremendous flexibility, but remember that you really want to be specific about the rules of content. Although you can use **ANY** whenever you want with whatever element you want to declare, if you use it all the time, you are really not following the proper XML document-development conventions. Those conventions strongly suggest that you declare elements that are as descriptive as possible to provide for a tight document that defines exactly where and which elements can be used in the various locations.

The EMPTY Elements

Using **ANY** to specify type of content is flexible, easy to do, and very simple to understand, as is parsed character data, so the idea of using **EMPTY** to specify content should be as easy to understand. However, its advantages and uses may not be as apparent as the **ANY** or parsed character data content declarations. Here, we'll outline how the *empty element* content specification can be used.

Many of your elements will have content, but there are times when you may want an element to have no content whatsoever. In that case, you declare empty element content by using the content keyword **EMPTY** in the element content specification. The following is an example of the code you would use to do just that:

```
<!ELEMENT LOGINFO EMPTY>
```

Table 7.1   An example of the content that can be used with the ANY keyword declaration.

Code	Description
`<BODYTEXT>` This is the bodytext `</BODYTEXT>`	This example demonstrates how any text can be referenced by using the element.
`<BODYTEXT><PARAGRAPH>` `</PARAGRAPH></BODYTEXT>`	This example demonstrates how you can nest another element within the `<BODYTEXT>` element because you've specified ANY as the content type.
`<BODYTEXT><PARAGRAPH>` This is the bodytext `</PARAGRAPH>` `</BODYTEXT>`	This example demonstrates how you can nest another element along with data.

In this example, we are defining an element called **LOGINFO** in preparation for a channel we are setting up with Microsoft's Channel Definition Format (CDF). We actually don't want to record any **LOGINFO** at this point, although later we may change our minds. In terms of content, we want to specify that this element records or contains no data, so we use the keyword **EMPTY** to turn off any content collection.

An empty element is one that actually has no textual context. Although empty elements can be used for just about anything, they are usually used as markers where something should occur. If we go backward a bit and look at HTML, the element **<HR>** is a prime example of an empty element and how the **EMPTY** content declaration works. The **<HR>** element paints a horizontal rule or line across a Web page. As with any empty element, there are attributes associated with the **<HR>** element. With its **SIZE** attribute, you can specify the width or length of the horizontal rule. For example, the following code

```
<HR SIZE=4>
```

specifies a horizontal rule that is four pixels high. Notice that there is no text following the element as there might be with structural elements we normally use in XML. In theory, if there was, the **<HR>** element declaration would look something like this:

```
<!ELEMENT HR EMPTY>
```

TIP: *Remember, with XML you must first declare the element name and then the content specification mode. With XML elements, attributes are specified later, after the element and its content model has been declared. We'll cover attributes a little later in this chapter (see "Element Attributes") and in detail in Chapter 8.*

As you can see, when you declare an element's content model empty, you do so by using the following syntax:

```
<!ELEMENT elementname EMPTY>
```

When you want to use these elements with the XML document, you can still use start- and end-tags. However, because they have no contextual information to envelop, empty elements can use a special format that standard elements don't allow. Although you *can* use start- and end-tags for the empty element within your document, there is no need to have them because there is nothing within the element to work with. Instead, when you use an empty element in your document, it's much easier to use just a single tag, the element name, and a single slash to indicate that the element is an empty tag. The following is an example of an empty tag used in an XML document:

```
<LOGFILE/>
```

Like standard elements, the tag is delimited by angle brackets, but the slash is placed after the element name to signal to the processor that there is no more content to follow. You'll see a great deal of empty elements when you set up Internet Explorer Channels. For example, you may not want to specify a start time for updating, so you would leave that element empty. As a matter of fact, CDF uses a great number of empty tags when defining channels. For more information about CDF and some of the empty elements used with CDF, see Chapter 20.

> **WARNING!** *Even though empty tags only need one tag, in order for XML processors to process your document correctly, make sure all your other elements have start-tags and end-tags. If you omit an element's end-tag, your document will return nothing but errors.*

Mixed Content

As its name implies, mixed content is a combination of element content and character data. Remember parsed character data? It also can be considered mixed content data. Why? The important distinction is between element content (content that doesn't include any character data) and mixed content (content that does include character data). If an element can contain any character data at all, it's considered to have a mixed content model, even if the content model includes only character data. Got that?

For example, suppose you were going to set up a database of people's birthdays in an XML document. The element content could be both character and date data. In the following example, the **ENTRY** element can contain elements such as name, birthdate, and phone. Plus, with the **#PCDATA** declaration, the **ENTRY** element can also contain parsed character data:

```
<!ELEMENT ENTRY (#PCDATA | name | birthdate | phone)*>
```

Notice that this example has an asterisk at the end of the content declaration. The asterisk indicates that each element's content can occur none or multiple times in the contents of the **ENTRY** element. The vertical bar or pipe (|) is a special character used to indicate the element content model rules. In this case, the vertical bar means that these elements—name, birthdate, and phone—can appear in any order and that any instances of these elements can appear.

> **TIP:** *If a parameter entity is used as part of a content model, it is considered mixed content instead of element content. For more on the role parameter entities play in content models, see Chapter 9.*

Symbols For Specifying Element Rules

Before we move on, let's examine the various rules you can impose when you use element content. Specifically, we'll explain a simple content model and the nomenclature used to specify rules. Let's start by dissecting this simple element example:

```
<!ELEMENT section (title, summary?, paragraph+)>
```

By now, you should know that **!ELEMENT** declares the rest to be an element declaration. The word **section** defines the name of the element. Next is the element content, or actually, in this example, a list of other elements that must be, could be, or might be included within the element. In this particular example, the section element must contain a title. We know this because the title element is listed without any additional trailing characters. The section element can include a summary element, but unlike the title element, it doesn't have to; the question mark following the summary element title tells us this. There must be paragraphs in the section element, but there is no limitation on the number of paragraphs that have to be included (like the limitation on the section element to include a title). We know this because the paragraph element has a plus sign (+) after it denoting that there can be more than one of these elements within the section element.

As you can see from this example, we've declared the element name, the content (which is actually the list of other elements than can be used), the order in which the content should be placed, and the rules by which the element content specification, or list of elements, should be used. Remember, however, when you declare the use of other elements within the content specification of an element declaration, these elements must have been previously defined. So if we went backward for a moment, the actual code defining all these elements would look like this:

```
<?XML version="1.0">
<BOOK>
<!ELEMENT title (#PCDATA)>
<!ELEMENT summary (#PCDATA)>
<!ELEMENT paragraph (#PCDATA)>
<!ELEMENT section (title, summary?, paragraph+)>
 .
 .
 .
</BOOK>
```

After you've declared the elements you want to use, you can include them in the content model in a list called the *content specification list*. It's in this list that you can specify the rules on how the elements can be used. You do this by mixing and matching various elements with various delimiters to come up with specific rules for when, how, and how many times the elements can be used.

As shown in the previous example, you may want to specify that the use of an element in the content is optional or that an element can be used more than once. The special symbols such as + and ? define those rules. Table 7.2 provides you with a partial list of the symbols you can use to specify certain rules within your element content.

TIP: *If you're familiar with these symbols because you've been using SGML, you might notice that the ampersand (&) is not listed. XML does not currently allow for AND operators in element content specifications. The ampersand would allow elements to be grouped. You can do this by mixing the symbols in Table 7.2.*

In the Immediate Solutions section of this chapter, we'll cover how to use the symbols to create some pretty complex rules for element usage. As you can see, you have an amazing array of rules you can structure for any element content declaration. But with all of these options comes the tendency to make things too complex. Make sure you keep things in check before you add too many rules and restrictions and complicate your documents.

Table 7.2 **Symbols that are available for specifying element structure rules.**

Symbol	Symbol Name	Description
|	Vertical bar (pipe)	Specifies an either/or condition.
?	Question mark	Specifies that the element listed is optional, but once listed, the element can appear only once.
,	Comma	Specifies that the element before the comma must be listed first and must be followed by the element after the comma.
*	Asterisk	Specifies that the element can be listed any number of times, including zero times.
+	Plus sign	At least one element specified must appear, but that element may appear more than once.
()	Parentheses	Groups elements together, specifying the order in which each element listed must appear. Any elements listed outside the parentheses are then specified.
	No symbol specified	Specifies that one and only one of these elements can appear.

Element Attributes

HTML offers some 70 elements and some 50 different attributes. In HTML, attributes extend the power of elements by specifying how the element can be formatted. Attributes further define how an element is to be used and what kind of content and information can be included within the element. For example, if you've declared the element **TIME** in this fashion

```
<!ELEMENT TIME (#PCDATA)>
```

the attribute **PM** can be added to it to further clarify the **TIME** element.

Attributes provide extra information about an XML element and its content. If an element is empty, attributes are generally used to provide additional content, but if the element has content, the attributes usually provide more information about the content. Either way, the attribute further defines the element in some fashion.

Defining attributes is slightly different than defining elements. When you define an attribute, you use the following syntax:

```
<!ATTLIST ElementName
AttributeName Type Default
(AttributeName Type Default...)>
```

TIP: *For a more detailed look at attributes, read Chapter 8.*

A Word About Exceptions And Exclusions

Full SGML element content models allow for what are called exceptions and exclusions, which do just what their names imply—explicitly forbid or allow instances of certain element types in the element or within the element's children. However, XML does not give its elements such functionality. Instead, all element content models must be complete and explicit to prevent ambiguity.

Unfortunately, this means that it can be difficult to convert SGML and HTML DTDs to XML because inclusions and exclusions are at a high level in the document structure. If you are converting SGML and HTML DTDs, you need to consider this one point. If an SGML DTD includes exclusions or exceptions, you'll need to reproduce the DTD with exactly the same properties, but without the exceptions or exclusions. To do so, you have to make your newly converted XML DTD more or less restrictive.

Immediate Solutions

Elements and attributes are the logical structures behind an XML document. It's important to know how to declare elements, how to nest them, and how to create empty elements. In this section, you'll create elements and define specific content model specification rules. You'll start by defining a simple element and then building on that definition. The next step will be to define that element's content rules, mixing and matching various types of rules that you might consider using with the variety of elements you declare.

TIP: *Examples for declaring and working with attributes are fully outlined in Chapter 8. In this chapter, we'll concentrate solely on elements and specifying element content model specifications.*

Declaring Elements

When you initially declare elements, you should have a good idea of the entire structure of your document content. You should also have an idea of the parent/child relationships your elements will have. Remember, too, that element names are case sensitive. It's best to use lowercase for identifying element names and uppercase for the actual declarations.

Declaring And Specifying A Single Element With Character Data Only

To declare a single element in the XML DTD, start with the element specification **!ELEMENT**, followed by the name of the element and the content model specification:

```
<!ELEMENT paragraph (#PCDATA)>
```

Here is an example of how to use this element in the document:

```
<paragraph>
now is the time for all good men to include character
data in this paragraph.
</paragraph>
```

Declaring And Specifying A Single Element With Element Content

To declare a single element in the XML DTD with element content as the content model specification, use the following code:

```
<!ELEMENT paragraph (#PCDATA)>
<!ELEMENT section (paragraph)>
```

The element used in the content model specification must first be defined in order for the element content to be valid and, in turn, for the parser to not return errors. When the element is used in the document, you would include the following code:

```
<section>
<paragraph>
now is the time for all good men to
include elements in their content.
</paragraph>
</section>
```

Declaring A Content Model With Both Character Data And Elements

When you want to include both content and elements, first specify the element and then list the character data and elements with vertical bars separating them. The * provides the repeatable option:

```
<!ELEMENT paragraph (#PCDATA | link | emphasis)*>
```

Declaring Element Types With The Same Content Specification

If you want to declare more than one element type with the same content specification and you are specifying element content, you must use a separate declaration for each one:

```
<!ELEMENT paragraph (#PCDATA)>
<!ELEMENT note (paragraph)>
<!ELEMENT section (paragraph)>
<!ELEMENT chapter (paragraph)>
```

Using The **ANY** Keyword To Declare Elements

Instead of specifying a content model specification, the content specification can include the keyword **ANY**. The **ANY** keyword allows for any character data or declared elements to be valid within the element content. You should use the **ANY** keyword sparingly, because you can end up with a document that is missing the rules and specifications that would make it tightly formed. To declare an element using the **ANY** keyword, use the following code:

```
<!ELEMENT paragraph ANY>
```

You could then use this element in any way you want, such as to nest other elements within this element. For example, the following code would be considered valid because the element paragraph has been defined to contain any data:

```
<paragraph>
<emphasis>
This paragraph uses both parsed character data and another
element labeled "emphasis", another element that has been
previously defined.
</emphasis>
</paragraph>
```

Using The **EMPTY** Keyword To Declare Elements

When you want to specify that an element may never contain any content, use the keyword **EMPTY** in the content model. The following code shows you exactly how you can create an empty element content model specification:

```
<!ELEMENT rule EMPTY>
```

In this example, the rule element may never contain character data or any other element data, although the element can be nested with other elements in other element content model rules. In your XML document, you can use one of two forms to specify an empty element. The first code example supplies a single empty element tag:

```
<rule/>
```

The second form is the same model you would use with any other element. It includes both a start-tag and an end-tag. The code in the XML document would look like this:

```
<rule></rule>
```

Remember, if you use the second form, you cannot place anything between the two tags; if you do, the document will be invalid and the parser will return an error.

7: Working With XML Elements

Specifying Element Rules And Order

When you want to specify what elements can be used, the order in which they should be used, and the number of times the elements can appear in a document, you need to specify rules in your element content model specification. Use a combination of elements, element declarations, and specialized content values and delimiters to outline exactly what rule you want imposed. You can mix and match rules, for the most part, creating specifications that tightly order your DTD and XML document. Use the parentheses, the vertical bar, the asterisk, and the plus sign operators to specify rules.

Rules help create the parent/child relationship and allow you to wrap elements around each other. The following sections explain some of the most popular rules you might want to invoke in your element declarations.

Requiring The Use Of Two Other Elements

To declare a single element, you must first specify the XML declaration and follow it with the document element. Following this initial information, all elements are declared, and all elements used in the XML document should be specified in the DTD or at the beginning of the XML document. To specify the element, you must first specify all the elements used in the content model if you plan to use the elements nested within the content model. Each element must contain the element declaration followed by the element name and the content model (which is specified in parentheses) or the element content keywords **ANY** or **EMPTY**. Here is the code you would use to declare elements in a newsletter XML document and to specify the order in which three elements can be used in the document:

```
<?XML version="1.0"?>
<NEWSLETTERDOC>
<!ELEMENT title (#PCDATA)>
<!ELEMENT content (#PCDATA)>
<!ELEMENT newsletter (title, content)>
```

After the elements are declared, you can use them in the document to allow either the title or content elements within the newsletter element. Use the comma between the element names to specify the requirement that both title and content must appear and that the content must follow the title element. The code for this element content model looks like this:

```
<newsletter>
<title>
XML Newsletter
</title>
```

```
<content>
Welcome to the first edition of the XML Newsletter.
In this newsletter we will outline all the various XML
applications that are currently available for parsing XML
documents.
</content>
</newsletter>
```

The newsletter element actually contains no data; instead, it contains the content of both the content element and the title element. Both elements can contain any type of parsed character data.

Declaring Optional Elements

In the previous example, the content model rules required that you use the elements, content, and title when specifying the newsletter element and that content follows the title element. This example allows you to make the title an optional element, so if the newsletter doesn't have a title, you don't have to include one. Here is the code for declaring such elements and rules:

```
<?XML version="1.0"?>
<NEWSLETTERDOC>
<!ELEMENT title (#PCDATA)>
<!ELEMENT content (#PCDATA)>
<!ELEMENT newsletter (title?, content)>
```

Just a simple question mark after the element name in the element's content model specification signifies to the parser that this element is optional. If it is missing, the parser will not return an error. However, the order rule still applies: The content must follow the title if, in fact, there is a title. Otherwise, the content element must be specified when the newsletter element is placed in the XML document.

Declaring Multiple Elements In A Group

If you want to create multiple content elements that could be used within a single newsletter element, simply add a plus sign to the element content model specification. For example, a newsletter, of course, would need more instances of paragraphs throughout the newsletter element. First, declare a simple XML DTD, but instead of using the element named content, use the element named paragraph so the code will make more sense:

```
<?XML version="1.0"?>
<NEWSLETTERDOC>
<!ELEMENT title (#PCDATA)>
<!ELEMENT paragraph (#PCDATA)>
<!ELEMENT newsletter (title?, paragraph+)>
```

This element content model specification tells the parser that the newsletter element can include a title; the title element is optional and not required. However, if there is a title element, the paragraph element must follow. If the title element is not specified, you can still specify the paragraph element, but instead of having only one instance of the paragraph element within the newsletter element, you can have multiple instances. Here's an example of how this would work:

```
<newsletter>
<title>
The XML Newsletter
</title>
<paragraph>
Welcome to the first edition of this newsletter.
We hope you enjoy it and find lots of valuable information.
</paragraph>
<paragraph>
XML is one of the most exciting markup languages available today.
</paragraph>
</newsletter>
```

Specifying One Element Or Another

When you want to specify that an element can contain either one element content specification or another, use the vertical bar to separate the two element choices from each other. In the following example, the document authors have the ability to include either paragraphs or lists of XML seminars in their newsletter. This example lets the author include either a list of information or a paragraph about XML. First, you need to declare the following:

```
<?XML version="1.0"?>
<NEWSLETTERDOC>
<!ELEMENT paragraph (#PCDATA)>
<!ELEMENT seminar (#PCDATA)>
<!ELEMENT seminarlist (seminars+)>
<!ELEMENT content (paragraph | seminarlist)>
```

You've declared the document element by specifying the document element name as **NEWSLETTERDOC**. Next, you've declared two simple elements, paragraph and seminar. Both of these elements are specified to include parsed character data. Then, you've created another element that uses just element content called seminarlist, which lets you list as many seminars as you please; you can list multiple seminars because the plus sign has been added. From there, you've defined the structure of the actual content you will add to the newsletter. This content can have either a paragraph or a list of seminars. Only one paragraph is allowed because nothing has been specified except the paragraph element in the content element model specification.

Now, when an XML author wants to include just a list of seminars, she would use the following code:

```
<content>
<seminarlist>
<seminar>Working with Elements</seminar>
<seminar>Adding Attributes to Your Elements</seminar>
<seminar>DTDs</seminar>
<seminar>Creating Well-Formed Documents</seminar>
</seminarlist>
</content>
```

If the author doesn't have a list of seminars to include in the newsletter, he could instead use a paragraph to fill up the spaces. In that case, the XML code would look something like this:

```
<content>
<paragraph>
When using XML elements you must make sure you declare all
the elements you want to include in the DTD. If you fail to do that,
you cannot use the start and end tags for an
element in the XML document.
</paragraph>
</content>
```

Chapter 8

Working With XML Attributes

By Natanya Pitts-Moultis

In Depth

This chapter takes a careful look at the role attributes play in a Document Type Definition (DTD) and in document development, the types of attributes DTD designers can include in their XML applications, and the ways attributes can be used to describe information.

Attributes provide information about elements in much the same way that adjectives modify nouns. Attributes allow DTD designers to provide developers with a wide range of information description choices. Document developers can even add their own attributes to the internal subset of a DTD to meet individual document needs. Attributes provide a mechanism for extending the meaning and value of XML elements and their content that is crucial to the effective dissemination of data across the world's networks.

The ability to define your own elements and use the markup generated from the elements with an XML processor to create a customized solution for a specific need is the very essence of the power XML affords developers. There are no limits to the number and type of elements you can create, and elements can be nested within each other in level after level (as the content models allows) to describe complex relationships between information. Still, the element mechanism alone isn't always enough; it must be extended to provide more information about the element or its content. Attributes are the extension. This introductory section examines the role attributes play and describes in detail the components that make up the attributes used in XML DTDs and documents. If you are well versed in the role and uses of attributes, you may turn directly to Immediate Solutions for instructions on creating and referencing attributes.

The Role Of Attributes In XML

In a nutshell, attributes provide extra information about an XML element and its content. If the element is empty, attributes are generally used to provide additional content, but if the element has content, the attributes usually provide more information about the content. Applications that incorporate empty tags—such as the Open Software Description (OSD) and the Channel Definition Format (CDF)—use a variety of attributes to allow developers to provide information to the processor in a controlled and standard way, as this snippet of example code from the CDF specification shows:

```
<SCHEDULE STARTDATE="1997-03-24">
    <INTERVALTIME HOUR="6" />
    <LATESTTIME HOUR="3" />
    <EARLIESTTIME HOUR="1" />
</SCHEDULE>
```

The **INTERVALTIME**, **LATESTTIME**, and **EARLIESTTIME** elements all use the **HOUR** attribute to provide scheduling information for a channel.

Other DTDs use attributes to help document developers provide more information about how the information described by the markup language should be presented. For example, the **mtable** element of the Mathematical Markup Language (MathML) can take up to 14 different attributes, all of which describe how the table should look when presented, including row and column alignment and spacing, as well as border information. By mixing and matching the attributes and their values, developers of MathML documents can create literally thousands of different table presentations. By itself, the **mtable** element only indicates that the information it contains is a table, but when the attributes are added, they bring the table to life.

Attribute Terminology

It is important to understand the meaning and specific uses of the following key attribute terms:

- *Attribute list declaration*—A listing in the DTD of all the attributes that can be used with a given element. This listing includes the attributes, their values and default value (if the values are fixed), and whether the attribute is required or optional.

- *Attribute specification*—An individual listing for a single attribute within the attribute list declaration.

- *Attribute name*—The name used to identify the attribute in the DTD and reference it in a document.

- *Attribute type*—The value that identifies the attribute as a string, tokenized, or enumerated attribute.

- *Attribute value*—A list in the specification of all the possible values an attribute can take; in a document, this is the specific value assigned to the attribute by the document developer.

In a DTD, the combination of a name, type, and value makes up a single attribute specification and a group of attribute specifications make up an attribute list declaration for an element. In a document, attributes and their values are part of a single instance of a tag. Attributes only apply to that single instance of the tag and must be referenced in every instance of a starting tag where they should be applied.

WARNING!   Attribute values in both DTDs and documents must be enclosed in quotation marks. Although both HTML and Standard Generalized Markup Language (SGML) are a bit more forgiving about the presence of quotation marks than XML is, if the quotation marks are missing in either the DTD or the document body, the document will be invalid and not well-formed. XML editors that are being developed should support the automatic insertion of quotation marks around values in both DTDs and documents. If you need to use quotation marks as part of an attribute's value, they must be escaped using the " entity. You may also use the entities ' and &aquote; as part of an attribute's value to indicate single and double quotation marks.

Types Of Attributes

XML provides for three different attribute types:

- String attributes
- Tokenized attributes
- Enumerated attributes

Each attribute type can only take specific kinds of values, and for a document to be valid, the value provided in the attribute specification must match the declared type. The following sections describe each of the three attribute types. For specific instructions on creating attributes of each type, turn to this chapter's Immediate Solutions section.

String Attributes

String attributes take string data and are used to create attributes that allow the user to define any value they would like for the attribute. The **HOUR** attribute for the **INTERVALTIME**, **LATESTTIME**, and **EARLIESTTIME** elements of the CDF application (these elements were discussed earlier in this chapter) is an example of a string attribute. Another example is the **HREF** attribute for the item tag from the same specification, shown in this example code taken from the specification:

```
<ITEM HREF="http://www.foosports.com/intro.htm">...<ITEM>
```

Tokenized Attributes

Tokenized attributes refer to seven different types of predefined attributes that play a specific role in XML documents and that must have a particular kind of value. These seven attributes can't be used for anything other than their express purposes in an XML document or the document will be invalid. The tokenized attributes include:

- *ID*—Provides a unique identifier for the element within the document. The value for an **ID** must always consist of a *name*—a letter or underscore followed by zero or more name characters. If two or more elements have the same **ID**, the document is invalid.

- *IDREF*—Points to an element with the specified **ID** value; if an element identified by the **ID** is not included somewhere in the document and an **IDREF** attribute attempts to point to it anyway, the document is invalid.

- *IDREFS*—Points to two or more elements within the documents by using multiple ID listings separated by spaces.

- *ENTITY*—Points to an external entity. The value must consist of a name and must match both the name and case constructs of the external entity it points to.

- *ENTITIES*—Points to two or more external entities by using multiple names separated by spaces.

- *NMTOKEN*—Takes a value that is a **NMTOKEN**—any mixture of name characters.

- *NMTOKENS*—Takes a value of two or more **NMTOKENS** separated by spaces.

Generally, the values of all tokenized attributes are character strings. Unlike string attributes, however, the strings used as values for tokenized attributes must conform to the rules of their specific tokenized types.

Enumerated Attributes

When an attribute includes a predefined list of options as its value, it is said to be *enumerated*. Enumerated attributes include a subset of attribute types that includes the notation type attribute and the general enumeration. A notation type attribute lists one of several notation types—defined elsewhere in the DTD—as values. A general enumeration takes a series of **NMTOKENS** as values. The value for any enumerated attribute in an XML document must match one of the values listed in the attribute specification.

TIP: *When you work with values of mixed case, the following rules apply: All **ID**, **IDREF**, **IDREFS**, **NMTOKEN,** and **NMTOKENS** values are automatically converted to uppercase by XML, so these values are not case sensitive. However, XML does not convert the values of string, **ENTITY**, or **ENTITIES** to uppercase, so these values are case sensitive. We recommend using lowercase for all values and file names wherever possible to avoid any accidental case incompatibilities.*

8: Working With XML Attributes

Additional Attribute Specifics

In addition to providing name, type, and value information in any given attribute specification, you can also provide answers to three important questions about any attribute:

- Is its value fixed?
- What is its default value?
- Is the attribute required or optional?

Attributes can have a fixed value assigned to them that the document developer cannot change. In addition, a default value can be declared for any attribute—especially commonly used attributes—so the document developer doesn't have to enter the attribute to reference it. Finally, an attribute can be defined as required and must be included each time its element is used in markup; if the attribute is missing or its value is incorrect, the entire document is invalid. "Adding Attribute Specifics To An Attribute Specification," in this chapter's Immediate Solutions section, provides more information on how to provide default values for an attribute, as well as designate it as fixed or required.

Uses Of Attributes

As already indicated, attributes provide an additional source of content and provide information about how an element's contents should be presented. Attributes are used in very different ways depending on whether the markup is presentation- or content-based. Presentation-based markup concerns itself with how the document's content is displayed, whereas content-based markup focuses on providing well-formatted and standardized content for an XML processor to read and manipulate.

Attributes are used quite differently in these two separate types of markup. In presentation-based markup, attributes provide document developers with a mechanism that allows them to customize the document's final display and appearance. In contrast, the attributes in content-based markup focus more on providing document developers with a list of possible standard values and less on describing content within elements. There's no rule that says a DTD has to lend itself to either presentation-based markup or content-based markup. Instead, a DTD can lend itself to both by including elements that are geared for both presentation and processing. The Mathematical Markup Language is a perfect example of a DTD that contains both presentation- and content-oriented elements, and it shows how their associated attributes play different roles depending on the role of each element.

Presentation Elements And Attributes In The MathML Application

Of the presentation elements included in the MathML specification, its creators have this to say: "Presentation elements correspond to the 'constructors' of traditional math notation—that is, to the basic kinds of symbols and expression-building structures out of which any particular piece of traditional math notation is built."

Notation is a physical representation of a mathematical function, so it makes sense that those elements that focus on notation should be presentation oriented. Among the list of presentation tags included in the MathML application are those that describe how elements should be grouped horizontally, how spaces and sub- and superscript should be addressed, and how square roots and fractions should be formed. These elements use attributes to allow the document developer to provide their own specifics about these notations as well. For example, the **mtable** element (mentioned in the opening paragraphs of the chapter) takes the following 14 attribute-value sets:

- *align*—top, bottom, center, baseline, axis, or row number
- *rowalign*—top, bottom, center, baseline, or axis
- *columnalign*—left, center, or right
- *groupalign*—group alignment list
- *alignmentscope*—true or false
- *rowspacing*—number
- *columnspacing*—number
- *rowlines*—none, solid, or dashed
- *columnlines*—none, solid, or dashed
- *frame*—none, solid, or dashed
- *framespacing*—horizontal and vertical numeric values
- *equalrows*—true or false
- *equalcolumns*—true or false
- *displaystyle*—true or false

Although none of these attributes contributes significantly to the way a MathML processor crunches numbers, they do have quite a bit to do with the way the results of the number crunching are displayed. Although processing numbers is very important, the presentation of the results has a great deal to do with their value to the end user. For the curious, the attribute list declaration for the **mtable** element looks like this:

```
<!ATTLIST mtable    %att-tableinfo;
                    %att-globalatts;>
```

This attribute list declaration makes use of parameter entities to assign the attributes within the **att-tableinfo** and **att-globalatts** attribute lists to the **mtable** element. For more information on the creation of parameter entities, consult Chapter 12. For instructions on how to use parameter entities in attribute list declarations, turn to "Using Parameter Entities In Attribute List Declarations" in this chapter's Immediate Solutions section.

On the content side of the fence, the **declare** element—clearly labeled as a content element—is used to set or change the default value of a mathematical object or to associate a name with an object. Its five attributes exist for the express purpose of assisting the element in its role; it does so by allowing the document developer to use a strict set of predetermined values, a number, or a URL to provide information about the mathematical object. The attributes and their values are:

- *type*—integer, rational, real, float, complex, complex-polar, complex-Cartesian, or constant
- *scope*—local or global
- *nargs*—numeric value
- *occurrence*—prefix, infix, function-model
- *definitionURL*—URL

The **type**, **scope**, and **occurrence** attributes force users to choose from a list of values that provide detailed information about the object's mathematical type, in what scope it can be applied, and the occurrence of any operator declarations. The **nargs** attribute specifies how many arguments there are for function declarations, whereas the **definitionURL** attribute links to an external definition of the element's syntax.

Even if you're not math-savvy, it's easy to see that these attributes provide information about the element that the processor will use in its calculations, but that probably won't have much effect on the final presentation of the MathML document. The attribute list declaration for the **declare** element is as follows:

```
<!ATTLIST declare          %att-type;
                           %att-scope;
                           %att-nargs;
                           %att-occurence;
                           %att-definition;
                           %att-globalatts;     >
```

This attribute declaration is made up of more of those pesky parameter entities. For practice, after you've read the parameter entity project in this chapter's Immediate Solutions section and reviewed its example from the same DTD, see if you can't detail all the attributes in the **declare** attribute list declaration based on the parameter entities included in the DTD.

Because the MathML DTD expressly defines content and presentation markup in separate categories, it is easy to see how the elements and their attributes act as a function of either content or presentation. It is likely that many of your DTDs will have both content- and presentation-oriented elements. Although you may not need to differentiate between them in the DTD in the same way the MathML DTD does, it's important to keep them separate in your own mind. As you begin to develop your elements, you'll notice that their role as either content or presentation markup will play a large part in what attributes you specify for the elements and how you define those attribute's values.

Immediate Solutions

It isn't difficult to create XML attributes, but once they are created, attributes can be a strong ally in the creation of quality XML DTDs and documents. This Immediate Solutions section lays out all of the different syntax and notation specifics and follows them up with some solid examples taken from DTDs at work on the Web and in the networking community. The topics in Immediate Solutions also include specifics on referencing attributes in the body of XML documents and using parameter entities in attribute list declarations. One section examines the attributes the XML linking mechanism uses, both as a teaser for what's to come in Chapter 10 and to showcase yet again the power of attributes. Finally, although the attribute syntax is easy, creating a set of attributes that form a vital cohesive portion of a functioning DTD is a bit more challenging. With that in mind, the final section in Immediate Solutions focuses on the process of creating an attribute list declaration for a single element and groups of related elements.

Specifying String Attributes

Use the following syntax to create string attribute specifications:

```
<!ATTLIST ELEMENT
     ATTRIBUTENAME CDATA #IMPLIED/#REQUIRED/#FIXED>
```

ELEMENT is the name of the element to which the attribute applies, and **ATTRIBUTENAME** is the name you give the attribute and the name by which it will be referenced in the body of an XML document. The **CDATA** label defines the attribute's type; it is required for every string attribute and indicates that the attribute's value will be text and numbers. The **#IMPLIED/#REQUIRED/#FIXED** label indicates to the XML processor that the attribute is either implied, required, or fixed. Each attribute specification is discussed in "Adding Attribute Specifics To An Attribute Specification" later in Immediate Solutions.

Here's an example from the Open Software Description (OSD) DTD of a string attribute:

```
<!ATTLIST SOFTPKG
     VERSION CDATA #IMPLIED>
```

The **SOFTPKG** element takes the **VERSION** attribute, whose value is string data. This particular attribute is used to provide version information for the software package that is described using OSD markup. The attribute takes a string value because it would have been impractical for the developers of OSD to try to provide a list of all the possible version values software developers might use. Instead, this information can be entered "freestyle" by the developer of the document as dictated by the software package version.

Specifying Tokenized Attributes

Tokenized attributes take string values closely controlled by type. Use the following syntax to create tokenized attribute specifications:

```
<!ATTLIST ELEMENT
    ATTRIBUTENAME TOKENTYPE #IMPLIED/#REQUIRED/#FIXED >
```

ELEMENT is the name of the element the attribute applies to, and *ATTRIBUTENAME* is the name you give the attribute and the name by which it will be referenced in the body of an XML document. The *TOKENTYPE* can be one of the following seven types (as described in the introductory sections of the chapter):

- **ID**
- **IDREF**
- **IDREFS**
- **ENTITY**
- **ENTITIES**
- **NMTOKEN**
- **NMTOKENS**

The *#IMPLIED/#REQUIRED/#FIXED* label indicates to the XML processor that the attribute is either implied, required, or fixed. Here is an example from David Megginson's novel DTD of a tokenized attribute specification:

```
<!ATTLIST chapter
  id ID #REQUIRED>
```

This attribute is used to assign a unique **ID** number to each chapter in a document and is a required part of any chapter element. If a chapter element doesn't have an **ID**, the document is invalid. Although the creator of the DTD could have made this a string value attribute instead of a tokenized attribute, a string attribute doesn't guarantee that its value must be unique. To make sure that each chapter has its own unique identifier, the DTD designer instead took advantage of the uniqueness requirement of the **ID** token and constructed a tokenized attribute instead of a string attribute.

Specifying Enumerated Attributes

Enumerated attributes include a set of possible values—each conforming to the **NMTOKEN** format—that the attribute can take rather than a string value. Use the following syntax to create an enumerated attribute specification:

```
<!ATTLIST ELEMENT
    ATTRIBUTENAME (A | B | C | ...) "DEFAULT"  #REQUIRED/#FIXED >
```

ELEMENT is the name of the element the attribute applies to and *ATTRIBUTE-NAME* is the name you give the attribute and the name by which it will be referenced in the body of an XML document. The list of possible values is enclosed within parentheses and separated by vertical lines. It's generally best not to list a value more than once within any given value list because this is redundant and incompatible with SGML standards. *DEFAULT* indicates which value should be the default if the user doesn't specify a value, and the *#REQUIRED/#FIXED* label indicates to the XML processor that the attribute is either required or fixed. Here is an example from the OSD DTD of an enumerated attribute specification:

```
<!ATTLIST DEPENDENCY
    ACTION (Assert|Install) "Assert">
```

This attribute assigns a value of either **Assert** or **Install** to the **DEPENDENCY** element, with **Assert** as the default. This attribute is not required, nor does it have a fixed value. Based on the presence of other application components, this attribute helps a client computer determine whether or not it should install the software package described by the OSD document. If **Assert** is the chosen value, the software package is installed only if other required components are already installed on the client computer. If these components are not installed on the client computer, the software package installation is skipped entirely. However, if the value of **ACTION** is **Install**, any missing required components are installed on the client machine, and then the described software package is installed. Because these two values provide the client machine with important information that can lead to the successful installation or intentional noninstallation of software, a consistent means of identifying the action had to be integrated into the DTD. By providing document developers with keywords to trigger different actions, the DTD designers guarantee that processing instructions will be transferred to the XML processor in a consistent and understandable manner. Neither a string nor a tokenized attribute could accomplish this.

A list of notations may also be used as values for an enumerated attribute, but each listed notation must be declared in the document's DTD using the syntax:

```
<!NOTATION NAME PUBLIC/SYTEM "location">
```

For more on notations, review Chapter 5. The following is an example of an enumerated attribute that takes a list of notations as possible values:

```
<!ATTLIST DOCUMENT
    TYPE NOTATION (DOC | TXT | RTF | WPF) "DOC">
```

This attribute defines the file type for the **DOCUMENT** element (the default value is **DOC**) and the options in the value list are described by the following notation statements in the DTD:

```
<!NOTATION DOC SYSTEM "/apps/docs/msword.exe">
<!NOTATION TXT SYSTEM "/apps/docs/pfe32.exe">
<!NOTATION RTF SYSTEM "/apps/docs/msword.exe">
<!NOTATION WPF SYSTEM "/apps/docs/wordperfect.exe">
```

If even one of the options listed in the value list wasn't declared by a notation statement in the DTD, the entire document would be invalid.

Adding Attribute Specifics To An Attribute Specification

In addition to providing name, type, and value information for an attribute, the attribute specification can include information that answers these three questions (as posed in the introductory portion of this chapter) about any given attribute:

- Is its value fixed?
- What is its default value?
- Is the attribute required or optional?

To answer these questions, attribute specifications use the following three mechanisms:

- **#IMPLIED/ "DEFAULT"**
- **#FIXED**
- **#REQUIRED**

Any attribute of any type can have a default value set for it by including that default value in quotation marks just prior to the end of the attribute specification. If the attribute doesn't have a default value, the label **#IMPLIED** is used instead to indicate to the XML processor that a default value wasn't assigned and the processor should ignore the attribute altogether. The document type attribute specification used in the previous section also provides an example of a default value being assigned to an attribute:

```
<!ATTLIST DOCUMENT
    TYPE NOTATION (DOC | TXT | RTF | WPF) "DOC">
```

The **DOC** inside of the quotation marks at the end of the specification indicates to both the document developer and the XML processor that the **DOC** notation is the default value for the attribute if the developer doesn't supply one at all.

If the label **#FIXED** precedes its default value, the default value of the attribute is considered fixed and must be referenced in the document body exactly as it is listed in the attribute specification. The **#FIXED** label is usually associated with string or tokenized attribute types and not enumerated types (What's the point of having choices if the choice is made for you?) and is always used in conjunction with a default value. Fixed attributes are created by DTD designers to ensure that vital information is passed to the XML processor even if the document developer forgets to include it. An example of a fixed attribute follows:

```
<!ATTLIST MSWDOC
    TYPE NOTATION CDATA #FIXED "DOC">
```

This example combines a notation with a string attribute and a fixed label to ensure that any document described by using the **MSWDOC** element is labeled as a Microsoft Word document, as declared in the **DOC** notation that would have been declared in the DTD. The document developer cannot change the value of the **TYPE** attribute without invalidating the document.

Finally, the **#REQUIRED** label can be used to indicate that the attribute must be included with each instance of its element. The example of a tokenized attribute declaration from an earlier section also serves as an example of a required attribute:

```
<!ATTLIST chapter
  id ID #REQUIRED>
```

Each time the **chapter** element is used in the document body, it must include the **ID** attribute. Because the **ID** attribute is tokenized, the attribute's value must meet the specifications set up for the ID token. The result is an attribute specification that requires each instance of the **chapter** element to have a unique identifier. This is a good example of how specific types of attributes and the additional specification labels can be combined to ensure that the document developer provides a required set of information to the XML processor.

Combining Attribute Specifications To Form An Attribute List Declaration

An attribute list declaration is simply a group of attribute specifications given for a single element. The list declaration may include as many or as few attribute specifications as necessary and can contain any combination of string, tokenized, and enumerated specifications. The syntax for forming an attribute list declaration is:

```
<!ATTLIST ELEMENT
attribute specification
attribute specification
attribute specification
...>
```

Here is an example from the OSD specification of an attribute list declaration for the **CODEBASE** element:

```
<!ATTLIST CODEBASE FILENAME CDATA #IMPLIED>
<!ATTLIST CODEBASE HREF CDATA #REQUIRED>
<!ATTLIST CODEBASE SIZE CDATA #IMPLIED>
```

Notice that the attribute list declarations contain one attribute per listing. These three attribute list declarations could be legally combined into one list declaration, like this:

```
<! ATTLIST CODEBASE
    FILENAME CDATA #IMPLIED
    HREF CDATA #REQUIRED
    CODEBASE SIZE CDATA #IMPLIED>
```

Referencing Attributes In Markup

XML attributes are referenced in markup in the exact same way as HTML attributes are referenced. The syntax is:

```
<ELEMENT ATTRIBUTE="VALUE">
```

The following rules apply to attributes referenced in markup:

- Attributes are listed after the element they modify and are separated from the element by a space.

- There are no spaces on either side of the equal sign in an attribute-value pair, and all attribute values in XML must be enclosed in quotation marks. If they are not, the document is invalid.

- Additional attributes may be assigned to an element (providing its attributed list declaration includes them) by listing them one after the other in attribute-value pairs separated by spaces.

- An attribute and its value can only appear once in any given instance of an XML markup element.

- An attribute-value pair only applies to the single instance of the XML markup element with which it is listed.

- Only those attributes and values assigned in an element's attribute list declaration can modify an element. Mixing and matching attributes is not allowed.

- One attribute can modify more than one tag as long as it has been declared in an attribute list declaration for each tag it modifies.

- Required attributes must be listed with each instance of their associated element. If they are not, the document is invalid.

- Fixed attribute values must be included exactly as specified by the attribute list declaration. If they are changed in any way or omitted, the document is invalid.

Using Parameter Entities In Attribute List Declarations

Parameter entities can be used in attribute list declarations as an aliasing mechanism for other lists of frequently used attributes. To utilize a parameter entity in attribute list declarations, you must first construct the entity by using the following syntax:

```
<!ENTITY % entity-name  'attribute specification
                         attribute specification' >
```

The entity can contain as many attribute specifications as necessary; the entire group must be enclosed in single quotation marks. The attribute specifications must adhere to all the rules established for each different type of attribute and can be of any type or combination of types. Parameter entities can also include other parameter entities as part of their declaration. For an extensive discussion of the creation of parameter entities, see Chapter 12.

To reference the entity in the attribute list declaration, use this syntax:

```
<!ATTLIST name %entity-name;>
```

More than one parameter entity can be used per attribute list declaration, and parameter entities can be mixed with standard attribute specifications to create one attribute list declaration. Parameter entities provide an excellent means for managing extensive and frequently used attribute lists in a complex DTD. The **mtable** presentation markup code from the introductory section of this chapter is a perfect example of how parameter entities may be used in a fairly extensive manner in attribute list declarations. Recall that the attribute list declaration for the **mtable** element in the MathML DTD is:

```
<!ATTLIST mtable    %att-tableinfo;
                    %att-globalatts;>
```

When the attribute list declaration is broken down, the two parameter entities that make it up are defined by these code snippets:

```
<!ENTITY % att-globalatts    'class CDATA #IMPLIED
                              style CDATA #IMPLIED
                              id    ID    #IMPLIED
                              other CDATA #IMPLIED' >

<!ENTITY % att-tableinfo     '%att-align;
                              %att-rowalign;
                              %att-columnalign;
                              %att-groupalign;
                              %att-alignmentscope;
                              %att-rowspacing;
                              %att-columnspacing;
                              %att-rowlines;
                              %att-columnlines;
                              %att-frame;
                              %att-framespacing;
```

```
                              %att-equalrows;
                              %att-equalcolumns;
                              %att-displaystyle;'          >
```

The **att-globalatts** parameter entity includes the **class**, **style**, **id**, and other attributes. These attributes are used frequently throughout the MathML DTD, so it was more efficient to assign them to a parameter entity instead of list them for each of the many elements to which they are assigned.

The **att-tableinfo** parameter entity, however, is made up of even more parameter entities, declared in these entity declarations:

```
<!ENTITY % att-align          'align CDATA #IMPLIED'>
<!ENTITY % att-rowalign       'rowalign CDATA #IMPLIED'>
<!ENTITY % att-columnalign    'columnalign CDATA #IMPLIED'>
<!ENTITY % att-groupalign     'groupalign CDATA #IMPLIED'>
<!ENTITY % att-alignmentscope 'alignmentscope CDATA #IMPLIED'>
<!ENTITY % att-rowspacing     'rowspacing CDATA #IMPLIED'>
<!ENTITY % att-columnspacing  'columnspacing CDATA #IMPLIED'>
<!ENTITY % att-rowlines       'rowlines CDATA #IMPLIED'>
<!ENTITY % att-columnlines    'columnlines CDATA #IMPLIED'>
<!ENTITY % att-frame          'frame (none | solid | dashed)#IMPLIED' >
<!ENTITY % att-framespacing   'framespacing CDATA #IMPLIED'>
<!ENTITY % att-equalrows      'equalrows CDATA #IMPLIED'>
<!ENTITY % att-equalcolumns   'equalcolumns CDATA #IMPLIED'>
```

Although these single line entities could have been declared as attribute specifications for the **att-tableinfo** parameter entity, they would have to be declared over and over again for any other elements that also needed them. Instead, the use of parameter entities means that these attributes can be linked to any number of other elements by simply including the parameter entity reference in the elements' attribute declaration lists.

If we were to remove all of the attribute specifications from the **att-tableinfo** and **att-globalatts** parameter entity declarations and instead create a single attribute list declaration for the **mtable**, it would look like this:

```
<!ATTLIST mtable
     class CDATA #IMPLIED
     style CDATA #IMPLIED
     id    ID    #IMPLIED
     other CDATA #IMPLIED
     align CDATA #IMPLIED
     rowalign CDATA #IMPLIED
     columnalign CDATA #IMPLIED
     groupalign CDATA #IMPLIED
```

```
alignmentscope CDATA #IMPLIED
rowspacing CDATA #IMPLIED
columnspacing CDATA #IMPLIED
rowlines CDATA #IMPLIED
columnlines CDATA #IMPLIED
frame (none | solid | dashed)#IMPLIED
framespacing CDATA #IMPLIED
equalrows CDATA #IMPLIED
equalcolumns CDATA #IMPLIED>
```

Evaluating The Special Linking Attributes Of XLink

Although DTD designers and document developers can define as many or as few attributes—each with its own relevant values—as the XML application requires, the XML linking mechanism (XLink) has a group of built-in attributes that it reserves for its own uses in any XML document. It is important to know what these attributes are so you don't accidentally use them in your own documents. They also provide a quick introduction to the XML linking mechanism, discussed in detail in Chapter 10. Table 8.1 lists each attribute, its values, and a brief description.

Table 8.1   XML linking mechanism (XLink) attributes.

Attributes	Value(s)	Description
XML-LINK	(SIMPLE | EXTENDED | LOCATOR | GROUP | DOCUMENT)	Defines the link's type
XML-ATTRIBUTES	String	Remaps attributes for linking elements
HREF	String	Specifies a link's resource
SHOW displayed	(INCLUDE | REPLACE | NEW)	Specifies how targeted resources are and processed
ACTUATE	(AUTO | USER)	Specifies when the link should be activated
ROLE	string	Describes the link's role to an XML processor
TITLE	string	Provides a title for the link to identify it to users
CONTENT-ROLE	string	Describes the linking element's role
CONTENT-TITLE	string	Provides a title for the linking element
INLINE	(TRUE | FALSE)	In extended links, indicates that the linking element is one of the link's resources

The XML Linking mechanism is an advanced and robust system of defining links among XML documents and resources, and it relies heavily on the attributes outlined in Table 8.1. Be sure to always reserve these attributes for links or your documents may be invalid.

Planning For Element Attributes

The following steps outline a good way to go about planning the attributes for a DTD. Index cards are a handy tool to have in this process. Use one for each element so you can group and regroup elements by type of function. To plan the attributes for a DTD, follow these steps:

1. Define the role and purpose of each element in as much detail as possible, one element to a card. This definition will be your first clue to what kind of attributes you'll need to assign to each element individually.

2. Compare all of the element definitions and group similar elements together.

3. Determine which, if any, attributes the elements will have in common and create lists of attributes that are common to several tags.

4. Use the lists of common attributes to create parameter entities to better organize your DTD.

5. Record the appropriate parameter entity or entities on the index cards of those elements that take attributes that are included in parameter entities.

6. Finalize the attribute lists for each element on the index cards.

7. Transfer the information from the index cards to attribute list definition statements and parameter entity declarations in your DTD.

Although the idea of using index cards may seem outdated, it will help you better define attributes for individual elements, as well as show the relationship between elements that have common attributes. The attributes for even the simplest DTD can be created from this process of definition and organization. The process also makes the creation and organization of complex DTDs easier.

Chapter 9

Creating Content In XML

By Natanya Pitts-Moultis

In Depth

Content and markup work hand in hand in an XML document to create a well-structured and useful information dissemination tool. Content in XML documents isn't limited to ASCII text and special character entities; it can also include other markup or no data at all. Document Type Definition (DTD) developers must define what content each element in a DTD can contain, so ultimately, DTDs define a strict set of content rules developers must adhere to when creating valid and well-formed documents. This chapter describes the three different types of content used in XML, discusses how to evaluate a DTD and understand the content models of each individual element, and provides instructions for declaring content rules for elements during DTD creation, including a section on how to use parameter entities as a shortcut to quick and easy content declaration.

Experienced Webmasters and Web-site developers are fond of the phrase, "Content is king," with good reason. Internet and Web technologies were created with the express goals of storing and sharing information with as many people as possible working in a wide variety of computing and networking environments. XML is no different. Markup describes a document's content, so in the end, markup is content driven. Although XML is robust and extensible enough to allow developers to create their own DTDs and processors, it has very strict rules about how content should be defined in DTDs and included in XML documents. Both DTD and document developers must follow these rules to create well-formed and valid documents.

Important Content-Related Terms

Before we jump into our discussion of XML content, there are a few words and phrases with which you must be familiar. The definitions go a long way toward explaining how the rules of content are used in XML DTD and document development. The following list includes the terms or phrases as we'll be using them throughout the chapter—indeed as they are used in the XML world—followed by their definitions:

- *content*—Anything found between the start and end tags of an element. Content can include element content, character data, or mixed content.

- *element content*—Other elements (tag pairs) that can be included within an element. The elements that can be nested within a tag (and the order in which they must appear) are defined for each element within the DTD.

- *character data*—The text (other than markup) included within document elements. Not all elements must necessarily allow character data as content; as with element content, character data content must be defined by the DTD as part of an element's content.

- *mixed content*—A combination of element and character data that can be included as content for any given element.

- *content model*—The definition in a DTD of what content is allowed for any given element.

- *parent element*—An element that has one or more elements as content. A parent element of a child element or elements may also be the child of another, higher-level element.

- *child element*—An element that is contained (nested) within another element. A child element may also be a parent of other, lower-level elements.

- *nesting*—A description of how elements are contained within one another.

- *empty element*—An element that has no content of any kind.

The projects in this chapter's Immediate Solutions section focus on such common tasks as evaluating the content of an element in a DTD, defining different types of content for elements while building a DTD, using parameter entities in a content model, and creating the content model for elements in a DTD. If you are familiar with XML content, these definitions should serve as a quick reminder of the components of XML content, and you can move on to the projects in the Immediate Solutions section for step-by-step instructions on creating content models in DTDs and content in XML documents. For those of you who are not as familiar with the topic of XML content, the remainder of the introductory section will prepare you to use the projects in the Immediate Solutions section by taking a closer look at the concepts and components defined in the previous definition list.

Different Types Of Content

As the definitions at the beginning of this chapter indicate, there is more than one kind of content that any given XML element can take. However, for an element to take any kind of content at all, the content and specific information about its order and requirement status must be included as part of the element's definition in the DTD. For a refresher on elements in general, refer to Chapter 7.

What Exactly Is Content Anyway?

Content is anything found between the open and close tags of an XML element. That's a pretty generic and almost vague statement, but it is entirely accurate. Developers tend to think of content as the text that shows up on the screen or the text that an application or user interacts with, but that's only the beginning of the important role content can play in an XML document. In addition to the text between open and close tags, other child elements can be included to provide additional information about the content of both the child and the parent elements. For example, let's examine these two lines from an XML document:

```
<TITLE>Dynamic HTML</TITLE>
<TITLE>Designing With JavaScript</TITLE>
```

Although we can intuit from the title tags that the text between each pair of open and close title tags is probably the title of something, we don't really know what. It could be a book title, a chapter title, an article title, or a even presentation title. However, when the title tags become child elements to two new sets of parent elements, we learn quite a bit more about these two unspecified titles:

```
<NOVEL>
    <FRONT>
        <TITLE>Designing With JavaScript</TITLE>
    </FRONT>
    <BODY>
        <CHAPTER>
            <TITLE>Dynamic HTML</TITLE>
        </CHAPTER>
    </BODY>
</NOVEL>
```

A glance at the markup—based on David Megginson's novel DTD first introduced in Chapter 7— reveals that "Designing With JavaScript" is the title of a book and "Dynamic HTML" is a chapter found in the book. (The book really does exist; it was written by Nick Heinle, and "Dynamic HTML" is the title of Chapter 9.) The inclusion of both text and element content within the **<FRONT>** and **<CHAP-TER >** elements demonstrates how one element (**<TITLE>**) can be used in more than one place in the document (which would be an example of an efficient DTD) but describe a different kind of text in each place.

XML content is much more than just the text that the user or application sees. Instead, it is a combination of text and other elements that not only includes text for users and applications to interact with, but also provides a mechanism for describing in detail the role of the text within the document.

An element's content model describes what kind of content can legally be included within its start and end tags. XML differentiates between four different kinds of content: element content, character data, mixed content, and any content. An element may also be specified as empty and not contain anything at all. The following sections provide a detailed look at each content type as well as empty elements.

Element Content

If an element's content model specifies that it can only contain other elements and no text, it is said to have element content. For example, this element content model, taken from the Open Software Description (OSD) DTD, indicates that the **ELEMENT DEPENDENCY** can include either the **<CODEBASE>** or **<SOFTPKG>** elements in its content, but it cannot contain other elements or text:

```
<!ELEMENT DEPENDENCY (CODEBASE|SOFTPKG)>
```

If we use this content model, the following XML markup is valid:

```
<DEPENDENCY>
    <CODEBASE />
    <SOFTPKG>...</SOFTPKG>
</DEPENDENCY>
```

<CODEBASE> is an empty element, so it doesn't have a closing tag or content. **<SOFTPKG>** has its own content model that defines which elements and/or character data may be included within it. This code, however, is not valid:

```
<DEPENDENCY>
    <CODEBASE />
    This is some text describing the dependency.
    <SOFTPKG>...</SOFTPKG>
</DEPENDENCY>
```

The content model for the **<DEPENDENCY>** tag does not include character data as part of the element's allowed content, so the line of text is not legal and the code snippet is invalid.

Nesting Elements Correctly

When you nest one element inside another, always remember to close first what you opened last. All child elements must be closed before a parent element is closed, and the end tags of child elements may not be switched around. For example, the following code is invalid

```
<DEPENDENCY>
      <CODEBASE />
      <SOFTPKG>...</DEPENDENCY>
</SOFTPKG>
```

because the parent, **<DEPENDENCY>**, is closed before the child, **<SOFTPKG>**. To correct this problem, the two closing tags must be reversed. Because many DTDs like OSD rely heavily on element content, it is important to be careful when nesting child elements within one another. Any number of XML and SGML editors, like those described in Chapter 22, can help you avoid this problem or catch it in document validation. However, it's always best to be aware of the open first, close last rule.

Another example, taken from the Web Interface Definition Language (WIDL) specification (yet another proposed XML application), includes the following content model for the **<BINDING>** element:

```
<!ELEMENT BINDING ( VARIABLE | CONDITION | REGION )* >
```

The parentheses and asterisk (*) indicate that the **<BINDING>** element can contain zero or more instances of the **VARIABLE**, **CONDITION**, and **REGION** elements. For a full explanation of the notation used in content models, refer to "Defining Element Content" in this chapter's Immediate Solutions section.

Based on the content model for the **<BINDING>** element, this code is valid:

```
<BINDING>
      <VARIABLE />
      <CONDITION />
      <CONDITION />
      <CONDITION />
</BINDING>
```

The code includes one **VARIABLE** element, three **CONDITION** elements, and no **REGION** elements. All three elements that may be included within the binding **ELEMENT** are empty tags, so they don't have content models; instead they have extensive attribute lists that provide information for the software package that is processing the WIDL document.

Character Data

Some elements can only contain character data—or text—and no other elements. In actuality, this is the simplest content model an element can contain. There's no need to worry about nesting elements correctly or which elements can be nested at all. The only thing you can include between the start and end tags is plain old text. Among existing XML applications, it's surprisingly difficult to find examples of content models that call for only character data. Neither the WIDL nor the novel DTDs have any such elements. (The novel DTD uses a parameter entity—which is described in the "Including Parameter Entities In Content Models" section in the Immediate Solutions section—as part of the content model instead of a simple character data listing.) The OSD DTD has this one:

```
<!ELEMENT TITLE (#PCDATA) >
```

The **<TITLE>** element can contain only text, as indicated by the **(#PCDATA)** notation in the element's content listing. Including any other elements within the title tag will render an OSD document invalid, but there's no limit to how much text can be included.

Mixed Content

As its name implies, mixed content is a combination of element content and character data. To make things even more complex, character data content can also be called mixed content. Why? The important distinction is between element content (content that doesn't include any character data) and mixed content (content that does include character data). If an element can contain any character data at all, it's considered to have a mixed content model, even if the content model includes only character data.

Imagine a calendar DTD created to facilitate the organization of staff member time. An entry could include information about people, places, times, project references, and more. And because there's no way to categorize everything included in a calendar entry, it's useful to be able to enter undefined text. The following code defines the content model for the **<ENTRY>** element:

```
<!ELEMENT ENTRY (#PCDATA | date | place | time | person | project | phone)*>
```

The **<ELEMENT ENTRY>** can contain character data in addition to the date, place, time, person, project, and phone entities. The asterisk indicates that each entity can occur zero or more times in the contents of the **<ENTRY>** element. Using this content model, we can create the following valid XML code:

```
<ENTRY>
<DATE>July 22, 1998</DATE>
<PLACE>Louis 106</PLACE>
<TIME PM>1:00PM</TIME>
<PERSON>Mr. Cooper
    <ORGANIZATION>Computers Inc.</ORGANIZATION>
</PERSON>
<PROJECT ID=14568 />
<PHONE>555-5555</PHONE>
Don't forget to take a revised training manual and
marketing materials.
</ENTRY>
```

This particular code snippet takes advantage of every available child element the entry element can contain. We also discover that the **<TIME>** element takes **PM** as an attribute, the **<PERSON>** element is parent to the **<ORGANIZATION>** element, and the **<PROJECT>** element is a singleton tag that uses the **ID** attribute to identify a project by number, possibly based on a companywide billing and project-tracking solution. The following code is also based on the same content model:

```
<ENTRY>
<DATE>November 3, 1998</DATE>
My birthday! Take myself to lunch.
</ENTRY>
```

In addition to the character data, the data element is the only child element we use from the content model list. Even so, it is still a valid bit of code, because the content model does not say that all of the listed elements must be included, only that they *can* be included.

If a parameter entity is used as part of a content model, it is considered mixed content instead of element content. For more on the role parameter entities play in content models, see "Including Parameter Entities In Content Models" in the Immediate Solutions section later in this chapter.

One of the most important differences between element content and mixed content is that content models that contain only element content can specify which child elements must be in the contents of the parent element (which are optional) and in what order. When you use mixed content, everything is optional and no order can be imposed. These two different approaches to defining content can greatly affect DTD design. For more on this topic, see "Planning Content Models For A DTD" in this chapter's Immediate Solutions section.

ANY Content

Instead of carefully specifying what content any given element can take, developers can declare the content of the element as empty. The syntax for this content model is

```
<!ELEMENT NNN ANY>
```

where *NNN* is the element's name. Although this may seem like the easy way out, remember that parent and child elements can provide useful information about each other, and there are times when you won't want one element to be included within another. For example, it would make no sense in the novel DTD to nest the **<BODY>** element within the **<CHAPTER>** element or the **<CHAPTER>** element within the **<TITLE>** element. The whole purpose behind XML is to provide structural information about data, and the ability to nest elements within elements at will defeats this purpose. Instead, carefully structured content models provide well-structured documents. In our search of existing XML DTDs, we couldn't find a single instance of any content being defined in an element's content model.

EMPTY Elements

There are some instances where an element is empty—that is, it can't contain any content at all—and it is listed as a singleton tag in an XML document. Examples from a familiar source, HTML, are the image (**<IMG>**) and line break (**
) tags. Logically, there is no reason why either tag should have content, because each tag exists to insert something into a document rather than to provide information about text or other elements. In XML, an **EMPTY element is defined in the DTD by using this notation:

```
<!ELEMENT NNN EMPTY>
```

Although the concept of an empty tag isn't new, the notation used to describe it is:

```
<ELEMENT />
```

All empty tags must end with a slash just before the greater-than sign or the document will be considered invalid.

Looking through the various XML DTDs already being developed, we found several instances where empty elements were used within regular elements to provide information in a structured way. Take this example from the OSD specification, as posted on the World Wide Web Consortium's (W3C) Web site at **www.w3.org/TR/NOTE-OSD**:

```
<IMPLEMENTATION>
    <OS VALUE="WinNT">
        <OSVERSION VALUE="4,0,0,0"/>
    </OS>
    <OS VALUE="Win95"/>
    <PROCESSOR VALUE="x86" />
    <LANGUAGE VALUE="en" />
    <CODEBASE HREF="http://www.foobar.org/solitaire.cab" />
</IMPLEMENTATION>
```

The operating system (**<OS>**), **<PROCESSOR>**, **<LANGUAGE>**, and **<CODEBASE>** elements all provide important information about the specific implementation of the software package being described. Except for the first instance of the **<OS>** element, all the other elements are empty, but they are hardly devoid of information. "Planning Content Models For A DTD" (in this chapter's Immediate Solutions section) discusses why it's often better to use empty entities with predefined attributes and values instead of allowing the document developer to provide structure information in regular character data.

Content-Based Markup Vs. Presentation-Based Markup

Because HTML provided many of us with our first introduction to markup languages, we tend to view markup with the idea that it is always based on presentation. Presentation-based markup describes data with the idea that it will be visually presented in some way, either on a computer screen, overhead, or on a printed page. Presentation-based markup, such as HTML, often focuses on the final look and feel of information, which leads to complex workarounds (such as using tables to control pages) and creating new methods for describing presentation-like style sheets.

However, XML was not created for the presentation of information alone. Instead, it is robust enough to describe information so it can be processed by one or more applications or delivered in ways other than traditional visual presentation (such as aurally or in Braille). This is known as content-based markup.

The novel and OSD DTDs are perfect examples of presentation-based and content-based paradigms. The whole point behind the description of a novel's content is so that people can read the novel on screen or in print. The DTD is compact and concerns itself mostly with describing author, title, and paragraph information. This approach lends itself quite easily to one of several visual presentations.

The OSD DTD, on the other hand, is designed to provide information (the OS and processor requirements as well as version and location information) about software packages. The goal of OSD is to facilitate the quick and easy download and update of software across a network without requiring the presence of a person at the computer while the installation or upgrade is being performed. This is not presentation-oriented information at all. Instead, the DTD concerns itself with describing the particulars of the software so the client computer can compare its parameters and installed software to determine if the package can be installed and, if so, which portions of the package it should download and from where.

The novel DTD leaves quite a bit of room for character data, and the OSD specification uses many empty elements with attributes that take one of several specified values. The novel DTD revolves around text, and the OSD DTD concerns itself with computer and software package information. The purpose that drives a DTD, whether it's based on content or presentation, will greatly affect how content models are defined for each element in the DTD.

There is no rule that says an XML application can't be both content and presentation based, but as the DTD develops, certain portions will be reserved for information that will be presented, and others for information that will be processed or analyzed. In the end, the content-based markup may affect the final display of the presentation-based markup. In general, presentation-based markup allows developers more room for including their own freeform character data, and there will be more of it. Content-based markup will more closely control the amount of character data allowed and may opt to use attributes and values instead of developer-supplied information.

The need for a markup language that supports both content- and presentation-based markup was one of the main motivations for the creation of XML. Although SGML is very good at creating both kinds of markup, its learning curve and implementation costs can be steep. Instead, XML provides the extensibility developers need to create DTDs to meet their needs (whether they are based on content, presentation, or both) without some of the complexities of SGML.

9: Creating Content In XML

Immediate Solutions

Both DTD and document developers work with XML content on a regular basis. If you're a DTD developer, you need to think through your content models carefully, ensuring that they don't step on one another's toes or violate each other's rules. If you're a document developer, you have to decipher the content model for each element as described in the DTD and then make sure you adhere to the rules they establish. This Immediate Solutions section focuses on the conventions used to define content models for elements in XML DTDs. Although creating DTDs and XML documents are two different tasks, they require the same knowledge base. If you can create a content model, you can implement one. Chapter 6 focuses on how to create a road map for a DTD, including how to evaluate the content model of every element. Visit the final project and checklist in that chapter for a refresher on analyzing a DTD. The projects in this Immediate Solutions section take you through the process of creating content models.

Defining Character Data Content

If an element can only contain character data content, its element description in the DTD takes this format:

```
<!ELEMENT NNN (#PCDATA)>
```

This is the simplest content an element can contain and indicates that the element cannot contain any other child elements. The following code provides an example of an element with a character-data-only content model and related markup:

```
<! ELEMENT note (#PCDATA)>
...
<NOTE>
This is some note text. This note can contain as much
text as necessary. It cannot contain any other markup.
</NOTE>
```

The following markup is not valid based on the content model for the **<NOTE>** element:

```
<NOTE>
This is some note text. <B>This markup is no longer valid</B>
because it contains additional elements nested inside of the
note element. The note element content model does not allow this.
</NOTE>
```

Because elements that can only contain character data cannot take advantage of the strengths offered by the ability to contain other elements or by recursion (the ability to nest elements within themselves), character data is very rarely the only content an element can contain. Instead, character data is often combined with element content in a mixed content model.

Defining Element Content

You can create element models that only allow other elements to be nested within the described element. Character data is not allowed in the contents of the elements. Elements contained within the described element are called child elements, and these child elements have their own content models, which may include other elements, character data, or both. Because of this, the content model only applies to the first nesting level within an element.

Element content can specify which elements can be included as content, as well as the order in which they must appear, which are required, and which are optional. To specify this information, the content model uses a special set of notations, as outlined in Table 9.1.

The notations within the element content notation system can be combined to create complex descriptions of the elements that are allowed as child elements within a parent element. For example, this content model

```
<!ELEMENT ENTRY ( date, place?, time, person+, project+, phone?)
```

indicates that the entry element must contain one instance of the **DATE** element—and it must be first—followed by zero or one optional **PLACE** element, a mandatory **TIME** element, one or more **PERSON** elements, one or more **PROJECT** elements, and an optional **PHONE** element. This carefully constructed content model ensures that important information like the date, time, person, and related project information is included, but it provides flexibility for the **PLACE** and **PHONE** elements because they might not be as necessary as the other information. Because the elements are separated by commas, they must occur in the order specified in the content model.

Table 9.1   The element content notation system.

Notation	Name	Description	Example
( )	Parentheses	Indicates a set of alternatives or a sequence of elements.	<!ELEMENT CAPTION (align | size)>
|	Vertical bar	Separates elements in a set of alternatives.	<!ELEMENT PERSON (organization | client | partner | staff)
,	Comma	Separates elements in a sequence; elements must occur in the order listed.	<!ELEMENT NOVEL (front, body)>
?	Question mark	Indicates that an element or set may occur zero or one time.	<!ELEMENT CAPTION (align, size?)
*	Asterisk	Indicates that an element or set may occur zero or more times.	<!ELEMENT PERSON (organization | client | partner | staff)*
+	Plus	Indicates that an element must occur one or more times.	<!ELEMENT ENTRY (date, place, time, person, project, phone)+>

The Channel Definition Format (CDF) specification found on the W3C's Web site at **www.w3.org/TR/NOTE-CDFsubmit.html** includes the item and schedule elements whose content models include only element content and use the element content notation:

```
<!ELEMENT Item ( LastMod, Title, Abstract, Author, Publisher,
     Copyright, PublicationDate, Keywords, Category, Rating,
     Schedule, Usage )* >
<!ELEMENT Schedule ( StartDate?, EndDate?, IntervalTime?,
     EarliestTime?, LatestTime? ) >
```

The item element can contain zero or more instances of several elements, and when it does, they must be included in the order listed in the content model. The **<SCHEDULE>** element can take one of five optional elements, but if the elements are included, they can only be included once and must be in the order listed.

Defining Mixed Content

Mixed content includes a combination of character data and element content. Unlike content models that include only element content, those that take mixed content cannot specify order or required values for the nested elements and data. Instead, a mixed data content model takes this format:

```
<!ELEMENT NNN (#PCDATA element | element | element |...)*>
```

The content list must be enclosed within parentheses, begin with the **#PCDATA** declaration, and be followed by an asterisk. Instead of using long lines of mixed content declarations, many DTDs include parameter entities in their mixed content. "Including Parameter Entities In Content Models" (later in this Immediate Solutions section) addresses this technique.

Defining **ANY** And **EMPTY** Elements

An element that can take any kind of content is said to have an any content model. Those that cannot take any content at all are considered empty. The syntax for describing these elements, respectively, is shown in the following code:

```
<!ELEMENT NNN ANY>
<!ELEMENT NNN EMPTY>
```

Elements that can contain any content must still adhere to the rules of nesting, but that is their only constraint. Empty elements require special notation in markup:

```
<ELEMENT />
```

The following is not considered an empty element:

```
<ELEMENT></ELEMENT>
```

If an element is defined as empty in the DTD but does not have its closing slash, the document is invalid.

Including Parameter Entities In Content Models

Parameter entities—entities that work only in the DTD to provide a shorthand notation for frequently used element groups—can be included in content models to make them more manageable and less cumbersome. For a detailed explanation of creating parameter entities, refer to Chapter 12. Parameter entities are included in an element's content model; they are prefaced by the percent sign (%) and followed by a semicolon (;), as shown in this syntax example:

```
<!ELEMENT NNN %entity;>
```

This sample code from the novel DTD provides an example of a parameter entity included in a content model:

```
<!ELEMENT item (%phrasal;)*>
```

This code indicates that the **item** element can include any content as defined by the phrasal parameter entity. The phrasal parameter entity is defined as:

```
<!ENTITY % phrasal "#PCDATA|emphasis">
```

So, the item **element** can contain either character data or the emphasis element. This example does not lend much weight to the argument for creating parameter entities instead of just listing content within a regular content model, but this example from the Technical Markup Language (TecML) found at **www.venus.co.uk/omf/cml-1.0/doc/dtd/index.html** does. The content model for the **relation** element looks like this:

```
<!ELEMENT relation ((array | xvar), (array | xvar), %x.content;)>
```

This content model indicates that the **relation** element can nest either **array** or **xvar** elements twice in any order, as well as any other elements included in the **x.content** entity. The **x.content** entity, shown in the following code, also references the **x.descrip** entity:

```
<!ENTITY % x.content '(%x.descrip;, (array | xlist| xvar)*)'>
<!ENTITY % x.descrip '(xhtml?)'>
```

These two entities add zero or more **array**, **xlist**, and **xvar** elements into the fray, as well as an optional **xhtml** element. If we put this all together, the content model for the relation **element** would look something like this:

```
<!ELEMENT relation ((array | xvar), (array | Xvar), (xhtml?),
    (array | xlist| xvar|)*)
```

Although this description isn't too long, keep in mind that you can use the **x.content** entity in the content model descriptions of as many other elements in the DTD as necessary. It's much easier to type %**x.content**; than its equivalent over and over again. Additionally, the TecML specification is included as an entity in the Chemical Markup Language (CML) and Molecular (MOL) DTDs, so you can use the **x.content** entity in the content models of all the elements in those two DTDs as well.

The use of entities is a powerful tool, as Chapter 12 discusses in detail, and when combined with content models, entities help DTD and document developers create well-structured and easy-to-read DTDs and documents.

Planning Content Models For A DTD

In many ways, content models can make or break an XML DTD. If the models contradict one another or do not work well together, the result could be invalid or unusable documents. Although it is the document developer's responsibility to follow the rules set forth in the element content models, it is up to the DTD developer to create a solid set of rules. Follow these steps to ensure your DTD's content models are viable:

1. Determine the goals and objectives of your DTD. This initial step helps you decide which elements you need in your DTD and which elements you don't need.

2. Make a list of all the elements you plan to include in the DTD and their descriptions. This process identifies the role each element will play in documents created for the DTD. For more information on elements, refer to Chapter 7.

3. Create a hierarchy showing how all the elements relate to one another. Make notes about initial ideas of what kind of content the elements might contain, but don't get too attached to your notes. In this phase, the roles and relationships among the elements will begin to become clearer than they were in Step 2.

4. Review your hierarchy and notes, paying close attention to those elements that will have child elements. Ask yourself:

   - In what order (if any) do the child elements need to appear?

   - Which child elements are required and which are optional?

   - How many times should you allow child elements to be included in content (only once or many times)?

   - Will the child elements have children of their own?

   - How will the children of child elements affect the parent element?

   - Can the element contain instances of itself as child elements (recurse)?

   These questions will no doubt lead to other, project-specific questions. The goal here is to keep examining your elements until you can see all the possible relations between them.

5. Create initial content models for each element and then take a break from your DTD development. After you've become intimately involved with a project, it becomes difficult to see your own mistakes. When you return to the project, you'll have a keener eye.

6. Develop a document for your DTD, focusing on using all the elements and their potential child elements. Document development helps flush out minor problems you couldn't see when you developed your content models. Make adjustments to your content models as necessary and keep working on your document until you have viable and solid content models.

7. Ask friends or colleagues to look over your content models and create documents for them. Be prepared to take criticism and remember that you asked for their help. Others will be able to find mistakes you might have missed or suggest a solution to a difficult problem. Even though your DTD isn't finished yet, errors at this stage in the game can be difficult to fix later on.

When you've developed your content models for an XML DTD account, you'll find that a large portion of your work is done. You'll still need to work on element attributes and entities, but the framework for your DTD will be firmly in place.

Chapter 10

Linking In XML: XLink

By Natanya Pitts-Moultis and Cheryl Kirk

In Depth

In addition to offering tremendous flexibility for structuring documents, XML offers advanced mechanisms for referencing and linking to other sources and documents and to internal cross-references. With XML, you can use various element attributes to cross-reference items within an XML document. And with XML's linking language, *XLink* (previously known as the Extensible Link Language and XML-Link), you can create powerful links in your XML documents.

Links overcome the boundaries imposed by localized file storage and add value to documents by simply linking them to other documents of similar content and value. Because XML extends the role of markup languages in document dissemination, it is necessary for it to have a specialized linking system that is as robust and extensible as the markup language itself. That linking system is XLink. XLink provides for multidirectional links among documents, the compilation and storage of link groups in a single folder, and other advanced linking mechanisms. This means you can create bidirectional links, links that point to multiple locations or files, and links that represent different views of the data. XML offers linking methods that allow you to specify links that have different types of behavior, links that can be typed, or links that can be used in different documents. This chapter explores the abilities and constructs of XLink.

TIP: *The XML linking specification is still in the working draft stage. Some of the information in this chapter may be subject to change. Check **www.w3.org/TR/WD-xlink** for the most up-to-date information.*

An Overview Of Linking In XML

XLink, XML's linking language, borrows some constructs—most notably the **HREF** attribute—from HTML, but it is in large part modeled on more advanced hypertext systems, such as HyTyme and the Text Encoding Initiative Guidelines. XLink also relies heavily on XPointer, a mechanism that provides strict but expansive guidelines for using XML links to point to the internal structures of XML documents. Together, XLink and XPointer are the XML linking mechanism.

TIP: *For a detailed discussion of XPointers, an extension of the XLink language, read Chapter 11.*

Like XML, because of its complexity, XLink has a specification all its own. Actually, it has two, both of which closely follow the XML recommendation. So, why didn't they include the linking portion of XML in the actual XML specification? Basically, there is a lot of ground to cover, because linking involves more than just declaring an element and the link resource. A separate specification is needed to explain both the linking mechanism and the mechanism used to reference sections of documents (XPointer). Also, the individual specifications provide information about how to create connections to hypertext and hypermedia. Before we go too far, let's first examine what hypertext is, how it works in HTML, and how linking in HTML extends to XML.

TIP: *If you're interested in reading more about the XPointer specification, check out **www.w3.org/TR/WD-xptr**.*

In the world of hypertext, a link is a connection to another resource. A resource can be anything that's accessible over the network. If you've developed any HTML Web pages, you're probably already familiar with links and the tag used to specify them. In HTML, you identify a link to another resource by using the anchor element **<A></A>** with the **HREF** attribute, which in turn specifies the location of the resource in the **HREF** value. As you can see in the following example, the anchor element represents a link to a resource, and the **HREF** attribute specifies the location of the resource (in this example, the resource is a Web page):

```
<A HREF="http://www.site.com/index.html">The Index of My Site</A>
```

The resource you specify could be another Web page, a file stored on a file transfer server, a script that allows you to query a remote database, or even a connection to a remote video camera. You could also specify other types of documents, fragments of documents, and even links to such multimedia resources as video or audio files. Instead of using http://, you can use a variety of protocols to connect to a variety of resources, including:

- *ftp://*—To connect to an FTP server
- *gopher://*—To connect to a Gopher server
- *nntp:// (or news://)*—To connect to a newsgroup server
- *file://*—To access a file on a local drive
- *javascript://*—To access a script
- *telnet://*—To connect to a remote computer system

In the previous example, the **HREF** attribute identifies exactly what the resource is, where it's located, and in a very elementary way, the action for the link. The action in the previous example is the user clicking on the link and moving forward in a single direction to a Web server. If we break down a standard HTML link, we would come up with the following parts:

- The element that defines that this code is, in fact, a link (**<A></A>**).

- The location of the resource that the link specifies (**http://www.site.com**).

- The action associated with the link, commonly referred to as traversing (clicking on the link).

- Also part of the action is the direction the link will take the user, be it forward, backward, up, down, and so on (with HTML, it's unidirectional; in other words, forward).

- Additional values that define the link (in the preceding example, the additional value is the content that specifies the text or graphics that serve to represent the link on the Web page—The Index of My Site).

When the developers of the XML Linking Language set out to create XLink, they knew they needed a language that was compatible with existing HTML documents but also powerful enough to support the many possible implementations of XML. XML links had to be able to—at the very least—support linking between XML and HTML documents as well as between two or more XML documents. With this in mind, XML links had to have the characteristics of basic HTML links, including:

- Links can be traversed from one end to the other.

- Links can be described at one end.

- The link goes to a single destination.

- The link's effect on the graphical user interface is determined by the GUI itself and not the link.

- The link is activated by the user.

These characteristics weren't difficult to include in XML, because they were a product of HTML. However, simple HTML links are limited, and XML needed additional functionality to include the following capabilities:

- Because XML allows developers to define their own links, they must be able to attach the linking mechanism to any element.

- Links need to have both human- and machine-readable labels.

- Links must be able to point to specific portions of an XML or HTML document. This ability must be based not only on name but on certain conditions, such as location or context.

- Developers must be able to provide the XML parser with specific information about how link content must be processed or displayed.

- Link transversal can be activated in ways other than by the user.

- Links don't have to be one-way links.

- Links can be described from outside of the resources they connect.

In XML, the link **<A HREF="http://www.site.com/index.html">The Index of My Site</A>** is referred to as a simple inline link; it connects the user to another document. In XML, simple links connect you to another Internet resource; it can be another XML document or any other resource accessible over the Internet. A simple XML link can include the following information:

- The element used to specify the link. In this case, it's the **<A>** element (like the one used in HTML), but it could actually be any element, such as **<BODY>**, **<SECTION>**, **<HEAD>**, and so on.

- The label (text or graphics) that indicates to the user that this is a link.

- Any instructions that specify to the browser or the software what the link should do, such as locate and display another document, open a new window, or display information in a different frame within the document.

- Whether a link has to be clicked on or whether the link is activated when the user moves the pointer over the link reference. This is similar to JavaScript; you can show information about the link as the user moves the mouse over the link.

- Whether the link will reference an entire document or a specific part of a resource. (In HTML, this type of link is either specified by a question mark or the **<A NAME>** tag references a particular search query or a particular portion of a document that is already specified in the **NAME** attribute.) XML links can specify not just a portion of an entire page, but also sections across multiple documents.

- Whether the linked document or fragment is cached on the linked document's server.

Let's look at the previous link again:

```
<A HREF="http://www.site.com/index.html">The Index of My Site</A>
```

All the linking information is included in the linking element. With simple links such as this one, there is no need for the application to search out other elements for information about the location (the information about the location is referred to as the locator). The locator is the URL, and in XML, the URL is specified. The URL can be a Web page or another external reference. The link in XML is self-contained. If we dissect this link further, we notice that it specifies one resource that moves the user in a single direction.

As with anything in XML, XLink offers much more than simple inline links. In fact, XLink offers a variety of link types, link actions, and link capabilities, many of which you define. In XML, you specify the element you want to use as a link. Unlike HTML, where the **<A>** element specifies that the information following the element is going to be a link, with XML there is no one element that specifies a link. Instead, you use the XLink language to define what elements or attributes will specify links. In this way, you are actually constructing your own links and linking action. XLink is defined in two subcomponents or parts, one called XLink and the other called XPointer.

XLink provides advanced linking capabilities, such as multidirectional and external linking. XPointer provides a convenient and easily understood way to describe locations in XML documents. Think of XLink as the package that combines hyperlinking and references in two parts, XLink and XPointer. Here's a longer definition of each:

• *XLink*—Specifies how you insert linking into your XML document and where the link may point. This component specifies that the links in your documents are recognized as links and not just content or other element or attribute information. It gives you the ability to link to objects or other resources internally or externally. It's a language that allows you to invent your own link elements and create a kind of link database.

TIP: *Think of XLink as the linking mechanism that you use in HTML.*

• *XPointer*—Lets you specify precise subparts of an XML document instead of just pointing to them. Part of this component includes advanced addressing you can use directly in the XML document structure. HTML limits pointing to parts of a document that have an ID or are named by using the anchor tag. XPointers are used with URLs and help define a series of steps that, in turn, define a particular path to a place in a document. Basically, XPointers govern the fragment identifier that goes into a URL when you are linking from another file to a resource in an XML document.

XML Linking Terms

Before we go any further, we should clearly define some of the terminology and components of the XLink language. XLinks are made up of several components, each with its own specific identifier and name. The following terms are used in the XLink specifications. You'll need to know and understand them to work with the Immediate Solutions section of this chapter as well as with new updates to the XLink specification:

- *Link*—A connection or relationship between two or more data objects or portions of data objects. A link defines a specific relationship between two or more resources or parts of those resources.

- *Linking element*—An element that specifies the existence of a link and describes its characteristics. Consider a linking element the element within an XML document that states the existence of a link and includes a description of the link. The anchor tag in HTML is a linking element. Any element in an XML document is a potential linking element.

- *Resource*—A service or object that is specified in a link. A resource can be a file, an image, documents, programs, database query results, or a sound file. More specifically, a resource can be anything that can be accessed via a URL or any object that can be referenced by a URI and is part of the link, including a part of a document.

- *Inline link*—A link that serves as one of its own resources. More specifically, an inline link is one where the content of the linking element acts as a resource. An example of such a link is the HTML **<A>** element.

- *Local resource*—The content of an inline linking element. An inline linking element's content is a local resource. If the document containing the link is one of the link's resources, then the document is considered to be a local resource.

- *Participating resource*—A resource that is part of a link. Any resource is a potential link and becomes a participating link when it is identified by a locator as part of the link.

- *Remote resource*—A participating resource that is part of a link and pointed to by a locator. A linking group can contain a list of links that include locators that point to other resources.

- *Subresource*—A portion of a resource that specifies another resource (such as an entire document that is specified for retrieval and display). A subresource is a section of a resource. It is the exact destination of a link and is identified by using XPointer notation.

- *Locator*—A piece of data (provided as part of a link) that identifies the resource and can be used to locate the resource. A locator is a resource's address, and it is used in a linking element to locate a resource.

- *Multidirectional link*—A link that can be traversed from more than one of its resources. It's more than just a link that provides a mechanism to go back to a previously visited resource or link. Instead, a multidirectional link gives the user the ability to move up, down, left, right, or backward—in other words, in just about any direction.

- *Out-of-line link*—A link whose content does not serve as one of the original link's resources. Out-of-line links don't even have to occur in the same document. They are used within multidirectional links and when read-only resources have outgoing links.

- *Traversal*—The action of using a link to access a resource. Traversals are usually initiated by a user action or by some sort of program control. Think of a traversal as a way to activate a link in order to access its resource.

All these link components are put together to form different types of links, which we'll cover in "The Details Of The XLink Language" later in this chapter. For now, you should be familiar with the following linking terms:

- *Simple link*—An XML link that uses the **HREF** attribute to point to only one resource. Simple links can take on several different attributes, including **ROLE** and **SHOW**, and are always inline links that connect the local resource to one remote resource. All HTML links are simple links.

- *Extended link*—An XML link that can point to several resources and doesn't have to be an inline link. Extended links can be broken down into two subgroups: out-of-line links and multidirectional links.

TIP: *XLink is extensive enough to provide for a variety of links to meet almost any document need, but it doesn't include a mechanism for pointing to specific places within documents. That job is left up to XML pointers, which are discussed in Chapter 11.*

The Origins Of XLink

Now that you know some of the basic terminology, it will be helpful to know where XLink came from and what previous linking technologies helped to form the XLink specification. XLink is actually derived from a variety of other linking specifications. The XLink specification was first called the Extensible Linking Language, and then it was XML-Link until the World Wide Web Consortium (W3C) decided on its final name, XLink. This linking language provides the mechanism to link objects to each other in XML and the mechanisms for backward compatibility with HTML. The three standards that have been instrumental are HTML, HyTyme, and the Text Encoding Initiative Guidelines (TEIP3). If you have had any previous experience with any of these standards, it will be relatively easy for you to understand what XLink offers.

In case you're not familiar with these linking technologies, which have been influential in helping to define XLink, here's a quick overview:

- *Hypertext Markup Language (HTML)*—HTML has helped to define several Standard Generalized Markup Language (SGML) element types that represent single directional links to resources regardless of the type of protocol (HTTP, FTP, Gopher, Telnet, and so on) used to connect to those resources.

- *HyTyme*—HyTyme, used within the SGML specification, defines the inline and out-of-line link structures and some semantic features, including traversal control and presentation of objects.

- *Text Encoding Initiative Guidelines (TEIP3)*—The TEIP3 guidelines provide structures for creating links, aggregate objects, and link collections.

But there are numerous other linking systems that have also contributed to the creation of the XLink specification, including Dexter, FRESS, MicroCosm, and InterMedia. More specifically, however, XML's linking specification builds upon HTML and actually works toward preserving the HTML linking structure. This ensures that XML documents can link to HTML documents and that the progression from HTML to XML is smooth.

As previously mentioned, the simple linking concept found in HTML—where you can specify various protocols, absolute and relative links, and fragment identifiers—is called an inline link in XML. The linking concept is used to connect to resources, including documents, graphics, and other file types. Using the same **<A>** element as is used in HTML, XML provides all the locator information in the element's **HREF** attribute. The **HREF** attribute works the same way it does in HTML, but with XML, whatever element (along with its attributes) you use to create a link has been extended. In XML, links can be bidirectional or multidirectional, and they can even be links that connect to two or more targets. These are just a few of the features of XLink. We'll take a closer look at each feature and how it performs in the "The Details Of The XLink Language" section later in this chapter. For now, let's look at the design principles that went into creating the XLink language and how linking should be used within XML.

TIP: *The XLink language has its own working draft, and soon it will have its own recommendation. Check it out at the W3C's site, **www.w3.org/TR/1998/WD-xlink-19980303**. Remember, this may be an older version of the language's specification. Make sure you follow the link for the most up-to-date specification.*

XLink Design Principles

When the governing body that put together the XLink syntax gathered, they had specific goals in mind in terms of how XLink should operate and function, not only on the Internet but also within XML documents. Now that you know the background and some of the terminology, you should also be familiar with the way in which links are designed in XML. Knowing these design principles will help you implement links within your documents. Following is the summary of the design principles governing XLink as defined by the W3C.

XLink shall be straightforwardly usable over the Internet. This simply means that, because you have no control over resources outside your own network, and because you cannot control the result each link provides, the linking feature should not be unusable in circumstances dictated by the Internet. Because sites move, pages are deleted, and information changes, XLink must accommodate broken links, resources that cannot be located, and links that take the user in the wrong direction. XLink must also support multidirectional links in software applications.

XLink shall be usable by a wide variety of link usage domains and of classes of linking application software. When you use linking in XML, there should be no favoritism of one domain over another. Regardless of where the link points or what type of document the link is stored in—for example, a cross-reference in a technical publication or a link to a Web page—there should be no preference. In addition, there should be no preference for various kinds of browsers, application software, or editing systems that are used to create or display the links. This means that linking in Microsoft Internet Explorer will be the same as linking in Netscape Navigator.

The XLink expression language shall be XML, meaning XLink follows the same rules and syntax. The premise here is that any link structure must follow the XML element and attribute syntax. Because you can use various elements— whereas in HTML, you use just a single element (such as the **<A>** element)— when you place a link within an element, you must follow the standard XML syntax regardless of the link you use. And because you can design your own link elements, you need to supply the attributes, content information, and parameters in the same way you do when you create and specify any element.

The XLink design shall be prepared quickly. Linking and the code used to create links should be able to be created without much effort. The code used to create the links should be straightforward and easy to understand. You should be able to create links quickly, because you already know how to create elements and attributes.

The XLink design shall be formal and concise. The link you specify should be explained in such a way that the explanation does not confuse the people who might read your code. And the code should be concise enough so that computers can understand it. The idea is that you don't confuse how the links relate to each other and the XML syntax used to define the links. For example, you might want to include specific information within your link element declaration about the number of resources needed in a link, thereby further defining the link topology.

XLink links shall be human-readable through their labels and understandable to the human. Don't you wish everything in the computer world followed this rule? Actually, it means more than just making sure links are readable. The link structures may be in compressed, encrypted, or binary form when transmitted or internally processed, but they must be in text form within the XML document to be considered XLinks.

XLink links may reside outside the documents in which the participating resources reside. Links can be stored inside or outside documents. To offer scalability and relief from HTML linking limitations, XLink must support sophisticated out-of-line linking. This means that some links may be out-of-line or inline. It's up to the developer to decide which link to use for which purpose.

XLink shall represent the abstract structure and significance of links. There should be some small indication about basic link behavior. The designers of the XLink specification didn't want to encourage procedural markup; they wanted to indicate what basic link behavior is acceptable.

XLink links must be feasible to implement. Although some of the features of linking will be difficult to implement because of their complexity, linking should at least be easy to manage and control and relatively easy to shape.

Knowing these design principles before you start creating links will help you design your links appropriately. If you want to read more about the XLink design guidelines, see the specification at **www.w3c.org/XML**. Next, we'll review the actual link process.

TIP: *The information about XLinks and XPointers is written in the Extended Backus-Naur Form (EBNF) notation, as described in the XML specification. If you need more information about how to use the EBNF notation to read the specification, see Chapter 2.*

An Overview Of XLink

XLink extends the concept of linking in several different ways. A link defined with XLink is an explicit relationship between two or more data objects or portions of data objects. Also, XLink provides not just one, but two types of link elements: the standard inline link that provides unidirectional connections to resources, and extended group links that can be either inline or out-of-line connections to resources that are used for multidirectional links. That means hyperlinking goes far beyond the basic linking mechanism HTML offers. Instead, XLink offers the ability to have smart links that require little or no additional programming. And with XLink, links now become objects, like almost everything else in XML.

One of the features of XLink is that you can create bidirectional links. Bidirectional links are more than just links that take the visitor forward to a particular location, as is the case with HTML. Also, a hyperlink might be an XML element itself, which means you can specify conditional behaviors that can be associated with the link. Moreover, XLink links can be grouped, searched, or activated based on certain behaviors. For example, you could create color-coded links based on the links' attributes. Or, you could create links that are summoned when the user requests them. Any XML element declared in a document can be converted into a hyperlink source or destination anchor.

When a developer creates a link with XLink, he or she can add behaviors to the link. XLink lets the developer create code that performs a variety of functions (for example, displaying a pop-up menu with a list of choices) without having to code any additional JavaScript to perform the action. XLinks reduce the amount of additional scripting required by allowing the developer to assign actions to links. The idea behind XLink is that the links and cross-references to other sources are scalable and maintainable.

In the next section, we'll examine the components of the XLink language and the design principles for creating links in an XML document.

The Details Of The XLink Language

The XLink specification provides for several different linking capabilities, all of which we'll demonstrate in this chapter's Immediate Solutions section. However, let's take a minute to outline the three types of linking elements XLink provides:

• *Simple links*—Are always unidirectional like they are in HTML.

• *Extended links*—Provide either inline or out-of-line links.

• *Extended link groups*— Provide groups of links that can be unidirectional, out-of-line, or inline links.

Each type of link can have various types of information associated with it. In addition, XLink offers a multitude of options within these different types of linking elements. Although we'll delve deeper into each of these options, XLink provides the following capabilities:

• Multidimensional links. That is, links that can point the user in more than one direction and can lead to multiple destinations.

• Filtered views of data and better connections to databases for remote querying without requiring a great deal of scripting (in some cases, requiring no scripting at all).

• The capability to have persistent links with semantics attached to them.

• The ability to assemble documents dynamically through linking.

• The ability to dynamically update software through links.

- The ability to annotate links so users and developers can get a clear picture of what the link offers.

- Links that offer special behaviors, such as opening up a new window, replacing a previous view with a new view, or cycling through windows, which are all things that Java or JavaScript could perform.

- Better link management and administration capabilities (including the ability to create link databases) that let you filter, sort, analyze, or process link collections.

One feature of a markup language such as XML is that you can define your own elements and attributes, and this is where XLink provides powerful linking capabilities. Unlike HTML, XML linking offers the ability to define any number of element types that can be used as links. XML extends the **HREF** attribute used within the **XML:LINK** element by allowing any element type to specify the existence of a link. Also, the **XML:LINK** element extends the linking capabilities by providing the ability to define a part of a URL fragment within an XML document. Let's examine each type of link and link fragment that allows this type of functionality.

In XML, a link is a relationship between two or more data objects. This means links can also be relationships between portions of data objects. The XLink specification outlines linking options and also provides for advanced hypertext linking capabilities. With XLink, you can use the various properties of XML, such as the elements and attributes, which in turn can define various relationships between objects in a document.

Dissecting A Simple Link

You need the XLink language, because, in XML, you can use whatever element you want as a link. XLink defines how you describe the links regardless of the element you use. Unlike HTML, there is no predetermined element used to specify a link. Your XML document simply doesn't know what elements will be used to define a linking element until you declare it. Therefore, you have to put some sort of marker in the form of a special attribute in your element so the XML parser and browser or other XML-enabled appliance will know that this particular element is, indeed, a link. In the following sections, we'll examine how a simple link looks and works. This link operates pretty much the same as a standard HTML link operates:

```
For more information about XML, <A XML:LINK="SIMPLE"
HREF="http://www.xml.com">check out this page.</A>
```

In this example, we used the **<A>** element, but we could have used any other element that had been defined in the Document Type Definition (DTD) or XML document. Let's look at how this is done and how defining elements and attributes actually makes the links in XML documents.

Defining A Simple Inline Link

As mentioned earlier, a simple inline link connects to resources. These resources are really anything that can be reached by using a locator and can include graphics, documents, database queries, and movies. The locator is defined in the same way URLs are defined in HTML. You can also use portions or fragments of URLs, just as you can with HTML.

When defining unidirectional external links in XML, you use the **SIMPLE** link type. This provides a unidirectional external link that includes a URL. Because of the compatibility between HTML and XML, links in XML actually have the same look and feel as HTML links. Simple links have only one locator, which combines the functions of a linking element and a locator into a single element. The **SIMPLE** link element provides both a locator attribute and a link and re-source semantic attribute. The following code would be valid in either an XML or HTML document:

```
<A HREF="http://www.site.com/links/default.html">
<A HREF="http://www.site.com/links/default.xml">
<A HREF="http://www.site.com/links/default.xml#sectiona">
```

In XML, a simple link carries all the linking information in the linking element itself. Although it sounds simple, creating a simple link in XML is a bit more time-consuming than creating one in HTML. It takes more than just the **<A>** element and the **HREF** attribute to specify a link.

Specifying Link Elements

Here's how the XML linking specification works. You can create a link by reserving an element, reserving an attribute, or leaving the whole matter of link recognition up to the style sheets and application software. That's pretty flexible. But the best way to define a link is to define an element and then specify the attribute as a link. You do so by specifying the **XML:LINK** attribute and then specifying the information about the link in the attribute.

Of course, when you specify a link, you must first specify the element that signifies the link. Then, you use that element and the attribute as you would any element within the XML document. For example, let's define an element called **LINK** and specify the attribute of the element. The following code would do just that:

```
<!ELEMENT LINK (#PCDATA)>
  <!ATTLIST LINK
    XML:LINK    CDATA    #FIXED    "simple"
    HREF    CDATA    #REQUIRED
    TITLE    CDATA    #IMPLIED>
```

First, we created an element called **LINK** that can use any parsable character data. Next, we defined the attribute list for the element. The first attribute is **XML:LINK**. This attribute specifies that the element is a link. Any element that contains this attribute clarifies that this element acts as a link because of the inclusion of the **XML:LINK** attribute. The link will also be a simple link because we declared it as a simple link instead of an extended link. Possible values for the **XML:LINK** attribute are either **SIMPLE** or **EXTENDED**, which identify linking elements, and **LOCATOR**, **GROUP**, and **DOCUMENT**, which identify other related types of elements. Simple links in XML are links that point forward to another single locator or URL. With a simple link, there are no restrictions on the contents of a simple linking element.

The **XML:LINK** attribute declaration signals to the XML processor that this will be a link. If you leave it out, some HTML browsers may pick up the **HREF** information and provide linking, but all XML parsers and processors will return an error. If you specify the attribute in the DTD as a fixed value, you don't have to specify it in every single instance of the element.

The **HREF** attribute works the same way the HTML **HREF** attribute works for the anchor tag, but it has been extended, as you'll see later. The **TITLE** attribute, which is optional because it has been marked **#IMPLIED**, contains the information that displays when the browsing visitor moves his or her mouse over the link. It's similar to the tool tips you see in almost every Windows application. You don't have to include it if you don't want to, but it can be useful for telling visitors where they will go if they click on the link.

There are a few more attributes we'll introduce to you, but for now, we've created all the attributes needed to create a link. Now, we're ready to pop a line of code in our document, using the **<LINK>** element and the declared attributes to specify the information about the link:

```
<LINK XML:LINK="simple" HREF="http://www.site.com/"
TITLE="This takes you to my site">going to my site</LINK>
```

Simple links can have only one locator. The locator combines the functions of the linking element you've defined and the locator into a single element. There are no constraints on the contents of a simple linking element. According to the XLink specification, for a document to be valid, every element that is significant to XLink must still conform to the constraints expressed in its governing DTD.

When you create a link, you specify a great deal about it, from the action used to the link the user will traverse. However, you leave the formatting of the link it-self—the way it will be displayed—up to the style sheet as you do everything else in XML. When you specify the format, you can indicate the link's appearance (or the way it is treated) before the user initiates any action. For example, because links can appear as standard text, you might want to specify the link's font or color just to indicate that a link is present in the document. You may also want to add special text that pops up when visitors move their mouse over the text.

Defining Link Behavior

After you've defined the format, you most likely will want to specify what behavior is initiated when the link is traversed. For example, you could specify that a window is opened, data from different resources is displayed in a separate window, or a program is executed when the user traverses the link.

With XLink, links can be specified to have attributes that are either remote or local. There are differences between the two attributes:

- *Remote resource*—Specifies the role, title show, actuate, and behavior attributes of the link

- *Local resource*—Specifies the content-role and content-title of the link

You should create the link's behavior based on what type of link it is, the resource to which it's connecting, the circumstances under which the user will come across the link, and what options you want to provide the user when the link is traversed. XLink provides some very basic behavioral options for links to meet the needs of some basic common link types.

The link's type is specified with two attributes, **SHOW** and **ACTUATE**. These attributes specify the link's behavior, not the mechanism. According to the XLink specification, any link-processing software is free to devise its own mechanism so it is best suited to a particular user environment and processing mode.

The SHOW Attribute

The **SHOW** attribute defines what will happen after the link has been traversed (clicked). You can assign three different values to the **SHOW** attribute:

- *EMBED*—Signifies that the resource should be embedded for the purpose of displaying or processing in the body of the resource at the exact location where the traversal started. In other words, after the link is clicked, the content of the link will be embedded at the location in which the link was specified. It's like embedding an image.

- *REPLACE*—After the link is traversed, the specified resource should replace the existing resource (in other words, the exiting resource is the location where the link started). The window will be replaced with the new window, just as when an HTML link is clicked.

- *NEW*—Indicates that upon traversal of the link, the designated resource should be displayed or processed in a new context, not affecting the context of the resource where the traversal started. In other words, the window where the link was located will not be replaced, and a new window will be displayed.

The ACTUATE Attribute

The **ACTUATE** attribute is used to specify when a link should be activated. It has two values:

- *AUTO*—Specifies that the resource or Web page should be retrieved when any of the other resources of the same link are encountered. All **AUTO** resources are retrieved in the order specified.

- *USER*—Specifies that the resource specified in the **HREF** attribute (the link, as it were) should not display until the user does something to request it, such as click on a link.

More Linking Attributes In Detail

In addition to the **SHOW** and **ACTUATE** attributes, there are numerous other attributes you can specify to define a simple link. We'll start by creating a linking element, an attribute, and their values. Here's our code snippet:

```
<!ELEMENT SIMPLE ANY>
<!ATTLIST SIMPLE
XML:LINK      CDATA      #FIXED "SIMPLE"
ROLE      CDATA      #IMPLIED
HREF      CDATA      #REQUIRED
TITLE      CDATA      #IMPLIED
INLINE      (TRUE|FALSE)      "TRUE"
CONTENT-ROLE          CDATA      #IMPLIED
CONTENT-TITLE      CDATA      #IMPLIED
SHOW      (EMBED|REPLACE|NEW)      "REPLACE"
ACTUATE      (AUTO|USER)      "USER"
BEHAVIOR      CDATA      #IMPLIED>
```

Probably the easiest way to explain each attribute in the attribute list and the accompanying values is to just go straight down the list. First, we define the element called **SIMPLE** by using the **ANY** notation to specify any and all kinds of markup. Next, we specify the attribute list, tying it to the **SIMPLE** element by specifying the name of the element to which the attribute is associated.

Then, we move on to the actual list of attributes. First, we need to specify that the attribute of this element is a link by declaring it as **XML:LINK**.

WARNING!   *You may have read other books that specify the XML:LINK attribute as xml-link. This was the notation used in the previous XLink specification, but it is now XML:LINK. Remember to keep checking the XLink specification for changes, additions, deletions, and updates on such important changes in syntax.*

Then more attributes are listed. The meaning of each attribute is as follows:

- *ROLE CDATA #IMPLIED*—Specifies the role of the link. The role of a link is what the link means to the application processing it. Because it's implied, it is optional.

- *HREF CDATA #REQUIRED*—Specifies the locator of the link's resource. Because we've specified that it is required, a locator must be indicated.

- *TITLE CDATA #IMPLIED*—Specifies the title you can use for the link. Again, because it's implied, it is optional. You can leave it out and not worry about the XML processor returning an error.

- *INLINE (TRUE\FALSE) "TRUE"*—Specifies that links built on this element are inline links. In a simple link, **INLINE** should always be set to **TRUE**.

- *CONTENT-ROLE CDATA #IMPLIED*—Performs a function similar to **ROLE**, but describes the content to which the locator points rather than the link; also describes the target resource.

- *CONTENT-TITLE CDATA #IMPLIED*—Specifies the **CONTENT-TITLE** for the **CONTENT-ROLE**.

- *SHOW (EMBED\REPLACE\NEW) "REPLACE"*—There are three defaults this attribute can have: **EMBED**, **REPLACE**, or **NEW**. If it's set to **REPLACE**, the window with the content of the linked-to locator is replaced. If the default is set to **EMBED**, the source of the locator is embedded within the current resource, much like the **EMBED** option in HTML. If set to **NEW**, a target resource—such as a window or an additional process that could operate in parallel to the current processing resource—is opened in a new context.

- *ACTUATE (AUTO|USER) "USER"*—Specifies either **AUTO** or **USER**. If the default is set to **USER**, the user must activate the link before it is traversed. If it's set to **AUTO**, the link is traversed by the processing application as soon as the resource is encountered. When you combine the **SHOW** attribute with an **EMBED** value and the **ACTUATE** attribute with **AUTO**, you can create a client-side type that requires the processing application to seek out the resource and include it in the linking element.

- *BEHAVIOR CDATA #IMPLIED*—With **BEHAVIOR**, you can direct the application displaying the XML document how to traverse the link. However, this attribute is not linked to a particular side of the connection.

TIP: *If you need help understanding what some of the terms (such as **#FIXED** or **CDATA**) mean when you are specifying element attributes, review Chapter 8. Chapter 8 gives you a clear understanding of the attribute terminology.*

Now, when we place the following code in our XML document

```
<SIMPLE HREF="http://www.site.com/info.html"
TITLE="A link to the information page."
SHOW="REPLACE" ACTUATE="USER">Click here to get
more information.</SIMPLE>
```

when the user moves his or her mouse over the link, the value of **TITLE**—A link to the information page—displays. Because we've specified the value of the **ACTUATE** attribute to be **"USER"**, the user must first initiate the link by clicking on it. Then, the user's current browser window will be replaced by the contents of the info.html document because we've specified the value of the **SHOW** attribute as **"REPLACE"**.

Extended Links

In this section, we'll show you how extended links work in XML. Extended links offer you a standardized, nonproprietary way to create relationships among different resources. If you've heard of Web rings, you already know how extended links work. A Web ring is a group of Web sites that share a common interest, such as genealogy. The user can move to the next or previous site in the ring. How does all this relate to extended links? Basically, you can use extended links in much the same way. Without using scripting, you can create a group of links to similar sites, a list of links that take the user from one site to another in a progression.

Here's an example of what an extended link looks like:

```
<moviereview XML:LINK="extended" inline="false">
    <locator href="movieinfo" role="Movie"/>
    <locator href="Siskel" role="Review"/>
    <locator href="Ebert" role="Rebuttal"/>
</moviereview>
```

As you can see, an extended link can connect to any number of resources, not just a single resource. And the progression of a link can take the visitor from one site or resource to the next in a logical order. Extended links are all about giving the visitor more choices in terms of links to various resources.

Creating Extended Links

Extended links are created in much the same way standard simple links are created, but instead of specifying "**SIMPLE**" in the **XML:LINK** attribute value, you should specify "**EXTENDED**". Here's the code you would place in the DTD to create an extended link:

```
<!ELEMENT ELINK ANY>
<!ATTLLIST ELINK
XML:LINK      CDATA #FIXED "EXTENDED"
ROLE        CDATA #IMPLIED
TITLE       CDATA #IMPLIED
INLINE      (TRUE|FALSE)"TRUE"
CONTENT-ROLE      CDATA      #IMPLIED
SHOW      (EMBED|REPLACE|NEW)      "REPLACE"
ACTUATE      (AUTO|USER)      "USER"
BEHAVIOR      CDATA      #IMPLIED>
```

Notice that this extended link code is similar to the element and attribute declarations for the simple link. But there are two major differences. The first is that we've specified the **XML:LINK** attribute as "**EXTENDED**", but we've also left out the **HREF** attribute. If we don't specify an **HREF** attribute, how do we specify the multiple link resources? We do so by creating another element that the **EXTENDED** element will rely on to create a subset of link locators. We'll create that element with the name **LOCATOR**, as shown in the following code:

```
<!ELEMENT LOCATOR ANY>
<!ATTLLIST LOCATOR
XML:LINK      CDATA #FIXED "LOCATOR"
ROLE       CDATA #IMPLIED
HREF      CDATA      #REQUIRED
TITLE      CDATA #IMPLIED
SHOW      (EMBED|REPLACE|NEW)      "REPLACE"
```

```
ACTUATE     (AUTO|USER)     "USER"
BEHAVIOR    CDATA     #IMPLIED>                                    \
```

The element we've just defined carries the linking information we need to create the extended link. The **TITLE** attribute specifies the information the browsing visitor will see, whereas the **ROLE** attribute specifies the information that will go to the processing software. When you use this element within a document, you can specify individual **SHOW**, **ACTUATE**, and **BEHAVIOR** values.

Now let's use this element, **ELINK**, within an XML document. To include an extended link, we first specify the first element we created, **ELINK**, and then use the **LOCATOR** element within the **ELINK** hierarchy. Here's an example:

```
<ELINK>Markup Languages
<LOCATOR TITLE="SMGL" HREF="http://www.w3c.org/SGML"/>
<LOCATOR TITLE="HTML" HREF="http://www.w3c.org/HTML"/>
<LOCATOR TITLE="XML" HREF="http://www.w3c.org/XML"/>
</EXTENDED>
```

When the user comes across the document that contains this reference and clicks on the Markup Languages link, the choices could display as a pop-up menu. When one of the menu items is selected, the user is taken to the location specified in the **HREF** attribute. It also links all these resources together so the user can move progressively from one link to the next. And it allows the user to traverse through the links both forward and backward or through the hierarchy in any direction possible.

However, this group of links may be difficult to manage, and the flexibility and possibilities really require more advanced link-management capabilities. XLink provides advanced link-management capabilities through a mechanism called *extended link groups*, which we'll discuss next.

Extended Link Groups

Extended link groups are a special kind of extended links. They are used to store a list of links to other documents. The linked documents constitute an interlinked group. Each document is identified by what is called an *extended link document element*, which actually is a special kind of locator element. These groups, which are actually elements, help manage links by telling the linked documents to check each other for relevant links and by providing a way to create a centralized link storage for sets of related data. The **XML:LINK** attribute value for an extended link group element must be **GROUP**, and the value for an extended link document element must be **DOCUMENT**.

A linking element for an extended link contains a series of child elements that serve as locators. Because an extended link can have more than one remote resource, it separates linking from the mechanisms used to locate each resource.

To define an extended link group, create two elements, one that defines a group and another that identifies the documents within the group. Here's what that declaration would look like:

```
<!ELEMENT GROUP (DOCUMENT*)>
<!ATTLIST GROUP
     XML:LINK CDATA #FIXED "GROUP"
     STEPS CDATA #IMPLIED>

<!ELEMENT DOCUMENT EMPTY>
<!ATTLIST DOCUMENT
     XML:LINK  CDATA  #FIXED  "DOCUMENT"
     HREF      CDATA  #REQUIRED>
```

Notice that, aside from the **HREF** and **XML:LINK** attributes, the only thing you need to really declare in the element is the **STEPS** attribute. The **STEPS** attribute tells the processing application how many layers of links it should follow before stopping on its search for the various related links. Use the **DOCUMENT** element to contain the link resources that will take the processing application to the documents that contain the links and that need to be searched.

The processing application will then check those documents for links to the original document and, in turn, build a table of links. You shouldn't specify large numbers in the **STEPS** value. If you do, the processing application will take a long time to load the document. For example, if a group of documents is organized in a single main document that contains all the out-of-line links, it would be better to have each nonhub document contain an extended link group that contains only one reference to the hub document. The **STEPS** attribute can be used by a developer to help deal with the situation where an extended link group directs application software to another document that contains an extended link group of its own. To use steps within a document, you would declare the following code, based on the previously defined extended link elements:

```
<GROUP STEPS=1>
<DOCUMENT HREF="http://www.w3c.org"/>
<DOCUMENT HREF="http://www.w3c.org/XML"/>
<DOCUMENT HREF="http://www.w3c.org/XML/XLink"/>
<DOCUMENT HREF="http://www.w3c.org/XML/XLink/Design"/>
</GROUP>
```

When the XML processor runs across this code, which could be stored in a document called xmlfiles.xml, the processor will first open the main W3C index, then the XML file, then the XLink file, and finally the design file. When these files are parsed, the parser will determine if there are any links to the main xmlfiles.xml document. If you didn't specify this code, the browsing visitor would see only those links that originated in the main xmlfiles.xml document. All links are centralized through this one main file in a hublike fashion.

Immediate Solutions

XLink uses very specific notation schemes to include links in XML documents. Incorrect notation will lead to broken and invalid XML documents. XML links rely heavily on the syntax for creating elements, attributes, and entities. To review these subjects, revisit Chapters 7, 8, and 12. In the following examples, we'll show you how to go from creating simple links to creating complex extended links.

Creating A Simple XML Link

A simple XML link takes the following syntax:

```
<ELEMENT XML:LINK="SIMPLE" HREF="URI">...</ELEMENT>
```

<ELEMENT> can be any element formally identified in the document's DTD. However, the **XML:LINK** attribute doesn't have to be defined as one of the element's attributes in an attribute declaration list because it is reserved for XML linking; neither does the **HREF** attribute, for the same reason. In fact, none of the XLink-specific attributes must be declared as attributes for an element that is going to act as a linking element. Technically, this means that you don't really need to plan for an element to be a linking element. Any element can become a linking element by adding the XLink attributes and values. However, we recommend that you decide in advance which elements are linking elements. Whether an element is a linking element might influence the other attributes it will take as well as its content rules.

Note that the **XML:LINK** attribute has its value defined as **SIMPLE**; hence, the link's classification as a simple link. Other link types include:

• *DOCUMENT*—Indicates that the link points to an extended link document.

• *EXTENDED*—Indicates that the link is an out-of-line or extended link.

• *GROUP*—Indicates that the link is an extended link group.

• *LOCATOR*—Indicates that the link is a locator that points to a resource.

Of the four, **EXTENDED** is the only actual linking element, whereas the other three provide support in extended link collections. These link types are discussed in more detail in "Creating An Extended XML Link" later in this Immediate Solutions section.

To create a simple link, you must first declare it as a link in the element declaration. To do so, create an element as you normally would, but specify the **XML:LINK** attribute. To create a simple link, follow these steps:

1. Start by declaring the element in your DTD or XML document, as shown in the following code:

```
<!ELEMENT SIMPLE ANY>
```

2. Next, specify the link attributes, making sure you define the first attribute as a link by using the **XML:LINK** attribute and specifying the value as "**SIMPLE**":

```
<!ATTLIST SIMPLE
XML:LINK      CDATA      #FIXED      "SIMPLE"
```

3. After the **XML:LINK** declaration, specify the **HREF** attribute:

```
HREF      CDATA      #REQUIRED
```

4. Following the **HREF** attribute, which signifies that this is a simple link instead of an extended link, specify the additional attributes:

```
TITLE        CDATA       #IMPLIED
INLINE       (TRUE|FALSE)        "TRUE"
CONTENT-ROLE            CDATA        #IMPLIED
CONTENT-TITLE      CDATA       #IMPLIED
SHOW       (EMBED|REPLACE|NEW)       "REPLACE"
ACTUATE       (AUTO|USER)       "USER"
BEHAVIOR       CDATA       #IMPLIED>
```

Using A Simple Link In The Document

To use the link in a document, specify the link by placing the **XML:LINK** attribute in the start-tag of the element, as shown in the following code:

```
<mylink XML:LINK="simple" title="Information on XML"
    href="http://www.site.com/info.xml" show="new"
    content-role="Reference">This is my link to XML.</mylink>
```

You can include any data you want, but you must specify the **XML:LINK** attribute, because its value is **FIXED**. All other elements, whose values are **#IMPLIED**, are optional.

Specifying A Link's Role

A link's meaning, or role, is defined by the **ROLE** attribute. Even the resources within a link can have individual and separate roles. Generally, the value of the **ROLE** attribute serves to provide more information about the relationship between the link's resources. It is specifically meant to be read, interpreted, and used by the application parsing and processing the XML document. Because the resources and the relationships between them will be different in every XML document, the **ROLE** attribute doesn't have a set of predetermined values. Instead, it is left to the DTD developer to establish meaningful and useful roles based on the resources with which the DTD works. In addition, the value of the **ROLE** attribute can be used as part of a search mechanism to provide more accurate results when large document collections are searched. A link's role is expressed using this syntax:

```
<ELEMENT XML:LINK="SIMPLE" HREF="URI" ROLE="ROLE">...</ELEMENT>
```

If our W3C **<RESOURCE>** link needed to be described as a general Web resource as opposed to an XML-specific resource (like **http://www.w3.org/XML** might be), its link might look like this:

```
<RESOURCE XML:LINK="SIMPLE" HREF="http://www.w3.org"
   ROLE="GENERAL-WEB">W3C</RESOURCE>
```

Controlling Link Behavior

Link behavior describes how and when a link is traversed and works with simple links as well as extended links. An HTML link can have user-invoked and replacing behavior. HTML links cannot be activated without a click from the user, and unless they are specified by the **<TARGET>** element, the contents of the linked resource generally replace the contents of the page where the link was initiated. XML provides a bit more flexibility via the **ACTUATE** and **SHOW** attributes.

The **ACTUATE** attribute specifies if the link is to be activated by the user or traversed as soon as it's found. The values for each of these actions are, respectively:

- **USER**

- **AUTO**

If the W3C link from the previous examples should only be activated by a user, it would take this code:

```
<RESOURCE XML:LINK="SIMPLE"  HREF="http://www.w3.org" ROLE="GENERAL-WEB"
   ACTUATE="USER">W3C</RESOURCE>
```

If, however, it should be traversed as soon as the parser or browser comes in contact with it, the code would be as follows:

```
<RESOURCE XML:LINK="SIMPLE"  HREF="http://www.w3.org" ROLE="GENERAL-WEB"
   ACTUATE="AUTO">W3C</RESOURCE>
```

The **SHOW** attribute controls how linked resources are both processed and displayed. It can have the following values:

- *INCLUDE*—Indicates that the target resource should be embedded directly into the body of the resource where the traversal began.

- *NEW*—Indicates that the target resource should be displayed in a new area (window, frame, and so on) and that the state of the resource where the transversal began shouldn't change.

- *REPLACE*—Indicates that the target resource should replace the resource where the traversal began. This is how standard HTML links function.

By combining the **ACTUATE="USER"** and **SHOW="NEW"** attributes and values in the following code, the link is set to open the W3C's home page in a new window:

```
<RESOURCE XML-LINK="SIMPLE" HREF="http://www.w3.org" ROLE="GENERAL-WEB"
   ACTUATE="USER" SHOW="NEW">W3C</RESOURCE>
```

If, however, those attributes were changed to **ACTUATE="AUTO"** and **SHOW="INCLUDE"**, the contents of the W3C's Web site would be directly embedded into the document where the link traversal began. Snippets of XML markup can be combined into one large XML document automatically by using this attribute combination. It is also useful for automatically embedding header and footer information into documents.

Labeling A Link

Just as the **ROLE** attribute provides a machine-readable identifier for a link, the **TITLE** attribute provides a human-readable one. The XML **TITLE** attribute is just like the HTML **TITLE** attribute and is added to a link using this syntax:

```
<ELEMENT XML:LINK="SIMPLE" HREF="URI" ROLE="ROLE"
    SHOW="(INCLUDE|NEW|REPLACE)"
    ACTUATE="(USER|AUTO)" TITLE="TITLE">...</ELEMENT>
```

To add a title of *The World Wide Web Consortium's home page* to our rapidly growing link, we would use this XML code:

```
<RESOURCE XML:LINK="SIMPLE" HREF="http://www.w3.org" ROLE="GENERAL-WEB"
    ACTUATE="USER" SHOW="NEW"
    TITLE="The World Wide Web Consortium's home page">W3C</RESOURCE>
```

Predefining Link Attributes And Values For Elements In The DTD

As discussed in previous sections, it's a good idea to know which of your elements will be linking elements. To facilitate the creation of links in an XML document, you can include any or all of the linking attributes in an element's attribute list declaration. When you include the linking attributes in the element's attribute list declaration, you can specify how these attributes will be used to control the links specified when using the element. For example, you can use the **XML:LINK** attribute in an element's attribute declaration list and include with it a fixed value of "**SIMPLE**", using this syntax:

```
<!ATTLIST ELEMENT
XML:LINK CDATA #FIXED "SIMPLE">
```

This attribute declaration indicates that the *ELEMENT* can take the **XML:LINK** attribute of type "**SIMPLE**" whose content is **CDATA**. Because the type is fixed, simple links made from this element must always be simple. If the element is used as a linking element in an extended resource, the document will be invalid. This presents yet another argument for planning your linking elements ahead of time. In the **<RESOURCE>** element example from the previous section, the link attribute can be affixed to the element by using this code:

```
<!ATTLIST RESOURCE
XML:LINK CDATA #FIXED "SIMPLE">
```

A link is now made with the **<RESOURCE>** element as the linking element in
this way:

```
<RESOURCE HREF="http://www.w3.org">W3C</RESOURCE>
```

About the only difference in the XML markup now is that the **XML:
LINK="SIMPLE"** attribute-value pair is missing. Still, if you're planning on making lots of links, the less typing you'll need to do, the better. If you use this convention, simple XML links begin to look much like HTML links, except of course
the linking elements are different.

Other attributes can also be fixed to ensure that a locator is named and default
values for the **SHOW** and **ACTUATE** attributes are set. This code specifies that,
in addition to a fixed simple link status, the **<RESOURCE>** element has a required **HREF** attribute, a required **ROLE** attribute, and the default values **EM-
BED** and **AUTO** specified for the required **SHOW** and **ACTUATE** attributes:

```
<!ATTLIST RESOURCE
XML-LINK CDATA #FIXED "SIMPLE"
HREF CDATA #REQUIRED
ROLE CDATA #REQUIRED
SHOW (EMBED|REPLACE|NEW) #REQUIRED "EMBED"
ACTUATE (AUTO|USER) #REQUIRED "AUTO">
```

Notice that the **TITLE** attribute is not included in this attribute declaration. Even
so, the document developer can still include it in the link as a valid attribute,
because it is predefined as a linking attribute even though it wasn't explicitly
defined in the element's attribute list.

Creating An Extended XML Link

Extended links are made possible by XLink's support of out-of-line links. Link
management and multidirectional linking are facilitated by XLink's ability to store
links in a document (or resource) that isn't actually part of any of the links listed
in the document. You can create and maintain a single linking document that
describes all the links in a set of documents, making the links easy to check, edit,
and update as necessary. Use the following syntax to create extended links:

```
<ELEMENT XML:LINK="EXTENDED">
    <ELEMENT XML:LINK="LOCATOR" HREF="URI" />
    <ELEMENT XML:LINK="LOCATOR" HREF="URI" />
    <ELEMENT XML:LINK="LOCATOR" HREF="URI" />
    ...
</ELEMENT>
```

The **<ELEMENT>** that is marked as an extended link must contain one or more **<ELEMENT>** tags that use a different linking element and actually provide the resource information. Imagine an extended link element called **<REFERENCE>** that takes locator elements of the type **<RESOURCE>**. Some XML linking code built with these two elements might look like this:

```
<REFERENCE XML:LINK="EXTENDED">
    <RESOURCE XML:LINK="LOCATOR" HREF="http://www.w3.org">
    <RESOURCE XML:LINK="LOCATOR" HREF="http://www.xml.com">
    <RESOURCE XML:LINK="LOCATOR" HREF="http://www.datachannel.com">
</REFERENCE>
```

This markup creates a set of extended XML links that link to a set of HTML resources. The XML document that contains the link listing isn't necessarily part of the links themselves—it is just a storage unit. Of course, how extended links are displayed and handled is ultimately up to the application that processes the XML documents. **ROLE**, **ACUATE**, **SHOW**, and **TITLE** attributes can also be added to the locator elements to provide the processor with more information about how to deal with the links.

Linking attributes can be included in the attribute declaration lists for linking elements of extended links just as they can for simple links. Using this approach, the attribute declaration list for the **<REFERENCE>** and **<RESOURCE>** elements might look like this:

```
<!ATTLIST REFERENCE
    XML:LINK CDATA #FIXED "EXTENDED">
<!ATTLIST RESOURCE
    XML:LINK CDATA #FIXED "LOCATOR"
    HREF CDATA #REQUIRED>
```

With these attribute lists in place, the previous example of an extended link list would look like this:

```
<REFERENCE>
    <RESOURCE HREF="http://www.w3.org">
    <RESOURCE HREF="http://www.xml.com">
    <RESOURCE HREF="http://www.datachannel.com">
</REFERENCE>
```

In addition, to ensure that one or more **<RESOURCE>** elements were included as content for each instance of the **<REFERENCE>** element, the **<REFERENCE>** element's content specification might use this code:

```
<!ELEMENT REFERENCE (RESOURCE)+
```

Extended links take three attributes:

- *INLINE*—Indicates that the linking element is one of the link's resources; takes the values **TRUE** or **FALSE**. The default is **FALSE**.
- *CONTENT-TITLE*—Provides role information for the linking element when it is one of the link's resources.
- *CONTENT-ROLE*—Provides title information for the linking element when it is one of the link's resources.

When you create an extended link, you need to declare the element as well as the attribute list. If you want to create an extended link group, you need to specify the locator group next. Follow these steps to create an extended link:

1. Start by declaring the element in your DTD or XML document, as shown in the following code:

```
<!ELEMENT EXTENDED ANY>
```

2. Next, specify the link attributes, making sure you define the first attribute as a link by using the **XML:LINK** attribute and specifying the value as **"EXTENDED"**:

```
<!ATTLIST SIMPLE
XML:LINK     CDATA     #FIXED "EXTENDED"
```

3. After the **XML:LINK** declaration, specify the additional attributes, making sure you don't include the **HREF** attribute:

```
TITLE     CDATA     #IMPLIED
INLINE     (TRUE|FALSE)     "TRUE"
CONTENT-ROLE     CDATA     #IMPLIED
CONTENT-TITLE     CDATA     #IMPLIED
SHOW     (EMBED|REPLACE|NEW)     "REPLACE"
ACTUATE     (AUTO|USER)     "USER"
BEHAVIOR     CDATA     #IMPLIED>
```

4. Next, create an element and attribute that specifies the locator for the group of resources:

```
<!ELEMENT LOCATOR ANY>
<!ATTLLIST LOCATOR
XML:LINK      CDATA #FIXED "LOCATOR"
ROLE       CDATA #IMPLIED
HREF       CDATA      #REQUIRED
TITLE      CDATA #IMPLIED
SHOW      (EMBED|REPLACE|NEW)     "REPLACE"
ACTUATE     (AUTO|USER)      "USER"
BEHAVIOR     CDATA      #IMPLIED>
```

Creating Extended Link Groups And Documents

An extended link group is nothing more than a list of documents that identify the
documents in which extended link sets are stored. The **GROUP** linking element
takes one or more **DOCUMENT** linking elements in much the same way **EX-
TENDED** and **LOCATOR** work together. Here is the syntax:

```
<ELEMENT XML:LINK="GROUP">
    <ELEMENT XML:LINK="DOCUMENT" HREF="URI" />
    <ELEMENT XML:LINK="DOCUMENT" HREF="URI" />
    <ELEMENT XML:LINK="DOCUMENT" HREF="URI" />
    ...
</ELEMENT>
```

XML code that uses the **<LINKS>** element as the extended linking element and
the **<DOC>** element as the **DOCUMENT** linking element might look like this:

```
<LINKS XML:LINK="GROUP">
    <DOC XML:LINK="DOCUMENT" HREF="extended1.xml">
    <DOC XML:LINK="DOCUMENT" HREF="extended2.xml">
    <DOC XML:LINK="DOCUMENT" HREF="extended3.xml">
</LINKS>
```

The **GROUP** and **DOCUMENT** link types can be assigned to elements in attribute
list declarations, as we've shown with the **SIMPLE**, **EXTENDED**, and **LOCA-
TOR** types. Assigning the **GROUP** and **DOCUMENT** link types to the **<LINKS>**
and **<DOC>** elements in the preceding example would condense the XML to:

```
<LINKS>
    <DOC HREF="extended1.xml">
    <DOC HREF="extended2.xml">
    <DOC HREF="extended3.xml">
</LINKS>
```

You can use standard DTD mechanisms and XLink to create an application-specific or document-specific linking specification. Because XML linking is so new, no real-life examples were available to show the extended link mechanism at work, so you'll just have to use your imagination (and since it's the most powerful tool you have, you're off to a good start).

Remapping Attributes

Attribute remapping allows you to alter existing XLink attributes if they interfere with attributes already established in your DTD, which is achieved in this manner in an element's attribute declaration list:

```
<!ATTLIST ELEMENT
      XML-ATTRIBUTES CDATA #FIXED "XML-ATTRIBUTE NEW-NAME">
```

The remapping is linked to the element, so it only applies to the individual element whose attribute list it occurs in. Therefore, if you wanted to change the name of the **SHOW** attribute to **INITIATE** for use with the **<RESOURCE>** element, you would use this code:

```
<!ATTLIST RESOURCE
      XML-ATTRIBUTES CDATA #FIXED "SHOW INITIATE">
```

It's really that simple. If you need to remap an XLink attribute in several different elements, you might want to consider using a parameter entity for quick and accurate results. To create a parameter entity from the preceding example for remapping, you would use this code:

```
<!ENTITY % show-remap 'XML-ATTRIBUTES CDATA #FIXED "SHOW INITIATE"'>
```

To include the attribute remapping in the **<RESOURCE>** element attribute declaration list, as well as in the **<REVIEW>** and **<TRAINING>** elements also found in the same fictional DTD, you would use this code:

```
<!ATTLIST RESOURCE %show-remap>
<!ATTLIST REVIEW %show-remap>
<!ATTLIST TRAINING %show-remap>
```

For a refresher on creating parameter entities, review Chapter 12, and for a discussion of using parameter entities with attributes, turn to Chapter 8.

Chapter 11

References Within Links: XPointers

By Natanya Pitts-Moultis and Cheryl Kirk

In Depth

Because pointing to various locations in documents can actually become rather complex, the World Wide Web Consortium (W3C) decided to create a separate but complementary piece to XLink that could specify fragments of documents. This complementary piece is called *XPointers*. XPointers are much more than just simple links. Basically, XPointers are references to locations within documents, much like you might find in HTML with the anchor tag and its accompanying **#NAME** reference.

As a matter of fact, XPointers are so much more extensive than simple links that the W3C decided to create an XPointer language, complete with its own specification. The XML pointer language, XPointer, was created to provide a way for the locators in XML links to point to specific places within resources. XPointers let the developer designate various resources by using terms that specify locations in documents or resources.

TIP: *The best way to learn about XPointers is to read the W3C's XPointer specification. You can find it at **www.w3.org/TR/1998/WD-xptr-19980303**. Although we cover much of the same information about XPointers in this chapter as the recommendation does, you should at least skim through the recommendation in case changes have been made.*

The places XPointers can identify go beyond sections identified by an **ID** or **NAME** attribute to those described by content, parent/child relationships, and more. XPointers add infinite value to the XLink mechanism, because they provide a degree of linking accuracy that is necessary for the robust documents described by XML. Without XPointers, you wouldn't be able to reference multiple resources within XML documents. In essence, XPointers are fragment identifiers that point to sub-resources of resources.

WARNING!   Don't confuse standard search engine query languages with the XPointer language. XPointers do not provide a mechanism for defining any type of query that would allow a user to retrieve information found in XML documents. XPointers do offer some options that may appear to refer to specific locations in documents, but the links created with XPointers are intended to focus on the actual location to which the XPointer refers and not on any type of query for finding references.

How XPointers Work

To understand how XPointers work, let's first consider how linking works in HTML. With HTML linking, you can do the following:

- Link to an entire Web page
- Link to a section of a Web page using the **#NAME** value of the **<A HREF>** element and attribute

But what do you do when you want to link to actual content within a document and not just a placeholder? With HTML, you're limited to only those two choices: pointing to an entire document or referencing a placeholder. If you wanted to point the browsing visitor to the fourth item in a list, for example, you need some sort of mechanism to reference content, not just locations.

With XML, you can create tree structures for documents, so you can easily create identifiers that you can use to help the visitor navigate to exactly what you want them to see. With XPointers, you can create such navigational controls by simply adding the location of the referenced content to the end of a URL (after the **#**). To do so, you must first define keywords and arguments. The syntax would look something like this:

```
keyword1(arg1,arg2).keyword2(arg1,arg2)
```

For example, if you want to link to the fourth item in a list (a list that offers a unique identifier called **seattle-hotspots**), you would specify the following link by using XPointer references:

```
href="http://www.site.com/seattle.xml#id(seattle-hotspots).child(4,item)"
```

Why would a separate language be created just for reference locating in links? Mainly to provide a more robust linking mechanism. If, for example, the actual list moves from **www.site.com** to **www.mysite.com**, the link will still be operational within the document.

XPointers And Locators

An XPointer can contain one or two locators. Using XPointers is very much like using fragment identifiers in HTML; they point to a section in a document or within a resource. The XPointer specification defines an XPointer as a sequence of *location terms* that are interpreted from left to right. When you specify an XPointer, the location you are specifying forms a kind of tree structure, much like the overall XML document into which you are placing the XPointer.

TIP: *XPointers are based on the Text Encoding Initiative Guidelines (TEIP3), upon which the entire XLink language is based. If you want to learn more about the mechanics behind XPointers, read through the TEI Guidelines. You can find them on the World Wide Web Consortium's Web site at* ***www.w3.org***.

XPointers aren't just simple references to subresources within documents. They can be a variety of types of links:

- Links that point to a place inside a document even if the document doesn't have an ID at the place to which you want to link

- Addressing to elements, character strings, and sections inside documents

- A clear syntax for defining locations and relationships in hierarchies in an effort to make the links readable by humans

The XPointer itself consists of a list of location terms that are basically used to address resources. Each item within the list specifies a location that is usually relative to the location specified by the prior location term. This is the reason XPointers create a kind of tree structure akin to XML documents. It's also the reason XPointers allow you to specify a precise location. XPointers aren't just individual links. Instead, they branch from a single root location. Each location is specified by a keyword (such as id, child, or ancestor). The keyword defines the location of the referencing material. Each term used as the keyword specifies a location, and that location can be relative to the prior location, if any, that has already been specified.

Each keyword can have arguments, such as an instance number, element type, or attribute. For example, the location term **child(2,MARKER)** refers to the second child element whose type is **MARKER**. Another example from the XPointer recommendation includes a location term **child(2,CHAP)** that refers to the second child element whose type is **CHAP**.

The easiest way to understand XPointers is to simply think of them as a kind of language you can add to the end of a URL, as you might in HTML, by adding a # after the URL and before the XPointer. But keep in mind that XPointers can actually build on themselves to make complex linking structures and that XPointers work with the standard Uniform Resource Identifier (URI) specifications that are at work every day on the Internet. If you've created URLs before, you shouldn't have trouble with URIs in XPointers.

XPointer Keywords

Let's take a look at the various types of keywords you'll use when creating an XPointer. You can use the following keywords within XPointers to specify a particular item within the hierarchy of the XPointer structure:

- *child*—Identifies direct child nodes of the location source

- *descendant*—Identifies nodes appearing anywhere within the content of the location source

- *ancestor*—Identifies element nodes containing the location source

- *preceding*—Identifies nodes that appear before (preceding) the location source

- *following*—Identifies nodes that appear after (following) the location source

- *psibling*—Identifies sibling nodes (sharing their parent with the location source) that appear before (preceding) the location source

- *fsibling*—Identifies sibling nodes (sharing their parent with the location source) that appear after (following) the location source

You can use these keywords in an XPointer to locate individual nodes in an element tree or a string matching a portion of a node. If you leave out one of these keywords when you define an XPointer, the XPointer is treated as if it contained the preceding keyword. However, you must not omit a keyword from the first location term of any XPointer, even if the XPointer is embedded within another XPointer.

When you specify an XPointer, you do so with the following type of code:

```
child(2,SECTION).(1,SUBSECTION)
```

Let's take this a little further. For example, the following code, which you'll find outlined in the XPointer specification, identifies the 29th paragraph of the 4th subdivision of the 3rd major division of the location source:

```
child(3,DIV1).child(4,DIV2).child(29,P)
```

As you can see, the key ingredient in an XPointer is its *location term*, or basic addressing information unit. Location terms can be combined to provide a highly specific locator for an XML link. Location terms can be defined in many ways, including:

- *Absolute location*—The keywords described in an absolute location do not require the existence of or dependence on a location source. Instead, absolute locations can be used to establish a source that can serve as a self-contained XPointer.

- *Relative location*—The keywords described in a relative location depend on the existence of a location source. If you don't specify one, the location source is then considered the root element of the containing resource.

- *Spanning location*—The spanning location locates a subresource starting at the beginning of the data selected by its first argument and continues through to the end of the data selected by its second argument.

- *Attribute location*—The attribute location takes only an attribute name as a selector and returns the attribute's value.

- *String location*—The string location selects one or more strings or positions between strings in the location source.

In this chapter's Immediate Solutions section, several of the projects that focus on defining location terms are based on each of these types. Before we get too far along, let's take a quick look at how an XPointer looks within a DTD. In this example, taken from the XPointer specification itself, we define various elements and attributes that will then be used with the XPointer we will declare. The DTD looks something like this:

```
<!DOCTYPE SPEECH [
  <!ELEMENT SPEECH (#PCDATA|SPEAKER|DIRECTION)*>
  <!ATTLIST SPEECH
         ID      ID      #IMPLIED>
  <!ELEMENT SPEAKER (#PCDATA)>
  <!ELEMENT DIRECTION (#PCDATA)>
  ]>
  <SPEECH ID="a27"><SPEAKER>Polonius</SPEAKER>
  <DIRECTION>crossing downstage</DIRECTION>Fare you well,
  my lord. <DIRECTION>To Ros.</DIRECTION>
  You go to seek Lord Hamlet? There he is.</SPEECH>
```

That means the following XPointers can select various subresources. For example:

- **id(a27).child(2,DIRECTION)**—Selects the second **DIRECTION** element. The content for this element is **To Ros**.

- **id(a27).child(2,#element)**—Selects the second child element. In this example, that would be the first direction, and that direction's content is **crossing downstage**.

- **id(a27).child(2,#text)**—Selects the second text region, which contains, **Fare you well, my lord**.

XPointer Design Guidelines

The developers of the XPointer specification knew they were creating a companion recommendation to work with XLink. To that end, they defined the following language design goals:

- *XPointers shall address into XML documents.* XPointers shall offer some form of interoperability between the client and server. Handling of strings should work not only across servers and documents, but also across countries, providing internationalization within the XPointer itself.

- *XPointers shall be straightforwardly usable over the Internet.* This means XPointers should be understandable when read by humans, and that XPointers references should be capable of being used and linked to over the Internet.

- *XPointers shall be straightforwardly usable in URIs.* XPointers should be used with URIs as part of an XLink used within a document. Also, you should keep XPointers simple and avoid any additional references that would refer to or allow for access directly into a URI.

- *The XPointer design shall be prepared quickly.* XPointers should be simple enough to be developed as quickly as possible.

- *The XPointer design shall be formal and concise.* Your XPointers should be constructed so they are self-contained and yet concise enough to specify the various locations you want to address in an XML document. In other words, your XPointer code shouldn't be sloppy or include extra elements or attributes.

- *The XPointer syntax shall be reasonably compact and human readable.* XPointers should not be lengthy in their declaration, and they should fit neatly into an XML attribute value. More importantly, the XPointer reference should be easily understood by the general XML user, and the reader should be able to interpret it just by looking at it.

- *XPointers shall be optimized for usability.* This is probably one of the most important concepts of XPointers. Your XPointer should easily mimic the way people think about finding information in a document. This may mean the XPointer actually references a single location multiple ways, as the user might if he or she were referencing the location.

- *XPointers must be feasible to implement.* Although the W3C understands that XPointers can become relatively complex, the entire goal is that the XPointer language is easy to implement in existing and new XML documents.

Notice that several of XPointer's language design goals are similar to those of XLink—they shall be prepared quickly and be feasible to implement. This cooperation among recommendations is important, because a large majority of your XML links will include XPointers. By following the design goals, you'll make your XML documents, links, and their pointers easier to understand and implement if other developers must work with your code.

TIP: *The language design goals list was taken from the XPointer working draft, edited by Eve Maler and Steve DeRose. They frequently contribute to the XML-Dev newsgroup and the site, XML.com. You can find many of their writings by checking www.xml.com.*

Immediate Solutions

In this section, you'll learn how to reference document fragments by using the XPointer language. You'll learn how to extend simple links into something much more sophisticated by using XPointers. Make sure you pay special attention to the code, because XPointers use different notations to indicate the fragments of links. Remember, however, that XPointers can't work without links; XPointers are an integral part of links. So if you haven't read about XLinks in Chapter 10, you should go back and read that chapter before reading this section.

Adding A Simple XPointer To An XML Link

To extend XML's **HREF** attribute to include XPointers, simply follow the URI with either the pound sign (#) or the vertical bar (|) and the pointer.

Both characters (# and |) indicate that what follows is an XPointer looking for a fragment identifier. The XPointer looks for the fragment or subresource inside of the containing resource defined by the URI locator, and the XPointer identifies the fragment as the true destination of the link. If a URI doesn't precede the # or | characters, the XPointer syntax assumes that the containing resource is the document that contains the XPointer. This is like the **<A NAME="top"></A>** marker in an HTML page called by the **<A HREF="#top">** anchor.

In general, any fragment identifier that follows the # or | character is treated as an XPointer and can be expressed in the XPointer notation. However, the pound sign (#) is an HTML-type connector, while the vertical bar (|) is an XML-specific connector. If the pound sign is present, the entire containing resource is delivered to the client, and it's up to the client to figure out how to process it. If the vertical bar is present, the processing application doesn't necessarily have to deliver the entire containing resource but instead can send just the subresource. This method provides for a quicker download of materials across a network, but it is restricted to XML resources.

A simple XPointer uses the pound sign followed by an XPointer that is the equivalent of a unique ID assigned to an element within the containing resource. For example, this code

```
<RESOURCE HREF="http://www.w3.org/Consortium/Legal/ipr-notice.html
    #Legal Disclaimer">
```

would point to the element marked with the **ID="Legal Disclaimer"** attribute within the **http://www.w3.org/Constortium/Legal/ipr-notice.html** document. Most likely, the **ipr-notice.html** document would be loaded into a display window and the "Legal Disclaimer" section brought into focus.

If this link code had used a vertical bar connector instead of the pound sign, as in the following code, it might have brought up only the disclaimer section instead of the entire document:

```
<RESOURCE HREF="http://www.w3.org/Consortium/Legal/ipr-notice.html
    |Legal Disclaimer">
```

The ultimate fate of the link would be determined by the XML processing application, of course, but imagine how powerful this excerpt retrieving tool could be when combined with the **<ACTUATE>** and **<SHOW>** elements of the link. Abstracts, titles, and other bits of information from a large group of documents could be collected and automatically displayed in a single document via a collection of links. The potential for outlining and mapping are enormous.

Of course, this method requires that elements within an XML document have assigned IDs. This is as good a time as any to get into the habit of assigning unique IDs to every major section of your documents and keeping a record of them so linking with XPointers will be easy to implement at any time.

Creating XPointers With Absolute Location Terms

It's entirely possible that a simple XPointer won't do the trick for you. Location terms use several different methods to describe elements within a resource. Absolute location terms describe fragment locations based on fixed positions within a document. An absolute location XPointer always begins with one of the following:

- *ROOT( )*—Indicates the origin of the initial location source in the document's root element. This is the default absolute location term.

- *HERE( )*—Indicates that the origin of the initial location source is the linking element containing the locator. This only works if the XPointer is pointing at a fragment in the current document.

- *ID(NAME)*—Indicates that the origin of the initial location source is an element with an **ID** of *NAME*.

- *DITTO( )*—In a pair of XPointers, indicates that the initial location source is the same as it is in the previous pointer.

- *HTML(NAMEVALUE)*—Indicates that the initial location source is the first anchor element with a value of *NAMEVALUE*.

Absolute location terms are just the beginning of XPointers. Once you've told the pointer where to start looking, you can use a combination of other location term types to be more specific about the fragment's location. The remaining sections of this chapter provide specific information on each type of location term.

Creating XPointers With Relative Location Terms

Relative location terms help you move around a document from the initial location source defined by an absolute term. A relative location term is created by using a keyword in combination with a number of steps, according to this syntax:

```
keyword(steps)
```

Keywords are used to limit the possible matching targets to a select few and then work with them. Elements that match the keyword are called candidates. Possible keywords include the following:

- *child*—Indicates child elements of the location source

- *descendant*—Indicates any elements contained within the location source

- *ancestor*—Indicates any elements the location source is contained within

- *preceding*—Indicates any elements that come before the location source

- *following*—Indicates any elements that come after the location source

- *psibling*—Indicates any sibling elements (share the same parent) that come before the location source

- *fsibling*—Indicates any sibling elements that come after the location source

Steps can take either a positive or negative number and indicate which direction to go from each candidate to ascertain if it is a final match. Positive counts forward from the first candidate location, and negative counts backward from the last candidate notation. The value **ALL** can also be used to select all candidate locations. For example, **(8)** indicates that the eighth candidate from the first should be selected, and **(-8)** means the eighth candidate before the last should be selected.

The step number is then followed by a comma and an element type of the following values:

- ***CDATA**—Indicates pseudoelements containing text

- *****—Indicates any element type

- **.**—Indicates only elements

- *NAME*—Indicates only elements of type *NAME*

So, **(8, LINK)** means select the eighth instance of all **LINK** candidates, and **(-2, *CDATA)** means choose the next-to-the-last plain text section from the candidate. Element types can be further described by attribute name and value information. The attribute name can be:

- *NAME*—Indicates an attribute of the name *NAME*

- *****—Indicates any attribute name

Element values can be:

- *NAME*—Indicates a value of *NAME*

- *"value"*—Indicates a quoted value

- ***IMPLIED**—Indicates attributes that have no specified value or default values

- *****—Indicates any value

Put all of these possible pieces together and you can come up with some pretty extensive XPointers. For example,

```
ROOT( )DESCENDANT(2, P, ALIGN, "LEFT")
```

is a pointer to all descendant elements of the second **P** element with an attribute of **ALIGN="LEFT"**.

Creating XPointers With Spanning Location Terms

The **SPAN** keyword used with XPointers is created by using absolute and relative terms to describe a subresource based on its start- and end-points. The syntax is:

```
SPAN(XPointer, Xpointer)
```

So, this XPointer

```
ID(BODY).span(descendant(CHAPT-TITLE), descendant(CHAPT-AUTHOR))
```

selects the information contained between the descendant **<CHAPT-TITLE>** and **</CHAPT-AUTHOR>** elements within the element with an ID of **BODY**.

Creating XPointers With String Location Terms

Finally, XPointers can also include a **STRING( )** keyword as their last location term to specify text within an element as the target of the pointer. The string keyword includes these three specifications, which must be included each time a string is used:

- *STEPS*—A required argument that specifies which occurrence of the string should be matched

- *STRING*—A character string that indicates the string to be matched

- *NUMBER*—The number of characters to count forward from the beginning of a matched string

The following code points to the letter *o* (15 characters in) in the fourth instance of the phrase **Just because you can...** in the **P** element with the ID **P5**:

```
ID(P5)STRING(4, "Just because you can...",15)
```

The string keyword only selects a single character. If you want to select an entire phrase, you would have to use a span, as described in the preceding section.

Because advanced XPointers are necessarily complex, look for a new wave of XPointer software to supply point-and-click or drag-and-drop pointer creation.

Chapter 12

Creating And Including XML Entities

By Natanya Pitts-Moultis

In Depth

An *entity* is a powerful XML tool that allows DTD and document developers to associate a text alias with non-ASCII text or binary resources and large or frequently used blocks of text and markup. Document Type Definitions (DTDs) that take advantage of the entity mechanism are well organized, easier to read and work with, and able to support literally thousands of nonstandard characters. Without entities, binary resources, such as image and audio files, cannot be included in Extensible Markup Language (XML) documents.

In this chapter, we'll examine the different kinds of entities XML supports and the crucial role each plays in DTD development. The Immediate Solutions section of this chapter provides instructions for constructing each kind of entity as well as a complete listing of the entities that are used in XML documents to include the most common special characters defined in the ISO-Latin-1 character set.

What Is An Entity?

An entity is essentially a unit of storage. In the XML world, almost anything can be stored in a entity, including:

• Binary resources

• Blocks of text or markup

• Other XML documents

• Lists of attributes

• Content models

• Characters that are not part of the ASCII character set

In HTML, entities play a superficial role in document development. Entities define non-ASCII characters using the following configuration: ampersand (&), text string, semi-colon (;). For example, this entity represents a less-than sign:

```
&lt;
```

Although entities play this role in XML as well, they can be used in a variety of other ways to simplify DTD organization and document construction. XML's sophisticated use of entities contributes in many ways to the extensibility and robustness so lacking in HTML.

The basic premise behind an entity is that the contents of the storage unit are associated with a name. Whenever the name is invoked in an XML document, the unit's contents are inserted in place of the name, just as a less-than sign (<) is displayed in place of the entity **<**. XML supports three types of entities—text, binary, and parameter—and the contents of the storage unit can be contained inside of the entity declaration (internal) or outside of the declaration (external).

The remainder of this introductory section discusses internal and external entities and provides a detailed description of each of the three types of entities. This chapter's Immediate Solutions section is devoted to instructions for referencing and creating entities and includes a listing of entities in common character sets.

Types Of Entities

Before any entity can be used in an XML document, it must be declared in either the internal or external subset of the DTD. DTD developers generally specify any general entities in the external subset, but individual document developers will declare document-specific entities in the internal DTD subset. Regardless of type, all entities are declared in the same way in the DTD:

```
<!ENTITY name "content">
```

External and parameter entities throw a few extra bits of information in for good measure, but they still include the basic entity name and content information.

Internal Entities

When the contents of the entity are included directly within the entity's declaration in the DTD, the entity is labeled an *internal entity*. Internal entities are self-contained and do not reference any content outside of the DTD. The following code is an example of a group of internal entities taken from David Megginson's novel DTD:

```
<!-- em-dash -->
<!ENTITY mdash "--">

<!-- left double quotation mark -->
<!ENTITY ldquo "``">

<!-- right double quotation mark -->
<!ENTITY rdquo "´´">

<!-- left single quotation mark -->
<!ENTITY lsquo "`">
```

```
<!-- right single quotation mark -->
<!ENTITY rsquo "´">

<!-- horizonatal ellipse -->
<!ENTITY hellip "...">
```

All of an entity's pieces—its name and complete content—are included within the declaration.

External Entities

Unlike internal entities, not all of the entity's pieces are stored within the declaration of an *external entity*. Instead, the content portion of the declaration refers to another storage unit, which is external to the declaration, by using either a system or public identifier. So, the declaration's content is really just a name of a file or other resource. An example from the Technical Markup Language (TecML) DTD, found at **www.venus.co.uk/omf/cml-1.0/doc/dtd/tecml.dtd**, references the HTML DTD created especially for the Chemical Markup Language (CML):

```
<!ENTITY % html20 PUBLIC "-//CML//DTD HTML (TecML)//EN">
```

This example references a file called mypict.gif stored on a local system:

```
<!ENTITY mypict SYSTEM "graphics/mypict.gif" NDATA gif>
```

Notice that the first entity (with a public identifier) doesn't include a specific file name or location, whereas the second entity (with the system identifier) does. The idea behind this identification system is that files labeled as public can be retrieved from one of many places because they are widely available, and it can be left up to the XML processor to figure out where best to get the file. System entities are usually specific to the document or set of documents, so there's no reason why they would be available on any place other than the local system. By differentiating between **PUBLIC** and **SYSTEM** when describing the entity, the DTD developer helps the XML processor know where to look for an entity.

Text Entities

A *text entity* is exactly what its name implies, character data assigned as content to an entity name. When a text entity is referenced, the content of the entity is inserted in the document in place of the entity reference. The examples of internal entities from David Megginson's novel DTD are also examples of text entities. These particular entities use names like **ldquo** and **hellip** as aliases for punctuation marks such as the left double quote (") and ellipsis (...).

Text entities are especially useful for creating aliases to frequently used phrases and blocks of text or markup, as well as for inserting special characters. Please see "Common Entity Uses" later in this chapter for more examples of using text entities in XML documents.

Binary Entities

Anything that's not an XML-encoded resource, like an audio or video file, is considered to be a *binary entity*. Binary entities don't necessarily have to be multimedia files; they can be plain text files that shouldn't be treated as XML-encoded files. In contrast to text entities, the storage contents called by a binary entity are not automatically treated as XML markup and text. For any external binary resource to be included in an XML file, it must first be declared as an entity.

In addition to the name and content portions, each binary entity declaration must have a notation that identifies the content's type. The only way to tell a binary entity from a text entity is by the notation. If you forget the notation, the XML processor will try to treat the entity as an XML-encoded resource, leading to invalid and virtually unusable files.

The example of an external system entity we used earlier is also an example of a binary entity:

```
<!ENTITY mypict SYSTEM "graphics/mypict.gif" NDATA gif>
```

The **NDATA** portion of the declaration indicates that there is notation information to follow and labels the entity as binary. In this example, the **gif** notation is assigned to the entity, so the XML processor will recognize the entity as a GIF file and not some XML-encoded data. If we change the example to

```
<!ENTITY mypict SYSTEM "graphics/mypict.gif" NDATA tiff>
```

the processor will treat the file as a TIFF file even though its extension says "gif." Although it's important to remember to include the notation information for a binary entity, it's just as important to include the *correct* notation information. For the declaration to be valid, the notation name must also be declared in the DTD. For more on this subject, see "Declaring Binary Entities" in this chapter's Immediate Solutions section.

How binary entities are handled or displayed is ultimately up to the XML processor. In general, the processor should know what to do with a binary entity based on its notation. The processor may have built-in mechanisms to handle the binary entity, just as Web browsers can display GIF and JPEG files in addition to other types of multimedia resources. If the processor can't support the entity type, it may automatically launch an external helper application to deal with the entity.

The types of binary entities you include in documents written for one DTD or another are driven by the purpose and functionality of the DTD itself. The OSD (Open Software Description) DTD is used strictly for describing software packages, so the chances that you'll want to embed an audio file in an OSD document are pretty slim. Knowing this, processors designed to work specifically with OSD probably won't know what to do with an audio file. When you include binary entities in your XML documents, always keep in mind the purpose and limitations of the DTD as well as those of the associated XML processor.

Parameter Entities

A parameter entity is created as an alias for a group of elements—usually attributes or element content—that are used frequently within the DTD. Parameter entities are only allowed inside of the external DTD subset and are reserved for use within the DTD to enhance organization and efficiency. Parameter entities take a slightly different format than the entities we've seen so far. In addition to the name and content portions of the declaration, a percent sign (%) is also included before the entity name. An example of a parameter entity from the novel DTD is:

```
<!ENTITY % phrasal "#PCDATA|emphasis">
```

The entity is invoked using the percent sign (instead of an ampersand) and its name is followed by a semicolon. Because parameter entities are reserved for use in the DTD, you will only see them included in other portions of the DTD. In the previous example, the parameter entity created an alias for a content model. Each time **%phrasal;** is included elsewhere in the DTD, it is an alias for the content model **#PCDATA|emphasis**, as shown in this element definition from the same DTD:

```
<!ELEMENT title (%phrasal;)*>
```

This element definition is the equivalent of:

```
<!ELEMENT title (#PCDATA|emphasis)*>
```

Because the phrasal content model is used repeatedly throughout the novel DTD, it was more efficient to assign it to a parameter entity.

Parameter entities can also be used to group frequently used attributes, as shown in this rather complex example from the TecML DTD. These entity declarations assign attributes to each entity name:

```
<!ENTITY % dictname '
        convention   CDATA      #IMPLIED
        dictname     CDATA      #IMPLIED
        '>

<!ENTITY % type '
        type         (%x.type;) #IMPLIED
        '>

<!ENTITY % fuzzy '
        fuzzy        (%x.fuzzy;) #IMPLIED
        '>

<!ENTITY % mime '
        mime         CDATA      #IMPLIED
        '>

<!ENTITY % targettype '
        targettype   CDATA      #IMPLIED
        '>

<!ENTITY % lang '
        lang         CDATA      #IMPLIED
        '>

<!ENTITY % units '
        units        CDATA      #IMPLIED
        '>
```

Parameter entities can also be included as content for other parameter entities, as the following example shows:

```
<!ENTITY % vararr '
        %dictname;
        %type;
        %fuzzy;
        %mime;
        %lang;
        %units;
        %targettype;
        '
```

The parameter entity **vararr** includes the attributes for the seven previously de-fined parameter entities in one parameter entity. For an exercise in unpacking parameter entities nested within parameter entities, visit the HTML 4 specification at **www.w3.org/TR/REC-html40** at your leisure. This spec demonstrates a masterful use of parameter entities in DTD organization.

Predefined Entities

XML has five predefined entities that are native to its specification. To use these entities, you won't have to define them in either your external or internal DTD subsets. These entities are shown in Table 12.1.

Future XML editors should include support for predefined entities as well as extensive support for text, binary, and parameter entities. In a perfect world, the editors will be able to read a DTD and provide a pull-down list of entities, automatically replace text with predefined entities, and show warning messages when an entity is referenced in a document that isn't defined by the internal or external subsets of the DTD.

Common Entity Uses

As our descriptions of entities show, entities lend themselves to a variety of uses. We'll discuss some of the more practical uses in this section.

Aliasing Frequently Used Text And Markup

Frequently used text can include:

• Company and division names

• Document header and footer information

• Authorship attribution

• Other strings or blocks of text used more than once or twice in a document or set of documents

Frequently used markup (entities that include both text and markup) can include:

• Copyright information

Table 12.1   XML's predefined entities.

Character	Entity	Description
>	&gt;	Greater-than sign
<	&lt;	Less-than sign
&	&amp;	Ampersand
'	&apos;	Apostrophe
"	&quot;	Quotation mark

- Document templates
- Press releases
- Product information

The benefits of using text entities to represent frequently used bits of text and markup include:

- *Consistency*—Because it is declared as an entity, the text that replaces the entity name will be the same every time. Much human error is avoided using this method.

- *Changeability*—If a block of text or markup needs to be altered universally among a group of documents, it is much easier to change the contents of an entity once and have the text automatically updated in every place where the entity is referenced. If the text isn't referenced by an entity, each instance must be altered individually, which opens the door to missed and incorrectly changed text.

- *Efficiency*—It's much easier to type a short entity name than large amounts of text and markup. Using entities is also faster than cutting and pasting, and the text is altered more easily, as indicated in the preceding bullet point.

Any text or markup can be used as the content of a text entity. These entities can be stored internally for short snippets and externally for longer chunks of text and markup. As with any portion of an XML DTD or document, plan your text entities carefully to make sure your entities nest properly and don't violate the content models established in the DTD.

Including XML Documents Within XML Documents

Lengthy documents are often easier to work with when they are split into a collection of smaller documents. By declaring each of the smaller documents as a text entity in the larger, final document, each one is imported into the main document in place of its entity reference. A document created for the novel DTD, darkness.xml, uses this approach to create one large document by embedding four smaller documents within it. The entities are defined like this:

```
<!ENTITY chapter.01
    PUBLIC "-//Megginson//TEXT Heart of Darkness, Chapter 1//EN"
    "chap01.xml">
<!ENTITY chapter.02
    PUBLIC "-//Megginson//TEXT Heart of Darkness, Chapter 2//EN"
    "chap02.xml">
<!ENTITY chapter.03
    PUBLIC "-//Megginson//TEXT Heart of Darkness, Chapter 3//EN"
    "chap03.xml">
```

```
<!ENTITY chapter.04
    PUBLIC "-//Megginson//TEXT Heart of Darkness, Chapter 4//EN"
    "chap04.xml">
```

They are then referenced in the body of the document using regular entity references:

```
<body>

&chapter.01;

&chapter.02;

&chapter.03;

&chapter.04;

</body>
```

When you use this method of document inclusion, remember that only the referring document can have a **<!DOCTYPE>** declaration. The included files can only contain text and XML markup, or you'll have dueling internal DTD subsets to contend with and a resulting invalid file.

Organizing The DTD

As our example from the TecML DTD shows, entities—parameter entities specifically—can be used to help better organize a DTD and make it more human-readable. In addition, using parameter entities in a DTD has the same advantages as using text entities to represent text and markup in a document. Large content models and blocks of attributes that are frequently used in the DTD can be referenced quickly and can be altered and extended just as quickly.

Including Non-XML Resources

Because the world of information is not limited to text and markup, there had to be a way to include non-XML resources in XML documents. Binary entities provide this mechanism. In effect, they extend XML's support of resources to every possible file type. Although XML allows you to define any binary entity in the internal or external DTD subset, always remember that the XML processor must know what to do with the entity or its inclusion is useless. DTDs and applications should be clear about what type of entities they require and support, and document developers should keep the purpose and goals of the DTD and application firmly in mind when defining and referencing binary entities.

Although XML has changed the way developers look at markup, it hasn't changed bandwidth issues. Large files still take a long time to download over a network, regardless of which markup language you are using. Because XML supports file types, the temptation to embed binary entity after binary entity may be great. Always keep download time firmly in mind when you reference external entity files. The extensibility and functionality of XML will be irrelevant if users have to wait three hours to download all the files they need in a document set.

Representing Non-ASCII Characters

Although the use of the ASCII character set in markup ensures that XML documents will be portable from one computer to another—because ASCII is the universal language of computers—it somewhat limits the characters developers can use in their document creation. Although all the computers in the world speak ASCII, it's not sufficient to describe every resource in the world. To extend the character set available to XML documents, entities are used as aliases for special characters.

XML supports the ISO 10646 (Unicode) character encoding scheme, which in turn supports a wide variety of character encoding schemes. You can use a character's Unicode number or hexadecimal code to reference it, but we prefer to use standard character entity sets defined in the DTD instead. The Immediate Solutions sections on declaring and encoding schemes and using character entities provide detailed information on extending your DTD and document character sets to support a wider variety of characters.

Immediate Solutions

This section provides instructions for constructing each kind of XML entity. The complete listing of entities used in XML documents includes the characters defined in the ISO-Latin-1 character set.

Referencing Entities

Use this syntax to reference text and binary entities in an XML document:

```
&name;
```

For example, this entity

```
<!ENTITY mypict SYSTEM "graphics/mypict.gif" NDATA gif>
```

is referenced by:

```
&mypict;
```

Use this syntax to reference parameter entities in an XML DTD:

```
%name;
```

For example, this entity

```
<!ENTITY % html20 PUBLIC "-//CML//DTD HTML (TecML)//EN">
```

is referenced by:

```
%html20;
```

Declaring Internal Entities

An internal entity stores all information about an entity inside the entity's declaration statement. Internal entities can be stored in either the external or internal

DTD subsets of a document and are used most often to define short text entities. Use the following syntax to declare internal entities:

```
<!ENTITY name "content">
```

The content must be enclosed within quotation marks, and each entity must have a name that is unique to both the internal and external subsets. If a name is used twice, the one listed last will have precedence over the one listed first. Examples of internal entities are as follows:

```
<!ENTITY html "Hypertext Markup Language">
<!ENTITY xml "Extensible Markup Language">
<!ENTITY sgml "Standard Generalized Markup Language">
```

This XML markup

```
The &html; (HTML) was the first markup language to be implemented
by the masses. The &xml; (XML) bridges the gap between HTML and
the more complex &sgml; (SGML).
```

is the equivalent of:

```
The Hypertext Markup Language (HTML) was the first markup
language to be implemented by the masses. The Exensible
Markup Language (XML) bridges the gap between HTML and the more
complex Standard Generalized Markup Language (SGML).
```

Declaring External Entities

An external entity stores its name and a reference to another container—usually a file—that holds its contents. Use the following syntax to declare external entities:

```
<!ENTITY name (PUBLIC|SYSTEM) "content">
```

The inclusion of the **PUBLIC** or **SYSTEM** identifier differentiates an external entity from an internal one, and the content points to a file stored either on a local system or a well-archived public file, such as a public DTD.

For example, this entity

```
<!ENTITY % html20 PUBLIC "-//CML//DTD HTML (TecML)//EN">
```

references the public version of the HTML 2.0 DTD. This entity

```
<!ENTITY % html20 SYSTEM "CML/HTML2.dtd">
```

references a system version of the same file. External entities with public identifiers don't usually provide exact file locations but allow the processor to use the most easily accessible copy. By contrast, external entities with system identifiers must provide location-specific file names so the processor can locate the file.

Declaring Text Entities

Text entities can be defined as either internal or external entities. Any content referenced by a text entity will be treated by the XML processor as XML content. To declare text entities, use either the internal or external declaration syntax:

```
<!ENTITY name "content">
<!ENTITY name (PUBLIC|SYSTEM) "content">
```

Text entities are the simplest form of XML entities and are used to reference non-ASCII characters, text strings, blocks of text, and marked-up text. An XML processor views the contents of a text declaration entity as a replacement for the entity references in the document.

Declaring Binary Entities

Binary entities are always defined as external entities, because their contents are always stored in external files and treated as non-XML content. Binary entity declarations must include a notation expression that describes what kind of resource the entity is referring to. Notations must also be declared elsewhere in the DTD in order for binary entities to be valid. The syntax for a binary entity is:

```
<!ENTITY name (PUBLIC|SYSTEM) "content" NDATA datatype>
```

Without the **NDATA** identifier and a data type matching a declared notation, the entity will be treated as a text entity. An example of a binary entity is:

```
<!ENTITY bp SYSTEM "docs/book-proposed.doc" NDATA DOC>
```

When you are working with binary entities, and entities in general, it is always important to remember that, for any entity to be referenced within an XML document, it must first be declared by using an entity declaration. However, once an entity has been declared, it can be referenced as many times as needed. An entity that is declared in the external subset of a DTD can be referenced by all documents that reference the DTD, but an entity that is declared in the internal subset of a DTD can only be referenced by the document.

Declaring Notations

Notation declarations take a form similar to that of an external entity. The purpose of a notation is to help the XML processor deal with non-XML entities like multimedia files and word processing documents. Notations can be declared in either the internal or external subset of the document's DTD. Use this syntax to declare notations:

```
<!NOTATION name (PUBLIC|SYSTEM) "location">
```

A notation that links Microsoft Word to the doc data type might look like this:

```
<!NOTATION doc (PUBLIC|SYSTEM)
"program_files/microsoft_office/office/winword.exe">
```

The XML specification is flexible enough to allow XML processors to treat binary entities in any way necessary, which means that the processor doesn't necessarily have to view the entity in the application referenced by the notation. The processor might just use the referenced application to provide a general idea of how the resource should be treated if it has its own built-in mechanism for handling the file. Alternately, users might be able to specify how certain entities are processed and thus override the notation references entirely.

Declaring A Text-Encoding Scheme For Entities

Because XML supports Unicode, there are a variety of encoding schemes available to DTD and document developers alike—including 8-bit, 16-bit, and 32-bit character encoding. The encoding scheme used in a particular document or DTD affects how non-ASCII characters are referenced using their Unicode decimal or hexadecimal code. If 8-bit encoding is specified and an entity declaration uses 16-bit encoding in its content, the XML processor might not be able to implement the entity when it is referenced.

A text entity must declare and adhere to a single encoding scheme, but that doesn't mean that several text entities, each with its own encoding scheme, can't be referenced by a single XML document. Using entities to represent large chunks of text or markup can be beneficial in this situation. Those blocks of text that need more advanced encoding systems, like 16- or 32-bit, can utilize entities, but those that only require 8-bit encoding do not have to. This makes for the most efficient use of character encoding. The more bits the encoding system includes, the more characters can be generated. However, the larger encoding systems also create large files that take more time to download.

In addition, if you only need a few of the 16- or 32-bit characters, you can reference them in individual entity declarations and use the smaller 8-bit encoding system for the entire document. For example, if you need to use the Cyrillic letter "palochak" in your document—but no other Cyrillic letters—it's easiest and most efficient to create a character entity reference that includes the letter's Unicode hexadecimal number (04C0) preceded by **&#x** and followed by a semicolon, as shown here:

```
&#x04C0;
```

The default encoding scheme assumed by XML processors is ISO 10646 UTF-8, which is 8-bit character encoding. To declare otherwise, you'll need to use a *processing instruction* (PI) that defines the character encoding scheme your document uses. Its syntax is:

```
<?XML encoding="[scheme name]" ?>
```

The ***scheme name*** can be one of the following:

- UTF-8
- UTF-16
- ISO-10646-UCS-2
- ISO-10646-UCS-4
- ISO-8859-1 to -9
- ISO-2022-JP
- Shift_JIS
- EUC-JP

The novel DTD includes this encoding PI:

```
<?xml version="1.0" encoding="UTF-8" standalone="no"?>
```

This example combines version and standalone information with encoding information, which is an effective and efficient way to provide three important pieces of information about the document to the XML processor at once.

The world of Unicode is complex, so much so that it's not supported by HTML yet but may possibly be in the future. Unicode covers a wide variety of languages (human and scientific alike)—including Cyrillic, Greek, Thai, and Box Drawing— and has had a two-volume tome written about it. For more information on Unicode, including charts and glyphs of characters and their hexadecimal codes, visit the Unicode site at **www.unicode.org**.

Using Character Entities In XML Documents

Character entity sets are large groups of text entities created to display non-standard characters in markup languages. Anyone familiar with HTML has used a character entity from one of these sets at least once in their coding career. Because Unicode is so complex and many developers would like to keep their documents within the 8-bit encoding system (and to help XML degrade gracefully to HTML), it is often useful to use the established ISO-Latin-1 character encoding sets, as well as a few others that are standard in HTML 4, with XML DTDs and documents. XML does not include native support for these specific entities. If you want to take advantage of a character set's entities, you'll have to use a regular text entity declaration to reference them in the DTD. You don't have to include all the entities, just the ones you think you'll need. You can also store them all in easily accessible external files and make a habit of referencing them in your DTDs, so you'll have a familiar and easy way to include nonstandard characters in your documents.

The remainder of the projects in the section are devoted to listings of five useful character sets, including:

- The ISO-Latin-1 character set
- A mathematical character set
- The Greek letter character set
- The miscellaneous technical character set
- The miscellaneous symbol character set

These five character sets are a part of HTML 4, but they certainly aren't the only entity sets you can include in your documents. They include some of the most commonly used non-ASCII characters as well as some useful math symbols and Greek letters. For each set, we've included the complete Unicode entity declaration list followed by a table that shows the characters, the numeric and/or character entity you can use to embed the character in a document, and a description of the character. (Listing 12.1 includes the ISO-Latin-1 character entity set, and Table 12.2 lists the ISO-Latin-1 character set. Listing 12.2 includes the mathematical, Greek, and miscellaneous character entity sets. Table 12.3 lists the mathematical character set, Table 12.4 lists the Greek character set, Table 12.5 lists the miscellaneous technical character set, and Table 12.6 lists the miscellaneous symbols character set.) Each entity declaration set includes a section on how to use an external entity declaration with a public identifier to reference the entity set, as seen in this example:

```
<!ENTITY % HTMLlat1 PUBLIC "ISO 8879-1986//ENTITIES Added
     Latin 1//EN//XML">
```

If you don't want to use a public identifier to reference an entire set of entity declarations, you can choose only those that you need, save them as internal entities or in a separate file, and reference them as an external text entity with a system identifier.

TIP: *All five of the character set entity declaration files are included on this book's CD-ROM for your cutting and pasting pleasure. They are referenced in the Code section of the CD's HTML files. These character sets are copyrighted by Unicode.*

Using The ISO-Latin-1 Character Entity Set

The most common special characters are defined in the ISO-Latin-1 character set. This character set includes common punctuation marks and frequently used symbols, such as the copyright and trademark indicators. The character set also contains entities for referencing accented characters in both lowercase and uppercase as well as ligatures important to languages such as Spanish and German that use the Latin character set.

Listing 12.1   The ISO-Latin-1 character entity set.

```
<!-- (C) International Organization for Standardization 1986
Permission to copy in any form is granted for use with
conforming SGML systems and applications as defined in
ISO 8879, provided this notice is included in all copies.
-->
<!-- Character entity set. Typical invocation:
<!ENTITY % HTMLlat1 PUBLIC
"ISO 8879-1986//ENTITIES Added Latin 1//EN//XML">
%ISOlat1;
-->
```

```
<!-- This version of the entity set can be used with any SGML
document which uses ISO 8859-1 or ISO 10646 as its document
character set. This includes XML documents and ISO HTML documents.
-->
<!-- The initial entries, up to numeric code 192, do not appear
     in the original version of this file. We've added them for
     completeness, to provide as complete an XML version of the
     ISO-Latin-1 set as possible
-->
<!ENTITY tab "&#09;"    ><!-- horizontal tab -->
<!ENTITY lf  "&#10;"    ><!-- linefeed or newline -->
<!ENTITY space "&#32;"  ><!-- space -->
<!ENTITY exclam "&#33;" ><!-- exclamation mark -->
<!ENTITY quot "&#34;"   ><!-- double quote mark -->
<!ENTITY hash "&#35;"   ><!-- number sign -->
<!ENTITY dlr "&#36;"    ><!-- dollar sign -->
<!ENTITY pct "&#37;"    ><!-- percent sign -->
<!ENTITY amp "&#38;"    ><!-- ampersand, already defined -->
<!ENTITY apos "&#39;"   ><!-- apostrophe -->
<!ENTITY lparen "&#40;" ><!-- left parenthesis -->
<!ENTITY rparen "&#41;" ><!-- right parenthesis -->
<!ENTITY ast "&#42;"    ><!-- asterisk -->
<!ENTITY plus "&#43;"   ><!-- plus sign -->
<!ENTITY comma "&#44;"  ><!-- comma -->
<!ENTITY hyph "&#45;"   ><!-- hyphen -->
<!ENTITY per "&#46;"    ><!-- period -->
<!ENTITY fwsl "&#47;"   ><!-- forward slash -->
<!ENTITY d0 "&#48;"     ><!-- digit zero (0) -->
<!ENTITY d1 "&#49;"     ><!-- digit one (1) -->
<!ENTITY d2 "&#50;"     ><!-- digit two (2) -->
<!ENTITY d3 "&#51;"     ><!-- digit three (3) -->
<!ENTITY d4 "&#52;"     ><!-- digit four (4) -->
<!ENTITY d5 "&#53;"     ><!-- digit five (5) -->
<!ENTITY d6 "&#54;"     ><!-- digit six (6) -->
<!ENTITY d7 "&#55;"     ><!-- digit seven (7) -->
<!ENTITY d8 "&#56;"     ><!-- digit eight (8) -->
<!ENTITY d9 "&#57;"     ><!-- digit nine (9) -->
<!ENTITY colon "&#58;"  ><!-- colon -->
<!ENTITY semi "&#59;"   ><!-- semicolon -->
<!ENTITY lt "&#60;"     ><!-- less than sign, already defined -->
<!ENTITY eq "&#61;"     ><!-- equal sign -->
<!ENTITY gt "&#62;"     ><!-- greater than, already defined -->
<!ENTITY ques "&#63;"   ><!-- question mark -->
<!ENTITY at "&#64;"     ><!-- at sign -->
<!ENTITY A "&#65;"      ><!-- Capital a (A) -->
```

```
<!ENTITY B "&#66;"        ><!-- Capital b (B) -->
<!ENTITY C "&#67;"        ><!-- Capital c (C) -->
<!ENTITY D "&#68;"        ><!-- Capital d (D) -->
<!ENTITY E "&#69;"        ><!-- Capital e (E) -->
<!ENTITY F "&#70;"        ><!-- Capital f (F) -->
<!ENTITY G "&#71;"        ><!-- Capital g (G) -->
<!ENTITY H "&#72;"        ><!-- Capital h (H) -->
<!ENTITY I "&#73;"        ><!-- Capital i (I) -->
<!ENTITY J "&#74;"        ><!-- Capital j (J) -->
<!ENTITY K "&#75;"        ><!-- Capital k (K) -->
<!ENTITY L "&#76;"        ><!-- Capital l (L) -->
<!ENTITY M "&#77;"        ><!-- Capital m (M) -->
<!ENTITY N "&#78;"        ><!-- Capital n (N) -->
<!ENTITY O "&#79;"        ><!-- Capital o (O) -->
<!ENTITY P "&#80;"        ><!-- Capital p (P) -->
<!ENTITY Q "&#81;"        ><!-- Capital q (Q) -->
<!ENTITY R "&#82;"        ><!-- Capital r (R) -->
<!ENTITY S "&#83;"        ><!-- Capital s (S) -->
<!ENTITY T "&#84;"        ><!-- Capital t (T) -->
<!ENTITY U "&#85;"        ><!-- Capital u (U) -->
<!ENTITY V "&#86;"        ><!-- Capital v (V) -->
<!ENTITY W "&#87;"        ><!-- Capital w (W) -->
<!ENTITY X "&#88;"        ><!-- Capital x (X) -->
<!ENTITY Y "&#89;"        ><!-- Capital y (Y) -->
<!ENTITY Z "&#90;"        ><!-- Capital z (Z) -->
<!ENTITY lsq "&#91;"      ><!-- Left square bracket -->
<!ENTITY bksl "&#92;"     ><!-- Reverse solidus (backslash) -->
<!ENTITY rsq "&#93;"      ><!-- Right square bracket -->
<!ENTITY crt "&#94;"      ><!-- Caret -->
<!ENTITY hbar "&#95;"     ><!-- Horizontal bar -->
<!ENTITY grav "&#96;"     ><!-- Grave accent -->
<!ENTITY a "&#97;"        ><!-- Lowercase a (a) -->
<!ENTITY b "&#98;"        ><!-- Lowercase b (b) -->
<!ENTITY c "&#99;"        ><!-- Lowercase c (c) -->
<!ENTITY d "&#100;"       ><!-- Lowercase d (d) -->
<!ENTITY e "&#101;"       ><!-- Lowercase e (e) -->
<!ENTITY f "&#102;"       ><!-- Lowercase f (f) -->
<!ENTITY g "&#103;"       ><!-- Lowercase g (g) -->
<!ENTITY h "&#104;"       ><!-- Lowercase h (h) -->
<!ENTITY i "&#105;"       ><!-- Lowercase i (i) -->
<!ENTITY j "&#106;"       ><!-- Lowercase j (j) -->
<!ENTITY k "&#107;"       ><!-- Lowercase k (k) -->
<!ENTITY l "&#108;"       ><!-- Lowercase l (l) -->
<!ENTITY m "&#109;"       ><!-- Lowercase m (m) -->
<!ENTITY n "&#110;"       ><!-- Lowercase n (n) -->
```

```
<!ENTITY o "&#111;"       ><!-- Lowercase o (o) -->
<!ENTITY p "&#112;"       ><!-- Lowercase p (p) -->
<!ENTITY q "&#113;"       ><!-- Lowercase q (q) -->
<!ENTITY r "&#114;"       ><!-- Lowercase r (r) -->
<!ENTITY s "&#115;"       ><!-- Lowercase s (s) -->
<!ENTITY t "&#116;"       ><!-- Lowercase t (t) -->
<!ENTITY u "&#117;"       ><!-- Lowercase u (u) -->
<!ENTITY v "&#118;"       ><!-- Lowercase v (v) -->
<!ENTITY w "&#119;"       ><!-- Lowercase w (w) -->
<!ENTITY x "&#120;"       ><!-- Lowercase x (x) -->
<!ENTITY y "&#121;"       ><!-- Lowercase y (y) -->
<!ENTITY z "&#122;"       ><!-- Lowercase z (z) -->
<!ENTITY lcb "&#123;"     ><!-- Left curly brace -->
<!ENTITY vbar "&#124;"    ><!-- vertical bar -->
<!ENTITY rcb "&#125;"     ><!-- Right curly brace -->
<!ENTITY til "&#126;"     ><!-- tilde -->
<!-- Note: codes 127 - 160 are currently unused -->
<!ENTITY ixl "&#161;"     ><!-- inverted exclamation mark -->
<!ENTITY cnt "&#162;"     ><!-- cent sign -->
<!ENTITY lbs "&#163;"     ><!-- pound sterling sign -->
<!ENTITY cur "&#164;"     ><!-- general currency sign -->
<!ENTITY yen "&#165;"     ><!-- yen symbol -->
<!ENTITY bvb "&#166;"     ><!-- broken vertical bar -->
<!ENTITY sec "&#167;"     ><!-- section sign -->
<!ENTITY uml "&#168;"     ><!-- umlaut sign -->
<!ENTITY cpy "&#169;"     ><!-- copyright symbol -->
<!ENTITY for "&#170;"     ><!-- feminine ordinal -->
<!ENTITY glf "&#171;"     ><!-- left angle quote, guillemot left -->
<!ENTITY not "&#172;"     ><!-- not symbol, logical negation -->
<!ENTITY shy "&#173;"     ><!-- soft hyphen -->
<!ENTITY trd "&#174;"     ><!-- trademark symbol -->
<!ENTITY mac "&#175;"     ><!-- macron accent -->
<!ENTITY deg "&#176;"     ><!-- degree symbol -->
<!ENTITY plm "&#177;"     ><!-- plus or minus symbol -->
<!ENTITY s2 "&#178;"      ><!-- superscript two -->
<!ENTITY S3 "&#179;"      ><!-- superscript three -->
<!ENTITY acc "&#180;"     ><!-- accute accent -->
<!ENTITY mic "&#181;"     ><!-- micro sign (lowercase mu) -->
<!ENTITY par "&#182;"     ><!-- paragraph symbol -->
<!ENTITY mdt "&#183;"     ><!-- middle dot -->
<!ENTITY ced "&#184;"     ><!-- cedilla -->
<!ENTITY s1 "&#185;"      ><!-- superscript one -->
<!ENTITY mor "&#186;"     ><!-- masculine ordinal -->
<!ENTITY glr "&#187;"     ><!-- right angle quote, guillemot right -->
<!ENTITY f4 "&#188;"      ><!-- fraction: one-fourth -->
```

```
<!ENTITY f2 "&#189;"    ><!-- fraction: one-half -->
<!ENTITY f34 "&#190;"   ><!-- fraction: three-fourths -->
<!ENTITY iqm "&#191;"   ><!-- inverted question mark -->
```

Table 12.2   The ISO-Latin-1 character set.

Character	Character Entity	Numeric Entity	Description
		&#00; - &#08;	Unused
		&#09;	Horizontal tab
		&#10;	Line feed
		&#11; - &#31;	Unused
	&space;	&#32;	Space
!	&exclam;	&#33;	Exclamation mark
"	&quot;	&#34;	Quotation mark
#	&hash;	&#35;	Number
$	&dlr;	&#36;	Dollar
%	&pct;	&#37;	Percent
&	&amp;	&#38;	Ampersand
'	&apos;	&#39;	Apostrophe
(	&lparen;	&#40;	Left parenthesis
)	&rparen;	&#41;	Right parenthesis
*	&ast;	&#42;	Asterisk
+	&plus;	&#43;	Plus
,	&comma;	&#44;	Comma
-	&hyph;	&#45;	Hyphen
.	&per;	&#46;	Period (full stop)
/	&fwsl;	&#47;	Slash
0-9	&d0; - &d9;	0 - 9	Digits 0 through 9
:	&colon;	&#58;	Colon
;	&semi;	&#59;	Semicolon
<	&lt;	&#60;	Less than
=	&eq;	&#61;	Equals
>	&gt;	&#62;	Greater than
?	&ques;	&#63;	Question mark
@	&at;	&#64;	Commercial at

(continued)

Table 12.2 The ISO-Latin-1 character set (continued).

Character	Character Entity	Numeric Entity	Description
A-Z		A - Z	Letters A through Z (capitals)
[	&lsq;	[	Left square bracket
\	&bksl;	\	Reverse solidus (backslash)
]	&rsq;	]	Right square bracket
^	&crt;	^	Caret
_	ℏ	_	Horizontal bar
`	&grav;	`	Grave accent
a-z		a - z	Letters a through z (lowercase)
{	&lcb;	{	Left curly brace
		&vbar;	|	Vertical bar
}	&rcb;	}	Right curly brace
~	&til;	~	Tilde
		&#127; -	Unused
¡	&ixl;	¡	Inverted exclamation mark
¢	&cnt;	¢	Cent
£	&lbs;	£	Pound sterling
¤	&cur;	¤	General currency
¥	¥	¥	Yen
¦	&bvb;	¦	Broken vertical bar
§	&sec;	§	Section
¨	¨	¨	Umlaut (dieresis)
©	&cpy;	©	Copyright
ª	&for;	ª	Feminine ordinal
«	&glf;	«	Left angle quote, guillemet, left
¬	¬	¬	Not
-	­	­	Soft hyphen
®	&trd;	®	Registered trademark
¯	&mac;	¯	Macron accent
°	°	°	Degree
±	&plm;	±	Plus or minus
²	&s2;	²	Superscript two
³	&s3;	³	Superscript three

(continued)

Table 12.2   The ISO-Latin-1 character set (continued).

Character	Character Entity	Numeric Entity	Description
´	&acc;	&#180;	Acute accent
µ	&mic;	&#181;	Micro
¶	&par;	&#182;	Paragraph
·	&mdt;	&#183;	Middle dot
¸	&ced;	&#184;	Cedilla
¹	&s1;	&#185;	Superscript one
º	&mor;	&#186;	Masculine ordinal
»	&glr;	&#187;	Right angle quote, guillemet right
1/4	&f4;	&#188;	Fraction one-fourth
1/2	&f2;	&#189;	Fraction one-half
3/4	&f34;	&#190;	Fraction three-fourths
¿	&iqm;	&#191;	Inverted question mark
À	&Agrave;	&#192;	Capital A, grave accent
Á	&Aacute;	&#193;	Capital A, acute accent
Â	&Acirc;	&#194;	Capital A, circumflex accent
Ã	&Atilde;	&#195;	Capital A, tilde
Ä	&Auml;	&#196;	Capital A, dieresis or umlaut
Å	&Aring;	&#197;	Capital A, ring
Æ	&AElig;	&#198;	Capital AE, diphthong (ligature)
Ç	&Ccedil;	&#199;	Capital C, cedilla
È	&Egrave;	&#200;	Capital E, grave accent
É	&Eacute;	&#201;	Capital E, acute accent
Ê	&Ecirc;	&#202;	Capital E, circumflex accent
Ë	&Euml;	&#203;	Capital E, dieresis or umlaut
Ì	&Igrave;	&#204;	Capital I, grave accent
Í	&Iacute;	&#205;	Capital I, acute accent
Î	&Icirc;	&#206;	Capital I, circumflex accent
Ï	&Iuml;	&#207;	Capital I, dieresis or umlaut
Ñ	&Ntilde;	&#209;	Capital N, tilde
Ò	&Ograve;	&#210;	Capital O, grave accent
Ó	&Oacute;	&#211;	Capital O, acute accent
Ô	&Ocirc;	&#212;	Capital O, circumflex accent

(continued)

Table 12.2   The ISO-Latin-1 character set (continued).

Character	Character Entity	Numeric Entity	Description
Õ	&Otilde	&#213;	Capital O, tilde
Ö	&Ouml;	&#214;	Capital O, dieresis or umlaut
×	&times;	&#215;	Multiply
Ø	&Oslash;	&#216;	Capital O, slash
Ù	&Ugrave;	&#217;	Capital U, grave accent
Ú	&Uacute;	&#218;	Capital U, acute accent
Û	&Ucirc;	&#219;	Capital U, circumflex accent
Ü	&Uuml;	&#220;	Capital U, dieresis or umlaut
Y	&Yacute;	&#221;	Capital Y, acute accent
ß	&szlig;	&#223;	Small sharp s, German (sz ligature)
à	&agrave;	&#224;	Small a, grave accent
á	&aacute;	&#225;	Small a, acute accent
â	&acirc;	&#226;	Small a, circumflex accent
ã	&atilde;	&#227;	Small a, tilde
ä	&auml;	&#228;	Small a, dieresis or umlaut
å	&aring;	&#229;	Small a, ring
æ	&aelig;	&#230;	Small ae, diphthong (ligature)
ç	&ccedil;	&#231;	Small c, cedilla
è	&egrave;	&#232;	Small e, grave accent
é	&eacute;	&#233;	Small e, acute accent
ê	&ecirc;	&#234;	Small e, circumflex accent
ë	&euml;	&#235;	Small e, dieresis or umlaut
ì	&igrave;	&#236;	Small i, grave accent
í	&iacute;	&#237;	Small i, acute accent
î	&icirc;	&#238;	Small i, circumflex accent
ï	&iuml;	&#239;	Small i, dieresis or umlaut
ñ	&ntilde;	&#241;	Small n, tilde
ò	&ograve;	&#242;	Small o, grave accent
ó	&oacute;	&#243;	Small o, acute accent
ô	&ocirc;	&#244;	Small o, circumflex accent
õ	&otilde;	&#245;	Small o, tilde
ö	&ouml;	&#246;	Small o, dieresis or umlaut

(continued)

Table 12.2   The ISO-Latin-1 character set (continued).

Character	Character Entity	Numeric Entity	Description
÷	&divide;	&#247;	Division
ø	&oslash;	&#248;	Small o, slash
ù	&ugrave;	&#249;	Small u, grave accent
ú	&uacute;	&#250;	Small u, acute accent
û	&ucirc;	&#251;	Small u, circumflex accent
ü	&uuml;	&#252;	Small u, dieresis or umlaut
y	&yacute;	&#253;	Small y, acute accent
ÿ	&yuml;	&#255;	Small y, dieresis or umlaut

Using Math, Greek, And Miscellaneous Character Entity Sets

The math, Greek, and miscellaneous character sets allow authors to include mathematical and scientific notation in their documents without having to resort to the overkill of the MathML or CML vocabularies. Although you can use these entities to toss assorted mathematical operators and Greek letters into the fray, they don't provide a way to describe mathematical or scientific notation. If you need advanced notation capabilities, consider using a graphic of the notation or working with one of the newly developed vocabularies that specialize in advanced notation.

Listing 12.2   The mathematical, Greek, and miscellaneous character entity sets.

```
<!-- Mathematical, Greek and Symbolic characters for HTML -->
<!-- Character entity set. Typical invocation:
<!ENTITY % HTMLsymbol PUBLIC
"-//W3C//ENTITIES Symbolic//EN//HTML">
%HTMLsymbol; -->


<!-- Portions © International Organization for Standardization 1986:
Permission to copy in any form is granted for use with
conforming SGML systems and applications as defined in
ISO 8879, provided this notice is included in all copies.-->


<!-- Relevant ISO entity set is given unless names are newly introduced.
New names (i.e., not in ISO 8879 list) do not clash with any
existing ISO 8879 entity names. ISO 10646 character numbers
are given for each character, in hex. CDATA values are decimal
conversions of the ISO 10646 values and refer to the document
character set. Names are Unicode 2.0 names. -->
```

```
<!-- Latin Extended-B -->
<!ENTITY fnof        CDATA "&#402;" -- latin small f with hook =
    function= florin-->


<!-- Greek -->
<!ENTITY Alpha       CDATA "&#913;" -- greek capital letter alpha-->
<!ENTITY Beta        CDATA "&#914;" -- greek capital letter beta-->
<!ENTITY Gamma       CDATA "&#915;" -- greek capital letter gamma-->
<!ENTITY Delta       CDATA "&#916;" -- greek capital letter delta-->
<!ENTITY Epsilon     CDATA "&#917;" -- greek capital letter epsilon-->
<!ENTITY Zeta        CDATA "&#918;" -- greek capital letter zeta-->
<!ENTITY Eta         CDATA "&#919;" -- greek capital letter eta-->
<!ENTITY Theta       CDATA "&#920;" -- greek capital letter theta-->
<!ENTITY Iota        CDATA "&#921;" -- greek capital letter iota-->
<!ENTITY Kappa       CDATA "&#922;" -- greek capital letter kappa-->
<!ENTITY Lambda      CDATA "&#923;" -- greek capital letter lambda-->
<!ENTITY Mu          CDATA "&#924;" -- greek capital letter mu -->
<!ENTITY Nu          CDATA "&#925;" -- greek capital letter nu -->
<!ENTITY Xi          CDATA "&#926;" -- greek capital letter xi-->
<!ENTITY Omicron     CDATA "&#927;" -- greek capital letter omicron-->
<!ENTITY Pi          CDATA "&#928;" -- greek capital letter pi-->
<!ENTITY Rho         CDATA "&#929;" -- greek capital letter rho-->
<!-- there is no Sigmaf, and no U+03A2 character either -->
<!ENTITY Sigma       CDATA "&#931;" -- greek capital letter sigma-->
<!ENTITY Tau         CDATA "&#932;" -- greek capital letter tau-->
<!ENTITY Upsilon     CDATA "&#933;" -- greek capital letter upsilon-->
<!ENTITY Phi         CDATA "&#934;" -- greek capital letter phi-->
<!ENTITY Chi         CDATA "&#935;" -- greek capital letter chi-->
<!ENTITY Psi         CDATA "&#936;" -- greek capital letter psi-->
<!ENTITY Omega       CDATA "&#937;" -- greek capital letter omega-->
<!ENTITY alpha       CDATA "&#945;" -- greek small letter alpha-->
<!ENTITY beta        CDATA "&#946;" -- greek small letter beta-->
<!ENTITY gamma       CDATA "&#947;" -- greek small letter gamma-->
<!ENTITY delta       CDATA "&#948;" -- greek small letter delta-->
<!ENTITY epsilon     CDATA "&#949;" -- greek small letter epsilon -->
<!ENTITY zeta        CDATA "&#950;" -- greek small letter zeta-->
<!ENTITY eta         CDATA "&#951;" -- greek small letter eta-->
<!ENTITY theta       CDATA "&#952;" -- greek small letter theta-->
<!ENTITY iota        CDATA "&#953;" -- greek small letter iota-->
<!ENTITY kappa       CDATA "&#954;" -- greek small letter kappa-->
<!ENTITY lambda      CDATA "&#955;" -- greek small letter lambda-->
<!ENTITY mu          CDATA "&#956;" -- greek small letter mu-->
<!ENTITY nu          CDATA "&#957;" -- greek small letter nu-->
<!ENTITY xi          CDATA "&#958;" -- greek small letter xi-->
<!ENTITY omicron     CDATA "&#959;" -- greek small letter omicron-->
```

```
<!ENTITY pi        CDATA "&#960;" -- greek small letter pi-->
<!ENTITY rho       CDATA "&#961;" -- greek small letter rho -->
<!ENTITY sigmaf    CDATA "&#962;" -- greek small letter final sigma-->
<!ENTITY sigma     CDATA "&#963;" -- greek small letter sigma-->
<!ENTITY tau       CDATA "&#964;" -- greek small letter tau-->
<!ENTITY upsilon   CDATA "&#965;" -- greek small letter upsilon-->
<!ENTITY phi       CDATA "&#966;" -- greek small letter phi-->
<!ENTITY chi       CDATA "&#967;" -- greek small letter chi-->
<!ENTITY psi       CDATA "&#968;" -- greek small letter psi-->
<!ENTITY omega     CDATA "&#969;" -- greek small letter omega-->
<!ENTITY thetasym  CDATA "&#977;" -- greek small letter theta symbol-->
<!ENTITY upsih     CDATA "&#978;" -- greek upsilon with hook symbol-->
<!ENTITY piv       CDATA "&#982;" -- greek pi symbol -->

<!-- Mathematical Operators -->
<!ENTITY forall    CDATA "&#8704;" -- for all -->
<!ENTITY part      CDATA "&#8706;" -- partial differential-->
<!ENTITY exist     CDATA "&#8707;" -- there exists, U+2203 ISOtech -->
<!ENTITY empty     CDATA "&#8709;" -- empty set = null set = diameter-->
<!ENTITY nabla     CDATA "&#8711;" -- nabla = backward difference-->
<!ENTITY isin      CDATA "&#8712;" -- element of -->
<!ENTITY notin     CDATA "&#8713;" -- not an element of-->
<!ENTITY ni        CDATA "&#8715;" -- contains as member-->
<!ENTITY prod      CDATA "&#8719;" -- n-ary product = product sign-->
<!-- prod is NOT the same character as U+03A0 'greek capital letter pi'
though the same glyph might be used for both -->
<!ENTITY sum       CDATA "&#8721;" -- n-ary sumation -->
<!-- sum is NOT the same character as U+03A3 'greek capital letter sigma'
though the same glyph might be used for both -->
<!ENTITY minus     CDATA "&#8722;" -- minus sign -->
<!ENTITY lowast    CDATA "&#8727;" -- asterisk operator-->
<!ENTITY radic     CDATA "&#8730;" -- square root = radical sign -->
<!ENTITY prop      CDATA "&#8733;" -- proportional to -->
<!ENTITY infin     CDATA "&#8734;" -- infinity-->
<!ENTITY ang       CDATA "&#8736;" -- angle-->
<!ENTITY and       CDATA "&#8743;" -- logical and = wedge-->
<!ENTITY or        CDATA "&#8744;" -- logical or = vee-->
<!ENTITY cap       CDATA "&#8745;" -- intersection = cap-->
<!ENTITY cup       CDATA "&#8746;" -- union = cup-->
<!ENTITY int       CDATA "&#8747;" -- integral-->
<!ENTITY there4    CDATA "&#8756;" -- therefore-->
<!ENTITY sim       CDATA "&#8764;" -- tilde operator
                   = varies with = similar to-->
<!-- tilde operator is NOT the same character as the tilde -->
<!ENTITY cong      CDATA "&#8773;" -- approximately equal to-->
<!ENTITY asymp     CDATA "&#8776;" -- almost equal to = asymptotic to-->
```

```
<!ENTITY ne      CDATA "&#8800;" -- not equal to-->
<!ENTITY equiv   CDATA "&#8801;" -- identical to-->
<!ENTITY le      CDATA "&#8804;" -- less-than or equal to-->
<!ENTITY ge      CDATA "&#8805;" -- greater-than or equal to-->
<!ENTITY sub     CDATA "&#8834;" -- subset of-->
<!ENTITY sup     CDATA "&#8835;" -- superset of-->
<!ENTITY nsub    CDATA "&#8836;" -- not a subset of-->
<!ENTITY sube    CDATA "&#8838;" -- subset of or equal to-->
<!ENTITY supe    CDATA "&#8839;" -- superset of or equal to-->
<!ENTITY oplus   CDATA "&#8853;" -- circled plus = direct sum-->
<!ENTITY otimes  CDATA "&#8855;" -- circled times = vector product-->
<!ENTITY perp    CDATA "&#8869;" -- up tack = orthogonal to =
perpendicular-->
<!ENTITY sdot    CDATA "&#8901;" -- dot operator-->
<!-- dot operator is NOT the same character as U+00B7 middle dot -->


<!-- Miscellaneous Technical -->
<!ENTITY lceil   CDATA "&#8968;" -- left ceiling = apl upstile-->
<!ENTITY rceil   CDATA "&#8969;" -- right ceiling-->
<!ENTITY lfloor  CDATA "&#8970;" -- left floor = apl downstile -->
<!ENTITY rfloor  CDATA "&#8971;" -- right floor-->
<!ENTITY lang    CDATA "&#9001;" -- left-pointing angle bracket = bra-->
<!-- lang is NOT the same character as U+003C 'less than'
or U+2039 'single left-pointing angle quotation mark' -->
<!ENTITY rang    CDATA "&#9002;" -- right-pointing angle bracket = ket-->
<!-- rang is NOT the same character as U+003E 'greater than'
or U+203A 'single right-pointing angle quotation mark' -->


<!-- Miscellaneous Symbols -->
<!ENTITY spades  CDATA "&#9824;" -- black spade suit-->
<!-- black here seems to mean filled as opposed to hollow -->
<!ENTITY clubs   CDATA "&#9827;" -- black club suit = shamrock-->
<!ENTITY hearts  CDATA "&#9829;" -- black heart suit = valentine-->
<!ENTITY diams   CDATA "&#9830;" -- black diamond suit-->
```

Table 12.3   The mathematical character set.

Character	Character Entity	Numeric Entity	Description
∀	&forall;	&#8704;	For all
∂	&part;	&#8706;	Partial differential
∃	&exist;	&#8707;	There exists
∅	&empty;	&#8709;	Empty set
∇	&nabla;	&#8711;	Nabla

(continued)

Table 12.3   *The mathematical character set (continued).*

Character	Character Entity	Numeric Entity	Description
∈	&isin;	&#8712;	Element of
∉	&notin;	&#8713;	Not an element of
∏	&prod;	&#8719;	n-ary product
∑	&sum;	&#8721;	n-ary summation
−	&minus;	&#8722;	Minus
∗	&lowast;	&#8727;	Asterisk operator
√	&radic;	&#8730;	Square root
∝	&prop;	&#8733;	Proportional to
∞	&infin;	&#8734;	Infinity
∠	&ang;	&#8736;	Angle
∧	&and;	&#8743;	Logical and
∨	&or;	&#8744;	Logical or
∩	&cap;	&#8745;	Intersection
∪	&cup;	&#8746;	Union
∫	&int;	&#8747;	Integral
∴	&there4;	&#8756;	Therefore
~	&sim;	&#8764;	Tilde operator
≅	&cong;	&#8773;	Approximately equal to
≈	&asymp;	&#8776;	Almost equal to
≠	&ne;	&#8800;	Not equal to
≡	&equiv;	&#8801;	Identical to =
≤	&le;	&#8804;	Less than or equal to
≥	&ge;	&#8805;	Greater than or equal to
⊂	&sub;	&#8834;	Subset of
⊃	&sup;	&#8835;	Superset of
⊄	&nsub;	&#8836;	Not a subset of
⊆	&sube;	&#8838;	Subset of or equal to
⊇	&supe;	&#8839;	Superset of or equal to
⊕	&oplus;	&#8853;	Circled plus
⊗	&otimes;	&#8855;	Circled times
⊥	&perp;	&#8869;	Up tack
•	&sdot;	&#8901;	Dot operator

Table 12.4   The Greek character set.

Character	Character Entity	Numeric Entity	Description
A	&Alpha;	&#913;	Capital letter alpha
B	&Beta;	&#914;	Capital letter beta
Γ	&Gamma;	&#915;	Capital letter gamma
Δ	&Delta;	&#916;	Capital letter delta
E	&Epsilon;	&#917;	Capital letter epsilon
Z	&Zeta;	&#918;	Capital letter zeta
H	&Eta;	&#919;	Capital letter eta
Θ	&Theta;	&#920;	Capital letter theta
I	&Iota;	&#921;	Capital letter iota
K	&Kappa;	&#922;	Capital letter kappa
Λ	&Lambda;	&#923;	Capital letter lambda
M	&Mu;	&#924;	Capital letter mu
N	&Nu;	&#925;	Capital letter nu
Ξ	&Xi;	&#926;	Capital letter xi
O	&Omicron;	&#927;	Capital letter omicron
Π	&Pi;	&#928;	Capital letter pi
P	&Rho;	&#929;	Capital letter rho
Σ	&Sigma;	&#931;	Capital letter sigma
T	&Tau;	&#932;	Capital letter tau
Y	&Upsilon;	&#933;	Capital letter upsilon
Φ	&Phi;	&#934;	Capital letter phi
X	&Chi;	&#935;	Capital letter chi
Ψ	&Psi;	&#936;	Capital letter psi
Ω	&Omega;	&#937;	Capital letter omega
α	&alpha;	&#945;	Small letter alpha
β	&beta;	&#946;	Small letter beta
γ	&gamma;	&#947;	Small letter gamma
δ	&delta;	&#948;	Small letter delta
ε	&epsilon;	&#949;	Small letter epsilon
ζ	&zeta;	&#950;	Small letter zeta
η	&eta;	&#951;	Small letter eta

(continued)

Table 12.4 **The Greek character set (continued).**

Character	Character Entity	Numeric Entity	Description
θ	&theta;	&#952;	Small letter theta
ι	&iota;	&#953;	Small letter iota
κ	&kappa;	&#954;	Small letter kappa
λ	&lambda;	&#955;	Small letter lambda
μ	&mu;	&#956;	Small letter mu
ν	&nu;	&#957;	Small letter nu
ξ	&xi;	&#958;	Small letter xi
ο	&omicron;	&#959;	Small letter omicron
π	&pi;	&#960;	Small letter pi
ρ	&rho;	&#961;	Small letter rho
σ	&sigma;	&#963;	Small letter sigma
τ	&tau;	&#964;	Small letter tau
υ	&upsilon;	&#965;	Small letter upsilon
φ	&phi;	&#966;	Small letter phi
χ	&chi;	&#967;	Small letter chi
ψ	&psi;	&#968;	Small letter psi
ω	&omega;	&#969;	Small letter omega
υ	&thetasym;	&#977;	Small letter theta
ϒ	&upsih;	&#978;	Upsilon with hook
Π	&piv;	&#982;	Pi

Table 12.5 **The miscellaneous technical character set.**

Character	Character Entity	Numeric Entity	Description
⌈	&lceil;	&#8968;	Left ceiling
⌉	&rceil;	&#8969;	Right ceiling
⌊	&lfloor;	&#8970;	Left floor
⌋	&rfloor;	&#8971;	Right floor
〈	&lang;	&#9001;	Left-pointing angle bracket
〉	&rang;	&#9002;	Right-pointing angle bracket

Table 12.6   The miscellaneous symbols character set.

Character	Character Entity	Numeric Entity	Description
♠	&spades;	&#9824;	Black spade suit
♣	&clubs;	&#9827;	Black club suit
♥	&hearts;	&#9829;	Black heart suit
♦	&diams;	&#9830;	Black diamond suit

Creating Parameter Entities

Parameter entities are reserved for use within the DTD itself and are not used in documents created for any XML DTD or application. Parameter entities provide a simple alias for groups of frequently used content models or attribute groups. To include a parameter entity in a DTD, use the following syntax:

```
<!ENTITY % nnn "content model or attribute list">
```

A sample parameter entity from the TecML DTD is:

```
<!ENTITY % x.content  '(%x.descrip;, (array | xlist| xvar)*)' >
```

As this examples shows, parameter entities can include other parameter entities in their content to create a nested effect that lends itself to clean and efficient DTD design. In a parameter entity, the single space to either side of the percent sign (%) is crucial. The spaces separate the sign from the entity declaration and the entity's name. If either space is missing, the entity will be invalid. To invoke a parameter entity within a DTD, simply use a percent sign (%) immediately followed by the entity's name and a semicolon (;), as shown here:

```
%x.descrip;
```

Chapter 13

Processing XML

By Cheryl Kirk

In Depth

To see the results of the markup and content of the XML documents and Document Type Definitions (DTDs) you've created, you must process the information contained within them. When an XML document is processed, it actually goes through several steps before the content is finally displayed. These steps—which include parsing, style-sheet formatting, and finally, displaying the XML content—make up the overall concept of XML document processing.

In this chapter, we'll examine the options you have for processing XML. We'll review parsers and how they work, and we'll look at the application programming interfaces (APIs) that are available for XML document objects so you can display or work with the contents of the document. In addition, we'll show you how you can use Java and C++ to create bridges to XML and browsers and objects within those XML documents. You'll learn exactly what you need to know about processing XML documents. In this chapter's Immediate Solutions section, we'll show you how to create the code used to help connect XML documents with browsers and other programs.

The Basics Of Processing XML Documents

What is an XML processor? It depends on whom you talk to and how they define processors. In the most basic terms, a processor is a software module that is used to read XML documents and provide access to their structure and content. Processing in the XML world can be done with parsers and processors, both of which survey the structure of the XML document and pass the results off to an XML application, which in turn does something with the content. The purpose of processing is to interpret the structure, report errors, and then pass along the interpretation to another XML application.

There are five basic steps you have to go through to get the structure and content you've created to the point where it can be displayed in a browser or sent to another application for further processing:

• Create the XML DTD and document.

TIP: *Remember that the DTD is optional, but we included it as part of the first step because we highly encourage you to create external DTDs for all your XML documents.*

- Run the DTD and document through a parser so it can gather the grammatical information it needs.

- Process the parsing results and check for errors.

- Provide the parsed results to any application that can interface with XML documents.

- Display (or send) the information according to the style-sheet formatting instructions to a browser or other XML application.

There is usually some piece of software that will help you accomplish each step involved in XML processing. First, let's evaluate each step in detail so you'll know the differences between a parser, a processor, and an XML software application.

When you create an XML file, you are actually creating a standard text file that can be interpreted by a variety of products, including browsers, Java applications, databases, and even page-layout programs. Which type of product you use to interpret the file depends on what you want to do with the content contained within the file. Do you want to send the information to a database? Perhaps you just want to display the information in a browser. Maybe you want to pull the content into a page-layout program. What you can do with the results of your processed XML file will depend on the steps you take when you process the XML files, related DTDs, and style sheets.

XML Editors

To create an XML file, you'll need to use some type of XML editor. Because XML files and DTDs are simply text files, you can use a simple text editor, such as Notepad.

TIP: *Notice that we recommended Notepad and not WordPad. WordPad natively saves its files with the .DOC extension (the Microsoft Word format), instead of the .TXT extension (text-only format). If you use WordPad, you must remember to change the file extension to .TXT when you save the document.*

But you don't have to use a simple text editor. More elaborate XML editors are available, and even more are slated for release over the next several years. Products such as XML Pro Editor by Vervet offer an easy-to-use interface that walks you through the process of creating XML elements, attributes, and entities and their related values. Such editors automatically put the correct brackets in the correct locations and include all the quotation marks, semicolons, and other grammatical notations. You simply provide the names of the elements and other XML components and XML Pro Editor does the rest.

In addition to performing the laborious tasks involved in marking up documents properly, editors such as XML Pro Editor offer wizards that help you write the XML DTDs and XML documents, then provide error checking to check the XML code. An XML editor is a great tool to keep in your XML software toolbox. You can find a list of other XML applications by checking out James Tauber's XMLInfo Web site at **www.xmlinfo.com**.

TIP: *There are now XML filters and plug-ins available for many word processors, including Microsoft Word. These additional pieces of code allow you to use the familiar interface of your word processor when you create XML files.*

Although we highly recommend you use such editors, here's what we recommend you do first. Create a few simple XML files in a text processor to get used to writing XML code and to learn how to form XML documents correctly. It's important that you understand how to construct a simple XML document before you use third-party editors; for example, it's easy to create an element when in fact the document requires an attribute. After you understand how to construct a simple XML document and the DTD, you can step up to the next level. Creating XML files manually will give you valuable experience and help you understand how XML elements, attributes, entities, and notations are formed. It will also help you troubleshoot the code you write in an XML editor because you'll understand exactly what is required where and when.

After you have some experience hand-coding a few pages, we recommend you explore and work with some of the XML editors on the market. They can help you quickly create XML documents and limit the amount of typing you have to do. Just make sure you carefully read and check the code generated by the XML editor you use. This will help prevent errors and allow you to add additional comments to your code if the XML editor does not include such an option.

Although there are many XML editors available, any XML editor you choose should have the following capabilities:

- The ability to display your document in a tree structure, which will help you visualize your document and quickly reference the elements and attributes that become objects in programming and scripting languages.

- The ability to quickly organize and reorganize your DTD and document.

- Support for both Unicode UTF-8 (8-bit Unicode) and Unicode UTF-16 (16-bit Unicode). Whichever encoding scheme you decide to use, your XML editor should be able to support it. Some only support 8-bit.

Here's a list of editors we highly recommend, all of which meet the preceding specifications:

- XML Pro by Vervet, available for download at **www.vervet.com**

- DynaBase from Inso Corporations, available for download at **www.inso.com**

- ADEPT by ArborText, located at **www.arbortext.com**

You can take XML document creation one step further and actually create documents based on other XML vocabularies, such as Microsoft's Channel Definition Format. You can choose from a variety of tools:

- Microsoft's Channel Wizard, located at **www.microsoft.com/channels**

- Cold Fusion's Channel Definition Wizard, located at **www.coldfusion.com**

- Bluestone Software's Sapphire/Web 4, available for download at **www.bluestone.com**

- Pictorius's iNet Developer, located at **www.pictorious.com**

XML Processors And Parsers

The processes of creating and then displaying XML data is very much akin to the process of writing a computer book. First, you write the text. Then, you send it to an editor who checks to make sure it's grammatically correct and warns you if there are any problems in the construction of your sentences. Next, you send it to a technical editor who checks it for technical accuracy. And finally, the whole thing goes to the designer who, with the help of style sheets, creates the final display of the book. Each step and each person's job ensures that the final product is as the original author intended it to be.

With XML files, software applications and components perform these functions. After you've created the XML file and/or the DTD, the next step is to check the file to ensure you've used the correct XML grammar. The XML counterpart to the editor is a software program called a *parser*. The Random House Dictionary defines the word *parse* as "the act of describing grammatically, or the telling of the part of speech." When you parse something, you are describing to something or someone what the various parts of XML speech you've created actually mean and that the correct grammar is used. On the most basic level, parsers break down the XML document into its element tree so either the processor or another application can do something with the content.

Before you can begin to think about displaying the content of your XML file, the document and its DTD must go through a parser. The parser reads the element tags and all other document components, checking to make sure the grammatical structure of the document conforms to the standards in the XML specification. If there are problems with your grammar, the processor will report errors. Without some sort of process-checking for proper XML syntax in your document or DTD, there would be no mechanism to alert you of structural and syntactical errors.

TIP: *Whether you decide to use an internal or external DTD is entirely up to you, but this choice will affect what type of parser you can use. Both validating and non-validating parsers are currently available. Validating parses check the accompanying DTD, but non-validating parsers will not check external or internal DTDs.*

XML documents can be parsed a variety of ways and with a variety of products. Usually, parsing is done on the client side, which means the server sending the XML document and data to the client performs little or no parsing of the data. And although you may assume parsing is done when the XML document processing starts, it can happen anywhere along the way. You can parse a document, process it, and then parse the links contained within it on a secondary level.

Which product or method you use to parse or when you parse the document is almost entirely left up to you. Some parsers are part of the final display application; others are separate pieces of software you load on your computer and use to evaluate your XML files. You'll find a variety of free XML parsers available on the Internet in such locations as Shareware.com (**www.shareware.com**). Microsoft also offers both a Java and C++ parser in both Internet Explorer 4 and Internet Explorer 5. The Java parser, called MSXML, is actually a Java code library. You can find out how to use these built-in parsers through Microsoft's XML site (**www.microsoft.com/xml**). IBM also offers a very good Java-based validating parser. You can find it at **www.alphaworks.ibm.com/Home**. Click the link titled "XML for Java" to download the code necessary to work with your Java browser.

TIP: *You'll see the terms* processor *and* parsing *mentioned a great deal in various XML-related documentation. Often, you'll find that these terms are interchangeable. In the general sense of the words, they are. But in this chapter, we define* parsing *as the act of checking the syntax of an XML document and* processing *as the overall group of steps used to get the final result you want.*

The parser compares the code in the XML document with the rules set forth in the XML specification. The parser must be able to read Unicode 8-bit and 16-bit characters and character entities. The parser must also read the internal XML document before interpreting internal or external DTDs. This ensures that local declarations are processed before external ones. If comments are stored within the document or within the external DTD, most parsers will ignore them, but some will report the context of the comment's text. When the parser encounters an attribute that is not defined in the DTD, an error will be reported, depending upon the type of parser used. An XML parser will also normalize any white space, character strings, or character references.

A parser will also send the XML application names of notations and the notations' external identifiers. When it encounters an entity, a parser warns the XML application of multiple entity declarations. The parser also tells the application where entity references have occurred and provides the application with the name of the entity. The parser replaces the reference with the actual character or text and passes this information to the application. The parser must recognize the five built-in entities used within XML, even if they aren't declared in the document. Parameter entity references are always expanded when the parser encounters them.

When the parser is interpreting the information in the XML document and/or DTD, it passes along specific information to the next application. Although you still have to check your document for errors, parsers will display errors so you don't have to hunt and peck through your document to find them. The parser application does that for you. Parsers are small programs that check not only the grammar of the XML file, but also the well-formedness and the validity of the document. There are two types of parsers and they know what rules are required for the document to be either well-formed or valid:

- *Non-validating parsers*—Software programs that check XML documents for well-formedness but not validity. This type of parser will ignore information provided in an accompanying DTD. If the document is missing a DTD, it will not report errors.

TIP: Non-validating parsers don't read DTDs. But, according to the XML 1 Specification, all parsers, whether they are validating or non-validating need to be able to read and properly interpret DTDs. The next time you use your parser, run one of your DTDs through it to see what happens. If it doesn't read the DTD, you may want to find another parser that can interpret the DTD. A parser that doesn't interpret DTDs may not interpret XML documents correctly.

- *Validating parsers*—Software programs check XML documents for validity, which means they check for the presence of the document's DTD and whether the document conforms to it. If a document doesn't have a DTD or if it has one but doesn't conform to its rules, the document is considered invalid.

Parsers usually take the form of some sort of code library usually written in C++ or Java. Both Netscape Navigator and Microsoft Internet Explorer use Java and C++ parsers. These parsers are actually made up of a code library that contains all the necessary programming to parse both valid and well-formed XML documents. If you don't have the code library, you would normally download it from the company that provides it and then reference it when you parse the document. Parsers can also be standalone applications from which you specify the file you want parsed and then get back the results of the parsing process. Figure 13.1 shows Microsoft's MSXML parser.

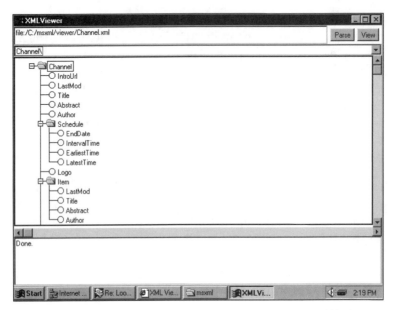

Figure 13.1 Microsoft's MSXML parser parses the XML document and, if it finds any errors, displays them in the bottom window.

Using Validating And Non-Validating Parsers

Which should you use to process your documents—a validating parser or a non-validating parser? It depends on the types of XML documents you are creating. If you use a non-validating parser, you can run the risk of sloppy XML code. If you use a validating processor, all code, regardless of whether it appears in the XML document or the DTD, must follow a specific set of defined rules. That's why using validating parsers is preferred. Because a validating parser reads and interprets both DTDs and XML documents, you can be sure the documents you create are correct in their structural content according to the XML 1 Specification.

But if speed is what you need, a non-validating parser will work faster than a validating parser, especially if you are using external DTDs stored on a remote site. A non-validating parser isn't required to check the DTD against the document, which can save processing time. All the information parsed is sent to the next processing application faster than if you were using a validating processor. Less computing resources are required with a non-validating parser, which most likely means that less bandwidth is required. Regardless of whether you use an external or internal DTD, you should consider using a non-validating parser if your computer resources are limited and you have network bandwidth constraints.

If you choose to use a non-validating parser, remember that a document must meet the following requirements to be considered well-formed:

- The beginning of the XML document must begin with a valid XML declarative statement.

- Only one element acts as the root element, which is the parent to all other elements.

- Elements cannot be empty. If no content is defined for an element—as in the **<IMG>** element where the location of the image is actually an attribute and not specified as content—the element must have both an open tag **<IMG>** and a close tag **</IMG>**. Or, you can indicate the close of the element within the tag, like this: **<IMG/>**.

- With the exception of the root element, all elements are contained within another element, which is referred to as the element's parent; all contained elements are referred to as the parent element's children.

- Character data that can be processed as XML is enclosed within **CDATA** sections.

- Documents can include comments, white space, and processing instructions.

XML Processors

After the XML document has been parsed, an XML processor takes over. It reads the document and offers other applications access to the XML components stored within the XML document. A processor could be a search application used to retrieve information from a database. Or, in the case of Mathematical Markup Language (MathML, an XML application), a processor could take the results of the parsed XML document, process the information through a statistical application, and pass along the results to another viewer that allows the client to see the results. A processor could also just pass along the results of the parsed file to a browser and let the browser display the data.

When a processor intercepts the parsed information, software developers can quickly access the structure of an XML document and work with the components in a variety of ways. All elements, attributes, entities, and notations are then considered objects, which can be further manipulated by other programs. Every XML development tool will have an XML parser at its core. After a document has been parsed, developers can take the parsed information and use additional editors, browsers, and databases to search or pull out XML objects from the parsed document. The various XML parsed objects can then be referenced, manipulated, or displayed by using additional programming languages or browsers.

With most XML processors and parsers, the role of the processor actually overlaps the role of the parser. The parser is responsible for checking the syntax of the DTD or XML document, and the processor is responsible for providing access to the content and structure of the document.

If a Web browser is capable of displaying or interpreting XML files, the browser must normally have an XML parser attached to it. The parser parses the data and then hands off the results to the processor. The built-in processor identifies the style formats specified in the file and displays the XML data in the format specified in the style sheet.

TIP: Current browsers, such as Netscape Navigator 5 and Microsoft Internet Explorer 5, have the ability to interpret and display XML files. In other words, they have built-in XML parsers. However, older browsers do not have the ability to display or parse XML documents. Remember that you must keep your audience in mind and identify whether their browsers have the capabilities to view the data you are offering.

Internet Explorer, versions 4 and 5, are good examples of how this parser/processor relationship works. Both offer a Java-based XML parser and also an ActiveX component that can be used to parse XML files. However, the ActiveX parser does not use external DTDs—only the built-in Java parser does. Older browsers, such as Internet Explorer 3 and Netscape Navigator 4, are limited because they don't include built-in parsers, but that doesn't mean they are incapable of displaying XML. They simply do not have the built-in programming code that enables XML files to be processed entirely. As a developer, you could display XML files by processing them through a Java interpreter that turns the results of a parsed XML file into HTML. As long as the browser offers a Java component, like those included in Internet Explorer 4 and 5 and Netscape Navigator 5, external Java-based parsers can be used to parse XML data and then display them in a Web browser window.

TIP: If you have one of the original versions of Internet Explorer 4, you need to download the latest Java class libraries in order for XML parsing to work. You can find them on Microsoft's XML site, **www.microsoft.com/xml**. Also note that the XML Java parser included with Internet Explorer 4 can also be used with Netscape Navigator. That's the glory of Java—never machine specific and, in most cases, portable across applications.

XML And Applications Such As Browsers

Most likely, you'll be creating XML documents so they can be browsed over the Internet. Because browsers can display XML content with the applicable defined styles, XML can be used on a wide scale. The browsers your visitors use must have XML capabilities. If they don't, the document will be displayed in text-only format or it will signal to the browser that the file should be downloaded and saved, usually as an EXE file. Figure 13.2 is an example of what happens when you use Netscape Communicator 4.05 to access an XML file. In this figure, Communicator 4.05 is unable to read or interpret an XML file because the definitions for XML and DTD files have been established or specified in the MIME/Types section of the browser. Based on these preferences established in the browser, Communicator must download the file and define it as an executable file on the Windows desktop.

Figure 13.2   Netscape Communicator 4.05 doesn't know what to do with XML or DTD files, so it assumes it's an executable and prompts you to specify a location to which the file should be downloaded.

A Brief History Of XML-Enabled Browsers

For the first two years of XML's existence, from 1996 to 1998, developers knew XML had great potential. But it was not quick to catch on because they couldn't demonstrate the results of their XML code and DTDs in any standard, widely used browser. Few, if any, Web browsers understood XML files, let alone offered built-in parsers and processors. Software developers quickly realized that, if all the hype about XML would be universally embraced, the masses must have a tool to view XML content.

Although native XML support was available in Microsoft Internet Explorer 4, there was no real support found in Netscape's Navigator browser as late as 1998. XML remained a relatively obscure markup language because there were far more Navigator users than Internet Explorer users in 1998, and Navigator users had to download additional Java code and code libraries that allowed them to use their Java-enabled browser to parse and then process the XML data into a tree-structured display. Even with Java-enabled parsers and processors, many Java implementations within the popular browsers were unstable, and users were still stymied by systems that regularly crashed when they tried to display XML files and structures.

It wasn't until early 1998 that Netscape announced widespread support of XML in its Navigator 5 browser. Although Internet Explorer 4 already had XML support, albeit on a limited basis, it wasn't until late 1998 with the release of both Navigator 5 and Internet Explorer 5, that users had not only a choice but also full XML support in the latest browsers.

Today's XML-Enabled Browsers

Today's browsers now fully implement all the features found in version 1 of the XML specification. They cannot only understand what XML and DTD files are, they can also parse, process, and display the content. Both Navigator and Internet Explorer offer the ability to view Cascading Style Sheets along with Dynamic HTML. Internet Explorer 4 and 5 also offer the ability to interface with XML documents through the Document Object Model, allowing developers the ability to use or display any of the objects found in an XML document.

TIP: See Chapter 23 for more information about how Microsoft Internet Explorer 4 and 5 and Netscape Navigator 5 utilize XML. Also, because new features are added almost monthly, make sure you visit both Netscape's and Microsoft's developer sites, located at **www.mozilla.org** and **www.microsoft.com/sitebuilder** respectively.

Browsers In Action: Parsing, Processing, And Displaying XML Data

Remember that the key component of XML is that the content is separate from the presentation. XML separates the presentation markup from the structural markup, and it is this feature that makes it easy for developers to embed specific instructions on how to display the same XML content in a variety of ways. The browser or display software is responsible for actually downloading and displaying the data in a format that best suits its needs. This allows the user to view the data in a variety of ways once it has been downloaded to the client computer. It also cuts down on the amount of server traffic, making it appear as if the browser is processing the information faster than it does for traditional HTML.

Because of this flexibility in content display, the developer must specify ways for the data to be presented. The developer must include in the code a style sheet (the markup language that defines how the content will look). Without a style sheet, the XML application won't know what to do with the parsed and processed data. A style sheet is the link to the content and the client. Let's look at how the parser, processor, and XML application use the document's structure, tree, and style sheet to display the content in a browser or through another XML-based application or vocabulary.

The XML Processing Instruction

By now, you should know the parts used to process XML documents. Let's take a look at how a simple XML document is processed. In this example, we'll use

Microsoft Internet Explorer 4 and its XML vocabulary called the Channel Definition Format (CDF). CDF reads, parses, and then processes the CDF file, which is actually an XML document. It all starts with the first line of code placed in the CDF file.

Remember how each XML document must first start with the XML processing instruction, **<?XML version="1.0"?>**? This processing instruction is placed at the top of XML files to tell the XML parser or processor component found in the XML-enabled application that this information is indeed meant to be processed as an XML file. Any application that is not XML aware, such as a standard HTML browser, would ignore this instruction.

The Document's Structure

In this section, we'll demonstrate how the XML processing instruction, document structure, and document elements are processed. We'll use Microsoft's Channel Definition Format to demonstrate this. Following the XML declaration, the actual document structure, the content of the channel, is created. With most XML documents, you can include an internal DTD or specify a reference to a DTD. In the case of CDF (an XML application) the CDF file (actually an XML file) does not contain any references to a DTD file. Instead, the structure of the document is defined within the declared element tags. In the next example, we've defined the structure of a channel.

The root element, from which all other elements branch, is defined by the **CHANNEL** element. Contained within the **CHANNEL** element are the elements that further describe the channel, including **ICON**, **ITEM**, and **ABSTRACT**. These elements create the tree structure from which Internet Explorer can parse and display the data. The code is as follows:

```
<?XML VERSION="1.0" ENCODING="UTF-8"?>
    <CHANNEL HREF="http://www.site.com/channels/index.htm"
        BASE="http://www.site.com/">

    <TITLE>The Channel
    </TITLE>

    <ABSTRACT>The Site's Channel
    </ABSTRACT>

        <LOGO HREF="http://www.site.com/logos/wide_logo.gif"
         STYLE="IMAGE-WIDE"/>
        <LOGO HREF="http://www.site.com/logos/logo.gif"
         STYLE="IMAGE"/>
        <LOGO HREF="http://www.site.com/logos/icon.gif"
         STYLE="ICON"/>
```

```
    <SCHEDULE>
      <INTERVALTIME DAY="1"/>
      <EARLIESTTIME HOUR="0"/>
      <LATESTTIME HOUR="12"/>
    </SCHEDULE>

    <ITEM HREF="http://www.site.com/channels/
     dailyupdate.htm">
        <LOGO HREF="http://www.site.com/logos/icon.gif"
         STYLE="ICON"/>

        <ABSTRACT>The Channel's Daily Update</ABSTRACT>

    </ITEM>

    <ITEM HREF="http://www.site.com/channels/info.htm">
        <LOGO HREF="http://www.site.com/logos/icon.gif"
         STYLE="ICON"/>

        <ABSTRACT>Information About the Channel
        </ABSTRACT>

    </ITEM>

</CHANNEL>
```

The structure of this document is defined by the main Web-page channel and other channel items included within the channel. Additional graphics help define the logos used to depict these various references to external Web pages. This is the XML document structure from which Internet Explorer can create a tree structure, thereby displaying the various channel elements we've created with our code.

TIP: *Notice that the previous code isn't really a document in the traditional sense; it contains no real content, only references to content. This mechanism to describe where the XML content can be found is called* metadata. *You'll hear Netscape use this term frequently when referring to XML-enabled applications.*

When you use Internet Explorer to access the CDF file, the browser parses the information knowing it is using XML instead of HTML. It then provides you with a dialog box asking you if you want to subscribe to the site's channel. The document was first parsed and then processed, and what you see in Figure 13.3 is an example of the processor's results.

Once the channel and all its elements have been loaded in the browser, you can see how channels show the tree structure of the XML document from which they

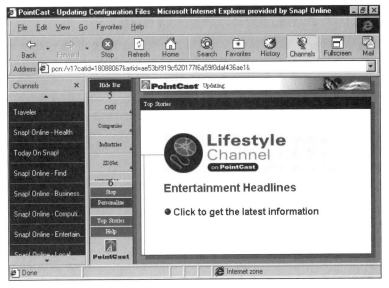

Figure 13.3   Our XML data file was parsed and processed, and the result is the channel in our Channels Explorer bar.

were based. You can then decide to view the individual channel elements or collapse the tree structure.

XML And Application Programming Interfaces

Application programming interfaces (APIs) are tools that work with XML processors. Some APIs might be included in the processor to provide additional processing functionality and services. In addition to numerous XML processors and parsers, API kits for XML have been popping up recently. With an API kit, you can use modules to process well-formed XML documents in a variety of ways. For example, you can use certain API modules to sort the data within an XML document. Other API modules might allow you to create reports from an XML data source. And still others can help you convert HTML documents to XML by cleaning up the HTML code so the file can successfully function as an XML document. Here is a partial list of available APIs (you can find more at **www.xmlsoftware.com**):

- *Free-Dom*—An API written in Java to sit on top of any XML parser.
- *Saxon*—An API written in Java for processing XML documents. This API assists in transforming XML documents to HTML and HTML to XML documents.
- *XAF*—A Java-based XML API for creating XML architectural forms.
- *Tidy*—An API written in the C programming language and used to clean up HTML documents so you can convert them to XML

Processing XML In Other Ways

After it is parsed, the XML document itself passes along the information to a processor. The processor can be a scripting language, such as JavaScript or VBScript, or it can be Java itself. It has been said by representatives of Sun Microsystems, the creators of Java, that XML finally gives Java something to do. With compatible structures, Java and XML complement each other, and Java helps extend the functionality you can incorporate with XML data sources. In the following sections, we'll describe how you can use scripting languages to process XML data sources. We'll start with a simple example that uses ActiveX (a component found in Internet Explorer) and Java components to present XML data within a browser.

Processing XML Documents With ActiveX And Java Components

As you know, presentation and data are separate in XML. Although the code to display XML is built in to newer browsers, many people are still using HTML-only browsers that cannot interpret your XML code. Therefore, you need some mechanism to display the content you've structured in XML. You can point to and display the XML content with either ActiveX or Java, both common methods used to get XML data to HTML-specific browsers. You can create your XML document, define a style sheet, and use a browser and additional programming code to marry the XML data to the browser, essentially processing the XML data into readable code an HTML-specific browser can handle.

First, you need to define the XML document from which the information will be parsed and then processed into the browser. Although such a document doesn't need a DTD, if you want valid XML code, you should include one. In the following example, we've included the DTD within the XML document itself:

```
<?XML VERSION = "1.0" ?>
<!DOCTYPE BOOKSTORE[
<!ENTITY BK "Borders Books">
<!ELEMENT BOOK (SUBJECT)*>
<!ELEMENT SUBJECT (TITLE,PUBLISHER,AUTHOR,PRICE,PAGES)>
<!ELEMENT TITLE (#PCDATA)>
<!ELEMENT PUBLISHER (#PCDATA)>
<!ELEMENT AUTHOR (#PCDATA)>
<!ELEMENT PRICE (#PCDATA)>
<!ELEMENT PAGES (#PCDATA)>
]>

<BOOKSTORE>
```

```
<BOOK>
    <TITLE>Supercharged Web Browsers</TITLE>
      <AUTHOR>Cheryl Kirk</AUTHOR>
      <PUBLISHER>Charles River Media</PUBLISHER>
      <PRICE>$34.95</PRICE>
    <PAGES>380</PAGES>
</BOOK>

<BOOK>
    <TITLE>Internet and Web Answers!</TITLE>
      <AUTHOR>Cheryl Kirk</AUTHOR>
      <PUBLISHER>Osborne</PUBLISHER>
      <PRICE>19.95</PRICE>
    <PAGES>400</PAGES>
</BOOK>

<BOOK>
    <TITLE>Dynamic HTML</TITLE>
      <AUTHOR>Natanya Pitts</AUTHOR>
      <PUBLISHER>Coriolis</PUBLISHER>
      <PRICE>$29.95</PRICE>
    <PAGES>700</PAGES>
</BOOK>

<BOOK>
    <TITLE>The Internet Phone Connection</TITLE>
      <AUTHOR>Cheryl Kirk</AUTHOR>
      <PUBLISHER>Osborne</PUBLISHER>
      <PRICE>$29.95</PRICE>
    <PAGES>380</PAGES>
</BOOK>

<BOOK>
    <TITLE>Getting Started with Netscape's Server</TITLE>
      <AUTHOR>Cheryl Kirk</AUTHOR>
      <PUBLISHER>Ziff Davis</PUBLISHER>
      <PRICE>$29.95</PRICE>
    <PAGES>400</PAGES>
</BOOK>

</BOOKSTORE>
```

After you've defined the XML data, you need to create the style sheet that will be referenced by the ActiveX parser. The code for such a style sheet will look something like this:

```
<xsl>
<rule>
     <root/>
     <HTML>
     <BODY font-family="Arial, helvetica,
          sans-serif" font-size="14pt"
         background-color="#FFFFFF">
       <children/>

          </BODY>

       </HTML>

    </rule>

<rule>
     <target-element type="BOOK"/>
     <DIV background-color="white" color="blue"
        padding="4px">

       Title: <:select-elements>
       <:target-element type="TITLE"/>
     </select-elements>; Author:

     <select-elements>
       <:target-element type="AUTHOR"/>
     </select-elements>
     </DIV>

      <DIV margin-left="20px" margin-bottom="1em"
        font-size="12pt">
     Publisher: <:select-elements>
     <target-element type="PUBLISHER"/>
     </select-elements>;

        <select-elements>
        <:target-element type="PAGES"/>
     </select-elements> pages;

        Price: <:select-elements>
        <:target-element type="PRICE"/>
     </select-elements>

    </DIV>
```

```
</rule>

</xsl>
```

The next step is to define code that points the ActiveX component or Java applet to the XML file. If you plan to use the ActiveX parser (a component shipped with Internet Explorer 4) to point to the style sheet and XML file, essentially marrying them together, the code you create would look like this:

```
<OBJECT ID="XSLControl"
CLASSID="CLSID:2BD0D2F2-52EC-11D1-8C69-0E16BC000000"
codebase="http://www.microsoft.com/xml/xsl/msxsl.cab"
style="display:none">

<PARAM NAME="documentURL" VALUE="xmldocument.xml">

<PARAM NAME="styleURL" VALUE="stylesheet.xsl">

</OBJECT>
```

The next step is to define a target in which the information can be placed. This information will be formatted using the style-sheet mechanism. The code looks like this:

```
<DIV id=styleTarget>
</DIV>
```

After you've define the target, you need to create a script that will specify to the parser that the information stored within the XML document, xmldocument.xml, will be displayed within the **DIV** target we've created. Here's how the code to do this would look:

```
<SCRIPT FOR=window EVENT=onload>
var xslHTML = XSLControl.htmlText;
document.all.item("styleTarget").innerHTML = xslHTML;
</SCRIPT>
```

Processing XML Data With JavaScript

But wait, there's more! Not only can we use this document to view channels if we're using Internet Explorer, we can also pass the XML document structure off to another processing language to do even more than just process the document structure. We could do something as simple as printing out what the contents of each **ITEM** element contains, or we could do something more complex, such as store the list of channels and their **ITEM** elements in a database.

We've used JavaScript in the following example to pull the information from the XML document and display it in another window. We might use this feature to give the visitor more information about what's contained in each channel or add additional banner advertising to a separate window. In the following example, we'll use JavaScript and the Microsoft MSXML processor to take the data contained in the previous XML CDF file, open a new window, and display more information about the channel. The JavaScript code to do just that could look like this:

```
<script language="jscript">
<!--
var doc = new ActiveXObject("msxml");
var wndw = null;

function DisplayElements(cdffile)
{
// This is where the new window opens to display the info
wndw = window.open("","CDFFile",
"resizable,scrollbars=yes");
wndw.document.open();
doc.URL = cdffile;

// The next line displays the elements or ITEMS
// starting with the root element
displayElement(doc.root);

wndw.document.write("</body>");
wndw.document.close();

}

function displayElement(elem) {
if (elem == null) return;
wndw.document.writeln("<p>");
if (elem.type == 0)
    wndw.document.writeln("Document with element: " + elem.tag);
else
    wndw.document.writeln("Document contains element with no tag.");
wndw.document.writeln("<br>Element is of type: " +
GetType(elem.type) +"<br>");
wndw.document.writeln("Element text: "
+ elem.text + "<br>");
wndw.document.writeln("Element href: "
+ elem.getAttribute("href") + "<br>");
wndw.document.writeln("Element base: "
+ elem.getAttribute("base") + "<br>");
wndw.document.writeln("Element style: "
```

```
      + elem.getAttribute("style") + "<br>");
wndw.document.writeln("Element day: "
      + elem.getAttribute("day") + "<br>");
wndw.document.writeln("Element hour: "
      + elem.getAttribute("hour") + "<br>");
wndw.document.writeln("Element minute: "
      + elem.getAttribute("min") + "<br>");

// Next we move to any children elements
var elem_children = elem.children;
if (elem_children != null)
   for (var i = 0; i < elem_children.length; i++) {
      element_child = elem_children.item(i);
         displayElement(element_child);
   }

}

// This is where we specify the element type
function GetType(type) {
if (type == 0)
        return "ELEMENT";
if (type == 1)
        return "TEXT";
if (type == 2)
        return "COMMENT";
if (type == 3)
        return "DOCUMENT";
if (type == 4)
        return "DTD";
else
        return "OTHER";
}

//-->
</script>
```

XML And The Document Object Model

To further explain how XML processing works, let's crank it up a notch and discuss something that for some people may be somewhat confusing—the Document Object Model (DOM). What is a DOM? It is a way to describe an XML document to another application or programming language in an effort to further manipulate the information the way you want it. You can use the DOM to place XML data sources with browsers. More specifically, however, you can use it to collect information about an XML document's structure and then use that information to create connections between the document's structure and other applications or data sources.

A relatively easy way to use DOM is to use scripting languages, such as JavaScript or VBScript, to load an XML document, manipulate it, and send the data or results back out to another application. Depending upon the application and scripting language you use, you can even use DOM to display the content of the XML file or to provide a mechanism to search the XML document.

You can create an XML document and load it into the Internet Explorer browser component by creating an ActiveX object and using the load method to load the document. Once it is loaded, you can then navigate or point to any component within the document by starting at the root element, which is commonly referred to as the *root node*.

> **WARNING!**   At the time this book was written, DOM was under review and discussion within the World Wide Web Consortium (W3C). Because there were multiple proposals for DOM submitted, some of the information presented here may have changed. Make sure you check the W3C's Web site (www.w3.org) for more information on DOM.

It's XML's tree structure that enables you to quickly retrieve the information or XML component you need. Everything in the tree is an object, from the first root node to the value of an entity. Being able to navigate this tree enables you to retrieve important information concerning the data source.

To help you further understand how DOM works in relationship to XML, let's look at how a simple script used in Internet Explorer 4 can access XML. After we've been able to access the objects we need, we can use JavaScript to display the final results in a Web page.

First, you should know that DOM uses three objects to access the XML file:

- The XML document
- The XML node
- The XML node list

The XML Document

Think of the XML document as an object. That object, although it represents the entire XML source document, can be accessed through the use of a script. That script can be placed in a Web page. The script can load the XML document, because to the scripting language, it's just an object. Once loaded, the script can then manipulate it, like any object. You can have the document load by creating an ActiveX object and using the **load** method, a scripting call available for ActiveX objects. Because XML requires you to follow a structured pattern to form your XML documents, DOM can access any XML document, and the document represents an object you can manipulate. In theory, that means you could use and reuse scripts to access XML documents, and because the structure of XML documents follow a pattern, with a few simple changes, your script would apply to just about any XML document.

The XML document, as defined in DOM, consists of the root element along with all of its descendants. For example, in the following code, **<NEWSPAPER>** is the root element, and the rest of the elements, such as **<SECTION>**, are considered its descendants or children. That means the entire XML document object is all the code contained in the following:

```
<NEWSPAPER>
    <SECTION>
        <STORY>
        </STORY>
    </SECTION>
</NEWSPAPER>
```

The XML Node

The XML node object represents a node within an XML document. The following are considered nodes in Internet Explorer 5:

- Element
- PCDATA
- Comment
- !DOCTYPE
- Any processing instructions
- CDATA sections
- Namespaces
- ENTITYREF
- White space
- Attributes
- The XML Declaration

The XML Node List

The node list in the XML document model represents a collection of nodes. There are several properties and methods used in the XML node list:

- *Property*—Length
- *Methods*—CurrentNode, Item, MoveTo, MoveToNode, NextNode, previousNode

Using XML DOM

When you use DOM, you can assign various XML objects to variables. The variables can then be accessed and manipulated by any number of applications. Once you have created an XML document object, you can access information about the object and manipulate the object by using DOM's properties and methods. A full reference to all the XML DOM properties and methods are available on Microsoft's Web site at **www.microsoft.com/DOM** or from the World Wide Web Consortium's site located at **www.w3c.org**. We would list them here, but DOM is still in the development stage, so you'll find the most up-to-date references online. Microsoft offers additional information about DOM on their XML Web site, located at **www.microsoft.com/xml**.

Database Processing

Until now, we've concentrated on processing XML data within a Web browser. But the beauty of XML is that it can also connect the data in XML documents with applications such as databases to make information more accessible. In this section, we'll give you an overview of how XML database processing works. We'll show you how a simple Access database can be interfaced with XML to create an interesting integrated database system.

The Problem

When you work with desktop databases such as Access or even Excel, the biggest problem is that only users who have Access or Excel stored on their systems can access the data. With XML, you can easily create a few simple scripts, an Active Server page (ASP), and an XML data source that would pull the information from the Access database and populate the XML database every time someone requests information from the database. This could all be done with the help of VBScript and the Open Database Connectivity (ODBC) found in Windows 95, 98, and NT.

After the scripts convert the data in the Access database into an XML source file, the information can easily be manipulated by other applications and shown within standard HTML Web pages. This makes the data accessible to anyone who has a Web browser, even if they don't have the Access application loaded on their computer. Let's step through the process and see how this all comes together and how ASP can help process XML data. In the following example, the actual act of processing the information into and out of XML involves more than just a simple browser application.

The Scenario

We have a database that lists all the employees in a particular department along with their phone numbers and addresses. We have this data stored in an Access database, so we can quickly find and sort whoever we are looking for at a particular time. But the problem is that not everyone has Access installed on their computer. We need to make the data accessible across your company's intranet. This will require our Access database, a few lines of code, the Microsoft Internet Information Server, Active Server pages, and XML.

Here's what the structure of our database looks like:

Name	Department	Phone
Jane Doe	Human Resources	555-2300
Harry Smith	Accounting	555-2301
Jeff North	Accounting	555-2310
Bobby Diggins	Information Systems	555-4458

We need to connect our database to the Web using an intranet server, running Microsoft's Internet Information Server with its accompanying Active Server Page technology, to make this information in the database accessible via a Web page. ASP will help us transform the Access data into an XML data source. The data source will reside on our intranet server in the form of an ASP file that can be accessed with the Internet Explorer browser. ASP does more than just transform the Access file into an ASP file—it actually converts the data to XML. The data can then be evaluated by using DOM or other XML-based technologies. It also makes it possible for scripts to access the file. Scripts can query the database, as well as populate it, if necessary. And because the XML data source is generated dynamically from the Access database, Access users can still use Access to add new information.

Creating The Data Source

Our first step is to create the XML data source on the server. We do this by creating an ASP file that is used to create the Access data and turn it into XML data. You might have seen this same type of thing done with ASP to generate HTML pages. The theory is the same, but the output will be XML instead of HTML. The code for generating an ASP file looks like this:

```
<%@LANGUAGE = VBScript%>
   <?XML VERSION="1.0">
   <Employees>
```

As you can see, the ASP file starts with a declaration that indicates what scripting language we will use. The next line indicates that XML version 1 will be used. The next line specifies what the main root element of the XML document will be.

The preceding code creates the structure we need. The next step is to name the Access database stored on the company's server. Because we are going to make a connection between Access, ASP, and VBScript, we need to invoke Open Database Connectivity (ODBC) and make the Access database accessible to the VBScript. We do that by opening the Control Panel's ODBC icon and adding the Access database to the list of ODBC-accessible items.

Next, we connect the Access database to the ASP script by using an Active Data Object declaration in another VBScript. This script will create an object from the Access database, which in turn will access a table we've created called **EMPLOYEELIST**. At that point, the following script will populate the XML data source:

```
<%
    Set Conn = Server.CreateObject("ADODB.Connection")
    Conn.Open "EMPLOYEES"
    Set EMPLOYEE = Conn.Execute("select * from EMPLOYEELIST")
    Do While Not Tape.EOF
    %>
```

Now, we need to create the basic structure of the elements. It's important that you pay special attention to the structure; if you don't, the information that is displayed could be incorrect or point to the wrong element. Working with data that is stored in tabular format makes it easier to create your XML structure. In our example, we have three subelements within the Employee Database: Employee Name, Department, and Phone. We can turn this information into an XML document structure with the following code to specify each employee's record:

```
<employee>
      <employeename></employeename>
      <department></department >
      <phone></phone>
</employee>
```

Now that we know the structure of the employee elements, the next step is to create an XML data source that contains the various elements. The idea is to have the script populate each of the employee elements in the XML document. The script would do this by pulling the information from the Access database and placing it in the XML document where the elements for the employees match up to the fields in the database. To do this, we simply need to create a framework for the employee element. Then, we populate the framework with declared variables representing the various fields in the employee database. The script would look something like this:

```
<EmployeeRecord>
      <employeename><%=Info("Name")%></employeename>
      <department><%=Info("Department")%></department>
      <phone><%=Info("Phone")%></phone>
</EmployeeRecord>
```

Now, we need to tell the Active Server Page to continue through each entry in the Access table. This will create a loop that pulls the information out:

```
<% Info.MoveNext
   Loop
   %>
   </Employees>
```

From the previous code listing, the accompanying script will create the following data source in well-formed XML structure:

```
<?XML VERSION="1.0">
   <Employees>
<Employee>
        <employeename>Jane Doe</employeename>
        <department>Human Resources</department>
        <phone>555-2300</Phone>
     </EmployeeRecord>

<EmployeeRecord>
        <employeename>Harry Smith</employeename>
        <department>Accounting</department>
        <phone>555-2301</phone>
     </EmployeeRecord>

<EmployeeRecord>
        <employeename>Jeff North</employeename>
        <department>Accounting</department>
        <phone>555-2310</phone>
</EmployeeRecord>

<EmployeeRecord>
        <employeename>Bobby Diggins</employeename>
        <department>Information Systems</department>
        <phone>555-4458</phone>
</EmployeeRecord>

<Employees>
```

Immediate Solutions

In this section, we'll show you the steps involved in parsing, processing, and displaying XML documents. In addition, we'll cover how to use and expose the XML DOM in Internet Explorer 5 to manipulate and display XML content.

Parsing An XML File

Parsing is simply reading through the document and checking to make sure the grammar conforms to the XML specification so the information can be passed along to the XML processor and finally to the intended application for display. Parsers can be written in a variety of languages, including Java and C++.

Using A Validating Parser To Parse An XML File

There are two types of XML parsers, validating and non-validating. We'll show you how to use both. Validating processors match the XML document structure to the referenced DTD to ensure all the elements, attributes, and entities specified in the XML document match those described in the DTD. In the following example, you'll use Microsoft's MSXML validating parser written in Java. Follow these steps for downloading, installing, and parsing your XML documents:

1. Make sure you are using Internet Explorer 4 or above. You need IE4 to use the classes you will download. You must have the Java Virtual Machine installed on your computer, and IE4 has this installed within it.

2. Connect to the Internet, and locate the following site: **www.microsoft.com/xml/parser/xmldl.asp**.

3. Click on the link to download the self-extracting installer, which will place the installer files in a directory called c:\msxml.

4. Double-click on the self-extracting installer icon to install the MSXML parser.

5. Double-click on the xmlparse HTML page, and then click on the link to the XML Viewer Applet. The MSXML parser is launched in a separate window.

6. Click in the first file path area, and type the full path name to the file you want to parse.

7. Click on the Parse button. A document tree structure displays. If there are any errors with this file, you'll see them in the window at the bottom of the screen. If you want to see the actual text that constructed the XML file, click the View button in the upper-right corner of the screen.

Using A Non-Validating Parser To Parse An XML File

A non-validating parser simply checks the document for well-formedness, meaning it checks to make sure the structure of the data uses the conventions set forth in the XML specification. The conventions include making sure each element start-tag has an accompanying end-tag, making sure elements with no content (empty elements) have some sort of notation specifying where the tag closes, and making sure content contained within the document is of character, CDATA, or element type.

To parse an XML document with a non-validating parser, you must have Internet Explorer 4 or above so you have the proper Java classes. Follow these instructions to view a non-validated parsed document online:

1. Locate the following Web site in your Internet Explorer browser:
   www.microstar.com/XML/AElfred.

2. Click on the link for the online demonstration. The Java-enabled non-validating parser loads within the right frame of the HTML page.

3. Click on the button to parse the XML document called "John Donne's Elegy XIX: To His Mistress Going to Bed," which is stored on Microstar's server.

4. As the parser moves through the document, you'll see the results of the parsed XML document.

Using The XML DOM To Access XML Objects

To access XML objects, you first have to create an instance of the parser. You can do this by using an ActiveX object. You can use the object model to walk the document tree structure. After creating this object, actually an object that is the document, you can access the information by calling the properties and methods that are associated with the XML document object we've created. To do so, follow these steps:

TIP: *The method for accessing an XML data source in Microsoft Internet Explorer 5 is similar to that of accessing an XML data source in Internet Explorer 4.*

---

1. Create an XML document object by creating a new ActiveX object. The code you use to create the document object will assign the XML document object to the variable **xml**, which you specify in the following code:

    ```
    var xml = new ActiveXObject("microsoft.xmldom");
    ```

2. Next, call the load method, and pass it a valid URL by including the following code in your document:

    ```
    xml.load("xmlDataSource.xml");
    ```

3. Next, use the document node property to identify the root element of the XML data source that you are pointing to in the URL in the preceding line of code:

    ```
    var docRoot = xml.documentNode
    ```

Once you have located the document root, you can move up and down the document's tree structure by using the node object, as we mentioned previously in this chapter, to navigate and manipulate the document's tree.

Creating A Script To Access The Object Model

After you've created the code to access an XML data source, you can create a JavaScript to reveal the contents of the XML document to a browser such as Internet Explorer 5. This script, an example from Microsoft's XML site, will create an ActiveX object that represents an XML data source. From there it will pass the root of the document to the function **output_doc**. The following code provides access to the object model:

```
<SCRIPT LANGUAGE="JScript" FOR=window EVENT=onload>
var indent_array = new String(" ");
var str = "";

var xml = new ActiveXObject("microsoft.xmldom");
xml.load("pdcxml.xml");

var docroot = xml.documentNode;

output_doc(docroot,0);
```

```
function output_doc(node,indents)
{
    var i;

    if (node.nodeType == 0)  // 0 is an ELEMENT node
    {
        document.all("results").insertAdjacentText("BeforeEnd",
            indent_array.substring(0,(4 * indents)) +
            "<" + elem.tagName + ">" + "\n");

    if (node.childNodes != null)
    {
        for (i = 0 ; i < node.childNodes.length ; i++)
        output_doc(node.childNodes.item(i),(indents + 1));
        }

        document.all("results").insertAdjacentText("BeforeEnd",
            indent_array.substring(0,(4 * indents)) +
            "</" + elem.tagName + ">" + "\n");
    }
    else if (node.nodeType == 1) // 1 is a TEXT node
    {
        document.all("results").insertAdjacentText("BeforeEnd",
            indent_array.substring(0,(4 * indents)) +
            "\"" + elem.text + "\"\n");
    }
    else
        alert("unknown element type: " + node.nodeType);
}
```

Part III

XML Style Sheets

Chapter 14

Stylin' XML: Cascading Style Sheets

By Natanya Pitts-Moultis

In Depth

This chapter focuses on the role style sheets play in the presentation of XML documents and provides in-depth coverage of Cascading Style Sheets (CSS)— one of the three style sheet methods that can be used with XML. It also contains a discussion of the pros and cons of using CSS with XML, a full reference for creating Cascading Style Sheets, and a complete rundown of all the CSS properties and values available to developers with the release of the latest version of CSS—CSS2.

Like any good markup language, XML exists to provide information about the structure and content of a document or set of documents. But XML leaves issues of document style and presentation to the software package used to parse and process it. To help these applications along, the creators of XML have considered some of the hard lessons learned during the development of HTML and implemented style sheet support as part of the overall XML strategy from the beginning. The markup governs content and structure, whereas associated style sheets govern how that content and structure is presented to the user.

The concept of style is not a new one, although the introduction of style sheets into the HTML world has been difficult at best. As with HTML, different browsers handle Cascading Style Sheets differently. To get a glimpse of the different implementations of style sheets among the various Web browsers, visit the Web site at **webreview.com/wr/pub/guides/style/mastergrid.html**. Because an XML document can be parsed by any application that can read its Document Type Definition (DTD) or any application that can read a well-formed document without a DTD, XML developers can't count on the application to take care of document display as HTML developers can. In the end, this is a good thing, as the differences in HTML rendering by various and sundry Web browsers have shown. HTML developers are constantly frustrated and stumped by the incompatible displays that are often the result of viewing a document with different browsers.

XML provides a much more complex, robust, and extensible set of markup options, and the final presentation is up to the browsers. This could prove to be almost disastrous. In this chapter, we'll make a case for XML style sheets, briefly discuss the three different style mechanisms available to XML developers, and spend the remainder of the chapter focusing on the first of the three mechanisms— Cascading Style Sheets.

The Case For Style Sheets

Because we have worked with Web documents both before and after style sheets were available, it seems obvious to us why anyone working with a markup language would want to use style sheets. But we realize that not everyone worked with Web documents back in the early days, and perhaps the use of style sheets isn't as much of a no-brainer as we seem to think it is. So, why should you use style sheets with XML when XML itself allows you to build in any page presentation tool you need? We have a three-part answer to that question:

- A single style sheet can govern an unlimited number of documents.

- When markup is separated from style presentation, rules are more efficiently created, more consistent, easier to update and change, and easier to manage.

- Multiple style sheets can easily be applied to the same document or set of documents as dissemination needs demand.

In following sections, we'll expand on each of these arguments so we can move on to the business of creating Cascading Style Sheets.

One Style Sheet, Unlimited Documents

Style information can be stored either internally or externally. Internal style rules—those listed only in the document they pertain to—are limited in application to the document in which they reside. However, external style rules—those that reside in a style-only document that is external to any other XML documents—apply to every document to which their document is linked. Therefore, in theory, a single external style sheet could be linked to, and define the style for, thousands of documents in a collection. Because an entire document collection relies on a single style sheet, you can change the style of the entire document collection by simply changing a single style sheet. Once the change is made to the style sheet, the style rules of the documents linked to it will change by extension.

Separate Style From Markup For Improved Efficiency, Consistency, And Maintenance

Imagine that you've written a DTD that provides eight different presentation-related attributes for each paragraph of your document and five for each heading. Whereas this DTD obviously takes advantage of the extensibility of XML, you'll have to set all of the attributes for every paragraph and heading every time they appear in your document or document collection. However, your paragraphs and headings probably fall into a variety of groups, or classes, because of their similar attribute settings. By adding a style sheet that defines the attribute settings for each class of paragraph or heading, you won't need to set them individually.

Instead, you only need to classify the paragraphs and headings and let the style sheet do the rest.

The ability to link multiple documents to a single style sheet provides a mechanism for ensuring consistency of style and presentation across an entire document collection. As the Internet, intranets, and extranets become the primary medium for the dissemination of documents, consistency of style and presentation is essential. Document designers can use style to provide readers with visual clues that help them familiarize themselves with the creators of the information they are browsing. For example, companies that have spent years creating a corporate image via logos and slogans can use those same elements to create familiarity with their Web content. Style can also be used to provide both nontextual content and emphasis to textual content. This makes the overall interaction with the information more enriching and interesting for the user. Without a simple, standard mechanism for ensuring the consistency of these visual and nontextual clues, document designers would not be able to easily implement advanced styles and presentation layouts. Style sheets allow developers to set up styles once and apply them to a large number of documents quickly and easily.

The development of XML documents is only the beginning of a long commitment to the upkeep and maintenance of a document collection. New information is generated constantly, and with solid XML DTDs and accompanying style sheets in place, adding the information to the collection is simple. Style and presentation needs change as well, and style information embedded in markup must be changed on a case-by-case and page-by-page basis. However, style information separated from markup and stored in style sheets can be changed for an entire document collection by simply changing the style sheet. This is an efficient method that ensures consistency and makes the maintenance of document collections quick and easy.

One Document, Many Styles

Very rarely is information created that won't be leveraged in some way and need to be presented in an entirely new light. Documents become bullet points. Bullet points become presentations. Presentations become outlines. Outlines become new documents. In addition, a single document may need to be presented across various media, such as Web pages, printed pages, Braille, and text read by a computer for the visually impaired. Public and private versions of documents are common, just as it is common for some portions of a document to be available only to those with the necessary access credentials.

Although it is possible to create a new iteration of a document to meet each need, it isn't an efficient or resource-effective method for disseminating information for a single document, much less a collection of thousands of documents. Instead, several different style sheets can be written for a document or collection of documents and be implemented as dissemination needs require. Once again, efficiency and consistency are achieved and a single iteration of a document can be manipulated to meet a wide variety of presentation and dissemination needs.

We could go on and on about why style sheets are useful; we could even write an entire book about them. Natanya actually did; see **www.lanw.com/books/ htmlcss.htm** for more information about the *HTML Style Sheets Design Guide* from The Coriolis Group. However, if you've spent any time developing content for dissemination, you'll see almost immediately why style sheets are a necessary and valuable tool. In the next section, we'll look briefly at the style alternatives available to XML developers and then move on to the Immediate Solutions section of this chapter.

XML Style Options

There are currently three different style sheet options available to XML developers. They include:

- Cascading Style Sheets levels 1 and 2 (CSS1 and CSS2)

- Document Style Semantics and Specification Language (DSSSL)

- Extensible Style Language (XSL)

CSS1 and DSSSL are existing standards, whereas CSS2 and XSL are under development by the World Wide Web Consortium (W3C) and related groups. The remainder of this chapter focuses on using CSS with XML; Chapters 15 and 16 focus on the other two style sheet mechanisms—DSSSL and XSL, respectively. Chapter 17 wraps up the coverage of XML style with a frank discussion of the realities of designing documents with XML.

The Pros And Cons Of Using CSS With XML

There are several reasons you would want to use CSS with XML, but there are also reasons you would not. As you work more and more with XML and related style sheet languages, you'll find that each has its appropriate uses, as do the various XML vocabularies. Luckily, you won't be obligated to try to force CSS, DSSSL, or XSL to do what you want them to because each provides a solution for very different needs. The following list includes some of the advantages of using CSS:

- CSS is easy to learn and implement. Because CSS was originally designed for HTML, it was created to be a simple yet elegant solution to the issues of style on the Web.

- CSS is already at work in the Web community. As CSS finds better implementation among Web-related vendors, it will naturally be implemented as an XML style solution as well as an HTML style solution.

- CSS works with HTML. While we wait for the integration of XML into the Web world, many XML documents will be translated into HTML for mass-market dissemination. Because CSS already works with HTML, it will be relatively simple to create style sheets for HTML documents that are produced from XML documents.

However, CSS does have a downside when it is implemented with XML (as described by Jon Bosak in his WWW6 presentation given in April 1997):

- CSS cannot generate text.

- CSS cannot grab an item from one place and use it again in another place.

- CSS is not a programming language; it does not support decision structures, and it cannot be extended by the style sheet designer.

- CSS is oriented toward Western languages and assumes a horizontal writing direction.

- CSS uses a simple box-oriented formatting model that works for current Web browsers but will not extend to more advanced applications of the markup, such as multiple column sets.

- CSS has no concept of sibling relationships.

Immediate Solutions

If you've ever used CSS with HTML, you'll take to using CSS with XML like a duck to water. All of the mechanisms are the same, selectors and property definitions take the same format, and the property/value combinations from which you have to choose are identical. If you treat HTML as an XML vocabulary, then you have used CSS with XML. The only difference in using CSS with other XML vocabularies is that the tags and content rules are different from those of HTML. If you've never used CSS for HTML or XML, the projects in this section will show you everything you need to know to create CSS style rules and style sheets and link them to existing documents.

Working With A Living Example

Throughout this Immediate Solutions section, we'll use David Megginson's novel DTD (previously dissected and discussed in Chapter 6) for all of our examples. Listing 14.1 contains the full version of the DTD.

Listing 14.1   The novel DTD.

```
<?xml encoding="UTF-8"?>

<!--
***********************************************************************
novel.dtd: A simple XML DTD for marking-up novels.
Copyright (c) 1997 by David Megginson.
***********************************************************************
-->

<!-- Content model for phrasal content -->

<!ENTITY % phrasal "#PCDATA|emphasis">

<!-- ******** -->
<!-- Elements -->
<!-- ******** -->

<!-- The top-level novel -->
```

```
<!ELEMENT novel (front, body)>

<!-- The frontmatter for the novel -->

<!ELEMENT front (title, author, revision-list)>

<!-- The list of revisions to this text -->

<!ELEMENT revision-list (item+)>

<!-- An item in the list of revisions -->

<!ELEMENT item (%phrasal;)*>

<!-- The main body of a novel -->

<!ELEMENT body (chapter+)>

<!-- A chapter of a novel -->

<!ELEMENT chapter (title, paragraph+)>
<!ATTLIST chapter
  id ID #REQUIRED>

<!-- The title of a novel or chapter -->
<!ELEMENT title (%phrasal;)*>

<!-- The author(s) of a novel -->
<!ELEMENT author (%phrasal;)*>

<!-- A paragraph in a chapter -->
<!ELEMENT paragraph (%phrasal;)*>

<!-- An emphasised phrase -->
<!ELEMENT emphasis (%phrasal;)*>

<!-- **************** -->
<!-- General Entities -->
<!-- **************** -->
<!--
  These really should have their Unicode equivalents.
-->
<!-- em-dash -->
<!ENTITY mdash "--">
```

```
<!-- left double quotation mark -->
<!ENTITY ldquo "´´">

<!-- right double quotation mark -->
<!ENTITY rdquo "``">

<!-- left single quotation mark -->
<!ENTITY lsquo "´">

<!-- right single quotation mark -->
<!ENTITY rsquo "`">

<!-- horizontal ellipse -->
<!ENTITY hellip "...">

<!-- end of DTD -->
```

The Simple Style Formula:
Selector+Declaration=Style Rule

Every style rule has two parts:

- *The selector*—The markup element to which the style rule is applied.

- *The declaration*—Specific information about how the element should be presented. (Declarations are made up of property and value combinations that define what aspect of the element's display is affected and how it is affected. The declaration margin-left: **.5in** indicates that the left margin of the element, which is affected by the declaration, should be half an inch. Declarations are enclosed in curly braces—{ and }. The property to be affected is listed first and is followed by a colon and the value the property should take.)

All style rules are created by using this syntax:

```
selector {property: value}
```

Therefore, a sample style rule that assigns a left margin of half an inch to a document (or to the chapter's authorship information) would be:

```
author {margin-left: .5in}
```

Case Doesn't Count, But Punctuation Does

CSS rules require a very specific syntax in which case is irrelevant but punctuation makes all the difference. Braces, colons, semicolons, periods, and commas all have defined roles in CSS rule notation. If you use a comma instead of a period, or a colon instead of a semicolon, your style sheets will break. When you debug Cascading Style Sheets, always check the accuracy of your punctuation. The section "Exploring The Role Of Punctuation In CSS" (later in this chapter) includes a table that details the meaning of each punctuation mark as it applies to CSS.

Grouping Selectors In Style Rules

Occasions will arise when you'll want to apply the same declaration (or set of declarations) to more than one selector. You could—with the help of cut and paste—generate a long series of style rules with different selectors but the same declarations, as shown in this code snippet:

```
author {margin-left: .5in}
title {margin-left: .5in}
revision-list {margin-left: .5in}
```

Thanks to the grouping mechanisms built into CSS, you can include all three selectors in one style rule. Simply separate them with commas and follow the entire group with the common declaration (or declarations, as discussed in the next project):

```
author, title, revision-list {margin-left: .5in}
```

Grouping Declarations In Style Rules

Just as it is convenient to group selectors in style rules to apply one declaration to many selectors, it is useful to be able to apply several different declarations to one selector, or to a group of selectors. More often than not, you will want to affect multiple aspects of an element's presentation. You could—once again, with the help of cut and paste—generate a long series of style rules with the same selector but different declarations:

```
author, title, revision-list {margin-left: .5in}
author, title, revision-list {color: navy}
```

```
author, title, revision-list {font-family: Arial}
author, title, revision-list {font-style: oblique}
```

This method quickly becomes cumbersome and lengthy. With CSS, you can group declarations. Separate multiple declarations within the curly braces of a single selector with semicolons, as shown here:

```
author, title, revision-list {margin-left: .5in;
                              color: navy;
                              font-family: Arial;
                              font-style: oblique;
                              }
```

The style rule takes on a slightly different format when it includes several declarations. Each declaration is moved to its own line, all are indented so they line up underneath the beginning of the first declaration, and the final curly brace resides on its own line. This formatting isn't required by CSS. We could have listed the entire rule on one line. However, listing each rule on its own line, with the final curly brace on the last line by itself, and adding white space makes it easier for the developer to read and change the rule.

Including Special Declaration Groupings For Individual Property Families

Some groups of property families have their own special rules for grouping declarations. This creates a type of CSS shorthand that allows you to create style rules quickly and easily. For example, box properties, such as margins, use the {1, 4} notation to indicate the values that should be assigned to each of the four sides of an element box. The syntax looks like this:

```
selector {margin: 1 2 3 4}
```

You can include up to four values after the colon in the declaration, but each number you add changes the way the values are applied to the element's box. The numbers are interpreted in this manner:

- *One number*—The value is applied to all four sides of the element's box.
- *Two numbers*—The first value is applied to the top and bottom of the element's box, and the second to the left and right sides.
- *Three numbers*—The first value is applied to the top, the second to the bottom, and the third to the right and left sides of the element's box.

- *Four numbers*—Each number is applied to a different side of the element's box in the order of top, bottom, left, and right.

The following style rules provide an example of this notation at work. Title elements will have a margin of 10 percent on all four sides:

```
title {margin: 10%}
```

Title elements will have a margin of 10 percent on the top and bottom and a margin of 20 percent on the left and right:

```
title {margin: 10% 20%}
```

Title elements will have a margin of 10 percent on the top, 20 percent on the bottom, and 15 percent on the left and right:

```
title {margin: 10% 20% 15%}
```

Title elements will have a margin of 10 percent on the top, 20 percent on the bottom, 15 percent on the left, and 5 percent on the right:

```
title {margin: 10% 20% 15% 5%}
```

Other property families also have their own built-in shorthand notation. For example, the background property combines the values of background-color, background-image, background-repeat, background-attachment, and background-position into one declaration. This long style rule

```
author {background-color: white;
        background-image: url(myback.gif);
        background-repeat: repeat-x;
        background-attachment: fixed;
        background-position: 50%;
```

can be reduced to this shorter rule and still retain the same meaning:

```
author {background: white url(myback.gif) repeat-x fixed 50%}
```

The projects found later in the section provide details of all of the properties and values, as well as the details of the property families that support special declaration groupings. All of them will take one of the two shorthand formats discussed in this project.

Using Class As A Selector

To create multiple instances of the same tag, each with its own style rule, CSS allows for the use of the **CLASS=** attribute as a selector. In a selector, follow the element name with a period and the class name. To link the rule to a specific instance of the tag, use **CLASS="*string*"**, where **"*string*"** is the same as the class name given after the element name in the style rule. The syntax for both the style rule and its invocation is:

```
selector.class {property: value}
<TAG CLASS="string">...</TAG>
```

If a selector includes class information and a tag is used without including the appropriate **CLASS=** attribute, the style rule will not be invoked for that instance of the element.

Megginson's novel DTD includes a title element that can be used to include either a title for the entire book or a title for a chapter. What if you wanted to create a separate style for each of the two titles based on the type of title (book or chapter)? Creating two separate style rules that are both linked to title, as follows, wouldn't work:

```
title {color: navy;
       font: 36pt Arial;
       background-color: teal;
       border-style: double;
       margin-top: 5%;
       margin-left: 10%;
       margin-right: 10%;
       }

title {color: teal;
       font: 18pt Arial;
       background-color: navy;
       border-style: groove;
       margin-left: 15%;
       margin-right: 15%;
       }
```

The second style rule would simply override the first, and the second rule would be used to present all instances of the title tag. We probably don't want to rewrite that DTD to have two separate types of titles. Instead, to create two separate style rules for two different instances of the same element, we will differentiate them by class. The new style rules would look like this:

```
title.book {color: navy;
     font: 36pt Arial;
     background-color: teal;
     border-style: double;
     margin-top: 5%;
     margin-left: 10%;
     margin-right: 10%;
     }

title.chapter {color: teal;
     font: 18pt Arial;
     background-color: navy;
     border-style: groove;
     margin-left: 15%;
     margin-right: 15%;
     }
```

This markup invokes the book and chapter style rules, respectively:

```
<TITLE CLASS="book">This is the book's title</TITLE>
<TITLE CLASS="chapter">This is a chapter title</TITLE>
```

If we use the title tag without specifying a class, neither style rule would be invoked.

The only drawback to using class as a selector when working with CSS and XML is that you must include **CLASS** as an attribute for every tag so the XML parser will recognize it. In the case of the novel DTD, **CLASS** isn't defined as a selector, so we would have to modify the DTD a bit by including this attribute for each tag:

```
class = cdata-list
```

This attribute allows a single class, or list of classes, to be specified for each element for which it is included as an attribute. When you use class as a selector, the individual rule is tied to a specific element as well as the class defined by the **CLASS=** attribute. Classes cannot be swapped between elements to apply the style rule from one element/class combination to another element/class combination. Instead, separate rules that use class as a selector must be created for each element.

Using Context As A Selector

Creating a class attribute for every element in a DTD is not the only way to create style rules that apply only to certain instances of a tag. Instead, an element's context can be used as a selector. To specify the context rules an element must meet before it can be considered a candidate for a style rule, simply list the elements included in the context in the order that they will appear. For example, this style rule

```
front title  {color: navy;
       font: 36pt Arial;
       background-color: teal;
       border-style: double;
       margin-top: 5%;
       margin-left: 10%;
       margin-right: 10%;
       }
```

specifies that only title elements nested within front elements should have this style rule applied to them. To invoke this style rule, the markup needs to take on this format:

```
<FRONT><TITLE>The book's title here</TITLE></FRONT>
```

In the same way, this style rule indicates that it should only be applied to title elements nested within chapter elements:

```
chapter title {color: teal;
       font: 18pt Arial;
       background-color: navy;
       border-style: groove;
       margin-left: 15%;
       margin-right: 15%;
       }
```

The following markup is required to invoke this style rule:

```
<CHAPTER><TITLE>The chapter's title here</TITLE></FRONT>
```

These two style rules work well with the novel DTD because both the front and chapter elements have required titles, and a title cannot stand alone outside of the front matter or chapter; therefore, we've covered all the title bases. We don't have to create a third title style without context information because we know there won't be (in a valid document) a title that doesn't fit one of our two pre-defined context models.

When you use context as a selector, the element names that make up the selector portion of the style rule are separated by spaces only, not by commas. If you include commas, you'll create a group of selectors instead of a single context-based selector. Elements linked to the style rules must be nested in the order defined by the style rule. Because DTDs must provide specific information about what content, in what order, is required or optional for all elements, you should study the DTD closely when you are creating rules that use context as a selector. Chapter 9 discusses element content in detail.

Exploring The Role Of Punctuation In CSS

The previous discussions of the syntax of style rules (including the different grouping and selector methods) show that CSS relies heavily on a variety of punctuation marks for the creation and interpretation of style rules. Table 14.1 recaps the role that each punctuation mark plays in creating style rules.

*TIP: For additional help in debugging your style sheets—especially to catch punctuation mistakes—run your Cascading Style Sheets through the Web Design Group's CSS validator, CSS Check, found at **www.htmlhelp.com/ tools/csscheck**.*

Table 14.1   Punctuation rules in CSS.

Character	Name	Role
{	Left curly brace	Begins a declaration
}	Right curly brace	Ends a declaration
:	Colon	Separates the property and its value in a declaration
,	Comma	Separates multiple selectors in a selector grouping
;	Semicolon	Separates multiple declarations in a declaration grouping
.	Period	Separates the element and the class name in a selector when class is used as a selector
	Space	Separates elements in the selector when context is used as a selector, or separates values in a declaration when certain property family shorthand notations are used

Using Measurement Units In CSS

CSS supports a wide variety of units, including standard measurements, percentages, and specific URL and color notation systems. This flexibility allows developers to assign the appropriate units, as dictated by the presentation aspect being defined, without having to perform laborious measurement conversions. In general, measurements in CSS are either absolute or relative. An example of an absolute measurement is 1 inch, whereas 75 percent is a relative measurement. One inch is one inch, no matter how you look at it, but a percentage changes as its whole changes; 75 percent of one inch is .75 inches, but 75 percent of 2 inches is 1.5 inches. Table 14.2 lists each measurement mechanism available in CSS with its abbreviation and its type (absolute or relative).

URLs are defined in CSS by using the syntax:

```
url(resource address)
```

The URL listed inside the parentheses can be a local URL, whose location is relative to the file the style sheet is attached to, or a fully qualified URL. Here is an example of a URL as a value for a CSS property:

```
title {background-image: url(background.gif)
```

Remember, for an image to be included as part of an XML document, it must be defined in the document's DTD as a binary entity.

CSS supports the hexadecimal color notation system used with HTML documents.

Table 14.2 Units of measure in CSS.

Name	Abbreviation	Type	Notes
Centimeter	cm	Absolute	
Em	em	Relative	Equal to the width of the display font's letter m.
Ex	ex	Relative	Equal to the height of the display font's letter x.
Inch	in	Absolute	
Millimeter	mm	Absolute	
Percentage	%	Relative	
Pica	pc	Absolute	
Pixel	px	Absolute	Pixels are different from device to device. A pixel on a screen that has a display resolution of 1024×768 is smaller than one with a screen resolution of 640×480.

14: Stylin' XML: Cascading Style Sheets

Reading Property Definitions

The next several projects provide a detailed discussion of the properties that are available for creating CSS style rules. For each property, we'll include the following:

- *Property name*—The property's name exactly as it should appear in the style rule.

- *Description*—A brief description of which aspect of an element the property affects.

- *Syntax*—The exact code used to call the property and the values it takes.

- *Values*—Lists all of the values that are valid for the property. (Refer to Table 14.3 for a description of value notation.)

Although CSS2 is being developed as a specification, what are currently listed as future CSS2 properties and values may not be around when the final specification is released. Because of the developmental state of CSS2, the following projects only cover the property families that are standard with CSS1. For a full view of the CSS2 recommendation, and to keep up with its development into a standard, visit the W3C's CSS site at **www.w3.org/Style/CSS**.

Using The Box Property Family

The box properties govern the margins, padding, height, width, and border aspects of any element. Table 14.4 lists each property and its description, syntax, and values.

Table 14.3   Descriptions of value notations for property values.

Value	Description	Example
<value>	A specific type of value	<percentage>; <length>
*Value**	A value that is repeated zero or more times	[[<family-name>I<generic-family>],]*
Value?	A value that is optional	[/<line-height>]?
Value{X, Y}	The value must occur at least X times and at most Y times	[<length>I<percentage>Iauto]{1,4}
Keyword	A keyword that must appear exactly as listed	thin
XIY	A list of possible keywords; only one may be used	thin I medium I thick
XIIY	A list of possible values; one or more may be used	<font-style> II <font-variant> II <font-weight>
[items]	Indicates a group of items	[thin I medium I thick I <length>] {1,4}

Table 14.4   Box properties.

Property	Description	Syntax	Values
Margin-Top	Sets the size of an element's top margin	margin-top: *<value>*	<length> I <percentage> I auto
Margin-Right	Sets the size of an element's right margin	margin-right: *<value>*	<length> I <percentage> I auto
Margin-Bottom	Sets the size of an element's bottom margin	margin-bottom: *<value>*	<length> I <percentage> I auto
Margin-Left	Sets the size of an element's left margin	margin-left: *<value>*	<length> I <percentage> I auto
Margin	Sets the size of all four element margins at one time	margin: *<value>*	[<length> I <percentage> I auto]{1,4}
Padding-Top	Sets the amount of space between an element's content and its top border	padding-top: *<value>*	<length> I <percentage>
Padding-Right	Sets the amount of space between an element's content and its right border	padding-right: *<value>*	<length> I <percentage>
Padding-Bottom	Sets the amount of space between an element's content and its bottom border	padding-bottom: *<value>*	<length> I <percentage>
Padding-Left	Sets the amount of space between an element's content and its left border	padding-left: *<value>*	<length> I <percentage>
Padding	Sets the padding size for all sides of an element at one time	padding: *<value>*	[<length> I <percentage>]{1,4}
Border-Top-Width	Sets the width of an element's top border	border-top-width: *<value>*	thin I medium I thick I <length>
Border-Right-Width	Sets the width of an element's right border	border-right-width: *<value>*	thin I medium I thick I <length>

(continued)

Table 14.4   Box properties (continued).

Property	Description	Syntax	Values
Border-Bottom-Width	Sets the width of an element's bottom border	border-bottom-width: <*value*>	thin | medium | thick | <length>
Border-Left-Width	Sets the width of an element's left border	border-left-width: <*value*>	thin | medium | thick | <length>
Border-Width	Sets the width of all four element borders at one time	border-width: <*value*>	[thin | medium | thick | <length>]{1,4}
Border-Color	Sets the color for all four sides of an element's border	border-color: <*value*>	<color>{1,4}
Border-Style	Sets the style for all four sides of an element's border	border-style: <*value*>	[none | dotted | dashed | solid | double | groove | ridge | inset | outset]{1,4}
Border-Top	Sets the width, color, and style of an element's top border	border-top: <*value*>	<border-top-width> | <border-style> | <color>
Border-Right	Sets the width, color, and style of an element's right border	border-right: <*value*>	<border-right-width> | <border-style> | <color>
Border-Bottom	Sets the width, color, and style of an element's bottom border	border-bottom: <*value*>	<border-bottom-width> | <border-style> | <color>
Border-Left	Sets the width, color, and style of an element's left border	border-left: <*value*>	<border-left-width> | <border-style> | <color>
Border	Sets the width, color, and style for all of an element's borders	border: <*value*>	<border-width> | <border-style> | <color>
Width	Defines an element's width	width: <*value*>	<length> | <percentage> | auto

(continued)

Table 14.4   Box properties (continued).

Property	Description	Syntax	Values
Height	Defines an element's height	height: *<value>*	<length> I auto
Float	Wraps text around an element	float: *<value>*	left I right I none
Clear	Identifies the sides on which text can be wrapped around an element	clear: *<value>*	none I left I right I both

Utilizing The Classification Property Family

The classification properties govern the way white space and lists are displayed. Table 14.5 lists each property and its description, syntax, and values.

Table 14.5   Classification properties.

Property	Description	Syntax	Values
Display	Defines how an element should be displayed	display: *<value>*	block I inline I list-item I none
White Space	Defines how white space within an element should be rendered	white-space: *<value>*	normal I pre I nowrap
List-Style-Type	Specifies the type of marker to be used within a list	list-style-type: *<value>*	disc I circle I square I decimal I lower-roman I upper-roman I lower-alpha I upper-alpha I none
List-Style-Image	Identifies an image to be used as a list-item marker	list-style-image: *<value>*	<url> I none
List-Style-Position	Defines whether text in a list should be displayed inside or outside of the list-item marker	list-style-position: *<value>*	inside I outside
List-Style	Defines the list-style type, position, and marker image URL	list-style: *<value>*	<list-style-type> II <list-style-position> II <url>

Using The Color And Background Property Family

The color and background properties govern the way color and background images are linked to elements, as well as the positioning and scrolling status of images. Table 14.6 lists each property and its description, syntax, and values.

Exploring The Font Property Family

The font properties provide font specifics for document elements. Table 14.7 lists each property and its description, syntax, and values.

Investigating The Text Property Family

The text properties provide text specifics for document elements. Table 14.8 lists each property and its description, syntax, and values.

Table 14.6   Color and background properties.

Property	Description	Syntax	Values
Color	Specifies an element's color	color: <*color*>	
Background-Color	Specifies an element's background color	background-color: <*value*>	<color> I transparent
Background-Image	Specifies an image to be attached as the background for an element	background-image: <*value*>	<url> I none
Background-Repeat	Defines how an element's background image should be repeated	background-repeat: <*value*>	repeat I repeat-x I repeat-y I no-repeat
Background-Attachment	Defines whether an element's background image is fixed in the browser window or scrolls with the element	background-attachment: <*value*>	scroll I fixed
Background-Position	Sets the position of an element's background image in relation to the element	background-position: <*value*>	[<percentage> I <length>]{1,2} I [top I center I bottom] II [left I center I right]
Background	Defines an element's background color and image, as well as how the image repeats its attachment, and its position	background: <*value*>	<background-color> I <background-image> I <background-repeat> I <background-attachment> I <background-position>

Table 14.7   Font properties.

Property	Description	Syntax	Values
Font Family	Specifies the font in which to display the element's text	font-family: [[<family-name> | <generic-family>],]* [<family-name> | <generic-family>]	<family-name> <generic-family> serif (ex: "Century Schoolbook") sans-serif (ex: Helvetica) monospace (ex: Courier) cursive (ex: Zapf-Chancery) fantasy (ex: Western)
Font Size	Sets the size of text	font-size: <absolute-size> | <relative-size>	<absolute-size> xx-small | x-small | small | medium | large | x-large | xx-large <relative-size> larger | smaller <length> <percentage>
Font Style	Defines the element's font style	font-style: *<value>*	normal | italic | oblique
Font Variant	Specifies whether the text should be rendered as normal or small caps	font-variant *<value>*	normal | small-caps
Font Weight	Defines how dark or light text should be	font-weight: *<value>*	normal | bold | bolder | lighter | 100 | 200 | 300 | 400 | 500 | 600 | 700 | 800 | 900
Font	Defines all of the font properties in one property/value set	font: *<value>*	[<font-style> | <font-variant> | <font-weight>]? <font-size> [/ <line-height>]? <font-family>

Table 14.8   Text properties.

Property	Description	Syntax	Values
Word-Spacing	Defines the amount of space between the words in an element	word-spacing: *<value>*	normal | <length>
Letter-Spacing	Defines the amount of space between the letters in an element	letter-spacing: *<value>*	normal | <length>

(continued)

Table 14.8   Text properties (continued).

Property	Description	Syntax	Values
Text-Decoration	Defines how the text in an element should be decorated	text-decoration: <value>	none | [underline | overline | line-through | blink]
Vertical-Align	Defines how an inline element should be positioned relative to its parent	element vertical-align: <value>	baseline | sub | super | top | text-top | middle | bottom | text-bottom | <percentage>
Text-Transform	Defines the case in which the text in an element should be rendered (regardless of the case it is typed in)	text-transform: <value>	none | capitalize | upper case | lowercase
Text-Align	Defines how text in an element should be aligned relative to its parent element and the page	text-align: <value>	left | right | center | justify
Text-Indent	Defines how much the first line of a block-level element should be indented	text-indent: <value>	<length> | <percentage>
Line-Height	Sets the amount of space between lines in an element	line-height: <value>	normal | <number> | <length> | <percentage>

Chapter 15

Stylin' XML: DSSSL

By Natanya Pitts-Moultis

In Depth

XML describes a document's structure but doesn't say much about how it should be processed or displayed. Those details are left up to the application processing the XML document. For content-based XML vocabularies, like Channel Definition Format (CDF) and Open Software Description (OSD), final display isn't much of an issue. However, if you're using XML with display-based DTDs, like Mathematical Markup Language (MathML) or Chemical Markup Language (CML), to display content in a browser, the final display is key to the user's ability to see, understand, and interact with your document.

Although some vocabulary-specific XML processors (such as Jumbo for MathML) have their own internal style sheets set up to govern the final display of an XML document specifically written for them, the vast majority of processors require information from the document developer on how to display the document. In Chapter 14, we showed you that Cascading Style Sheets, the style mechanism created for HTML, can be used with XML to govern the final display of XML documents. We also showed you that CSS is really too simplistic to work well with XML. Enter DSSSL.

The *Document Style Semantics and Specification Language* (DSSSL) was written to work with Standard Generalized Markup Language (SGML). It is a standard governed by the ISO that provides a mechanism to associate processing for display with SGML documents. Because XML is a subset of SGML, DSSSL works just as smoothly with it as it does with SGML. In theory, DSSSL could also work with HTML if any of the existing HTML browsers supported it. DSSSL is both amazingly powerful and complex, and it doesn't look anything like its younger cousin CSS. If you begin to feel a bit overwhelmed by DSSSL, keep in mind that it is still just a way of providing display information for documents described with markup.

DSSSL itself has been the topic of several books, and the specification that governs it is just over 300 pages long. Because of the relative complexity of DSSSL, we can't show you all its little nooks and crannies. Instead, this chapter focuses on describing the basic structures and constructs of DSSSL and includes a discussion of how to decide if DSSSL is the best style solution for your XML documents. The Immediate Solutions section of this chapter walks you through the creation of some of the basic DSSSL elements and evaluates some existing DSSSL style sheets to show you how DSSSL can be used to convert one type of SGML (and hence XML) document to another.

What Is DSSSL?

DSSSL is a style sheet mechanism that works with documents that are described by markup as a hierarchy of elements. Formatting and processing specifications are linked to document elements, and a display is created for the document as the document and its style sheet are processed by an XML parser and a DSSSL parser. DSSSL is designed to work with the many different media in which SGML documents can be disseminated, including print and various electronic formats. For this reason, it has some mechanisms that are only appropriate for one media or another—such as pagination properties—but not to all possible media through which the document might be disseminated. In fact, DSSSL can be used to create different style sheets for the same document. The style sheets can be geared toward a variety of media, and depending on how the document is disseminated, they could share common styles but take advantage of media-specific properties in their final display.

DSSSL recognizes that a document can be processed in several different ways, including:

• Transformation

• Formatting

• Querying

• Expression

The DSSSL specification is in fact separated into four discreet standard areas, each specializing in one of the four processing possibilities. The four sections that follow describe the goals and focus of each area in more detail.

Transformation

DSSSL can be used to convert an XML document from one DTD to another. This change is governed by a transformation specification. An example of such a transformation is the conversion of a document written for David Megginson's novel DTD into an HTML document that can be viewed on the Web. Because XML is not fully supported by existing Web browsers and—more importantly—isn't backward compatible with earlier browser versions, this particular aspect of DSSSL will be very useful to XML document developers. A standard DSSSL transformation specification can be written for XML DTDs that will convert their documents to HTML. It can be applied globally to a collection of documents for easy publication to the current Web and still take advantage of XML as a technology.

15: Stylin' XML: DSSSL

Basically, a transformation specification is a list of associations that comprise:

- *Query-expressions*—Used to create a list of which elements in one DTD may possibly be transformed into a specific element in the second DTD.

- *Transform-expressions*—Used to evaluate the elements in the list generated by the query-expression and, if they meet the transformation specification requirements, transform them into the element designated by the second DTD.

- *Priority-expressions*—An optional expression that assigns priorities to elements in the second DTD for matching to elements in the first DTD. If two elements in the second DTD potentially match a single element in the first DTD, the one with the higher priority is used in the transformation.

The transformation specification provides developers with a mechanism for taking existing structures from one DTD and duplicating, reorganizing, and regrouping them in another and for creating new structures as necessary to convert a document from one DTD to the other. "Transforming A Document From One DTD To Another With A Transformation Specification" in this chapter's Immediate Solutions section examines an existing DocBook-to-HTML style sheet.

Formatting

Formatting is a key issue in how documents should be displayed. Formatting governs page size, margins, font size, and so on, and one of DSSSL's primary objectives is to provide a standard way to supply formatting information for XML documents. In DSSSL terms, this is called the *formatting process*, and it's controlled by the style specification. Whereas transformation specifications are made up of associates, style specifications consist of construction rules. Although there are several types of construction rules, they all serve to map document elements to formatting information.

Because most XML processors and browsers won't have their own built-in style sheets, the majority of XML developers will probably use DSSSL to create style specifications for their documents. For that reason, the majority of the projects in the Immediate Solutions section focus on the creation and implementation of style specifications.

Querying

DSSSL can be used to identify specific sections in an XML document just as XPointers can, although in a much different way (XPointers are discussed in Chapter 11). The Standard Document Query Language (SDQL) is part of both the DSSSL transformation language and the DSSSL style language and is used to locate specific parts of document contents to process them. Because SDQL components blend naturally into the transformation and style languages, we'll discuss them in that context instead of splitting them out into their own group.

Expression

Like SDQL, the DSSSL expression language is used in both the transformation and style languages to create and manipulate objects. The components of the expression language will be discussed in the context of developing transformation and style specifications.

It's All About Tranformation And Style

As you can tell, the real focus of DSSSL is on the transformation and style languages. The query and expression languages are the supporting cast. The remainder of this portion of the chapter will be devoted to the transformation and style languages.

The Transformation Language

As noted earlier, the transformation language regulates the conversion of one document from one DTD into another as prescribed by the transformation specification. After a document has been through the transformation process, a style specification can be applied to it, but the two processes are separate otherwise. To transform a document from one DTD to another, the developer identifies the part of the document to be transformed—some or all—and a new document is created based on the transformation specification.

While a document is being transformed, one of several things can happen:

- New document structures or element attributes can be created to facilitate the change from one DTD to the other. A document from a DTD that nests a **<TITLE>** element within a **<CHAPTER>** element can, as a document that conforms to a new DTD, have **<TITLE>** attributes added to all **<CHAPTER>** elements instead.

- Document structures are reorganized and regrouped into new structures based on the demands of the DTD. For example, author bylines listed with individual articles in one DTD can be moved to the attributing author's section when the document is converted to a new DTD.

- Elements can be changed based upon sequence within the documents. For example, a paragraph immediately following a title or heading might be classified as a **<BODYA>** paragraph (and hence have different formatting), while all others in the document are automatically classified as **<BODYB>**.

- New structures or elements can be added to document-based text strings. For example, any link that refers to a Web page by using the **http://** string might be preceded by a Web icon.

For a transformation to occur, the following steps must be completed by the XML processor:

1. The XML document to be transformed is read by an XML parser with DSSSL capabilities.

2. The parser parses the document and creates a grove (a treelike representation of a document's elements, as well as their attributes and values) representation of the nodes of the document.

3. The grove and the transformation specification are processed together by the parser, which uses the associations in the transformation specification to convert the current grove into a new grove that represents the structures of a second DTD.

4. A result grove is created and converted back into an XML document.

This process may actually require several initial XML documents and may also create several XML documents from the result grove. Obviously, the more complex the documents and DTDs involved in the transformation, the more likely a larger number of documents will be needed to make the transformation. There is, however, only one transformation specification that governs the entire transformation process.

The Style Language

The style language is used to apply formatting to an XML document and can include:

- The application of presentation styles to a document
- The generation of new elements and content in the document based on instructions from the style specification
- The reorganization of elements and content based on instructions from the style specification
- The removal of elements and content based on instructions from the style specification

The formatting characteristics of a styled document are expressed in a flow-object tree. This tree describes the document as a series of flow-objects—paragraphs, graphics, columns, and so on—and links those objects to the document's elements to dictate the final formatting of the document. A style specification governs a document's formatting.

Formatting is applied to a document in these steps:

1. The XML document to be formatted is read by an XML parser with DSSSL capabilities.

2. The parser parses the document and creates a grove representation of the nodes of the document.

3. The construction rules defined in the style specification are applied to the document to create the flow-object tree.

4. Page and column specifics are established.

5. The page is physically laid out as described by the style specification.

The two most important components of the style specification are construction rules and flow-objects. The projects in the Immediate Solutions section focus on how to create and use each of these elements in DSSSL style sheet design.

Immediate Solutions

As you've probably come to realize, DSSSL is a rather complex mechanism for creating style sheets. It is complex because it was originally designed to work with SGML, perhaps the world's most complex document definition system. This Immediate Solutions section cannot attempt to cover every aspect of creating a DSSSL style sheet. Instead, it focuses on the primary constructs used in DSSSL (with examples from real-life style sheets) and how to use a style sheet to transform an XML document of one DTD into another. The projects are designed to give you a good idea of what DSSSL can do for you and your XML documents and help you decide if DSSSL is the right style solution for you.

Declaring A DTD For A DSSSL Style Sheet

It probably won't come as a surprise to learn that DSSSL specifications are actual SGML documents. This means you can use entities and comments in them, but it also means they must conform to a DTD and declare that DTD in their prologue. One of the most commonly used DSSSL DTDs is James Clark's publicly available DSSSL Style Sheet. Linking to it will provide you with all the DTD you need to create most DSSSL style sheets. To link to it, use this line of code at the beginning of your document:

```
<!doctype style-sheet PUBLIC "-//James Clark//DTD DSSSL Style Sheet//EN">
```

Defining A Construction Rule

Construction rules make up the guts of DSSSL style sheets, and flow-objects are the key to construction rules.

The syntax for a basic construction rule is:

```
(element ELEMENT-NAME
 (make flow-object
```

```
flow-object-characteristic: value
flow-object-characteristic: value
flow-object-characteristic: value
...))
```

ELEMENT-NAME is the name of the element in the DTD with which the style should be linked. The ***flow-object*** is one of several predefined objects that can be defined for any given element to create paragraphs, columns, boxes, and more. A ***flow-object-characteristic*** provides detailed information about the flow-object, such as margin height and width or font size. The following example of a construction rule is taken from the HTML 3.2 DSSSL style sheet by Jon Bosak (discussed in detail in a later project):

```
(element P
(make paragraph
     use: para-style
     space-before: %para-sep%
     start-indent: %body-start-indent%
     quadding: (PQUAD)
     (process-children-trim)))
```

This construction rule was created for the paragraph tag (**P**) and uses the flow-object **paragraph** with the characteristics of **use**, **space-before**, **start-indent**, and **quadding**. The values for these characteristics may look a bit strange, but that's only because they are definitions (as discussed in the next project) instead of straight values. The **process-child-trim** is a child-processing instruction, discussed later in this Immediate Solutions section.

As elements are dictated by the DTD, so are flow-objects dictated by the DSSSL specification. There are 46 flow-object classes, some with characteristics and others without. Table 15.1 lists each class, its characteristics (if any), and a brief description of the class. For complete descriptions of the characteristics and their values, see pages 198-293 of the DSSSL specification included on this book's companion CD-ROM.

Build construction rules using the flow-object that best fits your needs. However, the flow-objects for all document elements must be either **simple-page-sequence** or **page-sequence** if the style sheet is for a print document. The flow-object for an online document must be **scroll**.

15: Stylin' XML: DSSSL

Table 15.1   The DSSSL flow objects.

Flow-Object Class	Characteristics	Description
Sequence	none	Joins a series of construction rules into a single flow-object
Display-group	coalesce-id, position-preference, space-before, space-after, keep-with-previous?, keep-with-next?, break-before, break-after, keep, may-violate-keep-before?, may-violate-keep-after?	Applies a single set of display specifications to a group of construction rules
Simple-page-sequence	page-width, page-height, left-margin, right-margin, top-margin, bottom-margin, header-margin, footer-margin, left-header, center-header, right-header, left-footer, center-footer, right-footer, writing-mode	Creates a sequence of paged areas; cannot be contained within any other construction rules
Page-sequence	initial-page-models, repeat-page-models, force-last-page, force-first-page, first-page-type, blank-back-page-model, blank-front-page-model, justify-spread?, page-category, binding-edge	Creates a sequence of paged areas; can be nested within other construction rules
Column-set-sequence	column-set-model-map, column-set-model, position-preference, span, span-weak?, space-before, space-after, keep-with-previous?, keep-with-next?, break-before, break-after, keep, may-violate-keep-before?, may-violate-keep-after?	Creates a series of columns within a page
Paragraph	line, first-line-align, alignment-point-offset, ignore-record-end?, expand-tabs?, line-spacing, line-spacing-priority, min-pre-line-spacing, min-post-line-spacing, min-leading, first-line-start-indent, last-line-end-indent, hyphenation-char, hyphenation-ladder-count, hyphenation-remain-char-count, hyphenation-push-char-count, hyphenation-keep, hyphenation-exceptions, line-breaking-method, line-composition-	Specifies the formatting for a paragraph

(continued)

Table 15.1   The DSSSL flow objects (continued).

Flow-Object Class	Characteristics	Description
	method, implicit-bidi-method, glyph-alignment-mode, font-family-name, font-weight, font-posture, font-structure, font-proportionate-width, font-name, font-size, numbered-lines?, line-number, line-number-side, line-number-sep, quadding, last-line-quadding, last-line-justify-limit, justify-glyph-space-max-add, justify-glyph-space-max-remove, hanging-punct?, widow-count, orphan-count, language, country, position-preference, writing-mode, start-indent, end-indent, span, span-weak?, space-before, space-after, keep-with-previous?, keep-with-next?, break-before, break-after, keep, may-violate-keep-before?, may-violate-keep-after?	
Paragraph-break	All paragraph flow-object character-istics + first-line-start-indent and last-line-end-indent	Describes a series of paragraphs
Line-field	field-width, field-align, writing-mode, inhibit-line-breaks?, break-before-priority, break-after-priority	Creates a named field within a paragraph
Sideline	sideline-side, sideline-sep, color, layer, line-cap, line-dash, line-thickness, line-repeat, line-sep	Creates a container for flow-objects that have parallel attachment areas
Anchor	anchor-keep-with-previous?, display?, span, span-weak?, inhibit-line-breaks?, break-before-priority, break-after-priority	Generates a synchronized flow-object
Character	char, char-map, glyph-id, glyph-subst-table, glyph-subst-method, glyph-reorder-method, writing-mode, font-family-name, font-weight, font-posture, math-font-posture, font-structure, font-proportionate-width, font-name, font-size, stretch-factor,	Generates a specified character

(continued)

Table 15.1   The DSSSL flow objects (continued).

Flow-Object Class	Characteristics	Description
	hyphenate?, hyphenation-method, kern?, kern-mode, ligature?, allowed-ligatures, space?, inline-space-space, escapement-space-before, escapement-space-after, record-end?, input-tab?, input-whitespace-treatment, input-whitespace?, punct?, break-before-priority, break-after-priority, drop-after-line-break?, drop-unless-before-line-break?, math-class, script, position-point-shift, language, country, color, layer, inhibit-line-breaks?	
Leader	length, truncate-leader?, align-leader?, min-leader-repeat, inhibit-line-breaks?, break-before-priority, break-after-priority	Describes a set of flow-objects to be repeated
Embedded-text	direction, language, country, inhibit-line-breaks?	Embeds left-to-right text in right-to-left text or vice versa
Rule	orientation, length, color, layer, line-cap, line-dash, line-thickness, line-repeat, line-sep, position-point-shift, inhibit-line-breaks?, break-before-priority, break-after-priority, position-preference, display-alignment, start-indent, end-indent, writing-mode, span, span-weak?, space-before, space-after, keep-with-previous?, keep-with-next?, break-before, break-after, keep, may-violate-keep-before?, may-violate-keep-after?	Creates hard rules (lines)
External-graphic	display?, scale, max-width, max-height, entity-system-id, notation-system-id, color, layer, position-preference, display-alignment, start-indent, end-indent, writing-mode, span, span-weak?, space-before, space-after, keep-with-previous?, keep-with-next?, break-before, break-after, keep, may-violate-keep-before?, may-violate-keep-after?, position-point-x, position-point-y, escapement-direction, inhibit-line-breaks?, break-before-priority, break-after-priority	Describes graphics stored in an external file

(continued)

Table 15.1   The DSSSL flow objects (continued).

Flow-Object Class	Characteristics	Description
Included-container	display?, filling-direction, width, height, contents-alignment, overflow-action, contents-rotation, scale, position-preference, display-alignment, start-indent, end-indent, writing-mode, span, span-weak?, space-before, space-after, keep-with-previous?, keep-with-next?, break-before, break-after, keep, may-violate-keep-before?, may-violate-keep-after?, position-point-x, position-point-y, escapement-direction, inhibit-line-breaks?, break-before-priority, break-after-priority	Creates a series of area containers
Score	type, score-spaces?, color, layer, line-cap, line-dash, line-thickness, line-repeat, line-sep, inhibit-line-breaks?, font-family-name, font-weight, font-posture, font-structure, font-proportionate-width, font-name, font-size	Adds a score (line) to the contents of the element
Box	display?, box-type, box-open-end?, background-color, background-layer, box-corner-rounded, box-corner-radius, box-border-alignment, box-size-before, box-size-after, color, layer, line-cap, line-dash, line-thickness, line-repeat, line-sep, line-miter-limit, line-join, writing-mode, position-preference, inhibit-line-breaks?, break-before-priority, break-after-priority, start-indent, end-indent, span, span-weak?, space-before, space-after, keep-with-previous?, keep-with-next?, break-before, break-after, keep, may-violate-keep-before?, may-violate-keep-after?	Adds a box to a sequence of flow-objects
Side-by-side	side-by-side-overlap-control, position-preference, space-before, space-after, keep-with-previous?, keep-with-next?, break-before, break-after, keep, may-violate-keep-before?, may-violate-keep-after?	Aligns a sequence of items side by side

(continued)

15: Stylin' XML: DSSSL

Table 15.1   The DSSSL flow objects (continued).

Flow-object Class	Characteristics	Description
Side-by-side-item	start-indent, end-indent, side-by-side-pre-align, side-by-side-post-align	Defines an object with a side-by-side flow-object
Glyph-annotation	annotation-glyph-placement, annotation-glyph-style, inhibit-line-breaks?, break-before-priority, break-after-priority	Associates a meaning or pronunciation with characters, words, and phrases
Alignment-point	first-line-align	Defines a specific alignment point for paragraphs
Aligned-column	display-alignment, start-indent, end-indent, writing-mode, position-preference, space-before, space-after, keep-with-previous?, keep-with-next?, break-before, break-after, keep, may-violate-keep-before?, may-violate-keep-after?	Groups externally aligned paragraphs
Multi-line-inline-note	open, close, inline-note-line-count, inline-note-style, inhibit-line-breaks?, break-before-priority, break-after-priority	Adds a note in a document
Emphasizing-mark	mark, mark-distribution, mark-style, inhibit-line-breaks?, break-before-priority, break-after-priority	Adds emphasis to characters, words, or phrases
Math-sequence	math-display-mode	Creates a mathematical sequence area
Unmath	writing-mode, glyph-alignment-mode, font-family-name, font-weight, font-posture, font-structure, font-proportionate-width, font-name	Adds regular expressions (nonmathematical) into a mathematical sequence
Subscript	none	Formats text as subscript
Superscript	none	Formats text as superscript
Script	script-pre-align, script-post-align, script-mid-sup-align, script-mid-sub-align, math-display-mode	Creates a seven-part area for more closely controlling subscript and superscript notation
Mark	math-display-mode	Creates a three-part area for positioning mathematical operators
Fence	math-display-mode	Creates a three-part area for adding fences to mathematical operators

(continued)

Table 15.1   The DSSSL flow objects (continued).

Flow-Object Class	Characteristics	Description
Fraction	fraction-bar, numerator-align, denominator-align, math-display-mode	Creates a three-part area for describing fractions
Radical	math-display-mode, radical	Creates a three-part area for describing radicals
Math-operator	math-display mode	Creates a four-part area for describing math operators
Grid	grid-position-cell-type, grid-n-columns	Arranges a series of areas in a grid
Grid-cell	column-number, row-number	Creates a grid cell
Table	table-width, table-auto-width-method, table-border, before-row-border, after-row-border, before-column-border, after-column-border, table-corner-rounded, table-corner-radius, position-preference, display-alignment, start-indent, end-indent, writing-mode, span, span-weak?, space-before, space-after, keep-with-previous?, keep-with-next?, break-before, break-after, keep, may-violate-keep-before?, may-violate-keep-after?	Creates a table
Table-part	table-part-omit-middle-header?, table-part-omit-middle-footer?, space-before, space-after, keep-with-previous?, keep-with-next?, break-before, break-after, keep, may-violate-keep-before?, may-violate-keep-after?	Defines a header and footer for a table
Table-column	column-number, n-columns-spanned, width, display-alignment, start-indent, end-indent	Sets cell characteristics by column
Table-row	starts-row?, ends-row?	Describes the boundaries of a row
Table-cell	column-number, n-columns-spanned, n-rows-spanned, cell-before-row-margin, cell-after-row-margin, cell-before-column-margin, cell-after-column-margin, cell-row-alignment, cell-background?, background-	Sets cell characteristics by cell

(continued)

Table 15.1   The DSSSL flow objects (continued).

Flow-Object Class	Characteristics	Description
	color, background-layer, cell-before-row-border, cell-after-row-border, cell-before-column-border, cell-after-column-border, starts-row?, ends-row?, cell-crossed, line-cap, line-dash, line-thickness, line-repeat, line-sep, float-out-sidelines?, float-out-marginalia?, float-out-line-numbers?	
Table-border	border-priority, border-alignment, border-present?, border-omit-at-break?, color, layer, line-cap, line-dash, line-thickness, line-repeat, line-sep, line-miter-limit, line-join	Describes the table border
Scroll	filling-direction, writing-mode, background-color, background-layer, background-tile, start-margin, end-margin	Defines a document to be output as online (Web) display instead of as paged media with breaks
Multi-mode	multi-modes, principal-mode-simultaneous?	Describes a document that can be presented in more than one way (in print and on the Web, for example)
Link	destination	Creates a hyperlink

Creating A Definition

Aliases are used throughout XML in the form of entities to create shorthand for frequently accessed attributes, content, or bits of text. DSSSL includes its own aliasing mechanism in the form of definitions. A definition attaches a unique name to an expression. When you use the definition name in other parts of the style sheet, it's like including the expression. The syntax for creating a definition is:

```
(define NAME VALUE)
```

An example of an expression from the HTML 3.2 style sheet is:

```
(define %page-width% 8.5in)
(define %page-height% 11in)
```

```
(define %left-right-margin% 6pi)

...

(define %text-width% (- %page-width% (* %left-right-margin% 2)))
(define %body-width% (- %text-width% %body-start-indent%))
```

In this sample, **%page-width%**, **%page-height%**, **%left-right-margin%**, **%text-width%**, and **%body-width%** are all defined with appropriate measures. The percent symbols don't have any special meaning but instead are included by the author to make the definitions easy to spot. The definitions for **%text-width%** and **%body-width%** reference the definitions for **%page-width%**, **%left-right-margin%**, **%text-width%**, and **%body-start-indent%** (another definition created elsewhere in the document). Using the values from the definitions instead of their aliases, the definitions for **%text-width%** and **%body-width%** become:

```
(define %text-width% (- 8.5in (* 6pi 2)))
(define %body-width% (- (8.5in (* 6pi 2)) 4pi))
```

In this case, it's much easier to assign values to definitions and then create rules or other definitions that describe the relationship between the definitions instead of describing it as a set of numbers. The two preceding definitions use some pretty interesting expression notation, which will be described in detail in the next section.

Another set of definitions from the HTML 3.2 DTD is:

```
(define page-style
  (style
       page-width: %page-width%
       page-height: %page-height%
       left-margin: %left-right-margin%
       right-margin: %left-right-margin%
       top-margin: %top-margin%
       bottom-margin: %bottom-margin%
       header-margin: %header-margin%
       footer-margin: %footer-margin%
       font-family-name: %body-font-family%
       font-size: %bf-size%
       line-spacing: %bf-line-spacing%))
...
(element HTML
  ...
    (make simple-page-sequence
     use: page-style
  ...
```

After omitting some code that is unnecessary to our current discussion, this example shows how the definition of page style is created (by using some other definitions) and then invokes the simple-page-sequence flow-object definition for the HTML element.

Creating An Expression

An expression in a construction rule is any character string that can be evaluated. For example, this expression

```
(define-unit pi (/ 1in 6))
```

which defines the unit of **pi** as 1 inch divided by 6, is really two expressions. The first is "define the unit pi as" and the second is "1 inch divided by 6." So the second expression, which divides 1 inch by 6, is both its own expression and a part of the larger unit definition expression. Expressions in DSSSL are delineated by parentheses, and as with markup elements, nesting must be complete. If you forget to close an expression with a right parenthesis, your entire style sheet will break. A good tool, as discussed in the "Employing DSSSL Software" later in this section, is useful for avoiding the little mistakes that cause breakage.

This sample expression is also a good example of how DSSSL deals with math expressions. The expression **(/ 1in 6)** means divide 1in by 6. If it were **(/ 6 1in)**, it would mean the converse—divide 6 by 1in. This is an example of parenthesized prefix notation and DSSSL's solution to mathematical notation. The mathematical operator is first followed by the numbers it affects, in the order it affects them.

In the end of the example from the previous section, the relationship between the parts of the definition becomes clearer:

```
(define %text-width% (- %page-width% (* %left-right-margin% 2)))
(define %body-width% (- %text-width% %body-start-indent%))
```

The definition of **%text-width%** is the **%page-width%** minus the results of the **%left-right-margin%** multiplied by 2. The definition of **%body-width%** is the value of **%text-width%** (defined previously) multiplied by the value of **%body-start-indent%**. If we replace names with numbers, the equations are:

```
(define %text-width% (- 8.5in (* 6pi 2)))
(define %body-width% (- (8.5in (* 6pi 2)) 4pi))
```

For the equations to work, the units have to be the same, so "pixels" has to be changed to "inches." Remember that the pixel definition from earlier in the project says that a pixel is equal to 1in divided by 6, or .167 in. So, the equations now look like:

```
(define %text-width% (- 8.5in (* (* 6 .167) 2)))
(define %body-width% (- (8.5in (*(* 6 .167) 2)) (* 4 .167))
```

When you do all the math, starting from the innermost parentheses and working out, the final values are:

```
(define %text-width% 6.496in)
(define %body-width% 5.828in)
```

It's a good thing the DSSSL parser knows how to do all of this in a split second or style sheets would never get past the math. This ability to create definitions and use mathematical expressions with them removes the numbers and instead expresses the relationships between the characteristics of an element. It also makes it easy to change one part of the overall layout of the document, such as the text-width, and have all other parts of the layout that are dependent upon the text-width change automatically instead of having to be calculated by hand.

Defining A Sosofo

A *Specification of a Sequence of Flow-objects* (sosofo) is the specification for a flow-object. It can be as simple as

```
(make paragraph font-family-name: "Times New Roman")
```

or as complex as

```
(make simple-page-sequence
    use: page-style
    left-header: (if-first-page
            (empty-sosofo)
            (if-front-page (empty-sosofo) page-header))
    right-header: (if-first-page
            (empty-sosofo)
            (if-front-page page-header (empty-sosofo)))
    left-footer: (if-first-page
            (empty-sosofo)
```

```
             (if-front-page (empty-sosofo) page-footer))
      right-footer: (if-first-page
             (empty-sosofo)
             (if-front-page page-footer (empty-sosofo)))
      input-whitespace-treatment: 'collapse
      quadding: 'justify
      (process-children-trim))))
```

The sosofo isn't tied to any one element but instead is just a blueprint for how a certain flow-object is described. Sosofos can be duplicated, created, and ignored by style specifications and are very useful in transforming a document from one DTD to the other. The difference between a flow-object and a sosofo is that the sosofo describes how the flow-object should look and a single instance of a flow-object is created based on a sosofo. Sosofos are created as part of the style sheet, so they can be created, changed, or ignored spontaneously. Flow-objects aren't actually created until the entire style sheet has been parsed, so they are unchangeable after they've been created.

Elements can be suppressed using the **(empty-sosofo)** expression, as in this code:

```
(element HEAD (empty-sosofo))
(element FORM (empty-sosofo))
(element APPLET (empty-sosofo))
(element PARAM (empty-sosofo))
(element TEXTFLOW (empty-sosofo))
(element MAP (empty-sosofo))
(element AREA (empty-sosofo))
```

These are the nonprinting elements of the HTML 3.2 specification, so they were assigned empty-sosofo expressions to keep their content from being accidentally printed.

Specifying Child Processing

Generally, all style processing commands are extended to the child (nested) elements of the element for which they are defined. This is the default for DSSSL. However, there are times when you might not want this to happen. In those cases, you can use one of three special child-processing expressions:

- **process-matching-children** *'element*—Processes only those children whose names match the string specified by *element*. The expression

(process-matching-children 'TITLE) will only apply a sosofo to **TITLE** child elements.

- **process-first-descendant** *'element*—Only processes the first instance of the element whose name matches *element*. The expression **(process-first-descendant 'TITLE)** looks for the first **TITLE** element after the parent element and applies the sosofo only to it even if there are other **TITLE** child elements.

- **process-children-trim**—Trims white space between the child elements and the parent element.

This code uses the **process-first-descendant** expression to move the title of an HTML document into a document header:

```
(element HTML
...
        (page-header
      (make sequence
            font-size: %hf-size%
            line-spacing: %hf-line-spacing%
            font-posture: 'italic
            (process-first-descendant "TITLE"))))
```

Because the **HTML** element is the document element for any HTML document, all other elements are its children. If the style sheet didn't limit the processing to only the first instance of title but instead let all children be processed by the header sosofo, the entire document would be included in the header.

This expression in the sosofo for the **BODY** element uses the **process-children-trim** expression to get rid of extra white space between child elements:

```
(element BODY (process-children-trim))
```

Evaluating A DSSSL Style Sheet

A DSSSL style sheet is pretty impressive when it is constructed by an expert working with a well-built DTD. The following style sheet example is an excerpt from a DSSSL style sheet written for the HTML 3.2 specification by Jon Bosak, one of the two creators of CSS. You'll find that if you spend some time with it, you'll be able to see the different DSSSL structures and begin to understand their functions even if you're a relative newbie to DSSSL. We've included a running description of what's going on in the various parts of the style sheet to help you work your way through it. The entire document can be found at **sunsite.unc.edu/pub/sun-info/standards/dsssl/stylesheets/html32/html32hc.dsl**.

```
<!doctype style-sheet PUBLIC "-//James Clark//DTD DSSSL Style Sheet//EN">
```

TIP: *Every DSSSL style sheet is an XML document, so a **doctype** declaration is a must. James Clark's is a good one to use for any DSSSL style sheet.*

```
;; ###############################################################
;;
;; DSSSL style sheet for HTML 3.2 print output
;;
;; 1996.11.17
;;
;; Base version, August 1996: Jon Bosak, Sun Microsystems, based on work
;;    by Anders Berglund, EBT, with critical assistance from James Clark
;; TOC section and recto/verso page treatments based on models by James
;;    Clark, October 1996
;;
;; ###############################################################
```

TIP: *This informative section gives credit where credit is due. Jon Bosak owns the copyright to this style sheet and created it with the help of those listed.*

```
;; Features in HTML 3.2 that are not implemented in the style sheet:
;;
;;    automatic table column widths
;;    % on width attribute for TABLE
;;    attributes on TH and TD: align, valign, rowspan, colspan
;;    attributes on TABLE: width, align, border, cellspacing, cellpadding
;;    start attribute on OL
;;    value attribute on LI
;;    noshade attribute on HR
;;
;;    See also "Non-Printing Elements" below
;;
;; Features in the style sheet that are not in HTML 3.2:
;;
;;    page headers that display the HEAD TITLE content
;;    page footers that display the page number
;;    autonumbering of heads and table captions
;;    support for named units (pt, pi, cm, mm) in size attributes
;;    automatic TOC generation
```

The following code includes more information about what the style sheet covers and what it does not. If you have tables in your HTML document that use the unsupported attributes and you want to use this DSSSL style sheet, you may have to write your own additional style rules.

```
;; =============================== UNITS ===============================

(define-unit pi (/ 1in 6))
(define-unit pt (/ 1in 72))
(define-unit px (/ 1in 96))

;; see below for definition of "em"
```

TIP: *Named units are not part of the HTML specification. Because Bosak wanted to use them in his style sheet, he had to create unit definitions for them.*

```
;; =========================== PARAMETERS ===========================

;; ......................... Basic "look" ...........................

;; Visual acuity levels are "normal", "presbyopic", and
;;    "large-type"; set the line following to choose the level
```

TIP: *The document can be viewed in one of three acuity levels: normal, presbyopic (for those who are far sighted), and large-type. A great deal of the style sheet's formatting is closely controlled by these three levels, and the overal size of any document described by this style-specification will be changed as the acuity level changes.*

```
(define %visual-acuity% "normal")
;; (define %visual-acuity% "presbyopic")
;; (define %visual-acuity% "large-type")
```

TIP: *The initial part of the document creates a whole host of definitions to be used in later definitions and in sosofos.*

```
(define %bf-size%
  (case %visual-acuity%
    (("normal") 11pt)
    (("presbyopic") 12pt)
    (("large-type") 24pt)))
```

```
(define %mf-size% (- %bf-size% 1pt))
(define %hf-size% %bf-size%)

(define-unit em %bf-size%)

(define %autonum-level% 6)          ;; zero disables autonumbering
(define %flushtext-headlevel%       ;; heads above this hang out on the left
  (if (equal? %visual-acuity% "large-type") 6 4))
(define %body-start-indent%         ;; sets the white space on the left
  (if (equal? %visual-acuity% "large-type") 0pi 4pi))
(define %toc?% #t)                  ;; enables TOC after H1

;; ..................... Basic page geometry ........................

(define %page-width% 8.5in)
(define %page-height% 11in)

(define %left-right-margin% 6pi)
(define %top-margin%
  (if (equal? %visual-acuity% "large-type") 7.5pi 6pi))
(define %bottom-margin%
  (if (equal? %visual-acuity% "large-type") 7.5pi 6pi))
(define %header-margin%
  (if (equal? %visual-acuity% "large-type") 4.5pi 3pi))
(define %footer-margin% 3.5pi)

(define %text-width% (- %page-width% (* %left-right-margin% 2)))
(define %body-width% (- %text-width% %body-start-indent%))

;; ....................... Spacing factors .........................

(define %para-sep% (/ %bf-size% 2.0))
(define %block-sep% (* %para-sep% 2.0))

(define %line-spacing-factor% 1.2)
(define %bf-line-spacing% (* %bf-size% %line-spacing-factor%))
(define %mf-line-spacing% (* %mf-size% %line-spacing-factor%))
(define %hf-line-spacing% (* %hf-size% %line-spacing-factor%))

(define %head-before-factor% 1.0)
(define %head-after-factor% 0.6)
(define %hsize-bump-factor% 1.2)

(define %ss-size-factor% 0.6)
(define %ss-shift-factor% 0.4)
```

```
(define %smaller-size-factor% 0.9)
(define %bullet-size-factor% 0.8)

;; ....................... Fonts and bullets ........................

;; these font selections are for Windows 95
```

TIP: *Because definitions are used to assign fonts to different types of content (title, body, mono, and so forth), it would be very easy to alter all the title fonts in just a few quick keystrokes rather than doing a global search-and-replace for every instance of the font Arial.*

```
(define %title-font-family% "Arial")
(define %body-font-family% "Times New Roman")
(define %mono-font-family% "Courier New")
(define %dingbat-font-family% "Wingdings")

;; these "bullet strings" are a hack that is completely dependent on
;;      the Wingdings font family selected above; consider this a
;;      placeholder for suitable ISO 10646 characters
```

TIP: *The code that follows defines bullets for HTML lists.*

```
(define %disk-bullet% "l")
(define %circle-bullet% "i")
(define %square-bullet% "o")

(define %bullet-size% (* %bf-size% %bullet-size-factor%))


;; ======================== COMMON FUNCTIONS ========================
```

TIP: *These common functions take advantage of the programming side of DSSSL. The DSSSL specification on this book's companion CD-ROM provides more information about the notations used in these functions.*

```
(define (expt b n)
  (if (= n 0)
      1
      (* b (expt b (- n 1)))))
```

```
;; per ISO/IEC 10179
(define (node-list-reduce nl proc init)
  (if (node-list-empty? nl)
      init
      (node-list-reduce (node-list-rest nl)
                        proc
                        (proc init (node-list-first nl)))))


;; per ISO/IEC 10179
(define (node-list-length nl)
  (node-list-reduce nl
                    (lambda (result snl)
                      (+ result 1))
                    0))


(define if-front-page
  (external-procedure "UNREGISTERED::James Clark//Procedure::if-front-
page"))

(define if-first-page
  (external-procedure "UNREGISTERED::James Clark//Procedure::if-first-
page"))
```

TIP: *Even the upper- and lowercase alphabet characters are defined.*

```
(define upperalpha
  '(#\A #\B #\C #\D #\E #\F #\G #\H #\I #\J #\K #\L #\M
    #\N #\O #\P #\Q #\R #\S #\T #\U #\V #\W #\X #\Y #\Z))

(define loweralpha
  '(#\a #\b #\c #\d #\e #\f #\g #\h #\i #\j #\k #\l #\m
    #\n #\o #\p #\q #\r #\s #\t #\u #\v #\w #\x #\y #\z))

(define (char-downcase ch)
  (case ch
    ((#\A) #\a) ((#\B) #\b) ((#\C) #\c) ((#\D) #\d) ((#\E) #\e)
    ((#\F) #\f) ((#\G) #\g) ((#\H) #\h) ((#\I) #\i) ((#\J) #\j)
    ((#\K) #\k) ((#\L) #\l) ((#\M) #\m) ((#\N) #\n) ((#\O) #\o)
    ((#\P) #\p) ((#\Q) #\q) ((#\R) #\r) ((#\S) #\s) ((#\T) #\t)
    ((#\U) #\u) ((#\V) #\v) ((#\W) #\w) ((#\X) #\x) ((#\Y) #\y)
    ((#\Z) #\z) (else ch)))
```

```
(define (LOCASE slist)
  (if (null? slist)
      '()
      (cons (char-downcase (car slist)) (LOCASE (cdr slist)))))

(define (STR2LIST s)
  (let ((len (string-length s)))
    (let loop ((i 0) (ln len))
      (if (= i len)
          '()
          (cons (string-ref s i) (loop (+ i 1) ln))))))

(define (STRING-DOWNCASE s)
  (apply string (LOCASE (STR2LIST s))))

(define (UNAME-START-INDEX u last)
  (let ((c (string-ref u last)))
    (if (or (member c upperalpha) (member c loweralpha))
      (if (= last 0)
          0
          (UNAME-START-INDEX u (- last 1)))
        (+ last 1))))

(define (PARSEDUNIT u) ;; this doesn't deal with "%" yet
 (if (string? u)
  (let ((strlen (string-length u)))
    (if (> strlen 2)
      (let ((u-s-i (UNAME-START-INDEX u (- strlen 1))))
        (if (= u-s-i 0) ;; there's no number here
            1pi          ;; so return something that might work
            (if (= u-s-i strlen)             ;; there's no unit name here
              (* (string->number u) 1px) ;; so default to pixels (3.2)
              (let* ((unum (string->number
                       (substring u 0 u-s-i)))
                    (uname (STRING-DOWNCASE
                       (substring u u-s-i strlen))))
                (case uname
                  (("mm") (* unum 1mm))
                  (("cm") (* unum 1cm))
                  (("in") (* unum 1in))
                  (("pi") (* unum 1pi))
                  (("pc") (* unum 1pi))
                  (("pt") (* unum 1pt))
                  (("px") (* unum 1px))
```

15: Stylin' XML: DSSSL

```
                    (("barleycorn") (* unum 2pi)) ;; extensible!
                    (else
                     (cond
                      ((number? unum)
                       (* unum 1px))
                      ((number? (string->number u))
                       (* (string->number u) 1px))
                       (else u)))))))))
            (if (number? (string->number u))
             (* (string->number u) 1px)
             1pi)))
      1pi))

(define (INLIST?)
  (or
    (have-ancestor? "OL")
    (have-ancestor? "UL")
    (have-ancestor? "DIR")
    (have-ancestor? "MENU")
    (have-ancestor? "DL")))

(define (INHEAD?)
  (or
    (have-ancestor? "H1")
    (have-ancestor? "H2")
    (have-ancestor? "H3")
    (have-ancestor? "H4")
    (have-ancestor? "H5")
    (have-ancestor? "H6")))

(define (HSIZE n)
  (* %bf-size%
    (expt %hsize-bump-factor% n)))

(define (OLSTEP)
  (case (modulo (length (hierarchical-number-recursive "OL")) 4)
    ((1) 1.2em)
    ((2) 1.2em)
    ((3) 1.6em)
    ((0) 1.4em)))

(define (ULSTEP) 1em)
```

```
(define (PQUAD)
  (case (attribute-string "align")
    (("LEFT") 'start)
    (("CENTER") 'center)
    (("RIGHT") 'end)
    (else (inherited-quadding))))

(define (HQUAD)
  (cond
    ((string? (attribute-string "align")) (PQUAD))
    ((have-ancestor? "CENTER") 'center)
    ((have-ancestor? "DIV") (inherited-quadding))
    (else 'start)))

(define (BULLSTR sty)
  (case sty
    (("circle") %circle-bullet%)
    (("square") %square-bullet%)
    (else %disk-bullet%)))

;; ======================= NON-PRINTING ELEMENTS =========================
```

TIP: *Empty sosofos are used to suppress the printing of these elements and their children.*

```
;; Note that HEAD includes TITLE, ISINDEX, BASE, META, STYLE,
;;    SCRIPT, and LINK as possible children

(element HEAD (empty-sosofo))
(element FORM (empty-sosofo))
(element APPLET (empty-sosofo))
(element PARAM (empty-sosofo))
(element TEXTFLOW (empty-sosofo))
(element MAP (empty-sosofo))
(element AREA (empty-sosofo))


;; ========================= TABLE OF CONTENTS ==========================
```

TIP: *The code that follows provides for an automatic generation of a table of contents based on headings.*

15: Stylin' XML: DSSSL

```
;; Container elements in which to look for headings
(define %clist% '("BODY" "DIV" "CENTER" "BLOCKQUOTE" "FORM"))

(mode toc
  (element h1 (empty-sosofo))
  (element h2 ($toc-entry$ 2))
  (element h3 ($toc-entry$ 3))
  (element h4 ($toc-entry$ 4))
  (element h5 ($toc-entry$ 5))
  (element h6 ($toc-entry$ 6))
  (default (apply process-matching-children
            (append %hlist% %clist%)))
)

(define %toc-indent% 1em)

(define ($toc-entry$ level)
  (make paragraph
    use: para-style
    start-indent: (+ %body-start-indent%
          (* %toc-indent% (+ 1 level)))
    first-line-start-indent: (* -3 %toc-indent%)
    quadding: 'start
    (literal (NUMLABEL level))
    (make link
          destination: (current-node-address)
          (with-mode #f (process-children-trim)))
    (make leader (literal "."))
    (current-node-page-number-sosofo)))

(define (MAKEBODYRULE)
  (make rule
    orientation: 'horizontal
    space-before: (* 2 %block-sep%)
    space-after: (* 2 %block-sep%)
    line-thickness: 1pt
    length: %body-width%
    start-indent: %body-start-indent%
    display-alignment: 'start))

(define (MAKETOC)
  (if %toc?%
      (sosofo-append
       (MAKEBODYRULE)
```

```
(make paragraph
   font-family-name: %title-font-family%
   font-weight: 'bold
   font-posture: 'upright
   font-size: (HSIZE 2)
  line-spacing: (* (HSIZE 2) %line-spacing-factor%)
   space-before: (* (HSIZE 2) %head-before-factor%)
   space-after: (* (HSIZE 2) %head-after-factor%)
   start-indent: %body-start-indent%
   quadding: 'start
   keep-with-next?: #t
   (literal "Table of Contents"))
(with-mode toc
    (process-node-list (ancestor "BODY")))
(MAKEBODYRULE))
(empty-sosofo)))


;; ========================= TOP LEVEL ============================
```

TIP: *The following section of code defines the general page setup for the printed document.*

```
(define page-style
  (style
      page-width: %page-width%
      page-height: %page-height%
      left-margin: %left-right-margin%
      right-margin: %left-right-margin%
      top-margin: %top-margin%
      bottom-margin: %bottom-margin%
      header-margin: %header-margin%
      footer-margin: %footer-margin%
      font-family-name: %body-font-family%
      font-size: %bf-size%
      line-spacing: %bf-line-spacing%))

(element HTML
 (let ((page-footer
    (make sequence
        font-size: %hf-size%
        line-spacing: %hf-line-spacing%
        font-posture: 'italic
        (literal "Page ")
        (page-number-sosofo)))
```

```
          (page-header
        (make sequence
              font-size: %hf-size%
              line-spacing: %hf-line-spacing%
              font-posture: 'italic
              (process-first-descendant "TITLE"))))
      (make simple-page-sequence
        use: page-style
        left-header: (if-first-page
                  (empty-sosofo)
                  (if-front-page (empty-sosofo) page-header))
        right-header: (if-first-page
                (empty-sosofo)
                (if-front-page page-header (empty-sosofo)))
        left-footer: (if-first-page
                  (empty-sosofo)
                  (if-front-page (empty-sosofo) page-footer))
        right-footer: (if-first-page
                (empty-sosofo)
                (if-front-page page-footer (empty-sosofo)))
        input-whitespace-treatment: 'collapse
        quadding: 'justify
        (process-children-trim))))


(element BODY (process-children-trim))

;; ========================== BLOCK ELEMENTS ==========================
```

```
;; ......................... Generic DIV .........................

(element DIV
 (let ((align (attribute-string "align")))
  (make display-group
    quadding:
      (case align
        (("LEFT") 'start)
        (("CENTER") 'center)
        (("RIGHT") 'end)
        (else 'justify))
    (process-children-trim))))
```

```
(element CENTER
 (make display-group
      quadding: 'center
      (process-children-trim)))



;; ......................... Headings ...........................

(define %hlist% '("H1" "H2" "H3" "H4" "H5" "H6"))

(define (NUMLABEL hlvl)
  (let ((enl (element-number-list
          (reverse (list-tail (reverse %hlist%) (- 6 hlvl))))))
    (let loop ((idx 1))
      (if (or (= idx %autonum-level%) (= idx hlvl))
          (if (= idx 2) ". " " ")
          (let ((thisnum (list-ref enl idx)))
            (string-append
            (if (> idx 1) "." "")
            (format-number thisnum "1")
            (loop (+ idx 1)))))))))

(define ($heading$ headlevel)
  (let ((headsize (if (= headlevel 6) 0 (- 5 headlevel))))
    (make paragraph
      font-family-name: %title-font-family%
      font-weight: (if (< headlevel 6) 'bold 'medium)
      font-posture: (if (< headlevel 6) 'upright 'italic)
      font-size: (HSIZE headsize)
      line-spacing: (* (HSIZE headsize) %line-spacing-factor%)
      space-before: (* (HSIZE headsize) %head-before-factor%)
      space-after: (if (and %toc?% (= headlevel 1))
                  4em ;; space if H1 before TOC
                  (* (HSIZE headsize) %head-after-factor%))
      start-indent:
        (if (< headlevel %flushtext-headlevel%)
            0pt
        %body-start-indent%)
      quadding: (HQUAD)
      keep-with-next?: #t
      break-before: (if (and
                  %toc?%
                  (= headlevel 2)
                  (= (child-number) 1))
                  'page #f) ;; if TOC on, break before first H2
```

423

```
            (literal
             (if (and (<= headlevel %autonum-level%) (> headlevel 1))
                 (NUMLABEL headlevel)
                 (string-append "")))
            (process-children-trim))))

(element H1
  (sosofo-append
    ($heading$ 1)
    (MAKETOC)))

(element H2 ($heading$ 2))
(element H3 ($heading$ 3))
(element H4 ($heading$ 4))
(element H5 ($heading$ 5))
(element H6 ($heading$ 6))



;; ......................... Paragraphs ...........................
```

TIP: *Notice how all the paragraph-type elements define the para-style initially. This makes it easy to change the overall look and feel of paragraphs throughout the document quickly and consistently.*

```
(define para-style
  (style
   font-size: %bf-size%
   font-weight: 'medium
   font-posture: 'upright
   font-family-name: %body-font-family%
   line-spacing: %bf-line-spacing%))

(element P
 (make paragraph
      use: para-style
      space-before: %para-sep%
      start-indent: %body-start-indent%
      quadding: (PQUAD)
      (process-children-trim)))

(element ADDRESS
  (make paragraph
     use: para-style
     font-posture: 'italic
```

```
       space-before: %para-sep%
       start-indent: %body-start-indent%
       (process-children-trim)))

(element BLOCKQUOTE
  (make paragraph
     font-size: (- %bf-size% 1pt)
     line-spacing: (- %bf-line-spacing% 1pt)
     space-before: %para-sep%
     start-indent: (+ %body-start-indent% 1em)
     end-indent: 1em
     (process-children-trim)))

(define ($monopara$)
  (make paragraph
     use: para-style
     space-before: %para-sep%
     start-indent: %body-start-indent%
        lines: 'asis
     font-family-name: %mono-font-family%
     font-size: %mf-size%
     input-whitespace-treatment: 'preserve
     quadding: 'start
        (process-children-trim)))

(element PRE ($monopara$))
(element XMP ($monopara$))
(element LISTING ($monopara$))
(element PLAINTEXT ($monopara$))

(element BR
  (make display-group
    (empty-sosofo)))


;; .................. Lists: UL, OL, DIR, MENU, DL ....................
```

TIP: *All the lists use the same base display group sosofo for consistency.*

```
(define ($list-container$)
 (make display-group
       space-before: (if (INLIST?) %para-sep% %block-sep%)
       space-after:  (if (INLIST?) %para-sep% %block-sep%)
```

```
              start-indent: (if (INLIST?)
                     (inherited-start-indent)
                        %body-start-indent%)))

(define ($li-para$)
  (make paragraph
     use: para-style
     start-indent: (+ (inherited-start-indent) (OLSTEP))
     first-line-start-indent: (- (OLSTEP))
     (process-children-trim)))

(element UL ($list-container$))

(element (UL LI)
  (let ((isnested (> (length (hierarchical-number-recursive "UL")) 1)))
    (make paragraph
       use: para-style
       space-before:
        (if (attribute-string "compact" (ancestor "UL")) 0pt %para-sep%)
       start-indent: (+ (inherited-start-indent) (ULSTEP))
       first-line-start-indent: (- (ULSTEP))
       (make line-field
          font-family-name: %dingbat-font-family%
          font-size: (if isnested
                      (* %bullet-size% %bullet-size-factor%)
                      %bullet-size%)
          field-width: (ULSTEP)
          (literal
            (let
                ((litype
                (attribute-string "type"))
                 (ultype
                (attribute-string "type" (ancestor "UL"))))
              (cond
                ((string? litype) (BULLSTR (STRING-DOWNCASE litype)))
                ((string? ultype) (BULLSTR (STRING-DOWNCASE ultype)))
                (else %disk-bullet%)))))
       (process-children-trim))))

(element (UL LI P) ($li-para$))

(element OL ($list-container$))
```

```
(element (OL LI)
 (make paragraph
      use: para-style
      space-before:
        (if (attribute-string "compact" (ancestor "OL")) 0pt %para-sep%)
      start-indent: (+ (inherited-start-indent) (OLSTEP))
      first-line-start-indent: (- (OLSTEP))
      (make line-field
         field-width: (OLSTEP)
         (literal
           (case (modulo
             (length (hierarchical-number-recursive "OL")) 4)
           ((1) (string-append
             (format-number (child-number) "1") "."))
           ((2) (string-append
             (format-number (child-number) "a") "."))
           ((3) (string-append
             "(" (format-number (child-number) "i") ")"))
           ((0) (string-append
             "(" (format-number (child-number) "a") ")")))))
      (process-children-trim)))

(element (OL LI P) ($li-para$))

;; Note that DIR cannot properly have block children.  Here DIR is
;;   interpreted as an unmarked list without extra vertical
;;   spacing.

(element DIR ($list-container$))

(element (DIR LI)
 (make paragraph
      use: para-style
      start-indent: (+ (inherited-start-indent) (* 2.0 (ULSTEP)))
      first-line-start-indent: (- (ULSTEP))
      (process-children-trim)))

;; Note that MENU cannot properly have block children.  Here MENU is
;;   interpreted as a small-bulleted list with no extra vertical
;;   spacing.

(element MENU ($list-container$))
```

```
(element (MENU LI)
 (make paragraph
      use: para-style
      start-indent: (+ (inherited-start-indent) (ULSTEP))
      first-line-start-indent: (- (ULSTEP))
      (make line-field
         font-family-name: %dingbat-font-family%
         font-size: %bullet-size%
         field-width: (ULSTEP)
         (literal %disk-bullet%))
      (process-children-trim)))

;; This treatment of DLs doesn't apply a "compact" attribute set at one
;;    level to any nested DLs.  To change this behavior so that nested
;;    DLs inherit the "compact" attribute from an ancestor DL, substitute
;;    "inherited-attribute-string" for "attribute-string" in the
;;    construction rules for DT and DD.


(element DL
  (make display-group
     space-before: (if (INLIST?) %para-sep% %block-sep%)
     space-after:  (if (INLIST?) %para-sep% %block-sep%)
     start-indent: (if (INLIST?)
                    (+ (inherited-start-indent) 2em)
                    (+ %body-start-indent% 2em))
     (make paragraph)))

(element DT
  (let ((compact (attribute-string "compact" (ancestor "DL"))))
    (if compact
      (make line-field
         field-width: 3em
         (process-children-trim))
       (make paragraph
          use: para-style
          space-before: %para-sep%
          first-line-start-indent: -1em
          (process-children-trim)))))

(element DD
  (let ((compact (attribute-string "compact" (ancestor "DL"))))
    (if compact
      (sosofo-append
        (process-children-trim)
```

```
        (make paragraph-break))
         (make paragraph
            use: para-style
            start-indent: (+ (inherited-start-indent) 2em)
            (process-children-trim)))))


;; ========================= INLINE ELEMENTS ============================
```

TIP: *All text-level markup is really a function of bold, italic, monospace, or underlined text. Subscript and superscript fall into this category as well. Rather than repeat the same sosofo for each element that generates bold text, Bosak created the **$bold-seq$** definition for easy sosofo creation.*

```
(define ($bold-seq$)
  (make sequence
    font-weight: 'bold
    (process-children-trim)))

(element B ($bold-seq$))
(element EM ($bold-seq$))
(element STRONG ($bold-seq$))

;; ------------

(define ($italic-seq$)
  (make sequence
    font-posture: 'italic
    (process-children-trim)))

(element I ($italic-seq$))
(element CITE ($italic-seq$))
(element VAR ($italic-seq$))

;; ------------

(define ($bold-italic-seq$)
  (make sequence
    font-weight: 'bold
    font-posture: 'italic
    (process-children-trim)))
```

```
(element DFN ($bold-italic-seq$))
(element A
  (if (INHEAD?)
      (process-children-trim)
      ($bold-italic-seq$)))


;; ------------

(define ($mono-seq$)
  (make sequence
     font-family-name: %mono-font-family%
     font-size: %mf-size%
     (process-children-trim)))

(element TT   ($mono-seq$))
(element CODE ($mono-seq$))
(element KBD  ($mono-seq$))
(element SAMP ($mono-seq$))

;; ------------

(define ($score-seq$ stype)
  (make score
     type: stype
     (process-children-trim)))

(element STRIKE ($score-seq$ 'through))
(element U      ($score-seq$ 'after))

;; ------------

(define ($ss-seq$ plus-or-minus)
  (make sequence
     font-size:
       (* (inherited-font-size) %ss-size-factor%)
     position-point-shift:
       (plus-or-minus (* (inherited-font-size) %ss-shift-factor%))
     (process-children-trim)))

(element SUP ($ss-seq$ +))
(element SUB ($ss-seq$ -))

;; ------------
```

```
(define ($bs-seq$ div-or-mult)
  (make sequence
    font-size:
      (div-or-mult (inherited-font-size) %smaller-size-factor%)
    line-spacing:
      (div-or-mult (inherited-line-spacing) %smaller-size-factor%)))

(element BIG ($bs-seq$ /))
(element SMALL ($bs-seq$ *))


;; ------------

(element FONT
 (let ((fsize (attribute-string "SIZE")))
   (make sequence
       font-size:
       (if fsize (PARSEDUNIT fsize) (inherited-font-size)))))



;; ============================= RULES ===================================
```

TIP: *There's a lot more to a hard rule than you would think. This extensive sosofo is required to create the hard rules we're accustomed to seeing on the Web and in print.*

```
(element HR
 (let ((align (attribute-string "ALIGN"))
       (noshade (attribute-string "NOSHADE"))
       (size (attribute-string "SIZE"))
       (width (attribute-string "WIDTH")))
   (make rule
     orientation: 'horizontal
     space-before: %block-sep%
     space-after: %block-sep%
     line-thickness: (if size (PARSEDUNIT size) 1pt)
     length: (if width (PARSEDUNIT width) %body-width%)
     display-alignment:
       (case align
          (("LEFT") 'start)
          (("CENTER") 'center)
          (("RIGHT") 'end)
          (else 'end)))))
```

```
;; ============================ GRAPHICS ============================

;; Note that DSSSL does not currently support text flowed around an
;;    object, so the action of the ALIGN attribute is merely to shift the
;;    image to the left or right.  An extension to add runarounds to DSSSL
;;    has been proposed and should be incorporated here when it becomes
;;    final.

(element IMG
  (make external-graphic
     entity-system-id: (attribute-string "src")
     display?: #t
     space-before: 1em
     space-after: 1em
     display-alignment:
       (case (attribute-string "align")
          (("LEFT") 'start)
          (("RIGHT") 'end)
          (else 'center))))

;; ============================ TABLES ============================
```

TIP: *For this style sheet to work correctly with tables, they have to be described correctly. The following sosofos reconcile the DSSSL way of making tables with the HTML way.*

```
(element TABLE
;; number-of-columns is for future use
  (let ((number-of-columns
      (node-list-reduce (node-list-rest (children (current-node)))
               (lambda (cols nd)
                 (max cols
                   (node-list-length (children nd))))
               0)))
  (make display-group
     space-before: %block-sep%
     space-after: %block-sep%
     start-indent: %body-start-indent%
;; for debugging:
;;     (make paragraph
;;          (literal
;;           (string-append
;;          "Number of columns: "
```

```
;;           (number->string number-of-columns)))))
     (with-mode table-caption-mode (process-first-descendant "CAPTION"))
     (make table
           (process-children)))))

(mode table-caption-mode
  (element CAPTION
        (make paragraph
           use: para-style
           font-weight: 'bold
           space-before: %block-sep%
           space-after: %para-sep%
           start-indent: (inherited-start-indent)
           (literal
            (string-append
             "Table "
             (format-number
              (element-number) "1") ". "))
           (process-children-trim))))

(element CAPTION (empty-sosofo)) ; don't show caption inside the table

(element TR
  (make table-row
     (process-children-trim)))

(element TH
  (make table-cell
     n-rows-spanned: (string->number (attribute-string "COLSPAN"))
     (make paragraph
           font-weight: 'bold
           space-before: 0.25em
           space-after: 0.25em
           start-indent: 0.25em
           end-indent: 0.25em
           quadding: 'start
           (process-children-trim))))

(element TD
  (make table-cell
     n-rows-spanned: (string->number (attribute-string "COLSPAN"))
     (make paragraph
           space-before: 0.25em
           space-after: 0.25em
```

```
          start-indent: 0.25em
          end-indent: 0.25em
          quadding: 'start
          (process-children-trim))))
```

Transforming A Document From One DTD To Another With A Transformation Specification

Creating a transformation specification is not for the faint of heart. To do so, you need to fully understand both of the DTDs involved and find a way to accommodate any major differences in elements. The main use for transformation specifications in the XML world right now is to transform XML documents into HTML documents. Many of the XML tools include XML-to-HTML support as part of the functionality. They should because it's simple enough for them to use a DSSSL style sheet to convert documents built for one XML DTD into HTML. Because these tools are available, and because some are inexpensive or even free (as discussed in Chapter 22), it's our recommendation that you let a tool help you take advantage of this powerful DSSSL technology. However, to give you a taste of what a transformation specification looks like, here's a snippet from one written by Norm Walsh to translate documents written for DocBook—a popular SGML DTD—into HTML. As always, the copyright belongs to Mr. Walsh.

```
;; $Id: dblink.dsl 1.0 1997/12/30 17:48:14 nwalsh Exp $
;;
;; This file is part of the Modular DocBook Stylesheet distribution.
;; See ../README or http://www.berkshire.net/~norm/dsssl/
;;

;; ======================== LINKS AND ANCHORS ========================

(element LINK
  (let* ((target (element-with-id
            (attribute-string "LINKEND"))))
    (if (node-list-empty? target)
    (process-children)
    (make element gi: "A"
          attributes: (list
                  (list "HREF" (href-to target)))
          (process-children)))))

(element OLINK ($charseq$))
```

```
(element ULINK
  (make element gi: "A"
     attributes: (list
               (list "HREF" (attribute-string "URL")))
     (process-children)))

(element ANCHOR
  (make element gi: "A"
     attributes: (list
               (list "NAME" (attribute-string "ID")))
     (empty-sosofo)))

(element BEGINPAGE (empty-sosofo))


;; ==================================================================

(element XREF
  (let* ((endterm (attribute-string "ENDTERM"))
      (linkend (attribute-string "LINKEND"))
      (target  (element-with-id linkend)))
    (if (node-list-empty? target)
    (literal "[xref to non-existent element '" linkend "']")
    (make element gi: "A"
          attributes: (list
                (list "HREF" (href-to target)))
          (if endterm
           (if (node-list-empty? (element-with-id endterm))
               (literal "[xref endterm to non-existent element '"
                    endterm "']")
               (with-mode xref-endterm-mode
            (process-node-list (element-with-id endterm))))
           (if (attribute-string "XREFLABEL" target)
               (xreflabel-sosofo (attribute-string "XREFLABEL" target))
               (auto-xref target)))))))

(mode xref-endterm-mode
  (default
    (make element gi: "I"
       (process-children-trim))))

(define (xreflabel-sosofo xreflabel)
  (make element gi: "I"
     (literal xreflabel)))
```

```
;; Returns the title of the element as a sosofo, italicized for xref.
;;
(define (element-title-xref-sosofo nd)
  (make element gi: "I"
    (element-title-sosofo nd)))

(mode xref-title-mode
  (default
    (process-children-trim)))


;; =====================================================================

(define (element-page-number-sosofo target)
  (with-mode pageno-mode
    (process-node-list target)))

(mode pageno-mode
  (default
    (current-node-page-number-sosofo)))


;; =====================================================================
```

In a nutshell, this style sheet converts the DocBook **LINK**, **OLINK**, **ULINK**, **ANCHOR**, and **XREF** elements into HTML **A** elements. Because DocBook's linking mechanism is a bit different than HTML's, some functionality is lost and the transformation specification does an elegant job of squeezing a round peg into a square hole.

Deciding If DSSSL Is Right For You

As the samples in the previous sections of this chapter show, the DSSSL style sheet language is not as simple, easy to learn, and quick to implement as Cascading Style Sheets. It is a complex, robust, extensible, programming-language-like tool for adding advanced formatting to SGML, and hence XML documents. The learning curve is steep, but the rewards are many. The ultimate question becomes: Is DSSSL the right style solution for you? The answers to the following questions may help you decide:

- *Are you using DSSSL as part of an SGML style solution?* If you are, then DSSSL is a strong contender for your XML style solution. You may even be able to take advantage of your existing DSSSL style sheets—as you have probably taken advantage of your SGML style sheets—for a quicker implementation of well-formatted XML.

- *Do you have a working knowledge of DSSSL but aren't currently using it as a style solution?* Even if you're not currently using DSSSL, learning DSSSL is half the battle. Because DSSSL is a standard and Extensible Style Language (XSL, the future style sheet mechanism for XML) isn't even expected to be released as a recommendation until May 1999, it might be best to brush up on your DSSSL for a better style implementation.

- *Are you new to both XML and DSSSL?* If so, DSSSL might not be the best style solution for you. Although XSL is in its infancy, there is already an abundance of tools and resources for it. XSL is technically a subset of DSSSL, as XML is a subset of SGML, and you may not need to know everything about DSSSL just to use it with your XML documents.

- *Do you need to convert documents from SGML to XML or from XML to HTML?* As discussed in the preceding section, DSSSL is the perfect mechanism for cross-DTD transformations. However, because of DSSSL's learning curve, it may be a while before you can implement transformation specifications. If you answered yes to either of the first two questions, then, once again, DSSSL is a strong possibility for your style solution. If you answered yes to the third, focus your attention on finding a quality tool that will help you implement valid DSSSL style and transformation specifications as quickly as possible.

Employing DSSSL Software

There are couple of standalone DSSSL software packages available for use with both SGML and XML documents:

- *Jade*—This free parser from James Clark (the developer of the well-known and loved SP SGML parser and XP XML parser) is the DSSSL developer's best friend. Jade fully supports the entire style subset of DSSSL but does not support the transformation subset. For more information or to download Jade, visit **www.jclark.com/jade**.

- *DSSSL Developer's Toolkit*—From Copernican Solutions, the DSSSL Developer's Toolkit is a set of Java-based DSSSL application programming interfaces (APIs). It can work alone or in concert with the DAE software development kit (SDK), which provides an environment for processing SGML and XML documents via DSSSL. Point your Web browser to **www.copsol. com/products** to learn more about these products.

In addition, many SGML and XML tools have built-in DSSSL development mechanisms as part of a larger document creation and management package.

Chapter 16

Stylin' XML: XSL

By Natanya Pitts-Moultis

In Depth

The Extensible Style Language (XSL) is a style sheet mechanism that is customized for XML. You can use XSL to convert an XML document to HTML, rich text format (RTF), and other XML vocabularies, or you can tell an XML processor or browser exactly how you want your XML documents displayed. XSL is the ultimate formatting language for XML and is easy to learn and implement.

Chapters 14 and 15 examine Cascading Style Sheets (CSS) and the Document Style Semantics and Specification Language (DSSSL) as options for creating style sheets for XML documents. Although both of these style mechanisms have solid strengths and qualities that make them suitable for working with XML, the bottom line is that they were created to work with two other markup languages—HTML and SGML, respectively. On the other hand, the Extensible Style Language (XSL) has been designed to work specifically with XML and the vocabularies created with it. XSL style sheets are in fact XML documents and are more easily created and implemented than DSSSL style sheets, yet they are more robust and capable than CSS style sheets. In many ways, XSL represents the happy medium between CSS and DSSSL that XML provides for HTML and SGML.

This chapter describes XSL as a style mechanism, addresses the issues raised by XSL's current existence as just a note to the World Wide Web Consortium (W3C) and not a specification, shows how XSL relates to both CSS and DSSSL, and prepares you to construct XSL style sheets of any level. This chapter's Immediate Solutions section provides detailed instructions for constructing the components of an XSL style sheet.

What Is XSL?

As discussed in previous style chapters, XML should be used strictly to provide information about the structure of a document. Formatting information is provided for a document by a style sheet. XSL is the style sheet mechanism used to create style sheets for XML documents. XSL associates formatting rules with the different elements in a document and instructs the browser or display software on how to format the element and its contents for viewing by the user.

As with other types of style mechanisms, more than one XSL style sheet can be created for a single XML document to provide for one of several final display scenarios. For example, imagine that a document needs to be displayed on a Web browser for a user, utilized by a presenter at a conference, and printed for use as a handout. Three separate style sheets could be created with formatting instructions appropriate to each type of dissemination method. Now imagine that a company has hundreds of documents that need to be presented in a consistent manner in all three scenarios. Three separate style sheets could govern all the documents for easy application and a consistent look and feel. The following design principals of XSL are listed in the W3C note at **www.w3.org/TR/NOTE-XSL.html**:

- XSL should be straightforwardly usable over the Internet.

- XSL should be expressed in XML syntax.

- XSL should provide a declarative language to do all common formatting tasks.

- XSL should provide an "escape" into a scripting language to accommodate more sophisticated formatting tasks and to allow for extensibility and completeness.

- XSL will be a subset of DSSSL based on a proposed amendment.

- A mechanical mapping of a CSS style sheet into an XSL style sheet should be possible.

- XSL should be informed by user experience with the formatting output specification instance (FOSI) style sheet language.

- The number of optional features in XSL should be kept to a minimum.

- XSL style sheets should be human-legible and reasonably clear.

- The XSL design should be prepared quickly.

- XSL style sheets shall be easy to create.

- Terseness in XSL markup is of minimal importance.

XSL's primary function at this stage will be transforming XML documents into documents that are valid for use with other document systems, such as HTML and RTF. In the future, XSL will also describe to XML processors and browsers how the XML documents they work with should be displayed.

XSL's style application mechanisms are specific to XML. An XSL document is a valid XML document, so you don't have to learn a new language to create XSL documents. This also means you can use existing XML parsers to check the validity of your XSL style sheets and XML documents. XSL isn't even to the Request For Comments (RFC) stage, and it already has a validation system in place.

The Status Of The XSL Specification

XSL's single largest weakness is its infancy. Currently, XSL is a working draft developed for the W3C by a group of authors from Microsoft, Inso, ArbortText, and the University of Edinburgh. For the current version of the working draft, point your browser to **www.w3.org/TR/WD-xsl**. The working draft was released in mid-August 1998, and according to the XSL page at the W3C Web site (**www.w3.org/Style/XSL**), the final XSL specification will be developed according to this schedule:

- *Second working draft of XSL 1*—November 1998

- *Third working draft of XSL 1*—February 1999

- *Proposed recommendation for XSL 1*—May 1999

As you can see, we can't expect a final recommendation until May 1999. A few months in Web time can seem like forever, so a year can seem endless. XML itself will change greatly in that time. Although the basic constructs of XSL will probably remain the same, you should expect significant additions to the specification as well as a whole host of fine-tuning activities.

What does this mean to the XML developer? The best advice we can give you is to be cautious in your development of extensive XSL style sheets. Don't get so attached to a style sheet that you aren't willing to modify it as XSL evolves. If you are desperate for a solid style sheet mechanism that won't change on you every few months and that will work with a large collection of XML documents, use DSSSL (discussed in Chapter 15) until XSL is more stable. By then, there are sure to be several DSSSL-to-XSL converters (there is already an XSL-to-DSSSL engine, which is discussed at the end of the Immediate Solutions section). Be warned: DSSSL is a complex language, and if you're going to use it, you'll need to invest a fair amount of resources in learning and developing DSSSL style sheets.

If, however, you're new to XML and looking at it as an alternative Web technology or as a way to describe an emerging set of documents, then XSL is probably your best bet for XML style sheets. Despite its relative youth, XSL is already seeing a great deal of support in vendor products, and it's likely that browsers will have more XSL support than DSSSL support built into them. Also, XSL provides for CSS integration, so you can use XSL to convert documents from XML to HTML for Web publication and link the documents to your favorite CSS style sheet, or you can embed CSS style rules directly in your HTML documents via XSL. XSL tools are emerging at a slower rate than XML tools, but this is still impressive considering XSL's status as a W3C note.

Learning XSL is going to be a prerequisite for disseminating XML documents effectively in Web pages. Eventually, you'll need to know it one way or the other, so it's best if you learn it now. Keep a close watch on the XSL page at the W3C Web site, and you might want to subscribe to the XSL mailing list maintained by Mulberry Technologies (**www.mulberrytech.com/xsl/xsl-list**).

Important XSL Terms

Any XSL discussion will include the repeated use of several key terms. They include:

- *Construction rule*—The cornerstone of an XSL style sheet. It contains the formatting instructions for any given document element.

- *Pattern*—The portion of a construction rule that identifies the document element to receive the formatting (action).

- *Action*—The portion of a construction rule that describes how the document element (pattern) should be formatted.

- *Flow object*—Structures used to describe how the content of a document should be formatted. Flow objects are linked to elements with construction rules.

- *Root rule*—The construction rule that describes how a document's document element should be formatted.

- *Default rule*—The construction rule that describes how all rules not governed by other constructions rules should be formatted.

XSL borrows the concepts of construction rules and flow objects from DSSSL. The Immediate Solutions section of this chapter discusses the creation of each of these XSL components in turn and describes the role they play in an XSL style sheet.

Resolving Conflicts: Rule Arbitration

Unlike Cascading Style Sheets, XSL does not provide a mechanism for resolving rule conflicts. In essence, XSL does not cascade. Instead, when an element in an XML document matches more than one construction rule, the construction rule that contains the most specific pattern wins and its action is applied to the element. For example, a construction rule that specifies a title element contained within a chapter heading has precedence over one that only specifies title elements without any additional context or content definitions. Both rules could legally be applied to the titles found within chapter elements, but the first is more specific and is therefore the applied rule.

Immediate Solutions

XSL is a style mechanism like many others found in document creation. What makes it different is its direct applicability to XML and its constructs. This Immediate Solutions section focuses on how to create the various constructs found in an XSL style sheet, combine them to form a cohesive style sheet, and integrate the style sheet with one or more XML documents. In addition, the Immediate Solutions section discusses how to choose an XSL tool and evaluate the current and upcoming XSL DTDs.

Presently, the most practical use of XSL is for the conversion of XML documents to HTML documents for Web-publishing purposes. Therefore, the Immediate Solutions section focuses on this use of XSL in the majority of its examples. We are not suggesting that XSL isn't good for anything other than XML-to-HTML conversions. We chose this approach because it is a useful way to create examples with a point of reference everyone can understand and a way to show the immediate uses of XSL. Because XSL is constantly under review and in a state of flux, this Immediate Solutions section only covers the most basic XSL constructs. Many specific constructs may be lost or changed as the specification evolves.

Defining Basic Style Sheet Constructs

Every XSL document is an XML document, so it must adhere to all of XML's syntactical rules that govern well-formed and valid documents. The XSL DTD (listed at the end of the chapter) is relatively short, and for a document to function as an XSL style sheet, it must be valid as described by the DTD. As mentioned earlier, you can validate XSL style sheets by using a validating XML parser. This also means that building XSL support into existing parsers won't be very difficult.

The document element for an XSL style sheet is the **<XSL>...</XSL>** element. Every XSL style sheet should begin and end with an open and close **XSL** tag. The **XSL** element defines the document as a style sheet and can also contain the following elements:

- **<IMPORT>**—Imports other style sheets into the current XSL document. This element is equivalent to the **@import** element in a CSS style sheet.

- **<DEFINE-MACRO>**—Combines a set of construction rules into a macro to be executed when called.

- **<DEFINE-SCRIPT>**—Contains one or more scripts to be executed later in the document.

- **<ID>** *and* **<CLASS>**—Link source elements to unique identification labels or classes.

Use this code to begin an XSL document that imports another style sheet and includes a **define-macro** element named **<HEADER>**:

```
<XSL>
    <IMPORT HREF="/styles/main-style.xsl" />
    <HEADER>
        Header text to be affected by the header macro
    </HEADER>
...
</XSL>
```

The **XSL** element declares that the document is an XSL document and sets up the remainder of the document to describe style rules for elements in the document to which the style sheet is linked. Use the **XML-STYLESHEET** processing instruction (PI) to reference an XSL style sheet in an XML document, as shown in this example:

```
<?XML-STYLESHEET HREF="/styles/main-style.xsl" TYPE="TEXT/XSL" ?>
```

Using DSSSL And CSS Core Flow Objects In XSL Documents

A styled XML document is made up of a series of flow objects. Flow objects describe the parts of a document as a combination of elements described by the XML document and the styles that should be applied to it as defined in an associated XSL document. Construction rules are used to create flow objects. You can't make up your own flow objects but instead must choose from one of several predefined for XSL. Flow objects were predefined to help ensure ease of style sheet creation and consistency among documents. The current suggested core flow objects for XSL are taken from both DSSSL and HTML. The DSSSL core flow objects that are used in XSL are (for the time being):

- **scroll**—Describes a page meant for online (Web) display

- **paragraph, paragraph-break**—Describes paragraphs and paragraph breaks

- **character**—Describes characters
- **line-field**—Describes lists
- **external-graphic**—Creates links to external images
- **horizontal-rule**, **vertical-rule**—Creates horizontal and vertical rules
- **score**—Creates underlines and scores through text
- **embedded-text**—Describes bidirectional text
- **box**—Creates borders around elements
- **table**—Describes a table
- **table-part**—Divides a table into sections
- **table-column**—Describes a column within a table
- **table-row**—Describes where a table row begins and ends
- **table-cell**—Describes a table cell
- **table-border**—Creates a table border
- **sequence**—Describes inherited characteristics
- **display-group**—Describes how display-group objects should be positioned
- **simple-page-sequence**—Describes a simple page layout
- **link**—Creates a hyperlink

For a more detailed description of how DSSSL works, revisit Chapter 15, or for a more detailed description of each of these flow objects, browse the DSSSL specification included on this book's companion CD-ROM.

In addition to the DSSSL flow objects, you can also use elements from the HTML Document Object Model (DOM) as XSL flow objects. The following HTML elements can be used as XSL flow objects:

A	AREA	BASE	BODY
CAPTION	COL	COLGROUP	DIV
FORM	FRAMESET	HR	HTML
IMG	INPUT	MAP	META
OBJECT	PARAM	PRE	SCRIPT
SELECT	SPAN	TABLE	TBODY
TD	TEXTAREA	TFOOT	THEAD
TITLE	TR		

Keep in mind that these elements are all taken from the HTML 3.2 specification because the XSL note was released before the formal recommendation for HTML 4 was released. This is one of the primary areas where there are sure to be changes as the XSL specification is refined. HTML support was included in XSL so it could support the transformation of XML documents into HTML. The remainder of the examples in the Immediate Solutions section use HTML elements to create flow objects so that those of you who aren't DSSSL savvy won't have to try to figure out two style sheet mechanisms at once.

Creating Construction Rules

Construction rules associate elements in a source document with a formatting structure of elements in an output document. Use this syntax to create a basic construction rule:

```
<rule>
    <pattern>
    <action>
</rule>
```

Patterns and actions are created by using their own syntactical constructs, as discussed later in this chapter. Once again, we turn to David Megginson's novel DTD and associated *Heart of Darkness* documents (**home.sprynet.com/sprynet/dmeggins/texts/darkness/index.html**) for a functional DTD to use as an example. The following construction rule maps the novel DTD element **<TITLE>** to a **<P>** element in an HTML document:

```
<rule>
    <target-element type="title" />
    <P font-size="36pt" font-style="italic">
        <children/>
    </P>
</rule>
```

This construction rule indicates that the **target-element**, **title**, should be rendered in the output document as a paragraph and that its children (that is, text and contents) should also be processed—as defined by the **<CHILDREN/>** element. The **font-size** and **font-style** attributes included with the paragraph element in the action will create a style attribute for the paragraph when the tag **style="font-size:36pt; font-style:italic** is rendered. This technique allows XSL developers to easily add CSS style to HTML documents created from XML documents. **P** is the flow object created for the **<TITLE>** element of the novel DTD.

We can apply this style rule to this chunk of text from Chapter 1 of *Heart of Darkness,* as described by the novel DTD

```
<title>I</title>
```

and this HTML would be created:

```
<P STYLE="font-size:36pt; font-style:italic>I</P>
```

Figure 16.1 shows this title rendered in a browser window.

Granted, it's only the letter *I,* but if we create a construction rule for the **<PARA-GRAPH>** element in the novel DTD, the results are a bit more obvious. A construction rule that formats the content of **<PARAGRAPH>** elements as **<P>** elements in HTML rendered in 14-point Comic Sans MS with a top margin of 1.5 inches and a left margin of 1 inch looks like this:

```
<rule>
    <target-element type="paragraph" />
    <P margin-top="1.5in" margin-left="1in" font="14pt "Comic Sans MS"">
        <children/>
    </P>
</rule>
```

If we apply the rule to this text from Chapter 1 of *Heart of Darkness*

```
<paragraph>
The Nellie, a cruising yawl, swung to her anchor without a
flutter of the sails, and was at rest. The flood had made, the wind
was nearly calm, and being bound down the river, the only thing for it
was to come to and wait for the turn of the tide.
</paragraph>
```

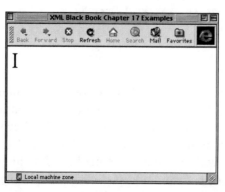

Figure 16.1   A title from an XML document is easily converted to HTML by using XSL.

we get this HTML:

```
<P
   STYLE="margin-top:1.5in;
   margin-left:1in;
   font="14pt Arial" >
The Nellie, a cruising yawl, swung to her anchor without a
flutter of the sails, and was at rest. The flood had made, the wind
was nearly calm, and being bound down the river, the only thing for it
was to come to and wait for the turn of the tide.
</P>
```

Figure 16.2 shows what this HTML looks like in a browser.

Figure 16.2   A paragraph from an XML document is easily converted to HTML by using XSL.

Declaring A Pattern

Patterns describe a source document's element or elements to which the action portion of a construction rule is applied. Create a basic pattern using this syntax:

```
<rule>
    <target-element type="element" />
    <action>
</rule>
```

The value of the **type=** attribute of the **target-element** element indicates which element from the source document should be affected by the action.

The title construction rule from the previous section is an example of the simplest form a pattern can have:

```
<rule>
    <target-element type="title" />
    <P font-size="36pt" font-style="italic">
        <children/>
    </P>
</rule>
```

A standalone **<TARGET-ELEMENT>** doesn't take into account the context of the element. So in this example, every instance of the **<TITLE>** tag would be formatted the same in the output document. However, the novel DTD allows titles to be assigned to the entire novel (via the **<FRONT>** element) or to each individual chapter. It makes sense to use different formatting for the book and chapter titles. The best way to do this is to differentiate between the types of titles based on their context. If the title appears within the **<FRONT>** tag, it takes one rule; if it appears within the **<CHAPTER>** element, it takes another. The XSL **<ELEMENT>** element provides contextual information within the patterns of construction rules to help make them more specific. Use the following syntax to provide contextual information about target elements:

```
<rule>
    <element type="element">
        <target-element type="element" />
    </element>
    <action>
</rule>
```

The value of the **type=** attribute of the **<ELEMENT>** element provides the context for the **<TARGET-ELEMENT>**. Nest **<ELEMENT>** within **<ELEMENT>** within **<ELEMENT>** tags as deeply as necessary to describe the context of the target element.

Using the **<ELEMENT>** element, these two rules define actions for each type of **title** found in the novel DTD:

```
<rule>
    <element type=front>
        <target-element type="title" />
    </element>
```

```
    <P font-size="36pt" font-style="italic">
        <children/>
    </P>
</rule>

<rule>
    <element type=chapter>
        <target-element type="title" />
    </element>
    <P font-size="30pt" font-style="bold">
        <children/>
    </P>
</rule>
```

Title elements contained in the **front** element create **p** flow objects with a font size of 36 points and a font style of italic. **Title** elements contained in **chapter** elements create **p** flow objects with a font size of 30 points and a font style of bold.

The rules of pattern creation state that there can only be one **<TARGET-ELEMENT>** element in any given pattern, but there can be as many **<ELEMENT>** elements as necessary to convey the appropriate contextual information for the **<TARGET-ELEMENT>** element. In addition to contextual specifications, patterns can also include wildcards, attributes, and qualifiers, as discussed in the next few sections.

Including Wildcards In A Pattern

Wildcards are used within patterns to make element matching easier. The available wildcards include:

- **<TARGET-ELEMENT/>**—Indicates that the pattern should extend to all elements. This can be refined by using **<ELEMENT>** elements to extend to all of the children of an element.

- **<ANY>...</ANY>**—Indicates that the pattern should extend to zero or more elements nested within the **<TARGET-ELEMENT>** regardless of how many levels down the element is listed.

This pattern references any element contained within the first level of an **HTML** element:

```
<rule>
    <element type="HTML">
        <target-element/>
    </element>
    <action>
</rule>
```

Because the pattern uses the blank **<TARGET-ELEMENT>** element, all children of the **HTML** element would be processed by the action. The action only extends to the children of the **HTML** element but not to the child element's children.

The following pattern references any **
** element contained within an **HTML** element, regardless of its ancestry:

```
<rule>
    <element type="HTML">
        <any>
            <target-element type="BR" />
        </any>
    </element>
    <action>
</rule>
```

Matching Attributes In A Pattern

Attributes are used to better define elements within an XML document, so XSL has access to an element's attribute as part of a pattern definition. The **<AT-TRIBUTE>** element works within the pattern to specify an element based on its attributes. **<ATTRIBUTE>** elements use this syntax:

```
<rule>
    <target-element type="element">
        <attribute name="attribute-name" value="attribute-value" />
    </target-element>
    <action>
</rule>
```

If attributes are used in pattern matching, the **<TARGET-ELEMENT>** element is no longer an empty tag but is used as a container. Notice that the **<ATTRIBUTE>** element is now an empty tag. This pattern matches only those instances of the anchor tag that have an attribute of **target** with a value of "**_blank**", as in the following code:

```
<rule>
    <target-element type="a">
        <attribute name="target" value="_blank" />
    </target-element>
    <action>
<rule>
```

Multiple attributes can be specified for either **<TARGET-ELEMENT>** or **<ELE-MENT>** elements to provide specific information about the pattern an element must match to be the target of an action.

Patterns can contain any combination of selection criteria, including context, wildcards, and attributes. This pattern matches any **a** element found at any level within a **<P>** element that has an attribute of **target** with the value of "**_blank**":

```
<rule>
    <element type="p">
        <any>
            <target-element type="a">
                <attribute name="target" value="_blank" />
            </target-element>
        </any>
    </element-type>
    <action>
</rule>
```

Using Qualifiers In A Pattern

There are two qualifiers included in XSL to assist in pattern matching. They are:

- **has-value**—Indicates whether a specified attribute has a value, regardless of what the value is

- **position**—Indicates an element's position as a first or last element in a grouping

These qualifiers provide a mechanism for pattern matching that can't be found anywhere else in XSL. Often, you don't really care what the value of an attribute is, especially if the attribute takes **CDATA** as its value. To inquire about the existence of an attribute's value, use this syntax:

```
<rule>
    <target-element type="element">
        <attribue name="attribute-name" has-value="yes" />
    </target>
    <action>
</rule>
```

As long as the *element* specified in the **type** attribute of the **<TYPE-ELEMENT>** element (or **<ELEMENT>** element) has an attribute of *attribute-name* with any value, the action will be applied to it.

The **position** element is used to create a flow object based upon an element's position in a list or grouping. The values for **position** are **last-of-type**, **first-of-type**, **last-of-any**, and **first-of-any**, and the **position** attribute can be used with either **<ELEMENT>** or **<TARGET-ELEMENT>** elements. The **of-type** values refer to one of several sibling elements of the same type, and the **of-any** values refer to one of any element of the same type regardless of the elements' relationships.

The following three patterns select the first, last, and middle elements in a listing of chapters:

```
<rule>
    <target-element type="chapter" position="first-of-type"/>
    <action>
</rule>

<rule>
    <target-element type="chapter" position="last-of-type"/>
    <action>
</rule>

<rule>
    <target-element type="chapter">
    <action>
</rule>
```

The first pattern applies an action to only the first item in a list of chapters, the second to the last item in the list, and the third to every item in between. This could allow you to apply different formatting to the first and last chapter listings as well as a third to all the other chapter listings in between. If the values had been **of-any** instead of **of-type**, the rules would apply to the first instance of the chapter element in the document and the last instance, respectively, and the third rule would apply to all other instances throughout the document body.

Including Multiple Patterns In A Construction Rule

To apply one action to several elements matching a variety of patterns, use this syntax to include several different **<TARGET-ELEMENT>** elements within the same style rule:

```
<rule>
    <target-element type="element" />
    <target-element type="element" />
    <target-element type="element" />
    <action>
</rule>
```

Each **<TARGET-ELEMENT>** element can contain one or more **<ATTRIBUTE>** elements.

Declaring An Action

An action in a construction rule describes how the element or elements that match the pattern should be formatted. Included in an action is information about:

- The final output flow object
- The formatting applied to the flow object
- Processing information for the children of the source element

The syntax for a basic action is:

```
<rule>
    <pattern>
    <flow-object>
</rule>
```

In its simplest form, the action maps the results of the pattern search to a flow object. The following example maps a **chapter** element to a **p** flow object:

```
<rule>
    <target-element type="chapter" />
    <p />
</rule>
```

Although this is the simplest form an action can take, it's probable that you'll need to create more advanced actions for source elements. Style information can be included in the action, as in this example:

```
<rule>
    <target-element type="title" />
    <P font-size="36pt" font-style="italic">
        <children />
    </P>
</rule>
```

This action maps all instances of the **title** element to a **p** element that has a **style** attribute with the value **font-size:36pt; font-style:italic**. In addition, this action includes the **<CHILDREN />** element that instructs the processor to include the processed results of the element's children after the element itself. In general, the empty children tag is used to keep the flow of the document going. This makes a bit more sense when you learn that the text contained within a document is considered part of its child content. If you don't reference an element's children, none of its textual content will be displayed within the output document.

Actions can be used in combination with advanced pattern matching to closely control the final output of an XML document. This set of style rules defines how a series of chapters should be formatted:

```
<rule>
     <target-element type="chapter" position="first-of-type"/>
     <P font="14pt blue Arial">
          <children />
          <HR />
     </P>
</rule>

<rule>
     <target-element type="chapter" position="last-of-type"/>
     <HR />
     <P font="14pt blue Arial">
          <children />
     </P>
</rule>

<rule>
     <target-element type="chapter">
     <P font="12pt Arial">
          <children />
     </P>
</rule>
```

The first style rule creates a **p** flow object for the first instance of a chapter in a group of chapters and renders it in 14-point blue Arial with a hard rule following the contents of the chapter element. The second style rule creates another **p** flow object for the last instance of a chapter in a group and also renders it in 14-point blue Arial, but the hard rule comes before the chapter's content in this flow object instead of after. Finally, the third style rule renders all other chapters within the chapter grouping in 12-point Arial in regular text color without hard rules.

Creating A Root Construction Rule

The root construction rule governs the formatting of the document's **<ROOT>** element (document element) and is created by using this syntax:

```
<rule>
     <root />
```

```
        <action>
</rule>
```

The **<ROOT>** element takes the place of the **<TARGET-ELEMENT>** or **<ELEMENT>** tags. This rule is automatically applied to the document element as defined in the DTD. The following markup assigns a conventional HTML document structure to the **<ROOT>** element of the source document, ensuring that the output document is a valid HTML document:

```
<rule>
        <root />
        <HTML>
                <HEAD>
                        <TITLE>
                                <target-element type="title">
                                <children/>
                                </target-element>
                        </TITLE>
                </HEAD>
                <BODY>
                        <children />
                </BODY>
        </HTML>
</rule>
```

Evaluating The XSL DTD

As stated earlier, XSL is an actual XML DTD, so for the curious, this final section includes the full text of the XSL DTD. Note that it is rather short. You'll also notice that there are some elements and attributes included in the DTD that aren't discussed in this chapter. That is due in large part to the forthcoming changes in XSL. The easiest way to find out what changes have been made to XSL will be to run through the new version of the DTD and compare it with the old version. Because this DTD is the first DTD, all others will grow from it, so this is the baseline for comparison. As XSL matures, keep an eye on the changes in the notes and specifications associated with it, but remember that the DTD is always the ultimate source of information about any XML document.

16: Stylin' XML: XSL

TIP: *This DTD is a portion of the XML note found on the W3C site at **www.w3.org/TR/NOTE-XSL.html**. Copyright is maintained by the W3C.*

```
<!-- This DTD is for exegesis only.  It assumes that the action parameter
entity has been defined as an or-group of flow object elements.
The style parameter entity is used to represent an or-group of the apply
element and styles defined with define-style. -->
<!ENTITY % pattern
        "(root | (target-element | element | any)*)">
<!ELEMENT rule
        (%pattern;, %action;) >
<!ELEMENT style-rule
        (%pattern;, %style)>
<!ELEMENT root  EMPTY>
<!ATTLIST (rule | style-rule)
        priority   NUMBER      #IMPLIED
        importance NUMBER      #IMPLIED
        mode       NAME        #IMPLIED>
<!ELEMENT target-element
        (attribute*, (element+ | any)?)    -(target-element)>
<!ELEMENT element
        (attribute*, (target-element | element | any)?) >
<!ELEMENT any  EMPTY >
<!ATTLIST (target-element | element)
        type       NAME        #IMPLIED
        id         NAME        #IMPLIED
        class      NAME        #IMPLIED
        only      (of-type|of-any) #IMPLIED
        position (first-of-type|last-of-type|first-of-any|last-of-any)
        #IMPLIED>
<!ELEMENT attribute EMPTY >
<!ATTLIST attribute
        name      NAME        #REQUIRED
        value     CDATA       #IMPLIED
        has-value (yes|no)    'yes'>
```

Chapter 17

Designing With XML

By Natanya Pitts-Moultis

In Depth

Although a strong knowledge of Extensible Markup Language (XML) elements, attributes, styles, and so on is a practical requirement for any XML document developer, a solid understanding of document design basics is also a prerequisite to document development. The usefulness and effectiveness of a document can be quickly compromised by hasty design, ineffectual navigation, or small mistakes scattered throughout a document that cause it to be invalid.

Moving away from the cut-and-dry world of syntax and coding requirements and into the more abstract world of document design, this chapter includes a look at browser and processor compatibility issues, a discussion of the different roles valid and well-formed documents play in information delivery, and a visit to the often-forgotten world of content. The chapter ends with a lesson on creating useful navigation schemes for electronic document collections.

A Brief History Of Documents

As evidenced by a quick foray into the vast amounts of information on the World Wide Web, poorly designed documents seem to be the norm rather than the exception in the rapidly growing world of electronic information dissemination. This is not a new phenomenon. Recall that ill-thought-out brochures and flyers seemed to proliferate in abundance with the advent of personal desktop publishing systems—like PageMaker and QuarkXPress—in combination with the creation of vast and inexpensive clip-art collections. Art, balance, color, and type have always been advanced issues, usually left to those with years of education and experience. Personal publishing systems didn't do away with the issues but instead pushed them to the background as untrained novices recklessly wielded the power their newly found desktop publishing tools provided. The addition of the affordable copier into the fray didn't help either.

The two prohibitive factors that stemmed the tide of unschooled and primitive documents were the cost of full-color printing and dissemination. Whereas fliers, brochures, and decorated documents could be created and copied in black and white by the score, full, four-color printing was expensive (and still is), and even two-color documents were often cost prohibitive. In addition, the cost of postage was steadily rising, and snail mail was the best way to send documents from one place to the other.

The Web made short work of these two final prohibitive factors. Color on the Web is free, and dissemination is no longer an issue worth discussing. WYSIWYG (What You See Is What You Get) editors help the same group of novices create full-color documents in which emphasis is placed on bells and whistles instead of on content. Internet Service Providers allow anyone in the United States who pays roughly $19.95 a month to post his or her creations for the entire world to see, even if the world doesn't necessarily want to see the creations.

Quick and easy document publishing solutions in combination with the Web have made the creation and dissemination of documents easier than ever before. This revolution in information sharing seems to have swept the issues of document design far under the carpet, if not vacuumed them up entirely and thrown them away forever. But, as Bart Simpson would say, "Au contraire mon freres." The issues of design are more important now than ever before.

The Role Of Design In Document Creation

XML is all about information. The same can be said for its parent, Standard Generalized Markup Language (SGML), and its distant cousin—or child, depending on how you look at it—Hypertext Markup Language (HTML). The Internet and the Web provide the creators of information with a powerful mechanism for sharing information with others around the world. No matter which way you look at it, the Internet—all of its services and protocols, hardware and software—is all about information.

But you knew that already, and that's probably why you've turned to XML as a document creation tool. Existing Internet and Web mechanisms don't provide you with the exact solution you need, but an XML application—your own or someone else's—does. So, why kill all these trees to talk about design? In the end, the design of a document can make or break its ability to convey the information it contains. Granted, good design is more important in presentation-based documents than in content-based documents, but half, if not more, of the documents created for XML applications will be presentation based. As a whole, a document's design includes:

- *Styles*—Fonts, colors, placement of page elements
- *Bells and whistles*—Images, multimedia components
- *Wayfinding toolkit*—The navigation system it employs
- *Well-formedness*—The correct use of markup
- *Congruity*—How well it fits with other documents in a document collection
- *Appropriateness*—How well it adheres to the spirit of the XML application for which it was created

Put together, these design elements form the *user interface* (UI) for the document as a whole, and the UI is guided entirely by the document's content. In a nutshell, the UI provides a way for the user to interact with the information in the document. Even colors and font selection can contribute to users' success or failure in getting what they need from a document. The remainder of this portion of the chapter examines the pieces and parts of a document's design (or UI) and is followed by an abbreviated Immediate Solutions section that provides step-by-step instructions to help you:

• Figure out when a document should be well-formed or valid

• Define the goal of an XML application as it relates to document design

• Design an effective document navigation system

• Plan the UI for a collection of XML documents

Throughout the chapter, we refer to several well-designed Web sites as examples of quality document design. Although this is a book on XML, the reality is that this technology is still in its infancy—with most developers focusing on Document Type Definition design—and real-life examples are few and far between. If you treat HTML as an XML application, then all Web documents are XML documents anyway. In the end, the elements of good document design aren't limited to one media or another, even though certain media make it easier to ignore them than others do.

Technical Design Elements

Design elements can be broken down into two categories: technical and interface. In this section, we'll look at some behind-the-scenes elements of document design. These elements don't affect how a document is displayed by the browser as directly as elements such as fonts and colors do. Nonetheless, their role is just as important. They include:

• Processor and browser specifics

• The goal and purpose of the XML application

• The requirement that a document be well-formed and/or valid

• The potential and limitations of the markup

At first glance, these elements are a bit more amorphous than the interface elements, but the following discussions should make them more concrete.

Processor And Browser Specifics

At the very least, XML documents are going to be evaluated, and possibly displayed, by an XML processor. The role of the processor is to evaluate the document, usually in relation to its specified DTD, and then do something with its content. For presentation-based markup, this "something" will usually be to display it with a browser of some sort. Both Netscape and Microsoft have committed to creating Web browsers that can view XML documents. The goal of the browser vendors and the developers of XML is for users to be able to move from an HTML document to an XML document and back again and never know the difference. This will allow for the full integration of XML documents into existing HTML document collections without the need to recode the HTML documents.

For every XML document you create, you'll need to know how an XML processor expects to deal with documents written for a specific application and what happens to the content of the document after it has been processed. For example, the XML application Channel Definition Format (CDF) was expressly designed to describe content for display in a Web browser. CDF files are processed by XML processors built into Web browsers that support CDF (specifically, Microsoft Internet Explorer 4), and the information inside the files is shown to the user in a Web browser. Armed with this knowledge, CDF document developers should realize that their CDF documents will be best viewed with IE4 and probably can't be viewed with Netscape Navigator. Also, because CDF was created specifically to work with a Web browser, any generic XML processor will be able to parse the XML document, but it won't necessarily be able to display it as a Web browser would.

Internet Explorer 4 is designed to work with CDF documents that allow users to specify how often channels should be updated, as well as set other specifications. The browser has a built-in interface that allows the user to set these options easily and quickly, as shown in Figures 17.1 and 17.2.

Once a subscription has been set for a user, the content described by the CDF markup is displayed in the browser, as shown in Figure 17.3.

The IE4 channel interface is designed specifically to work with CDF files. The channel manager on the left side of the browser window uses a gold diamond icon to alert the user to areas in subscribed channels where new information has been downloaded. The user can easily move from area to area and view the content in the larger right-hand portion of the screen.

Although the CDF files used to create channels could easily be parsed by a generic XML processor, they are best processed and displayed by a software package—Internet Explorer 4—that was designed to work with the content after processing.

As the Web has developed, we've all learned some important lessons about the role browsers play in the development of Web technology. CDF was one of the

17: Designing With XML

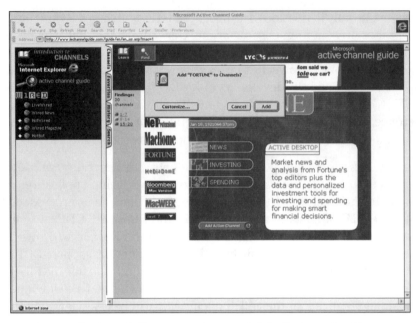

Figure 17.1   Internet Explorer 4 allows users to accept default channel settings or customize their own when they subscribe to a channel.

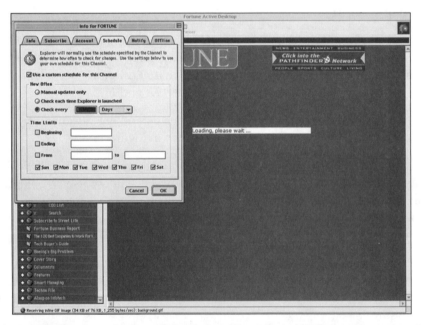

Figure 17.2   The IE4 channel information window lets users set their own channel-update schedule and other channel-related information through an easy-to-use dialog box. Any channel information set by the user must conform to the rules set forth in the CDF DTD.

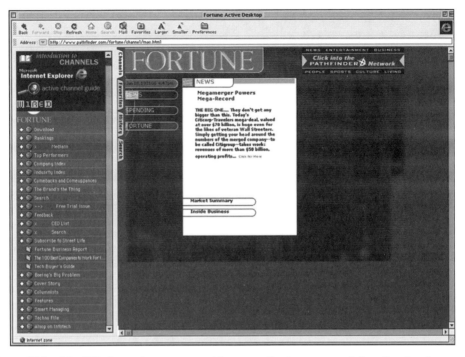

Figure 17.3   The IE4 channel manager and browser display area work together to allow users to sort through and view information downloaded from a subscribed channel.

first XML applications to be developed and has had quite a bit of research and development resources thrown at it because it is backed by a powerful investor—Microsoft. As major vendors begin to implement XML support in their browsers, their implementation specifics will bring a strong force to bear on how the future of XML shapes up. As a document developer, you'll need to think long and hard about how the content of your XML documents will be viewed by your intended audience after it has been processed.

If you are developing documents for an XML application associated with a specific software package or packages, such as CDF, make sure your audience has access to the tools needed to access and view your documents, or your efforts will have been for naught. For all the nitty-gritty details about CDF, refer to Chapter 20.

The Goal And Purpose Of The XML Application

Because XML allows DTD designers to create markup to provide a solution to a specific problem, each XML application is going to have its own specific purpose. A quick look at a handful of existing applications in Table 17.1 shows how the purpose can change drastically from one application to another.

Table 17.1   Various XML applications and their purposes.

Application	Acronym	Purpose	Presentation or Content Based
Channel Definition Format	CDF	To facilitate the delivery of Internet content via server-side push	Presentation format
Open Software Description	OSD	To guide the installation of software over a network via server-side push	Content
Resource Description Framework	RDF	To describe Internet resources in a standard metadata format that is usable by a wide variety of clients and servers	Content
Meta Content Framework	MCF	To describe collections of documents residing on a network in a standard metadata format	Content
Web Interface Definition Language	WIDL	To describe Web APIs	Content
Mathematical Markup Language	MathML	To describe and process mathematical data	Presentation and content
Chemical Markup Language	CML	To describe and process chemical compound data	Presentation and content

Obviously, a document written for the MathML application would be very different from one written for the OSD application. Currently, the purposes behind each of the existing XML applications are clear almost at first glance. However, as XML becomes a more prevalent technology, applications that are more similar in purpose will begin to arise. It will be necessary for you to examine the documentation and resources that support each application to discover its exact purpose and make sure your documents reflect it. "Defining The Goal Of An XML Application," in this chapter's Immediate Solutions section, provides instructions on how to do so.

The Requirement That A Document Be Well-Formed And/Or Valid

For an XML processor to work with any XML document, it must be at least well-formed. Well-formed documents have the following characteristics:

• All entities used in the document body are declared in the internal DTD.

• All formal rules for the physical document structure are followed.

Basically, a well-formed document is not checked against any DTD except the internal one that specifies the entities for the document. A valid XML document is a well-formed document that also adheres to all the rules set down in its associated DTD.

Each XML document that you create must be either well-formed or valid. If it is not, the document is considered invalid, and all other design issues are irrelevant. This is an important issue for those coming to XML from an HTML background. Because Web browsers are so forgiving, HTML documents are created that contain numerous markup errors that wouldn't be so easily forgiven by an XML parser. Often, document authors aren't even aware of their mistakes because "well-formed" and "valid" are not part of the vocabulary of the HTML world. HTML authors are used to doing whatever it takes with the markup to achieve a desired affect, even it means bending—or outright breaking—the formal rules of HTML. This just won't work with XML.

Many XML parsers are designed to check for well-formedness and will help you find errors in your markup based on the rules of XML in general and the DTD specifically. Visit Chapter 22 for a complete listing of XML tools, including this type of parser.

The Potential And Limitations Of The Markup

As discussed in the previous section, HTML authors who come to the world of XML comfortable with defying all the rules to achieve an end result might have some adjusting to do. XML markup can't be forced to do what it wasn't created to do, so it's important to know both the potential and the limitations of any given XML application. By researching an application, as described in detail in Chapter 6, you can put together a reasonably accurate picture of how the elements in the application are supposed to function. By all means, use them to their full potential, but don't try to force them beyond their capabilities.

An example of forcing markup can be easily seen in the proliferation of tables as precise placement tools in Web pages. HTML tables were created to format tabular information by using rows and columns. Tabular information includes mathematical data and other kinds of information you might want to put into a table. However, some enterprising Web developers discovered that table markup could be extended to divide a Web page into sections and thereby force the placement of text and objects on a page. However, these same developers were confounded when different screen and window sizes, coupled with the users' abilities to change their base font size, led to strange and convoluted Web page displays. Is this surprising? Not really. After all, when was the last time you used Excel as a page layout program?

Interface Design Elements

Whereas technical design elements work almost invisibly in the background of a document, interface design elements work up front in center stage. They include:

- Content

- Style components

- Images and other multimedia components

- Navigation tools

Each element is at work in individual documents as well as in document collections. Put together, they guide users through the information you present, creating an interface for them. In the following sections, we'll examine each one in turn and look at some examples of quality design on the Web today.

Content

Content is king, and it should always be so (even if some Web pages lead you to think otherwise). Content is what it's all about, and all the other design elements on a page, both technical and interface, should be created with the content in mind. The best advice we can give any document developer in any media is this: Never loose sight of the content.

All your design elements should be crafted so they make content easy to find, navigate, and understand. Colors, images, and navigation are all supporting cast members that make your content shine. Because pictures often speak louder than words, we've included Figures 17.4, 17.5, and 17.6 as examples of content-driven design.

The design elements all three sites have in common are clean lines, useful graphics, intuitive navigation, and a strong focus on content. Graphics on the page are related directly to the content, and often they serve double duty as navigation tools. Any bells and whistles are integrated into the entire document so they don't distract the reader. The sites are visually pleasing, yet they never loose sight of their initial goal—to provide the reader with information.

Style Components

Font faces, heading levels, and colors are all components of page and site styles. They should always be created to reflect the purpose and content of the site. For example, the *HTML 4 For Dummies* site, shown in Figure 17.7, is a good example of styles driven by content.

This site makes use of the familiar Dummies yellow in the navigation bar, and uses a typeface—Comic Sans MS—that is both fun and functional, true to the

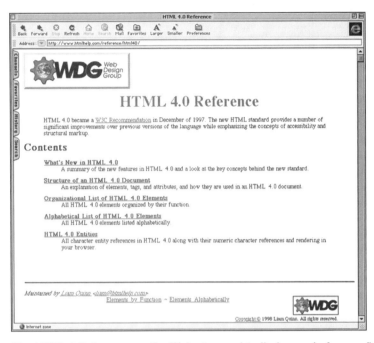

Figure 17.4   The HTML 4 Reference on the Web at www.htmlhelp.com/reference/html40.

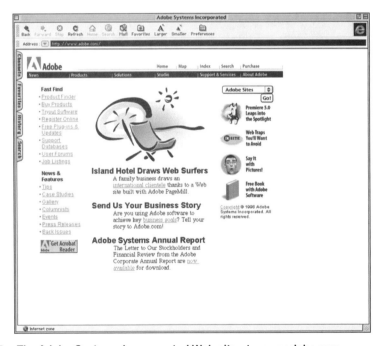

Figure 17.5   The Adobe Systems Incorporated Web site at www.adobe.com.

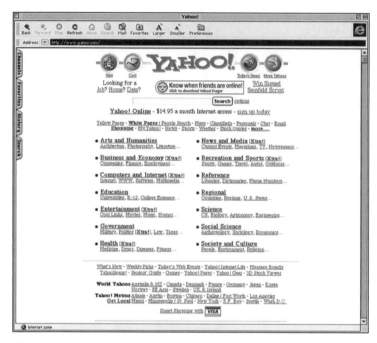

Figure 17.6   The Yahoo search site at **www.yahoo.com**.

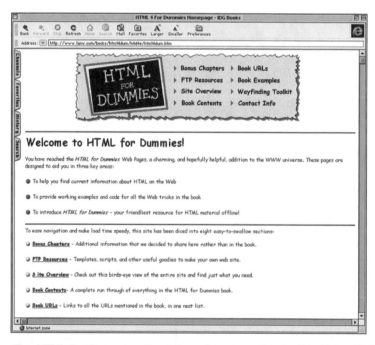

Figure 17.7   The *HTML For Dummies* site at **www.lanw.com/books/html4dum/h4d4e/ html4dum.htm**.

nature of the Dummies series. The site's look and feel takes it cue from the book's content and the book series itself. These same observations can be made of the *Dynamic HTML Black Book* site shown in Figure 17.8.

The black-and-white motif used extensively throughout the Black Book series was adapted for use on this site. The fonts—Verdana and Arial—have a technical feel to them and reflect the basic premise behind the Black Book series.

Images And Other Multimedia Components

Images and multimedia components can be a useful addition to a Web site, or they can drag it down so quickly that users won't get past the time it takes to download the components. Because adding color and pictures to a Web site doesn't cost anything, it's easy to go overboard. In fact, we've come across Web pages that are nothing but images. This is fine if you're on a T1 line, but if you surf at 33.6 Kbps or lower, it's generally best to keep images turned off. Unless your pages are devoted to showing pictures, as a gallery or artists site might need, use images judiciously.

Multimedia components, such as audio and video files, can also add a nice touch to your documents, especially because XML isn't limited in the type of binary files

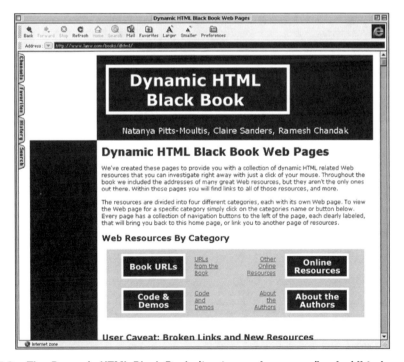

Figure 17.8   The *Dynamic HTML Black Book* site at **www.lanw.com/books/dhtml.**

it can support. Affordable tools for creating multimedia are abundant, and free canned audio and video files are available on hundreds of sites around the Web. As with graphics, use audio and video files judiciously, and remember that, unless they *are* the content, don't let them overwhelm the content.

Navigation Tools

The user's ability to navigate between documents in a collection is perhaps the most important element of a Web site to consider. Navigation needs to be intuitive, well thought-out, and consistent. Returning to another page on the Adobe Web site discussed earlier in this chapter, you'll notice that the black navigation bar is at the top of every page of the site, as shown in Figures 17.9 and 17.10.

Even though the content on these two pages is very different, users see the same navigation bar on both pages and can quickly and easily navigate the site. This makes users more comfortable with a site and also makes it easier for them to find what they are looking for.

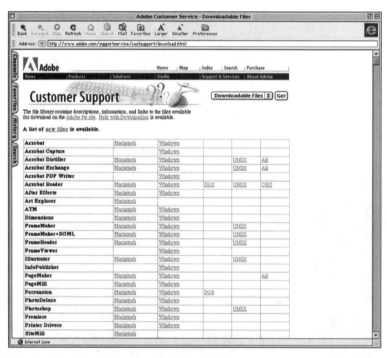

Figure 17.9   The free plug-ins page at www.adobe.com.

Figure 17.10   The Adobe Tips page at www.adobe.com.

Site maps are another useful navigation tool. They can help users move through your documents directly to the information they want. XML's advanced linking mechanism makes the creation of a site map easier than ever before. For complete information on using XML links, turn to Chapter 10.

Immediate Solutions

A well-designed document is based on good sense, good taste, and some time spent analyzing documents that successfully convey their content. Because every XML document will be just a bit different, this Immediate Solutions section speaks in generalities, not in specifics. If you let your common sense guide you and keep your content firmly in sight, you can't help but come out on top in the document design world.

Defining The Goal Of An XML Application

The goal of an XML application drives document creation and design. If an application and its documents are largely content-based, there won't be much design work to do except for ensuring that the document is well-formed and/or valid and that it doesn't try to stretch the bounds of the application's markup. For those applications and documents that are presentation-based, design extends past well-formedness to the documents' look and feel. Of course, before you begin developing a document for an application, you should make sure its goals match your own. Follow these steps to match an application to your needs:

1. Define your goals. Answer the following questions to help you determine them:
   a. What kind of information are you trying to describe with an XML application?
   b. What other applications have you looked to as a solution and where have they fallen short?
   c. Who is your audience?
   d. What do you want your audience to get/learn from your information?
   e. Is your information based on content or presentation?
2. Define the goal of the application. Turn to application documentation and other XML documents to see how the application has been used as a solution by others. Take the time to create a road map for the application (as described in Chapter 6) if you think it might meet your needs.

3. Compare the road map you've created for the XML application with your findings about your own goals and see if they are compatible. Remember that you must play by the rules set down by the DTD for creating documents for the application. If you think you might have to bend the rules, the application might not be your best choice.

4. In the end, if you can't find an existing application that meets your needs, consider building your own.

Planning An Effective Navigation System For A Document Collection

If users can't move easily through your documents, you've already lost the information dissemination war. Although content is always your first focus, users must be able to move from document to document or they'll never be able to access all of your content. A navigation system for a collection of documents can be as simple or as complex as the documents themselves. The following steps outline how to plan your navigation system:

1. Create a hierarchical outline of all the documents in the collection.

2. The top-level headings in your document collection outline should provide the content for a standard navigation system that will appear on each and every page. No matter where they are in the collection, users should be able to get to each of its major areas.

3. Analyze each group of second-level headings under each top-level heading in the collection to create subnavigation systems that will function only within an individual area of the document collection. These navigation links may be used in addition to the standard navigation system or as a simple extension of it.

4. Create a series of common, easy-to-use navigation tools that direct users:

   • Up

   • Down

   • To the next page

   • To the previous page

   These common tools can be used in smaller subsections of the collection to direct users from page to page in a regular manner. Remember that your standard navigation scheme should occur on every page, even if certain portions of the collections have their own unique navigation tools.

5. Create a standard look and feel for your navigation scheme. If you are going to rely on intuitive images, make sure to provide text-only navigation for users who don't or can't see graphics. Because the navigation scheme is going to be included on every page, you'll want to make sure it fits in with the other styles you've included in your document collection.

6. Create a site overview or search area that is accessible from all pages in the collection and placed prominently on the entry page of the document collection. The site overview provides users with a general idea of what is contained in the document collection as well as how resources on the site are related to one another. A good search area should help users jump right to where they want to be in your site.

7. Always link to home. Users should always be able to get to the entry point of the document or resource collection from anywhere in the collection.

Part IV

XML Applications

Chapter 18

XML Applications

By Cheryl Kirk

In Depth

XML offers the flexibility to create new vocabularies, which are actually applications that use the XML language. This means organizations and industries can create their own elements, attributes, and entities that fully explain the structure of the specific types of data they use. Already a handful of applications have been created for either industry-specific or subject-specific document types. For example, OpenMLS has created Document Type Definitions (DTDs) for real estate agents that specify the structure of data documents that hold information about properties for sale.

In this chapter, we'll explore the various special-purpose applications that are available and describe how they work. This chapter is not, however, meant to be a complete reference of each XML application. Each application is meant to solve a particular problem, and we'll show you how you can use them to your advantage. If you are thinking of creating your own application, you may find that you can instead use one of the applications described in this chapter.

What Is An XML Application?

By now, you know that XML gives you the ability to create your own set of elements, your own attributes, and even your own entities. XML defines how a vocabulary can be structured. Vocabularies are sets of XML components that can be used to define specific document structures. In the example of one very popular vocabulary, Channel Definition Format (CDF), XML provided the structure to define channels and their accompanying channel elements, called items. In other words, you can use the XML language to create your own language of sorts, and this language can be used to do a variety of things, from displaying mathematical equations to pushing information to a user's computer desktop.

With XML, you can construct your own set of components that define the structure of a document. As you've seen, you define this structure in the DTD. That DTD lists all the elements, attributes, entities, and notation declarations, and it can be stored in a separate file outside of the XML document or it can be included at the top of an XML content document. You determine where the DTD is placed. When you really think about it, XML allows you to construct entirely new applications, not through conventional programming methods, but rather by defining the contextual structure of the document.

It hasn't taken much time for XML applications to start showing up. There already are more than a handful of XML applications you can use for a variety of functions, and a dozen more are under development or up for consideration with the World Wide Web Consortium (W3C). Some, such as the Channel Definition Format, are already part of the Internet Explorer browser, whereas others are still just in the development phase. In this chapter, we will highlight the most popular applications, but we'll also point you to those that are more industry specific.

Types Of XML Applications

XML applications follow the XML syntax, so all you have to do to learn how to use them is familiarize yourself with the specific elements and their attributes. Most of the XML applications available today use less than 20 different element tags, and most of these element tags have only 1 or 2 attributes, so the learning curve is relatively small.

As mentioned in Chapter 2, XML applications fall within one of three types of applications:

- *Horizontal-industry applications/vocabularies*—Push-based delivery, software distribution, searching/filtering, electronic commerce, and so on
- *Vertical-industry applications/vocabularies*—Pharmaceuticals, telecommunications, aerospace, and so on
- *Internal applications/corporate vocabularies*—Internal data processes

The three different types of XML applications can be placed in one of these seven categories:

- Web and Internet applications
- Metadata and archival applications
- Multimedia, including graphics and speech applications
- Finance/commerce and business-oriented applications
- Scientific applications
- Education-oriented applications
- Language-oriented applications

Web And Internet Applications

As their name implies, Web and Internet XML applications work over the Internet or through the Web to either deliver content and programming information or enhance communication between computers over the Internet. The following are considered Web-oriented XML applications:

- *Channel Definition Format (CDF)*—Developed by Microsoft, CDF is an XML application that lets a developer use a variety of delivery mechanisms to publish collections of information called channels from any Web server to any Internet-compatible appliance. CDF is included in the Internet Explorer browser and can be accessed through Netscape's Communicator software. More information about this application can be found in the official specification at **www.microsoft.com/standards/cdf.htm**.

- *Open Software Description (OSD)*—Also developed by Microsoft, OSD is used to describe software components, software versions, and the underlying structure of software packages and their components for delivery over a network. OSD can work in conjunction with CDF to update software over the Internet or over an intranet. More information about this application can be found on Microsoft's Web site (**www.microsoft.com/standards/osd/ osdspec.htm**).

- *Distributed Authoring and Versioning on the World Wide Web (WebDAV)*— WebDAV is still in the draft stage, but it should be an application shortly. It is an application specification that is intended to define Hypertext Transfer Protocol (HTTP) methods and semantics for creating, removing, querying, and editing Web pages remotely. WebDAV will offer overwrite protection of files, structured views of sites, and the ability for more than one author to collaborate on a single site. More information can be found on the working group's Web site (**www.ics.uci.edu/~ejw/authoring**).

- *HTTP Distribution and Replication Protocol (DRP)*—The DRP protocol is an application aimed at improving the efficiency and reliability of using the HTTP protocol for data distribution over the Internet. It is meant to be a backward-compatible application that will work with existing standards but provide better caching of servers and proxies and efficient replication of data and content. It is still in the note phase at the W3C, meaning there may or may not be any further work done on this application. More information about the note can be found on the W3C's Web at **www.w3.org/TR/NOTE-drp-19970825.html**.

- *Wireless Application Protocol*—This protocol offers standards for wireless network transmissions and scaling across various transport options and device types. It was created by some of the leaders in the wireless communication industry, including Ericsson, Motorola, and Nokia. Information about this application can be found on the Wireless Application Protocol organizing committee's Web site (**www.wapforum.org**).

- *UML eXchange Format*—The UML eXchange Format application was created for software developers as a mechanism for transferring Unified Modeling Language (UML) models. The application format is powerful enough to allow developers to express, publish, and exchange UML models universally. DTDs have already been created for this particular application and are available on the UML eXchange's Web site (**www.yy.cs.keio.ac.jp/~suzuki/project/uxf**).

• *Web Interface Definition Language (WIDL)*—WIDL is an object-oriented, soon-to-be standard XML application that uses the WIDL protocol to automate many functions of the Web, including document data input, document distribution, and interchange between various applications. You can define and design various services that interface with various applications—including C++, Java, or VBScript applications—to provide data automation between Web pages, Web servers, and database systems. You can find out more information about WIDL from the company that has proposed this protocol, WebMethods (**www.webmethods.com**).

Metadata And Archival Applications

Metadata and archival applications handle certain kinds of data sets (data sets that may be specific to a particular industry, such as library sciences), multiple sets of data information, and data interchange between systems. The following XML applications are available, although they are in different stages of development:

• *Resource Description Framework (RDF)*—RDF is a framework specification that supports metadata and Web-based activities such as site maps, content ratings, search engine data collections, and distributed authoring. You can read the official RDF specification on the W3C's site (**www.w3.org/RDF**).

• *Meta Content Framework (MCF)*—Developed first by Apple and then enhanced by Netscape, this framework uses XML to describe information-organization structures. You can read the note on this framework at the W3C's site (**www.w3.org/TR/NOTE-MCF-XML.html**).

• *Web Interface Definition Language (WIDL)*—WIDL, which is based on XML, is a metadata syntax that defines application programming interfaces (APIs) for Web data and services. We include it in this category as well as in the "Web And Internet Applications" category because, in addition to being an Internet application, it handles other types of data and allows developers to connect XML data to other types of data or Internet-based applications. It's used with the WebMethods servers as a method for Web automation. You can read more about WIDL on the WebMethods Web site (**www.webmethods.com/technology/widl_description.html**).

• *IMS Metadata Specification*—This specification uses XML to offer effective delivery of high-quality training materials over the Internet. It also supports the management of materials and types of data relating to Web sites. Basically, this specification is meant to track students online, create reports of students' progress, exchange student records over the Internet, and work

18: XML Applications

with various administrative learning systems. You can read more about this specification at the IMS official Web site (**www.imsproject.org**).

- *Encoded Archival Description (EAD)*—This XML application, a full DTD, is used to develop a nonproprietary encoding standard for library documents, including indexes, archives, and any other type of holdings that may be found in libraries and museums. You can learn more about the EAD DTD at the Library of Congress Web site (**www.loc.gov/ead**).

- *Genealogical Data in XML (GedML)*—The GedML DTD was created to provide a standard method for presenting, exchanging, and manipulating genealogical data across a network and with other users. The intent is to make genealogical data exchange and searching easier. You can find out more information about GedML at **home.iclweb.com/icl2/mhkay/gedml.html**.

- *XML-Data*—The XML-Data specification is for exchanging structured and networked data on the Web. For example, it could be used to describe digital signatures, remotely located Web resources, or how data transfers work. This specification was created by Microsoft and several other large organizations. You can read more about the XML-Data specification on Microsoft's Web site (**www.microsoft.com/standards/xml/xmldata.htm**).

Multimedia Applications

Multimedia XML-based applications use the XML language and syntax to create standardized ways to present information over the Web, particularly graphics, video, and digitized speech. Applications such as the Synchronized Multimedia Integration Language (SMIL) give developers the ability to work from a common development platform to use the interactive features of the Web to deliver feature-rich video and audio. These XML-based applications are in various stages of specification completion, but look for them to gain widespread support over the next year or two if they haven't already been approved and recommended by the W3C. The following XML-based applications fall into this category:

- *Synchronized Multimedia Integration Language (SMIL)*—The SMIL specification was recently approved by the W3C and is meant to help deliver multimedia content to the Web. SMIL lets developers create and deliver television-like content with low bandwidth requirements. It also adds hyperlinking capabilities to the multimedia content, making it possible for users to quickly move to other Web-based content, and it gives developers the ability to synchronize presentations. You can read more about SMIL at **www.w3.org/TR/PR-smil**.

- *Precision Graphics Markup Language (PGML)*—PGML, still in the W3C's note stage, is a 2D scalable graphics language designed to offer vector graphics and precision graphic specifications to artists. Using image modeling common to both the PostScript format and the Portable Document Format (PDF), it offers features that integrate fully with the Web (linking, for example).

- *Java Speech Markup Language (JSML)*—The JSML specification is intended to allow developers to create applications that annotate text for playback through speech synthesizers via the Java Speech API. This data format provides detailed information on how the text should be spoken through the synthesizer. It describes the structure of the document, the pronunciations of words, and the phrasing and punctuation in the text. Also, it indicates how pitch, speaking rate, and other spoken characteristics should be noted. JSML uses the Unicode character set and follows XML standards for marking up text, so most languages can be processed to the API and then through the speech synthesizer.

Finance/Commerce And Business-Oriented Applications

Finance and commerce XML-based applications open up a whole world for consumers, financial institutions, and businesses. They allow consumers and businesses to use a standardized language to communicate. Consumers can transfer funds, check on accounts, and use their financial applications to track their investments regardless of the financial institution they are dealing with. Without standardized XML applications, consumers and financial institutions would be forced to work with proprietary information and applications. The following XML-based applications are currently available or are in the process of being finalized:

- *Open Financial Exchange (OFX)*—OFX is a data format used to represent how financial information can be exchanged between an online financial services server and client software, such as a browser. This format makes it possible for Microsoft's Money or Intuit's Quicken to connect to financial servers and exchange information about transactions and financial data stored on a user's computer. It allows banks, credit card companies, brokerage firms, and mutual fund markets to transmit and receive data over the Internet in a standardized fashion. It allows customers to pay bills, transfer funds, keep track of investments online, and buy mutual funds, stocks, and bonds regardless of the financial application they use. For more information about this financial exchange standard, check out Microsoft's Web site at **www.microsoft.com/ofx**.

- *XML/Electronic Data Interchange (XML/EDI)*—XML/EDI offers vendors a standard framework and format for describing different types of data used in processing invoices, payments, and project information. For example, a vendor could use the XML/EDI format to transmit an invoice to a customer electronically. The information in the invoice could then be searched, de-coded, encoded, or manipulated so it could be displayed or printed. Using EDI dictionaries and XML ensures that information is displayed consistently and correctly regardless of the vendor or the customer. For more information on XML/EDI, check out the official home page at **www.xmledi.net**.

- *Open Trading Protocol (OTP)*—OTP was developed by a group of compa-nies—including AT&T Universal Card Services, Canadian Imperial Bank of Commerce, CyberCash, DigiCash, Fujitsu, and others—to make widespread Internet trading of securities and stocks both convenient and secure. OTP offers an interoperable message protocol intended to encourage development of software products that will permit interoperability for electronic purchases over the Internet regardless of the payment mechanism. OTP encapsulates the payment with the invoice, offer, or receipt. You can find out more about the Open Trading Protocol by checking out the official Web site at **www.otp.org**.

- *Information & Content Exchange (ICE)*—This proposed protocol is based on the XML standard and is intended to provide automatic, controlled ex-change and management of online assets between business partners. ICE gives businesses a standard way to set up online relationships with other business and to transfer and share information. With ICE, businesses can easily partner with any number of affiliates to create online destinations such as syndicated publishing networks, Web superstores, and online reseller channels. You can find out more about ICE from its official Web site at **www.vignette.com/Products/ice**.

Scientific Applications

Scientific XML-based applications allow scientists and mathematicians to ex-change data in a standardized way. The applications set the language and syntax that can be used to specify such things as the constructs of an atom or how to properly display mathematical equations. The following scientific XML-based applications are some of the most recent entrants into this category:

- *Mathematical Markup Language (MathML)*—MathML is now a W3C recom-mendation that provides a standard way to describe mathematical symbols and equations and how mathematical expressions should be displayed in Web pages. It is also meant to facilitate the use and reuse of mathematical and scientific content on the Web and in other applications, such as print typesetters and voice synthesizers. MathML can be used to encode both mathematical notation (for high-quality visual display) and mathematical content. You can find out more about the Mathematical Markup Language at **www.w3.org/Math**.

- *Chemical Markup Language (CML)*—CML was created to provide a way to describe molecular information and manage a wide range of chemical equa-tion problems within a single language. It was also created to help chemists manipulate atoms and molecules as elements. CML offers standard document elements, such as footnotes, citations, and glossary terms, for inclusion in scholarly papers. On the CML Web site, the developers of the language (which was originally derived from SGML) say CML is "HTML with chemistry added." CML provides the data format needed to represent chemical equations, molecules, formulas, and scientific data in a single standardized way regardless of the application used. You can find out more about CML from its Web site at **www.venus.co.uk/omf/cml**.

• *Bioinformatic Sequence Markup Language (BSML)*—BSML is still in the comment phase, but it is intended to provide a standard method for encoding and displaying DNA, RNA, and protein sequence information between programs and data over the Internet. Although many proprietary software packages can display such information, there is currently no publicly available standard for graphic displays of sequences such as chromosomes and genetic material as well as physical maps of a variety of sequences. You can find out more about BSML and comment on the application by visiting the BSML Web site at **visualgenomics.com/sbir/rfc.htm**.

• *Telecommunications Interchange Markup (TIM)*—The TIM language is used to provide a standard mechanism for offering industry standards associated with the provision, procurement, and use of telecommunications equipment, products, and services. The group that is working on TIM, the Telecommunications Industry Forum (TCIF), was founded in June 1986 in an effort to promote understanding and implementation of global standards, guidelines, and emerging technologies involving electronic data interchange, electronic commerce, and bar coding. You can find out more about TIM from the TCIF Web page (**www.atis.org/atis/tcif/index.htm**).

Education-Oriented Applications

Actually, some of the XML applications listed previously could fall within this category, but the only educational application we'll discuss at this time is the Tutorial Markup Language (TML). At the time of this writing, TML is the only markup language that functions as a markup language specifically for creating or working with educational applications. As instruction, test-taking and -tracking, and educational development moves more and more toward the Web, you will soon find more and more XML-based educational applications springing up.

The Tutorial Markup Language was originally an SGML application, but it has recently been converted to XML to provide flexibility over the Internet. TML is an interchange format designed to separate the semantic content of a question from its screen layout or formatting. This will allow questions and answers to be searched, cataloged, and calculated easily. TML allows questionnaire developers to specify such things as how many attempts a test-taker can make to answer a question correctly, what the questions are, what choices you want to include for the answers, what the correct answers are, and what, if any, hints are available for the question. For more information about TML, check out the official TML Web site, which offers the full language set and examples (**www.ilrt.bris.ac.uk/ netquest/about/lang**).

Language-Oriented Applications

Language-oriented XML-based applications are not for spoken language but rather for computer language and interchange between computer systems. They are by far the most "out there" in terms of XML-based applications because they are the applications that help machines make decisions about the data stored in Web pages and in databases. If you are looking to develop true machine-based intelligent systems, you'll want to delve deeper into some of the following XML applications:

- *Translation Memory eXchange (TMX)*—TMX's purpose is to allow easier exchange of translation memory data between tools and/or translation vendors with little or no loss of critical data during the process. You can find out more about TMX through its official Web site (**www.lisa.org/tmx**).

- *Ontology Markup Language (OML)*—OML allows Web-page authors to annotate their Web pages so they can be read by machines and processed with intelligent agent software. You can read more about OML and the elements and attributes used with it at **asimov.eecs.wsu.edu/WAVE/Ontologies/OML/ OML-DTD.html**. Make sure you check out the references pointing to the language on which OML is based—Simple HMTL Ontology Examples (SHOE). You'll learn more about what OML really offers by reading the SHOE examples.

- *Conceptual Knowledge Markup Language (CKML)*—CKML follows the philosophy of Conceptual Knowledge Processing (CKP). This processing language is used to represent knowledge and data analysis, which serves to create models for rational thinking, judgement, and decision making. It is an extension of the OML application. You can find out more about CKML from its Web site (**asimov.eecs.wsu.edu/WAVE/Ontologies/CKML/CKML-DTD.html**).

- *OpenTag*—The OpenTag format helps to create a standardized way to code diverse file types through the use of a common markup method. For example, suppose you have two files, one saved in RTF format and another saved in HTML format. Both files contain the same text and are formatted in the same fashion. Although the information and layout are the same, the encoding methods used to save the files are different. With OpenTag, you can use identical tags to output the files and display the data, but the formatting codes that were used to save the files originally are saved and later used to encode the files in their native formats. You can find out more about OpenTag from the official OpenTag Web site (**www.opentag.org**).

XML Applications In Detail

Now, let's take a closer look at some of the more popular XML applications. This section is not meant as a full tutorial for each application. Instead, it's meant to introduce you to the application, what it offers, and some of the element tags used most often within the application. We recommend that you visit the official Web site for applications you're interested in for more information and examples.

We'll concentrate on the applications that have already been standardized and have a range of practical uses, such as exchanging financial data, software, mathematical information, or multimedia files. You will undoubtedly see some of these applications incorporated into many new browsers and servers. We'll examine the following five XML applications here and in this chapter's Immediate Solutions section. (CDF is only covered briefly here. Because it's a widely used XML application, Chapter 20 presents a complete discussion of CDF.):

- Channel Definition Format (CDF)
- Chemical Markup Language (CML)
- Mathematical Markup Language (MathML)
- Open Software Description (OSD)
- Synchronized Multimedia Integration Language (SMIL)

Channel Definition Format (CDF)

The Channel Definition Format provides developers with a way to automatically publish Web-based content to subscribers through a variety of methods, such as through a Web browser, through an Active Desktop component, through HTML-formatted email, or through Web crawlers. A channel is a set of HTML-formatted documents that can be sent to individual clients or groups of clients. XML is used to define the channel. Information including the subelements contained within the channel, the update schedule, and the delivery mechanism are part of the definition. (See Chapter 20 for a complete discussion of CDF.)

Chemical Markup Language (CML)

The Chemical Markup Language was invented by British chemists specifically for exchanging descriptions of formulas, molecules, and other chemical specifications between people and computers within intranets or on the Internet. You can use CML for accomplishing such tasks as rendering 2D and 3D molecules or creating and publishing scientific papers.

CML lets you specify and represent very specific types of data (molecules) within a structured format. Although CML is an XML application, you need a specialized viewer to see the results of the data CML represents.

Why would you want to use CML? Because it's based on XML, a platform-independent markup language, it doesn't matter whether you develop the data on a Mac, PC, or Unix box. The information will still display granted you are using a browser that supports XML.

Just as with all other XML applications, the best way to understand CML (aside from getting a degree in chemistry) is to understand the CML DTD and the CML elements and their attributes. But first, let's take a quick look at molecular technology and some of the terminology you might need know to understand this application.

With CML, you can represent the following molecular information:

• Molecular structure

• Molecular sequence

• Quantum chemistry

• Inorganic crystallography

• Organic molecules

• Spectra

You create CML files as you would any other XML-based file, through the use of a text processor, such as Notepad or Emacs. When you create your CML file and save it, you then must parse the data file and view the results with a specialized CML viewer, such as CMLViewer, which was written in Java and can be used with Java-enabled browsers or as a standalone application. As with any XML application, you must first declare the document to be a CML document in the **!DOCTYPE** statement at the beginning of the CML file. Then, every element you place must have a start-tag and end-tag and all attribute values must be in quotes. In this chapter's Immediate Solutions section, you'll write a CML data file and include a few formulas. When you write your CML document, you can include any of the nine main CML DTD elements, which are explained in the following paragraphs.

<ARRAY>

The **<ARRAY>** element specifies an array of variables. You can use the **<ARRAY>** element to specify both one- and two-dimensional arrays. As is the case with every XML element, the **<ARRAY>** element must have a matching ending **</ARRAY>** tag. The following is an example of how the **<ARRAY>** tag can be used to declare a simple one-dimensional array:

```
<ARRAY>
1 3 5 7 9 10 11
</ARRAY>
```

<ATOMS>

The **<ATOMS>** element is used to represent an atom or a list of atoms contained within a molecule. The element has a following of attributes:

- **ATOMNO**—Specifies the atom's serial number
- **ATID**—Specifies the atom's unique identifier
- **ATTYPE**—Specifies the atom type
- **ELSYM**—Specifies the atom's elemental symbol
- **ISOTOPE**—Specifies the atom's isotope
- **X2**—Details the atom's 2D X coordinate

<BONDS>

The **<BONDS>** element represents the chemical bond or connection between two atoms. You can specify an arbitrary number of arrays for carrying the bond information. The **<BONDS>** element uses the following attributes:

- **ATID1**—Specifies the atom identifier of the first atom within the bond
- **ATID2**—Specifies the atom identifier of the second atom stored within the bond
- **BONDID**—Represents the unique identifier for the bond
- **CYLIC**—Represents the bond's cyclicity
- **ORDER**—Specifies the bond's order
- **PARITY**—Represents the parity of the bond

<CML>

You use the **<CML>** element to represent to the parser or browser that the document is a CML document, as shown in the following code:

```
<!DOCTYPE CML PUBLIC "-//CML//DTD CML//EN">
<CML TITLE="This is a CML Document">
</CML>
```

Notice that the element requires a closing tag, but additional elements can be placed between the CML title declaration and the closing **</CML>** tag. Every CML document needs to include the **!DOCTYPE** declaration, which specifies that the document is a CML document. The preceding example specifies a CML document with no content.

<FORMULA>

The **<FORMULA>** element is used to create a formula. You can use the following attributes to further represent the formula:

18: XML Applications

- **MOLWT**—Represents the element's molecular weight

- **STOICH**—Represents the element's chemical composition or stoichiometry

Here's an example of how the formula for water, H_2O, might be written:

```
<FORMULA>
<XVAR BUILTIN="STOICH">
H H O
</XVAR>
</FORMULA>
```

<MOL>

The **<MOL>** element represents the molecule, including the atoms, the bonds between the atoms if there are any, and the molecule's formula. The **<ATOMS>** and **<BONDS>** elements can be used as subelements or children within the molecule element.

<XADDR>

The **<XADDR>** tag is the easiest tag of the bunch. It specifies the address of the person or organization who created the document. You can use the **<XVAR>** element to separate out the various elements of the address if you need to.

<XLIST>

You can use the **<XLIST>** element as a generic container of information. It can include arrays, xvariables, or even xlists to specify such things as chemical elements and compounds, lists of dates, lists of values, or anything else that needs to be specified in a list string.

<XVAR>

When you want to specify an individual generic container of information, you use the **<XVAR>** element. You can use **<XVAR>** to specify formulas, additional address information, reference pointers to external information sources, or anything else that is considered a container of generic information.

Mathematical Markup Language (MathML)

The MathML vocabulary was created primarily for supporting the need to display and exchange mathematical formulas and symbols. This language is useful if you need to include mathematical formulas in your Web site. It's also an excellent XML application for learning how elements and subelements work and how attributes further explain the elements. Be forewarned, however, that there is a lot to the MathML vocabulary, and we cannot outline all the features here. We highly recommend that you check out the official MathML Recommendation at **www.w3.org/TR/REC-MathML**.

It may sound strange to hear that MathML is an XML application, because XML is more about structuring data than displaying it. However, think about standard mathematical equations and how they are structured and you'll soon realize that you first need to create the structures in order to construct a formula. MathML data files, like CML data files, require that you use a specialized viewer to see the parsed data, because the current browsers do not support the MathML results.

MathML can be used to create mathematical formulas as well as represent such advanced mathematical equations as polynomials, calculus, and geometric and trigonometric equations on the Web. MathML has two sets of markup elements, one for content and the other for presentation.

MathML Presentation And Content Tags

When you use MathML to create mathematical expressions, follow the guidelines specified in XML. Each element must have an end-tag. To code your equation properly, follow the mathematical expression from left to right.

All MathML elements are contained in one of three categories:

- *Presentation*—Presentation elements describe mathematical notation structures. For example, **<MROW>** is used to indicate a horizontal row of characters. As a general rule, each presentation element corresponds to a single kind of notation schema, such as a row, subscript, or superscript. Currently, the MathML presentation markup consists of 28 elements that have more than 50 attributes assigned. Each element corresponds to a two-dimensional notational device, such as a super- or subscript, a fraction, or a table. In addition, there are the presentation token elements **<MI>**, **<MN>**, and **<MO>**. The remaining few presentation elements are empty elements and are used mostly in connection with alignment.

- *Content*—Content elements describe mathematical objects instead of just describing the notation that represents them. The **<PLUS/>** element is an example of a content element. Each content element corresponds to a carefully defined mathematical concept.

- *Interface*—Interface elements are elements that don't fall into the category of either a content or a presentation element. The **<MATH>** element is an example of an interface element.

In the following sections, we'll describe some MathML elements (both presentation and content elements) that are used to define mathematical equations.

Arithmetic And Algebraic Elements

Most of the arithmetic and algebraic element tags are relatively easy to understand and are either empty element tags (meaning they have no content) or have no attributes. The empty element tags are specified by following the name of the element with the forward slash.

- *Addition*—**<PLUS/>**
- *Subtraction*—**<MINUS/>**
- *Division*—**<OVER/>**
- *Multiplication*—**<TIMES/>**
- *To the power of*—**<POWER/>**
- *Exponentiation*—**<EXP/>**
- *Remainder*—**<REM/>**
- *Factorial*—**<FACTORIAL>**
- *Maximum*—**<MAX>**
- *Minimum*—**<MIN>**

Presentation Elements

Presentation elements give you the ability to specify a notation's expression structure. The presentation elements come in two flavors—elements that declare the type of data and elements that denote the layout definition. The layout definition may include tags that specify rows, scripts, or fractions. Here are several presentation elements you might want to familiarize yourself with:

- **<MF>**—Represents a fence (a set of parentheses). The *F* in MF stands for fence.
- **<MI>**—Specifies variables, function names, and constants.
- **<MN>**—Represents numerical data.
- **<MO>**—Represents a mathematical operator.
- **<MROW>**—Groups together a number of subexpressions in a horizontal fashion.
- **<MSUP>**—Represents the superscript notation to a base number.

Using Content Elements

The **<APPLY>** element is perhaps the single most important content element. It is used to apply a function to a collection of arguments. If we used the **<APPLY>** element to present the formula a − b, the code would look something like this:

```
<apply>
<minus/>
<ci>a</ci>
<ci>b</ci>
</apply>
```

Open Software Description (OSD)

Microsoft and Marimba understood that there was a need to create a standard for distributing software over the Internet. Their standard, called the Open Software Description, uses unique XML element tags to describe such things as the version of the product, the platform the product should work on (such as a Macintosh or Windows 95 operating system), and the upgrade mechanism. The Channel Definition Format can be used to deliver software packages over the Internet.

OSD is an XML application because it uses XML to create the elements and attributes it uses to describe how the software will be distributed over an intranet or the Internet. The OSD elements and attributes have the same rules and restrictions that XML elements and attributes have. As with any XML document, OSD should have a single root element from which all other subelements branch.

Why would you use OSD to distribute software over a network? Most software now comes on multiple disks or even multiple CD-ROMs, so the installation process is time-consuming. The cost of employing software technicians to keep up with the never-ending software upgrades increases the cost of software ownership substantially. With so many computers, networks, and systems running the same type of software (such as Windows 95, Internet Explorer, Microsoft Office, or Windows NT), offering a quick way to upgrade software over a network without the need to employ additional resources is paramount for most networked corporations and many individuals.

Remote software distribution provides the end user and the corporation with the following features:

- The ability for hands-off installation. The end user does not need to manually install software or pop disks into disk drives.

- Software can be updated in a timely fashion from a single designated source. End users no longer have to seek out upgrades.

- Upgrades can work across platforms. The right software gets to the right platform based on the version and operating system used.

OSD can not only be used to upgrade standalone commercial software packages, it can also be used to deploy Java packages, Java standalone applications, and platform-native code across a network.

Each OSD data file specifies a particular archive file (which can be a JAR or CAB file) in the URL attribute of the **\<CODEBASE\>** element. You can also embed the OSD vocabulary within the archived files. Examples of how to implement OSD can be found in this chapter's Immediate Solutions section.

18: XML Applications

There are major and minor elements available in the OSD. The minor elements are children of one of the major elements and are used to further clarify the OSD package. In the following sections, we'll cover the OSD elements you need to be familiar with before you create an OSD file.

Major OSD Elements

You need to understand the following major elements before creating OSD files:

- **<SOFTPKG>**—The **<SOFTPKG>** element is the document element for any OSD document. It defines the general software package and the overall features of that package. All other elements are subelements to the **<SOFTPKG>** element.

- **<IMPLEMENTATION>**—The **<IMPLEMENTATION>** tag is used to describe an implementation of the client-specific software package.

- **<DEPENDENCY>**—The **<DEPENDENCY>** element is used to indicate the dependency between software distributions or components.

  The **ACTION= (Assert | Install)** attribute can be used with the **<DEPEN­DENCY>** element. If the **ACTION** value is **Assert**, the software package should be ignored entirely if the dependency is not already present on the client machine. If the value is **Install** and the dependency is not already present on the client machine, the browser should get the package and install it on the client machine.

Minor OSD Elements

You need to understand the following minor elements before creating OSD files:

- **<IMPLTYPE>**—The **<IMPLTYPE>** element nests within the **<IMPLEMEN­TATION>** major element and describes the type of implementation.

- **<TITLE>**—The **<TITLE>** element is the name of the software package, usually the consumer-oriented name.

- **<ABSTRACT>**—The **<ABSTRACT>** is used to provide a short description summarizing the nature and purpose of the software distribution. This alerts the user to what the software package contains.

- **<LICENSE>**—The **<LICENSE>** tag indicates where the user can retrieve the license agreement or copyright notice. It usually indicates a Web site, which can be used to verify that the user has read the license agreement.

- **<DISKSIZE>**—The **<DISKSIZE>** element specifies how much disk space is required by the software package as specified in the **VALUE** attribute of the **<DISKSIZE>** element. All sizes are specified in kilobytes.

- **<CODEBASE>**—The **<CODEBASE>** element indicates where an archive of the software distribution exists. Basically, it sets up the location of the software package. Multiple URLs can be specified to load-balance when software packages are updated on an intranet or on the Internet. The following attributes can be used with the **<CODEBASE>** element:

- *SIZE*=**<max-KB>**—Specifies the maximum allowable size for the software as measured in kilobytes.

- *HREF*=**<URL>**—Points to the archive of the software package to be downloaded.

- *FILENAME*=**<string>**—Specifies a file contained within the archive that contains the OSD. If the OSD file is a standalone file, this attribute is ignored.

- **<OS>**—The **<OS>** element indicates which operating system the software package requires. You can leave this element set to zero and the existing software platform will be used and specified to run on all operating systems, as is the case with Java applets.

- **<OSVERSION>**—The **<OSVERSION>** element, working in conjunction with **<OS>**, specifies the operating system version required to use the software package. If no version is specified, it is assumed that the software package will run on all versions.

- **<PROCESSOR>**—The **<PROCESSOR>** element indicates the computer processor required to run the software package. If no **<PROCESSOR>** value is specified, the particular implementation of the software is assumed to run on all processors.

- **<LANGUAGE>**—The **<LANGUAGE>** element indicates the natural language used in the software user interface. If none is specified, it is assumed that the software package will use all languages.

- **<VM>**—The **<VM>** element defines the virtual machine used by the software package.

- **<MEMSIZE>**—The **<MEMSIZE>** element specifies how much memory (runtime) is required by the software package. If the machine does not meet the specifications, the software package is not sent.

Synchronized Multimedia Integration Language (SMIL)

With SMIL, developers can create Web sites with multimedia-rich content. SMIL allows sites to have almost TV-like content with low bandwidth requirements for transmitting content over the Internet. Once SMIL becomes more widely used, there will be no need for users to configure their browsers to use specific helper or plug-in applications. Instead, SMIL will provide a cross-platform, standardized way to deliver multimedia without the need for specialized proprietary software. It also means that additional programming languages won't be required to create

18: XML Applications

multimedia documents. Like any XML application, all that is needed is a simple text processor.

SMIL also allows the developer to create and embed hyperlinking within the multimedia file. This means the developer can create time-based Web presentations, and media objects can be reused again and again.

TIP: *If you don't want to hard-code your SMIL files, you can download Real Networks SMIL Presentation Wizard application. This application is located at **www.real.com/g2/developer/smilwizard.html** and contains 11 layout templates. It's a great application for learning SMIL, because it offers a View Source option for viewing the SMIL code.*

Design Principles For SMIL

Like all XML applications, SMIL follows the standard design principles, but it also has a set of design principles all its own:

- All objects specified in any URLs must be available online.

- All objects specified in SMIL files must have a start and end time based on temporal parameters.

- User options, such as stop, play, forward, and reverse, should be made available, and all components must react to these options in a synchronized fashion.

Hyperlinking is a key component to SMIL, and you should develop SMIL files with hyperlinks embedded in the files. However, SMIL doesn't just use simple hyperlinks. Instead, SMIL uses the advanced hyperlinking mechanisms used in XML.

TIP: *For more information on the hyperlinking options available in XML, check out Chapter 10.*

SMIL Elements

The following list includes some of the SMIL elements you'll use to create a SMIL document. They follow the same convention used in any XML-based application. Each element needs a start-tag and an end-tag. The SMIL elements include:

- **<HEAD>**—Specifies head information, such as meta content and layout

- **<BODY>**—Specifies the section where the multimedia elements are displayed

- **<SMIL>**—Specifies that the document will be a SMIL document

- **<AUDIO>**—Specifies an audio object

- **<VIDEO>**—Specifies a video object

- **<TEXT>**—Specifies a text object

- **<IMG>**—Specifies an image object

- **<PAR>**—Specifies that the objects will play in a parallel fashion
- **<SEQ>**—Specifies that the objects will play in a sequence (for example, first A, then B)

TIP: *Both the **<PAR>** and **<SEQ>** elements can have begin and end attributes to specify when one object will begin playing and when one will end.*

- **<SWITCH>**—Specifies that the user has the ability to switch between certain attributes, such as bitrate, language, multimedia objects, and even various screen resolutions
- **<A>**—Specifies a link to a multimedia file (used just as the **<A>** in HTML is used)

TIP: *Remember, there is a lot more to SMIL than the simple elements we've just listed. Although Real Networks has created some powerful design tools, if you want to know more about SMIL, make sure you check out **www.justsmil.com**. The site includes additional information about how you can put this multimedia XML-based application to good use.*

SMIL In Depth

To give you a better idea of how SMIL works, let's examine how to create a SMIL file. First, like HTML files, a SMIL file has two parts: a head and body. The head specifies metacontent such as copyright, author, and comment information. The head section is used to define various layout features of the document. If no layout information is specified in the head section, the application playing the SMIL file will control the layout of the media. A SMIL head section looks something like this:

```
<HEAD>
<LAYOUT>
<ROOT-LAYOUT HEIGHT="252" WIDTH="340"
BACKGROUND-COLOR="White"/>
<meta name="author" content="C. Kirk"/>
<meta name="title" content="My Summer Vacation"/>
<meta name="copyright" content="(c)1999 Cheryl Kirk"/>
</head>
```

Information about the various multimedia elements and the synchronization of these objects is specified in the body of the SMIL document. Three presentation styles can be defined within the body of the SMIL document. Parallel presentation styles define how objects can be presented at the same time and how each object relates to another. The code for specifying parallel presentations looks like this:

18: XML Applications

499

```
<par>
<audio src="audio.wav"/>
<img src="video.avi"/>
</par>
```

Sequence is another presentation style. Sequence specifies the order of two individual multimedia objects. In a sequence presentation, the first object will start displaying or playing at the time specified. The rest of the objects listed in the body of a sequence presentation will start whenever the preceding object ends. The code to specify a sequence of multimedia elements looks like this:

```
<body>
<seq>
<audio src="audio/songone.wav"/>
<audio src="audio/songtwo.snd"/>
</seq>
</body>
```

It's amazing to see the tremendous support XML has garnered, and nowhere is it more evident than in the number of XML-based applications that have been created in a relatively short period of time. You can use XML to do just about anything you can think of, including delivering software updates remotely, transmitting multimedia objects in a standard way, and designing and displaying mathematical equations. In this chapter, we've examined what applications are available, the types of elements used in the most popular XML-based applications, and how some of these elements can be put to good use.

Immediate Solutions

In this section, you'll learn where you can get more information about new XML applications and how to put that information to good use. You'll also learn how to create four different specific XML-application files: CDF, MathML, SMIL, and OSD.

Locating New XML Applications

The most important thing to do in your XML development career is to keep abreast of all the new XML applications that seem to pop up. One of the best places to find new XML applications is James Tauber's XML Info site (**www.xmlinfo.com**). You can also find information about other XML activities at the W3C site (**www.w3c.com/XML**).

Creating A Channel

To create a channel, the first thing you need to do is create the CDF file that will contain the information about the channel. Next, you need to place the CDF file on a Web server and reference a link to it through a Web page. To create the channel file, follow these steps:

1. Open your XML editor or a text editor, such as Notepad.

2. In the first line of the document, create the XML declaration to specify that this is an XML document by typing the following code into the XML document:

```
<?XML Version="1.0"?>
```

3. Next, specify where top-level main page of the channel is located by typing the following code (this identifies the main page of the channel):

```
<CHANNEL HREF="http://www.site.com/channels/default.htm">
```

4. Use the **<ABSTRACT>** element to define the text that displays before the user subscribes to the channel, as shown in the following code:

18: XML Applications

501

```
<ABSTRACT>This Channel provides up-to-date news and information.
</ABSTRACT>
```

5. Specify the title for the channel by typing the following code:

```
<TITLE>The Channel Title</TITLE>
```

6. Specify the logo graphics for the channel's icons by typing the following code:

```
<LOGO HREF="channel.ico" STYLE="icon" />
<LOGO HREF="channel.gif" STYLE="image" />
<LOGO HREF="http://channel-w.gif" STYLE="image-wide" />
```

7. Use the **<ITEM>** element to specify the channel subpages. The **<ITEM>** element defines the subpage and specifies the various **<ITEM>** information and the location of the pages that provide the content. These elements can be nested or kept on the same level, as shown in this code example:

```
<ITEM HREF="http://www.site.com/channels/subpage.html">
<ABSTRACT>This is the news page</ABSTRACT>
<TITLE>News Page</TITLE>
</ITEM>
<ITEM HREF="http://www.site.com/channels/subpage2.html">
<ABSTRACT>This is the sports page</ABSTRACT>
<TITLE>Sports Page</TITLE>
</ITEM>
```

8. You'll also need to specify the channel's delivery schedule. You can set the frequency for updates to the channel content by using the **<SCHEDULE>** element to specify the schedule. The code for setting the schedule is as follows:

```
<SCHEDULE STARTDATE="1999-01-01">
<INTERVALTIME DAY="7" />
<EARLIESTTIME HOUR="0" />
<LATESTTIME HOUR="12" />
</SCHEDULE>
```

This specifies that the channel content will be updated once a week between midnight and noon starting January 1, 1999. **LATESTTIME** is definitely an element you should include. If you omit it, all users will have their channels updated at exactly the same local time, which may overload the server.

9. Complete the XML file by specifying the channel end-tag:

```
</CHANNEL>
```

10. Save the file as a CDF file (use the .CDF extension) and then use standard file transfer methods to upload the file.

11. Place a reference to the CDF file in a Web page by specifying a URL to the file:

```
<A HREF="http://www.site.com/channels/channel.cdf">
```

Creating A Mathematical Equation With MathML

In this example, you'll use the **<MROW>** element to create the equation $x^2 + 4x + 4 = 0$. You'll need to start from the left-hand side of the equation and nest the **<MROW>** elements to denote the terms specified in the equation. The **<MSUP/>** element specifies the superscript notation and the **<MO>** and **<MN>** elements specify the mathematical operator and the mathematical numeric data respectively. The code for this equation would look like this:

```
<mrow>
  <mrow>
    <msup>
      <mi>x</mi>
      <mn>2</mn>
    </msup>
    <mo>+</mo>
    <mrow>
      <mn>4</mn>
      <mo>&InvisibleTimes;</mo>
      <mi>x</mi>
    </mrow>
    <mo>+</mo>
    <mn>4</mn>
  </mrow>
  <mo>=</mo>
  <mn>0</mn>
</mrow>
```

Creating An OSD Software Package

To use OSD to create a software package, you need to know several things about the software package and the intended audience or program you are distributing. The first thing you should do is create the main element that will define the application and where the application is located. To do that, follow these steps:

1. Create the main element by using the **<SOFTPKG>** element to define where the program is located:

```
<SOFTPKG NAME="wwww.site.com/solitaire" VERSION="1,0,0,0">
```

2. Next, specify the title of the package by supplying the **<TITLE>** element like this:

```
<TITLE>Solitaire</TITLE>
```

3. You can add additional abstract information specifying what's contained in the package by adding this line of code next:

```
<ABSTRACT>Solitaire by FooBar Corporation</ABSTRACT>
```

4. Next, specify the location of the licensing agreement by adding the **<LICENSE>** element along with the URL of the location where the license is stored:

```
<LICENSE HREF="http://www.foobar.com/solitaire/license.html" />
```

5. Next, specify the implementation of the software, which will include the OS versions, the processor required, and the location of the CAB or JAR files of the actual application. You can also specify the language required for the application within the **<IMPLEMENTATION>** section. You can specify more than one implementation for different types of code and the dependencies required for the other types of code implementations to run. The code would look something like this:

```
<!-- Solitaire is implemented in native code for Win32,
Java code for other platforms -->
<IMPLEMENTATION>
<OS VALUE="WinNT"><OSVERSION VALUE="4,0,0,0"/></OS>
<OS VALUE="Win95"/>
<PROCESSOR VALUE="x86" />
<LANGUAGE VALUE="en" />
```

```
<CODEBASE HREF="http://www.site.com/solitaire.cab" />
</IMPLEMENTATION>

<IMPLEMENTATION>
<IMPLTYPE VALUE="Java" />
<CODEBASE HREF="http://www.site.com/solitaire.jar" />

<!-- The Java implementation needs the DeckOfCards object -->
<DEPENDENCY>
<CODEBASE HREF="http://www.site.com/cards.osd" />
</DEPENDENCY>
</IMPLEMENTATION>
```

6. To complete the software package, add the following end-tag element:

```
</SOFTPKG>
```

Creating A SMIL Data File

A SMIL file has the .SMI extension and can be created with any text editor. Within the **<SMIL>** root element, you define how the file will be displayed, how the video will be synchronized with the audio, and how it will play other multimedia files within the file itself.

To create a SMIL file, follow these steps:

1. First, declare the file as a SMIL file by adding this code to your blank text-only file:

```
<SMIL>
```

2. Next, specify the header information. The header information sets the size dimensions and the background color along with the text and image areas. It can also include the meta-information about the presentation. To create the header section, include the following code after the **<SMIL>** element:

```
<HEAD>
<LAYOUT>
<ROOT-LAYOUT HEIGHT="252" WIDTH="340"
BACKGROUND-COLOR="White"/>
<REGION ID="REGION_IMAGES" LEFT="0" TOP="32"
HEIGHT="180" WIDTH="300"/>
```

18: XML Applications

```
<meta name="author" content="C. Kirk"/>
<meta name="title" content="My Summer Vacation"/>
<meta name="copyright" content="(c)1999 Cheryl Kirk"/>
</head>
```

3. Next, specify the body of the SMIL document. In the body, you'll determine what elements will be shown together in a parallel-play sequence. In the following example, the video window, the narrative audio track, the main image area, and the text region show when the file loads. Notice how these elements are nested in the proper order:

```
<BODY>
<PAR>
<SEQ>
<PAR>
<!--This shows the intro screen-->
<IMG SRC="TITLE.IMF" REGION="REGION_IMAGES" FILL="REMOVE"/>
</PAR>
<PAR>
<!--This starts the narrative track-->
<AUDIO SRC="AUDIO.RM"/>
<!--This starts the main image track-->
<IMG SRC="IMAGES.IMF" REGION="REGION_IMAGES" FILL="REMOVE"/>
</PAR>
<SEQ>
</PAR>
</BODY>
```

Playing Files In Sequence

If you want to play files in sequence instead of specifying a parallel-play sequence, you would use the following code in the body of your SMIL file:

```
<body>
<seq>
<audio src="audio/songone.wav"/>
<audio src="audio/songtwo.snd"/>
</seq>
</body>
```

This code would play the first song (songone), which is a WAV file, and when that song finished, it would play the second song, which is a SND file. Files played in sequence do not have to be of the same type.

Specifying Bandwidth Options

You can use the **<SWITCH>** element to allow users to switch to different bandwidth options. Based on the bitrate used, you could provide several video files stored with different compression methods, or you could use different file types specified in the URL of the type of multimedia file. The code would look something like this:

```
<smil>
<head>
<meta name="author" content="Cheryl Kirk"/>
<meta name="title" content="Switchable Content"/>
<meta name="copyright" content="(c)1999 Cheryl Kirk"/>
</head>
<body>
<switch>
<par system-bitrate=75000>
<!--for dual isdn and faster-->
<audio src="audio/song.snd"/>
<video src="video/song.avi"/>
<image src="lyrics/song.gif"/>
</par>
<par system-bitrate=47000>
<!--for single isdn-->
<audio src="audio/song.snd"/>
<video src="video/song.avi"/>
<image src="lyrics/song.gif"/>
</par>
<par system-bitrate=28000>
<!--for 28.8kpbs modem-->
<audio src="audio/song28.snd"/>
<video src="video/song28.avi"/>
<image src="lyrics/song28.gif"/>
</par>
</switch>
</body>
</smil>
```

18: XML Applications

507

Chapter 19

Working With RDF:
An Advanced XML Case Study

By Natanya Pitts-Moultis

In Depth

Throughout the chapters in this book, we rely heavily on relatively simple Document Type Definitions (DTDs) to provide the majority of our examples. We do this in part to isolate examples of one particular element of XML or another so it won't get lost in the fray of a complex DTD. Although DTDs are solid teaching tools, they truly understate the possibilities XML has locked within its seemingly simple constructs. To demonstrate the true potential of XML as an advanced data description and dissemination tool, this chapter is devoted entirely to the discussion of one of XML's most advanced XML applications—the *Resource Description Framework* (RDF).

What Is RDF?

The Resource Description Framework (RDF) is a basis for processing metadata. Its primary goal is to facilitate the exchange of machine-understandable information among applications via the Web. An important cornerstone of RDF is its ability to automate the processing of Web resources.

Why Do We Need RDF?

If you've tried to search the Web lately for any kind of information, you already know the answer to this question. Current search techniques revolve around full-text search and retrieval by unintelligent agents. All search engines do is match text strings with text strings, not descriptions with other descriptions. HTML's **<META>** tag is available, but it is not widely used by HTML developers, and even less by search engines.

The number and types of resources on the Web are growing at an exponential rate, and soon it will be impossible for anyone to find anything in any reasonable length of time, as evidenced by a Reuters news article, published in April 1998, that said:

"If you use a search engine like Lycos or HotBot to search the Internet, you may not get as much coverage as you think, computer science researchers said. Steve Lawrence and Lee Giles of the NEC Research Institute in Princeton, New Jersey, said their study found that people who rely on the major search engines to find information on the Web only get a small proportion of the available documents. 'The engines index only a fraction of the total number of documents on the Web;

the coverage of any one engine is significantly limited,' they wrote in a report in the journal *Science*."

The Web is in desperate need of a way to describe resources, and XML is extensible enough that it has been used to create an application that can do so. Because RDF is not designed to work with one or two specific types of resources, but instead with all kinds of electronic data, it has a variety of applications, including:

- Consistent labeling of copyright, trademark, and other intellectual property information in Web resources
- Advanced cataloging of resources and their relationships within a single system or across multiple systems
- More accurate searching of data archives because the data itself is better labeled
- More precise filtering of data for more viable content-rating systems
- The ability to depict entire document collections as a single large document when appropriate
- Establishing safe trust relationships among documents and computers to facilitate the exchange of ideas and resources, as well as electronic commerce

RDF As An XML Application

RDF is an XML application that is still in development by the World Wide Web Consortium (W3C). RDF uses XML notation as an encoding syntax for metadata descriptions. You won't find an RDF DTD *per se*. Instead, XML constructs are used to describe the RDF data model. This allows the descriptions to be parsed by XML parsers and passed to XML-aware applications, but that doesn't mean RDF can only be implemented in XML. RDF developers intend to make it flexible enough that its data model can be described by using other vocabularies besides XML. But, because this is an XML book, we're primarily concerned with RDF as an XML application.

Important Terminology And Concepts

Before we delve into the intricacies of RDF, there are a few terms and advanced concepts you need to understand:

- Metadata
- Graphs
- Nodes

- ISO 10646
- Namespaces
- Schemas
- The Dublin Core

All of these terms and concepts will play a role in our discussion of RDF, so it's best to get them out of the way.

Metadata

In general, *metadata* is data about data. Card catalogs contain metadata entries for books and other literary resources. When applied specifically to the RDF context, metadata is data about Web resources. Describing metadata consistently is the whole focus of RDF. Just to complicate things a bit, metadata for one resource can have metadata of its own. For example, here is some metadata for this chapter's contents:

- *Title*—Working With RDF: An Advanced XML Case Study
- *Author*—Natanya Pitts-Moultis
- *Description*—An in-depth look at the XML application RDF.

Now, here's some metadata about the chapter itself:

- *Title*—The XML Black Book
- *Authors*—Natanya Pitts-Moultis and Cheryl Kirk
- *Publisher*—The Coriolis Group

The first set of metadata is specific to this chapter, whereas the second set describes the book that contains the chapter. If we wanted to, we could further describe the book as part of the Black Book series, as a Coriolis publication, as an XML book, as a technical publication, and as a book.

The same can be said of a Web page. The images in a Web page can have their own metadata, followed by the page itself, the collection of pages the individual page belongs to, the entire site, and the World Wide Web. You can peel metadata layers almost as you can peel an onion (with as many tears, as well, without a consistent description method).

Graphs

Remember graphs from college math? Take them one step further into the world of computing for the definition of graphs in the RDF context. *Graphs* are used in the RDF world (and in the larger world of computer science) as a physical map of data. Graphs show the relationships between bits of data by using connectors. A noncomputer example of a graph is a map used by an airline to show destination cities and the routes airplanes take to get from one city to the other. The entire map is a graph, and the routes are connections. The cities on the map are the graph's nodes. When you're representing data in a binary tree, the tree is the graph, and the data points are nodes.

Nodes

Nodes are instances of data on a graph. In the previous example, each city on the map (graph) is a node. Graphs contain points of data (nodes) and represent the relationships between them.

ISO 10646

ISO 10646 is the International Organization for Standards's official name for the Universal Character Set (UCS), which is equivalent to Unicode.

Namespaces

A *namespace* is an advanced XML technology that uses processing instructions (PIs) to assign unique names in a document to Uniform Resource Identifiers. Namespaces allow a common naming scheme to be used throughout a collection of documents. They also allow you to use portions of well-written DTDs again and again. Namespaces in XML are still in the draft recommendation stage, and the most current version of the namespace recommendation can be found at **www.w3.org/TR/1998/WD-xml-names-19980327**. "Creating Namespaces In XML," in this chapter's Immediate Solutions section, provides specific instructions on how to create namespace declarations.

Schemas

A *schema* is made up of concepts gathered from DTDs, object-oriented programming, and relational databases. Although schemas can describe the structure of an XML document, they can also be used to describe the structures of databases, graphs, and other kinds of organized data. Schemas go beyond DTDs in that they provide additional information about inheritance and data types in documents. Because schemas use the same syntax data types use but aren't limited to the creation of DTDs, a single schema can be used across many different sets of organized data. Schemas use namespaces to create reusable components that can be transferred from one schema to another.

The Dublin Core

The *Dublin Metadata Core Element Set* (or Dublin Core for short) is a list of 13 key metadata elements created by the participants of the OCLC/NCSA Metadata

Workshop, which was held in March 1995 and attended by experts from such fields as library science, computer science, and text encoding. The group's goal was to create a metadata description tool that was easy to use. The Dublin Core was the result. The Dublin Core does not have a specific syntax and it is not a direct component of RDF, but it is one of the first schemas being tested with RDF. It isolates many of the metadata components that RDF uses in its description of Web resources, and it is used in this chapter in further examples of how RDF might be implemented.

The 13 key metadata elements of the Dublin Core are:

- *Title*—The title an author or publisher assigns to the work.

- *Subject*—What the work is about; defined with keywords or topical linformation.

- *Author*—The person or persons responsible for the work's content.

- *Publisher*—An agent or agency responsible for making the work available in its current form; usually a publishing house or an educational institution.

- *OtherAgent*—People other than the author(s) who have contributed substantially to the work (for example, artists and editors).

- *Date*—When the work was made available in its described form.

- *ObjectType*—What the object is; examples include books, poems, Web pages, and artists' sketches.

- *Form*—The data type the work takes; usually a file type.

- *Identifier*—A string unique to the object and used for identification purposes; examples include ISBN numbers and URIs.

- *Relation*—What relationship, if any, the work has with other works; usually describes a work as part of a larger collection.

- *Source*—Other sources, if applicable, from which the work is derived.

- *Language*—The language of the work.

- *Coverage*—The geographic area the work covers, if applicable.

Immediate Solutions

RDF's nucleus is an archetype for depicting named properties and their values. The properties are representations of resource attributes as well as the relationships between resources. This data model provides a syntax-independent means of representing RDF expressions. XML is just one way to represent the RDF data model. However, regardless of how the data model is represented, all the representations have equivalent meanings. This Immediate Solutions section focuses on using XML to describe RDF.

Comparing Apples And Oranges

Because RDF expressions can be represented in more than one way, it's possible that two expressions that use completely different syntaxes mean the same thing. One of the primary tasks of RDF is to compare resources (most especially for searching). So, it's important that the syntax used to describe the RDF expression does not matter when the expressions are compared. In the end, RDF expressions are rendered down from whatever syntax they are in to the ISO 10646 string values, and those string values are compared. The RDF expressions are the same if the string values match.

Exploring The RDF Grammar

The description of a Web resource is made up of property and value sets and is called an *expression*. For example, for the Web page **www.w3.org**, the property author has the value World Wide Web Consortium. Descriptions are created using the RDF grammar.

A conceptual framework for describing and using metadata is provided in the RDF data model, but to write and exchange metadata, there must be a concrete syntax. This syntax is XML. However, RDF requires a DTD for the descriptions of metadata to actually function. So without a DTD, RDF descriptions really only have to be well-formed, because they don't necessarily have to be validated against a DTD. The schemas used by RDF descriptions can be XML DTDs, but they can also be schemas for other entities, such as databases or graphs.

RDF provides two syntactical versions for describing the data model:

- The *serialization syntax* describes the full abilities of the data model by using a set of typical constructs.

- The *abbreviated syntax* uses an additional set of constructs to describe a subset of the data model with a much smaller footprint.

Any RDF interpreter should implement each syntax equally well.

Because the RDF specification is still in the development phases, it's important to be able to read new versions of the specification as they are released. The specification used the Extended Backus-Naur Form (EBNF) notation to describe the elements of the RDF syntax. Table 19.1 lists the major EBNF notation elements and a description of each. Table 19.2 describes how expressions can be substituted for A and B in EBNF notations.

The RDF specification also makes use of the abbreviation ***rdf*** to represent the RDF variable namespace. Because the RDF specification is described in XML,

Table 19.1   The Extended Backus-Naur Form (EBNF) notation system.

Notation	Description
#xN	Represents character encoding with the ISO 10646 standard, where *N* is an integer and corresponds to the ISO 10646 character code.
[a-zA-Z], [#xN-#xN]	Represents any character with a value in the range(s) indicated (inclusive).
[^a-z], [^#xN-#xN]	Represents any character with a value *outside* the range indicated.
[^abc], [^#xN#xN#xN]	Represents any character with a value not among the characters given.
"string"	Represents a literal string given inside the double quotation marks.
'string'	Represents a literal string given inside the single quotation marks.
(expression)	A combination of symbols treated as a unit. Expressions can be substituted for A and B in the notations listed in Table 19.2.

Table 19.2   In EBNF notation, expressions can be substituted for A and B.

Notation	Description
A?	Represents A or nothing; optional A
A B	Represents A followed by B
A	B	Represents A or B but not both
A - B	Represents any string that matches A but does not match B
A+	Represents one or more occurrences of A
A*	Represents zero or more occurrences of A

other important XML rules are observed when RDF descriptions are created, including those that govern:

- Start- and end-tags (their names must match)
- The use of quotation marks (either single or double quotation marks are acceptable)
- White space
- Case sensitivity
- Escape characters (all of XML's are recognized)

Finally, the schema that governs a given RDF description or set of descriptions must be declared via a URI that uses XML namespaces. So even though RDF is not strictly part of the XML vocabulary, it makes use of XML's syntax and flexibility to describe Web resources.

Creating Namespaces In XML

XML namespaces are important to RDF as well as to other up-and-coming XML applications. They are created by using this syntax:

```
<?xml:namespace name="some-uri" as="some-abbreviation"?>
```

Using this syntax, the name **w3c** can be applied to the URI **http://www.w3.org**:

```
<?xml:namespace name="http://www.w3.org" as="w3c"?>
```

Keep in mind that the namespace recommendation is just that, a recommendation, and it may be a while before it is a full specification. For more detailed information about XML namespaces, point your browser to **www.w3.org/TR/1998/NOTE-xml-names-0119**.

Using The Serialization Syntax To Create RDF Elements

First things first. The actual RDF serialization syntax looks like this:

```
[1] RDF            ::= '<rdf:RDF>' expression* '</rdf:RDF>'
[2] expression     ::= description | collection
```

```
[3]  description    ::= '<rdf:Description' idRefAttr? bagIdAttr? '>'
                        '</rdf:Description>'
[4]  collection     ::= sequence | bag | alternatives
[5]  sequence       ::= '<rdf:Seq' idAttr? '>' collMember* '</rdf:Seq>'
[6]  bag            ::= '<rdf:Bag' idAttr? '>' collMember* '</rdf:Bag>
[7]  alternatives   ::= '<rdf:Alt' idAttr? '>' collMember+ '</rdf:Alt>'
[8]  collMember     ::= hrefItem | valueItem
[9]  hrefItem       ::= '<rdf:LI' hrefAttr '/>'
[10] valueItem      ::= '<rdf:LI>' value '</rdf:LI>'
[11] idRefAttr      ::= idAttr | hrefAttr
[12] hrefAttr       ::= 'rdf:HREF="' resourceURI '"'
[13] idAttr         ::= 'ID="' IDsymbol '"'
[14] bagIdAttr      ::= 'rdf:BAGID="' IDsymbol '"'
[15] resourceURI    ::= (see RFC1738)
[16] IDsymbol       ::= (any legal XML name symbol)
```

TIP: *All specification information is taken from the RDF working draft maintained by the W3C at **www.w3.org/TR/ WD-rdf-syntax**. All excerpts from the working draft are copyrighted by the W3C.*

Okay, so what does this really mean in English, or at least techie English? The RDF expression can be either one of two expressions—**description** or **collection**. The **collection** expression is further broken down into **sequence**, **bag**, and **alternatives** (indicated by the strings **Seq**, **Bag**, and **Alt** respectively). The expression is represented with this syntax:

```
<RDF:DESCRIPTION>...</RDF:DESCRIPTION>
```

You can also use this syntax:

```
<RDF:SEQ>...</RDF:SEQ>
<RDF:BAG>...</RDF:BAG>
<RDF:ALT>...</RDF:ALT>
```

If the expression is a description, it can take an **ID** or an **HREF** attribute and a **BAGID** attribute. The **ID** attribute assigns a unique ID to the description, and an **HREF** attribute associates the description with the Web resource it describes. Use **ID** with new descriptions you create (to be referenced by other descriptions) and **HREF** when you are describing existing Web resources. The **BAGID** attribute labels the bag node created by the description.

TIP: *A bag is an unordered list of nodes associated with a property.*

By adding these attributes, we get this code:

```
<RDF:DESCRIPTION RDF:HREF="http://www.w3.org" BAGID="w3c">
...
</RDF:DESCRIPTION>
```

If the expression is a collection, its type (**SEQ**, **BAG**, or **ALT**) indicates what kind of collection it is. Collection types are:

- *SEQ*—An ordered list of nodes
- *BAG*—An unordered list of nodes
- *ALT*—A list of alternative values for a single variable

Use the **ID** attribute to assign a unique name to a collection. The nodes in any type of collection are marked by the **<LI>...</LI>** tag pair. The **<LI>...</LI>** tags can include an **HREF** attribute to identify other Web resources as nodes, or it can contain string values as content to create the node values. Both sequence and bag collections can have zero or more occurrences of an **<LI>...</LI>** element, but alternative collections must have one or more. A sample collection expression might look like this:

```
<RDF:SEQ ID="XMLResources">
    <LI RDF:HREF="http://www.w3.org/XML"></LI>
    <LI REF:HREF="http://www.xml.com"></LI>
    <LI>The XML Black Book</LI>
</RDF:SEQ>
```

An example of a collection from the RDF note is:

```
<?xml:namespace name="http://www.w3.org/TR/WD-rdf-syntax#" as="RDF"?>
<RDF:RDF>
  <RDF:Seq ID="JSPapersByDate">
    <RDF:LI RDF:HREF="http://www.dogworld.com/Aug96.doc"/>
    <RDF:LI RDF:HREF="http://www.webnuts.net/Jan97.html"/>
    <RDF:LI RDF:HREF="http://www.carchat.com/Sept97.html"/>
  </RDF:Seq>
  <RDF:Seq ID="JSPapersBySubj">
    <RDF:LI RDF:HREF="http://www.carchat.com/Sept97.html"/>
    <RDF:LI RDF:HREF="http://www.dogworld.com/Aug96./doc"/>
    <RDF:LI RDF:HREF="http://www.webnuts.net/Jan97.html"/>
  </RDF:Seq>
</RDF:RDF>
```

This collection describes a set of papers, first by date and then by subject. Because the elements use the **SEQ** label, the elements in the collection are not only listed as part of the collection, but a specific order is indicated, first by date and then by subject.

Once you've identified an expression as a description or collection, you can create one or more property elements to provide more information about the resource defined by the expression. The official specification for an RDF property is:

```
[17] property        ::= '<' propName idAttr? '>' value '</' propName '>'
                         '<' propName idRefAttr '/>'
[18] propName        ::= 'rdf:Value' | 'rdf:InstanceOf' | name
                         | NSname ':' name
[19] value           ::= expression | string
[20] name            ::= (any legal XML name symbol)
[21] NSname          ::= (any legal XML namespace prefix)
[22] string          ::= (any XML text, with "<", ">", and "&" escaped)
```

Once again in English, property elements are created by defining the schema that governs the property. One example of such a schema might be the Dublin Core (**DC** in the namespace definition) metadata format. Before the schema can be used in the property's name, it must be declared by using the XML namespace syntax.

Once you've defined the schema, use its abbreviation combined with the name of the property. The basic syntax looks like this:

```
<SCHEMA:PROPERTY>...</SCHEMA:PROPERTY>
```

If we use an example from the Dublin Core, the title property for this book would be defined this way:

```
<DC:TITLE>The XML Black Book</DC:TITLE>
```

Now, we'll put it all together. The following example is taken from the Dublin Core In RDF Examples Web page at **www.dstc.edu.au/RDU/RDF/dc-in-rdf-ex.html**. This (and any other Dublin Core examples in the Immediate Solutions section) was created by Eric Miller and Renato Iannella. The Dublin Core examples were the only real-life, working examples of RDF to be found on the Web when this book was written. This example is a simple description of the Dublin Core Elements Web page:

```
<?xml:namespace href="http://www.w3c.org/RDF/" as="RDF"?>
<?xml:namespace href="http://purl.org/RDF/DC/" as="DC"?>
<RDF:RDF>
```

```
<RDF:Description RDF:HREF="http://purl.org/metadata/dublin_core_elements">
    <DC:Title>
          Dublin Core Metadata Element Set: Reference Description
    </DC:Title>
    <DC:Creator>Stuart Weibel</DC:Creator>
    <DC:Creator>Eric Miller</DC:Creator>
    <DC:Subject>
          Metadata, Dublin Core element, resource description
    </DC:Subject>
    <DC:Description>
       This document is the reference description of the
       Dublin Core Metadata Element Set designed to facilitate resource
       discovery.
    </DC:Description>
    <DC:Publisher>OCLC Online Computer Library Center, Inc.
    </DC:Publisher>
    <DC:Format>text/html</DC:Format>
    <DC:Type>Technical Report</DC:Type>
    <DC:Language>en</DC:Language>
    <DC:Date>1997-11-02</DC:Date>
</RDF:Description>
</RDF:RDF>
```

The two namespace declarations assign the values **RDF** and **DC** to the RDF and DC schemas respectively. The DC schema name is fictitious, but if this were a real RDF document, the link to the schema would be valid. The **<RDF:DESCRIPTION>** element declares that this is a description, and the **RDF:HREF** attribute names the resource (**http://purl.org/metadata/dublin_core_elements**) being described. The remainder of the property elements provide information about the document's creators, subject, publisher, format, type, native language, and date. The example would provide someone who hadn't seen the reference with quite a bit of valuable information.

Borrowing their code, we created this description of a book from The Coriolis Group:

```
<?xml:namespace href="http://www.w3c.org/RDF/" as="RDF"?>
<?xml:namespace href="http://purl.org/RDF/DC/" as="DC"?>
<RDF:RDF>
<RDF:Description>
    <DC:Title>HTML Style Sheets Design Guide</DC:Title>
    <DC:Creator>Natanya Pitts-Moultis</DC:Creator>
    <DC:Creator>Steven Nelson James</DC:Creator>
    <DC:Creator>Ed Tittel</DC:Creator>
```

```
<DC:Subject>
    Style sheets, Cascading Style Sheets, CSS, Web design
</DC:Subject>
<DC:Description>
    Covers how to add CSS1 style sheets to Web pages
    with a special emphasis on design techniques.
</DC:Description>
<DC:Publisher>Coriolis</DC:Publisher>
<DC:Format>text/MSWord</DC:Format>
<DC:Type>Technical Book</DC:Type>
<DC:Language>en</DC:Language>
<DC:Date>1997-11-15</DC:Date>
</RDF:Description>
</RDF:RDF>
```

Using The Abbreviated Syntax To Create RDF Elements

The abbreviated syntax can be used with a property if it only appears once and its value is a string, or it can be used if the property value is a node and the values of the properties of that node are strings. The abbreviated syntax looks like this:

```
[1] RDF          ::= '<rdf:RDF>' expression* '</rdf:RDF>'
[2] expression   ::= description | collection
[3] description  ::= '<rdf:Description' idRefAttr? bagIdAttr? propAttr* '/>'
                     | '<rdf:Description' idRefAttr? bagIdAttr? propAttr* '>'
                       property* '</rdf:Description>' | typedNode
[4] collection   ::= sequence | bag | alternatives
[5] sequence     ::= '<rdf:Seq' idAttr? '>' collMember* '</rdf:Seq>'
[6] bag          ::= '<rdf:Bag' idAttr? '>' collMember* '</rdf:Bag>
[7] alternatives ::= '<rdf:Alt' idAttr? '>' collMember+ '</rdf:Alt>'
[8] collMember   ::= hrefItem | valueItem
[9] hrefItem     ::= '<rdf:LI' hrefAttr '/>'
[10] valueItem   ::= '<rdf:LI>' value '</rdf:LI>'
[11] idRefAttr   ::= idAttr | hrefAttr
[12] hrefAttr    ::= 'rdf:HREF="' resourceURI '"'
[13] idAttr      ::= 'ID="' IDsymbol '"'
[14] bagIdAttr   ::= 'rdf:BAGID="' IDsymbol '"'
[15] resourceURI ::= (see RFC1738)
[16] IDsymbol    ::= (any legal XML name symbol)
```

```
[17] property      ::= '<' propName idAttr? '>' value '</' propName '>'
                    | '<' propName idRefAttr? bagIDAttr? propAttr* '/>'
[18] propName      ::= 'rdf:Value' | 'rdf:InstanceOf' | name
                        | NSname ':' name
[19] value         ::= expression | string
[20] name          ::= (any legal XML name symbol)
[21] NSname        ::= (any legal XML namespace prefix)
[22] string        ::= (any XML text, with "<", ">", and "&" escaped)
[23] typedNode     ::= '<' typeName idRefAttr? bagIDAttr? propAttr* '/>'
                    | '<' typeName idRefAttr? bagIDAttr? propAttr* '>'
                        property* '</' typeName '>'
[24] typeName      ::= NSname ':' name
[25] propAttr      ::= propName '="' string '"'
                    (with embedded quotes escaped)
```

The major changes to the syntax are the addition of lines 23 through 25 and the changes found in lines 3 and 17. Line 3 now uses this specification:

```
[3] description   ::= '<rdf:Description' idRefAttr? bagIdAttr? propAttr* '/>'
                    | '<rdf:Description' idRefAttr? bagIdAttr? propAttr* '>'
                        property* '</rdf:Description>' | typedNode
```

The description element can now be either an empty tag with the usual **HREF** or **ID** attributes and a **BAG** attribute. In this iteration, the description element can also take a property attribute. The property attribute (**propAttr**) is formed in almost the same way as a property element, taking the syntax:

```
SCHEMA:PROPERTY-NAME="Value"
```

The property attribute for the Dublin Core title label would be:

```
DC:TITLE="Value"
```

The description element can also still be used as a regular tag pair that takes property elements, but even the tag pair can take a property attribute as well. Remember that a property can only be abbreviated if it appears only once and if its value is a string, so there may be a need for both property attributes and property elements. The description element can also contain a new kind of element—the **typedNode** element. A **typedNode** element is used to describe nodes of specific types and to provide more information about them.

The new specification for line 17 is:

```
[17] property       ::= '<' propName idAttr? '>' value '</' propName '>'
                      | '<' propName idRefAttr? bagIDAttr? propAttr* '/>'
```

As with the description element, the property element can now be either a single-ton or tag pair, and a property element pair can take property attributes. This provides for nesting of metadata and more-specific descriptions of properties.

New line 23 defines the **typedNode** element:

```
[23] typedNode      ::= '<' typeName idRefAttr? bagIDAttr? propAttr* '/>'
                      | '<' typeName idRefAttr? bagIDAttr? propAttr* '>'
                            property* '</' typeName '>'
```

This element looks like the original description element and can take an **ID** or **HREF** attribute, a **BAG** attribute, and one or more property attributes. Because the **typeName** portion of the element gives it the name, it is identified by the element.

New lines 24 and 25 provide information about the **typeName** identifier used in the new **typedNode** element and define the property attribute used with the new description and property tags:

```
[24] typeName       ::= NSname ':' name
[25] propAttr       ::= propName '="' string '"'
                        (with embedded quotes escaped)
```

An example (from the RDF working draft) of RDF elements condensed from the serialization syntax to the abbreviated syntax is:

```
<?xml:namespace name="http://www.w3.org/TR/WD-rdf-syntax#" as="RDF"?>
<?xml:namespace name="http://mycorp.com/my-schema#" as="LOCAL"?>
<RDF:RDF>
   <RDF:Description RDF:HREF="http://www.webnuts.net/">
    <LOCAL:Abstract>
     <RDF:Description>
      <RDF:InstanceOf href="http://mycorp.com/my-schema#Sitemap"/>
       <LOCAL:Title>Map of our Site</LOCAL:Title>
       <LOCAL:ValidUntil>1999-02-01T00:00Z</LOCAL:ValidUntil>
     </RDF:Description>
    </LOCAL:Abstract>
   </RDF:Description>
</RDF:RDF>
```

The preceding code can be abbreviated as:

```
<?xml:namespace name="http://www.w3.org/TR/WD-rdf-syntax#" as="RDF"?>
<?xml:namespace name="http://mycorp.com/my-schema#" as="LOCAL"?>
<RDF:RDF>
   <RDF:Description RDF:HREF="http://www.webnuts.net/">
     <LOCAL:Abstract>
       <LOCAL:Sitemap
        LOCAL:Title="Map of our Site"
        LOCAL:ValidUntil="1999-02-01T00:00Z"/>
     </LOCAL:Abstract>
   </RDF:Description>
</RDF:RDF>
```

Our earlier example from the Dublin Core RDF examples can also be abbreviated. Here is the code in the RDF serialization syntax:

```
<?xml:namespace href="http://www.w3c.org/RDF/" as="RDF"?>
<?xml:namespace href="http://purl.org/RDF/DC/" as="DC"?>
<RDF:RDF>
<RDF:Description RDF:HREF="http://purl.org/metadata/dublin_core_elements">
    <DC:Title>
        Dublin Core Metadata Element Set: Reference Description
    </DC:Title>
    <DC:Creator>Stuart Weibel</DC:Creator>
    <DC:Creator>Eric Miller</DC:Creator>
    <DC:Subject>
        Metadata, Dublin Core element, resource description
    </DC:Subject>
    <DC:Description>This document is the reference description of the
        Dublin Core Metadata Element Set designed to facilitate resource
        discovery.</DC:Description>
    <DC:Publisher>OCLC Online Computer Library Center, Inc.
    </DC:Publisher>
    <DC:Format>text/html</DC:Format>
    <DC:Type>Technical Report</DC:Type>
    <DC:Language>en</DC:Language>
    <DC:Date>1997-11-02</DC:Date>
</RDF:Description>
</RDF:RDF>
```

The preceding code can be abbreviated as:

```
<?xml:namespace href="http://www.w3c.org/RDF/" as="RDF"?>
<?xml:namespace href="http://purl.org/RDF/DC/" as="DC"?>
```

```
<RDF:RDF>
   <RDF:Description RDF:HREF="http://purl.org/metadata/dublin_core_elements"
    DC:Title = "Dublin Core Metadata Element Set: Reference Description"
    DC:Creator = "Stuart Weibel, Eric Miller"
    DC:Subject = "Metadata, Dublin Core element, resource description"
    DC:Description = "This document is the reference description of the
        Dublin Core Metadata Element Set designed to facilitate resource
        discovery."
    DC:Publisher = "OCLC Online Computer Library Center, Inc."
    DC:Format = "text/html"
    DC:Type = "Technical Report"
    DC:Language = "en"
    DC:Date = "1997-11-02" />
</RDF:RDF>
```

And as a final exercise, here is a description of the *HTML Style Sheets Design Guide*:

```
<?xml:namespace href="http://www.w3c.org/RDF/" as="RDF"?>
<?xml:namespace href="http://purl.org/RDF/DC/" as="DC"?>
<RDF:RDF>
<RDF:Description>
    <DC:Title>HTML Style Sheets Design Guide</DC:Title>
    <DC:Creator>Natanya Pitts-Moultis</DC:Creator>
    <DC:Creator>Steven Nelson James</DC:Creator>
    <DC:Creator>Ed Tittel</DC:Creator>
    <DC:Subject>
        Style sheets, Cascading Style Sheets, CSS, Web design
    </DC:Subject>
    <DC:Description>Covers how to add CSS1 style sheets to Web pages
        with a special emphasis on design techniques. </DC:Description>
    <DC:Publisher>Coriolis</DC:Publisher>
    <DC:Format>text/MSWord</DC:Format>
    <DC:Type>Technical Book</DC:Type>
    <DC:Language>en</DC:Language>
    <DC:Date>1997-11-15</DC:Date>
</RDF:Description>
</RDF:RDF>
```

It can be abbreviated as:

```
<?xml:namespace href="http://www.w3c.org/RDF/" as="RDF"?>
<?xml:namespace href="http://purl.org/RDF/DC/" as="DC"?>
<RDF:RDF>
   <RDF:Description
    DC:Title = " HTML Style Sheets Design Guide "
```

```
       DC:Creator = "Natanya Pitts-Moultis, Steven Nelson James, Ed Tittel"
       DC:Subject = " Style sheets, Cascading Style Sheets, CSS, Web design "
       DC:Description = " Covers how to add CSS1 style sheets to Web pages
           with a special emphasis on design techniques."
       DC:Publisher = "Coriolis"
       DC:Format = "text/MSWord"
       DC:Type = "Technical Book"
       DC:Language = "en"
       DC:Date = "1997-11-15" />
   </RDF:RDF>
```

Associating Descriptions With The Resources They Describe

There are four ways for a description to be associated with its resources:

- The resource can contain an embedded version of the description. This will most certainly be the initial way RDF descriptions will be associated with HTML files and other XML files.

- The description will be stored external to the resource but retrieved along with the resource. The XML linking mechanism will support this type of piggyback retrieval.

- The description will be stored either internal or external to the resource but is retrieved independently of the resource. Search and catalog applications will use this feature most often.

- The description will be wrapped around the resource so that the resource is actually part of the description.

Chapter 20

Implementing CDF

By Cheryl Kirk

In Depth

In this chapter, we'll get pushy. In other words, we're going to delve into the world of push technology. Specifically, we'll examine Microsoft's implementation of push technology, which is called the Channel Definition Format (CDF). CDF is actually an XML application, meaning CDF relies on the Extensible Style Language to create an information-delivery system. In this chapter, you'll learn what the Channel Definition Format is, how to use the correct syntax, how to create a CDF file, and how to create your own channels to push content to subscribers through applications such as screen savers, HTML-formatted email, and the standard Active Desktop channel.

Microsoft introduced the Active Channel technology and its structural base, CDF, when it introduced Internet Explorer 4. Push technologies that use XML (such as CDF) give you, the developer, a way to organize and deliver specific personalized Web-based information at predetermined times to users who request it. It is one of the easiest XML applications to learn and implement within a site, regardless of whether the site is on the Internet or is part of an intranet. With CDF, developers can create content for distribution to a wide range of users and through a variety of delivery formats. For example, current stock prices could be sent to subscribers of a CDF push channel via HTML-formatted email, Web pages, or a desktop screen saver. This push technology allows users to get the information they need by simply subscribing to the content source. The information is automatically delivered to the users' computers based on a predetermined schedule or upon connection to the Internet. Once sent, the information can be viewed offline, because all of the graphics and textual content are delivered together in a single subscription package.

CDF provides a standard set of tags for defining channels, which automatically send data from a Web server to a Web browser. CDF also lets you create a schedule for downloading updated content from the Web server to the browser. The content is labeled with a brief description and includes navigational buttons to allow the user to move through it easily. Let's examine how CDF relates to XML, the design concepts used in developing channels, and the XML vocabulary.

A Closer Look At Channels

The concept of channels is relatively easy to understand. In its most basic form, a channel is a collection of Web-page information the developer has defined for delivery to those users who have subscribed to receive it. The easiest way to explain channels and their potential is to step out of the computer world for a minute and think about the television world, specifically, cable television. When you subscribe to cable television, you normally get access to an option called pay-per-view. Pay-per-view channels are channels you can subscribe to for specific content that is aired at a specific time. The cable company tells you what's available, most often through a preview channel. You subscribe to the content that appeals to you—the latest boxing match or a movie, for example—by dialing the phone, entering your cable account number, and selecting the program identification number shown on the preview channel. At a predetermined time, the cable company delivers the content you requested directly to your cable box.

With Web channels, the theory is much the same, except you normally don't have to pay. Content is usually free and can be accessed by a click of a button. On television, a channel is basically a collection of content, such as movies, delivered to the subscriber at a predetermined time. However, on the computer, channels deliver a collection of Web pages, graphics, sounds, and possibly movie files. The file that outlines what's available in the channel is called the CDF file, and like any XML application, the CDF file provides an outline of the resources available within the channel. Included in the channel index is a schedule that outlines when the information in the channel will be updated. Depending upon how the channel is coded, the subscriber can specify whether that information is pushed to his or her email address, computer's desktop, or screen saver. After the content is received, the user can then view, manipulate, or print the information without connecting to the Internet, because all the content is sent to the user's computer.

Advantages Of Channels For The User

For the user, channels offer easy access to information. The Channels button on the Internet Explorer toolbar gives single point-and-click access to the channels that are available. If the user has installed the Active Desktop, channels are also accessible through the Channels button on the QuickStart toolbar. Once activated, the Channels Guide displays the list of channels to which the user has subscribed. Channels offer the same accessibility that Web pages offer by offering the same navigational controls. Links are still incorporated within the content, and depending on the level of the subscription, the information can be more than just a single Web page deep. The user is not required to learn new navigational techniques, special commands, or other controls in order to subscribe to, gather, or read the information. Since the information pushed to the user's desktop is presented in standard HTML format, the subscriber uses the information supplied in the channel in the same fashion he or she would use the information in a standard Web page.

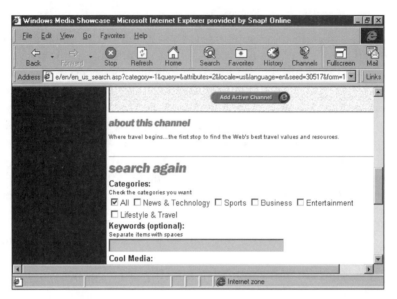

Figure 20.1   To subscribe to a site, all a user has to do is click on the channel logo.

For the user, subscribing to channels is about as simple as clicking on an icon on a Web page, such as the icon shown in Figure 20.1. The icon, called the channel logo, can reside on a Web page positioned somewhere on your site, or it can be added to the user's Active Desktop or the Explorer pane in Internet Explorer. Subscribers can use either Internet Explorer's Active Desktop or Navigator's Netcaster technology. As long as the developer has followed the Channel Definition Format, it shouldn't matter which browsing mechanism is used to view the data.

All the information the user subscribes to is automatically updated. The user does nothing in terms of seeking or finding the new information on your site. And better still, the updating is done at a predetermined time, which means the user doesn't have to download content or wait for Web pages to load. Simply viewing the channel will bring up the latest information. Because the information is downloaded automatically, the user can view it offline.

Advantages Of Channels For The Developer

All of this automation provides plenty of advantages to the Web-site developer. With CDF, the developer can extend the content on a Web site by delivering it to users who may not know about the content or who don't have the time to browse. As mentioned earlier, CDF is an excellent mechanism for delivering content through Web pages, email, and screen savers. It offers developers the following benefits:

- *Full control over the delivery of information*—You can specify exactly what and how much information is pushed to the user. This ensures that the user at least sees the information you want them to see, unlike just posting it on a Web page that may or may not be accessed by the users you want to target.

- *The ability to personalize content for the subscriber*—Subscribers can pick and choose what content will be delivered to their desktops.

- *The ability to provide access to authorized users only through password protection*—Because you can request a login name and password within the CDF file you create, you can request that only users who have login names and passwords subscribe to the content information. This option, however, does not provide full digital certification.

- *The ability to track and log page hits*—You can track users to learn what pages are being viewed and what pages are downloaded but never touched. This helps you determine what information should be updated and what information users aren't interested in reading.

- *Options to deliver information based on subscriber's preference*—You can give the user a choice to view the information through a Web page, email, or a desktop screen saver, or an Active Desktop channel.

- *More exposure of content to subscribers through category folders and through Microsoft's channel Authors Site*—Located at **www.microsoft.com/ workshop/delivery/contents.htm**, you can place your information within the Microsoft Channel, giving you exposure to people who want to subscribe to additional channels. This site is what users see when they first install the Channel option in their Internet Explorer application.

When you employ CDF files within your site, you are basically setting up Web pages that are targeted to an interested audience, which means the information is more likely to be read. When users subscribe to your channel, they know the information will be updated on a regular basis.

In terms of development, you can use the knowledge you already have to develop channel content:

- No new development tools or knowledge is needed to create the content. Because channels are simply HTML pages, you can use your development skills and current layout, graphics, and programming in the channel content.

- The CDF file can be customized with Active Server Page technology and other CGI scripting—plus client-side scripting such as cookies—to extend and customize the content of the channel.

- You can automate the production of CDF files with such products as Microsoft FrontPage 98 or Microsoft CDF Generator, which is a separate application that allows you to create CDF files without using FrontPage.

TIP: *You can download the CDF Generator at Microsoft's Site Builder Network site at* **www.microsoft.com/gallery/tools/contents.htm** *or* **www.microsoft.com/gallery/tools/liburnia/liburnia.asp**.

- CDF files let you organize your information in a hierarchy—the same structure as any other XML document. That means CDF files can be viewed through many of today's parsers. This makes it easy to organize your information and present it to your subscribers in a logical order.

- When you package content in channels, you can target different sets of audiences for different types of information.

- Because CDF files are XML applications, you can start implementing XML in your site quickly and easily.

XML's Relationship With CDF

All content sent to the subscriber through a channel is created in HTML. XML doesn't format the content. So, how does CDF relate to XML? XML provides the framework through which the browser finds, describes, and delivers the content based on the schedule provided. CDF is an XML application, which means Microsoft has developed a list of specific CDF elements that follow the XML syntax and conventions but have been defined with their own attributes. These elements are used to create a channel. When you create an XML document that defines the channel, its content, and its delivery mechanism, you use the XML document declaration and follow the XML concepts of nesting elements within other elements. The only difference is that you use the predefined elements Microsoft has created to outline a channel.

TIP: *If you're a little fuzzy about the concept of elements, Chapters 7 and 8 outline exactly what elements and attributes are.*

To put it more succinctly, because CDF is an application of XML, the CDF specification relies heavily on the definition of XML. Elements, entities, attributes, and element rules are all part of CDF, as are nested elements, XML declarations, and the use of URL linking. Know XML and you already know CDF. XML parsers parse the information specified in the CDF.

Specifically, CDF is based on a Document Type Definition (DTD) containing information that points the user's browser to the information source, descriptive information about the content, and the schedule for downloading the information. The CDF application consists of a single root element, an element from which all other items within the channel branch. This single root element is called the **<CHANNEL>** element. The branches from this root element are called **<ITEM>** elements.

You can have multiple **<ITEM>** elements, but you can only have one **<CHAN-NEL>** element to describe the channel. The **<ITEM>** elements specify the individual pages or subpages that are the children of the channel root. With CDF, only the **<CHANNEL>** element and its content are defined in the CDF specification.

In this chapter's Immediate Solutions section, you'll learn how to create both the CDF file that specifies the XML declaration and the CDF elements that create the channel information. Because the information is automatically sent to the user at a predetermined time, when the user clicks the Channel button in Internet Explorer 4 (see Figure 20.2), the content is automatically available. There is no waiting for the text, pictures, sounds, or even movies to download.

The Development Of Channels

There are five major steps for developing the CDF file and the accompanying images and information needed for a user to subscribe to your channel. Here are the steps in the order in which they should be performed:

1. Design the channel.
2. Create the channel logo icons and images.
3. Create the CDF file.
4. Upload or post the CDF file to the HTTP server.
5. Offer the channel to potential subscribers.

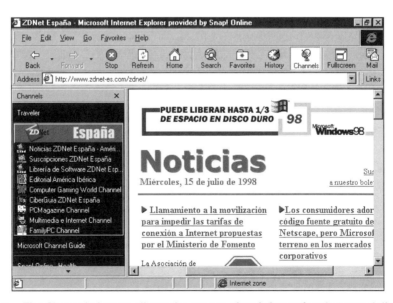

Figure 20.2   The Channels button allows the user to view information that was delivered to the computer at a predetermined time.

Designing The Channel

Before you start creating the logos and the content or telling potential subscribers about your channel, you should design its structure. It doesn't matter if your channel is simply a re-creation of your Web site, a subset of it, or new content altogether, you need to sketch out the channel content hierarchy. The hierarchy is the actual structure of your channel and is created in the CDF file by using the **<CHANNEL>** and **<ITEM>** elements, which will represent the channel's content as well as its hierarchy.

When you design your channel, make sure there are no more than eight subitems within the first level. Not only will this prevent information overload for the subscriber, it will also reduce the download time needed to send the information. In addition, make sure your channels fall into one of the channel types, which will make it easier for the potential subscriber to understand exactly what type of content you're making available. After you've outlined the hierarchy and the type of channel your content falls into, you're ready to design the logos that will represent it.

Creating The Channel Logo Icons And Images

Channels rely on three different types of icons that appear in various locations within your Web site and within the user's desktop and Internet Explorer application. These logo icons and images make it easier for the subscriber to identify and locate the information within your channel both online and offline. Each of the following icons needs to be designed within a certain size to match the design of Internet Explorer:

- *Channels Explorer Bar*—Must be 32 pixels high by 192 pixels wide and appear in the Internet Explorer Channel pane. An example of this image is shown in Figure 20.3.

- *Desktop Channels Explorer Bar*—Must be 80 pixels high by 32 pixels wide and, as the name implies, appear on the user's Windows desktop. This image is shown in Figure 20.4.

- *Icons for each item in the channel subcategory*—Each icon must be 16 pixels high by 16 pixels wide. These icons appear in the Internet Explorer Channel pane to display the additional subcategories when the channel is expanded. This type of icon is shown in Figure 20.5.

Figure 20.3   The Channels Explorer Bar appears in the Channel pane located in the user's Internet Explorer application.

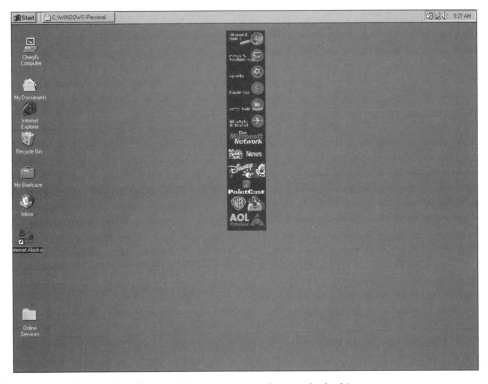

Figure 20.4   The desktop Channel Bar appears on the user's desktop.

Figure 20.5   These icons appear in the Internet Explorer Channel pane when the channel
is expanded.

It's imperative that you create these images and icons so your channel will display properly on the user's computer and within the user's version of Internet Explorer. Without them, the default icons Microsoft supplies will show instead, and your channel won't look much different than other channels. Each icon should have a transparent color background. The icons and images should also be fairly simplistic in design because they will occupy only a small amount of screen real estate. The code for including these elements is outlined in the CDF file in the following fashion:

```
<CHANNEL HREF="http://www.site.com/topchannel.html">
<LOGO HREF="http://www.site.com/explorerlogo.gif" STYLE="IMAGE-WIDE"/>
<!--This Logo is for the Channels Explorer Bar -->
<LOGO HREF="http://www.site.com/desktoplogo.gif" STYLE="IMAGE"/>
<!--This Logo is for the Desktop Channel Bar -->
<LOGO HREF="http://www.site.com/icon.gif" STYLE="ICON"/>
<!--This Logo is for the Channels Category Folder -->
    .
    .
    .
</CHANNEL>
```

Notice that you specify the images for each category. And for each top-level **<CHANNEL>** element, there should be three **LOGO** child elements. Each child element should contain a style attribute that defines the type of icon. Again, if you don't specify these images and icons, Microsoft supplies default images for each category.

Also, note that you supply the **STYLE="ICON"** attribute just in case the subscriber puts your Active Channel in a category folder. The icon then displays properly in the subscriber's Channel pane by appearing in the list of available channels in the Channels Explorer Bar when the group it represents is selected.

Creating The CDF File

After you have created the structure of your channel and designed all the logos and icons, you're ready to create the actual CDF file. This file, which describes the channel itself, is an XML application even though the syntax is very similar to HTML. Remember, however, that XML is extremely particular about syntax, and each tag must have a closing tag in order to make the CDF file a well-formed document. You also need to make sure all the quotes and slashes are in the right place and that you close out any open quotes.

Each CDF file must have at least one **<CHANNEL>** element that declares the channel and its elements. The **<CHANNEL>** element is used to define the top-level channel and any subitems that are nested below the main channel and are part of it. The **<CHANNEL> </CHANNEL>** tags are actually defining the hierarchy of the channel and its elements. Within the **<CHANNEL>** element, **<ITEM>** elements are used to specify which Web pages are part of the channel's content. You can update this information when you want to redefine or update the channel content.

After you specify the hierarchy with the **<CHANNEL>** element and the content with the **<ITEM>** elements, you must include the proper **<LOGO>** elements for each icon and image. The order in which you specify them is not important. Remember, however, if you don't specify them, Internet Explorer will use the default icons.

Notice that the following simple CDF file is declared as an XML file. Also notice where the icons and images are outlined with the **<LOGO>** element and the items for the channel content are tagged with the **<ITEM>** element:

```
<?XML Version="1.0"?>
  <CHANNEL HREF="http://www.site.com/mainpage.html">
  <ABSTRACT>This is a sample channel </ABSTRACT>
  <TITLE>Sample Channel</TITLE>
     <LOGO HREF="http://www.site.com/.ico" STYLE="icon" />
     <LOGO HREF="http://www.site.com/.gif" STYLE="image" />
     <LOGO HREF="http://www.site.com/-w.gif" STYLE="image-wide" />
      <ITEM HREF="http://www.microsoft.com/workshop/author/dhtml/">
       <ABSTRACT>Site Builder articles about
        Dynamic HTML</ABSTRACT>
       <TITLE>Dynamic HTML Articles</TITLE>
      </ITEM>
      <ITEM HREF="http://www.microsoft.com/workshop/prog/ie4/">
        <ABSTRACT>Site Builder articles about
         authoring for Internet Explorer 4.0</ABSTRACT>
       <TITLE>Internet Explorer 4.0 Technologies</TITLE>
      </ITEM>
</CHANNEL>
```

Uploading Or Posting The CDF File To The Web Server

To make it possible for people to subscribe to your Channel, you need to place the CDF file, the logo and graphics, and the content on a Web server and make sure the directory in which the files are stored is available to the public. Placing the CDF file along with the accompanying logo and graphic files and content is as simple as transferring a single file via FTP. You can upload files in a batch format using a standard FTP client, such as the one included with Windows 95 and Windows 98. Locate the directory where you'll place the files, and use the **MPUT** command to place multiple files on the Web server.

You can also use your Web browser to upload the files one at a time. Using the FTP protocol in the address of the URL, you can log on and specify the password and directory location. The URL would look like this:

```
ftp://username:password@ftp.site.com/directory/
```

You should replace *username* with the logon name you use to access the Web server. *Password* is the password assigned to your logon name. Replace *ftp.site.com* with the name of the Web server you are logging on to. The directory location where you will place the files is specified by */directory/*. Once you are logged on to the server, you can use the Web browser's File|Upload File command to upload files individually.

This chapter's Immediate Solutions section outlines the steps required to upload your CDF files. See "Adding The Channel To The Web Site."

Offering The Channel To Potential Subscribers

After you've placed the CDF file and the content on a publicly accessible Web server, you need to provide a mechanism for potential subscribers to not only find but also subscribe to the channel. Normally, subscribers can find your channel subscription button in one of the following formats:

- As a button image placed on one of your Web pages or sent via HTML email that links directly to the CDF file

- Through the Channel Guide, a guide offered by Microsoft that lists available channels

- Through the preinstalled set of channels listed in the Channel Bar in Internet Explorer

Microsoft recommends you use their Add Active Channel or Add To Active Desktop logo button to maintain a level of consistency. You can find these predefined logos on Microsoft's Site Builder Network site at **www.microsoft.com/snbmemeber/ielogo/default.asp**.

Channel Features

Channel content can be identical to standard Web page content. When you are designing channels, however, there are several guidelines you can follow to take advantage of the slightly different delivery mechanisms that Internet Explorer and Windows 98 offer through the Channel feature. Because you don't have control of the subscriber's bandwidth, the first thing to remember is that the information you deliver should accommodate the users who want to subscribe to the channel. This might mean sending information at non-peak hours, compacting information as much as possible, and warning users about large downloads.

CDF offers three features developers can use with Internet Explorer and Windows 98 to design channels that take advantage of the capabilities of CDF:

- Notification channels

- Site map options

- Offline content-caching features

Notification Channels

Notification channels do what their name implies: They notify the user that the channel information has changed and that new information is available. In addition to sending notifications of new information, notification channels send, via the CDF file, a site map of the channel in which the new information is located. The site map can be viewed offline, because the **PRECACHE** value for notification channels is set to **YES**. This lets the subscriber glimpse what that new data is without having to download all the channel content.

To indicate changes in channel content, you can use a red "gleam" flag that flashes, or you can make the logos or icons of the channel flash. You can also make the Windows toolbar flash if the Channel icon is displayed.

Subscribers can also request that an email message be sent to them when channel content has been updated. They can make the request through the Subscription wizard when they first subscribe to the channel or later when they change the options of the channel subscription. If the subscriber is using Microsoft Outlook, the main page of the channel content will be sent as well as notification of the changed content.

Site Map Options

Most Windows users are familiar with the Windows Explorer interface that displays directory content in a treelike structure. Because CDF is an XML application, and because XML uses the same type of tree structure, the Channels Explorer Bar can display an outline of all the available page URLs that are specified in the CDF file. The tree structure/outline is fully navigational and displays the **<ABSTRACT>** information for each **<ITEM>** element found in the CDF file. The subscriber can navigate through the channel and pick and choose what content to download. All the user needs to do is subscribe to the channel; the CDF file specifies what will be cached to the user's computer, and specifies what will be displayed in the channel's site map.

Offline Content-Caching Features

With CDF, the developer can specify that channel content be downloaded for offline or off-site viewing. By caching or downloading not only Web pages but also all graphics and scripts, the entire page will render properly even though the subscriber isn't connected to the Internet. The user can browse through the entire content of a channel regardless of whether he or she is connected to the Internet or to the intranet that served the original channel content. However, the user must specify during the subscription process that caching is allowed. This is done by selecting the Download Content option in the channel's Subscription Wizard.

Active Channel Types

You can create a variety of channel types to facilitate delivery of information. Microsoft recommends that you fit your channel content into one of four categories:

- Immersion channels
- Notification channels
- News channels
- Hybrid channels

TIP: *For more information about channel content development, make sure you check out Microsoft's Site Builder Network at **www.microsoft.com/sitebuilder**. Click the link for content information at the bottom of the screen or in the toolbar at the top of the screen.*

Immersion Channels

Immersion channels are not too difficult to explain because their name clarifies exactly what this type of channel should provide—an immersion into the total content of the channel. You could use an immersion channel for an online game, a serialized soap opera, or a report on a particular topic.

Typically, all of an immersion channel's content will be precached to the subscriber's site so the channel can be browsed offline. Therefore, you should consider the subscriber's bandwidth constraints when you are designing the content.

> **WARNING!**   *Because you can specify other resources, such as ActiveX controls, Dynamic HTML (DHTML), scripts, and graphic files, all channel content should be designed for offline browsing and not have external references that need to be shown.*

Because the channel is meant to immerse the subscriber into all of its content, its items and subchannels should not appear in the Channels Explorer Bar. However, all the elements should be precached so the subscriber is not required to reconnect to the Internet to continue exploring the channel. The CDF file is used mainly to specify what content needs to be downloaded and when the subscriber will be notified that the content is updated. In the CDF file, the developer should specify a list of items that need to be updated and the schedule to update them. Each item in the CDF file must include the following child element:

```
<USAGE VALUE="None"></USAGE>
```

It's this child element that tells the browser not to display the channel's subchannel or any other item in the Channels Explorer Bar. However, the element does allow for the subchannel items to download and cache the content to the subscriber's computer. See "Creating An Immersion Channel" in this chapter's Immediate Solutions section for instructions on how to define an immersion channel.

Notification Channels

Notification channels also do what their name implies: They notify the user that content has been updated for a particular channel. A site map is sent to the subscriber when the notification is sent, so the subscriber can quickly access the desired content. However, the site map does not include the actual content. Instead, the **PRECACHE** attribute of each subchannel is set to **"NO"** because a notification channel is only meant to notify.

When you create a notification channel, each item and subchannel should be displayed in the Channels Explorer Bar. Either the **<ABSTRACT>** or subscription information should alert the subscriber that only the outline of the notification channel is sent to his or her computer, not the entire content of each subchannel. This type of channel is only set to notify the subscriber of the updated content. For instructions on how to create this type of channel, see "Creating A Notification Channel" in this chapter's Immediate Solutions section.

News Channels

This channel type is also self-explanatory. According to Microsoft, a news channel provides breaking news to its subscribers. It should provide a hierarchical structure with a list of other channel items available through the CDF file. This information can be cached to the subscriber's machine for offline viewing.

News channels can use all three channel capabilities: notification, a site map, and offline caching content. The site map capability provides an overview of all the late-breaking news available in the channel. The offline caching content allows the subscriber to view both the site map and the channel content offline. You would use the notification capabilities to place a gleaming icon on the subscriber's desktop or to send the subscriber an email message.

TIP: *A good example of a news channel is Microsoft's own MSNBC channel. You can subscribe to MSNBC's news channel at **www.msnbc.com**.*

Microsoft suggests the following guidelines for developing a news channel:

- Each news item page should be small and consist of only the most important text. Each page should have minimal graphics or reuse existing graphics.

- Each news item should be self-contained and dedicated to a single news story. Instead of using frames, you should use DHTML whenever possible.

Also, the **<TITLE>** elements of the story should specify the news item headline, and the **<ABSTRACT>** element should summarize the content of the story.

For more information, see "Creating A News Channel" in this chapter's Immediate Solutions section.

Hybrid Channels

Hybrid channels are a mix between news, immersion, and notification channels. For example, you can create a notification channel that provides news. Or you can create a Web site that is an immersion channel that also provides news. When you define a hybrid channel, you do so using the **<CHANNEL>** element, the **<ITEM>** element, and nested **<CHANNEL>** and **<ITEM>** elements.

When you develop a hybrid channel, you should remember to minimize the strain on bandwidth. You should also define those items that can be browsed offline and those that should only be accessed online.

Channel Delivery Mechanisms

You can use three different delivery mechanisms to push data to the user:

• Screen savers

• HTML email

• Desktop items

Screen Savers

Screen savers can deliver limited channel information to the user's screen. Internet Explorer allows HTML pages and files saved in the SCR format to be displayed on the subscriber's screen in the form of a screen saver. Any type of HTML tag can be used to define the content shown on the user's screen. Animated GIFs, DHTML, and even JavaScript can be used in the channel content and viewed through the screen saver.

When the user subscribes to a channel that offers a screen saver as an **<ITEM>** of the **<CHANNEL>** element, the Channel Screen Saver dialog box appears. The user can then select to have the information delivered through the screen saver or through another method.

The option to replace the existing screen saver with the channel's screen saver can be selected at any time, not just during the subscription process. The Channel Screen Saver can be selected as the default screen saver. First, you would right-click on the Windows desktop, then select Properties from the pop-up menu.

Next, you select Display Properties and click the Screen Saver tab. Select the Channel option in the list of screen savers. When the user selects the Channel Screen Saver as the default screen saver, Internet Explorer will rotate through all the screen savers provided by the channel.

In order to identify the HTML page content as a screen saver, the developer must identify it as an **<ITEM>** element in the CDF file. The **USAGE** value of **<ITEM>** is what determines that the **<ITEM>** element will be a screen saver. The **<US-AGE>** value is actually considered an empty element. The **USAGE VALUE** attribute describes the content as a screen saver. There is no content for the **<USAGE>** element. Here's the code you would use:

```
<ITEM
HREF="http://www.site.com/screensavers/default.htm">
<USAGE VALUE="ScreenSaver">
</USAGE>
</ITEM>
```

HTML Email

Subscribers have the option of receiving email notifications when the channel's content has been updated. The user can choose this option through the Subscription wizard, and by default, Internet Explorer will send an HTML-formatted email. The HTML message will include a link to the top-level channel page. If the subscriber's email client is Outlook Express, the actual top-level page will be sent and will load when the content is updated.

As with screen savers, HTML email is specified in the **<ITEM>** element in the top-level channel in the CDF file. The code for HTML email looks almost identical to the code for specifying a screen saver, with one exception: the **USAGE VALUE**. In the **USAGE VALUE** attribute, you simply specify that the value is **"Email"**. Here's the code snippet:

```
<ITEM
HREF="http://www.site.com/screensavers/default.htm">
<USAGE VALUE="Email">
</USAGE>
</ITEM>
```

Desktop Items

With the introduction of Internet Explorer and Windows 98, a new option called the Active Desktop now gives developers the ability to code information directly to the user's Windows desktop. This feature, called *desktop items*, lets the user receive information without launching a browser or opening an email client. Desktop items, previously called desktop components, require a separate CDF file. The **<USAGE>** element takes on a number of child elements that are specific to desktop items.

Users subscribe to desktop items the same way they would subscribe to any channel, through a Subscription wizard. As with channels, the top-level **<ITEM>** element's **HREF** value specifies the main page of the desktop item's content.

Elements for a desktop item help define the size of the item, the ability of the item to move, and whether the item can be resized. They also specify how the item will be interpreted and opened if the user double-clicks on it. The following elements are specific to desktop items:

- **OPENAS**—Specifies the file format in which the item opens. The two allowed values for this element are **"HTML"**, which is the default if no value is specified, or **"Image"**.

- **HEIGHT**—Specifies the height of the item as it appears on the Active Desktop.

- **WIDTH**—Specifies the width of the item as it appears on the Active Desktop.

- **CANRESIZE**—Specifies whether the user can resize the item once it has been loaded onto the user's Active Desktop.

Other elements that can be used for—but are not specific to—desktop items include **<SCHEDULE>**, **<TITLE>**, and **<ITEM>**. You can use the **<SCHEDULE>** element to specify the schedule for updating content to the user's desktop. **<TITLE>** specifies the title that appears in the Web tag of the Desktop Properties dialog box and the Favorites|Subscription window.

TIP: *As you may have already guessed, the DesktopCompoment value is what determines whether an element will be a screen saver, desktop item, or email message.*

The code for defining a desktop item would look something like this (notice that **USAGE VALUE** is set to **"DesktopComponent"**):

```
<?XML version="1.0"?>
<CHANNEL>
<SCHEDULE STARTDATE="1999-01-01">
<INTERVALTIME DAY="7"/>
<EARLIESTTIME HOUR="0"/>
<LATESTTIME HOUR="5"/>
</SCHEDULE>

<ITEM HREF="http://www.site.com/channels/items/default.htm"
PRECACHE="YES">
```

```
<TITLE>Daily Stock Quotes</TITLE>
<USAGE VALUE="DesktopComponent">
<OPENAS VALUE="HTML"/>
<HEIGHT VALUE="200"/>
<WIDTH VALUE="420"/>
<CANRESIZE VALUE="YES"/>
</USAGE>
</ITEM>
</CHANNEL>
```

TIP: The **PRECACHE** element you've seen in the various delivery mechanism code examples specifies whether items other than the HTML page will be downloaded to the user's cache. For example, you might have several logo files, a photo, and an animated GIF that make up the top-level main page of the channel. If you set this element's value to **YES**, all the items associated with the Web page are cached locally and the page can be viewed offline.

Design Guidelines For Channels

According to Microsoft, to take advantage of CDF, which is a true push technology, you should follow several guidelines for developing channels. These guidelines include:

- Develop channels so that they conform to the type of Active Channels outlined by Microsoft and described in "Active Channel Types" earlier in this chapter.

- Match the size of the content to the delivery capabilities of the subscribers. You should figure out how much data an average user can download in a few minutes. For example, if a subscriber is using a modem, the amount of data you supply should be far less than if the user were on an Ethernet network, passing data at 10 to 100 megabits per second.

- Ensure that the channels are self-contained and don't require content from other sources that may not be online all the time.

- Use one of the three channel capabilities: notification, offline caching, or site map. This allows you to create channels and deliver the information in the way the user requests it.

Let's examine each channel design guideline in more detail.

Channels Should Conform To Active Channel Types

The channel you design should conform to one of the Active Channel types: news, immersion, notification, or hybrid. If you follow the guidelines, the channel can be categorized properly in Microsoft's Channel Guide.

Channels Content Should Match Bandwidth Constraints

Because the content of so many different types of channels can be viewed offline, you need to be aware of the bandwidth constraints your channel imposes, not only on your subscriber's connections, but also on your own connections. For example, if you set up a news channel, you need to ensure that it doesn't contain so much graphics and content that you end up overloading your network and your subscribers end up spending hours downloading your channel content to their computers. Remember that 1MB of data takes about 6 minutes to download using a 28.8Kbps modem. On its Site Builder Network (**www.microsoft.com/sitebuilder**), Microsoft has included a table that outlines the size and speed at which various channels can be downloaded with a simple 28.8Kbps dial-up connection. We've included their estimates in Table 20.1.

Channels Should Be Self-Contained

All content in a channel should be self-contained so it can be browsed offline. If it's not self-contained, subscribers may find that subitems are unavailable or their system is constantly reconnecting to fetch the content that isn't cached. According to Microsoft, you should minimize, hide, or consider not including links to noncached resources, particularly for content meant to be browsed offline. CGI scripting, DHTML, or JavaScript can be used to determine when the subscriber is offline. If the subscriber is offline, the script could perform functions to redisplay the data and check to see when the subscriber gets back online so the information could then be updated automatically.

You should reuse as many graphic elements as possible throughout the channel's site map. Use highly minimized graphics when you can. If you don't know how to strip colors out of graphic files or compress photos so they are optimized for downloading, you should consider either learning how or buying graphic-optimizing programs such as Emblaze.

Table 20.1   Average download times for channels.

Number of Channels	500K Content	1MB Content
2	From 6 to 10 minutes	From 12 to 20 minutes
4	From 12 to 20 minutes	From 24 to 40 minutes
8	From 24 to 39 minutes	From 49 to 80 minutes
12	From 36 to 59 minutes	From 73 to 120 minutes

Channels Should Be Personalized

With the use of cookie technology, it is relatively easy to create a personalized browsing experience for each subscriber. According to Microsoft, you should personalize channels whenever possible so that subscribers feel they are getting more than just content they could get by browsing a typical Web site. By using HTTP cookies to generate a personalized CDF file, channel information can be sent faster, because content that is not applicable to the subscriber is not sent. Only pertinent information is sent. See "Using Cookies To Create Personalized Channels" in this chapter's Immediate Solutions section for more information.

Developing For Netcaster

In theory, because CDF and HTML are so similar, browsers other than Microsoft Internet Explorer (such as Netscape Navigator) should be able interpret the information found in the CDF file and parse it to the subscriber. However, as you may have guessed, there are issues that prevent full cross-browser compatibility. Netscape uses its own push technology—called Netcaster—to accommodate push information. When you are designing the CDF file and its accompanying content, you should be aware of the compatibility issues between the two browsers.

First, Netcaster cannot use the CDF file for full processing, because it does not fully implement CDF as an XML application. However, Netcaster can use the CDF file to crawl the site, which means it retrieves and processes information for the user. The process differs only slightly from the process of retrieving information for a channel subscription:

1. An HTML page is retrieved.
2. The page is cached locally on the user's system.
3. The browser locates the links in the page.
4. For each link specified in the page, the browser retrieves and caches pages until all links have been followed or when the process has been repeated enough times, which is specified by certain criteria.
5. Non-HTML documents are retrieved for each link that specifies either an image file or a text file.

Netcaster uses the CDF file as if it was a standard HTML page to gather the information about where to crawl the site but not for full CDF processing. For Netcaster to know where to start, however, an anchor element must be placed within the **<ITEM>** and **<CHANNEL>** elements of the CDF file. You specify this anchor element as you would any other normal anchor element. For example, the following anchor element would provide Netcaster with the information needed to start crawling the site:

```
<A HREF="http://www.site.com/netcaster/default.html">Welcome to Our Site</a>
```

The anchor element defines which links Netcaster should follow. The rest of the information found in the CDF file is normally ignored. The anchor element is nested inside the **<ITEM>** and **<CHANNEL>** elements of the CDF file. The anchor element identifies which pages are displayed when the items and channels are selected. The CDF file would look something like this:

```
<CHANNEL>
<A HREF="http://www.site.com/netcaster/mainpage.htm"></A>
<ITEM>
<A HREF="http://www.site.com/netcaster/page1.htm"></A>
<TITLE>This is Page 1 of the Site</TITLE>
</ITEM>
<ITEM>
<A HREF="http://www.site.com/netcaster/page2.htm"></A>
<TITLE>This is Page 2 of the Site</TITLE>
</ITEM>
</CHANNEL>
```

To use a CDF file to crawl a site, Netcaster must process the file as an HTML file. The CDF file must have either the .HTML or .HTM extension, and the server storing the CDF file must return the MIME (content) type as "**text/html**" to the non-CDF-enabled browser. Also, the browser must be configured so that the MIME type for CDF files—specified in the browser as the "**cdf**" file type needing the "**application/x-cdf**" definition—is set to open as HTML.

TIP: *In order for CDF files to be processed correctly to CDF-enabled browsers, the MIME (content)* **"application/x-cdf"** *must be set on the server.*

When the browser uses the CDF file, it identifies the links in the **<ITEM>** element—such as mainpage.htm, page1.htm, and page2.htm—and crawls these pages. Much of the CDF file will be ignored. For example, Netcaster will not use the **BASE** attribute of the CDF file. Relative URLs are resolved by Netcaster against the base URL instead of the **BASE** attribute. You may decide to omit the **BASE** attribute or, if you want, use the **BASE** attribute to make sure the name is the same as the base URL of the CDF file.

Once these options have been set on both the server and browser, the user can use Netcaster to subscribe to a channel defined by the CDF file. The subscription process is the same as the one used with Internet Explorer, with one exception. The user doesn't enter the URL for the CDF file. If the user specifies the URL of a CDF file, the initial page for the channel is not a normal HTML page. Instead, it is an HTML file rendered as an HTML page. The page will probably not appear correctly because the CDF file is not formatted for displaying HTML-formatted information.

Subscribing To CDF Files With Netcaster

The process of subscribing to a CDF-defined channel with Netcaster is the same as the process of subscribing to a channel, which is actually a Web page or Web site in Netcaster. However, if the user specifies the URL of the CDF file, the initial page of the channel is obviously not an HTML file. This means the page will not render properly in Netcaster. You can fix this problem by creating a transitory Web page that represents the channel content and contains a reference to the CDF file.

To make this transitory page and have it display properly in Netcaster, you can use Netscape's **<LAYER>** tag. With a hidden **<LAYER>** tag that references the new CDF file, users can use the transitory page rather than the URL of the CDF file when they subscribe. Use the following code to create the reference to the CDF file using the **<LAYER>** tag:

```
<LAYER SRC="cdf_file.html" VISIBILTY =HIDDEN></LAYER>
```

To subscribe to the channel automatically, the user clicks the Subscription button on the transitory page. See "Creating A CDF File For Netcaster Users" in this chapter's Immediate Solutions section for the code and instructions on how to create the CDF file and the transitory page.

Examining The CDF Vocabulary

The best way to learn the CDF vocabulary is to look at an example of a CDF file. The CDF file serves to define the structure of the channel in much the same format HTML defines a Web page. Remember, however, because CDF is an XML application, all tags must have ending tags and all quotes must have closing quotes. There are four main elements in each CDF file:

- *The document header*—Defines the file as an XML file and specifies the version of XML used.
- *The channel element*—Identifies the main page of the channel and all information about the subpages contained within the channel.
- *The software*—Uses the **SoftwareUpdate** value for the **<USAGE>** element to specify what software will be downloaded.

- *The <ABSTRACT> and <TITLE> elements*—Provide navigational aides. The **<TITLE>** element helps the user identify the title of the channel (which is displayed in the list of channels). The **<ABSTRACT>** element defines the tooltip that displays when the user moves the mouse over the channel logo in the Channels Explorer Bar in Internet Explorer.

- *The logo element*—Defines the two different logos and the individual icon displayed in the Channels Explorer Bar, Active Desktop, and the Channel listing.

- *The item element*—Defines the subpages used in the channel.

The Individual Elements And Their Attributes

In Chapter 1, you learned about markup languages and how they work. Now, you can put that information to good use. The following elements (and their attributes) were created by Microsoft developers using the XML syntax. These elements, which define the CDF XML application, are relatively simple, and their attributes are fairly limited. We've alphabetized the elements and noted in their definitions where they would be placed in the CDF file.

<ABSTRACT> Tag

The **<ABSTRACT>** tag represents what is displayed in the tooltip, the pop-up text that displays when the user moves the mouse over the channel logo in the Channels Explorer Bar in Internet Explorer. The tooltip is displayed when the user moves the cursor over the channel or item title.

The **<ABSTRACT>** tag

```
<ABSTRACT="VALUE"></ABSTRACT>
```

has no attributes and is placed within the **<CHANNEL>** element section or within the **<ITEM>** subsection.

You should always place the **<ABSTRACT>** element after the channel element or before any nested **<ITEM>** or **<CHANNEL>** children, and you should follow every start **<ABSTRACT>** tag with an end tag, **</ABSTRACT>**. The following code is an example of how the **<ABSTRACT>** tag is used:

```
<ABSTRACT>This article describes how to create a CDF file.</ABSTRACT>
<CHANNEL>
<ABSTRACT>This channel provides information about my Web site.</ABSTRACT>
</CHANNEL>
```

<CHANNEL> Tag
The **<CHANNEL>** tag identifies the main page of the channel:

```
<CHANNEL BASE=URL HREF=URL
LASTMOD=DATE LEVEL=Number
PRECACHE=YES or NO></CHANNEL>
```

The **<CHANNEL></CHANNEL>** section contains the information about the channel's subpages. The channel attributes include:

- **BASE**
- **HREF**
- **LASTMOD**
- **LEVEL**
- **PRECACHE**

The **<CHANNEL>** element defines the channel, all its subchannels, and other elements and attributes. The channel is defined by whatever is placed within the first occurrence of the start- and end-tags, **<CHANNEL></CHANNEL>**. Every channel element contained within the top-level channel represents a subchannel, which is actually a subfolder. Subchannels are used to create the hierarchy of the channel items.

The **BASE** attribute is used to specify the relative URL that the **<ITEM>** and **<CHANNEL>** subelements might use. If declared, the **BASE** attribute applies to all the child elements within the current channel. If a URL has already been specified by a parent **<CHANNEL>** element, the **BASE** value supersedes the defined URL. The URL must end with a trailing **/** or the last word will be removed.

The **HREF** attribute specifies a location and instructs the browser to navigate to that location when the user activates the channel. This attribute should be omitted if the **<CHANNEL>** element contains an anchor **<A>** as a child element.

The **LASTMOD** attribute specifies the date and time the page indexed by the **HREF** attribute was modified. This date is specified in Greenwich mean time (GMT), also known as Universal Time Coordinated (UTC). The **LASTMOD** value is the time the page was last modified. This time may or may not be your local time depending upon whether you are in the same time zone as the system that is modifying the page. This attribute is used to help the client determine whether the content has changed since the last time the channel content was downloaded. The item is downloaded only if the date associated with the cached item is older than the **LASTMOD** value in the CDF file. The date format used in the **LASTMOD** attribute is yyyy-mm-dd hh:mm, such as 1999-01-01 12:01.

The **LEVEL** attribute value specifies the number of links deep the client should crawl the site and precache the content specified in the **HREF** attribute of the channel. If no value is set, the default is zero, which specifies that the browser should only cache the top-level content of the channel.

The **PRECACHE** attribute specifies whether the content should be downloaded and cached on the subscriber's computer. The content will be downloaded only if subscribers specify when they first subscribe to the channel that channel content should cached. If the value is set to **NO**, the content is not cached. If the value is set to **YES** or omitted, the content is cached to the subscriber's computer.

TIP: *For additional information about any CDF element, check out Microsoft's Site Builder Network, located at* ***www.microsoft.com/sitebuilder****.*

Here is an example of how the channel element code looks:

```
<CHANNEL>
<A HREF="http://www.site.com/netcaster/mainpage.htm"></A>
<ITEM>
<A HREF="http://www.site.com/netcaster/page1.htm"></A>
<TITLE>This is Page 1 of the Site</TITLE>
</ITEM>
<ITEM>
<A HREF="http://www.site.com/netcaster/page2.htm"></A>
<TITLE>This is Page 2 of the Site</TITLE>
</ITEM>
</CHANNEL>
```

<EARLIESTTIME> Tag

The **<EARLIESTTIME>** element specifies the earliest time the channel content can be updated:

```
<EARLIESTTIME DAY=Value HOUR=Value MIN=Value/>
```

If no value is set, the time is based on the value of **INTERVALTIME**. The days, hour, and minutes are then totaled to determine the offset value of **INTERVALTIME**.

The **DAY** attribute specifies the first day within the schedule you've created using the **INTERVALTIME** attribute. The **HOUR** attribute specifies the first hour within the schedule you've created using the **INTERVALTIME** attribute. The **MIN** attribute specifies the minute used in the schedule you've specified.

<HTTP-EQUIV> And <LOGTARGET> Tags

The **<HTTP-EQUIV>** tag would be used in creating the channel much like the following example:

```
<HTTP-EQUIV NAME=HEADERPARAMETER VALUE=TEXT/>
```

You can supply information to the server through the HTTP response headers via the **<LOGTARGET>** element. This element indicates that an HTTP header parameter should be added. The **NAME** attribute specifies the name of the HTTP header parameter that should be sent with the log file. For example, you may want to send the value **"encoding-type"** when you are sending back a compressed log file to the server. The **VALUE** attribute specifies the value of the corresponding parameter. The following example shows how to send a compressed log file back to the server:

```
<LOGTARGET HREF="http://www.mysite.com/logging/" METHOD="POST">
    <HTTP-EQUIV NAME="encoding-type" VALUE="gzip" />
</LOGTARGET>
```

<INTERVALTIME> Tag

The **<INTERVALTIME>** element specifies the period of time that should pass before the schedule is repeated:

```
<INTERVALTIME DAY=VALUE HOUR=VALUE MIN=VALUE/>
```

The days, hours, and minutes are totaled to determine the length of the interval. **DAY** specifies the number of days that should pass, and the **HOUR** and **MIN** values are added. Any **<INTERVALTIME>** value greater than half a day but less than a day will always be rounded up to a day. This element is a required child element of **<SCHEDULE>** and must always contain a value to be considered valid.

The following code demonstrates how a channel will be updated every day between 10 A.M. and 2 P.M. during the month of December:

```
<SCHEDULE STARTDATE="1997-12-01" STOPDATE="1997-12-31">
<INTERVALTIME DAY="1" />
<EARLIESTTIME HOUR="10" />
<LATESTTIME HOUR="14" />
</SCHEDULE>
```

<ITEM> Tag

The **<ITEM>** element defines an item within a channel:

```
<ITEM HREF=URL LASTMOD=DATE LEVEL=VALUE PRECACHE="YES" | "NO" ></ITEM>
```

<ITEM> can represent any type of information, but it is almost always a Web page. In the Channels Explorer bar, an **<ITEM>** will appear in a hierarchy pertaining to the child/subelement relationships of the **<CHANNEL>**. If you do not want the **<ITEM>** to show up in the Active Channels Explorer Bar, you can specify the **<USAGE>** element included as a child element of the **<ITEM>** by setting the attribute **VALUE** to **"NONE"**.

The **HREF** attribute is required and represents the channel. When the subscriber clicks on the channel item, which was created using the <**ITEM**> element, the browser navigates to the location specified in the attribute of the <**ITEM**> element. There can only be one **HREF** attribute with each <**ITEM**> element.

The **LASTMOD** attribute specifies the date and time the Web page specified in the **HREF** attribute was last modified. The **LASTMOD** attribute is specified in the form yyyy-mm-ddThh:mm.

The **LEVEL** attribute specifies the number of links or levels deep the client should crawl and cache the Web site and graphics from within the location specified in the **HREF** attribute. If the default of "**NONE**" is specified, the client will cache only the Web page of the item and the images it references. If the Web page contains frames, the client also retrieves all content inside the frames. The **PRECACHE** specification indicates whether the content should be cached on the subscriber's computer.

> **WARNING!** *You must specify the end-tag </ITEM> for the <ITEM> element to be processed properly.*

The following code shows how the <**ITEM**> element could be used:

```
<ITEM HREF="http://www.site.com/mainpage.html" LASTMOD="1999-10-11T10:30">
<TITLE>
Welcome to this page.
</TITLE>
<ABSTRACT>Information on this page.
</ABSTRACT>
</ITEM>
```

<LATESTTIME> Tag

The <**LATESTTIME**> element specifies the latest time during <**INTERVALTIME**> that the schedule will be applied and updated:

```
<LATESTTIME DAY=VALUE HOUR=VALUE MIN=VALUE/>
```

This element totals the days and minutes to determine the value from <**INTERVALTIME**> that represents the latest valid time to update a channel. If you omit it, the latest time is set to the beginning of the <**INERVALTIME**> value.

The **DAY** attribute specifies the number of days to which the schedule applies. The **HOUR** attribute specifies the number of hours, and the **MIN** attribute specifies the number of minutes. If you specify **VALUE="document:view/">**, the URL of the parent <**ITEM**> element should be recorded as a page hit in the log.

The following code outlines how the **<LATESTTIME>** element would be used in a channel:

```
<ITEM  HREF="http://www.foosports.com/promotion.htm">
<LOG VALUE="document:view"/>
</ITEM>
```

<LOGIN> Tag

The **<LOGIN>** element specifies that the channel requires authentication for updates. A CDF file containing this element will prompt the user for a name and password during the channel subscription process. The way in which you would specify this element is demonstrated in the following code:

```
<LOGIN />
```

<LOGO> Tag

The <**LOGO**> element specifies an image that can be used to represent a channel or channel item:

```
<LOGO HREF=URL STYLE="ICON" | "IMAGE" | "IMAGE-WIDE" />
```

The **HREF** attribute specifies the URL associated with the channel log or the icon image. Table 20.2 lists the values that can be associated with the **STYLE** attribute.

TIP: *GIF, JPEG, and other standard image formats supported by Internet Explorer can be used for logo images. However, animated GIF files are not supported with this element. Image formats and styles are subject to change.*

Here is an example of the code used to specify a logo image:

```
<LOGO HREF="http://www.site.com/images/logo.gif" STYLE="IMAGE"/>
```

Table 20.2   STYLE values you can specify.

Value	Size	What The Image Represents
ICON	16H×16W	Appears in the Channels Explorer Bar hierarchy.
IMAGE	32H×80W	Placed in the desktop Channels Bar to provide a quick launching mechanism for the main channel page.
IMAGE-WIDE	32H×194W	Wide logos are displayed in the Channels Explorer Bar to provide a link to the main channel page. When clicked on, this image will also expand or contract the channel's hierarchy (if one exists) in the Channels Explorer Bar.

More On <LOGTARGET> And The <LOG> Tag

The **<LOGTARGET>** and **<LOG>** tags provide you with a mechanism for track-ing the number of hits to the individual channel pages you've created:

```
<LOGTARGET HREF="url" METHOD="POST" SCOPE="ALL" | "OFFLINE" | "ONLINE" >
```

Pages are tracked even while they are being viewed offline. Viewing is logged with the World Wide Web Consortium (W3C) Standard Extended Log File For-mat, which is initially stored on the user's machine and later sent back and posted to the server during subsequent channel updates. These two tags, **<LOGTARGET>** and **<LOG>**, are required in order for page-view logging to be enabled.

The **<LOGTARGET>** tag is always located in the top-level **<CHANNEL>** ele-ment and defines where the logged information is stored. There are three attributes used with this tag: **HREF**, **METHOD**, and **SCOPE**. The **<LOGTARGET>** tag's **HREF** attribute specifies the directory where the log file is posted. The **METHOD** attribute then specifies the transmission method used to post the file. At the time of this writing, **"POST"** is the only method supported, although that may change in the future. The **SCOPE** attribute specifies whether logging will occur when pages are viewed offline (**"OFFLINE"**), online (**"ONLINE"**), or both (**"ALL"**). In the following code example, the page is tracked, even though it's viewed offline:

```
<LOGTARGET HREF="http://www.site.com/logs/channelog.pl"
METHOD="POST" SCOPE="OFFLINE">
<PURGETIME=HOUR="12" />
</LOGTARGET>
```

TIP: *You can use a variety of methods to process log files, including Perl scripts or Microsoft Internet Information Server's ISAPI DLL.*

Each individual item to be logged needs to be marked with a **<LOG>** child ele-ment. At the time of this writing, only **"DOCUMENT:VIEW"** is a loggable user activity. Specify the **<LOG>** item as follows:

```
<LOG VALUE="DOCUMENT:VIEW"/>
```

<PURGETIME> Tag

The **<PURGETIME>** element would look something like this when placed within a CDF file:

```
<PURGETIME HOUR=VALUE/>
```

When the log file is being uploaded, any page hits older than the value specified by **<PURGETIME>** will not be reported. The **HOUR** attribute specifies the number of hours for which the logging information is considered valid.

The **<SCHEDULE>** element used within a CDF file would look something like this:

```
<SCHEDULE STARTDATE="1999-09-22">
```

The **<SCHEDULE>** tag allows you to set the frequency and time for subscribers to receive channel updates. Channel updates involve downloading and saving or precaching the content specified in the **<CHANNEL>** and **<ITEM>** elements on a client machine. Updating also includes sending page-hit logging information to the target server specified in the **<LOGTARGET>** element. The following attributes can be included with the **<SCHEDULE>** tag:

- **STARTDATE**—Specifies the day on which the schedule starts. If you omit this attribute, updating will start on the current day.

- **STOPDATE**—Specifies the day on which the updating expires.

- **TIMEZONE**—Specifies the time zone in which the update will occur.

- **INTERVALTIME**—Declares how often the update will occur.

- **EARLIESTTIME**—When used with the **INTERVALTIME** value, specifies the earliest time the updating schedule applies.

- **LATESTTIME**—When used with the **INTERVALTIME** value, specifies the latest time the updating schedule applies.

Place the **<SCHEDULE>** tag within the CDF file and specify the **<STARTDATE>**, **<INTERVALTIME>**, **<EARLIESTTIME>**, and **<LATESTTIME>** elements. The **<SCHEDULE>** tag must be placed within the top-level channel. Once the schedule is designated, all the channel items are updated at the same date and time according to the schedule outlined in the **<SCHEDULE>** elements. You can only set one schedule for a CDF file, and it's important to schedule the update for when your server load is lightest and the most bandwidth is free.

One element of the **<SCHEDULE>** tag, **<LATESTTIME>**, is a very important element to include if you want to reduce server overload. With **<LATESTTIME>**, you can set an interval, basically the latest time (**<LATESTTIME>**) minus the earliest time (**<EARLIESTTIME>**), during which subscribers' channel content will be updated at random. This prevents all subscribers from having all their channel content updated at exactly the same local time.

TIP: *Dates are specified as year-month-day, as in 1999-09-22.*

Speaking of time, the schedule is set to use the subscriber's local time zone. If you want to force updates of channel content to occur at a specific absolute time when you know the server is not in use, for example, you can use the optional **TIMEZONE** attribute of the **<SCHEDULE>** tag. **TIMEZONE** is expressed relative to Greenwich mean time.

The following code snippet gives you an example of a schedule that updates content weekly between midnight and noon starting on September 22, 1999:

```
<SCHEDULE STARTDATE="1999-09-22">
<INTERVALTIME DAY="7" />
<EARLIESTTIME HOUR="0"/>
<LATESTTIME HOUR="12" />
</SCHEDULE>
```

TIP: For those subscribers on local area networks (LANs), the AutoSchedule option will apply, but dial-up users may find that their systems, if left on, dial into the Internet unless they specify manual or custom-scheduled updates in the Channel Properties dialog box when they subscribe to your channel. Also remember that the end-tag **</SCHEDULE>** is required in order for the code to be valid.

After an update has taken place, if the CDF file has changed, the channel icon in the Channels Explorer Bar gleams. Figure 20.6 is an example of gleaming channel icons.

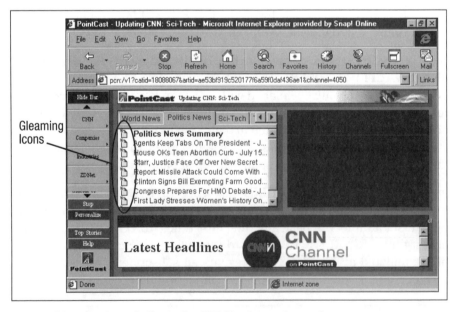

Figure 20.6   Gleaming icons indicate the CDF files have changed.

Again, a gleaming icon only appears if the CDF file has changed, indicating something has changed within the CDF file. No gleaming icon appears if the content has changed. If you want to use the gleaming icon as an indication of new content, you'll also need to modify the CDF file. But this doesn't mean you have to change the entire CDF file. Something as simple as adding a blank space to your CDF file and then saving it back to the server will cause the gleaming icon to appear. This is just one way to notify subscribers that the CDF file has changed. If the subscriber has requested an email notification in the Channel Properties dialog box, the email message will also receive a gleaming icon indicator.

<TITLE> Tag

The **<TITLE>** element when placed within a CDF file would look something like this:

```
<TITLE>A Day in the Life...</TITLE>
```

The **<TITLE>** tag defines the title of the channel content. There are no attributes to this tag. It's used much like the **<TITLE>** tag in an HTML document. For example, if you want to name your channel, "A Day In The Life...," you would include the following code within the **<CHANNEL>** element:

```
<CHANNEL>
<TITLE>A Day in the Life...</TITLE>
.
.
.
</CHANNEL>
```

<USAGE> Tag

The **<USAGE>** tag appears as the following:

```
<USAGE VALUE="Channel" | "Email" |
"DesktopComponent" | "NONE" | ScreenSaver"
| "SoftwareUpdate" >
```

There may be times when you want to specify additional files—such as sound or video files—to be downloaded and placed in the user's cache for later viewing offline. To do so, you would use the **USAGE VALUE="None"** element. This tells the browser that this item should be downloaded, but no usage is assigned to it at this point. The following code caches an AVI movie that can be played later:

```
<ITEM HREF="http://www.site.com/channel/movie.avi">
<USAGE VALUE="NONE"></USAGE>
</ITEM>
```

If you want to specify additional files for downloading, set the child items for the subchannel's **<USAGE>** tag to "**NONE**", outline each item, and set the **ITEM PRECACHE** attribute to "**YES**". The following code caches multiple items:

```
<CHANNEL>
<USAGE VALUE="NONE">
<ITEM HREF="http://www.site.com/channel/sound.wav" PRECACHE="YES">
<ITEM HREF="http://www.site.com/channel/movie.avi" PRECACHE="YES">
<ITEM HREF="http://www.site.com/channel/moresound.wav" PRECACHE="YES">
</USAGE>
</CHANNEL>
```

Table 20.3 contains a list of values for the **<USAGE>** element. Each value specifies the delivery-type mechanism you can use to deliver your content to the subscriber.

By now, you should realize exactly how pushy you can be, particularly with your Web-site content. The Channel Definition Format is one of the most exciting and easy-to-implement XML applications available. It extends the possibilities of your site by allowing users to receive information with little involvement. Channels are better than mailing lists because they offer the full content of a site instead of just the text, and they offer that content for offline browsing.

You can use the various predefined elements in the Channel Definition Format in the same fashion you would use any other XML elements. All the conventions used in XML are applicable, because CDF is an XML application. If you have a good grasp of XML, you can quickly and easily implement channel technology within your site and start offering personalized content to visitors you probably never knew you had.

Table 20.3   <USAGE> values.

Value	What The Value Does
Email	Specifies that the item listed is emailed when the channel content has been updated.
None	When used within an <ITEM> element, the <ITEM> element will not appear in the Channels Explorer Bar.
DesktopComponent	Specifies that items will be displayed in a frame on the subscriber's Active Desktop. You can only use this value within the context of an Active Desktop item. You need to use a separate CDF file when you use this value.
ScreenSaver	Specifies that the item will be displayed as a screen saver on the subscriber's computer.
SoftwareUpdate	Specifies that the CDF file is being used for a Software Update channel. Software Update channels let you send automatic software updates over the Web to the subscriber. You can only specify this value in a top-level channel.

Immediate Solutions

In this chapter, you learned what channels are, how CDF is actually an XML application, and both the user's and developer's perspectives in terms of implementing CDF. In this section, you'll create single-level and multilevel channels of various types. You'll also learn how to post your channel to your Web site. You'll learn how to check your channel to make sure the information is pushed to the subscriber's desktop. Then, you'll move on to more advanced topics, such as optimizing your channel for delivery over an HTTP sever.

Creating A Channel

In this section, you'll learn how to create a CDF file that will house all the items the user can subscribe to. You will set the intervals at which the channel will update the subscriber's machine with new content, and specify what logos will be used to indicate what your channel content contains.

Creating The CDF File

The CDF file defines the structure of the channel. You need to create the CDF file after you have created the content and know exactly what options you will offer your subscribers. The syntax of a CDF file is much like the syntax in any XML or HTML document. Remember, however, that XML files require the proper syntax to make sure elements have start- and end-tags, and references to attributes must be in the right case.

To create a CDF file, follow these steps:

1. Open your XML editor or a text editor, such as Notepad.

2. In the first line of the document, create the XML declaration that specifies that this is an XML document by typing the following code:

```
<?XML Version="1.0"?>
```

3. Next, specify where the top-level main page of the channel is located by typing the following code:

```
<CHANNEL HREF="http://www.site.com/channels/default.htm">
```

4. Use the **<ABSTRACT>** element as shown in this following code to define the text that displays for subscribers to see before they subscribe to the channel:

```
<ABSTRACT>This is a sample channel,
used in the CDF 101 article, which has
some Dynamic HTML information
</ABSTRACT>
```

5. Specify the channel's title:

```
<TITLE>The Channel Title</TITLE>
```

6. Specify the logo graphics for defining the channel's icons by typing the following code:

```
<LOGO HREF="channel.ico" STYLE="icon" />
<LOGO HREF="channel.gif" STYLE="image" />
<LOGO HREF="http://channel-w.gif" STYLE="image-wide" />
```

7. Use the **<ITEM>** element to specify the channel's subpages (the **<ITEM>** element defines the subpage and various **<ITEM>** information):

```
<ITEM HREF="http://www.site.com/channels/subpage.html">
<ABSTRACT>This is the subpage for the Channel</ABSTRACT>
<TITLE>Subpage Title</TITLE>
</ITEM>
```

8. Complete the XML file by specifying the channel end-tag:

```
</CHANNEL>
```

9. Use the .CDF extension to save the files as a CDF file.

TIP: *Remember to include references for pages if you plan to offer this channel to Netcaster users.*

Identifying The Main Page Or Channel Element

The main page of the channel is identified by the **<CHANNEL>** element, and the information about the channel's subpages is contained between the start-tag,

\<CHANNEL\>, and the end-tag, **\</CHANNEL\>**. In the opening **\<CHANNEL\>** tag, identify the URL of the channel's main page with the **HREF** attribute:

```
<CHANNEL HREF="http://www.site.com/channels/mainpage.html">
```

Describing The Channel And Its **\<ABSTRACT\>** And **\<TITLE\>** Elements

The **\<ABSTRACT\>** element appears as a tooltip when the subscriber moves the mouse over the channel logo in the Channels Explorer bar. It also helps relay information about what's contained in the channel. The **\<TITLE\>** element is a short description of what is displayed in the list of channels provided in the Favorites menu. The **\<ABSTRACT\>** and **\<TITLE\>** elements are used with both the **\<CHANNEL\>** element and the **\<ITEM\>** element. To define **\<ABSTRACT\>** and **\<TITLE\>** elements, type the following code after either the **\<CHANNEL\>** or **\<ITEM\>** element:

```
<TITLE>The Channel Title</TITLE>
<ABSTRACT>This is the abstract information.</ABSTRACT>
```

Describing The **\<ITEM\>** Element

The **\<ITEM\>** element helps define the channel's subpage. Within the **\<ITEM\>** element, specify the **HREF** attribute, which points to the URL of the subpage. The **\<ABSTRACT\>** and **\<TITLE\>** elements further define for the subscriber the information held within each **\<ITEM\>** by giving short descriptions of what will appear in the channel, via the Channels Explorer Bar and the tooltip. The code snippet used to define an **\<ITEM\>** subpage looks like this:

```
<ITEM HREF="http://www.site.com/channels/subpage.html">
  <ABSTRACT>The subpage for the Channel would be listed here.</ABSTRACT>
  <TITLE>The Channel Subpage</TITLE>
</ITEM>
```

Specifying The Logos For The Channels Explorer Bar

The **\<LOGO\>** element identifies the two logo images and one icon that will be used within the Channels Explorer Bar. The logo images should be saved in GIF format and the icon should be saved in ICO format. You should use images no more than 194×32 pixels wide and 80×32 high for the images and 16×16 pixels high and wide for the icon. The **\<LOGO\>** element does not have a content model specification, which means it does not have an end-tag. It is closed by placing a **/** at the end of the tag declaration.

TIP: *Microsoft recommends that you use a standard GIF file. If you don't have one or you don't want to make one, you can use theirs. You'll find the icons and graphics files at **www.microsoft.com/workshop/prog/ie4/channels/ addChan.gif**. The logo icon is the standard Add Channel GIF you might have seen on other Web sites.*

Here is the code you should use to specify both the images and icon graphics:

```
<LOGO HREF="http://www.site.com/channels/icon.ico" STYLE="icon" />
<LOGO HREF="http://site.com/channels/image1.gif" STYLE="image" />
<LOGO HREF="http://www.site.com/channels/image-w.gif" STYLE="image-wide" />
```

Specifying Content To Be Precached

Information that should be cached (such as content used with immersion channels) or any content that should be available for offline viewing needs to be specified by using the **<ITEM>** element's **PRECACHE** attribute. To define content that should be downloaded and cached on the subscriber's computer, use the following code:

```
<ITEM HREF="http://www.site.com/channels/subpage.html"
PRECACHE="YES">
<ABSTRACT>Abstract information for the page</ABSTRACT>
<TITLE>Page Title Information</TITLE>
</ITEM>
```

You can precache individual files by using the **USAGE VALUE** element/attribute. For example, you can precache sound files with the following code:

```
<ITEM HREF="http://www.site.com/channels/sound.wav">
  <USAGE VALUE="NONE"></USAGE>
</ITEM>
```

You can also precache multiple items by setting a subchannel's **USAGE VALUE** to "**NONE**" and then specifying the various child items:

```
<CHANNEL>
<USAGE VALUE="NONE">
<ITEM HREF=http://www.site.com/channels/sound1.wav PRECACHE="Yes">
<ITEM HREF=http:// www.site.com/channels/sound2.wav PRECACHE="Yes">
<ITEM HREF=http:// www.site.com/channels/sound3.wav PRECACHE="Yes">
</USAGE>
</CHANNEL>
```

Specifying The Delivery Schedule

You can set the frequency for channel-content updates by using the **<SCHEDULE>** element to specify the schedule. The code for setting the schedule is as follows:

```
<SCHEDULE STARTDATE="1999-01-01">
<INTERVALTIME DAY="7" />
<EARLIESTTIME HOUR="0" />
<LATESTTIME HOUR="12" />
</SCHEDULE>
```

This code defines a schedule to update the channel content once a week between midnight and noon starting January 1, 1999. **<LATESTTIME>** is definitely an element you should include. If you omit it, all users will have their channels updated at exactly the same local time, which can result in server overload.

You can set an interval by using the equation **<LATESTTIME>** minus **<EARLIESTTIME>**. This will update the content randomly, thereby reducing server load. All channel items are updated at the same date and time according to the schedule you've outlined. Only one schedule may be specified in a CDF file. After an update has taken place, the channel icon in the Channels Explorer Bar will gleam or an email message will be sent to the subscriber if the CDF file has changed.

TIP: *LAN-connected users will automatically adhere to the schedule for content updates that is defined in the CDF file. Dial-up users will need to update their channels manually or create a custom schedule in the Channel Properties dialog box when they subscribe to a channel.*

Adding The Channel To The Web Site

After you've created the CDF file, have the graphics for your various channel logos, and know where you want to place the channel, all that's left is to place the file on a Web (HTTP) server. Users can then subscribe to the channel by clicking on a link to the CDF file. Again, the link can be a text link or an icon with the **HREF** attribute specifying its value. It should be apparent to the user that the icon or text is a link to subscribe to the channel.

If you are not using a FrontPage-enabled Web server, you can use an FTP program or Internet Explorer to connect to your Web server and upload the channel. Specify the login name, password, FTP location, and directory in the Address field of the browser or open the folder for the site and it will open a new window.

Follow these steps to use Internet Explorer to upload the CDF file and all the accompanying graphics to the Web site:

1. Store CDF file, graphics, and content in a folder or subfolder. You may want to store the CDF file and the graphics in the main folder, and the actual content in the subfolder.

2. Connect to the Internet and launch Internet Explorer.

3. Type "ftp://login:password@ftpsite.com/directory/" in the Address field, substituting the login name, password, and directory locations with your own information.

4. Next, upload your CDF file, your icon graphic, your channel graphics, and the content. You'll have to upload your files individually, because browsers do not offer batch uploading options at this point.

Creating Various Types Of Channels

In this section, you'll learn how to create the various types of channels that Microsoft specifies. We will create immersion, notification, and news channels. You'll see how the channel types differ and what each channel does.

Creating An Immersion Channel

Each item in the CDF file of an immersion channel must include child elements with the **USAGE VALUE** element set to **"None"**. The following code is an example of a simple maze game. Different Web pages serve as the various hallways subscribers move through to find their way out. Here is the code for the CDF file:

```
<?XML version="1.0"?>
<CHANNEL HREF="startpage.html"
BASE="http://www.site.com/games/maze">

<TITLE>The Maze Game</TITLE>
<ABSTRACT>Find your way out of our maze!</ABSTRACT>
<LOGO HREF="maze16x16.gif" STYLE="ICON"/>
<LOGO HREF="maze32x80.gif" STYLE="IMAGE"/>

<SCHEDULE STARTDATE="1999-10-10" STOPDATE="1999-10-10">
<INTERVALTIME DAY="1"/>
</SCHEDULE>
```

```
<ITEM HREF="hallway1.html" LASTMOD="1999-10-10T11:00">
<USAGE VALUE="None"></USAGE>
</ITEM>

<ITEM HREF="hallway2.html" LASTMOD="1999-10-10T11:00">
<USAGE VALUE="None"></USAGE>
</ITEM>

<ITEM HREF="hallway3.html" LASTMOD="1999-10-10T11:00">
<USAGE VALUE="None"></USAGE>
</ITEM>

<ITEM HREF="hallway4.html" LASTMOD="1999-10-10T11:00">
<USAGE VALUE="None"></USAGE>
</ITEM>

<ITEM HREF="roomNN.html" LASTMOD="1999-10-10T11:00">
<USAGE VALUE="None"></USAGE>
</ITEM>

</CHANNEL>
```

We started this CDF file by declaring the channel, and then we declared the various items within the channel. The **<TITLE>** element specifies the game's title, and the **<ABSTRACT>** element displays descriptive information about the game. The **<SCHEDULE>** element specifies when new hallways will be updated. Each item defined specifies a hallway in the maze. Each time the CDF file is updated, the developer dynamically generates a new CDF file that creates new hallways. The developer could also modify existing hallways.

Creating A Notification Channel

The only purpose of a notification channel is to notify the subscriber of new content. Therefore, all items should display abstracts, but content should not be precached to the subscriber's computer. Suppose, for example, that you work in the human resources department and you want to notify employees about new employee benefits, changes in the payroll process, and upcoming company holidays. You can use a notification channel to tell employees there is new information in the human resources section on the company Web site. The following code is an example of how a CDF file for a notification channel is constructed:

```
<CHANNEL HREF="main.html"
<BASE-"http://www.site.com/notify/hr/" PRECACHE="NO">
```

```
<TITLE>Available HR Info</TITLE>
<ABSTRACT>Information about your human resources department.</ABSTRACT>
<LOGO HREF="logo16x16.gif" STYLE="ICON"/>
<LOGO HREF="logo32x80.gif" STYLE="IMAGE"/>

<SCHEDULE STARTDATE="1999-12-12" STOPDATE="1999-12-12">
<INTERVALTIME DAY="1"/>
</SCHEDULE>
</CHANNEL>
```

Creating A News Channel

News channels deliver information to subscribers in the form of stories. They are different than notification channels, because the content is actually cached to the subscribers computer and subchannels are used to define the various stories. You can use the **<ABSTRACT>** element to identify the information that is contained in the channel. The **<TITLE>** element defines the news story headline. Also, each page contains the same graphics, which creates the consistent look of a newspaper but alleviates the bandwidth requirement.

The CDF file creates the hierarchy and serves to organize the channel's items into subchannels, which are actually the individual stories. In this example, there is one channel, the Business Channel, and within it are the stories for one section. The CDF file looks like this:

```
<?XML version="1.0"?>
<CHANNEL HREF="news.html">
<BASE-"http://www.site.com/channels/news/">

<TITLE>Today's News</TITLE>
<ABSTRACT>Today's News delivered to your electronic doorstep.</ABSTRACT>
<LOGO HREF="logo16x16.gif" STYLE="ICON"/>
<LOGO HREF="logo32x80.gif" STYLE="IMAGE"/>

<SCHEDULE STARTDATE="1999-12-12" STOPDATE="1999-12-12">
<INTERVALTIME DAY="1"/>
</SCHEDULE>

<CHANNEL HREF="news1.html">
<TITLE> Business News</TITLE>
<ABSTRACT>Today's Business News</ABSTRACT>
<LOGO HREF="street.gif" STYLE="ICON"/>

<ITEM HREF="news2.html" LASTMOD="1999-10-10T11:00">
<TITLE>
<ABSTRACT>
```

```
<LOGO HREF="bizlogo.gif" STYLE="ICON"/>
</ITEM>

<ITEM HREF="news3.html" LASTMOD="1999-10-10T11:00">
<TITLE>
<ABSTRACT>
<LOGO HREF="bizlogo.gif" STYLE="ICON"/>
</ITEM>
</CHANNEL>
</CHANNEL>
```

In this example, "Today's News" is shown in the Channels Explorer Bar. Because we have not included a **PRECACHE ITEM** attribute, all the content will be cached on the subscriber's computer. This allows the subscriber to view the news offline.

Creating Various Delivery Channels

In this section, you'll learn how to create the various types of delivery channels, including desktop channels, desktop screen savers, and HTML email.

Creating A Desktop Channel

Desktop channels require a separate CDF file. The file's **<USAGE>** element uses a number of child elements to specify various attributes for the desktop item channel. These attributes include **OPENAS**, **HEIGHT**, **WIDTH**, and **CANRE-SIZE**. See "Desktop Items" earlier in this chapter for explanations of the attributes used with desktop items.

The CDF files for desktop items can also have a **<SCHEDULE>** element to specify when automatic updating can occur. The following code creates a desktop item:

```
<?XML version="1.0"?>
<CHANNEL>
  <SCHEDULE STARTDATE="1999-01-01">
    <INTERVALTIME DAY="7" />
    <EARLIESTTIME HOUR="0" />
    <LATESTTIME HOUR="5" />
  </SCHEDULE>

  <ITEM
   HREF="http://www.site.com/channels/desktopitem.htm"
    PRECACHE="YES">
```

```
<TITLE>The Desktop Item</TITLE>
<USAGE VALUE="DesktopComponent">
  <OPENAS VALUE="HTML" />
  <HEIGHT VALUE="200" />
  <WIDTH VALUE="320" />
  <CANRESIZE VALUE="NO" />
</USAGE>
</ITEM>

</CHANNEL>
```

In this example, the **HREF** attribute in the top-level **<ITEM>** element specifies which page to display on the subscriber's Active Desktop. When the subscriber opens the item, the page will be displayed in HTML format.

Creating A Desktop Screen Saver

You can present your channel content as a screen saver on the subscriber's computer. In the CDF file, specify which page you want to turn into a screen saver and specify the **USAGE VALUE** as "**ScreenSaver**", as shown in the following code:

```
<ITEM
HREF="http://www.site.com/channels/screensaver.html"
PRECACHE="yes">
<USAGE VALUE="ScreenSaver"></USAGE>
</ITEM>
```

The screen saver item must be placed in the top-level **<CHANNEL>** element. When the user subscribes to the channel, a dialog box that provides a choice between the channel screen saver and the existing (nonchannel) screen saver will be presented.

Internet Explorer will rotate through all screen savers provided by the subscriber's channels. All screen saver behavior can be controlled through the Screen Saver Properties dialog box.

Creating HTML Email

To create an HTML email message that notifies subscribers of changes to your channel, set **USAGE VALUE** to "**Email**". If the subscriber elects to receive email notifications, Internet Explorer will send a link to the main top-level channel page as HTML mail to the subscriber. If the subscriber is using Microsoft Outlook, the main channel content page will load in the email message. Here is the code used to create an HTML email notification:

```
<ITEM
HREF="http://www.site.com/channels/emailchannel.htm">
<USAGE VALUE="Email"></USAGE>
</ITEM>
```

Creating Advanced Channel Features

In this section, you'll learn how to create some advanced channels, including a multilevel channel and a channel that crawls a site for new content. You'll also learn how to track the usage of a particular channel. These advanced features go beyond the creation of a simple channel with a few channel items.

Creating A Multilevel Channel

To create multiple levels within your channel, place the **<CHANNEL>** elements within the main **<CHANNEL>** declaration and then place the **<ITEM>** elements within the subchannels, as shown in the following code:

```
<CHANNEL>
    <ITEM>
    <ITEM>
    <CHANNEL>
        <ITEM>
        <ITEM>
    </CHANNEL>
    <CHANNEL>
        <ITEM>
        <ITEM>
        <ITEM>
    </CHANNEL>
</CHANNEL>
```

Make sure every start-tag has an accompanying end-tag. Also, remember that you can only have one **<CHANNEL></CHANNEL>** element to create the CDF file. This document would be invalid and only the first **<CHANNEL>** element would be recognized:

```
<CHANNEL>
<ITEM>
</CHANNEL>
<CHANNEL>
<ITEM>
```

```
</ITEM>
</CHANNEL>
```

The preceding code creates second-level subchannels. The first subchannel contains two items, and the second contains three items. Unlike the top-level channel, subchannels containing items do not require an associated page. In other words, you do not have to specify an **HREF** attribute. This is what happens when you don't specify an **HREF** page:

- If a **BASE** parameter has not been declared for the top-level channel, the page that is displayed in the subscriber's current browser window is shown when the subscriber clicks on the subchannel's folder.

- If you have defined a **BASE** parameter, the base page will be displayed in the browser window when the subscriber clicks on the subchannel's folder.

- If you specify the **HREF** attribute for the subchannel, the page to which the **HREF** attribute refers will load in the subscriber's browser window when the subscriber clicks on the subchannel folder.

The graphic used to signify subchannels is a simple default "book" graphic unless you use the **<LOGO>** tag to specify another one. The following code specifies a specific icon instead of the default icon:

```
<LOGO HREF="http://www.site.com/channels/logo.gif" STYLE="icon" />
```

Creating Crawling Options

Internet Explorer can connect to the Internet and check Web pages during channel updates. This process is called *site crawling*. The CDF file can specify the number of link levels deep the browser should crawl as it works its way through the channel. Within the CDF file, the developer can specify whether the pages that are crawled should be cached.

You can set the level of crawling by specifying the **LEVEL** attribute of the **<CHANNEL>** and **<ITEM>** elements. A value of "**0**" indicates that Internet Explorer should visit only the page defined in the **<CHANNEL>** or **ITEM HREF** attribute. A value of "**1**" tells Internet Explorer to crawl the **HREF** page and all the pages to which **HREF** links. The higher the number, the deeper Internet Explorer will crawl.

You can mix and match the precache options to specify which pages should and shouldn't be cached as the site is crawled. The code for instructing a browser to crawl a site follows this format in the CDF file:

```
<ITEM
HREF="http://www.site.com/channels/mainpage.htm"
```

```
PRECACHE="yes" LEVEL="0">
<ABSTRACT>Channel Abstract Information</ABSTRACT>
<TITLE>Channel Title Information</TITLE>
</ITEM>
```

The preceding code tells the subscriber's browser to precache the page mainpage.htm. There are no other pages or links that will be crawled because the **LEVEL** value is set to zero.

Tracking Channel Usage

If you want to know who is getting the information you are sending, you can use the mechanisms in the CDF language to track hits to individual channel pages. Tracking allows you to find out who is viewing what pages, even if the pages are normally set to cache offline. Logging is done through the W3C Standard Extended Log File Format. The log file is initially stored on the subscriber's computer and then later posted to the server when the channel updates are performed.

To track usage, you need to use two elements, **<LOGTARGET>** and **<LOG>**. The **<LOGTARGET>** element should be located in the top-level **<CHANNEL>** element because it specifies where the log file will be placed. The **HREF** attribute of the **<LOGTARGET>** element specifies the directory or location of the log file. The **METHOD** attribute specifies the method of transmission. Currently, the only method you can use is the POST method, but that may change soon. The **SCOPE** attribute specifies whether offline ("**OFFLINE**"), online ("**ONLINE**"), or all ("**ALL**") page views should be logged in the log file. The following code specifies that all page views should be logged:

```
<LOGTARGET HREF="http://www.site.com/channels/log.pl"
METHOD="POST" SCOPE="ALL">
<PURGETIME=HOUR="12" />
</LOGTARGET>
```

Each individual item to be logged must be marked as such with a **<LOG>** child element. Currently, only "**DOCUMENT:VIEW**" is supported as loggable user activity. The following line of code causes an entry to be made in the log file every time the page is viewed:

```
<LOG VALUE="DOCUMENT:VIEW" />
```

You can use a number of methods to process log files, including Perl scripts or the ISAPI DLL (if you are running your channels off IIS server). Logs of individual **<ITEM>** elements are stored on your server, so you should specify what you wanted logged with some care.

Creating A CDF File For Netcaster Users

To make CDF files available for Netcaster users, you need to create both the CDF file and a transitory page that gives them the ability to subscribe to and view the content in Netcaster. To make this clearer, let's take a look at some more code. First, we'll look at the code for the CDF file. Then, we'll examine the code for the transitory page that enables the user to subscribe to the channel. The CDF file code should have the .CDF extension. The file that included the following code is named cdf_file:

```
<?XML VERION="1.0"?>
<CHANNEL HREF="http://www.site.com/netcaster/mainpage.htm">
<ABSTRACT>This is the main page of the Channel</ABSTRACT>
<LOGO HREF="http://www.site.com/netcaster/logos/logo.gif"> STYLE="IMAGE">
<SCHEDULE>
<INTERVALTIME DAY="1"/>
</SCHEDULE>
<!--These items allow the Netcaster user
to view the Channel content offline. -->
<ITEM><A HREF="http://www.site.com/
netcaster/page1.htm"></A></ITEM>
<ITEM><A HREF="http://www.site.com/
netcaster/page2.htm"></A></ITEM>
<ITEM><A HREF="http://www.site.com/
netcaster/page3.htm"></A></ITEM>
</CHANNEL>
```

Notice that the **<ITEM>** elements specifies the additional pages that will be downloaded to the client and made available for offline browsing. The next step is to create a copy of this file and name it cdf_file.htm so the CDF file can be viewed and used by Netcaster users.

Now, we need to create a section of code for the transitory Web page that allows the Netcaster user to subscribe to the channel. Notice that the **<LAYER>** tag is used. You should name this second file something like channel.htm and it should reference the cdf_file.cdf. The code for this transitory page contains not only HTML but also JavaScript to display the pages accurately:

```
<HTML>
<BODY>
<LAYER SRC="cdf_file.htm" VISIBILITY=HIDDEN></LAYER>

<SCRIPT language="Javascript 1.2">
var nc - components["netcaster"];
nc.activate();
```

```
var chan = nc.GetChannelObject();
chan.url="http://www.site.com/netcaster/channel.htm";
chan.name = "My Channel";
chan.desc = "This is a JavaScript
generated Channel using the JavaScript
API extensions";
chan.cardURL = "http://www.site.com/netcaster/logos/logo.gif";
function openDialog() { nc.AddChannelObject (chan);}
</SCRIPT>

</BODY>
</HTML>
```

Using Cookies To Create Personalized Channels

It's possible to customize channel content based upon user preferences saved in HTTP cookies. You can integrate CDF files with Internet Explorer browser cookies to present specific information to each of your subscribers. This is done using the subscriber's browser preferences to create a dynamically generated, customized CDF file.

To create a personalized channel, you should be familiar with cookies. If you don't know how to create cookies, check the Microsoft Web site, located at **www.microsoft.com** for more information. Just use the link to Support and then use the search option to search for cookies.

You need to perform the following steps to create personalized channel content:

1. Create a form to request specific information from a visitor to your site who is a potential subscriber. The information will be used to customize the content for the user.

2. Save the information in the form to the Web server or within a cookie on the user's computer.

3. When the subscriber's Internet Explorer browser requests an updated CDF file from the server, the server downloads an existing CDF file specified by the preferences stored in the cookie file. The other option is to create a dynamically generated file to match the user's profile.

If you are using a Microsoft IIS server to dynamically generate personalized CDF files, you must insert the following line of code at the top of your CDF file so the server will send the personalized CDF file. This code returns the correct MIME content type to the browser and will perform the expected actions for CDF files:

```
<% Response.ContentType = "application/x-cdf"%>
```

Optimizing The Delivery Of Active Channels

Aside from cutting down on the amount of content pushed to a subscriber and making sure you only cache that content that is required, there are a few more steps you should do to ensure that delivery of your channel is optimized. These steps support various HTTP headers. These headers check to make sure the server is not unnecessarily transferring data when it shouldn't be. Specifically, you should follow these suggestions for your HTTP headers:

- Use the **<ITEM>** element's **LASTMOD** attribute. This prevents Internet Explorer from hitting the server again and again trying to retrieve content based on the last modified date for each item you reference in your channel's CDF file. This will cause the browser to download only the changes you've made. If your Web pages don't change often, using **LASTMOD** won't be a problem. Of course, if your content changes frequently, a dynamically generated CDF is in order.

- Use the "**If-Modified-Since**" request header in the CDF file.

- Make sure you use the "**EXPIRES**" response header to indicate the lifetime of the response (the length of time the resource should remain active).

- Within the CDF file, make sure you use the **HEAD** and **GET** requests in the "**Last-Modified**" response header. By specifying these elements in the response header, the CDF client can monitor changes made to the channel without having to download any channel resources.

- Make sure you don't send the "**Pragma:no-cache**" response header unless you absolutely have to.

- Make sure you consider scheduling. The **<SCHEDULE>** element dictates the server load. It is important to manage schedules if you are to facilitate your subscribers demand for information. Make sure you list the update schedule near the beginning of your CDF file. The most effective update interval is once a day. Make sure you set the **<INTERVALTIME>** and **<LATESTTIME>** elements properly. Also make sure you schedule your updates for when your subscribers are most likely going to be connected if your content is of an important nature. Stock quote updates need to be scheduled during the day, not at night or on the weekends.

- Let the client browser do the load balancing. Internet Explorer updates your channel randomly with the **INTERVALTIME** attribute. This means you would have no control over when the content updates. If you specify it in the **INTERVALTIME** attribute, you can control exactly what time the content should be updated. Scheduling the updates to download during wide time frames helps reduce server load. You could create a 23-hour interval to accomplish a wide time-frame parameter.

- Make sure you keep your updates less than 250K and no larger than 500K in size. Most subscribers will be using 28.8Kbps modems.

Internet Explorer can handle your updates and you should let it. Because many subscribers may not have their machines on all the time, Internet Explorer will queue up the next updates. However, be aware of the following problems associated with allowing the client to update content automatically:

- If a user cancels the update, the browser will not attempt the update again until the next scheduled update.

- Updates interrupt the subscriber's computer, which could confuse or annoy subscribers who might decide to cancel the update or even the subscription.

- If the auto dialer connection fails to update the CDF file, it will not try again during that update. It will wait until the next update is scheduled.

- If the browser gets a time-out error during a scheduled update, it will not try to reconnect to the server, which is why it's important to balance the load and keep the size of updates small.

- If the browser is able to connect to the server but there's a download failure, it will not attempt the update again during that scheduled update.

Optimizing A Channel For The Subscriber

Here are a few tips for optimizing your CDF file and channel content for the subscriber:

- Change the CDF file so the subscriber is notified of new content. This will cause the channel to gleam. Changing the CDF file can be as simple as adding a blank space somewhere and saving the file on the server.

- Make sure you personalize your Web site for the subscriber. This will give your subscribers more of what they are looking for. Give the subscriber options for specifying content and delivery mechanisms.

- Use Active Server Pages to give the subscriber a uniform and simple interface.

Part V

The XML Users Guide

Chapter 21

Converting To XML

By Cheryl Kirk

In Depth

The process of converting to XML requires a tremendous amount of examination and planning. You need to examine what kind of documents you have, whether they are candidates for conversion, and what additional software, if any, the people who will read and use them will need. You also need to examine how XML might fit in with other systems to create a cohesive document-management system.

In this chapter, you'll learn how to convert your existing documents from HTML to XML. Remember, not all documents should be converted to XML documents. Some documents are prime candidates for establishing connections with XML documents. For other documents, you may decide to keep your data right where it is and simply create an interface between XML and other applications, such as Web browsers or database systems. We'll explore some reasons to convert documents to XML and some reasons to stick with what you have.

Today's Corporate Documents

Take a look at any corporation and you'll find a plethora of different types of documents, including HTML, Word, PowerPoint, database, and Adobe Portable Document Format (PDF) files. When a corporation decides to implement XML, they must first consider the range of document types and determine which would be candidates for conversion to XML. Some documents may simply work better in their native format, while others are well suited for conversion to XML.

So, how do you decide which documents are best suited for conversion? First, you'll need to determine what the future holds for the documents you already have. You also have to consider whether there are benefits to making them accessible through your intranet (or on the Internet) and whether converting them will save time and money.

What Documents Can Be Converted?

Just about anything can be converted to XML, including Word, Excel, and Access data files. It doesn't matter whether the file is a simple ASCII file or a Web page with frames. Some applications—Microsoft Office, for example—will soon offer XML filters and conversion features; creating XML documents will be as easy as selecting the Save As option under the File menu and saving files as XML documents.

Web pages are prime candidates for conversion because the markup theory for HTML and XML is similar. Even data files and databases, because of their structured format, could easily be converted to XML or accessed via XML. What is required is a different way of thinking about data and how you create and store it. Here's a quick list of document types you might consider converting to XML or interfacing with XML:

- *HTML (Web) pages*—Although not every page should be converted, Web pages that have dependencies on other data collections are prime candidates. Groups of HTML pages that you change repeatedly, especially if those changes are design changes, are prime candidates for XML conversion.

- *Adobe PDF (Portable Document Format) files*—Files that store large groups of data or require the user to search through them—such as catalogs and technical documentation—are excellent candidates for XML conversion. On the other hand, documents such as brochures, which need to retain their look, may not be worth converting.

- *Excel documents*—You can convert information stored in tabular format in Excel documents to XML, or you can use XML to pull the information from the documents. When information is repeated within several rows in an Excel spreadsheet, you should consider using XML to provide more structure for the data. Also, if you need to share information with other users who don't have Excel, you can use XML to display the Excel information on Web pages.

- *Access database files*—You can use XML as an interface with Access databases so users can use Web browsers to view data. Or, if your Access database consists of a relatively large amount of text within various fields, you can use XML to store it. Also, if you need to share the information with users who don't have Access on their computers, you can use Windows Open Database Connectivity (ODBC). ODBC allows you to link between the Access database file and a Web browser and use XML to transfer the information from the database to a Web browser.

- *Text or Word documents*—Although you may think that converting all your Word or text documents to XML would be a laborious task, consider creating a standardized structure for your files. You could then search across documents for specific information or offer documents to visitors who are using Internet Explorer 4 or Navigator 5.

Determining The Needs Of The Document

Next, you should think about the actual needs of the document to determine whether you should convert it to XML. When we discuss document conversions, we are actually discussing a wide range of issues that involve processing and managing documents. Consider the following requirements of just about any type of document:

- Document creation
- Document distribution
- Accessibility
- Maintenance
- Overall costs

Let's review each one of these document requirements as they relate to the conversion process.

Document Creation

When you decide to convert a group of documents or files from one type to another, you must consider who created them, what programs they used to create those documents, and what programs and processes will be used to create subsequent documents. When you consider converting, you need to ensure the following:

- Those responsible for document creation should be well versed in XML.
- Editing and parsing tools should be made available to those who will be creating the documents.
- Training should be provided to understand how to use the tools.
- Standardized Document Type Definitions (DTDs), elements, entities, and attributes should be made available to those who will be creating new XML documents.

Document Distribution

After documents have been created or converted, the next step is to distribute them to those who need them. Some mechanism must be put in place for document distribution. You could use a standard Web server on an intranet, or you might consider using push mechanisms—XML vocabularies such as Channel Definition Format (CDF) or Open Software Description (OSD)—to send them to the appropriate people. You can also distribute the documents through email. Whatever distribution method you select, you should make sure it is capable of handling XML documents. It is important that external references or links that are placed within the XML documents are always available if the files are to be placed and accessed on a server.

Accessibility

Documents you've converted to XML must be accessible. That is, users must have the tools to access them. If you convert HTML documents to XML, you must use Web browsers that are capable of displaying XML files, have built-in XML parsers or processors, and can work with the style sheets you've created. Your company may need to change direction in terms of the browser it uses. Or the information systems department may need to upgrade the browser on each employee's desktop. You should ensure that all machines on your network can access XML files before you jump into the conversion process. Otherwise, you'll find that the conversion may not be beneficial for your company.

Maintenance

Computer hardware requires maintenance, and so do XML documents. The topic of site maintenance actually encompasses a wide range of components that you must consider. For example, here is a list of some of the XML components you'll need to maintain and why:

- *DTDs*—DTDs often require updating, or you may need to point your documents to newly defined DTDs. Also, you'll sometimes create new DTDs that can then be applied to existing documents.

- *Entities*—You may need to replace information contained within entities with new information if, for example, the company changes its name, a manager's name changes, or new entities are created.

- *Style sheets*—Style sheets may need to be changed, updated, or revised. Because they are part of the overall XML document, you'll need to include style sheets in your list of documents that need to be maintained.

- *Links*—Because links are part of any XML document, and because they change, you'll need to maintain them. Although XML's linking mechanism, XLink, offers multilinking capabilities and helps fix the broken-link problem that has hampered HTML, you'll still need to pay attention to the links stored in any XML document.

- *Servers*—You may need to reconfigure server files to serve up XML files, DTDs, and external resources. It can be as simple as adding a line such as "text/xml xml XML" to your MIME files or as complex as adding new hardware to accommodate larger databases that may interface with XML.

Overall Costs

Although there are good tools for converting files, you may need to pay someone to examine the documents, hand-code additional XML code that conversion software doesn't provide, and test the results.

You may also need to purchase new XML editing software, pay for the use of DTDs, and possibly pay a designer to create style sheets for your particular needs. In addition, you'll need to consider the cost of upgrading the software required to view XML documents and training employees to use the new software. In addition, you may need to update your server software to accommodate the new technology. Most Web servers can easily be changed to handle XML files, but if you're using older Web-server software, it's possible that you'll need to buy additional patches or update the software entirely.

Don't forget to include training as part of your overall document costs. You'll want to train those developing the new documents as well as those who will view them, particularly if you plan to use new software products. Without proper training, standards cannot be fully implemented and the full capabilities of the new documents will not be realized.

TIP: *Remember, you are actually restructuring your entire document process in addition to your documents. This means you need to break down and rebuild, which is never a quick, easy, or inexpensive process.*

The Process Of Converting XML

When you convert any type of document, the process will follow certain steps. We'll examine the conversion process in detail in this chapter's Immediate Solutions section. The following steps can be considered standard in any conversion process:

1. Determine what documents and processes you already have.
2. Examine the documents that may require conversion.
3. Create a time frame for conversion.
4. Assign the resources (including people) required to convert the documents.
5. Standardize the tools you'll use to convert the documents.
6. Create prototypes and test them within a test group.
7. Convert the documents as outlined in the time frame specified.
8. Document the process.
9. Train the users.
10. Implement the converted files throughout the workgroup by distributing them to the users who will use them.
11. Isolate, troubleshoot, and fix problems.

Document Conversion Pitfalls

From choosing the wrong documents to convert to creating the wrong elements for your DTD, you'll find the road to conversion can often be fraught with problems. Here's a glimpse of some of the problems (and solutions) you may run into.

The software you use on both the client and server side doesn't understand XML. This is by far the most frequent problem developers run into, but it's also the easiest to solve. Before you consider moving existing documents to XML, first inventory the systems and servers you have on your network. Investigate whether additional configuration data has to be updated or if patches or new versions of software are required in order to interpret your XML documents. Some of the software you currently use may need to be updated to work with XML version 1 files and the current linking specification. You may also need to update your Web browser software (so it can understand style sheets and display XML data files) and your server software (so it can serve up XML documents). Once you know what server- and client-side software you need, test the files on your local server and on several workstations connected to your network to ensure that the server and browser software work properly with your XML files.

You underestimate the time it takes to convert documents. In the wonderful world of computers, this is a pretty standard problem. Even the best project managers can run into problems when documents are being converted. There may be technical glitches, or there may simply be problems with staffing resources. The best solution for underestimating the time it will take is to either add an additional one to three months to your project schedule or have a contingency plan ready in case problems arise. Another method is to figure out the total time the project should take, and then add a percentage of the total time to compensate for problems or delays. Keep a list of contractors who can help you complete a project, itemize additional hardware resources or software tools that will help you complete the job, or convert higher-priority documents first. Good project-management software can help guide you through the trouble spots. Consider putting your project in Microsoft Project or some other project-management software program so you can keep track of all the variables.

You use the wrong software tools for document conversion. With the rush to meet a relatively large demand for XML tools, numerous software manufacturers have published software that is, shall we say, less than stable. Consider all the possible software titles available and put them through relatively rigorous testing before you use them for your project. Make sure you test the following types of software tools before you use them:

- XML editors
- XML parsers and processors
- Servers and additional server products
- Browsers
- Automated tools for checking links and syntax

The converted documents don't work or display as well as the originals. If you've done any software conversions, you already know many users will find change hard to swallow. If you convert documents and find that users are complaining that the original versions worked better than the converted versions, you must ask the following questions:

- Should you have left the document in its original format?
- Does the user need more training, or is the user having a hard time coping with change?
- Does the software for viewing the document need to be updated?
- Is there is a problem with the style sheet, a group of links, or the DTD?
- Is the parser or processor working properly and reporting errors?

Converting From HTML To XML

HTML documents are the most common type of documents you'll want to convert. In fact, you may want to convert most of your HTML files to XML before you convert other documents for one simple reason—HTML documents closely resemble XML documents and, for the most part, can easily be converted. With software conversion products, such as Tidy, now becoming available, conversion may be easier than you think.

Yet, because so many Web browsers are so forgiving of sloppy HTML code, you may find that most of the conversion process consists of cleaning up HTML code so it conforms to the rigid standards XML imposes. Let's first examine when and where HTML works best and when it's best to convert your HTML pages to XML.

Why HTML Isn't The Best Solution For Web Pages

Although you should never consider XML a replacement for HTML, you should realize some of the limitations HTML has when you compare the two languages. This will help you further identify which HTML pages you should convert and which pages will work fine as they are. In this section, we'll identify the major reasons HTML fails to meet the needs of document creators.

To understand HTML's limitations, you need a relatively good understanding of what HTML does, what it does well, and what it does poorly. Once HTML became popular, its capabilities were stretched to the max, and its limitations started to show.

The problem with HTML lies in the fact that HTML handles the display of data relatively well, but it has no clue about how to handle the structure of the data. And when you start to design a Web site, you'll quickly come to realize, although displaying data is what HTML does best, it is limited in its ability to display data on a variety of platforms. We'll delve deeper into the differences and similarities between XML and HTML, but first, let's take a look at a simple illustration.

Suppose you have a chunk of data—corporate manuals and brochures—that you need to display on a variety of platforms. You've got the on-the-road sales-people using handheld Windows CE-enabled computers. You've also got the corporate businesspeople sitting at their desks using Netscape Navigator. Plus, you have a variety of customers using a multitude of different computers from Macs to Windows-based PCs. If you use HTML to deliver this data to everyone, you would most likely do what thousands of other Web-site designers have done in the past—create separate pages that contain the same data for each type of user. You would set up pages specifically for the Navigator users, you would set up a site specifically for those users who can take advantage of the special features Internet Explorer offers, and you would condense more pages into something the palm-portable computer users can view quickly. Then, when the data changes, you would have to make the same changes to all the different versions of the pages. This is a laborious process and one that leaves a huge door open for mistakes. HTML does not offer any real standards for document structure. Just about anything goes because browsers are so forgiving. Also, HTML development tools often don't follow exact standards for HTML construction, meaning document code created in FrontPage will most likely be different than code written in Claris Home Page. Are you starting to get the picture? Let's take a closer look at why HTML doesn't work for everything you will do on the Web or within an intranet.

Why HTML Doesn't Work For All Intranet And Internet Documents

HTML was created to provide a quick and simple solution for displaying documents on a variety of platforms. Initially, the documents consisted mainly of text, but they often included a few graphics and maybe a link or two that pointed to a single document or a particular section of a document. Because of a variety of factors—including bandwidth, incompatibility between file formats, and lack of multimedia PCs—the idea of offering up video, sound, and access to databases wasn't even a consideration. HTML was meant more for accessibility to relatively bland text-based documents than to diverse files, formats, and data. It wasn't created as a page-description language; it could display text and relatively simplistic formatting, but it couldn't do what page-description languages such as PostScript can do. As the Web started to gain popularity around 1994, developers and designers quickly realized these limitations. Specifically, they found HTML couldn't or didn't offer the following:

- The ability to publish one chunk of data in a variety of ways and to a variety of display devices
- More complex linking options other than simple one-way links

- Flexibility to structure and describe different types of data

- Control over how the data was displayed

Developers who wanted to design pages like they designed in page-layout programs, such as PageMaker, found that HTML simply didn't have the capabilities.

Using HTML To Complement XML

XML is an excellent vehicle for manipulating structured data on the Web. When it is accompanied by HTML's ability to present data, the two markup languages actually complement each other. XML's ability to handle structure rather than presentation makes it an excellent markup language for building complex Web applications. And your knowledge and background in HTML will make the transition easier and the concepts outlined in the XML specification easier to understand.

Also, because Internet Explorer supports XML and Navigator offers similar support, you can use style sheets to present XML data, or in the case of Internet Explorer, you can use the data-binding capability of Dynamic HTML for displaying XML files. In addition, both browsers support the Document Object Model, so all elements become objects, which in turn allows them to be programmable through scripting languages.

As a developer, you can present dynamic content on your site and you don't have to worry about HTML's limitations. XML not only lets you create dynamic data, it also enables you to create data sources that can be used for a variety of purposes, which in turn makes interoperability between applications on a server or client machine and your site a reality.

XML is very much like HTML. Both languages use or are made up of elements. You may be more familiar with the term *tags*. But as you learned in Chapter 1, tags are actually parts of elements. They are either start-tags or end-tags, not just tags as they're called in HTML. In technical terms, a tag is a singular entity that opens or closes an element. For example, the **<P>** tag is an opening tag (or start-tag), and it opens a paragraph element in HTML. The **</P>** tag is a closing tag (or end-tag), and it is used to close the paragraph element. The two tags and the content enclosed within them represent the entire element. Both XML and HTML use tags, which are part of the bigger unit called elements.

Like HTML, XML's main purpose is to describe the content of a document. But this is where the big difference between HTML and XML becomes apparent. Unlike HTML, XML does not describe how the content should be displayed. Instead, XML describes what the content *is*. With XML, the Web author can mark up the contents of a document by describing it in terms of its relevance as data.

The easiest way to explain the difference is by looking at a simple example. The following HTML code snippet should be pretty familiar to you by now:

```
<P>Gone With the Wind</P>
```

This line of code is simply describing the content of a paragraph. When it is processed through an HTML browser, we see the text in relationship to whatever HTML content is included in the page. Specifically, HTML *displays* the content of the paragraph element.

This is fine if all we want to do is display information. But consider what else you might want to do with this information. You might want to create a searchable database of your favorite movies. In other words, you may want to access the information as *data* instead of *display* information. In that case, you would need to use XML to mark up the words *Gone With the Wind* so they mean something. In XML, instead of specifying the words as simple paragraph content, you can specify them as something more meaningful, as shown in this example:

```
<FILM>Gone With the Wind</FILM>
```

You could then use a style sheet to display the content of the **<FILM>** element in any way you choose.

Differences Between HTML And XML

To understand when it would be appropriate to convert from HTML to XML, you need to know the differences between the two markup languages. Table 21.1 provides a quick overview of the major differences you should be aware of. Think about your current documents as you look through this list.

Table 21.1 Differences between HTML and XML.

HTML	XML
Mainly used for display purposes; has little knowledge about the structure of the information contained within.	Used exclusively for structuring data, not displaying it.
A closed language that does not give the developer the flexibility to create tags for specific uses. Each new set of tags is created through the World Wide Web Consortium.	Entirely open to new elements, and browsers will be able to incorporate them into pages.
Relatively easy to learn.	Not as easy to learn; requires more planning.
Tags are not case sensitive.	Elements, attributes, and everything else is case sensitive.
White space in a document is ignored.	White space is not ignored.

(margin) 21: Converting To XML

Syntactical Differences Between XML And HTML

Let's examine the differences, as well as the similarities, between XML and HTML, so you'll know what needs to be changed in order to move from one markup language to the next and why some documents should stay in their native HTML format. You'll see that there are plenty of similarities between the two languages, especially if you've tried to follow the rules of good HTML coding. In the following paragraphs, we'll examine XML's requirements and whether they also exist in HTML.

XML does not limit you to a set library of elements. When you create an XML document, you must first create your own elements and attributes and then use them to structure the document. HTML has a predefined set of tags that you are required to use. You cannot manipulate or change the attributes, the types of values that can be placed within the element content, or even the names of the element tags you use to format the document.

In HTML, you can get away with sloppy documents. How many times have you viewed the source of an HTML document and found a dizzying array of mistakes, missing elements, and just downright sloppy code? Some of the problems occur because people don't know proper HTML syntax, and others occur because HTML editors simply haven't kept up with HTML. Because most of today's browsers are relatively forgiving, most of these faux pas are glossed over and the data is displayed. With HTML, you can be sloppy without great fear of retribution. For example, if you don't add the **</A>** to the **<ANCHOR>** element when you specify a link to another document, the rest of the text from that point forward will turn into one big hypertext link, but the information will still display. It may not display the way you had intended, but it will display.

You *can't* be sloppy with your XML code. The first objective for any XML document is well-formedness. Tags must be nested properly. Start-tags must have end-tags. One missing end-tag and your XML processor will return an error—you can't get away with sloppy code as you can with HTML. The end user won't be left wondering if the page appears as it should. The data and information is displayed properly, and the structure of the data is clearly and accurately defined.

XML requires you to tell the parser that it's an XML document. Another type of sloppiness HTML browsers let you get away with is not declaring what markup language will be used in your document. Whether you're using HTML 2 or HTML 4, the browser usually figures out how to display the data. You may often find HTML documents that are missing the document type declaration at the top of the HTML file. With XML, you must declare that your document is an XML document and what version of the XML specification you plan to use. To do so, you must use the XML declaration, a small piece of code that appears at the top of any XML document:

```
<?XML version="1.0"?>
```

In XML, all elements must have a start-tag and an end-tag. If you've created even a single Web page, you've used at least one element. For example, you may have used the **<TITLE>** element to specify the title of the Web page. To tell the browser where the title begins and ends, you must use a start-tag and an end-tag, as shown in this example:

```
<TITLE>This is the title of my Web page</TITLE>
```

Maybe you've slacked off and used the **PARAGRAPH** element, **<P>**, without its end-tag, **</P>**, in your HTML pages. You'll find that many HTML developers are guilty of this, and plenty of HTML page-creation programs insert the **<P>** element without a closing **</P>** to accompany it. XML, however, doesn't allow you to slide. Every element must have a start-tag and an end-tag. Look through your HTML code to see how many end-tags you've used. You may be surprised, as we were.

In XML, empty elements must be formatted correctly. Lots of developers have created thousands of HTML pages and probably never knew there was such a thing as the empty element. But they abound, not only in HTML, but also in XML. One empty element you might have encountered in HTML is the image element, specified as **<IMG>**. In HTML, you would type the following code to specify a link to a particular image file:

```
<IMG SRC="file.gif">
```

This is considered an empty element because it has no content associated with it. The **file.gif** is the **SRC** attribute value and is not considered the **<IMG>** element's content. But **<IMG SRC="file.gif">** is still a tag. The only problem is that it has no content, so the concept of adding an end-tag to this element declaration is probably foreign to you. But remember, in XML, every start-tag must have an end-tag. So, what do you do with elements that don't normally offer content but require you to specify an end-tag? You can do one of two things. You can specify that this element is an empty element, sans content, by doing what comes naturally:

```
<IMG SRC="file.gif"></IMG>
```

Or you can do what comes naturally in XML (something you'll find you do a lot if you use the Channel Definition Format to develop Internet Explorer Channels).

You can specify the empty element in this fashion—the preferred way to specify empty elements in XML documents:

```
<IMG SRC="file.gif"/>
```

Go through your HTML documents and you'll start to realize how many empty elements exist in your code. This will give you an indication of how much work you'll have to do to convert HTML documents to XML documents.

XML requires quotes around all attribute values. While we're on the subject of elements, and because we just looked at one empty element that included an attribute, let's talk about how XML requires quotes around attribute values. In HTML, only certain attribute values, such as text strings and URLs, need to be quoted, whereas other values don't require such formatting. Take, for example, the following code snippet:

```
<FONT SIZE=+1>This is one size larger</FONT>
```

The **<FONT>** element's **SIZE** attribute value of **+1** will work in HTML. It will signal the browser that the default font used to display the text should be one size larger for the enclosed content of the element. HTML does not require you to place quotes around the **SIZE** attribute value, but if this were an XML document, it would be required. For an XML document to be well-formed, we would need to do this to the previous code snippet:

```
<FONT SIZE="+1">This is one size larger</FONT>
```

It doesn't matter whether you use single or double quotes as long as you use the same type of quotes around the attribute value and the use of quotes is consistent throughout your document. Also, if an attribute has a single value (a default value), such as in the following example, you need to include quotes around the value:

```
<ELEMENT ATTRIBUTE="default">
```

With XML, tags need to be nested correctly. If you're a picky developer, you probably nested your tags correctly in your HTML documents. If so, you're halfway to being a top-notch XML developer. But many people don't, and if you have to work with HTML documents created by others, you should check for properly nested tags by using a conversion-checking program or by reading through the code yourself. To nest tags properly in XML, you must close first what you opened last. For example, although this code listing would usually work in HTML, it wouldn't work in XML:

```
<I><B>This is bold and italics</I></B>
```

The **<B>** tag should be closed first because it was opened last. XML is picky about this because so much of the XML document depends on you showing the parser where things begin and end. The following code illustrates the proper way to nest bold and italic elements in an XML document:

```
<I><B>This is bold and italics</B></I>
```

Without proper nesting, the XML parser wouldn't know how to structure your document. Remember, the key to XML is structure, not format. If you're just formatting your document, you can be somewhat sloppy, just as you can be somewhat sloppy with the paint you put on the exterior of a house. But when you're structuring your document, you need to be more careful, just as you need to be more careful when you're structuring a house. If you mess up the foundation, don't frame the house properly, or leave out a two-by-four here or there, the walls will eventually fall down around you.

Also, you cannot overlap elements. The following code, for example, would be considered invalid:

```
<publisher>Coriolis<publishertype>Computer Book
publisher</publisher></publishertype>
```

This is the proper way to construct the code:

```
<publisher>Coriolis<publishertype>Computer Book
publisher</publishertype></publisher>
```

In HTML, white space is ignored. You may have used white space within your HTML document to separate the HTML code and to make it more readable. You could do this because HTML simply ignored any additional white space other than a single space character. However, XML recognizes white space as data and does not ignore it when the document is put through the parser and then processed, which means this code

```
<film>Pretty
 Woman starring
Julia Roberts</film>
```

is not the same as this code:

```
<film>Pretty Woman starring Julia Roberts</film>
```

When you convert HTML documents to XML documents, you need to remove any extra spaces and extra carriage returns you've placed in the HTML source code.

You can easily use simple find-and-replace options in text editors to remove extra white space in your documents.

In XML, you need to specify when characters are data. There will be times when you will want certain character data to be treated as such. For instance, if the contents of an XML element consists of some sample XML code, rather than replacing each reserved character with its decimal code equivalent, you can simply mark it as character data:

```
<![CDATA[Rope]]>
```

With HTML, just about everything is considered character data, so there is no need to specify when data is character data and when it is not. In HTML, you simply format how the text will look, not whether it is character data or not.

Unlike HTML, XML is case sensitive. Case-sensitivity is important in XML, but not in HTML. You must use the same case when you declare and use elements within XML documents. This code

```
<director>Alfred Hitchcock</director>
```

is not the same as this code:

```
<DIRECTOR>Alfred Hitchcock</DIRECTOR>
```

You can use the find-and-replace option in any text editor to change elements from lowercase or uppercase so the cases match.

Converting HTML To XML

As you've seen, there are certain things you need to pay attention to when you convert HTML documents to XML documents. In this section, we'll convert the simple HTML document in Listing 21.1 to XML.

Listing 21.1   A simple HTML document ready for conversion.

```
<!DOCTYPE HTML PUBLIC "-//IETF//DTD HTML//EN">

<HTML>
<HEAD>
    <TITLE>Domains</TITLE>   </HEAD>
<BODY TOPMARGIN="0" LEFTMARGIN="40"
BGCOLOR="#FFFFFF" LINK="#000066"
VLINK="#666666" TEXT="#000000"
BACKGROUND="../images/backgrnd.gif"
BGPROPERTIES="fixed">
```

```
<!--Questions and Answers Start here-->
<H1>Domains</H1>
<P><A NAME="domain1"><STRONG>
Q. How do I change Domain Names?</STRONG></A></P>
<P><STRONG>A.</STRONG>Make sure everyone is logged
off the computer. The computer will prompt for a reboot
and select &quot;Reboot Now&quot;.<P>
<HR>

<P><STRONG>Q. How do I move a Workstation to
another Domain?</STRONG></A></P>
<P><STRONG>A.</STRONG>Logon to the Workstation locally
as Administrator and go to Control Panel. Double click Network and
click change. Enter the new Domain name and click OK.
You will receive a message &quot;Welcome to Domain x&quot;.
Reboot the machine and you are part of the new domain.</P></BODY>
</HTML>
```

Notice that this document has many things that need to be changed to make it a valid and well-formed XML document. There are entities that need to be defined, tags that need to be nested correctly, and elements that need to be further defined to create the structure. Before we get into the actual conversion process, let's look at what needs to be done to all HTML documents before you can convert them to XML (the following points are listed in the order in which you should consider them):

1. Create a DTD if the HTML document you are converting requires one. Remember, HTML documents don't have DTDs of their own associated with them. First determine if a DTD is necessary and, if so, how it will be constructed.

2. Examine the document for empty elements that need to be closed with the **/>** delimiter or with a closing tag element. It's preferable to use a closing tag element so your XML documents are backward compatible. A list of the empty tags you'll need to convert are included in Table 21.2. By closing out empty tags, you'll be creating a well-formed document, assuming the elements are also properly nested.

3. Examine the document for characters that need to be turned into entity references, such as the & and the < symbols.

4. Change the names of all tags to uppercase so you can easily discern what are elements and attributes and what is content. This also forces you to use the same case throughout the document. Although you can use any case, case-sensitivity is an important aspect of XML.

5. Check the documents for overall structure, and determine the nesting order of the elements.

Table 21.2   Empty tags that need conversion.

Tag Name	Location	Convert To
AREA	Located in the body	<AREA></AREA> or <AREA/>
ATOP	Located in the body	<ATOP></ATOP> or <ATOP/>
AUDIOSCOPE	Located in the body	<AUDIOSCOPE></AUDIOSCOPE> or <AUDIOSCOPE/>
BASE	Located in the header	<BASE></BASE> or <BASE/>
BASEFONT	Located in the body	<BASEFONT></BASEFONT> or <BASEFONT/>
BR	Located in the body	 </BR> or
CHOOSE	Located in the body	<CHOOSE></CHOOSE> or <CHOOSE/>
COL	Located in the body	<COL></COL> or <COL/>
FRAME	Located in the body but can appear in the header	<FRAME></FRAME> or <FRAME/>
HR	Located in the body	<HR></HR> or <HR/>
IMG	Located in the body	<IMG></IMG> or <IMG/>
ISINDEX	Located in the header	<ISINDEX></ISINDEX> or <ISINDEX/>
KEYGEN	Located in the body	<KEYGEN></KEYGEN> or <KEYGEN/>
LEFT	Located in the body	<LEFT></LEFT> or <LEFT/>
LIMITTEXT	Located in the body	<LIMITTEXT></LIMITTEXT> or <LIMITTEXT/>
LINK	Located in the header	<LINK></LINK> or <LINK/>
META	Located in the header	<META></META> or <META/>
NEXTID	Located in the header	<NEXTID></NEXTID> or <NEXTID/>
OF	Located in the body	<OF></OF> or <OF/>
OVER	Located in the body	<OVER></OVER> or <OVER/>
PARAM	Located in the body	<PARAM></PARAM> or <PARAM/>
RANGE	Located in the header	<RANGE></RANGE> or <RANGE/>
RIGHT	Located in the body	<RIGHT></RIGHT> or <RIGHT/>
SPACER	Located in the body	<SPACER></SPACER> or <SPACER/>
SPOT	Located in the body	<SPOT></SPOT> or <SPOT/>
TAB	Located in the body	<TAB></TAB> or <TAB/>
WBR	Located in the body	<WBR></WBR> or <WBR/>

6. Identify where single-pixel white GIF images are specified. They will be turned into white space in XML. All references to these types of "spacer" images need to be replaced.

7. Delete or remove empty tables that were used as spacers in the document.

Creating The Elements, Attributes, And Entities

We won't go into the entire process of creating elements, attributes, and entities here; Chapters 7, 8, and 9 cover those components. Instead, we'll give you some insight into what elements will be declared for our example HTML document (see Listing 21.1). First, because this is a question-and-answer document, we need to define elements specifically for this document and use them to create a document structure:

```
<OVERALLSUBJECT>
<TOPIC>
    <TITLE>
    </TITLE>
      <QUESTION>
            <EXAMPLE>
            </EXAMPLE>
      </QUESTION>
      <ANSWER>
            <EXAMPLE>
            </EXAMPLE>
      </ANSWER>
   </TOPIC>
<OVERALLSUBJECT>
```

We'll leave the formatting that is prevalent in our example HTML file for the style sheet. For now, the preceding code lists the major elements for this question-and-answer format.

Specifying The XML Processing Declaration

The first thing we need to do is convert the document from HTML to XML by specifying the XML processing declaration. This code

```
<HTML>
.
.
.
</HTML>
```

becomes this in XML

```
<?XML version="1.0"?>
```

Now, we're ready to move on through the rest of the code, replacing some of the HTML code with appropriate XML code, converting empty elements to valid XML elements, defining new types of links, and linking style sheets to the document. At this point, we assume you've already created the DTD and are simply using the elements and attributes defined within the DTD throughout your XML document.

Specifying The DOCTYPE Declaration

After we've identified which element tags need to be converted, our first step is to move toward XML validity and well-formedness by specifying the document type declaration right after the XML declaration. The document type declaration outlines what DTD is used to construct the tree structure of the document. The declaration can point to an external DTD or it can specify the DTD internally.

In our HTML example, this code

```
<!DOCTYPE HTML PUBLIC "-//IETF//DTD HTML//EN">
```

specifies that this is an HTML document and that it will use the HTML DTD. We need to change this so that we use the DTD that has been created for this type of document. The XML document type declaration is made the same way it's made in HTML. The document type declaration in our HTML document looks like this in our XML document:

```
<!DOCTYPE DOCUMENT SYSTEM "QANDA.DTD">
```

This, of course, follows the XML processing declaration. Our converted HTML file looks like this so far:

```
<?XML version="1.0"?>
<!DOCTYPE DOCUMENT SYSTEM "MEMO.DTD">
```

Converting Characters To General Entities

The next step is to identify the general elements we need to convert. In this document, we will need to convert the ampersand, but there are other characters that also need conversion:

- <—Open bracket
- >—Close bracket
- &—Ampersand
- '—Single open quote
- '—Single close quote
- "—Double open quote
- "—Double close quote

If they are used within the content of the XML document, these characters need to be converted to the predefined entities that XML offers. For example, the ampersand would be defined in the DTD like this

```
<!ENTITY amp "&#38;">
```

and would be referenced within the XML document like this

```
&amp;
```

Converting Attribute Values To Include Quotes

In our HTML example in Listing 21.1, we have numerous tag attributes that specify values. Yet those values are not enclosed in quotes. We'll need to add quotes to all the attribute values in our document. For example, this code

```
<BODY BGCOLOR=RED>
```

would be converted to

```
<BODY BGCOLOR="RED">
```

You'll find a lot of HTML code with inconsistencies in the use of the quoted attribute values. You could use a text editor's find-and-replace feature to assist you in converting all attribute values to quoted attribute values, but you may have to do a lot of the work by hand.

Reformatting Links To The XLink Specification

One important aspect of converting HTML documents to XML is converting the links so they take advantage of the advanced XML linking features. Chapter 10 outlines how the XLink specification allows you to create all sorts of elaborate links. It will provide you with valuable information about XLinks and XPointers, the two linking mechanisms used in XML documents.

When you convert HTML links to XML links, you need to consider the following:

- Do the links need to be multidirectional?
- Will the links require some sort of behavior to be attached to them?
- Do the links reference internal or external resources within documents? If they reference resources internally, you would need to create XPointers for the referenced sections of documents.
- Are all the links listed in the HTML document going to be valid references in the XML document?

- What element or elements and their attributes will you use to define the link? Are those definitions already specified in the DTD?

You should answer these questions about each individual link contained within your XML document. Then, you need to convert them individually, using the elements specified as linking elements. Here is a quick example of the conversion of a simple HTML link. This particular type of link is specified as an inline link in XML. In this example, we use the XML linking specification, XLink, to create a link that opens in a new window. The old link looks like this:

```
<A HREF="http://www.alaska.net/~ckirk/">My Page</A>
```

And the new XLink link that opens into a new window looks like this, assuming we have defined the **<A>** element to be a linking element in the document's DTD:

```
<A HREF=http://www.alaska.net SHOW="NEW"
ACTUATE="USER">My Page</A>
```

This link now opens up into a new window when the user clicks on it because we've specified the **SHOW** attribute's value to be **NEW**, as in new window.

Specifying The Style Sheet

Because most of our HTML document is actually going to concentrate on format, not structure, a fair bit of your HTML file will be moved to the style sheet we'll specify within our XML document in the XML declaration. For example, if we had already created a style sheet titled brochure, we would include the reference to the brochure style sheet in our XML document so it will be used to display the content of the XML document. We could then reference it in the XML document or within the resulting HTML file that would be used to eventually display the information. The code for the style sheet will look something like this:

```
<brochurestyle>
<!--
h1 {font-family: Arial, sans-serif;
font-size: 14pt; font-weight: bold; color:#0279C8}
h1.title {font-size:150%; color:black}
h2 {font-size: 12pt; font-style: italic; color:#0279C8}
P {font-family: Arial,sans-serif; font-size:10pt}
table {font-family: Arial,sans-serif; font-size:10pt}
table.text {background-color=white; border-style:ridge;
border-color:#0279C8; border-width:medium}
table.bhs {background-color=#BCE3FE; border-style:outset;
border-width:thin}
a.toc1 {font-family: Arial, sans-serif; font-size:10pt;
```

```
font-weight: bold; color:#0279C8}
a.toc2 {font-family: Arial, sans-serif; font-size:9pt;
color:#0279C8}
ul {font-family: Arial, sans-serif; font-size: 10pt}
#indent {position:relative; left:.1in}

-->
</brochurestyle>
```

The conversion from HTML document to style sheet is a complex one. You must consider all the formatting rules you want to apply to the document and where those rules should be applied. Chapter 14 outlines how you construct style sheet rules and how to apply them to the XML document you want to format. It also outlines how to convert standard HTML formatting conventions to XML.

Cleaning Up Comments

In addition to cleaning up the major components of your HTML documents, you should also clean up the comments or add them if they aren't already included. Comments, which are specified by a pair of hyphens, cannot be placed within the XML declarations. Instead, they must be placed after the declaration.

You should also refine the comments so they provide more information about elements, attributes, entities, and the DTDs that you include in your XML documents. Comments are also a great way to break up the markup text and make it more readable. Consider using comments liberally throughout your XML documents and DTDs. Most HTML code you see uses comments sparingly. With XML, you need to explain as much of the code as possible, particularly if you are creating DTDs that will be used by others.

Immediate Solutions

In this section, you'll learn how to convert all the various elements found in HTML to XML. We'll take you step by step through the process of converting an HTML document to an XML document. Then, you'll create a DTD for that document. To perform the conversion, all you need is a simple text editor, an HTML file, attention to detail, and some patience.

Converting From HTML To XML

Because you can create XML documents that don't have DTDs, converting HTML documents to XML can be relatively easy as long as you create a well-formed XML document. However, because HTML is forgiving in terms of the constructs of the document, there will be some cleanup duties you'll need to perform. We'll outline some of them, but can you spot some of the more simplistic problems?

WARNING!   Regardless of whether it's internal or external, we highly recommend you create a DTD for every document you create.

Here is the HTML document you'll convert:

```
<!DOCTYPE HTML PUBLIC "-//W3C//DTD HTML 3.2//EN">
<HTML>
<HEAD>
   <TITLE>Converting to XML</TITLE>
</HEAD>
<BODY BGCOLOR=#FFFFFF>

<CENTER><P><A HREF="../index.html">Home</A>
<CENTER><P>
<HR></P></CENTER>

<H1 ALIGN=CENTER><B>
Converting and Formatting XML Documents</B></H1>
<P>
<HR WIDTH=100%>
This document outlines how to convert XML
```

Documents. We can use it as a guideline to help us
understand the steps used in the process.

```
<H2><B>The Steps Involved</H2></B> </H2>
.
.
.
.
<HR><P>Last updated: 2/1/99
<A HREF="http://www.site.com/convert.html">
Copyright &copy; 1999
<br>Comments or problems to <A HREF =
"mailto:webmaster@site.com">webmaster</a></P></body>
</HTML>
```

Adding A Processing Declaration

First, you need to add a processing declaration at the top of the HTML file. This
will indicate to the processor or browser that this document should be processed
according to the XML 1 specification. The declaration looks like this:

```
<?XML version="1.0"?>
```

Changing The Document Type Declaration

Most HTML documents don't include document type declarations, although you
may run into some that do. Many of the HTML browsers are forgiving and don't
require document type declarations, but XML does. If you don't have a document
type declaration in your HTML file, you'll have to add it. If you do have a document type declaration that defines the document as using HTML, you'll have to
change it to reflect the new document type declaration for XML. In our example,
we'll change ours from

```
<!DOCTYPE HTML PUBLIC "-//W3C//DTD HTML 3.2//EN">
```

to

```
<!DOCTYPE CONVERT SYSTEM "CONVERT.DTD">
```

Converting Missing Or Mismatched End-Tags

There are a few mismatched tags and missing tags. For example, the following
code includes mismatched tags:

```
<H2><B>The Steps Involved</H2></B> </H2>
```

It should be changed to the following:

```
<H2><B>The Steps Involved</B></H2>
```

Also, the **\<BR\>** tag and the **\<HR\>** tag used throughout need to be converted to

```
<BR></BR>
```

and

```
<HR></HR>
```

Adding Missing Quotes Around Attribute Values

The following code requires quotes around the attribute values:

```
<BODY BGCOLOR=#FFFFFF>
```

You need to add quotes around the value specified for the body color:

```
<BODY BGCOLOR="#FFFFFF">
```

Making Cases Match

In the document, we can see that some of the element tags use different cases some of the time. This will not work with XML. For example, the following code snippet includes several tags that will not work properly when converted to XML:

```
<br>Comments or problems to
<A HREF = "mailto:webmaster@site.com">
webmaster</a></P></body>
```

Notice that the **\<BR\>** tag is specified throughout the document as **\<BR\>**, and in the preceding code, it's specified as **\<br\>**. Also, the **\<A\>** tag in this code example ends with **\</a\>**. In XML, this would bring about an error in processing. To make this a well-formed XML document, you need to match cases for every element specified.

Removing Or Repeating Empty Paragraph Elements And Line Breaks

Notice that the document has numerous empty paragraph elements **\<P\>** and line breaks **\<BR\>**. They need to be removed, or end-tags need to be added. You should also remove the additional blank lines in the code because XML treats white space as character data, unlike HTML, which ignores it.

Indenting Text

Finally, you need to indent the text to make it easier to read the code. Here is the result of converting the HTML document to XML:

```
<?XML version="1.0"??
<!DOCTYPE CONVERT SYSTEM "CONVERT.DTD">

<STYLE>
<!--
<BODY BGCOLOR="#FFFFFF">
</STYLE>

<SECTION>
   <TITLE>Converting to XML
   </TITLE>
      <LINK>
            <A HREF="../index.html">Home</A>
         </LINK>
    <SUBTITLE>Converting and Formatting XML Documents
    <SUBTITLE>

      <HR WIDTH="100%"><HR>
    <CONTENT>
    This document outlines how to convert XML
      Documents. We can use it as a guideline to help us
      understand the steps used in the process.
      </CONTENT>
    .
    .
    .
    .

   <UPDATE>Last updated: 2/1/99</UPDATE>
   <COPYRIGHT>Copyright &copy; 1999</COPYRIGHT>
   <COMMENTS>Comments or problems to
  <COMMENTLINK><A HREF = "mailto:webmaster@site.com">
    webmaster</A></COMMENTLINK>
</SECTION>
```

Chapter 22

The XML Toolbox

By Natanya Pitts-Moultis

In Depth

Although XML applications and documents can be created by using a simple text editor, complex Document Type Definitions (DTDs) and extensive document collections are better managed using tools specifically created for XML. Because XML is a child of Standard Generalized Markup Language (SGML), tool vendors are already in place and quality XML tools have been cropping up left and right. This chapter examines the types of XML development tools available and provides descriptions and links to important Web resources for each tool. The Immediate Solutions section focuses on choosing the right XML tool to meet your needs.

There's nothing like a good tool to make a tough job easier. The same holds true for the design and development of XML DTDs and documents. Because XML is so robust and can be used to create complex and extensive documents, it is easy to see why the right set of tools can be an XML developer's best friend. Grounded in the strong history of quality SGML development tools, the first generation of XML development tools is proving to be an excellent bunch.

XML tools generally fall into these categories:

• Parsers

• Browsers

• Development tools

In this chapter, we'll look at the role each type of tool plays in the development of XML applications and documents and provide you with specifics about the tools currently available on the market in each category. The Immediate Solutions section at the end of this chapter provides a set of diagnostic tools you can use to determine which tools are right for you.

XML Parsers

An XML parser is the most basic XML tool. Its main job is to ensure that XML documents are valid or at least well-formed. Because an XML document has to be well-formed and/or valid to function properly, the parser plays an important role in the implementation of an XML solution. In addition, any application that is XML aware has a parser built into it to ensure well-formedness, if not validity. Often, these parsers only check to see if a document is well-formed but not if it is valid. Although this approach saves processing time and energy, it assumes that the document creator adhered strictly to the rules set down by the DTD when the document was constructed.

Parsing isn't new to the SGML world; therefore, when XML was first created, there were plenty of SGML parsers around to parse XML documents. However, they were often too large or too slow to process an XML document properly, and they were written to work with proprietary SGML software on single platforms. Because XML is intended to be an Internet technology, a large number of the XML parsers that have appeared in the last few months are Java based and can run in any Web browser on any platform that supports Java.

The remainder of this section is dedicated to a discussion of the various XML parsers available as of press time. Table 22.1 provides a quick reference to the parsers and includes vendor, language, type, and version information.

Ælfred

- *Vendor*—Microstar
- *Language*—Java
- *Type*—Non-validating
- *Version*—1.1
- *URL*—**www.microstar.com/XML**
- *What the vendor says*—"We've designed Ælfred for Java programmers who want to add XML support to their applets and applications without doubling their size: Ælfred consists of only two core class files, with a total size of about 26K, and requires very little memory to run" (Ælfred home page).

Table 22.1   XML parsers.

Parser	Vendor	Language	Type	Version
Ælfred	Microstar	Java	Non-validating	1.1
DXP	DataChannel	Java	Validating	1 beta1a
Expat	James Clark	C	Non-validating	N/A
Lark	Textuality	Java	Non-validating	1 final beta
Larval	Textuality	Java	Validating	0.8
MSXML	Microsoft	Java	Validating	1.8
TclXML	Steve Ball	Tcl	Non-validating	N/A
Xparse	Jeremie	JavaScript	Non-validating	0.91
xmlproc	Lars Marius Garshol	Python	Non-validating	0.3
XP	James Clark	Java (JDK 1.1)	Non-validating	Alpha

This compact parser, shown in Figure 22.1, is one of the new class of Java-based parsers with a small footprint and a large number of abilities. Ælfred is a non-validating parser, so it will only check documents for well-formedness, but its primary goal is to provide Java programmers with a same-type implementation of XML. The developers of Ælfred set for themselves the goal of creating a small, fast, and multiplatform-compatible XML parser, and they have achieved their goal. One of the developers of Ælfred is David Megginson, the author of the novel DTD utilized as an example in several of this book's chapters.

To see Ælfred at work for yourself, point any Java-enabled Web browser on any platform to **www.microstar.com/XML/browser-test.html**. Figure 22.2 shows Ælfred parsing an XML document. Ælfred is SAX compatible, and it is freeware.

TIP: *The Simple API For XML (SAX) is an event-based interface specifically created for XML parsers written in object-oriented applications like Java. Fore more information on SAX, visit the SAX page at* **www.microstar.com/xml/sax***.*

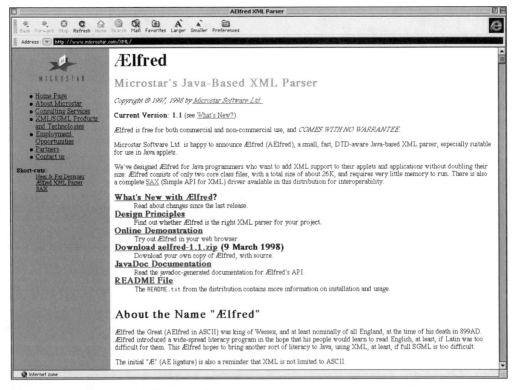

Figure 22.1   The Ælfred XML parser home page.

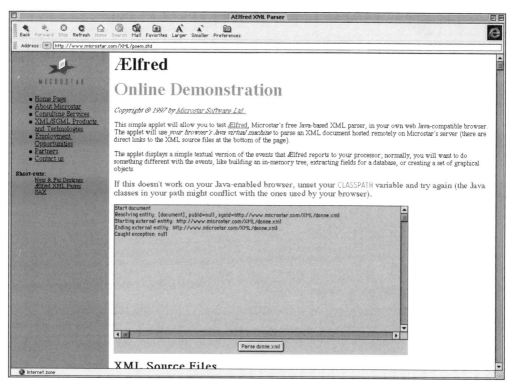

Figure 22.2   The Ælfred XML parser at work in a Web page.

DXP

- *Vendor*—DataChannel

- *Language*—Java

- *Type*—Validating

- *Version*—1 beta 1a

- *URL*—**www.datachannel.com/products/xml/DXP**

- *What the vendor says*—"DXP is specifically aimed at providing a utility for server-side applications that need to integrate XML capabilities into existing systems and for out-of-the-browser Java-based software. DXP, in its final version (due in March), will provide the highly sophisticated error-checking mechanisms required for XML-based data interchange" (DXP home page).

DataChannel XML Parser (DXP), formerly known as NXP (Norbert's XML Processor), is shown in Figure 22.3. DXP is a product of DataChannel, one of the first major XML-based vendors to appear in the last year. Although DataChannel's initial XML offerings focused on the Channel Definition Format (CDF) XML

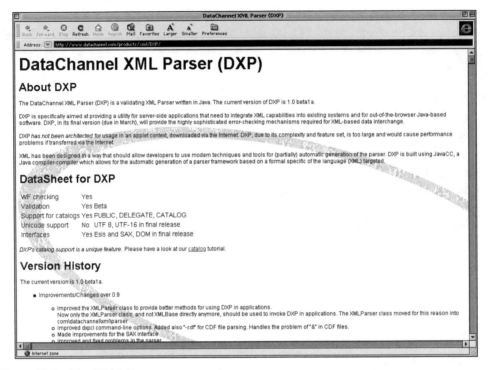

Figure 22.3   The DXP home page.

application, they have since developed a strong suite of tools that is quite useful for all aspects of XML development.

As the vendor statement indicates, DXP is focused on facilitating data exchange. Even though it is Java based, it isn't intended to be embedded in a Web document as Ælfred is, because it is so large. DXP is a validating parser that is SAX compliant, and it is available for free at **www.datachannel.com/products/xml/DXP/ download.html**.

Expat

- *Vendor*—James Clark
- *Language*—C
- *Type*—Non-validating
- *Version*—None
- *URL*—**www.jclark.com/xml/expat.html**
- *What the vendor says*—"Expat is an XML 1 parser written in C. It aims to be fully conforming. It is currently not a validating XML processor" (James Clark's Expat page).

James Clark, the author of one of the most widely used SGML parsers, SP, brings us XMLTok, a C-based XML parser tool kit. Clark doesn't have much to say about the tool kit on his Web page except that it is subject to the Mozilla Public License, version 1. This is a pretty lengthy licensing agreement. Anyone who wants to use Expat should read it at **www.jclark.com/xml/MPL-1_0.html**. To download Expat, point your browser to **ftp://ftp.jclark.com/pub/xml/expat.zip**.

Lark

- *Vendor*—Textuality
- *Language*—Java
- *Type*—Non-validating
- *Version*—1 final beta
- *URL*—**www.textuality.com/Lark**
- *What the vendor says*—"Lark is a non-validating XML processor implemented in the Java language; it attempts to achieve good tradeoffs among compactness, completeness, and performance" (Lark and Larval home page).

Lark was one of the first Java-based non-validating XML parsers available. Lark began as Tim Bray's personal project and experiment in both Java and XML and has turned into a valuable tool for XML developers. However, because Lark was a personal project, it doesn't have a snazzy interface. In fact, it doesn't have an interface at all (but it *is* SAX compatible). Instead, Lark is made up of a series of Java class files that an experienced Java hacker can manipulate and edit. Because it is written in Java, Lark can be easily integrated into other Java projects to provide fast and easy XML handling.

Regardless of its simplicity, Lark is still a quality tool that you can download for free at **www.textuality.com/Lark/lark.tar.gz**. The Lark home page is shown in Figure 22.4.

Larval

- *Vendor*—Textuality
- *Language*—Java
- *Type*—Validating
- *Version*—0.8
- *URL*—**www.textuality.com/Lark**
- *What the vendor says*—"Larval is a validating XML processor built on the same code base as Lark" (Lark and Larval home page).

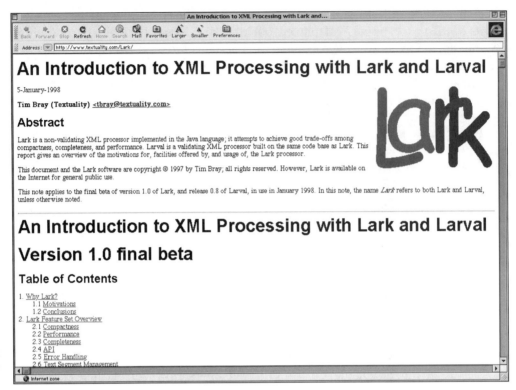

Figure 22.4   The Lark and Larval home page.

As Bray's statement about Larval indicates, it is simply a validating version of Lark. Built on the same source code as Lark, Larval provides a simple Java-based validating XML parser to Java developers who need to include XML support in their applications. Because both Lark and Larval exist, developers can choose a parser that best meets their needs, and they are both free.

MSXML

- *Vendor*—Microsoft
- *Language*—Java
- *Type*—Validating
- *Version*—1.8
- *URL*—**www.microsoft.com/workshop/author/xml/parser**
- *What the vendor says*—"The Microsoft XML Parser is a validating XML parser written in Java. The parser checks for well-formed documents and optionally permits checking of the documents' validity. Once parsed, the XML document is exposed as a tree through a simple set of Java methods, which we are

working with the World Wide Web Consortium (W3C) to standardize. These methods support reading and/or writing XML structures, such as the Channel Definition Format (CDF) or other text formats based on XML, and thereby enable building applications using XML" (Microsoft's XML parser page).

Microsoft's XML parser offering, shown in Figure 22.5, is Java based, just as DXP, Lark, and Larval are. Microsoft jumped on the XML bandwagon early, and it seems as if it's going to be around for the long haul. Cosponsoring XML initiatives such as CDF and Open Software Description (OSD) with such big industry names as Marimba indicates that it is committed to XML as a new Web technology.

The MSXML parser is just another example of Microsoft's commitment to XML. It is freeware, but it only works well on PCs running Windows 95 or NT. MSXML is a validating parser and was constructed to work with other Microsoft proprietary technologies, such as data binding. Developers who work closely with Internet Explorer or Microsoft's Internet Information Server (IIS) may find that MSXML is their parser of choice, because it is well suited to integration with other Microsoft products.

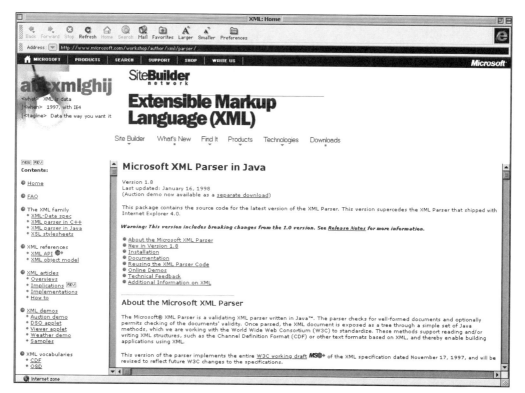

Figure 22.5   The MSXML home page.

The Microsoft XML parser pages also include several XML demos and links to valuable articles and XML tools. You can download the MSXML parser at **www.microsoft.com/xml/parser/xmldl.htm**.

TclXML

- *Vendor*—Steve Ball
- *Language*—Tcl
- *Type*—Non-validating
- *Version*—None
- *URL*—**tcltk.anu.edu.au/XML**
- *What the vendor says*—"It goes without saying that there is a lot more testing and development to be done" (TclXML home page).

TclXML, shown in Figure 22.6, is an experimental version of a non-validating XML parser specifically written for the Tcl (pronounced "tickle") environment. If you are a Tcl programmer and you want to learn more about XML and integrate it into your Tcl documents, this is the parser for you. Steve Ball has tested the parser on a DTD and several documents. To install this specialized parser, point your Web browser to **tcltk.anu.edu.au/XML/XML-1.0a1.tcl**.

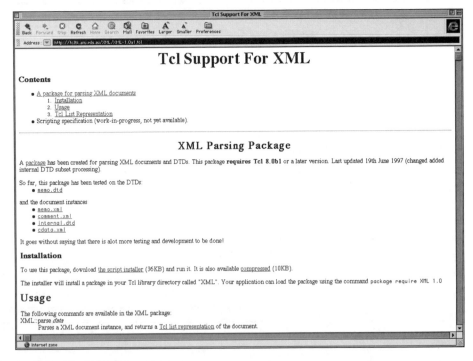

Figure 22.6   The TclXML home page.

Xparse

- *Vendor*—Jeremie
- *Language*—JavaScript
- *Type*—Non-validating
- *Version*—0.91
- *URL*—**www.jeremie.com/Dev/XML**
- *What the vendor says*—"Xparse is a fully compliant well-formed XML parser written in less than 5K of JavaScript" (Xparse home page).

Xparse, shown in Figure 22.7, is the first XML parser to be written in JavaScript. Because it is written in JavaScript, with an eye toward integrating it with the ECMAScript Core application programming interface (API), this parser could play an important role in creating dynamic Web pages that integrate XML documents, which is both challenging and exciting. This parser is definitely for the avid JavaScripter who wants to learn something about a new technology. The author is working on a companion Extensible Style Language (XSL) parser that is also written in JavaScript. To download this free non-validating parser, visit **www.jeremie.com/Dev/XML/download.html**.

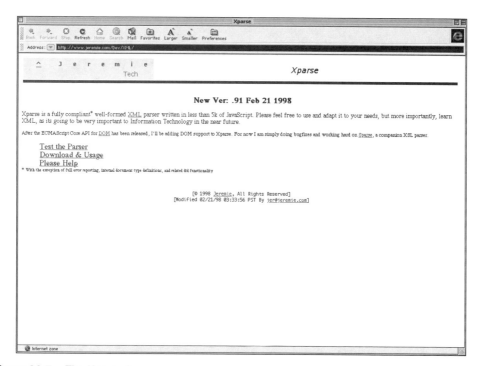

Figure 22.7   The Xparse home page.

xmlproc

- *Vendor*—Lars Marius Garshol
- *Language*—Python
- *Type*—Non-validating
- *Version*—0.3
- *URL*—**www.stud.ifi.uio.no/~larsga/download/python/xml/xmlproc.html**
- *What the vendor says*—"xmlproc is an XML parser written in Python. It is a fairly complete validating parser, but it does not do everything required of a validating parser or even a well-formedness parser. The average user should not run into any omissions, though" (xmlproc home page).

Just as TclXML was written specifically for the Tcl environment, xmlproc (shown in Figure 22.8) has been designed by Lars Marius Garshol to run in the Python environment. xmlproc is designed to either be a command-line parser or function as an API for developing XML applications. Of course, you must be running

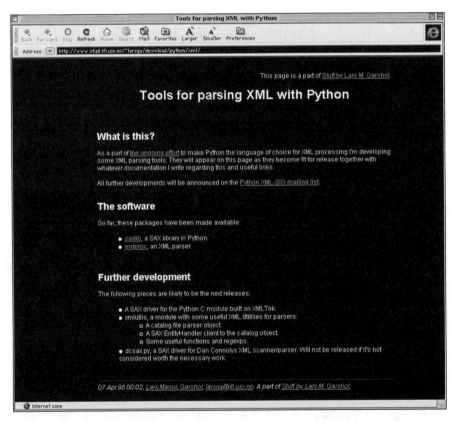

Figure 22.8   The xmlproc home page.

Python to use this processor. You can download xmlproc for free from **www.stud.ifi.uio.no/~larsga/download/python/xml/xmlproc.zip**.

XP

- *Vendor*—James Clark
- *Language*—Java (JDK 1.1)
- *Type*—Non-validating
- *Version*—Alpha
- *URL*—**www.jclark.com/xml/xp/index.html**
- *What the vendor says*—"XP is an XML 1 parser written in Java. It is fully conforming: It detects all non well-formed documents. It is currently not a validating XML processor. However, it can parse all external entities: external DTD subsets, external parameter entities and external general entities" (the XP Web page).

XP, James Clark's XML version of SP, is a Java-based non-validating XML parser. This particular parser uses the Java 1.1 software development kit (SDK), so it may not work well with Java 1. True to form, Clark is pretty close-mouthed on his Web site about the inner workings of his parser. He warns users that the parser wasn't meant for applet creation but rather for production use, so the class file is large and the error handling is "brutal." Because Clark is such an established player in the SGML game, we can say with confidence that his parser will be a quality tool that will serve any XML developer. To download it, visit **ftp://ftp.jclark.com/pub/xml/xp.zip**. This tool is very much in the alpha stage, so keep tabs on the tool's home page to watch its development.

XML Browsers

XML browsers are designed to display XML content in a graphical interface that is navigable by users. Generally, browsers are developed with a specific XML application in mind, such as the Jumbo viewer created expressly for viewing Chemical Markup Language (CML) documents. Currently, there are only two such XML viewers available on the market: Jumbo and DataChannel's Tree Viewer. The following descriptions use much the same format the previous section does to examine these two viewers.

Jumbo

- *Vendor*—Peter Murray-Rust
- *Language*—Java

- *Version*—1

- *URL*—**www.venus.co.uk/~pmr/README**

Jumbo is an XML viewer created specifically for viewing Chemical Markup Language (CML) documents. It is robust enough to render complex molecule models and show extensive chemical formulas. Although it was written for one XML application, it is a good learning tool for anyone interested in XML and also serves as a model for future viewer developers.

Tree Viewer

- *Vendor*—DataChannel

- *Language*—Java

- *Version*—None

- *URL*—**xml.datachannel.com/XMLTreeViewer/demo.html**

The Tree Viewer, shown in Figure 22.9, is a Java applet designed to work with CDF to display the contents of a set of Web documents in a hierarchical tree. Users can navigate from page to page using the tree. This is a cool way to create a site map for your Web site, but it must be viewed using Internet Explorer 4 and

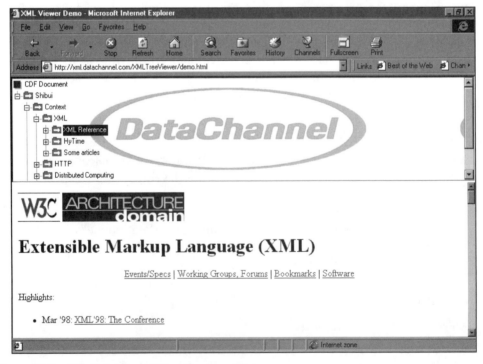

Figure 22.9   The DataChannel Tree Viewer applet.

doesn't work well on the Mac. If you're designing an intranet made up of PCs running IE4, you'll want to add this XML tool to your site at your earliest convenience. DataChannel provides an excellent tutorial on integrating the viewer into an existing site and allows you to download the viewer deployment kit at **xml.datachannel.com/XMLTreeViewer/deploy/xmlviewerappletkit.zip**.

XML Development Tools

The remainder of the XML tools fall into the general XML development tools category. Although many of them include parsers and viewers, they serve as components of a larger development kit. Many of these tools are based on SGML development tools, and some are very expensive, whereas others are freeware or shareware. Although we won't quote specific prices for any given tool, we'll let you know if it is an expensive solution or a relatively inexpensive one. We've included demo versions of many of these tools on this book's companion CD-ROM. Others that aren't included on the CD-ROM often have demos that you can download from their associated Web sites.

ADEPT·Editor

- *Vendor*—ArborText

- *Version*—7

- *Platform(s)*—Windows NT, Windows 95/98

- *URL*—**www.arbortext.com/editor.html**

- *What the vendor says*—"Based on SGML and XML, ArborText's ADEPT·Editor software offers organizations more than just another way to create documents. With ADEPT·Editor, you can capture knowledge in a format that's easily reusable, easily automated, and easily shared across hardware platforms and on multiple media—paper, online, the Web, and CD-ROM" (ADEPT·Editor home page).

The ADEPT·Editor, shown in Figure 22.10, is a high-end SGML development environment that has been adapted to also support XML. With a fully graphical interface and its own proprietary API, ADEPT is a powerful tool for advanced XML document development. This is the kind of tool designed for use in enterprise and advanced technology situations. It is as robust and extensible as the languages it was built to work with. Although it is a more costly solution, it is a solid one if you have thousands of documents to create and manage. For more information on pricing and demo versions, contact ArborText at **www.arbortext.com/ info@arbortext.html**.

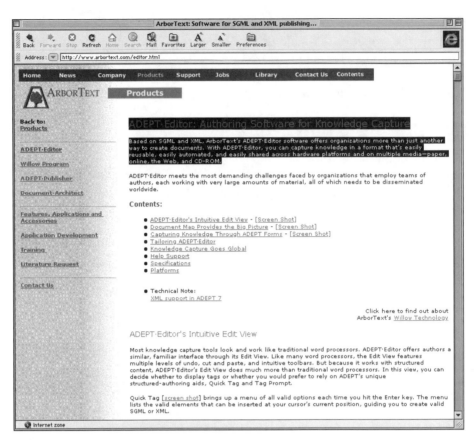

Figure 22.10   The ADEPT·Editor home page.

DataChannel XML Development Kit

- *Vendor*—DataChannel
- *Version*—None
- *Platform(s)*—Any with a Java Virtual Machine
- *URL*—**www.datachannel.com/press_room/wp_xdk_pro.html**
- *What the vendor says*—"The DataChannel product suite was designed as an aid to create next generation systems and to integrate existing systems into the new world of open information exchange based on XML" (Development Kit home page).

The DataChannel XML Development Kit, shown in Figure 22.11, includes three much-needed tools:

- DataChannel XML Parser (discussed in a previous section)

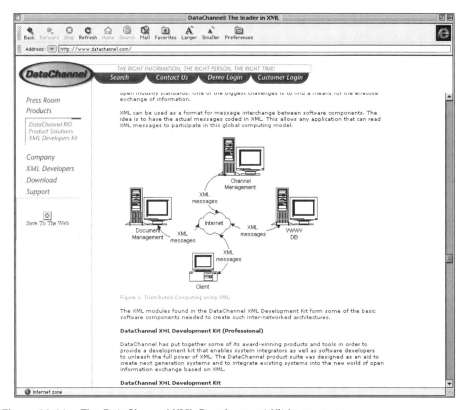

Figure 22.11   The DataChannel XML Development Kit home page.

- DataChannel DOM Module
- DataChannel XML Generator

Combined, these three tools provide you with a complete environment for developing and processing XML documents. The DOM Module acts as an API for the parser, and you can use it to export data in XML format from any application to the parser. Much of DataChannel's focus for XML is as a database connectivity medium. Although the tools are built with this purpose in mind, they can be used for any practical application of XML. Download demo versions of the tools at **www.datachannel.com/download/xdk_downlo.html**.

LT XML

- *Vendor*—Language Technology Group
- *Version*—.0.9.5
- *Platform(s)*—Windows 95, Windows NT, Macintosh, Unix (Solaris, Sunos, FreeBSD, Linux)

- *URL*—**www.ltg.ed.ac.uk/software/xml**

- *What the vendor says*—"The LT XML tool kit includes standalone tools for a wide range of processing of well-formed XML documents, including searching and extracting, down-translation (e.g., report generation, formatting), tokenizing, and sorting" (LT XML home page).

LT XML is the XML tool kit being developed under the watchful eye of the W3C, so it has some strong backing and you can be sure it will be a good tool. LT XML is also one of the few tool kits to run on a wide variety of platforms. It has a C-based API and its own built-in parser. Download a noncommercial use version for free at **www.ltg.hcrc.ed.ac.uk/software/research_xml.html**.

Symposia doc+

- *Vendor*—Grif SA

- *Version*—3

- *Platform(s)*—Windows 3.x, Windows 95, Windows NT, SunOS 4.1.x, Solaris 2.x, HP-UX 9.05, AIX 3.2.x

- *URL*—**www.grif.fr/prod/symposia/sympro.html**

- *What the vendor says*—"Symposia pro combines a fully functional Web browser and a WYSIWYG-structured HTML editor in a single, easy-to-use package that lets you create and maintain multimedia documents directly on the World Wide Web or on a corporate intranet....Symposia doc+ offers all the features of Symposia pro 3, plus graphical site management and ODBC database connectivity tools and now includes support for the XML standard" (Symposia doc+ home page).

Symposia doc+, shown in Figure 22.12, is an XML-enabled WYSIWYG Web page editor and document-management system. Symposia doc+ represents the future of editors. Document editors will replace HTML and XML editors and will support multiple markup languages and their many applications. Symposia doc+ is a good and reasonably priced tool for document developers who want a smooth path to valid XML documents.

Web Automation Toolkit

- *Vendor*—webMethods

- *Version*—2.1

- *Platform(s)*—Windows 95/98, Windows NT, Macintosh, Unix (with JDK installed)

- *URL*—**www.webmethods.com/products/index.html#ToolKit**

- *What the vendor says*—"The Web Automation Toolkit is an integrated development, testing, and management environment for Web Interface Definition

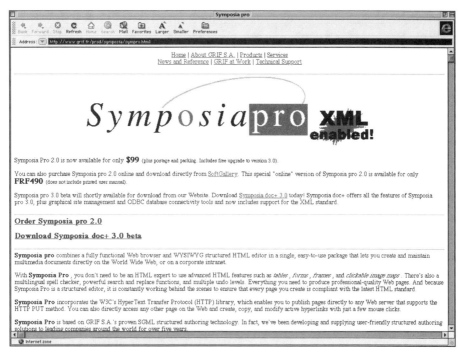

Figure 22.12   The Symposia doc+ home page.

Language (WIDL) files; it allows developers to specify Web data sources, manage service relationships, and generate C/C++, Java, JavaScript and ActiveX 'WebLets,' which allow Web access functionality to be integrated directly into business applications. New languages and middleware environments are supported via a rapidly extensible template-driven code generator" (Web Automation home page).

The Web Automation Toolkit, shown in Figure 22.13, is better described as a Web document-development kit that uses XML instead of an XML development kit. The tool kit uses XML to facilitate data exchange, and the folks at webMethods have created their own XML application WIDL for this very purpose. This product is an excellent example of how XML can be used with existing Web infrastructure to create flexible and robust documents. Of course, the Web Automation Toolkit generates all your code for you, from HTML to Java. You can download a free 365-day demo at **www.webmethods.com/products/toolkit/userguide/download.html**.

WebWriter

- *Vendor*—Stilo
- *Version*—None

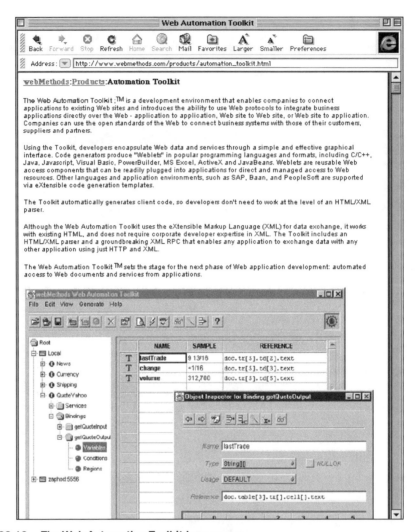

Figure 22.13   The Web Automation Toolkit home page.

- *Platform(s)*—Windows 95/98 and Windows NT

- *URL*—**www.stilo.com/products/xmlbody.htm**

- *What the vendor says*—"WebWriter captures the essential simplicity and flexibility of XML in an authoring tool that everybody will be able to use" (WebWriter home page).

The WebWriter from Stilo, shown in Figure 22.14, is the kind of XML editor every document developer dreams of. It supports both well-formed and valid documents, allowing you to edit with or without a DTD. The graphical DTD display shows how element content is laid out for a particular DTD, and the dynamic DTD builder helps you edit existing XML DTDs.

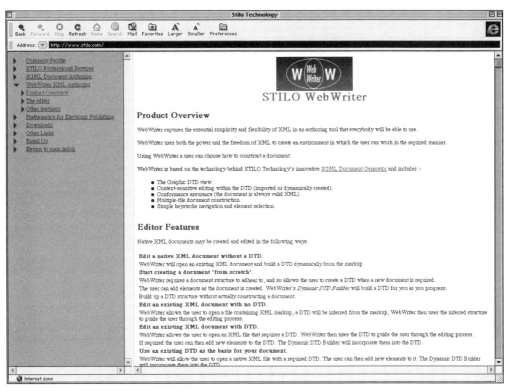

Figure 22.14   The WebWriter home page.

XPublish

- *Vendor*—Media Design in Progress
- *Version*—1
- *Platform(s)*—Macintosh
- *URL*—**interaction.in-progress.com/xpublish/index**
- *What the vendor says*—"XPublish is a professional Macintosh XML publishing system for efficient development and maintenance of Web sites" (XPublish home page).

XPublish, shown in Figure 22.15, is the kind of tool current Web developers need to bridge the gap between HTML and XML in the coming months. XPublish is an XML development tool kit that also generates HTML from your XML for immediate publishing on the Web. In addition, XPublish facilitates DTD development and has a Cascading Style Sheets development tool for adding styles to your XML and HTML documents. This is a Macintosh-only product, a rarity in today's computing world, and moderately priced. A 30-day demo can be downloaded for free at **interaction.in-progress.com/xpublishindex?download=xpublish.random&id=56OIG**.

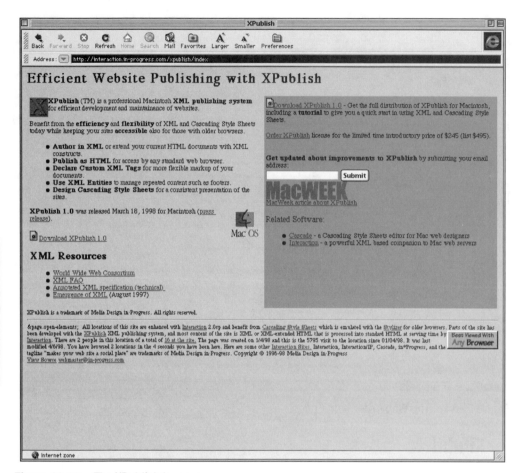

Figure 22.15   The XPublish home page.

Finding New Tools

Although this chapter couldn't contain an exhaustive list of all the XML tools available today, we've attempted to provide a good sampling of what's out there to aid you in application and document development. To keep up with new tool developments, we suggest keeping weekly tabs on the following three sites:

- James K. Tauber's XML site software list at **www.jtauber.com/xml/software.html**

- Robin Cover's XML site at **www.sil.org/sgml**

- The World Wide Web Consortium's XML site at **www.w3.org/XML**

Immediate Solutions

As the survey of tools in this chapter's In Depth section shows, a great number of quality XML tools are already available, and the ranks are quickly swelling as it becomes evident that XML is not just a passing fad. But how do you choose which tools are right for you? This Immediate Solutions section provides a series of questions you can ask yourself about your own needs. Compare your answers to the specs for each tool and you'll soon find the tool that best fits your needs.

Identifying Your Tool Needs

Answer the following questions to help identify your needs and wade through the swamp of available XML tools to find the best match.

Step 1: What Is Your Budget?

XML tools come with a variety of prices, from free to extremely expensive. Usually, the free tools are under development or are part of an initiative by the W3C, as is the case with the LT XML development kit. The high-priced development tools are often part of a larger SGML document-management suite. They can be powerful and provide you with slick interfaces and custom APIs. The middle-of-the-road tools are a bit better than the free ones but don't have the advanced management capabilities of the high-end ones. If you are working in an enterprise or intranet environment and are planning a wholesale move to XML as your document type of choice, you'll want to invest in a high-end tool. If you're a serious but small Internet developer on a budget, go for a middle-of-the-road tool. You'll enjoy its frills, but you won't pay for advanced capabilities you'll never need. Finally, if you're just learning XML or aren't sure that it's the right solution for you, take advantage of one of the many free XML tools available today.

Step 2: What Is Your Platform?

This is almost a no-brainer, but it had to be mentioned. Make sure the tool you are interested in is available for your primary platform. Those running Windows and Unix have a few more choices than the Mac crowd. Also, if a tool claims to work well on all platforms, see if you can't do a bit of research to find out if the claim is true or not. If a tool is constantly crashing your system, it's not doing you much good, regardless of its XML development qualities.

Step 3: Do You Need A Parser Or A Development Kit?

Are you looking for just an XML parser to add to existing applications (Java, C, and so forth), or do you want an entire development kit devoted to document and application development? Many of the existing XML parsers are compact and fast and designed that way specifically. Most of them are Java based, so they will fit neatly with existing Web applications. If, however, you need a full document-development kit, you'll want more than just a parser. In general, these development kits have XML-specific editors and tools to make document generation easier. They'll probably have a small parser, as well, to help you check your documents, but it's not a requirement in a good development tool.

Step 4: Do You Need Manuals And A Lot Of Tech Support?

Free software packages generally don't come with extensive manuals or tech support. Often a readme file is the only material you'll get in addition to the code package. You can email the developer, but it could be weeks before you get a reply, if ever. However, middle-of-the-road and high-end tools usually come with solid manuals and tech support. Generally, the more expensive the product, the more extensive the manuals and tech support. If you're not used to working with beta or test-bed freeware, you might want to consider a midrange tool. Although it will cost you a bit, the headaches you'll avoid while trying to use it will be well worth the cost.

Chapter 23

XML And Web Browsers

By Cheryl Kirk

In Depth

Mention XML to any Web designer who isn't familiar with the topic and the first question he or she will probably ask is, "Which Web browsers currently support XML?" That's a good question and one that needs close examination if you plan to implement XML on the Web for public consumption or within an intranet for more private perusal of corporate data. Before you start converting all your HTML documents into XML files and applications, you need to know exactly how well today's browsers recognize and integrate XML. It's also important to know what kind of future XML support you might expect from the browser manufacturers. Knowing which direction the browser world is going will help you to better plan the design and implementation of your site.

In this chapter, we'll take a look at how XML is integrated into Web browsers. We'll also explore which browsers interpret XML now, how they do it, and the plans both Microsoft and Netscape have for future integration into Internet Explorer and Navigator respectively. At the end of this chapter, we'll discuss the role the Web server plays in transmitting XML data to browsers. But first, let's take a look at how XML found its way into browsers, and then we'll discuss how XML is implemented in various browsers.

A Little Browser History

Let's go back in time a bit to understand the evolutionary process browsers have gone through. Although HTML is actually an application of XML, try pulling up any well-formed XML document with older versions of browsers like Netscape's Navigator 3 or Microsoft's Internet Explorer 3 and see what you get—nothing! All things are not created equal, including markup languages, and even though older browsers can handle HTML tags just fine, interpreting XML is another story. These browsers don't understand Document Type Definitions (DTDs), styles sheets, or other XML-related code.

The simple fact is that these earlier browsers don't include an XML parser, which is an interpreter that translates the XML code. Still mired in the constraints of HTML, early browsers simply aren't capable of understanding exactly how to handle XML and accompanying DTDs. When the discussion of XML started back in 1996, there was simply no XML browser on the market to display XML data.

But there was support for Java within the early browsers, and that paved the way for a Java-enabled parser. As XML started to gain widespread support in early 1997, along came Jumbo, the first widely available freeware XML browser written completely in Java capable of being used by anyone with a Java-enabled browser. Jumbo's author, Peter Murray-Rust, wrote Java to work in concert with browsers like Navigator and Internet Explorer. This gave those who wanted access to XML data and applications the ability to work with, develop, and in limited context, display XML data.

Jumbo allows users to view XML documents without having to download or modify the actual browser software. Users only need to activate the Java Virtual Machine. Jumbo runs as a Java applet, providing access to any type of XML document available. Armed with this Java applet, XML was available to any Java-enabled browser.

TIP: *Jumbo can also be used as a standalone browser, although it lacks the features of Explorer or Navigator.*

In 1997, Microsoft released Internet Explorer 4, which included support for XML in both its internal XML parser and its XML application called channels. At that point, Internet Explorer became the first widespread, commercially available browser to implement XML, although in a somewhat limited fashion.

With Microsoft's Channel Definition Format, developers could then use some of XML's capabilities through the use of Channels, which is actually an XML application. Soon, more Web-server and Web-browser software manufacturers announced support for XML, and the groundswell started. Because CDF is so relatively easy to use—it can be added to any Web site with just a few lines of code—soon many site developers were creating links to channels. These XML applications "pushed" data to subscribers automatically, allowing the user to pick the display option for the data.

TIP: *Chapters 18 and 20 explore how CDF works and how you can implement channels in your Web site. Refer to these chapters to learn more about how to implement an XML application on your Web site.*

Then, it finally happened. At XML 98 (an XML developer's conference held in Seattle in spring 1998), Netscape displayed its support of XML within its widely popular Navigator browser. Netscape's support of XML was crucial, because Navigator was still holding on to a large share of the market. With support for XML in both browsers, Web site developers now knew XML was here to stay and therefore a language worth implementing on their sites.

It was during that developer's conference that Netscape engineer Ramanathan Guha demonstrated Netscape's first incantation in Mozilla, Netscape's development

23: XML And Web Browsers

version of the latest Navigator browser. In this version, Netscape demonstrated how Navigator could display XML data as easily as it displayed HTML code, making it seem as if XML was a native part of the Navigator browser. For those in attendance, it was obvious that Netscape went much further in its support of XML than the development community had previously thought it would. Not only did Netscape add a parser, it also included linking support and the use of Cascading Style Sheets (CSS) for the display of XML data.

Now that both major browser manufacturers were fully behind XML, all that was left was for the XML specification to be approved by the World Wide Web Consortium (W3C). This happened in May 1998. From this point forward, the movement toward implementing XML in browsers is gaining tremendous momentum.

How Do Browsers Work?

To understand the level of XML support found in today's popular browsers, first you have to understand what goes on behind the scenes when a browser displays a file. Let's start by dissecting a standard Web browser to see how information is fetched and displayed. Then, we'll examine how the most popular browsers use various components, such as scripts, a Java Virtual Machine, and style sheets to transfer and display information to the user.

If we break the browser down to its most basic parts (setting aside for a moment some of the integrated elements, such as newsgroup and email readers), it consists of four main processing components. Each browser component plays an integral part in the process of displaying Web pages:

- *The communications engine*—A communications engine is any piece of code that transmits data from the client (the browser) to a server and receives data from a server. The engine could be an HTTP communications engine or another type of engine, such as a Gopher, FTP, or newsgroup engine. In every browser, the HTTP communication engine sends HTTP requests to the server, receives data from the server, and passes it along to a parser. So when the user types a URL, the HTTP communications engine interprets the address and then sends the request to the intended Domain Name Server (DNS), which in turn looks up the IP address of the server and locates it either on the Internet or in an intranet. The Web server fetches the file and transmits it back to the HTTP communications engine, which then sends it on to the parser.

- *The parser*—The parser is a built-in application that reads and interprets the markup language sent from the communications engine. When the communications engine sends a file that contains XML to the parser, the parser checks the syntax. For example, it may check the file for well-formedness. If the code fits within a set of standardized rules, the parser converts the serialized markup text found in the file into an element tree structure. Once a page has been received and cached in memory, the parser is responsible for taking that file, creating the element tree structure, and sending it on to the presentation engine so the presentation engine can display the results of the parsed data.

- *A processor application*—The processor application could be a presentation engine. The application takes the information and/or elements the parser has processed and formats the elements based on the information supplied by the parsed file, recognizing and interpreting how the data should be displayed or processed. An application could take the data and print it, search it, or automatically read it to the blind user, or it could present the data on a computer screen. The data is displayed according to the rules set forth in the application. After the application takes the parsed data and displays it, the control is passed to the user through the user interface.

- *The user interface*—The user interface controls interaction between the user and the information that has been fetched, parsed, and displayed. The user interface includes menu bars, scroll bars, buttons, and so on. It allows the user to move through the parsed, presented data on the screen.

As you can see, these four main parts handle the data coming from Web (HTTP) servers and pass it along from one engine or processor to another until it is finally displayed. Of course, that's the most elemental way to explain how browsers take data and display it.

These days, however, browsers are actually much more complex and contain other engines, such as scripting engines, virtual machines, and plug-in interfaces. For example, the Netscape Navigator browser contains Netscape's Java Virtual Machine. This engine interprets and displays the results of Java code within the browser. Also, many of today's browsers have a plug-in interface, a processor that, when armed with the right plug-in, adds functionality to the browser by handling and displaying various MIME types that the browser's built-in parser and presentation engines cannot handle. Every engine included in any browser extends the capabilities of displaying, manipulating, and interfacing with the data presented to the user.

So, what does all this talk about processors and engines have to do with XML? First, as with HTML, every language needs some sort of parser to parse the data found in the file. A parser can be written as a component of the browser, or it can be added as a Java applet as long as the browser has a Java interpreter. The current versions of both Navigator and Internet Explorer not only include an HTML parser but also an XML parser, which allows any XML file to be displayed. The process of how that data is parsed varies from one browser to the next.

TIP: *We'll delve a little deeper into the differences between Navigator and Internet Explorer and how each parses XML data later in this chapter in "Netscape's Support For XML" and "Microsoft's Support For XML."*

XML is actually a markup language that serves only to describe the structure of the data, not the presentation of it. Therefore, displaying XML data is a little more complex than displaying HTML. After the data has been parsed into an element tree structure, the XML parser must pass along the process of displaying the resulting data to another presentation mechanism. XML does not offer tags for describing how the data should be presented, so after the XML parser has interpreted the data into an element tree structure, that task can be passed along to other processors, such as Cascading Style Sheets, which are found in both Navigator and Internet Explorer.

TIP: *What's the difference between a validating and non-validating parser? A non-validating parser checks the XML documents for well-formedness. A validating processor checks to make sure the documents are valid and that they conform to the rules found in their accompanying DTD. A validating processor also checks to make sure the code matches the XML language specification.*

The style sheet language is responsible for describing the element tree structure based upon the rules set out in the style sheet. XML relies on style sheets—either in the form of Cascading Style Sheets found in Navigator and Internet Explorer or the Extensible Style Language (XSL) found in Internet Explorer—to display the data. Think for a minute about how much more advantageous this process is than the process HTML offers. With HTML, the data and the formatting is all done in a single file. If Web-page designers want to design for a particular screen size, a particular browser, or in a particular format, they have to decide to possibly exclude those who don't use that particular browser or have a particular monitor size.

By relying on style sheets for presentation, XML source data can be written once and displayed in an amazing variety of ways. For example, to create data that could be viewed by a whole host of people, the designer could use different types of hardware and different style sheets to accommodate different viewing platforms. That means the same data could be displayed on a computer screen, on a cell-phone display, or through hand-held personal information management devices. The data stays the same, only the style sheet changes. Each device would use the proper style sheets to display the same data on its particular screen format.

TIP: *At present, to see the contents of an XML document, you first have to create a script that can read the content and then turn it into HTML. Then that content has to be manipulated by scripting again to display data in style sheets. XML documents are still not presented as part of the regular browser interface.*

Style sheets also allow for centralized control. With style sheets, the designer has full control over the look of a site without having to worry about changing the design and inadvertently changing the data. Currently, the W3C is working to standardize the XSL format, so you may see Netscape's implementation of style sheets, CSS, slowly fade away.

As you can see, XML and HTML work in concert: XML defines the structure of the data, and HTML defines how the data is displayed. Browsers, both now and in the future, will be able to process XML and HTML as they have processed just HTML in the past.

Netscape's Support For XML

With Navigator 5, Netscape is quickly adding support by including an XML delivery component, code-named Aurora, which uses the Resource Description Framework (RDF). Through RDF, Aurora appears on the user's desktop as what Netscape calls a *windowpane*. This windowpane is a menu interface that takes the links to documents, whether they are XML or HTML documents, and pull them together so, even though they may point to different resources, they actually create a single current project. Through RDF, the Aurora navigation bar points to local files of varying data types (such as word processing files, email messages, database files, or even spreadsheet files) and to resources that are available through internal or external network servers. RDF will also assist Aurora in storing other important user files, such as bookmarks, mail preferences, and channel definition formats.

Netscape's Focus For Navigator

"We want to turn Navigator into an XML platform."—Ramanathan Guha, Netscape principal engineer, speaking at the XML 98 conference.

Within this Aurora component is actually an XML parser based on XML guru James Clark's XP parser. Aside from parsing XML data, this parser can also parse files stored in the Chemical Markup Language (CML) and those files utilizing the MathML, a mathematical markup language. Both languages are now accepted by the World Wide Web Consortium.

The Aurora component also includes application support for XLink, the XML linking specification still in draft status at the W3C at the time of this writing. And Navigator 5 includes support for XML namespaces as well as transclusions, which are tags that mark an object that will be included by reference. In order to format parsed XML data, Netscape makes use of Cascading Style Sheets (CSS) to format all text encoded with XML tags. The Netscape browser's rendering engine not only works with XML, it also works with HTML.

TIP: *At the time of this writing, Netscape currently displays XML pages using CSS, XMLLink, and elements from the HTML namespace.*

Figure 23.1 outlines how Netscape incorporates the XML architecture in the latest version of its browser. The arrows represent the C, Java, and JavaScript application programming interfaces (APIs).

Microsoft's Support For XML

Microsoft started showing its support for XML back in the summer of 1996 when it helped found the XML Working Group. From that point forward, Microsoft was the first browser vendor to aggressively start implementing XML. As a matter of fact, Internet Explorer was the first commercial browser to offer true XML support by adding an XML parser and an XML application through Internet Explorer's Channel Definition Format. Microsoft offers support for XML through a pair of XML processors. One parser is written in C++ and comes with the browser. The second is a Java parser with source code that Web builders can download and incorporate into their own applications. Both are generalized and not dependent upon any particular XML application, such as CDF.

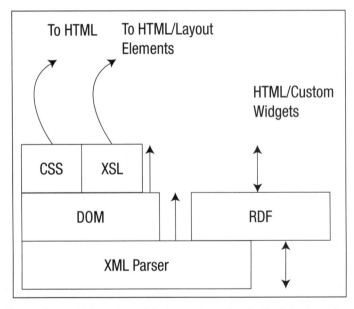

Figure 23.1   How Netscape integrates XML and various APIs in the latest version of its browser. The arrows represent the C, Java, and JavaScript APIs.

In the simplest form, support of XML documents in Internet Explorer 4 works like this: Explorer accesses the XML document, queries it for data, and then displays it as HTML. Because XML does not handle the presentation side of things, Microsoft uses what it calls the XML Data Source Object, or XML DSO. This model uses the data binding capability of Dynamic HTML in an effort to link the XML data to HTML.

Internet Explorer also uses the XML Object Model (XML OM) to let developers interact with XML. With this model, developers can interact with XML data within the browser by exposing HTML as objects based on the Document Object Model (DOM). With DOM, developers can access structured XML data through scripts and other programs.

But Microsoft didn't stop there. In addition to support for DOM, Internet Explorer supports XSL. XML transforms XML into HTML in an effort to format XML directly. XSL is compatible with CSS and is derived from the Document Style Semantics and Specification Language (DSSSL). Microsoft feels CSS is not suitable for presenting XML data properly, because it lacks the ability to redesign data in a different order than how it was received. The company views XSL as offering more functionality than CSS because of its inherent scripting capabilities, and Microsoft is pushing to have the W3C standardize on this style sheet language.

TIP: *For more information about Microsoft's view on the XSL standard, check **www.microsoft.com/standards/xsl**.*

Microsoft has also gotten behind the Resource Description Framework (RDF). This initiative takes features from the XML-Data and Meta Content Format, a technology originally created by Apple and then acquired by Netscape. Although RDF's underlying syntax is still XML, it provides a complementary view of XML data by using what Netscape calls "graphs" and "nodes" instead of the element tree structure.

With these technologies in place, and because it is tightly integrating browser technology within Windows 98, Microsoft has vowed to offer wide-ranging support for XML. Already, you'll find XML support in the Microsoft Commerce Server and limited support in Microsoft Office.

Support For XML In Internet Explorer 4

The support you'll find in Microsoft Internet Explorer 4 includes:

- *Two parsers*—One written in C++ that comes with Internet Explorer and the source code to a Java parser that developers can download and incorporate into their applications. The Java parser is a validating parser that checks against a Document Type Definition (DTD).

TIP: *The C++ parser is a non-validating parser. The only reason it is a non-validating parser is to improve performance. Also, note that both parsers included in Internet Explorer 4 are not dependent on specific XML applications.*

- *XML Data Source Object (XML DSO)*—It uses the data-binding facility found in Dynamic HTML to bind structured XML data to HTML.

- *XML Object Model support*—This model turns all XML data elements into programmable objects.

Within the Internet Explorer application, you'll find support for two document-based file formats:

- *Channel Definition Format*—The CDF file provides an index of resources available in a channel the user has subscribed to. Also within the CDF file is a recommended schedule for when the channel should be updated on the local computer.

- *Open Software Description (OSD)*—OSD is a format for describing Cabinet Files, Java packages, and other interactive file types. This new file format is meant to supersede INF files.

Most likely, you'll see much more support for XML at more than just the browser level. Already you can find XML support in Microsoft's Commerce Server and in such desktop applications as Microsoft Office and Outlook and new releases of Microsoft's FrontPage site-management application.

The Future Of XML

XML has certainly fostered a great deal of interest over the past few years. But unlike HTML, with all its complexity, XML will take more time to catch on. Once developers fully integrate XML in not only Web browsers but also a myriad of publishing applications, you should see XML used in a variety of applications and within a variety of industries.

Already corporations, such as Cisco Systems, use XML to distribute news and information within the corporate network, culling that information from multiple sources both inside and outside the company. Hewlett-Packard is in the testing phase of a new XML-based business system that relies on software from WebMethods (a vendor of server software) that, through the use of XML, lets users exchange data with each other, other Web sites, proprietary internal systems, and various desktop applications.

It's rumored too that the government is jumping on the XML bandwagon by making some governmental information and catalogs available, and Citibank has reported that it is currently working on a billing and payment system based primarily on XML.

You should see a variety of personalized and customizable applications for the Web hit the market, such as Microsoft's Internet Explorer Channels. For example, larger newspapers in the United States are now working with XML to create customizable, push-deliverable news, weather, and sports. And with XML's ability to connect databases to documents, you should see a wide range of accessible applications that bring together internal corporate and external client information in a single interface, provided in a relatively automatic fashion.

XML should also help jump-start the electronic commerce industry, which has lagged behind for so many years because of the constraints of HTML. With XML, vendors can now create industry-specific tags for products through a common format, providing a consistent way for electronic shoppers to access and find the information about products they need.

XML will also speed up the acceptance of Electronic Data Interchange (EDI). EDI takes existing paper documents and turns them into electronic verifiable documents. With standardized XML tags for EDI, hospitals, insurance companies, and doctors' offices can all exchange information about a patient, and the proper forms can easily be transferred through the Internet or through a separate secure intranet.

And just as XML/EDI hopes to change the future of paperwork, XML and the Open Software Description format will give developers the ability to automate software distribution both on the Internet and through an intranet. OSD, a set of tags created by Microsoft and Marimba, describes how software packages can be distributed across multiple software platforms. So instead of walking into CompUSA to pick up the latest version of Windows, you'll be able to use the power of XML to not only purchase the software, but also to install it without a CD-ROM. This also means corporations will be able to easily update all users on a network without having to manually install the software updates on each individual machine.

But all of these possibilities will require that Netscape and Microsoft continue to update, expand, and standardize XML browser support, style sheet implementations, and linking options. Both companies have shown that they want to quickly adopt XML within their browsers, but actual full implementation may not happen for a year or two.

23: XML And
Web Browsers

Immediate Solutions

In this section, you'll view XML data using several browsers that implement XML through somewhat different methods. You'll explore how Microsoft Internet Explorer displays XML files and how the Java-enabled Jumbo browser displays XML data with either Internet Explorer or Navigator.

Viewing XML Data With The Jumbo Java Browser

In this project, you'll use the Jumbo Java browser to view XML data. You should already have a Java-enabled browser, such as Netscape Navigator version 4 or above or Microsoft Internet Explorer version 4 or above. You can find Jumbo at **ala.vsms.nottingham.ac.uk/vsms/java/jumbo** in the form of a zipped file. The file contains all the Java classes needed to run the Jumbo browser. However, at the time of this writing, Jumbo does not include an XML parser, so you need to download an XML parser of your choice.

Enabling Java To Work With Your Browser

To enable Java to work with your browser, follow these steps:

1. Connect to the Internet, and launch Navigator or Internet Explorer.

2. If you are using Netscape Navigator 4, select Preferences from the Edit menu, and click on the Advanced option. Do not expand this option—only click on the word *Advanced*. (If you are using Internet Explorer, skip to Step 5.)

3. Look at the right-hand side of the Preferences tab and make sure the Enable Java checkbox is checked (see Figure 23.2). Java won't be enabled if you select only Enable JavaScript. JavaScript is Netscape's implementation of a scripting language, but it does not allow you to run Java applets.

4. Click on the Apply button, and then click on OK.

5. If you are using Internet Explorer 4, select Internet Options from the View menu.

6. Scroll down and click on the Java Console Enabled checkbox under the Java VM section.

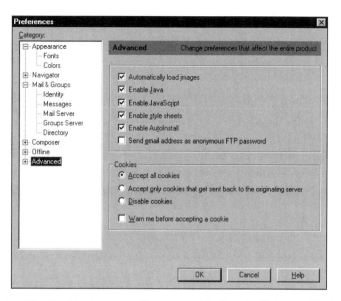

Figure 23.2   Select the Enable Java checkbox to enable Java in Netscape Navigator.

7. Click on OK, and exit Internet Explorer.

8. Click on the Start button on the Windows Taskbar, and select Shut Down. Select the option to shut down and restart the computer in order for the installation of Internet Explorer to complete.

Downloading The Jumbo Java Browser

To download the Jumbo Java browser, follow these steps:

1. Enter "http://ala.vsms.nottingham.ac.uk/vsms/java/jumbo" in your browser's address field, and press Enter.

2. Click on the link to download the latest version of the Jumbo browser. Make sure you select the zipped file, which is the correct file format for Windows-based systems.

3. After you've downloaded the file, create a folder on your desktop labeled Jumbo, and place the zipped file in it. Unzip the file to this folder. You should see the following files:

   • jumbo (directory, with subdirectories for class files)

   • icons (directory for icons on a per-package basis)

   • scene1.sgm (Act 1, Scene 1 from *Julius Caesar*)

   • install.xml (the installation documentation)

- jumbo/mimetypes.xml (MIME types read by Jumbo)
- jumbo/config.xml (this is the configuration file for Jumbo, and it can be used with other parsers)

Warning: Make sure your CLASSPATH includes the directory where you've placed all your demo files. Otherwise, Jumbo may not be able to find all the files it needs to display XML files.

Running The Jumbo Browser

To run the Jumbo browser, follow these steps:

1. Open the browser, and select File|Open menu. In the Jumbo folder, locate the file scene1.sgm.

2. Click on the Open button to open the file. At this point, the browser window opens, and you will notice a progress message stating that Jumbo is reading the file.

3. The Jumbo browser and Java reads the file, parses it, and converts it into a tree that displays the file's table of contents in the element tree structure format. Figure 23.3 shows the Jumbo Object Browser window displaying the TOC. The root node is listed as #DOCROOT.

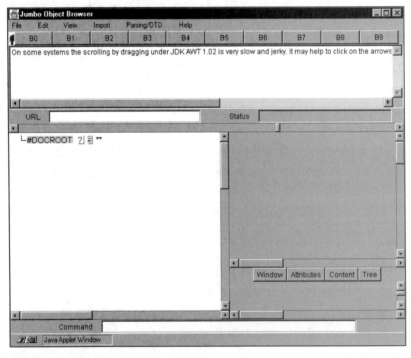

Figure 23.3   The Jumbo Object Browser window.

4. To view the tree, click on the folder icon just as you would in Windows Explorer. Your screen should look like Figure 23.4.

5. You can also use the command line to open files and at the same time specify the parser you would like to use. For example, if you are using the Lark parser, you would type "java jumbo.sgml.Jumbo scene1.sgm PARSER=SAX:Lark".

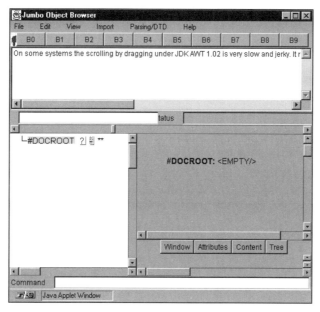

Figure 23.4   The #DOCROOT provides an element tree structure for the files listed in the XML application.

Viewing XML Data With Internet Explorer 4

Microsoft has done an excellent job with its first attempt to integrate XML into its browser. And with the examples Microsoft offers, you can quickly get a feel for how XML works to display metadata. The actual procedure for viewing XML files is the same as viewing any file or page, especially if you are using Windows 98. Microsoft includes a C++ parser in the latest version of Internet Explorer 4. This parser is a non-validating parser and supports most of the W3C XML specifications. Make sure you update your version of Explorer before you attempt to access any of the examples. You can update your browser at **www.microsoft.com/ie**.

Accessing Microsoft's XML Demonstration Files

To view the Microsoft demonstration files, follow these steps:

1. Launch the Internet Explorer browser. If you are using the Active Desktop option found with Windows 98, you can simply open any folder or volume window and type "microsoft.com/xml" in the Address field. Assuming you are connected to the Internet, this will provide access to the site, or it will initiate the dial-up network option and connect you to the Internet. The Active Desktop provides immediate access to Internet Explorer from any window on your desktop.

2. Type "http://www.microsoft.com/xml" in the Address field of the browser window. This is Microsoft's main page for everything relating to XML (see Figure 23.5).

3. Locate the list of XML sample files in the list of links displayed in the left frame. You may need to scroll down to see the list of demo files.

4. Click on the link for the XML samples. The first quick sample you might want to view is the Weather sample. It takes data and parses it into a format. It also displays the XML code used to create the page.

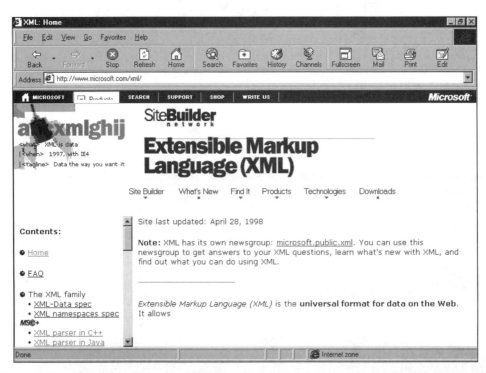

Figure 23.5   Microsoft's XML page. The XML demo files are located under The XML Family, in the left frame.

5. In the Weather sample, the right frame changes to display two buttons for you to choose whether you would like use the C++ parser or the Java parser. The C++ parser button may already be highlighted if the page has already loaded.

6. Click on the button for the parser you want to use, then scroll down to view the result of the parsed file. Figure 23.6 shows what your screen will look like.

Figure 23.6   Microsoft's Internet Explorer displays the results of the XML file for the Weather sample.

Chapter 24
How People Are Using XML

By Cheryl Kirk

In Depth

There are literally thousands of corporations, libraries, small businesses, and even individuals whose Web sites and intranets can benefit from deploying XML. XML is extensible and flexible and is quickly becoming the next wave of the Web. Soon, you'll find Web-site developers using XML to serve up dynamic documents. Because of the flurry of user interest, a large collection of software—including browsers, specialized server products, and development tools—are also quickly hitting the market.

In this chapter, we'll examine how various industries are using XML. We'll start with an overview and move on to specific examples. We'll also show you how real people are using XML. On Web sites for the healthcare industry, in online newspapers, and on simple Web sites, XML is handling data that used to be handled by complex and intricate scripting languages.

TIP: *An excellent place to find out how others are using XML is James Tauber's XML.Info site, located at* ***www.xmlinfo.com****.*

Who Is Using XML?

Major corporations are already beginning to use XML within their networks. Some are replacing older HTML-based systems for data structure and delivery, and others are using XML to enhance their existing networks and reduce the cost of coding specialized programs. In this section, we'll examine how DHL, the Wall Street Journal Interactive Edition, Ziff-Davis's ZDNet online service, and an oil company all use XML in one form or another to structure and deliver information to their employees, customers, clients, and other corporations. Some of these organizations are using XML-based applications. Some are using XML with programming languages, such as JavaScript, to create automated dynamic documents that are delivered over the Internet and through intranets.

In this section, we'll show you the software these organizations are using to integrate XML into their networks. This section is meant to give you ideas concerning the variety of systems XML can work within. Because many of these sites are complex and employ a tremendous amount of code, we'll concentrate on how XML is being used, not the specifics of the code. In this chapter's Immediate Solutions section, we'll focus on two sites—a simple Web site about weeds and another that demonstrates a real estate system—and show you the DTDs and code they used to create their XML documents.

The Wall Street Journal Interactive Edition

The Wall Street Journal Interactive Edition was one of the first electronic newspapers on the Web and one of the first to start making money right away. With more than 200,000 paid subscribers, the Wall Street Journal (WSJ) Interactive Edition is now handling some 40 million page views a month. Figure 24.1 shows the main page.

To keep up with such expansive growth and demand, the WSJ uses a variety of languages (such as JavaScript and Perl) to interface with their SGML- and now XML-based systems to produce dynamic pages on the fly for all their subscribers. The Journal can deliver information to Web-based desktop users and Palm Pilot users and will be able to deliver information to users of pagers and other types of mobile technology in the future.

How The System Works

Here's how the system works. First, Microsoft Word is used to input the text. The files are saved in Word's Rich Text Format (RTF). Then, the staff runs the customized Visual Basic scripts that they created for Word. These macros take the text in the Microsoft Word file and turn the file into a SGML/XML-tagged file. From there, a JavaScript conversion program is used to format the text to look like the print edition of *The Wall Street Journal.*

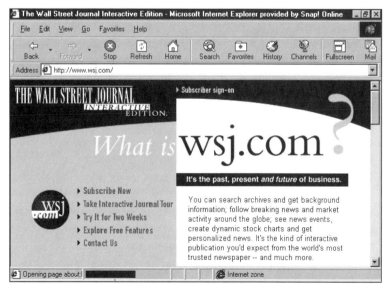

Figure 24.1   The WSJ Interactive Edition's Welcome screen.

The interactive edition of the Journal is created by using a combination of XML and Microsoft Word. They used the Visual Basic macro programming language to customize Word. Macros were created to tag elements such as headline, byline, and company name within the document with the XML element tags specified for those types of entries. When editors or reporters need to tag a section of a document with a specific XML tag, they simply click on an icon that represents the appropriate tag on the Microsoft Word toolbar that has been customized with Word's macro language.

From there, the file is saved in RTF format. The format allows another utility to read the file—a standard text file at this point—and convert it into XML text. The utility they use is the Konstructor Suite from OmniMark Technologies Corporation. It inserts the proper XML elements and attributes and the XML processing instructions needed to transform the RTF document into an XML document. Konstructor Suite uses a batch process to convert the documents into HTML pages that can then be formatted for various delivery options, including standard Web pages and Palm Pilot pages that use the AvantGo format (which lets Palm Pilot users download the interactive edition into their Palm Pilots for later reading).

Specialized formatting for a wide variety of users isn't the only thing XML offers the interactive edition. It also helps the Journal create archives of its articles that can easily be searched. For example, if you want to read stories written by Walter Mossberg, you can search by byline. The search would return exactly what you want, because you can base your search on an element instead of content, as you would in an HTML-based search. If you're searching for articles written about IBM, you could search by the **<COMPANY NAME>** element. You wouldn't find documents that mention IBM, only those written about IBM because the **<COMPANY NAME>** element specifies what company the article is about. The interactive edition uses a full-text search feature that Verity Incorporated supplies. It runs on four servers dedicated to full-text searching for its subscribers.

The Future Of The Interactive Edition

When all popular browsers fully incorporate XML, the Wall Street Journal Interactive Edition will move toward full delivery of XML documents to the desktop. Various style sheets will be used to format the stories in whatever format the reader specifies. And readers will be able to specify how their front pages are delivered and what is included. The Journal will complement its existing scripting capabilities by adding more client-side scripts that let readers organize their front pages on the fly.

Using XML In The Oil Patch

Keeping an Alaskan-based major oil-drilling operation running is no easy task. Downtime means lost income, and high maintenance costs can cut into the profits at an alarming rate. Different computing systems to serve a variety of specific purposes have been developed over time. Over the years, however, this has caused more problems because of the lack of integration between the systems. More paperwork is generated just to keep an audit trail of where parts and orders are and where back orders currently stand. Some of the systems are flat-file databases, and others are relational databases. They don't, however, offer any type of data interchange, which means reentering information is common.

Now that the Internet is available and accessibility of outside data sources is becoming a priority, the information technology (IT) group needs to find a solution that will help tie in all these different systems and at the same time offer a simple interface for users. Parts suppliers are offering parts catalogs over the Internet, as well as some order and back-order checking capabilities, so the IT group is also charged with bringing inside and outside sources of information together. As it stands, each system has its own unique keystrokes and menu options, and training new employees takes considerable time. The idea is to not only integrate the systems, but to create a simple flow-through system that provides a standard interface to the user and minimizes training requirements.

The idea is to eventually have everything integrated. Although each piece of equipment comes from a different manufacturer and has its own user's manual, the IT group would like to meld this paper library into an electronic one that can easily be searched from any networked system in the plant. Presently, there is a large library full of manuals on how to repair everything from the microwave oven to the flanges and valves used to keep the oil flowing. Just to figure out what's wrong with a certain piece of equipment, a repairperson has to search these manuals by hand, which is both time-consuming and difficult. The ideal solution is to create a computer system that provides repair information to staff members who enter a few simple keywords describing the problem.

As it stands, after a repairperson figures out what's wrong with a piece of equipment by searching through the manuals and checking previous repair logs, he or she has to access the company's inventory database to find out if the needed part is in stock. If it is, the repairperson has to switch over to another system to order it. If it isn't in stock, the repairperson has to create an order and send it to the warehouse where yet another system is used to order the part from the supplier. None of the information is automated, nor is the information staff members supply to either database. Employees must type in the information each time they work with each system. Because of this nonintegration of data, the following problems arise:

- Ordering and servicing a piece of equipment can take a long time, which means more downtime for the crew.

- A tremendous amount of time is spent searching for the right information and processing paperwork so there is a paper trail in case information is lost, which happens frequently.

- Information within the different systems is inconsistent—one part may be referenced in a variety of ways. Unless the repairperson and the suppliers are familiar with the nomenclature, the repairperson may never find the right part or may end up ordering the wrong part.

When the IT department decided to tackle this problem, they realized they had a big job on their hands. First, they decided to examine each system to see how the information flowed and in what order. They also paid specific attention to how each field of data was identified. From there, they created a flow chart, complete with field names and requirements for each system.

At that point, they realized they needed an integrated database and a delivery system that required only a few keystrokes to find information and a few more keystrokes to place an order. Because the information in the database doesn't change, they needed a transport mechanism to bring it through from one database system to the next. These separate pieces of data—the manuals, the service logs, the on-hand inventory system, the supplier's parts database, and the ordering system—needed to be integrated in some fashion.

The idea was to create a DTD that encompassed all the different fields and their required attributes that would work across systems. Because it allows developers to create customized element tags, and because it can communicate between various data sources and then deliver the data through any browser, the IT department used XML as the standard. They started by forming a committee to create the DTD. The committee included the repair staff, the warehouse personnel, and even the outside vendors. The various committee members' involvement helped the IT department figure out exactly what information needed to flow and how it needed to be referenced. After they had a DTD in place, they set about finding exactly how the order processing worked, so they could identify what databases needed to be integrated and in what fashion.

The Ideal Process

The repairman is called to check on a valve that is malfunctioning. He discovers that a simple retaining clip is broken. He goes over to the terminal in the repair shop, enters his login information, brings up the Web browser, and enters the search term *retaining clip*. He's looking for the actual part number for this particular type of retaining clip. Instead of flipping through a parts catalog book like he used to, he can quickly locate the information he needs when he queries the parts inventory database.

The information he is looking for is retrieved, and a list of different retaining clips is shown in both text and picture form. He clicks on the picture that represents the retaining clip he needs, and the information he needs is automatically generated in a separate window. Information, such as the description of the part, installation instructions, and special alerts about using this retaining clip in various valves, is listed. Also included in this dynamic page is a series of buttons; one of which allows the repairman to get the inventory count and pricing information.

When the repairman clicks on the button to check on-hand inventories, he is informed that the part is in stock in the company's warehouse in aisle 4, bin 32. There are only two of this particular retaining clip in stock, and this level has been determined to be the reorder point, so a reorder alert message is flashed on the Web page. Because this is the part he needs, the repairman clicks on the button to order it. The order is sent to the parts warehouse employee, who knows where to deliver it because of the location from which the order was placed and the logon ID. Because an order has been placed, and because on-hand inventories are low, the system has also been instructed—by the value of the attribute for the on-hand quantity, and by the value of the attribute of the **<PART-NUM>** element—to place an order with the manufacturer for more retaining clips.

When the warehouse employee gets the order, she clicks on a button to verify that more retaining clips should be ordered. This button brings up a form with most of the information already filled in. All the parts warehouse employee has to do is verify the order and provide any additional delivery instructions in the fields provided. Once she clicks on the Submit button, the order is electronically delivered to the supplier and confirmation that the order has been received is electronically mailed to the parts person.

How The System Was Created

After the committee members identified the problems, they identified the tools that were necessary to accomplish the ideal process. This is what they came up with:

- For the user interface format, the company decided to use Internet Explorer as the standard because of its existing and soon-to-be-revamped XML capabilities and because of the Dynamic HTML (DHTML) features it offers.

- They standardized on the Microsoft Internet Information Server (IIS), because it could interpret and store XML files and because the programmers could easily interface with the Active Server Page technology that is part of IIS.

- To connect disparate databases together, they selected Insight, a product developed by Enigma (**www.enigmainc.com**).

The programmers can use Insight and XML DTD elements and attributes to create information for the various systems and match it up with an HTML-based form. Consider, for example, a parts search. The programmer can create a part-number tag and specify it as **<PART-NUM>** in the XML data set. When the part number is passed to the company's material inventory database via Insight, the software program, Insight instructs the materials inventory database system to be automatically searched. But that's not all. After **<PART-NUM>** has been found in the database, if the **<PART-NUM>** attribute's **QTY-ON-HAND** value is less than two, inventory is automatically ordered. The XML-based parts document looks something like this:

```
<?XML version="1.0"?>
    <PART>
      <PARTLIST>
       <PART-NUM>32-A-Valve</PART-NUM>
       <PART-NAME>Valve</PART-NAME>
       <UNITS-PER-ASSEMBLY>1</UNITS-PER-ASSEMBLY>
      </PARTLIST>
      <INSTALL-INFO>
         <SUPPLIER-NOTE>Make sure the pressure valve is in
         the off position when installing this part.
         </SUPPLIER-NOTE>
         <ADDITIONAL-NOTES>Contact the OCC before installing
         or bringing off-line any valves. Extension 6345
         </ADDITIONAL-NOTES>
      </INSTALL-INFO>
    </PART>
```

The Internet Explorer browser and Microsoft's Internet Information Server use XML to store the information and transfer it back and forth from user to supplier to parts person. The information is stored in XML format on the server, and when it is requested, Dynamic HTML formats it for the browser. The IIS server uses the Data Source Object scripting on the browser end to generate the DHTML. Because all the data is sent to the client at the time it is requested, the user can switch between a view of how to install the part to a view of the inventory status without having to make another request to the server. This off-loads a lot of server connection requirements and provides a speedier way to do business.

By using Enigma's Insight database, the IT department of this oil company was able to create a system whereby the parts catalog is stored in the Insight database along with a customized subset of maintenance data that lists the service logs, parts descriptions, and supporting documentation. This information is delivered in XML format to the parts warehouse. Additional information can then be stored in a variety of formats, including XML, Adobe's PDF for the manual information, and Microsoft Word for correspondence about the various parts, orders, and processes. The XML document for the inventory system looks something like this:

```
<?XML version="1.0"?>
    <INVENTORY>
        <PART-NUM>32-A-Valve</PART-NUM>
        <PART-NAME>Valve</PART-NAME>
        <LOCAL-INVENTORY>
            <AVAILABLE>10</AVAILABLE>
            <LOCATION>BIN Warehouse A-47</LOCATION>
        </LOCAL-INVENTORY>
          <SUPPLIER>
            <NAME>Rolls Royce</NAME>
            <COMMERCE-SERVER-URL>http://commerce.rollsroyce.com
            </COMMERCE-SERVER-URL>
          </SUPPLIER>
    </INVENTORY>
    </PART>
```

All this data is then loaded into the Insight database. First, the Insight database creates a structure map of any Word documents and turns them into XML files that contain the element tag information, the assigned style sheet references, and any summary information about the Word files. Then, it checks the PDF files and adds meta information about them and what's contained within the XML document. After all the information is loaded and turned into XML data, it becomes available for any user to query by using a standard HTML Web page form.

The major parts inventory database and the parts availability information are maintained in a relational database stored within the company's intranet. When the repairperson performs a query against the database, the query is gathered up by the form and sent to the Insight search engine, which in turn uses ODBC to generate an SQL query against the actual database server. After the pertinent information is gathered, the results are turned into XML, which is then parsed and displayed back to the repairperson's browser through the use of style sheets.

The repairperson is actually using Insight's search capabilities, the predefined XML DTD, and its elements to create a search query. If the repairperson cannot find the information through a search, he or she can use the standard XML hierarchy, which is displayed in a kind of table of contents, to navigate to the information needed.

Ziff-Davis's ZiffNet

Ziff-Davis has a lot of Web-based content, and the amount of content just keeps growing. Long known for its stable of computer magazines and its book-publishing ventures, Ziff-Davis (the company that owns ZDNet, an online informational service) has branched out onto the Web, becoming one of the preeminent sources of computer news and information. But the company had to figure out a way to stay one step ahead of the ever-increasing competition. They plan to do that with the help of StoryServer, an XML-based product created by Vignette Corporation.

Using The XML-Based StoryServer

StoryServer allows readers to customize the news and information ZDNet offers. Users can customize their home pages, and StoryServer will track and find the stories that match users' particular interests. Eventually, the system will "learn" what readers' preferences are and will seek out corresponding information, including information about special product promotions or even assistance with their computer systems. Advertisers will be able to notify readers of special sales and promotions for products in which readers have indicated interest. Ads will appear less randomly and be targeted to the reader. For example, readers on the East Coast will see ads for companies in their area, or Mac users will see more advertisements for Mac products than for PC products.

The advertisements are also customizable, but readers don't have to customize their preferences for ads. Instead, StoryServer customizes ads by keeping track of the types of articles they read and the type of banner advertising they respond to.

The system creates a template for the type of articles that need to be placed on the site. The templates provide a structure for the content in an XML-based format. The content is then fed into the templates, and the information is stored in a relational repository. When a user requests content stored within the repository, the Web page is generated dynamically. The repository database is actually an Oracle-based system that uses scripting to generate the Web pages.

DHL

DHL Worldwide Express is the world's largest shipper. The company ships to more than 635,000 destinations in more than 220 countries worldwide. Its business is package delivery, a business that continues to be fiercely competitive. DHL knew it needed a competitive advantage. Knowing that its clients used several package shipping outfits instead of just one, DHL decided to offer them the ability to do something none of its competitors were letting them do—track packages regardless of the shipper they used. They asked the people at Netscape if they thought they could create a system that would let any customer with access to the Web check multiple shipping companies from a single site. Netscape proposed a system that was based on their server technology and would have cost DHL around $30,000.

Instead, DHL decided to use an XML-based product called the webMethod Automation ToolKit, produced by a company called webMethods; webMethods produced the system in a couple of hours for only a couple thousand dollars. The overall software solution, DHL Connect, uses the XML-based server tool, a software program that reads and manipulates XML data, to streamline tracking of international deliveries regardless of whether customers are using DHL, FedEx, United Parcel Service, or Airborne Freight.

The server finds the information requested by customer, analyzes it, and creates a structure of Java objects that are then relayed to a Web page. It interfaces with DHL's existing Oracle, Informix, and DB2 databases to extract the information requested by the customer. The system will also notify the customer of an incoming shipment by using an interface that connects with the XML-based server to deliver notifications by email, fax, downloadable Web page, or just about any other format the customer specifies.

24: How People Are Using XML

Immediate Solutions

In this section, you'll learn how XML was used to develop two Web sites. The first example is a relatively elaborate database-driven site that displays the various types of weeds found in El Limon. The second outlines how the real estate industry can use XML to create a customized search engine for displaying real estate inventories.

Creating The Weeds Of El Limon Site

The idea behind the Weeds of El Limon site (**www.honeylocust.com/limon**) is simple. Put information about and drawings of 32 different weeds on a Web site and format it so that anyone with a Web browser can easily investigate what kind of wild foliage grows native in the village of El Limon, which is located in the Dominican Republic. Anyone browsing the site can view the weeds by Latin name or common name.

The authors of the site—Olivia Direnzo, the illustrator, and Paul Houle, the self-styled Informatician, as he calls himself—realized that making this information available on the Web would be a horrendous task if they had to create HTML pages. It would be difficult to achieve a consistent look across pages, and they were concerned that they might leave something out or that the site might not work with all browsers. In addition, if they wanted to re-create the site for their Spanish-speaking friends, they would have to re-create the content. So, the authors decided to use XML to create the site. With XML, they figured they could create their own element tags and wouldn't have to worry about a consistent look, adding new elements, or repurposing the content in a variety of ways. XML would also make it easier for visitors to search for information.

Paul decided to bypass the standard method of using Java to intercept the XML data and create Web pages, a method many developers use to display XML files. Instead, he decided to write a program that would compile the XML files into somewhat plain but standard static HTML pages and serve them up as requested.

Creating A Java-Based XML Conversion System

The system Paul created is actually a three-tiered system. First, he created the XML DTD and the XML content document. Then, he used the XML parser to collect the objects of the XML document. He used MSXML as his parser, although he admits if he had to do it over again, he might use IBM's XML for Java parser. Nevertheless, after the information is parsed, the output is true XML. He developed a Java-based parsing system that would create another class of objects, which includes a species object and a text chunk object that are both used to pass along data that describes the entire plant. This allows him to easily transform the data from XML format to HTML format. Finally, he used a Java-based HTML generator to create the page. The source code for the generator is in Listing 24.1.

Listing 24.1 The source code for the generator.

```java
package honeylocust.limon;

import honeylocust.limon.representation.*;

import java.io.PrintWriter;
import java.io.FileWriter;
import java.io.IOException;
import java.io.File;
import java.io.FileNotFoundException;
import java.text.DateFormat;
import java.util.Vector;
import java.util.Date;


public abstract class GenerateHtml {

  String p_htmlPath;
  String p_imagePath;

  public GenerateHtml() {

    p_htmlPath="";
    p_imagePath="images/";
  };

  public void setHtmlPath(String s) {
    p_htmlPath=s;
  };

  public void setImagePath(String s) {
    p_imagePath=s;
  };

  public String getLanguage() {
    return "en";
  };
```

```
      public String getRobotInfo() {
        return "ALL";
      };

      public String getAuthor() {
        return "Olivia S. Direnzo and Paul A. Houle";
      };

      public Date getDate() {
        return new Date();
      };

      public String getCopyright() {
        return "&copy; 1998 Honeylocust
Media Systems
(http://www.honeylocust.com/)";
      };

      public String getKeywords() {
        return "El Limon,Weeds,Botany,xml";
      };

      public String getDescription() {
        return "A collection of descriptions and illustrations
        of weeds observed in El Limon,  a small village in the
        Dominican Republic during January 1998. ";
      };

      public String getVersion() {
        return "0.9a";
      };

      public abstract String computeTitle();

      public void generateHead(PrintWriter w) {
        w.println("<HTML lang='"+getLanguage()+"'>");
        w.println("<HEAD><TITLE>"+computeTitle()+"</TITLE>");
        generateMetaInformation(w);
        w.println("</HEAD>");
        w.println("<BODY BGCOLOR=#FFFFFF>");
      };

      public void
      generateMeta(PrintWriter w,String name,String content) {
        if (content==null || content.length()==0)
          return;
```

```
    w.println("<META name='"+name+"' content='"+content+"'
lang='"+getLanguage()+"'>");
  };


  public void generateLink(PrintWriter w,String rel,String href )
  {
    if (href==null || href.length()==0)
      return;

    w.println("<LINK rel='"+rel+"' href='"+href+"'>");
  };

  public void generateMetaInformation(PrintWriter w) {
    generateMeta(w,"ROBOTS",getRobotInfo());
    generateMeta(w,"Author",getAuthor());
    generateMeta(w,"Date",getDate().toGMTString());
    generateMeta(w,"Copyright",getCopyright());
    generateMeta(w,"Keywords",getKeywords());
    generateMeta(w,"Description",getDescription());
    generateLink(w,"Index","../common/");
    generateLink(w,"Index","../family/");
    generateLink(w,"Index","../latin/");
    generateLink(w,"Begin","1.html");
    generateLink(w,"Top","..");
    generateLink(w,"Contents","..");
    generateLink(w,"Start","..");
  };

  public void generateTopBar(PrintWriter w) {
    w.println("<TABLE CELLSPACING=0 WIDTH=100%>
    <TR><TD BGCOLOR=#000000><FONT COLOR=#FFFFFF>
    <FONT SIZE=+2><FONT FACE='sans-
    serif'>"+computeTitle()+"</FONT></FONT></FONT>
    </TD></TR></TABLE>");
  };

  void generateNavLink(PrintWriter w,String text,String url)
  {
    w.print("<A STYLE='text-decoration:none' HREF='"+url+"'>
    <FONT COLOR=white>"+text+"</FONT></A>");
  };

  void generateNavSpacer(PrintWriter w) {
    w.print(" | ");
  };
```

```
public void generateNavInsert(PrintWriter w) {
  generateNavLink(w,"TOP","..");
  generateNavSpacer(w);
};

public void generateNavBar(PrintWriter w) {
  w.println("<BR CLEAR=ALL>");

  w.println("<TABLE CELLSPACING=0 WIDTH=100%><TR>
  <TD BGCOLOR=#000000><FONT COLOR=#FFFFFF><FONT SIZE=+1>
  <FONT FACE='sans-serif'>");
  generateNavInsert(w);
  generateNavLink(w,"FAMILY","../family");
  generateNavSpacer(w);
  generateNavLink(w,"LATIN","../latin");
  generateNavSpacer(w);
  generateNavLink(w,"COMMON","../common");
  w.println("</FONT></FONT></FONT></TD></TR></TABLE>");

};

void generateTail(PrintWriter w) {
  w.println("<BR CLEAR=all><hr>");
  w.print("<I>Version "+getVersion()+" ");
  w.println("&copy; 1998
  <A HREF='http://www.honeylocust.com/'>
  Honeylocust Media Systems.</A>");
  w.println(" Contact: <A HREF='mailto:houle@msc.cornell.edu'>
houle@msc.cornell.edu</A>");
  w.println("</BODY></HTML>");
};

public void outputTwoCol(PrintWriter w,Vector v) {
  int half=v.size()/2;
  w.println("<TABLE WIDTH=100% COLS=2>");
  w.println("<TR><TD WIDTH=50% valign=top>");
  for(int i=0;i<half;i++)
  w.println(v.elementAt(i).toString());

  w.println("</TD><TD WIDTH=50% valign=top>");
  for(int i=half;i<v.size();i++)
  w.println(v.elementAt(i).toString());

  w.println("</TD></TR></TABLE>");

};
```

```
public void ensureDirectory(String s) throws IOException{
  File f=new File(s);
  if (f.exists()) {
    if (!f.isDirectory())
  throw new IOException("File "+f.toString()+"
  already exists and is not a directory.");

    return;
  }

  f.mkdirs();
};



};
```

TIP: *The source code for the generator is just one piece of Paul's XML puzzle. To get a peek at all the Java source code he used to generate the HTML pages from XML data, make sure you download his source code files. You can find them at **www.honeylocust.com/limon/xml/limonsrc.zip**.*

Creating A DTD

The XML DTD for describing the structure of each document that will contain the information about the weeds looks like this:

```
<!ELEMENT PLANTDATA ( SPECIES )+>
 <!ELEMENT SPECIES ( FAMILY?,LATIN*,COMMON*,TEXT*,CITE*)>
 <!ATTLIST SPECIES ID CDATA #REQUIRED>

 <!ELEMENT FAMILY ( #PCDATA )>
 <!ELEMENT LATIN ( #PCDATA )>
 <!ELEMENT COMMON ( #PCDATA )>

 <!ELEMENT TEXT ( #PCDATA | A | CM | REF )*>
 <!ATTLIST TEXT TYPE CDATA #REQUIRED>
 <!ATTLIST TEXT SOURCE CDATA #REQUIRED>
 <!ATTLIST TEXT LANGUAGE CDATA "ENGLISH">

 <!ELEMENT A (#PCDATA)>
 <!ATTLIST A HREF CDATA #REQUIRED>

 <!ELEMENT CM (#PCDATA)>
```

```
<!ELEMENT REF EMPTY>
<!ATTLIST REF ID CDATA #REQUIRED>

<!ELEMENT IMAGE (#PCDATA)>
<!ATTLIST IMAGE HREF CDATA #REQUIRED>
<!ATTLIST IMAGE SOURCE CDATA "">
<!ATTLIST IMAGE TYPE CDATA "PHOTO">

<!ELEMENT CITE EMPTY>
<!ATTLIST CITE SOURCE CDATA #REQUIRED>
<!ATTLIST CITE PAGE CDATA "">

<!ENTITY Agrave '&#192;'>
<!ENTITY Aacute '&#193;'>
<!ENTITY agrave '&#224;'>
<!ENTITY aacute '&#225;'>
```

Creating The XML Document

After Paul created the DTD, he had to create the code to describe the weeds. He created a separate file for each weed he wanted to list. That code looks something like this:

```
<?XML VERSION="1.0"?>
<!DOCTYPE PLANTDATA SYSTEM "limon.dtd">
<PLANTDATA>
 <SPECIES ID="6">
<FAMILY>Cucurbitacea</FAMILY>
<LATIN>Momordica charantia L.</LATIN>
<COMMON>balsam pear</COMMON>
<COMMON>balsam apple</COMMON>
<COMMON>cerasee bush</COMMON>
<COMMON>archucha</COMMON>
<COMMON>balsamina</COMMON>
<COMMON>achochilla</COMMON>
<COMMON>pepinillo</COMMON>
<COMMON>cunde amor</COMMON>
<COMMON>melao de Sao Caetano</COMMON>
<COMMON>carcilla</COMMON>

<TEXT TYPE="DESCRIPTION" SOURCE="Direnzo98">
Vine, climbs by tendrils. Leaves are alternate, soft and lightly
hairy. Leaves are deeply lobed with five lobes. (Length about <CM>3</CM>)
Yellow flowers arise from leaf axils as do tendrils. Flower has five
petals, bright orange small clusters of pistils and stamen at center.
```

```
(Diameter about <CM>1.5</CM>) Pods are oval tapering to a point with rows
of little spikes, green turning orange as they mature.  Exploded
pods show bright orange peels and four red seeds.  Inside is sticky.
Pod length (about <CM>2.5</CM>)  Stem is hairy, very hairy at terminal
end.  Found growing on fence along main road in full sun.
</TEXT>

  </SPECIES>
</PLANTDATA>
```

He then parsed the information and passed it to on to his Java-based HTML generator. The Java code contains all the references that actually take the data and turn it into an HTML page; such code includes the **<HEAD>** and **<BODY>** sections. The generator then created the results you see in Figure 24.2.

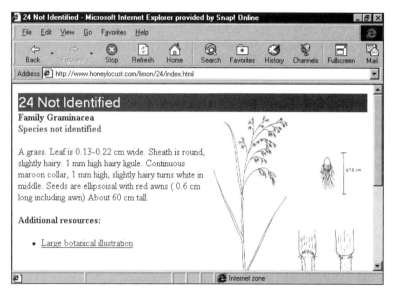

Figure 24.2   The results created by the Java-based HTML generator. The text describing this weed was originally formatted with XML.

Creating A Real Estate DTD

No matter where you live, there's one thing that's almost universal—the real estate market. There are buyers, sellers, and real estate agents, and there are real estate listings. But there is no universal system that allows agents nationwide to exchange information over the Internet about their particular properties or that allows their clients quick access to the real estate inventory they carry.

The real estate industry needs a standard format for listings so they can easily be viewed—and more importantly, searched—with a Web browser. Currently, listings are stored in the nationwide Multiple Listing Service (MLS), which is a directory that is available to real estate agents, although individual systems are stored separately. The problem, however, is that there are no formatting standards within the MLS system, and real estate brokers don't usually format the MLS data in the same way. Although they contain almost all the same type of data, each localized MLS system uses its own format and structure and runs on existing legacy systems that may not be compatible with other systems. Worse yet, although many real estate companies are now offering their inventories on the Web, there is no centralized MLS database.

With XML, realtors could continue to use their existing MLS system software in addition to a new method to connect systems together and gather data in a single repository that would be accessible over the Internet. A company called OpenMLS is working toward that centralized XML-based system. In collaboration with 4thWORLD Telecom, it is developing the Real Estate Listing Markup Language (RELML). The idea is to use the OpenMLS software to create a system that will work with existing systems to generate XML data that can then be used to search.

OpenMLS has also developed a search engine to work with these XML files. The search engine software, Xsearch, can use the RELML DTD or any other existing DTD. It searches XML data and sends results to an HTML Web page. Although the search engine resides on a Microsoft Index Server, which uses Active Server Pages, there are no additional scripts used to generate the HTML page from the search engine.

Creating The RELML DTD

Listing 24.2 shows the proposed DTD for the Real Estate Listing Markup Language that was developed by OpenMLS (**www.openmls.com**) and John Petit of 4thWORLD Telecom (**www.4thworldtele.com**).

Listing 24.2   The RELML DTD.

```
RESIDENTIAL LISTING DTD
<!--    Parameter Entities -->
  <!ENTITY % OTHER "OTHER">
  <!ENTITY % NAME "NAME">
  <!ENTITY % ACZ "ADDRESS?,CITY?,ZIP?">
  <!ENTITY % PFW "PHONE?,FAX?,WEB?">
  <!ENTITY % BA "BUILDING-AREA|ADD-INFO" >
  <!--    Notation Declarations    -->
   <!--    Should point to media viewers at a universalsite    -->
  <!NOTATION gif SYSTEM "gview.exe">
  <!NOTATION jpeg SYSTEM "jview.exe">
  <!NOTATION mov SYSTEM "Movie Player">
  <!ELEMENT RESIDENTIAL-LISTING
```

```
(GENERAL,FEATURES,FINANCIAL,
REMARKS,CONTACTS)>
   <!ATTLIST RESIDENTIAL-LISTING
   VERSION CDATA #FIXED "080698">

   <!-- ********************************************************** -->
   <!ELEMENT GENERAL
   (IMAGE*,APN?,MLS?,TYPE,PRICE,
AGE,LOCATION,STRUCTURE,DATES,
LAND-AREA,STATUS,(%OTHER;)?,TERMS*)>

   <!--The IMAGE element does not
include X and Y positions for the
placement will more than-->
   <!--likely be handled by XSL or CSS.-->
   <!ELEMENT IMAGE EMPTY>
   <!ATTLIST IMAGE
   WIDTH    CDATA    #REQUIRED
   HEIGHT   CDATA    #REQUIRED
   SRC     CDATA    #REQUIRED
   NAME CDATA #IMPLIED
   DESCRIPTION CDATA #IMPLIED>
<!ELEMENT APN (#PCDATA)>
   <!ATTLIST APN
   SECURITY  (MLS-Only|Restricted|Public) "MLS-Only">
<!ELEMENT MLS (MLS-CODE,MLS-SOURCE?)>
<!ELEMENT MLS-CODE (#PCDATA)>
   <!ATTLIST MLS-CODE
   SECURITY  (MLS-Only|Restricted|Public) "MLS-Only">
<!ELEMENT MLS-SOURCE (%NAME;,%PFW;)>
   <!ATTLIST MLS-SOURCE
   SECURITY  (MLS-Only|Restricted|Public) "MLS-Only">
<!ELEMENT TYPE (#PCDATA)>
   <!ELEMENT PRICE (#PCDATA)>
<!ATTLIST PRICE
 UNITS    (PESO|USDOLLAR|CANDOLLAR) "USDOLLAR">
   <!ELEMENT AGE (#PCDATA)>
   <!ATTLIST AGE
   UNITS    (YEARS|MONTHS) "YEARS">
   <!ELEMENT LOCATION (%ACZ;,ROUGH?)>
   <!ATTLIST LOCATION
   COUNTRY   CDATA   #REQUIRED
   STATE    CDATA   #REQUIRED
   COUNTY   CDATA   #REQUIRED
   SECURITY  (MLS-Only|Restricted|Public) "Public">
   <!ELEMENT ROUGH (#PCDATA)>
```

```
<!ELEMENT STRUCTURE ((NUM-BEDS|NUM-BATHS|SUPER-STRUCTURE|%BA;)*)>
<!ELEMENT NUM-BEDS (#PCDATA)>
<!ELEMENT NUM-BATHS (#PCDATA) >
<!-- If the property in question
is a condo or such,
SUPER-STRUCTURE is used -->
<!-- to describe the building containing that property-- >
<!ELEMENT SUPER-STRUCTURE ((NUM-UNITS|NUM-FLOORS|%BA;)*)>
<!ELEMENT BUILDING-AREA (#PCDATA)>
 <!ATTLIST BUILDING-AREA
 UNITS    (SQ-METRES|SQ-FEET) "SQ-FEET">
 <!ELEMENT NUM-UNITS (#PCDATA)>
 <!ELEMENT NUM-FLOORS (#PCDATA)>
<!ELEMENT ADD-INFO (#PCDATA)>
 <!ELEMENT DATES (LISTING-DATE,LAST-MODIFIED,EXPIRATION-DATE)>
 <!ELEMENT LISTING-DATE (#PCDATA)>
<!ELEMENT LAST-MODIFIED (#PCDATA)>
 <!ELEMENT EXPIRATION-DATE (#PCDATA)>
<!ELEMENT LAND-AREA (#PCDATA)>
 <!ATTLIST LAND-AREA
 UNITS    (HECTARES|ACRES) "ACRES">
 <!ELEMENT STATUS (#PCDATA)>
 <!ELEMENT TERMS (#PCDATA)>
 <!ATTLIST TERMS
 SECURITY  (MLS-Only|Restricted|Public) "MLS-Only">


 <!-- ********************************************************** -->
 <!ELEMENT FEATURES (DISCLOSURES,
UTILITIES,EXTRAS,
CONSTRUCTION,ACCESS,(%OTHER;)?)>

 <!ELEMENT DISCLOSURES (#PCDATA)>
 <!ELEMENT UTILITIES (#PCDATA)>
 <!ELEMENT EXTRAS (#PCDATA)>
 <!ELEMENT CONSTRUCTION (#PCDATA)>
 <!ELEMENT ACCESS (#PCDATA)>




 <!-- ********************************************************** -->
 <!ELEMENT FINANCIAL
 (ASSUMABLE,OWNER-CARRY,
ASSESMENTS,DUES,TAXES,
LENDER,EARNEST,DIRECTIONS,(%OTHER;)?)>
```

```
<!ELEMENT ASSUMABLE (#PCDATA)>
<!ATTLIST ASSUMABLE
SECURITY  (MLS-Only|Restricted|Public) "MLS-Only">
<!ELEMENT OWNER-CARRY (#PCDATA)>
<!ATTLIST OWNER-CARRY
SECURITY  (MLS-Only|Restricted|Public) "MLS-Only">
<!ELEMENT ASSESMENTS (#PCDATA)>
<!ATTLIST ASSESMENTS
SECURITY  (MLS-Only|Restricted|Public) "MLS-Only">
<!ELEMENT DUES (#PCDATA)>
<!ATTLIST DUES
SECURITY  (MLS-Only|Restricted|Public) "MLS-Only">
<!ELEMENT TAXES (#PCDATA)>
<!ATTLIST TAXES
SECURITY  (MLS-Only|Restricted|Public) "MLS-Only">
<!ELEMENT LENDER (#PCDATA)>
<!ATTLIST LENDER
SECURITY  (MLS-Only|Restricted|Public) "MLS-Only">
<!ELEMENT EARNEST (#PCDATA)>
<!ATTLIST EARNEST
SECURITY  (MLS-Only|Restricted|Public) "MLS-Only">
<!ELEMENT DIRECTIONS (#PCDATA)>
<!ATTLIST DIRECTIONS
SECURITY  (MLS-Only|Restricted|Public) "MLS-Only">


<!-- ************************************************************ -->
<!--This is the freeform description
section, the general impressions of the
property-->
<!--The aspects of the property that
make it special. The PROPERTY-REFERENCE
attribute-->
<!--is for naming the property (by what
 title do you want people to refer to
the property). -->
<!ELEMENT REMARKS (#PCDATA)>
 <!ATTLIST REMARKS
PROPERTY-REFERENCE CDATA #IMPLIED>


<!-- ************************************************************ -->
<!ELEMENT CONTACTS (COMPANY?,AGENT+,OWNER?,TENANT?,COMMISSION+)>
<!ELEMENT COMPANY (%NAME;,%ACZ;,%PFW;)>
<!ELEMENT AGENT (%NAME;,%ACZ;,%PFW;)>
```

```
<!ELEMENT OWNER (%NAME;,%ACZ;,%PFW;)>
<!ATTLIST OWNER
SECURITY   (MLS-Only|Restricted|Public) "MLS-Only">
<!ELEMENT TENANT (%NAME;,%ACZ;,%PFW;)>
<!ATTLIST TENANT
SECURITY   (MLS-Only|Restricted|Public) "MLS-Only">
<!ELEMENT COMMISSION (RECIPIENT,AMOUNT)>
<!ATTLIST COMMISSION
SECURITY   (MLS-Only|Restricted|Public) "MLS-Only">

<!ELEMENT RECIPIENT (#PCDATA)>
<!ATTLIST RECIPIENT
SECURITY   (MLS-Only|Restricted|Public) "MLS-Only">
<!ELEMENT AMOUNT (#PCDATA)>
<!ATTLIST AMOUNT
SECURITY   (MLS-Only|Restricted|Public) "MLS-Only">
<!ELEMENT OTHER (#PCDATA)>
<!ATTLIST OTHER
SECURITY   (MLS-Only|Restricted|Public) "MLS-Only">
<!ELEMENT NAME (#PCDATA)>
<!ELEMENT ADDRESS (#PCDATA)>
 <!ATTLIST ADDRESS
SECURITY   (MLS-Only|Restricted|Public) "Public">

<!ELEMENT CITY (#PCDATA) >
 <!ATTLIST CITY
SECURITY   (MLS-Only|Restricted|Public) "Public">

<!ELEMENT ZIP (#PCDATA)>
 <!ATTLIST ZIP
SECURITY   (MLS-Only|Restricted|Public) "Public">

<!ELEMENT PHONE (#PCDATA)>
<!ELEMENT FAX (#PCDATA)>
<!ELEMENT WEB (E-MAIL,SITE)>

<!ELEMENT E-MAIL (#PCDATA)>
<!ELEMENT SITE (#PCDATA)>

<!ENTITY lt "<">
<!ENTITY gt "">
<!ENTITY apos "'">
<!ENTITY amp "&">
```

The developers of this DTD want to ensure that the element tags are used for their intended purpose. But the problem is that some of the element tags need further defining, so users will understand exactly what type of content needs to be included within them. For example, they need to specify whether data included in the **<PRICE>** element should include the dollar sign, decimal points, or other special notations. This is specified through the use of the element attributes. The elements that need further defining include the following:

- **<IMAGE>**—This element will include a description attribute that specifies whether an optional single paragraph description, such as a photo caption, should be included with the image of the property.

- **<TYPE>**—This element requires further clarification by specifying what type of property it is. This element would include attributes such as **Residential-Type**, which would specify whether the home is a mobile home or a condo.

- **<STRUCTURE>**—This element needs additional information to specify all the things that have to do with the structure of the residence.

Reviewing How The System Works

Using the previously outlined RELML DTD, the Xsearch engine works off of a Microsoft Index Search server and searches the XML document that stores the real estate listings. Users input the information they are looking for in the Xsearch Web page and then click the button for the results. The index server crawls the XML document looking for matching results. The search page is show in Figure 24.3. The following code shows the HTML used to create the page (notice the form posts to the Active Server):

Figure 24.3   Using Xsearch and the RELML to search.

```
<!DOCTYPE HTML PUBLIC "-//IETF//DTD HTML 3.0//EN" "html.dtd">
<html>
<head>

    <!--
        option explicit
      -->

    <title>OpenMLS Search Form</title>
    <meta NAME="DESCRIPTION"
CONTENT="OpenMLS query form
for Residential Listings">
    <meta NAME="AUTHOR" CONTENT="Doug Greenwood">
    <meta NAME="KEYWORDS" CONTENT="query, content, hit, asp">
    <meta NAME="SUBJECT" CONTENT="sample form">
    <meta NAME="MS.CATEGORY" CONTENT="Internet">
    <meta NAME="MS.LOCALE" CONTENT="EN-US">
    <meta HTTP-EQUIV="Content-Type" CONTENT="text/html; charset=Windows-
      1252">

</head>
<body background="
images/sys_images/pmap22.gif"
text="#FFFFFF" link="#FFFFFF"
vlink="#FFFFFF">
<font face="Garamond, Times New Roman, Helvetica">

<center>

<table>
    <tr>
        <td><center><img
SRC="Channel/imagewide.gif"
VALIGN="MIDDLE" ALIGN="LEFT"
border="0" WIDTH="194" HEIGHT="32">
</td>
    </tr>
</table>

<form ACTION="/OpenMLS_Demo/aIndexSearch_3x.asp" METHOD="POST">
<table>

    <tr><td><h1><center>Real Estate Listings Search</h1></td></tr>
      <tr>
          <td><center>
```

```
<input TYPE="SUBMIT" NAME="Action"
 VALUE="Search!"></center></td>
      </tr>

</table>

<hr WIDTH="75%" ALIGN="center" SIZE="3">

 <table WIDTH="70%">
     <tr>
         <td><center>Select your criteria below:</td>
     </tr>
  </table>

 <table WIDTH="500">
  <!-- *****Dynamically create listing status from DB -->

   <tr>


    <td width="100">Listing Status:</td>
       <td><select name="Status" value="" size="1">
      <option value = "All">All</option> 
         <option value = "Active">Active</option> 
         <option value = "Contingent">Contingent</option> 
         <option value = "Pending">Pending</option> 
         <option value = "Expired">Expired</option> 
         <option value = "Withdrawn">Withdrawn</option> 
         <option value = "Temp Withdrawn">Temp Withdrawn</option> 
         <option value = "Sold">Sold</option> 

     </select></td>
  <!-- *****END Dynamically create age from DB -->

    <td width="100">Property Type:</td>
       <td><select name="PropType"  value="" size="1">
          <option value = "All">All</option> 
        <option value = "Residential">Residential</option> 
         <option value = "Commercial">Commercial</option> 
         <option value = "Vacant">Vacant</option> 
         <option value = "Land">Land</option> 

     </select>
    </td>
  </tr>
```

```
<tr>
    <td width="100">Number Bedrooms:</td>
        <td><select name="Bedrooms"  value="" size="1">
            <option value = "All">All</option> 
        <option value = "One">One</option> 
         <option value = "Two">Two</option> 
         <option value = "Three">Three</option> 
         <option value = "Four">Four</option> 
         <option value = "Five">Five</option> 
         <option value = "Six">Six</option> 
         <option value = "Seven">Seven</option> 

    </select>
    </td>

    <td width="100">Price  Between:</td>
        <td><select name="Price"  value="" size="1">
            <option value = "All">All</option> 
         <option value = "Price0">0 - 49999</option> 
            <option value = "Price50">50000 - 99999</option> 
         <option value = "Price100">100000 - 124999</option> 
         <option value = "Price120">125000 - 149999</option> 
         <option value = "Price150">150000 - 199999</option> 
         <option value = "Price200">200000 - 224999</option> 
         <option value = "Price225">225000 - 249999</option> 
         <option value = "Price250">250000 - 274999</option> 
         <option value = "Price275">275000 - 299999</option> 
         <option value = "Price300">300000 - 324999</option> 
         <option value = "Price325">325000 - 349999</option> 
         <option value = "Price350">350000 - 374999</option> 
         <option value = "Price375">375000 - 399999</option> 
         <option value = "Price400">400000 - 499999</option> 
         <option value = "Price500">500000 - 599999</option> 
         <option value = "Price600">600000 - 699999</option> 
         <option value = "Price700">700000 - 799999</option> 
         <option value = "Price800">800000 - 899999</option> 
         <option value = "Price900">900000 - 999999</option> 
         <option value = "Price1000">1000000 - 4999999</option> 
         <option value = "Price5000">5000000 - 9999999</option> 
         <option value = "Price10000">10000000 and above</option> 

    </select>
    </td>

</tr>
```

```
   <tr>
<td width="100">Number Baths:</td>
      <td><select name="Baths" value="" size="1">
         <option value = "All">All</option> 
      <option value = "One">One</option> 
       <option value = "Two">Two</option> 
       <option value = "Three">Three</option> 
       <option value = "Four">Four</option> 
       <option value = "Five">Five</option> 
       <option value = "Six">Six</option> 
       <option value = "Seven">Seven</option> 

    </select>
   </td>

   <td width="100">Size (Sq Ft)
  Between:</td>
      <td><select name="Sqft"  value="" size="1">
         <option value = "All">All</option> 
       <option value = "Sqft0">0 - 499</option> 
          <option value = "Sqft50">500 - 999</option> 
       <option value = "Sqft100">1000 - 1249</option> 
       <option value = "Sqft120">1250 - 1499</option> 
       <option value = "Sqft150">1500 - 1999</option> 
       <option value = "Sqft200">2000 - 2249</option> 
       <option value = "Sqft225">2250 - 2499</option> 
       <option value = "Sqft250">2500 - 2749</option> 
       <option value = "Sqft275">2750 - 2999</option> 
       <option value = "Sqft300">3000 - 3249</option> 
       <option value = "Sqft325">3250 - 3499</option> 
       <option value = "Sqft350">3500 - 3749</option> 
       <option value = "Sqft375">3750 - 3999</option> 
       <option value = "Sqft400">4000 - 4999</option> 
       <option value = "Sqft500">5000 - 5999</option> 
       <option value = "Sqft600">6000 - 6999</option> 
       <option value = "Sqft700">7000 - 7999</option> 
       <option value = "Sqft800">8000 - 8999</option> 
       <option value = "Sqft900">9000 - 9999</option> 
       <option value = "Sqft1000">10000 - 49999</option> 
       <option value = "Sqft5000">50000 - 99999</option> 
       <option value = "Sqft10000">100000 and above</option> 

    </select>
   </td>
```

24: How People Are Using XML

```
        </tr>

          <tr>
          <td width="30%">Listings Per Page:</td>
        <td><select name="PageSize"    size="1">
            <option value = "10">10</option> 
          <option value = "20">20</option> 
           <option value = "30">30</option> 
           <option value = "40">40</option> 
           <option value = "50">50</option> 
         </select>
       </td>
          <td width="30%">Include Photos?</td>
          <td><input NAME="Photos" TYPE="CHECKBOX"
             >
       </td>
       </tr>

       </table>


<hr WIDTH="75%" ALIGN="center" SIZE="3">
Add special keywords here!
                <table WIDTH="65%">
                  <tr>
                   <td><input TYPE="TEXT"
NAME="SearchString" SIZE="65" MAXLENGTH="100" VALUE=""></td>
                  </tr>
                </table>

                <table WIDTH="65%">
                  <tr>
<!--
                  <td align=left>
                   <input NAME="FreeText"
            TYPE="CHECKBOX"
          >
          Use <a href="ixtiphlp.htm#FreeTextQueries"
color=blue>Free-Text Query</a>.
                  </td>
-->

                    <td ALIGN="CENTER">
<a HREF="ixtiphlp.htm" color=blue>
```

```
                Tips for searching</a></td>
                        </tr>
                <tr>
            <td><center> </td>
                </tr>


                <tr>
            <td><center><input
TYPE="SUBMIT" NAME="Action"
VALUE="Search!"></center></td>
                </tr>
                    </table>



<hr WIDTH="75%" ALIGN="center" SIZE="3">
<p>
<table border="0" width="95%">
<center><a HREF="../aHome.asp">
<img src="Channel/chanimage.gif" border="0"
WIDTH="80" HEIGHT="32"></a>

<tr>

<td>

<font style="font-size: 8pt; font-weight: bold">

<center><sup>©</sup>1997,
1998 OpenMLS Software. All rights reserved.
Photo credits courtesy of
OpenMLS Software</font>
</td>

</tr>

</table>

</body>
</html>
```

The server returns a results page that matches the specifications, as shown in Figure 24.4. The results page has a link to both an HTML page and an XML page. The HTML page actually picks up the information from the XML data file specified in the individual listing.

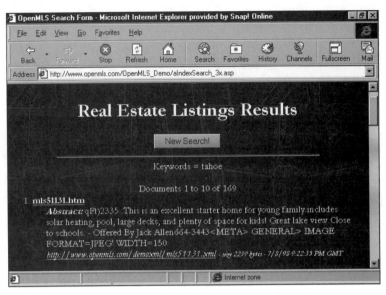

Figure 24.4   The results page lists both HTML- and XML-related links.

Click on the HTML link and you'll see the specifics of the property. Click on the link to the XML data and you'll see the XML document specified for that particular property. This is the file used to generate the HTML page (the XML document looks similar and uses the previously listed DTD to formulate the document content):

```
<?XML version='1.0'?>
<RESIDENTIAL-LISTING VERSION='A1'>
<REMARKS>Price:194900
Size (SqFt):2400 :Beautiful Mountain
Chalet w/ lots of Lake views and trees,
even has fruit trees, close to town and
bus stop, good afternoon sun, plenty of
summer gardening for your green
thumb! </REMARKS>
<GENERAL>
<IMAGE FORMAT='JPEG' WIDTH='150' HEIGHT='150'
SRC='/images/photos/Untitled-7.jpg'/>
<APN SECURITY='PUBLIC'>44-050-12</APN>
<MLS>
<MLS-CODE SECURITY='PUBLIC'>61051</MLS-CODE>
<MLS-SOURCE SECURITY='PUBLIC'>
<NAME>OpenMLS</NAME>
<WEB>www.openmls.com</WEB>
<EMAIL>greenwd@inreach.com</EMAIL>
```

```
</MLS-SOURCE>
</MLS>
<TYPE>SINGLE-FAMILY</TYPE>
<PRICE>194900</PRICE>
<AGE UNITS='YEARS'>23</AGE>
<LOCATION COUNTRY='USA' STATE='CA' COUNTY= 'Placer'>
<ADDRESS>13570 Marlett</ADDRESS>
<CITY>Tahoe City</CITY>
<ZIP>96145</ZIP>
</LOCATION>
<STRUCTURE>
<NUM-BEDS>Three</NUM-BEDS>
<NUM-BATHS>Two</NUM-BATHS>
<BUILDING-AREA UNITS='SQ-FEET'>2400</BUILDING-AREA>
</STRUCTURE>
<DATES>
<LISTING-DATE>4/19/96</LISTING-DATE>
<EXPIRATION-DATE></EXPIRATION-DATE>
<LAST-MODIFIED>7/24/98</LAST-MODIFIED>
</DATES>
<LAND-AREA UNITS='ACRES'>Parcel</LAND-AREA>
<STATUS>Active</STATUS>
<TERMS SECURITY='Public'></TERMS>
<OTHER TITLE='One Up'>aXSLTransport.asp?mlsValue=61051</OTHER>
<OTHER TITLE='Days On Market'>826</OTHER>
</GENERAL>
<FEATURES>
<OTHER TITLE='Arc'>Old Tahoe</OTHER>
<OTHER TITLE='Area'>Area 06</OTHER>
<OTHER TITLE='Garage'>Two; Attached; Boat Storage</OTHER>
<OTHER TITLE='H_0amenities'>Pool;
Tennis; Golf; Sauna; Hot tub or
Spa; Equestrian; Ski Area; Beach
</OTHER>
<OTHER TITLE='PropTypeRES'>Single Family</OTHER>
<OTHER TITLE='SubArea'>Sub Area North Star; Sub Area Alpine Meadows</OTHER>
</FEATURES>
<CONTACTS>
<COMPANY>
<NAME>Mac Realtors of Tahoe</NAME>
</COMPANY>
<AGENT>
<NAME>Jason Salamander</NAME>
<PHONE>412-4643</PHONE>
```

```
<WEB>www.Anonymous.com</WEB>
<EMAIL>Anonymous@openmls.com</EMAIL>
</AGENT>
</CONTACTS>
<OTHER TITLE='PriceBracket'>Price150</OTHER>
<OTHER TITLE='AreaBracket'>Sqft225</OTHER>
</RESIDENTIAL-LISTING>
```

Part VI

Appendixes

Appendix A

Online Resources

XML and its associated specifications—Extensible Style Language (XSL), XLink, and XPointer—will grow and change rapidly in the coming months. Although we are confident that this book provides you with the most current and up-to-date information about XML, as veteran Web developers, we are aware that nothing in this industry stays the same for long. The best way to stay abreast of the most current developments in XML, or any Web technology, is to visit those Web sites with the most reliable and current information and to visit them regularly.

To help you get started, we've sorted through the growing collection of online XML resources to provide you with a list of the best XML sites. If you take the time once a week or so to visit these sites and read about the latest updates and changes to XML, you'll always be aware of the developments in the XML world. In addition to a list of general XML sites that you can always count on for reliable information, this appendix includes links to information on the majority of XML vocabularies under development at press time. The appendix ends with a list of links to information on many of the XML parsers and development applications currently available. This list of software links serves as a companion to the more detailed descriptions of software packages in Chapter 22.

General Resources

The following sections describe general XML resources.

W3C's XML Page

www.w3.org/XML

The World Wide Web Consortium's XML page, shown in Figure A.1, is the ultimate resource for any XML developer. This site includes links to current and past XML specifications as well as useful resources, information on works in progress, and the most up-to-date news about XML. Although it is the most current and accurate, the information at the W3C site is also the most technical. Once you've got the XML lingo down, though, the information on this site will be invaluable.

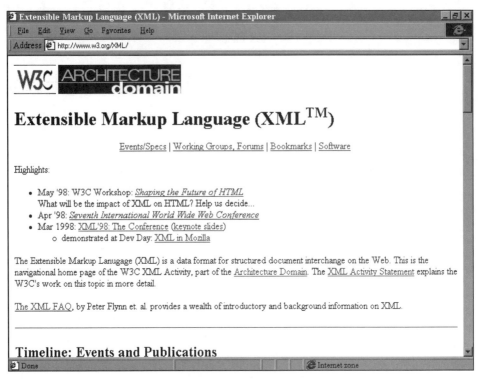

Figure A.1   The W3C's XML page is the official XML Web site.

XLink Specification

www.w3.org/TR/1998/WD-xlink-19980303

XML's linking element is separate from XML proper and has its own specification—XLink. The XLink working draft on the Web includes the most current information about the status of XLink. When XLink is finally released as an official specification, all the particulars will be posted to this site first. Because XLink will be the mechanism you use to connect your XML documents, this site is a resource you will want to visit time and again.

XPointer Specification

www.w3.org/TR/1998/WD-xptr-19980303

XPointers work with XLinks to create internal references in an XML document. As with XLink, XPointer has been removed from the general XML specification so it can be more fully developed. The XPointer specification is the most accurate account of the mechanisms and syntax specifics that make XML references tick. XPointers are a powerful tool, and as you begin to integrate them into your own

XML documents, you'll find that this Web site is the best way to learn all you need to know.

XSL Specification

www.w3.org/TR/NOTE-XSL.html

Style sheets for XML are being developed as the Extensible Style Language (XSL) specification. This Webified version of the specification is the best place to begin learning about XML style sheets and will always contain the most current information about XSL. Because XSL is the bridge that will allow many XML documents to be served on the Web, you'll want to visit this site frequently to catch up on the latest XSL news.

XML FAQ

www.ucc.ie/xml

Got questions about XML? The XML FAQ (shown in Figure A.2), maintained by Peter Flynn on behalf of the W3C's XML Working Group, answers many of the most commonly asked XML questions. The FAQ is regularly maintained, and it contains basic questions and answers about XML as well as the most current and hot XML topics. Once you're XML savvy, you'll want to keep an eye on this site for quick, concise, and accurate descriptions of what's new in XML.

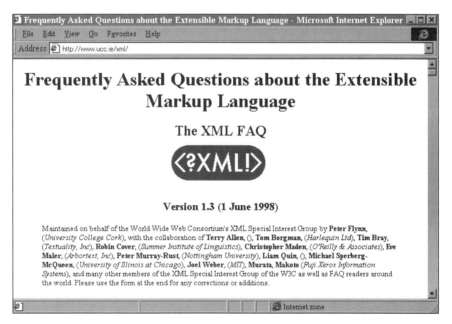

Figure A.2   The XML FAQ contains questions and answers that are useful to XML newbies and veterans.

Robin Cover's XML/SGML Pages

www.sil.org/sgml/xml.html

Robin Cover has compiled *the* list of XML resources. This site includes links to virtually every XML-related resource on the Web. Linked resources are grouped under the following categories:

- Overview
- Specifications
- Links To Other WWW Sites
- Proposed Applications And Industry Initiatives
- Articles And Books
- Mailing Lists, Discussion Groups, Newsgroups
- Software
- XML And HTML
- Examples
- Conferences, Seminars, Workshops

The list of links is contained within a single Web page and may take a few minutes to load over a slow modem connection, but it's well worth the wait. XML developers should visit Cover's site at least once a week.

XML.com

www.xml.com

Produced by the folks at Seybold Publications, a subsidiary of O'Reilly & Associates, XML.com (shown in Figure A.3) is one of the best independent sources of XML information available on the Web. The site includes a wonderfully annotated version of the XML 1 specification, articles about XML, and the Are You Well Formed? (RUWF) XML validator. As XML develops as a Web technology, look to this site for interesting and useful information.

XML Info

www.xmlinfo.com

Created by James Tauber, XML Info (shown in Figure A.4) is yet another site chock-full of useful and up-to-date information. The site includes links to general XML information, books about XML, sample XML documents, and more. The site is frequently updated and keeps pace with the almost daily happenings in the world of XML. Bookmark this must-visit site, and check it regularly for important XML developments.

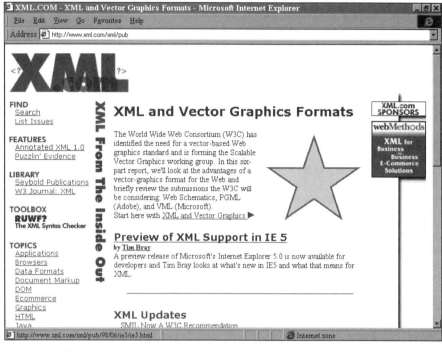

Figure A.3   The XML.com site is an excellent resource for any XML developer.

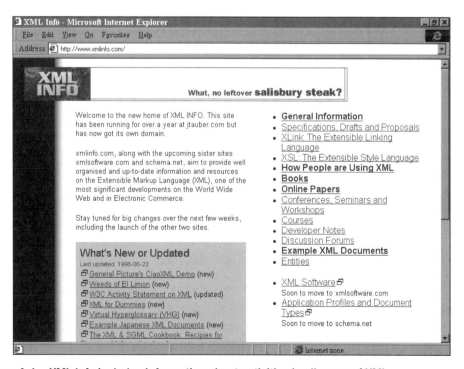

Figure A.4   XML Info includes information about activities in all areas of XML.

Application Profiles And Document Types

www.schema.net

Also from James Tauber, schema.net focuses specifically on XML vocabularies that are both standard and under development. If you're searching for the right vocabulary for your documents, or if you're searching for examples of the work others have already done with XML, this site is a virtual gold mine of information.

XML Software

www.xmlsoftware.com

Yet another exceptional site from James Tauber (this makes three in a row), xmlsoftware.com is the best place on the Web to find out about the software available to XML developers. The site includes a parser comparison chart and a frequently updated list of XML software. When you're looking for the right tool for the job, turn to xmlsoftware.com.

XML Exchange

www.xmlx.com

XML Exchange, shown in Figure A.5, is a Web site specifically for those developers who are designing their own Document Type Definitions (DTDs). Visitors can check out examples of good DTDs, exchange information, and swap solutions. If you're working hard to get your own XML vocabulary up and running, this site is an invaluable resource.

XML Resources At Textuality

www.textuality.com/xml

Tim Bray has created a set of XML links that are useful to every XML developer, as shown in Figure A.6. Although it is not as extensive as some of the other sites listed in this appendix, Bray's collection of resources and information is highly selective and useful. You won't have to sort through any fluff to get right to what you need, and because Bray is the primary editor of the XML 1 specification, the information on these pages is truly from the proverbial horse's mouth.

WebReview's XML Reference Guide

webreview.com/xml

WebReview, a solid Web information resource in general, has some excellent XML resources. Included are source code, articles about implementing XML, and links to other resources. All in all, this is a good resource for any XML developer.

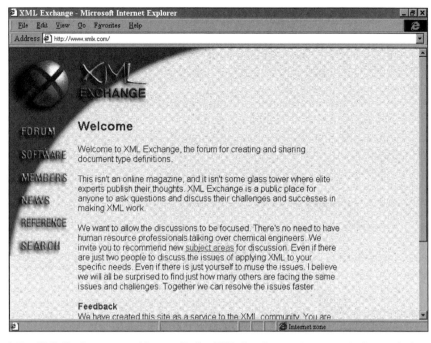

Figure A.5   XML Exchange provides a site for DTD developers to swap stories and share solutions.

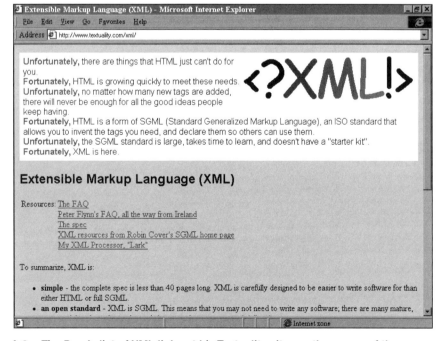

Figure A.6   Tim Bray's list of XML links at his Textuality site are the cream of the crop.

Microsoft XML Pages

www.microsoft.com/xml

Microsoft is on the XML bandwagon and has created a set of extremely useful Web pages housed at the Microsoft site and shown in Figure A.7. You'll find an XML FAQ and information about Channel Definition Format (CDF) and Open Software Description (OSD)—two Microsoft-sponsored XML vocabularies—as well as links to demos and other related information. This site focuses its implementation information on Internet Explorer, but even so, the information is factual and usable without a lot of marketing hype.

Support For XML In Internet Explorer

www.microsoft.com/sitebuilder/features/ie5over.asp

Unlike the general XML resources on the Microsoft site, this set of Web pages specifically discusses the use of XML in Internet Explorer 5. Issued as a developer's release at the time of publication, IE5 includes a much broader implementation of XML than is found in IE4. Because Web browsers are users' windows to the Web, it's important to keep up with their level of support for XML.

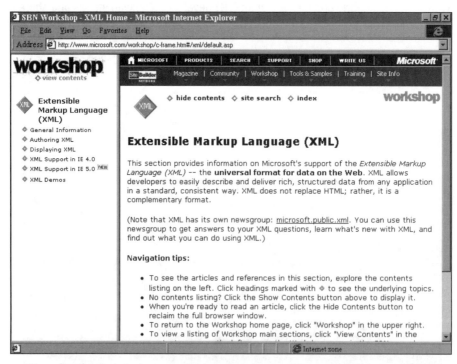

Figure A.7   The Microsoft XML site hosts a wealth of XML information useful to any XML developer.

XML In Mozilla
www.mozilla.org/rdf/doc/xml.html

When the Mozilla source code for what would have been Navigator 5 was released, many were surprised to find support for XML. You never know which browser your users may be using to view the Web, so you'll want to know as much as you can about how XML is implemented in Navigator 5.

DataChannel's XML Information
www.datachannel.com/ChannelWorld/XML/XMLIndex.htm

DataChannel was one of the first organizations to focus on the development of software for XML—specifically the CDF vocabulary. Although DataChannel's main concern is the development of tools for the delivery of channel data over the Web, it has many XML resources that are beneficial to any developer. DataChannel is a good example of how future groups may develop tools for one specific XML vocabulary, and much can be learned from the site, which is shown in Figure A.8.

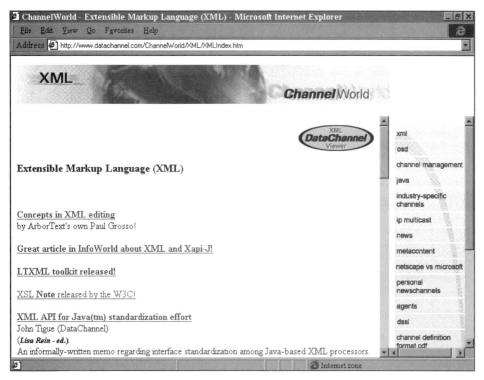

Figure A.8   DataChannel's XML resources provide a glimpse into the future of XML.

XML Vocabularies

An XML vocabulary is an implementation of XML for a specific application. The following list contains URLs to resources for XML vocabularies:

- *Bioinformatic Sequence Markup Language (BSML)*—**www.topogen.com/sbir/rfc.html**

- *Channel Definition Format (CDF)*—**www.microsoft.com/standards/cdf.htm**

- *Chemical Markup Language*—**www.venus.co.uk/omf/cml**

- *Conceptual Knowledge Markup Language (CKML)*—**asimov.eecs.wsu.edu/WAVE/Ontologies/CKML/CKML-DTD.html**

- *Encoded Archival Description (EAD)*—**www.loc.gov/ead**

- *Genealogical Data in XML (GedML)*—**home.iclweb.com/icl2/mhkay/gedml.html**

- *HTTP Distribution and Replication Protocol*—**www.w3.org/TR/NOTE-drp-19970825.html**

- *IMS Metadata Specification*—**www.imsproject.org/md_overview.html**

- *Information and Content Exchange (ICE)*—**www.vignette.com/Products/ice/Item/0,1669,5226,00.html**

- *Java Speech Markup Language (JSML)*—**java.sun.com/products/java-media/speech/forDevelopers/JSML**

- *Mathematical Markup Language (MathML)*—**www.w3.org/Math**

- *Meta Content Framework (MCF)*—**www.w3.org/TR/NOTE-MCF-XML.html**

- *Ontology Markup Language (OML)*—**asimov.eecs.wsu.edu/WAVE/Ontologies/OML/OML-DTD.html**

- *Open Financial Exchange (OFX)*—**www.ofx.net**

- *Open Software Description (OSD)*—**www.microsoft.com/standards/osd**

- *Open Trading Protocol (OTP)*—**www.otp.org:8080**

- *OpenTag*—**www.opentag.org/otspecs.htm**

- *Precision Graphics Markup Language (PGML)*—**www.w3.org/TR/1998/NOTE-PGML**

- *Resource Description Framework (RDF)*—**www.w3.org/RDF**

- *Synchronized Multimedia Integration Language (SMIL)*—**www.w3.org/AudioVideo/Activity.html**

- *Telecommunication Interchange Markup (TIM)*—**www.atis.org/atis/tcif/ipi/5tc60hom.htm**

- *Translation Memory eXchange (TMX)*—**www.lisa.org/tmx/tmx.htm**
- *Tutorial Markup Language (TML)*—**www.ilrt.bris.ac.uk/mru/netquest/ tml/about/aboutlang.html**
- *UML eXchange Format*—**www.yy.cs.keio.ac.jp/~suzuki/project/uxf**
- *Web Interface Definition Language (WIDL)*—**www.webmethods.com/ technology/widl_description.html**
- *WebDAV: Distributed Authoring and Versioning on the World Wide Web*— **www.ics.uci.edu/~ejw/authoring**
- *Wireless Application Protocol (WAP)*—**www.wapforum.org**
- *XML/EDI (Electronic Data Interchange)*—**www.xmledi.net**
- *XML-Data*—**www.microsoft.com/standards/xml/xmldata.htm**

XML Software

The following sections contain links to XML parsers and document-development software.

Parsers

- *Ælfred*—**www.microstar.com/XML/AElfred**
- *DXP*—**www.datachannel.com/products/xml/DXP**
- *Expat*—**www.jclark.com/xml**
- *Lark*—**www.textuality.com/Lark**
- *Larval*—**www.textuality.com/Lark**
- *MSXML*—**www.microsoft.com/workshop/author/xml/parser**
- *TclXML*—**tcltk.anu.edu.au/XML**
- *XML for Java*—**alphaworks.ibm.com/formula/xml**
- *xmlproc*—**www.stud.ifi.uio.no/~larsga/download/python/xml/ xmlproc.html**
- *XP*—**www.jclark.com/xml/xp/index.html**
- *Xparse*—**www.jeremie.com/Dev/XML**

Document Development Software

- *AgentSoft's XML Technology Demonstration*—**www.agentsoft.com/xml**
- *Jumbo: A Java XML Browser*—**ala.vsms.nottingham.ac.uk/vsms/java/ jumbo/index.html**

- *Prototype*—**www.pierlou.com/prototype**
- *SAXON*—**home.iclweb.com/icl2/mhkay/saxon.html**
- *SP-Grove*—**ftp://ftp.uu.net/vendor/bitsko/gdo**
- *Visual XML*—**www.pierlou.com/visxml**
- *webMethods Automation Toolkit*—**www.webmethods.com/products/automation_toolkit.html**
- *Woodstock Fastlane/XML*—**www.vtopia.com**
- *Woodstock Markup*—**www.vtopia.com**
- *XED (alpha 0.3.1)*—**www.ltg.ed.ac.uk/~ht/xed.html**
- *XML <PRO> (beta 2)*—**www.vervet.com**
- *XML Styler*—**www.arbortext.com/xmlstyler/index.html**
- *XPublish*—**interaction.in-progress.com/xpublish/index**
- *xslj*—**www.ltg.ed.ac.uk/~ht/xslj.html**
- *Zydeco: An XML Browser and Development Environment*—**www.dn.net/zydeco**

Appendix B

The XML 1 Specification

The XML specification is the ultimate resource for any Web developer using XML, because it is the XML rule book. Although you can find the most current version of the specification at the World Wide Web Consortium's (W3C's) Web site, we decided to include a copy of it here for quick reference. Tim Bray, the primary editor of the specification, has compiled a Web-based annotated version of it that is available at **www.xml.com/xml/pub/axml/axmlintro.html**. This annotated version of the specification serves as a guide to its many parts and includes extended explanations of terminology as well as historical information. You may want to visit the annotated version and mark down in this appendix those annotations that are most relevant to your needs or that you think you'll want to remember. Regardless of which version of the specification you're using for reference—annotated or not—remember that the specification is the first and best source for questions about XML rules and syntax.

> *WARNING!*   *The World Wide Web Consortium owns the copyright for the XML 1 specification. It was written by Tim Bray, Jean Paoli, and C. M. Sperberg-McQueen and can be found online at* **www.w3.org/TR/1998/REC-xml-19980210**.   .

Extensible Markup Language (XML) 1.0
REC-xml-19980210

W3C Recommendation 10-February-1998

This version:

http://www.w3.org/TR/1998/REC-xml-19980210

http://www.w3.org/TR/1998/REC-xml-19980210.xml

http://www.w3.org/TR/1998/REC-xml-19980210.html

http://www.w3.org/TR/1998/REC-xml-19980210.pdf

http://www.w3.org/TR/1998/REC-xml-19980210.ps

Latest version:

http://www.w3.org/TR/REC-xml

Previous version:

http://www.w3.org/TR/PR-xml-971208

Editors:

Tim Bray (Textuality and Netscape) **<tbray@textuality.com>**

Jean Paoli (Microsoft) **<jeanpa@microsoft.com>**

C. M. Sperberg-McQueen (University of Illinois at Chicago) **<cmsmcq@uic.edu>**

Abstract

The Extensible Markup Language (XML) is a subset of SGML that is completely described in this document. Its goal is to enable generic SGML to be served, received, and processed on the Web in the way that is now possible with HTML. XML has been designed for ease of implementation and for interoperability with both SGML and HTML.

Status Of This Document

This document has been reviewed by W3C Members and other interested parties and has been endorsed by the Director as a W3C Recommendation. It is a stable document and may be used as reference material or cited as a normative reference from another document. W3C's role in making the Recommendation is to draw attention to the specification and to promote its widespread deployment. This enhances the functionality and interoperability of the Web.

This document specifies a syntax created by subsetting an existing, widely used international text processing standard (Standard Generalized Markup Language, ISO 8879:1986(E) as amended and corrected) for use on the World Wide Web. It is a product of the W3C XML Activity, details of which can be found at **http://www.w3.org/XML**. A list of current W3C Recommendations and other technical documents can be found at **http://www.w3.org/TR**.

This specification uses the term URI, which is defined by [Berners-Lee et al.], a work in progress expected to update [IETF RFC1738] and [IETF RFC1808].

The list of known errors in this specification is available at **http://www.w3.org/XML/xml-19980210-errata**.

Please report errors in this document to **xml-editor@w3.org**.

Extensible Markup Language (XML) 1.0

Table Of Contents

F. Autodetection Of Character Encodings (Non-Normative)

G. W3C XML Working Group (Non-Normative)

1. Introduction

Extensible Markup Language, abbreviated XML, describes a class of data objects called XML documents and partially describes the behavior of computer programs which process them. XML is an application profile or restricted form of SGML, the Standard Generalized Markup Language [ISO 8879]. By construction, XML documents are conforming SGML documents.

XML documents are made up of storage units called entities, which contain either parsed or unparsed data. Parsed data is made up of characters, some of which form character data, and some of which form markup. Markup encodes a description of the document's storage layout and logical structure. XML provides a mechanism to impose constraints on the storage layout and logical structure.

A software module called an *XML processor* is used to read XML documents and provide access to their content and structure. It is assumed that an XML processor is doing its work on behalf of another module, called the *application*. This specification describes the required behavior of an XML processor in terms of how it must read XML data and the information it must provide to the application.

1.1 Origin And Goals

XML was developed by an XML Working Group (originally known as the SGML Editorial Review Board) formed under the auspices of the World Wide Web Consortium (W3C) in 1996. It was chaired by Jon Bosak of Sun Microsystems with the active participation of an XML Special Interest Group (previously known as the SGML Working Group) also organized by the W3C. The membership of the XML Working Group is given in an appendix. Dan Connolly served as the WG's contact with the W3C.

The design goals for XML are:

1. XML shall be straightforwardly usable over the Internet.

2. XML shall support a wide variety of applications.

3. XML shall be compatible with SGML.

4. It shall be easy to write programs which process XML documents.

5. The number of optional features in XML is to be kept to the absolute minimum, ideally zero.

6. XML documents should be human-legible and reasonably clear.

7. The XML design should be prepared quickly.

8. The design of XML shall be formal and concise.

9. XML documents shall be easy to create.

10. Terseness in XML markup is of minimal importance.

This specification, together with associated standards (Unicode and ISO/IEC 10646 for characters, Internet RFC 1766 for language identification tags, ISO 639 for language name codes, and ISO 3166 for country name codes), provides all the information necessary to understand XML Version 1.0 and construct computer programs to process it.

This version of the XML specification may be distributed freely, as long as all text and legal notices remain intact.

1.2 Terminology

The terminology used to describe XML documents is defined in the body of this specification. The terms defined in the following list are used in building those definitions and in describing the actions of an XML processor:

- *may*—Conforming documents and XML processors are permitted to but need not behave as described.

- *must*—Conforming documents and XML processors are required to behave as described; otherwise, they are in error.

- *error*—A violation of the rules of this specification; results are undefined. Conforming software may detect and report an error and may recover from it.

- *fatal error*—An error which a conforming XML processor must detect and report to the application. After encountering a fatal error, the processor may continue processing the data to search for further errors and may report such errors to the application. In order to support correction of errors, the processor may make unprocessed data from the document (with intermingled character data and markup) available to the application. Once a fatal error is detected, however, the processor must not continue normal processing (i.e., it must not continue to pass character data and information about the document's logical structure to the application in the normal way).

- *at user option*—Conforming software may or must (depending on the modal verb in the sentence) behave as described; if it does, it must provide users a means to enable or disable the behavior described.

- *validity constraint*—A rule which applies to all valid XML documents. Violations of validity constraints are errors; they must, at user option, be reported by validating XML processors.

- *well-formedness constraint*—A rule which applies to all well-formed XML documents. Violations of well-formedness constraints are fatal errors.

- *match*—(Of strings or names:) Two strings or names being compared must be identical. Characters with multiple possible representations in ISO/IEC 10646 (e.g., characters with both precomposed and base+diacritic forms) match only if they have the same representation in both strings. At user option, processors may normalize such characters to some canonical form. No case folding is performed. (Of strings and rules in the grammar:) A string matches a grammatical production if it belongs to the language generated by that production. (Of content and content models:) An element matches its declaration when it conforms in the fashion described in the constraint "Element Valid".

- *for compatibility*—A feature of XML included solely to ensure that XML remains compatible with SGML.

- *for interoperability*—A non-binding recommendation included to increase the chances that XML documents can be processed by the existing installed base of SGML processors which predate the WebSGML Adaptations Annex to ISO 8879.

2. Documents

A data object is an *XML document* if it is well-formed, as defined in this specification. A well-formed XML document may in addition be valid if it meets certain further constraints.

Each XML document has both a logical and a physical structure. Physically, the document is composed of units called entities. An entity may refer to other entities to cause their inclusion in the document. A document begins in a "root" or document entity. Logically, the document is composed of declarations, elements, comments, character references, and processing instructions, all of which are indicated in the document by explicit markup. The logical and physical structures must nest properly, as described in "4.3.2 Well-Formed Parsed Entities".

2.1 Well-Formed XML Documents

A textual object is a well-formed XML document if:

1. Taken as a whole, it matches the production labeled `document`.

2. It meets all the well-formedness constraints given in this specification.

3. Each of the parsed entities which is referenced directly or indirectly within the document is well-formed.

Document

```
[1]  document::= prolog element Misc*
```

Matching the `document` production implies that:

1. It contains one or more elements.

2. There is exactly one element, called the **root**, or document element, no part of which appears in the content of any other element. For all other elements, if the start-tag is in the content of another element, the end-tag is in the content of the same element. More simply stated, the elements, delimited by start- and end-tags, nest properly within each other.

As a consequence of this, for each non-root element C in the document, there is one other element P in the document such that C is in the content of P, but is not in the content of any other element that is in the content of P. P is referred to as the *parent* of C, and C as a *child* of P.

2.2 Characters

A parsed entity contains *text*, a sequence of characters, which may represent markup or character data. A *character* is an atomic unit of text as specified by ISO/IEC 10646 [ISO/IEC 10646]. Legal characters are tab, carriage return, line feed, and the legal graphic characters of Unicode and ISO/IEC 10646. The use of "compatibility characters", as defined in section 6.8 of [Unicode], is discouraged.

Character Range

```
[2] Char::= #x9 | #xA | #xD | [#x20-#xD7FF] | [#xE000-#xFFFD] |
    [#x10000-#x10FFFF]    /* any Unicode character, excluding the
    surrogate blocks, FFFE, and FFFF. */
```

The mechanism for encoding character code points into bit patterns may vary from entity to entity. All XML processors must accept the UTF-8 and UTF-16 encodings of 10646; the mechanisms for signaling which of the two is in use, or for bringing other encodings into play, are discussed later, in "4.3.3 Character Encoding In Entities".

2.3 Common Syntactic Constructs

This section defines some symbols used widely in the grammar.

S (white space) consists of one or more space (#x20) characters, carriage returns, line feeds, or tabs.

White Space

```
[3]   S::= (#x20 | #x9 | #xD | #xA)+
```

Characters are classified for convenience as letters, digits, or other characters. Letters consist of an alphabetic or syllabic base character possibly followed by one or more combining characters, or of an ideographic character. Full definitions of the specific characters in each class are given in "B. Character Classes".

A *Name* is a token beginning with a letter or one of a few punctuation characters, and continuing with letters, digits, hyphens, underscores, colons, or full stops, together known as name characters. Names beginning with the string "xml", or any string which would match ((('X'|'x') ('M'|'m') ('L'|'l'))), are reserved for standardization in this or future versions of this specification.

TIP: *The colon character within XML names is reserved for experimentation with name spaces. Its meaning is expected to be standardized at some future point, at which point those documents using the colon for experimental purposes may need to be updated. (There is no guarantee that any name-space mechanism adopted for XML will in fact use the colon as a name-space delimiter.) In practice, this means that authors should not use the colon in XML names except as part of name-space experiments, but that XML processors should accept the colon as a name character.*

An `Nmtoken` (name token) is any mixture of name characters.

Names And Tokens

```
[4] NameChar::= Letter |Digit |'.' |'-' |'_' |':' |CombiningChar |Extender
[5] Name::= (Letter |'_' |':') (NameChar)*
[6] Names::= Name (S Name)*
[7] Nmtoken::= (NameChar)+
[8] Nmtokens::= Nmtoken (S Nmtoken)*
```

Literal data is any quoted string not containing the quotation mark used as a delimiter for that string. Literals are used for specifying the content of internal entities (`EntityValue`), the values of attributes (`AttValue`), and external identifiers (`SystemLiteral`). Note that a `SystemLiteral` can be parsed without scanning for markup.

Literals

```
[9] EntityValue::= '"' ([^%&"] |PEReference |Reference)* '"'
|  "'" ([^%&'] |PEReference |Reference)* "'"
[10] AttValue::= '"' ([^<&"] |Reference)* '"'
|  "'" ([^<&'] |Reference)* "'"
[11] SystemLiteral::= ('"' [^"]* '"') |("'" [^']* "'")
[12] PubidLiteral::= '"' PubidChar* '"' |"'" (PubidChar - "'")* "'"
[13] PubidChar::= #x20 |#xD |#xA |[a-zA-Z0-9] |[-'()+,./:=?;!*#@$_%]
```

2.4 Character Data And Markup

Text consists of intermingled character data and markup. Markup takes the form of start-tags, end-tags, empty-element tags, entity references, character references, comments, CDATA section delimiters, document type declarations, and processing instructions.

All text that is not markup constitutes the *character data* of the document.

The ampersand character (&) and the left angle bracket (<) may appear in their literal form only when used as markup delimiters, or within a comment, a processing instruction, or a CDATA section. They are also legal within the literal entity value of an internal entity declaration; see "4.3.2 Well-Formed Parsed Entities". If they are needed elsewhere, they must be escaped using either numeric character references or the strings "&" and "<" respectively. The right angle bracket (>) may be represented using the string ">", and must, for compatibility, be escaped using ">" or a character reference when it appears in the string "]]>" in content, when that string is not marking the end of a CDATA section.

In the content of elements, character data is any string of characters which does not contain the start-delimiter of any markup. In a CDATA section, character data is any string of characters not including the CDATA-section-close delimiter, "]]>".

To allow attribute values to contain both single and double quotes, the apostrophe or single-quote character (') may be represented as "'", and the double-quote character (") as """.

Character Data

```
[14] CharData::= [^<&]* - ([^<&]* ']]>' [^<&]*)
```

2.5 Comments

Comments may appear anywhere in a document outside other markup; in addition, they may appear within the document type declaration at places allowed by the grammar. They are not part of the document's character data; an XML processor may, but need not, make it possible for an application to retrieve the text of comments. For compatibility, the string "--" (double-hyphen) must not occur within comments.

Comments

```
[15] Comment::= '<!--' ((Char - '-') |('-' (Char - '-')))* '-->'
```

An example of a comment:

```
<!--declarations for <head> & <body> -->
```

2.6 Processing Instructions

Processing instructions (PIs) allow documents to contain instructions for applications.

Processing Instructions

```
[16] PI::= '<?' PITarget (S (Char* - (Char* '?>' Char*)))? '?>'
[17] PITarget::= Name - (('X' | 'x') ('M' | 'm') ('L' | 'l'))
```

PIs are not part of the document's character data, but must be passed through to the application. The PI begins with a target (`PITarget`) used to identify the application to which the instruction is directed. The target names "`XML`", "`xml`", and so on are reserved for standardization in this or future versions of this specification. The XML Notation mechanism may be used for formal declaration of PI targets.

2.7 CDATA Sections

CDATA sections may occur anywhere character data may occur; they are used to escape blocks of text containing characters which would otherwise be recognized as markup. CDATA sections begin with the string "`<![CDATA[`" and end with the string "`]]>`":

CDATA Sections

```
[18] CDSect::= CDStart CData CDEnd
[19] CDStart::= '<![CDATA['
[20] CData::= (Char* - (Char* ']]>' Char*))
[21] CDEnd::= ']]>'
```

Within a CDATA section, only the `CDEnd` string is recognized as markup, so that left angle brackets and ampersands may occur in their literal form; they need not (and cannot) be escaped using "`&lt;`" and "`&amp;`". CDATA sections cannot nest.

An example of a CDATA section, in which "`<greeting>`" and "`</greeting>`" are recognized as character data, not markup:

```
<![CDATA[<greeting>Hello, world!</greeting>]]>
```

2.8 Prolog And Document Type Declaration

XML documents may, and should, begin with an *XML declaration* which specifies the version of XML being used. For example, the following is a complete XML document, well-formed but not valid:

```
<?xml version="1.0"?>
<greeting>Hello, world!</greeting>
and so is this:
<greeting>Hello, world!</greeting>
```

The version number "`1.0`" should be used to indicate conformance to this version of this specification; it is an error for a document to use the value "`1.0`" if it does not conform to this version of this specification. It is the intent of the XML working group to give later versions of this specification numbers other than "`1.0`", but this intent does not indicate a commitment to produce any future versions of XML, nor if any are produced, to use any particular numbering scheme. Since future versions are not ruled out, this construct is provided as a means to allow the possibility of automatic version recognition, should it become necessary. Processors may signal an error if they receive documents labeled with versions they do not support.

The function of the markup in an XML document is to describe its storage and logical structure and to associate attribute-value pairs with its logical structures. XML provides a mechanism, the document type declaration, to define constraints on the logical structure and to support the use of predefined storage units. An XML document is *valid* if it has an associated document type declaration and if the document complies with the constraints expressed in it.

The document type declaration must appear before the first element in the document.

Prolog

```
[22]   prolog ::=   XMLDecl? Misc* (doctypedecl Misc*)?
[23]   XMLDecl ::=   '<?xml' VersionInfo EncodingDecl? SDDecl? S? '?>'
[24]   VersionInfo ::=   S 'version' Eq (' VersionNum ' | " VersionNum ")
[25]   Eq ::=   S? '=' S?
[26]   VersionNum ::=   ([a-zA-Z0-9_.:] | '-')+
[27]   Misc ::=   Comment | PI | S
```

The XML *document type declaration* contains or points to markup declarations that provide a grammar for a class of documents. This grammar is known as a document type definition, or *DTD*. The document type declaration can point to an external subset (a special kind of external entity) containing markup declarations, or can contain the markup declarations directly in an internal subset, or can do both. The DTD for a document consists of both subsets taken together.

A *markup declaration* is an element type declaration, an attribute-list declaration, an entity declaration, or a notation declaration. These declarations may be contained in whole or in part within parameter entities, as described in the well-formedness and validity constraints below. For fuller information, see "4. Physical Structures".

Document Type Definition

```
[28]   doctypedecl ::=   '<!DOCTYPE' S Name (S ExternalID)? S? ('['
(markupdecl | PEReference | S)* ']' S?)? '>' [ VC: Root Element Type ]
[29]   markupdecl ::=   elementdecl | AttlistDecl | EntityDecl | NotationDecl
| PI | Comment  [ VC: Proper Declaration/PE Nesting ]
     [ WFC: PEs in Internal Subset ]
```

The markup declarations may be made up in whole or in part of the replacement text of parameter entities. The productions later in this specification for individual nonterminals (`elementdecl`, `AttlistDecl`, and so on) describe the declarations after all the parameter entities have been included.

Validity Constraint: Root Element Type

The `Name` in the document type declaration must match the element type of the root element.

Validity Constraint: Proper Declaration/PE Nesting

Parameter-entity replacement text must be properly nested with markup declarations. That is to say, if either the first character or the last character of a markup declaration (`markupdecl` above) is contained in the replacement text for a parameter-entity reference, both must be contained in the same replacement text.

Well-Formedness Constraint: PEs In Internal Subset

In the internal DTD subset, parameter-entity references can occur only where markup declarations can occur, not within markup declarations. (This does not apply to references that occur in external parameter entities or to the external subset.)

Like the internal subset, the external subset and any external parameter entities referred to in the DTD must consist of a series of complete markup declarations of the types allowed by the non-terminal symbol `markupdecl`, interspersed with white space or parameter-entity references. However, portions of the contents of the external subset or of external parameter entities may conditionally be ignored by using the conditional section construct; this is not allowed in the internal subset.

External Subset

```
[30]    extSubset ::=   TextDecl? extSubsetDecl
[31]    extSubsetDecl ::=   ( markupdecl | conditionalSect | PEReference | S )*
```

The external subset and external parameter entities also differ from the internal subset in that in them, parameter-entity references are permitted within markup declarations, not only between markup declarations.

An example of an XML document with a document type declaration:

```
<?xml version="1.0"?>
<!DOCTYPE greeting SYSTEM "hello.dtd">
<greeting>Hello, world!</greeting>
```

The system identifier "hello.dtd" gives the URI of a DTD for the document.

The declarations can also be given locally, as in this example:

```
<?xml version="1.0" encoding="UTF-8" ?>
<!DOCTYPE greeting [
  <!ELEMENT greeting (#PCDATA)>
]>
<greeting>Hello, world!</greeting>
```

If both the external and internal subsets are used, the internal subset is considered to occur before the external subset. This has the effect that entity and attribute-list declarations in the internal subset take precedence over those in the external subset.

2.9 Standalone Document Declaration

Markup declarations can affect the content of the document, as passed from an XML processor to an application; examples are attribute defaults and entity declarations. The standalone document declaration, which may appear as a component of the XML declaration, signals whether or not there are such declarations which appear external to the document entity.

Standalone Document Declaration

```
[32]  SDDecl ::=  S 'standalone' Eq (("'" ('yes' | 'no') "'") | ('"'
('yes' | 'no') '"'))  [ VC: Standalone Document Declaration ]
```

In a standalone document declaration, the value "yes" indicates that there are no markup declarations external to the document entity (either in the DTD external subset, or in an external parameter entity referenced from the internal subset) which affect the information passed from the XML processor to the application. The value "no" indicates that there are or may be such external markup declarations. Note that the standalone document declaration only denotes the presence of external declarations; the presence, in a document, of references to external entities, when those entities are internally declared, does not change its standalone status.

If there are no external markup declarations, the standalone document declaration has no meaning. If there are external markup declarations but there is no standalone document declaration, the value "no" is assumed.

Any XML document for which standalone="no" holds can be converted algorithmically to a standalone document, which may be desirable for some network delivery applications.

Validity Constraint: Standalone Document Declaration

The standalone document declaration must have the value "no" if any external markup declarations contain declarations of:

- Attributes with default values, if elements to which these attributes apply appear in the document without specifications of values for these attributes, or

- Entities (other than amp, lt, gt, apos, quot), if references to those entities appear in the document, or

- Attributes with values subject to normalization, where the attribute appears in the document with a value which will change as a result of normalization, or

- Element types with element content, if white space occurs directly within any instance of those types.

An example XML declaration with a standalone document declaration:

```
<?xml version="1.0" standalone='yes'?>
```

2.10 White Space Handling

In editing XML documents, it is often convenient to use "white space" (spaces, tabs, and blank lines, denoted by the nonterminal S in this specification) to set apart the markup for greater readability. Such white space is typically not intended for inclusion in the delivered version of the document. On the other hand, "significant" white space that should be preserved in the delivered version is common, for example in poetry and source code.

An XML processor must always pass all characters in a document that are not markup through to the application. A validating XML processor must also inform the application which of these characters constitute white space appearing in element content.

A special attribute named xml:space may be attached to an element to signal an intention that in that element, white space should be preserved by applications. In valid documents, this attribute, like any other, must be declared if it is used. When declared, it must be given as an enumerated type whose only possible values are "default" and "preserve". For example:

```
<!ATTLIST poem   xml:space (default|preserve) 'preserve'>
```

The value "default" signals that applications' default white-space processing modes are acceptable for this element; the value "preserve" indicates the intent that applications preserve all the white space. This declared intent is considered to apply to all elements within the content of the element where it is specified, unless overridden with another instance of the xml:space attribute.

The root element of any document is considered to have signaled no intentions as regards application space handling, unless it provides a value for this attribute or the attribute is declared with a default value.

2.11 End-Of-Line Handling

XML parsed entities are often stored in computer files which, for editing convenience, are organized into lines. These lines are typically separated by some combination of the characters carriage-return (#xD) and line-feed (#xA).

To simplify the tasks of applications, wherever an external parsed entity or the literal entity value of an internal parsed entity contains either the literal two-character sequence "#xD#xA" or a standalone literal #xD, an XML processor must pass to the application the single character #xA. (This behavior can conveniently be produced by normalizing all line breaks to #xA on input, before parsing.)

2.12 Language Identification

In document processing, it is often useful to identify the natural or formal language in which the content is written. A special attribute named xml:lang may be inserted in documents to specify the language used in the contents and attribute values of any element in an XML document. In valid documents, this attribute, like any other, must be declared if it is used. The values of the attribute are language identifiers as defined by [IETF RFC 1766], "Tags for the Identification of Languages":

Language Identification

```
[33]   LanguageID ::=  Langcode ('-' Subcode)*
[34]   Langcode ::=  ISO639Code | IanaCode | UserCode
[35]   ISO639Code ::=  ([a-z] | [A-Z]) ([a-z] | [A-Z])
[36]   IanaCode ::=  ('i' | 'I') '-' ([a-z] | [A-Z])+
[37]   UserCode ::=  ('x' | 'X') '-' ([a-z] | [A-Z])+
[38]   Subcode ::=  ([a-z] | [A-Z])+
```

The Langcode may be any of the following:

- A two-letter language code as defined by [ISO 639], "Codes for the representation of names of languages"

- A language identifier registered with the Internet Assigned Numbers Authority [IANA]; these begin with the prefix "i-" (or "I-")

- A language identifier assigned by the user, or agreed on between parties in private use; these must begin with the prefix "x-" or "X-" in order to ensure that they do not conflict with names later standardized or registered with IANA

There may be any number of `Subcode` segments; if the first subcode segment exists and the Subcode consists of two letters, then it must be a country code from [ISO 3166], "Codes for the representation of names of countries." If the first subcode consists of more than two letters, it must be a subcode for the language in question registered with IANA, unless the `Langcode` begins with the prefix "x-" or "X-".

It is customary to give the language code in lower case, and the country code (if any) in upper case. Note that these values, unlike other names in XML documents, are case insensitive.

For example:

```
<p xml:lang="en">The quick brown fox jumps over the lazy dog.</p>
<p xml:lang="en-GB">What colour is it?</p>
<p xml:lang="en-US">What color is it?</p>
<sp who="Faust" desc='leise' xml:lang="de">
  <l>Habe nun, ach! Philosophie,</l>
  <l>Juristerei, und Medizin</l>
  <l>und leider auch Theologie</l>
  <l>durchaus studiert mit heiflem Bem,h'n.</l>
  </sp>
```

The intent declared with `xml:lang` is considered to apply to all attributes and content of the element where it is specified, unless overridden with an instance of `xml:lang` on another element within that content.

A simple declaration for `xml:lang` might take the form

```
xml:lang   NMTOKEN  #IMPLIED
```

but specific default values may also be given, if appropriate. In a collection of French poems for English students, with glosses and notes in English, the `xml:lang` attribute might be declared this way:

```
<!ATTLIST poem    xml:lang NMTOKEN 'fr'>
    <!ATTLIST gloss  xml:lang NMTOKEN 'en'>
    <!ATTLIST note   xml:lang NMTOKEN 'en'>
```

3. Logical Structures

Each XML document contains one or more *elements*, the boundaries of which are either delimited by start-tags and end-tags, or, for empty elements, by an empty-element tag. Each element has a type, identified by name, sometimes called its "generic identifier" (GI), and may have a set of attribute specifications. Each attribute specification has a name and a value.

Element

```
[39] element::= EmptyElemTag
                        | STag content ETag[ WFC: Element Type Match ]
                                          [ VC: Element Valid ]
```

This specification does not constrain the semantics, use, or (beyond syntax) names of the element types and attributes, except that names beginning with a match to (('X' | 'x') ('M' | 'm') ('L' | 'l')) are reserved for standardization in this or future versions of this specification.

Well-Formedness Constraint: Element Type Match

The Name in an element's end-tag must match the element type in the start-tag.

Validity Constraint: Element Valid

An element is valid if there is a declaration matching elementdecl where the Name matches the element type, and one of the following holds:

1. The declaration matches EMPTY and the element has no content.

2. The declaration matches children and the sequence of child elements belongs to the language generated by the regular expression in the content model, with optional white space (characters matching the nonterminal S) between each pair of child elements.

3. The declaration matches Mixed and the content consists of character data and child elements whose types match names in the content model.

4. The declaration matches ANY, and the types of any child elements have been declared.

3.1 Start-Tags, End-Tags, And Empty-Element Tags

The beginning of every non-empty XML element is marked by a *start-tag*.

Start-tag

```
[40] STag::= '<' Name (S Attribute)* S? '>'[ WFC: Unique Att Spec ]
[41] Attribute::= Name Eq AttValue[ VC: Attribute Value Type ]
                                  [ WFC: No External Entity References ]
                                  [ WFC: No < in Attribute Values ]
```

The Name in the start- and end-tags gives the element's *type*. The Name - AttValue pairs are referred to as the *attribute specifications* of the element, with the Name in each pair referred to as the *attribute name* and the content of the AttValue (the text between the ' or " delimiters) as the *attribute value*.

Well-Formedness Constraint: Unique Att Spec

No attribute name may appear more than once in the same start-tag or empty-element tag.

Validity Constraint: Attribute Value Type

The attribute must have been declared; the value must be of the type declared for it. (For attribute types, see "3.3 Attribute-List Declarations".)

Well-Formedness Constraint: No External Entity References

Attribute values cannot contain direct or indirect entity references to external entities.

Well-Formedness Constraint: No < in Attribute Values

The replacement text of any entity referred to directly or indirectly in an attribute value (other than "<") must not contain a <.

An example of a start-tag:

```
<termdef id="dt-dog" term="dog">
```

The end of every element that begins with a start-tag must be marked by an *end-tag* containing a name that echoes the element's type as given in the start-tag:

End-tag
```
[42] ETag::= '</' Name S? '>'
```

An example of an end-tag:

```
</termdef>
```

The text between the start-tag and end-tag is called the element's *content*:

Content Of Elements
```
[43] content::= (element | CharData | Reference | CDSect | PI | Comment)*
```

If an element is *empty*, it must be represented either by a start-tag immediately followed by an end-tag or by an empty-element tag. An *empty-element tag* takes a special form:

Tags For Empty Elements
```
[44] EmptyElemTag::= '<' Name (S Attribute)* S? '/>'[ WFC: Unique Att Spec ]
```

Empty-element tags may be used for any element which has no content, whether or not it is declared using the keyword EMPTY. For interoperability, the empty-element tag must be used, and can only be used, for elements which are declared EMPTY.

Examples of empty elements:

```
<IMG align="left" src="http://www.w3.org/Icons/WWW/w3c_home" />

<br></br>
<br/>
```

3.2 Element Type Declarations

The element structure of an XML document may, for validation purposes, be constrained using element type and attribute-list declarations. An element type declaration constrains the element's content.

Element type declarations often constrain which element types can appear as children of the element. At user option, an XML processor may issue a warning when a declaration mentions an element type for which no declaration is provided, but this is not an error.

An *element type declaration* takes the form:

Element Type Declaration

```
[45] elementdecl::= '<!ELEMENT' S Name S contentspec S? '>'
                         [ VC: Unique Element Type Declaration ]
[46] contentspec::= 'EMPTY' | 'ANY' | Mixed | children
```

where the Name gives the element type being declared.

Validity Constraint: Unique Element Type Declaration

No element type may be declared more than once.

Examples of element type declarations:

```
<!ELEMENT br EMPTY>
<!ELEMENT p (#PCDATA|emph)* >
<!ELEMENT %name.para; %content.para; >
<!ELEMENT container ANY>
```

3.2.1 Element Content

An element type has *element content* when elements of that type must contain only child elements (no character data), optionally separated by white space (characters matching the nonterminal S). In this case, the constraint includes a content model, a simple grammar governing the allowed types of the child elements and the order in which they are allowed to appear. The grammar is built on content particles (`cps`), which consist of names, choice lists of content particles, or sequence lists of content particles:

Element-Content Models

```
[47] children::= (choice | seq) ('?' | '*' | '+')?
[48] cp::= (Name | choice | seq) ('?' | '*' | '+')?
[49] choice::= '(' S? cp ( S? '|' S? cp )* S? ')'
             [ VC: Proper Group/PE Nesting ]
[50] seq::= '(' S? cp ( S? ',' S? cp )* S? ')'[ VC: Proper Group/PE Nesting ]
```

where each `Name` is the type of an element which may appear as a child. Any content particle in a choice list may appear in the element content at the location where the choice list appears in the grammar; content particles occurring in a sequence list must each appear in the element content in the order given in the list. The optional character following a name or list governs whether the element or the content particles in the list may occur one or more (+), zero or more (*), or zero or one times (?). The absence of such an operator means that the element or content particle must appear exactly once. This syntax and meaning are identical to those used in the productions in this specification.

The content of an element matches a content model if and only if it is possible to trace out a path through the content model, obeying the sequence, choice, and repetition operators and matching each element in the content against an element type in the content model. For compatibility, it is an error if an element in the document can match more than one occurrence of an element type in the content model. For more information, see "E. Deterministic Content Models".

Validity Constraint: Proper Group/PE Nesting

Parameter-entity replacement text must be properly nested with parenthesized groups. That is to say, if either of the opening or closing parentheses in a `choice`, `seq`, or `Mixed` construct is contained in the replacement text for a parameter entity, both must be contained in the same replacement text. For interoperability, if a parameter-entity reference appears in a `choice`, `seq`, or `Mixed` construct, its replacement text should not be empty, and neither the first nor last non-blank character of the replacement text should be a connector (| or ,).

Examples of element-content models:

```
<!ELEMENT spec (front, body, back?)>
<!ELEMENT div1 (head, (p | list | note)*, div2*)>
<!ELEMENT dictionary-body (%div.mix; | %dict.mix;)*>
```

3.2.2 Mixed Content

An element type has *mixed content* when elements of that type may contain character data, optionally interspersed with child elements. In this case, the types of the child elements may be constrained, but not their order or their number of occurrences:

Mixed-Content Declaration

```
[51] Mixed::= '(' S? '#PCDATA' (S? '|' S? Name)* S? ')*'
            | '(' S? '#PCDATA' S? ')'
                [ VC: Proper Group/PE Nesting ]

                [ VC: No Duplicate Types ]
```

where the `Names` give the types of elements that may appear as children.

Validity Constraint: No Duplicate Types

The same name must not appear more than once in a single mixed-content declaration.

Examples of mixed content declarations:

```
<!ELEMENT p (#PCDATA|a|ul|b|i|em)*>
<!ELEMENT p (#PCDATA | %font; | %phrase; | %special; | %form;)* >
<!ELEMENT b (#PCDATA)>
```

3.3 Attribute-List Declarations

Attributes are used to associate name-value pairs with elements. Attribute specifications may appear only within start-tags and empty-element tags; thus, the productions used to recognize them appear in "3.1 Start-Tags, End-Tags, And Empty-Element Tags". Attribute-list declarations may be used:

- To define the set of attributes pertaining to a given element type.
- To establish type constraints for these attributes.
- To provide default values for attributes.

Attribute-list declarations specify the name, data type, and default value (if any) of each attribute associated with a given element type:

Attribute-list Declaration

```
[52] AttlistDecl::= '<!ATTLIST' S Name AttDef* S? '>'
[53] AttDef::= S Name S AttType S DefaultDecl
```

The `Name` in the `AttlistDecl` rule is the type of an element. At user option, an XML processor may issue a warning if attributes are declared for an element type not itself declared, but this is not an error. The `Name` in the `AttDef` rule is the name of the attribute.

When more than one `AttlistDecl` is provided for a given element type, the contents of all those provided are merged. When more than one definition is provided for the same attribute of a given element type, the first declaration is binding and later declarations are ignored. For interoperability, writers of DTDs may choose to provide at most one attribute-list declaration for a given element type, at most one attribute definition for a given attribute name, and at least one attribute definition in each attribute-list declaration. For interoperability, an XML processor may at user option issue a warning when more than one attribute-list declaration is provided for a given element type, or more than one attribute definition is provided for a given attribute, but this is not an error.

3.3.1 Attribute Types

XML attribute types are of three kinds: a string type, a set of tokenized types, and enumerated types. The string type may take any literal string as a value; the tokenized types have varying lexical and semantic constraints, as noted:

Attribute Types

```
[54] AttType::= StringType | TokenizedType | EnumeratedType
[55] StringType::= 'CDATA'
[56] TokenizedType::= 'ID'[ VC: ID ]
                                              [ VC: One ID per Element Type ]
                                              [ VC: ID Attribute Default ]
              | 'IDREF'[ VC: IDREF ]
              | 'IDREFS'[ VC: IDREF ]
              | 'ENTITY'[ VC: Entity Name ]
              | 'ENTITIES'[ VC: Entity Name ]
              | 'NMTOKEN'[ VC: Name Token ]
              | 'NMTOKENS'[ VC: Name Token ]
```

Validity Constraint: ID

Values of type `ID` must match the `Name` production. A name must not appear more than once in an XML document as a value of this type; i.e., ID values must uniquely identify the elements which bear them.

Validity Constraint: One ID Per Element Type

No element type may have more than one ID attribute specified.

Validity Constraint: ID Attribute Default

An ID attribute must have a declared default of #IMPLIED or #REQUIRED.

Validity Constraint: IDREF

Values of type IDREF must match the Name production, and values of type IDREFS must match Names; each Name must match the value of an ID attribute on some element in the XML document; i.e. IDREF values must match the value of some ID attribute.

Validity Constraint: Entity Name

Values of type ENTITY must match the Name production, values of type ENTI-TIES must match Names; each Name must match the name of an unparsed entity declared in the DTD.

Validity Constraint: Name Token

Values of type NMTOKEN must match the Nmtoken production; values of type NMTOKENS must match Nmtokens.

Enumerated attributes can take one of a list of values provided in the declaration. There are two kinds of enumerated types:

Enumerated Attribute Types
```
[57] EnumeratedType::= NotationType | Enumeration
[58] NotationType::= 'NOTATION' S '(' S? Name (S? '|' S? Name)* S? ')'
                          [ VC: Notation Attributes ]
[59] Enumeration::= '(' S? Nmtoken (S? '|' S? Nmtoken)* S? ')'
                          [ VC: Enumeration ]
```

A NOTATION attribute identifies a notation, declared in the DTD with associated system and/or public identifiers, to be used in interpreting the element to which the attribute is attached.

Validity Constraint: Notation Attributes

Values of this type must match one of the notation names included in the declaration; all notation names in the declaration must be declared.

Validity Constraint: Enumeration

Values of this type must match one of the Nmtoken tokens in the declaration.

For interoperability, the same Nmtoken should not occur more than once in the enumerated attribute types of a single element type.

3.3.2 Attribute Defaults
An attribute declaration provides information on whether the attribute's presence is required, and if not, how an XML processor should react if a declared attribute is absent in a document.

Attribute Defaults

```
[60] DefaultDecl::= '#REQUIRED' | '#IMPLIED'
                              | (('#FIXED' S)? AttValue)
[ VC: Required Attribute ]

[ VC: Attribute Default Legal ]

[ WFC: No < in Attribute Values ]

[ VC: Fixed Attribute Default ]
```

In an attribute declaration, #REQUIRED means that the attribute must always be provided, #IMPLIED that no default value is provided. If the declaration is neither #REQUIRED nor #IMPLIED, then the AttValue value contains the declared *default* value; the #FIXED keyword states that the attribute must always have the default value. If a default value is declared, when an XML processor encounters an omitted attribute, it is to behave as though the attribute were present with the declared default value.

Validity Constraint: Required Attribute

If the default declaration is the keyword #REQUIRED, then the attribute must be specified for all elements of the type in the attribute-list declaration.

Validity Constraint: Attribute Default Legal

The declared default value must meet the lexical constraints of the declared attribute type.

Validity Constraint: Fixed Attribute Default

If an attribute has a default value declared with the #FIXED keyword, instances of that attribute must match the default value.

Examples of attribute-list declarations:

```
<!ATTLIST termdef
        id      ID      #REQUIRED
        name    CDATA   #IMPLIED>
<!ATTLIST list
        type    (bullets|ordered|glossary)  "ordered">
<!ATTLIST form
        method  CDATA   #FIXED "POST">
```

3.3.3 Attribute-Value Normalization

Before the value of an attribute is passed to the application or checked for validity, the XML processor must normalize it as follows:

- A character reference is processed by appending the referenced character to the attribute value

- An entity reference is processed by recursively processing the replacement text of the entity

- A whitespace character (#x20, #xD, #xA, #x9) is processed by appending #x20 to the normalized value, except that only a single #x20 is appended for a "#xD#xA" sequence that is part of an external parsed entity or the literal entity value of an internal parsed entity

- Other characters are processed by appending them to the normalized value

If the declared value is not CDATA, then the XML processor must further process the normalized attribute value by discarding any leading and trailing space (#x20) characters, and by replacing sequences of space (#x20) characters by a single space (#x20) character.

All attributes for which no declaration has been read should be treated by a non-validating parser as if declared CDATA.

3.4 Conditional Sections

Conditional sections are portions of the document type declaration external subset which are included in, or excluded from, the logical structure of the DTD based on the keyword which governs them.

Conditional Section

```
[61] conditionalSect::= includeSect | ignoreSect
[62] includeSect::= '<![' S? 'INCLUDE' S? '[' extSubsetDecl ']]>'
[63] ignoreSect::= '<![' S? 'IGNORE' S? '[' ignoreSectContents* ']]>'
[64] ignoreSectContents::= Ignore ('<![' ignoreSectContents ']]>' Ignore)*
[65] Ignore::= Char* - (Char* ('<![' | ']]>') Char*)
```

Like the internal and external DTD subsets, a conditional section may contain one or more complete declarations, comments, processing instructions, or nested conditional sections, intermingled with white space.

If the keyword of the conditional section is INCLUDE, then the contents of the conditional section are part of the DTD. If the keyword of the conditional section is IGNORE, then the contents of the conditional section are not logically part of the DTD. Note that for reliable parsing, the contents of even ignored conditional sections must be read in order to detect nested conditional sections and ensure that the end of the outermost (ignored) conditional section is properly detected. If a conditional section with a keyword of INCLUDE occurs within a larger conditional section with a keyword of IGNORE, both the outer and the inner conditional sections are ignored.

If the keyword of the conditional section is a parameter-entity reference, the parameter entity must be replaced by its content before the processor decides whether to include or ignore the conditional section.

An example:

```
<!ENTITY % draft 'INCLUDE' >
<!ENTITY % final 'IGNORE' >

<![%draft;[
<!ELEMENT book (comments*, title, body, supplements?)>
]]>
<![%final;[
<!ELEMENT book (title, body, supplements?)>
]]>
```

4. Physical Structures

An XML document may consist of one or many storage units. These are called *entities*; they all have *content* and are all (except for the document entity, see below, and the external DTD subset) identified by *name*. Each XML document has one entity called the document entity, which serves as the starting point for the XML processor and may contain the whole document.

Entities may be either parsed or unparsed. A *parsed entity's* contents are referred to as its replacement text; this text is considered an integral part of the document.

An *unparsed entity* is a resource whose contents may or may not be text, and if text, may not be XML. Each unparsed entity has an associated notation, identified by name. Beyond a requirement that an XML processor make the identifiers for the entity and notation available to the application, XML places no constraints on the contents of unparsed entities.

Parsed entities are invoked by name using entity references; unparsed entities by name, given in the value of ENTITY or ENTITIES attributes.

General entities are entities for use within the document content. In this specification, general entities are sometimes referred to with the unqualified term entity when this leads to no ambiguity. Parameter entities are parsed entities for use within the DTD. These two types of entities use different forms of reference and are recognized in different contexts. Furthermore, they occupy different namespaces; a parameter entity and a general entity with the same name are two distinct entities.

4.1 Character And Entity References

A *character reference* refers to a specific character in the ISO/IEC 10646 character set, for example one not directly accessible from available input devices.

Character Reference

```
[66] CharRef::= '&#' [0-9]+ ';'
                            | '&#x' [0-9a-fA-F]+ ';'[ WFC: Legal Character ]
```

Well-Formedness Constraint: Legal Character

Characters referred to using character references must match the production for Char.

If the character reference begins with "&#x", the digits and letters up to the terminating ; provide a hexadecimal representation of the character's code point in ISO/IEC 10646. If it begins just with "&#", the digits up to the terminating ; provide a decimal representation of the character's code point.

An *entity reference* refers to the content of a named entity. References to parsed general entities use ampersand (&) and semicolon (;) as delimiters. *Parameter-entity references* use percent-sign (%) and semicolon (;) as delimiters.

Entity Reference

```
[67] Reference::= EntityRef | CharRef
[68] EntityRef::= '&' Name ';'[ WFC: Entity Declared ]
                                                [ VC: Entity Declared ]
                                                [ WFC: Parsed Entity ]
                                                [ WFC: No Recursion ]
[69] PEReference::= '%' Name ';'[ VC: Entity Declared ]
                                            [ WFC: No Recursion ]
                                                [ WFC: In DTD ]
```

Well-Formedness Constraint: Entity Declared

In a document without any DTD, a document with only an internal DTD subset which contains no parameter entity references, or a document with "standalone= 'yes'", the Name given in the entity reference must match that in an entity declaration, except that well-formed documents need not declare any of the following entities: amp, lt, gt, apos, quot. The declaration of a parameter entity must precede any reference to it. Similarly, the declaration of a general entity must precede any reference to it which appears in a default value in an attribute-list declaration. Note that if entities are declared in the external subset or in external parameter entities, a non-validating processor is not obligated to read and process their declarations; for such documents, the rule that an entity must be declared is a well-formedness constraint only if standalone='yes'.

Validity Constraint: Entity Declared

In a document with an external subset or external parameter entities with "standalone='no'", the Name given in the entity reference must match that in an entity declaration. For interoperability, valid documents should declare the entities amp, lt, gt, apos, quot, in the form specified in "4.6 Predefined Entities". The declaration of a parameter entity must precede any reference to it. Similarly, the declaration of a general entity must precede any reference to it which appears in a default value in an attribute-list declaration.

Well-Formedness Constraint: Parsed Entity

An entity reference must not contain the name of an unparsed entity. Unparsed entities may be referred to only in attribute values declared to be of type ENTITY or ENTITIES.

Well-Formedness Constraint: No Recursion

A parsed entity must not contain a recursive reference to itself, either directly or indirectly.

Well-Formedness Constraint: In DTD

Parameter-entity references may only appear in the DTD.

Examples of character and entity references:

```
Type <key>less-than</key> (&#x3C;) to save options.
This document was prepared on &docdate; and
is classified &security-level;.
```

Example of a parameter-entity reference:

```
<!-- declare the parameter entity "ISOLat2"... -->
<!ENTITY % ISOLat2
        SYSTEM "http://www.xml.com/iso/isolat2-xml.entities" >
<!-- ... now reference it. -->
%ISOLat2;
```

4.2 Entity Declarations

Entities are declared thus:

Entity Declaration

```
[70] EntityDecl::= GEDecl | PEDecl
[71] GEDecl::= '<!ENTITY' S Name S EntityDef S? '>'
[72] PEDecl::= '<!ENTITY' S '%' S Name S PEDef S? '>'
```

```
[73] EntityDef::= EntityValue | (ExternalID NDataDecl?)
[74] PEDef::= EntityValue | ExternalID
```

The Name identifies the entity in an entity reference or, in the case of an unparsed entity, in the value of an ENTITY or ENTITIES attribute. If the same entity is declared more than once, the first declaration encountered is binding; at user option, an XML processor may issue a warning if entities are declared multiple times.

4.2.1 Internal Entities

If the entity definition is an EntityValue, the defined entity is called an *internal entity*. There is no separate physical storage object, and the content of the entity is given in the declaration. Note that some processing of entity and character references in the literal entity value may be required to produce the correct replacement text: see "4.5 Construction Of Internal Entity Replacement Text".

An internal entity is a parsed entity.

Example of an internal entity declaration:

```
<!ENTITY Pub-Status "This is a pre-release of the specification.">
```

4.2.2 External Entities

If the entity is not internal, it is an *external entity*, declared as follows:

External Entity Declaration

```
[75] ExternalID::= 'SYSTEM' S SystemLiteral
                  | 'PUBLIC' S PubidLiteral S SystemLiteral
[76] NDataDecl::= S 'NDATA' S Name[ VC: Notation Declared ]
```

If the NDataDecl is present, this is a general unparsed entity; otherwise, it is a parsed entity.

Validity Constraint: Notation Declared

The Name must match the declared name of a notation.

The SystemLiteral is called the entity's *system identifier*. It is a URI, which may be used to retrieve the entity. Note that the hash mark (#) and fragment identifier frequently used with URIs are not, formally, part of the URI itself; an XML processor may signal an error if a fragment identifier is given as part of a system identifier. Unless otherwise provided by information outside the scope of this specification (e.g., a special XML element type defined by a particular DTD, or a processing instruction defined by a particular application specification), relative URIs are relative to the location of the resource within which the entity declaration occurs. A URI might thus be relative to the document entity, to the entity containing the external DTD subset, or to some other external parameter entity.

An XML processor should handle a non-ASCII character in a URI by representing the character in UTF-8 as one or more bytes, and then escaping these bytes with the URI escaping mechanism (i.e., by converting each byte to %HH, where HH is the hexadecimal notation of the byte value).

In addition to a system identifier, an external identifier may include a *public identifier*. An XML processor attempting to retrieve the entity's content may use the public identifier to try to generate an alternative URI. If the processor is unable to do so, it must use the URI specified in the system literal. Before a match is attempted, all strings of white space in the public identifier must be normalized to single space characters (#x20), and leading and trailing white space must be removed.

Examples of external entity declarations:

```
<!ENTITY open-hatch
        SYSTEM "http://www.textuality.com/boilerplate/OpenHatch.xml">
<!ENTITY open-hatch
        PUBLIC "-//Textuality//TEXT Standard open-hatch boilerplate//EN"
        "http://www.textuality.com/boilerplate/OpenHatch.xml">
<!ENTITY hatch-pic
        SYSTEM "../grafix/OpenHatch.gif"
        NDATA gif >
```

4.3 Parsed Entities

4.3.1 The Text Declaration
External parsed entities may each begin with a *text declaration*.

Text Declaration
```
[77] TextDecl::= '<?xml' VersionInfo? EncodingDecl S? '?>'
```

The text declaration must be provided literally, not by reference to a parsed entity. No text declaration may appear at any position other than the beginning of an external parsed entity.

4.3.2 Well-Formed Parsed Entities
The document entity is well-formed if it matches the production labeled docu-ment. An external general parsed entity is well-formed if it matches the production labeled extParsedEnt. An external parameter entity is well-formed if it matches the production labeled extPE.

Well-Formed External Parsed Entity
```
[78] extParsedEnt::= TextDecl? content
[79] extPE::= TextDecl? extSubsetDecl
```

An internal general parsed entity is well-formed if its replacement text matches the production labeled `content`. All internal parameter entities are well-formed by definition.

A consequence of well-formedness in entities is that the logical and physical structures in an XML document are properly nested; no start-tag, end-tag, empty-element tag, element, comment, processing instruction, character reference, or entity reference can begin in one entity and end in another.

4.3.3 Character Encoding In Entities

Each external parsed entity in an XML document may use a different encoding for its characters. All XML processors must be able to read entities in either UTF-8 or UTF-16.

Entities encoded in UTF-16 must begin with the Byte Order Mark described by ISO/IEC 10646 Annex E and Unicode Appendix B (the ZERO WIDTH NO-BREAK SPACE character, #xFEFF). This is an encoding signature, not part of either the markup or the character data of the XML document. XML processors must be able to use this character to differentiate between UTF-8 and UTF-16 encoded documents.

Although an XML processor is required to read only entities in the UTF-8 and UTF-16 encodings, it is recognized that other encodings are used around the world, and it may be desired for XML processors to read entities that use them. Parsed entities which are stored in an encoding other than UTF-8 or UTF-16 must begin with a text declaration containing an encoding declaration:

Encoding Declaration

```
[80] EncodingDecl::= S 'encoding' Eq ('"' EncName '"' |  "'" EncName "'" )
[81] EncName::= [A-Za-z] ([A-Za-z0-9._] | '-')
     */* Encoding name contains only Latin characters */
```

In the document entity, the encoding declaration is part of the XML declaration. The `EncName` is the name of the encoding used.

In an encoding declaration, the values "`UTF-8`", "`UTF-16`", "`ISO-10646-UCS-2`", and "`ISO-10646-UCS-4`" should be used for the various encodings and transformations of Unicode / ISO/IEC 10646, the values "`ISO-8859-1`", "`ISO-8859-2`", ... "`ISO-8859-9`" should be used for the parts of ISO 8859, and the values "`ISO-2022-JP`", "`Shift_JIS`", and "`EUC-JP`" should be used for the various encoded forms of JIS X-0208-1997. XML processors may recognize other encodings; it is recommended that character encodings registered (as charsets) with the Internet Assigned Numbers Authority [IANA], other than those just listed, should be referred to using their registered names. Note that these registered names are defined to be case-insensitive, so processors wishing to match against them should do so in a case-insensitive way.

In the absence of information provided by an external transport protocol (e.g., HTTP or MIME), it is an error for an entity including an encoding declaration to be presented to the XML processor in an encoding other than that named in the declaration, for an encoding declaration to occur other than at the beginning of an external entity, or for an entity which begins with neither a Byte Order Mark nor an encoding declaration to use an encoding other than UTF-8. Note that since ASCII is a subset of UTF-8, ordinary ASCII entities do not strictly need an encoding declaration.

It is a fatal error when an XML processor encounters an entity with an encoding that it is unable to process.

Examples of encoding declarations:

```
<?xml encoding='UTF-8'?>
<?xml encoding='EUC-JP'?>
```

4.4 XML Processor Treatment Of Entities And References

The table below summarizes the contexts in which character references, entity references, and invocations of unparsed entities might appear and the required behavior of an XML processor in each case. The labels in the leftmost column describe the recognition context:

- *Reference in Content*—As a reference anywhere after the start-tag and before the end-tag of an element; corresponds to the nonterminal `content`.

- *Reference in Attribute Value*—As a reference within either the value of an attribute in a start-tag, or a default value in an attribute declaration; corresponds to the nonterminal `AttValue`.

- *Occurs as Attribute Value*—As a `Name`, not a reference, appearing either as the value of an attribute which has been declared as type `ENTITY`, or as one of the space-separated tokens in the value of an attribute which has been declared as type `ENTITIES`.

- *Reference in Entity Value*—As a reference within a parameter or internal entity's literal entity value in the entity's declaration; corresponds to the nonterminal `EntityValue`.

- *Reference in DTD*—As a reference within either the internal or external subsets of the DTD, but outside of an `EntityValue` or `AttValue`.

4.4.1 Not Recognized

Outside the DTD, the % character has no special significance; thus, what would be parameter entity references in the DTD are not recognized as markup in `content`. Similarly, the names of unparsed entities are not recognized except when they appear in the value of an appropriately declared attribute.

	ENTITY TYPE				
	Parameter	**Internal General**	**External Parsed General**	**Unparsed**	**Character**
Reference in Content	Not recognized	Included	Included if validating	Forbidden	Included
Reference in Attribute Value	Not recognized	Included in literal	Forbidden	Forbidden	Included
Occurs as Attribute Value	Not recognized	Forbidden	Forbidden	Notify	Not recognized
Reference in EntityValue	Included in literal	Bypassed	Bypassed	Forbidden	Included
Reference in DTD	Included as PE	Forbidden	Forbidden	Forbidden	Forbidden

4.4.2 Included

An entity is *included* when its replacement text is retrieved and processed, in place of the reference itself, as though it were part of the document at the location the reference was recognized. The replacement text may contain both character data and (except for parameter entities) markup, which must be recognized in the usual way, except that the replacement text of entities used to escape markup delimiters (the entities `amp`, `lt`, `gt`, `apos`, `quot`) is always treated as data. (The string "`AT&amp;T;`" expands to "`AT&T;`" and the remaining ampersand is not recognized as an entity-reference delimiter.) A character reference is *included* when the indicated character is processed in place of the reference itself.

4.4.3 Included If Validating

When an XML processor recognizes a reference to a parsed entity, in order to validate the document, the processor must include its replacement text. If the entity is external, and the processor is not attempting to validate the XML document, the processor may, but need not, include the entity's replacement text. If a non-validating parser does not include the replacement text, it must inform the application that it recognized, but did not read, the entity.

This rule is based on the recognition that the automatic inclusion provided by the SGML and XML entity mechanism, primarily designed to support modularity in authoring, is not necessarily appropriate for other applications, in particular document browsing. Browsers, for example, when encountering an external parsed entity reference, might choose to provide a visual indication of the entity's presence and retrieve it for display only on demand.

4.4.4 Forbidden

The following are forbidden and constitute fatal errors:

- The appearance of a reference to an unparsed entity.

- The appearance of any character or general-entity reference in the DTD except within an `EntityValue` or `AttValue`.

- A reference to an external entity in an attribute value.

4.4.5 Included In Literal

When an entity reference appears in an attribute value, or a parameter entity reference appears in a literal entity value, its replacement text is processed in place of the reference itself as though it were part of the document at the location the reference was recognized, except that a single or double quote character in the replacement text is always treated as a normal data character and will not terminate the literal. For example, this is well-formed:

```
<!ENTITY % YN '"Yes"' >
<!ENTITY WhatHeSaid "He said &YN;" >
```

while this is not:

```
<!ENTITY EndAttr "27'" >
<element attribute='a-&EndAttr;>
```

4.4.6 Notify

When the name of an unparsed entity appears as a token in the value of an attribute of declared type `ENTITY` or `ENTITIES`, a validating processor must inform the application of the system and public (if any) identifiers for both the entity and its associated notation.

4.4.7 Bypassed

When a general entity reference appears in the `EntityValue` in an entity declaration, it is bypassed and left as is.

4.4.8 Included As PE

Just as with external parsed entities, parameter entities need only be included if validating. When a parameter-entity reference is recognized in the DTD and included, its replacement text is enlarged by the attachment of one leading and one following space (#x20) character; the intent is to constrain the replacement text of parameter entities to contain an integral number of grammatical tokens in the DTD.

4.5 Construction Of Internal Entity Replacement Text

In discussing the treatment of internal entities, it is useful to distinguish two forms of the entity's value. The *literal entity value* is the quoted string actually present in the entity declaration, corresponding to the non-terminal `EntityValue`. The *replacement text* is the content of the entity, after replacement of character references and parameter-entity references.

The literal entity value as given in an internal entity declaration (`EntityValue`) may contain character, parameter-entity, and general-entity references. Such references must be contained entirely within the literal entity value. The actual replacement text that is included as described above must contain the replacement text of any parameter entities referred to, and must contain the character referred to, in place of any character references in the literal entity value; however, general-entity references must be left as-is, unexpanded. For example, given the following declarations:

```
<!ENTITY % pub    "&#xc9;ditions Gallimard" >
<!ENTITY   rights "All rights reserved" >
<!ENTITY   book   "La Peste: Albert Camus,
&#xA9; 1947 %pub;. &rights;" >
```

then the replacement text for the entity "`book`" is:

```
La Peste: Albert Camus,
© 1947 …ditions Gallimard. &rights;
```

The general-entity reference "`&rights;`" would be expanded should the reference "`&book;`" appear in the document's content or an attribute value.

These simple rules may have complex interactions; for a detailed discussion of a difficult example, see "D. Expansion Of Entity And Character References".

4.6 Predefined Entities

Entity and character references can both be used to *escape* the left angle bracket, ampersand, and other delimiters. A set of general entities (`amp`, `lt`, `gt`, `apos`, `quot`) is specified for this purpose. Numeric character references may also be used; they are expanded immediately when recognized and must be treated as character data, so the numeric character references "`&#60;`" and "`&#38;`" may be used to escape < and & when they occur in character data.

All XML processors must recognize these entities whether they are declared or not. For interoperability, valid XML documents should declare these entities, like any others, before using them. If the entities in question are declared, they must be declared as internal entities whose replacement text is the single character being escaped or a character reference to that character, as shown below.

```
<!ENTITY lt      "&#38;#60;">
<!ENTITY gt      "&#62;">
<!ENTITY amp     "&#38;#38;">
<!ENTITY apos    "&#39;">
<!ENTITY quot    "&#34;">
```

Note that the < and & characters in the declarations of "lt" and "amp" are doubly escaped to meet the requirement that entity replacement be well-formed.

4.7 Notation Declarations

Notations identify by name the format of unparsed entities, the format of elements which bear a notation attribute, or the application to which a processing instruction is addressed.

Notation declarations provide a name for the notation, for use in entity and attribute-list declarations and in attribute specifications, and an external identifier for the notation which may allow an XML processor or its client application to locate a helper application capable of processing data in the given notation.

Notation Declarations

```
[82] NotationDecl::= '<!NOTATION' S Name S (ExternalID |  PublicID) S? '>'
[83] PublicID::= 'PUBLIC' S PubidLiteral
```

XML processors must provide applications with the name and external identifier(s) of any notation declared and referred to in an attribute value, attribute definition, or entity declaration. They may additionally resolve the external identifier into the system identifier, file name, or other information needed to allow the application to call a processor for data in the notation described. (It is not an error, however, for XML documents to declare and refer to notations for which notation-specific applications are not available on the system where the XML processor or application is running.)

4.8 Document Entity

The *document entity* serves as the root of the entity tree and a starting-point for an XML processor. This specification does not specify how the document entity is to be located by an XML processor; unlike other entities, the document entity has no name and might well appear on a processor input stream without any identification at all.

5. Conformance

5.1 Validating And Non-Validating Processors

Conforming XML processors fall into two classes: validating and non-validating.

Validating and non-validating processors alike must report violations of this specification's well-formedness constraints in the content of the document entity and any other parsed entities that they read.

Validating processors must report violations of the constraints expressed by the declarations in the DTD, and failures to fulfill the validity constraints given in this specification. To accomplish this, validating XML processors must read and process the entire DTD and all external parsed entities referenced in the document.

Non-validating processors are required to check only the document entity, including the entire internal DTD subset, for well-formedness. While they are not required to check the document for validity, they are required to *process* all the declarations they read in the internal DTD subset and in any parameter entity that they read, up to the first reference to a parameter entity that they do not read; that is to say, they must use the information in those declarations to normalize attribute values, include the replacement text of internal entities, and supply default attribute values. They must not process entity declarations or attribute-list declarations encountered after a reference to a parameter entity that is not read, since the entity may have contained overriding declarations.

5.2 Using XML Processors

The behavior of a validating XML processor is highly predictable; it must read every piece of a document and report all well-formedness and validity violations. Less is required of a non-validating processor; it need not read any part of the document other than the document entity. This has two effects that may be important to users of XML processors:

- Certain well-formedness errors, specifically those that require reading external entities, may not be detected by a non-validating processor. Examples include the constraints entitled Entity Declared, Parsed Entity, and No Recursion, as well as some of the cases described as forbidden in "4.4 XML Processor Treatment Of Entities And References".

- The information passed from the processor to the application may vary, depending on whether the processor reads parameter and external entities. For example, a non-validating processor may not normalize attribute values, include the replacement text of internal entities, or supply default attribute values, where doing so depends on having read declarations in external or parameter entities.

For maximum reliability in interoperating between different XML processors, applications which use non-validating processors should not rely on any behaviors not required of such processors. Applications which require facilities such as the use of default attributes or internal entities which are declared in external entities should use validating XML processors.

6. Notation

The formal grammar of XML is given in this specification using a simple Extended Backus-Naur Form (EBNF) notation. Each rule in the grammar defines one symbol, in the form

```
symbol ::= expression
```

Symbols are written with an initial capital letter if they are defined by a regular expression, or with an initial lower case letter otherwise. Literal strings are quoted.

Within the expression on the right-hand side of a rule, the following expressions are used to match strings of one or more characters:

- #xN—Where N is a hexadecimal integer, the expression matches the character in ISO/IEC 10646 whose canonical (UCS-4) code value, when interpreted as an unsigned binary number, has the value indicated. The number of leading zeros in the #xN form is insignificant; the number of leading zeros in the corresponding code value is governed by the character encoding in use and is not significant for XML.

- [a-zA-Z], [#xN-#xN]—Matches any character with a value in the range(s) indicated (inclusive).

- [^a-z], [^#xN-#xN]—Matches any character with a value outside the range indicated.

- [^abc], [^#xN#xN#xN]—Matches any character with a value not among the characters given.

- "string"—Matches a literal string matching that given inside the double quotes.

- 'string'—Matches a literal string matching that given inside the single quotes.

These symbols may be combined to match more complex patterns as follows, where A and B represent simple expressions:

- (expression)—expression is treated as a unit and may be combined as described in this list.

- A?—Matches A or nothing; optional A.

- A B—Matches A followed by B.

- A | B—Matches A or B but not both.

- A - B—Matches any string that matches A but does not match B.

- A+—Matches one or more occurrences of A.

- A*—Matches zero or more occurrences of A.

Other notations used in the productions are:

- /* ... */—Comment.

- [wfc: ...]—Well-formedness constraint; this identifies by name a constraint on well-formed documents associated with a production.

- [vc: ...]—Validity constraint; this identifies by name a constraint on valid documents associated with a production.

Appendices

A. References

A.1 Normative References

IANA

(Internet Assigned Numbers Authority) Official Names for Character Sets, ed. Keld Simonsen et al. See **ftp://ftp.isi.edu/in-notes/iana/assignments/character-sets**.

IETF RFC 1766

IETF (Internet Engineering Task Force). RFC 1766: Tags for the Identification of Languages, ed. H. Alvestrand. 1995.

ISO 639

(International Organization for Standardization). ISO 639:1988 (E). Code for the representation of names of languages. [Geneva]: International Organization for Standardization, 1988.

ISO 3166

(International Organization for Standardization). ISO 3166-1:1997 (E). Codes for the representation of names of countries and their subdivisions—Part 1: Country codes [Geneva]: International Organization for Standardization, 1997.

ISO/IEC 10646

ISO (International Organization for Standardization). ISO/IEC 10646-1993 (E). Information technology—Universal Multiple-Octet Coded Character Set (UCS)—Part 1: Architecture and Basic Multilingual Plane. [Geneva]: International Organization for Standardization, 1993 (plus amendments AM 1 through AM 7).

Unicode

The Unicode Consortium. The Unicode Standard, Version 2.0. Reading, Mass.: Addison-Wesley Developers Press, 1996.

A.2 Other References

Aho/Ullman

Aho, Alfred V., Ravi Sethi, and Jeffrey D. Ullman. Compilers: Principles, Techniques, and Tools. Reading: Addison-Wesley, 1986, rpt. corr. 1988.

Berners-Lee et al.

Berners-Lee, T., R. Fielding, and L. Masinter. Uniform Resource Identifiers (URI): Generic Syntax and Semantics. 1997. (Work in progress; see updates to RFC1738.)

Brüggemann-Klein

Brüggemann-Klein, Anne. Regular Expressions into Finite Automata. Extended abstract in I. Simon, Hrsg., LATIN 1992, S. 97-98. Springer-Verlag, Berlin 1992. Full Version in Theoretical Computer Science 120: 197-213, 1993.

Brüggemann-Klein and Wood

Brüggemann-Klein, Anne, and Derick Wood. Deterministic Regular Languages. Universität Freiburg, Institut für Informatik, Bericht 38, Oktober 1991.

Clark

James Clark. Comparison of SGML and XML. See **http://www.w3.org/TR/NOTE-sgml-xml-971215**.

IETF RFC1738

IETF (Internet Engineering Task Force). RFC 1738: Uniform Resource Locators (URL), ed. T. Berners-Lee, L. Masinter, M. McCahill. 1994.

IETF RFC1808

IETF (Internet Engineering Task Force). RFC 1808: Relative Uniform Resource Locators, ed. R. Fielding. 1995.

IETF RFC2141

IETF (Internet Engineering Task Force). RFC 2141: URN Syntax, ed. R. Moats. 1997.

ISO 8879

ISO (International Organization for Standardization). ISO 8879:1986(E). Information processing—Text and Office Systems—Standard Generalized Markup Language (SGML). First edition—1986-10-15. [Geneva]: International Organization for Standardization, 1986.

ISO/IEC 10744

ISO (International Organization for Standardization). ISO/IEC 10744-1992 (E). Information technology—Hypermedia/Time-based Structuring Language (HyTime). [Geneva]: International Organization for Standardization, 1992. Extended Facilities Annexe. [Geneva]: International Organization for Standardization, 1996.

B. Character Classes

Following the characteristics defined in the Unicode standard, characters are classed as base characters (among others, these contain the alphabetic characters of the Latin alphabet, without diacritics), ideographic characters, and combining characters (among others, this class contains most diacritics); these classes combine to form the class of letters. Digits and extenders are also distinguished.

Characters

```
[84] Lettet::= BaseChar | Ideographic
[85] BaseChar::=  [#x0041-#x005A] | [#x0061-#x007A] | [#x00C0-#x00D6] |
[#x00D8-#x00F6] | [#x00F8-#x00FF] | [#x0100-#x0131] | [#x0134-#x013E] |
[#x0141-#x0148] | [#x014A-#x017E] | [#x0180-#x01C3] | [#x01CD-#x01F0] |
[#x01F4-#x01F5] | [#x01FA-#x0217] | [#x0250-#x02A8] | [#x02BB-#x02C1] |
#x0386 | [#x0388-#x038A] | #x038C | [#x038E-#x03A1] | [#x03A3-#x03CE] |
[#x03D0-#x03D6] | #x03DA | #x03DC | #x03DE | #x03E0 | [#x03E2-#x03F3] |
[#x0401-#x040C] | [#x040E-#x044F] | [#x0451-#x045C] | [#x045E-#x0481] |
[#x0490-#x04C4] | [#x04C7-#x04C8] | [#x04CB-#x04CC] | [#x04D0-#x04EB] |
[#x04EE-#x04F5] | [#x04F8-#x04F9] | [#x0531-#x0556] | #x0559 |
[#x0561-#x0586] | [#x05D0-#x05EA] | [#x05F0-#x05F2] | [#x0621-#x063A] |
[#x0641-#x064A] | [#x0671-#x06B7] | [#x06BA-#x06BE] | [#x06C0-#x06CE] |
[#x06D0-#x06D3] | #x06D5 |
[#x06E5-#x06E6] | [#x0905-#x0939] | #x093D |
[#x0958-#x0961] | [#x0985-#x098C] | [#x098F-#x0990] | [#x0993-#x09A8] |
[#x09AA-#x09B0] | #x09B2 |
[#x09B6-#x09B9] | [#x09DC-#x09DD] | [#x09DF-#x09E1] | [#x09F0-#x09F1] |
[#x0A05-#x0A0A] | [#x0A0F-#x0A10] | [#x0A13-#x0A28] | [#x0A2A-#x0A30] |
[#x0A32-#x0A33] | [#x0A35-#x0A36] | [#x0A38-#x0A39] | [#x0A59-#x0A5C] |
#x0A5E |
[#x0A72-#x0A74] | [#x0A85-#x0A8B] | #x0A8D |
[#x0A8F-#x0A91] | [#x0A93-#x0AA8] | [#x0AAA-#x0AB0] | [#x0AB2-#x0AB3] |
[#x0AB5-#x0AB9] | #x0ABD | #x0AE0 | [#x0B05-#x0B0C] | [#x0B0F-#x0B10] |
[#x0B13-#x0B28] | [#x0B2A-#x0B30] | [#x0B32-#x0B33] | [#x0B36-#x0B39] |
#x0B3D |
[#x0B5C-#x0B5D] | [#x0B5F-#x0B61] | [#x0B85-#x0B8A] | [#x0B8E-#x0B90] |
[#x0B92-#x0B95] | [#x0B99-#x0B9A] | #x0B9C |
[#x0B9E-#x0B9F] | [#x0BA3-#x0BA4] | [#x0BA8-#x0BAA] | [#x0BAE-#x0BB5] |
[#x0BB7-#x0BB9] | [#x0C05-#x0C0C] | [#x0C0E-#x0C10] | [#x0C12-#x0C28] |
```

```
[#x0C2A-#x0C33] | [#x0C35-#x0C39] | [#x0C60-#x0C61] | [#x0C85-#x0C8C] |
[#x0C8E-#x0C90] | [#x0C92-#x0CA8] | [#x0CAA-#x0CB3] | [#x0CB5-#x0CB9] |
#x0CDE |
[#x0CE0-#x0CE1] | [#x0D05-#x0D0C] | [#x0D0E-#x0D10] | [#x0D12-#x0D28] |
[#x0D2A-#x0D39] | [#x0D60-#x0D61] | [#x0E01-#x0E2E] | #x0E30 |
[#x0E32-#x0E33] | [#x0E40-#x0E45] | [#x0E81-#x0E82] | #x0E84 |
[#x0E87-#x0E88] | #x0E8A | #x0E8D | [#x0E94-#x0E97] | [#x0E99-#x0E9F] |
[#x0EA1-#x0EA3] | #x0EA5 | #x0EA7 | [#x0EAA-#x0EAB] | [#x0EAD-#x0EAE] |
#x0EB0 | [#x0EB2-#x0EB3] | #x0EBD | [#x0EC0-#x0EC4] | [#x0F40-#x0F47] |
[#x0F49-#x0F69] | [#x10A0-#x10C5] | [#x10D0-#x10F6] | #x1100 |
[#x1102-#x1103] | [#x1105-#x1107] | #x1109 |
[#x110B-#x110C] | [#x110E-#x1112] | #x113C | #x113E | #x1140 | #x114C |
#x114E | #x1150 | [#x1154-#x1155] | #x1159 | [#x115F-#x1161] | #x1163 |
#x1165 | #x1167 | #x1169 |
[#x116D-#x116E] | [#x1172-#x1173] | #x1175 | #x119E | #x11A8 | #x11AB |
[#x11AE-#x11AF] | [#x11B7-#x11B8] | #x11BA | [#x11BC-#x11C2] | #x11EB |
#x11F0 | #x11F9 | [#x1E00-#x1E9B] | [#x1EA0-#x1EF9] | [#x1F00-#x1F15] |
[#x1F18-#x1F1D] | [#x1F20-#x1F45] | [#x1F48-#x1F4D] | [#x1F50-#x1F57] |
#x1F59 | #x1F5B | #x1F5D |
[#x1F5F-#x1F7D] | [#x1F80-#x1FB4] | [#x1FB6-#x1FBC] | #x1FBE |
[#x1FC2-#x1FC4] | [#x1FC6-#x1FCC] | [#x1FD0-#x1FD3] | [#x1FD6-#x1FDB] |
[#x1FE0-#x1FEC] | [#x1FF2-#x1FF4] | [#x1FF6-#x1FFC] | #x2126 |
[#x212A-#x212B] | #x212E |
[#x2180-#x2182] | [#x3041-#x3094] | [#x30A1-#x30FA] | [#x3105-#x312C] |
[#xAC00-#xD7A3]
[86] Ideographic::= [#x4E00-#x9FA5] | #x3007 | [#x3021-#x3029]
[87] CombiningChar::= [#x0300-#x0345] | [#x0360-#x0361] |
[#x0483-#x0486] | [#x0591-#x05A1] | [#x05A3-#x05B9] | [#x05BB-#x05BD] |
#x05BF | [#x05C1-#x05C2] | #x05C4 | [#x064B-#x0652] | #x0670 |
[#x06D6-#x06DC] | [#x06DD-#x06DF] | [#x06E0-#x06E4] | [#x06E7-#x06E8] |
[#x06EA-#x06ED] | [#x0901-#x0903] | #x093C | [#x093E-#x094C] | #x094D |
[#x0951-#x0954] | [#x0962-#x0963] | [#x0981-#x0983] | #x09BC | #x09BE |
#x09BF |
[#x09C0-#x09C4] | [#x09C7-#x09C8] | [#x09CB-#x09CD] | #x09D7 |
[#x09E2-#x09E3] | #x0A02 | #x0A3C | #x0A3E | #x0A3F | [#x0A40-#x0A42] |
[#x0A47-#x0A48] | [#x0A4B-#x0A4D] | [#x0A70-#x0A71] | [#x0A81-#x0A83] |
#x0ABC |
[#x0ABE-#x0AC5] | [#x0AC7-#x0AC9] | [#x0ACB-#x0ACD] | [#x0B01-#x0B03] |
#x0B3C |
[#x0B3E-#x0B43] | [#x0B47-#x0B48] | [#x0B4B-#x0B4D] | [#x0B56-#x0B57] |
[#x0B82-#x0B83] | [#x0BBE-#x0BC2] | [#x0BC6-#x0BC8] | [#x0BCA-#x0BCD] |
#x0BD7 |
[#x0C01-#x0C03] | [#x0C3E-#x0C44] | [#x0C46-#x0C48] | [#x0C4A-#x0C4D] |
[#x0C55-#x0C56] | [#x0C82-#x0C83] | [#x0CBE-#x0CC4] | [#x0CC6-#x0CC8] |
[#x0CCA-#x0CCD] | [#x0CD5-#x0CD6] | [#x0D02-#x0D03] | [#x0D3E-#x0D43] |
[#x0D46-#x0D48] | [#x0D4A-#x0D4D] | #x0D57 | #x0E31 | [#x0E34-#x0E3A] |
```

```
[#x0E47-#x0E4E] | #x0EB1 |
[#x0EB4-#x0EB9] | [#x0EBB-#x0EBC] | [#x0EC8-#x0ECD] | [#x0F18-#x0F19] |
#x0F35 | #x0F37 | #x0F39 | #x0F3E | #x0F3F |
[#x0F71-#x0F84] | [#x0F86-#x0F8B] | [#x0F90-#x0F95] | #x0F97 |
[#x0F99-#x0FAD] | [#x0FB1-#x0FB7] | #x0FB9 | [#x20D0-#x20DC] | #x20E1 |
[#x302A-#x302F] | #x3099 | #x309A
[88] Digit::= [#x0030-#x0039] | [#x0660-#x0669] | [#x06F0-#x06F9] |
[#x0966-#x096F] | [#x09E6-#x09EF] | [#x0A66-#x0A6F] | [#x0AE6-#x0AEF] |
[#x0B66-#x0B6F] | [#x0BE7-#x0BEF] | [#x0C66-#x0C6F] | [#x0CE6-#x0CEF] |
[#x0D66-#x0D6F] | [#x0E50-#x0E59] | [#x0ED0-#x0ED9] | [#x0F20-#x0F29]
[89] Extender::= #x00B7 | #x02D0 | #x02D1 | #x0387 | #x0640 | #x0E46 |
#x0EC6 | #x3005 | [#x3031-#x3035] | [#x309D-#x309E] | [#x30FC-#x30FE]
```

The character classes defined here can be derived from the Unicode character database as follows:

- Name start characters must have one of the categories Ll, Lu, Lo, Lt, Nl.

- Name characters other than Name-start characters must have one of the categories Mc, Me, Mn, Lm, or Nd.

- Characters in the compatibility area (i.e., with character code greater than #xF900 and less than #xFFFE) are not allowed in XML names.

- Characters which have a font or compatibility decomposition (i.e., those with a "compatibility formatting tag" in field 5 of the database—marked by field 5 beginning with a "<") are not allowed.

- The following characters are treated as name-start characters rather than name characters, because the property file classifies them as alphabetic: [#x02BB-#x02C1], #x0559, #x06E5, #x06E6.

- Characters #x20DD-#x20E0 are excluded (in accordance with Unicode, section 5.14).

- Character #x00B7 is classified as an extender, because the property list so identifies it.

- Character #x0387 is added as a name character, because #x00B7 is its canonical equivalent.

- Characters ':' and '_' are allowed as name-start characters.

- Characters '-' and '.' are allowed as name characters.

C. XML And SGML (Non-Normative)

XML is designed to be a subset of SGML, in that every valid XML document should also be a conformant SGML document. For a detailed comparison of the additional restrictions that XML places on documents beyond those of SGML, see [Clark].

D. Expansion Of Entity And Character References (Non-Normative)

This appendix contains some examples illustrating the sequence of entity- and character-reference recognition and expansion, as specified in "4.4 XML Processor Treatment Of Entities And References".

If the DTD contains the declaration

```
<!ENTITY example "<p>An ampersand (&#38;#38;) may be escaped
numerically (&#38;#38;#38;) or with a general entity
(&amp;amp;).</p>" >
```

then the XML processor will recognize the character references when it parses the entity declaration, and resolve them before storing the following string as the value of the entity "example":

```
<p>An ampersand (&#38;) may be escaped
numerically (&#38;#38;) or with a general entity
(&amp;amp;).</p>
```

A reference in the document to "&example;" will cause the text to be reparsed, at which time the start- and end-tags of the "p" element will be recognized and the three references will be recognized and expanded, resulting in a "p" element with the following content (all data, no delimiters or markup):

```
An ampersand (&) may be escaped
numerically (&#38;) or with a general entity
(&amp;).
```

A more complex example will illustrate the rules and their effects fully. In the following example, the line numbers are solely for reference.

```
1 <?xml version='1.0'?>
2 <!DOCTYPE test [
3 <!ELEMENT test (#PCDATA) >
4 <!ENTITY % xx '&#37;zz;'>
5 <!ENTITY % zz '&#60;!ENTITY tricky "error-prone" >' >
6 %xx;
7 ]>
8 <test>This sample shows a &tricky; method.</test>
```

This produces the following:

- In line 4, the reference to character 37 is expanded immediately, and the parameter entity "xx" is stored in the symbol table with the value "%zz;".

Since the replacement text is not rescanned, the reference to parameter entity "zz" is not recognized. (And it would be an error if it were, since "zz" is not yet declared.)

- In line 5, the character reference "<" is expanded immediately and the parameter entity "zz" is stored with the replacement text "<!ENTITY tricky "error-prone" >", which is a well-formed entity declaration.

- In line 6, the reference to "xx" is recognized, and the replacement text of "xx" (namely "%zz;") is parsed. The reference to "zz" is recognized in its turn, and its replacement text ("<!ENTITY tricky "error-prone" >") is parsed. The general entity "tricky" has now been declared, with the replacement text "error-prone".

- In line 8, the reference to the general entity "tricky" is recognized, and it is expanded, so the full content of the "test" element is the self-describing (and ungrammatical) string. This sample shows an error-prone method.

E. Deterministic Content Models (Non-Normative)

For compatibility, it is required that content models in element type declarations be deterministic.

SGML requires deterministic content models (it calls them "unambiguous"); XML processors built using SGML systems may flag non-deterministic content models as errors.

For example, the content model ((b, c) | (b, d)) is non-deterministic, because given an initial b the parser cannot know which b in the model is being matched without looking ahead to see which element follows the b. In this case, the two references to b can be collapsed into a single reference, making the model read (b, (c | d)). An initial b now clearly matches only a single name in the content model. The parser doesn't need to look ahead to see what follows; either c or d would be accepted.

More formally: a finite state automaton may be constructed from the content model using the standard algorithms, e.g., algorithm 3.5 in section 3.9 of Aho, Sethi, and Ullman [Aho/Ullman]. In many such algorithms, a follow set is constructed for each position in the regular expression (i.e., each leaf node in the syntax tree for the regular expression); if any position has a follow set in which more than one following position is labeled with the same element type name, then the content model is in error and may be reported as an error.

Algorithms exist which allow many but not all non-deterministic content models to be reduced automatically to equivalent deterministic models; see Brüggemann-Klein 1991 [Brüggemann-Klein].

F. Autodetection Of Character Encodings (Non-Normative)

The XML encoding declaration functions as an internal label on each entity, indicating which character encoding is in use. Before an XML processor can read the internal label, however, it apparently has to know what character encoding is in use—which is what the internal label is trying to indicate. In the general case, this is a hopeless situation. It is not entirely hopeless in XML, however, because XML limits the general case in two ways: each implementation is assumed to support only a finite set of character encodings, and the XML encoding declaration is restricted in position and content in order to make it feasible to autodetect the character encoding in use in each entity in normal cases. Also, in many cases other sources of information are available in addition to the XML data stream itself. Two cases may be distinguished, depending on whether the XML entity is presented to the processor without, or with, any accompanying (external) information. We consider the first case first.

Because each XML entity not in UTF-8 or UTF-16 format must begin with an XML encoding declaration, in which the first characters must be '<?xml', any conforming processor can detect, after two to four octets of input, which of the following cases apply. In reading this list, it may help to know that in UCS-4, '<' is "#x0000003C" and '?' is "#x0000003F", and the Byte Order Mark required of UTF-16 data streams is "#xFEFF".

- 00 00 00 3C: UCS-4, big-endian machine (1234 order)

- 3C 00 00 00: UCS-4, little-endian machine (4321 order)

- 00 00 3C 00: UCS-4, unusual octet order (2143)

- 00 3C 00 00: UCS-4, unusual octet order (3412)

- FE FF: UTF-16, big-endian

- FF FE: UTF-16, little-endian

- 00 3C 00 3F: UTF-16, big-endian, no Byte Order Mark (and thus, strictly speaking, in error)

- 3C 00 3F 00: UTF-16, little-endian, no Byte Order Mark (and thus, strictly speaking, in error)

- 3C 3F 78 6D: UTF-8, ISO 646, ASCII, some part of ISO 8859, Shift-JIS, EUC, or any other 7-bit, 8-bit, or mixed-width encoding which ensures that the characters of ASCII have their normal positions, width, and values; the actual encoding declaration must be read to detect which of these applies, but since all of these encodings use the same bit patterns for the ASCII characters, the encoding declaration itself may be read reliably

- 4C 6F A7 94: EBCDIC (in some flavor; the full encoding declaration must be read to tell which code page is in use)

- other: UTF-8 without an encoding declaration, or else the data stream is corrupt, fragmentary, or enclosed in a wrapper of some kind

This level of autodetection is enough to read the XML encoding declaration and parse the character-encoding identifier, which is still necessary to distinguish the individual members of each family of encodings (e.g., to tell UTF-8 from 8859, and the parts of 8859 from each other, or to distinguish the specific EBCDIC code page in use, and so on).

Because the contents of the encoding declaration are restricted to ASCII characters, a processor can reliably read the entire encoding declaration as soon as it has detected which family of encodings is in use. Since in practice, all widely used character encodings fall into one of the categories above, the XML encoding declaration allows reasonably reliable in-band labeling of character encodings, even when external sources of information at the operating-system or transport-protocol level are unreliable.

Once the processor has detected the character encoding in use, it can act appropriately, whether by invoking a separate input routine for each case, or by calling the proper conversion function on each character of input.

Like any self-labeling system, the XML encoding declaration will not work if any software changes the entity's character set or encoding without updating the encoding declaration. Implementors of character-encoding routines should be careful to ensure the accuracy of the internal and external information used to label the entity.

The second possible case occurs when the XML entity is accompanied by encoding information, as in some file systems and some network protocols. When multiple sources of information are available, their relative priority and the preferred method of handling conflict should be specified as part of the higher-level protocol used to deliver XML. Rules for the relative priority of the internal label and the MIME-type label in an external header, for example, should be part of the RFC document defining the text/xml and application/xml MIME types. In the interests of interoperability, however, the following rules are recommended:

- If an XML entity is in a file, the Byte-Order Mark and encoding-declaration PI are used (if present) to determine the character encoding. All other heuristics and sources of information are solely for error recovery.

- If an XML entity is delivered with a MIME type of text/xml, then the charset parameter on the MIME type determines the character encoding method; all other heuristics and sources of information are solely for error recovery.

- If an XML entity is delivered with a MIME type of application/xml, then the Byte-Order Mark and encoding-declaration PI are used (if present) to determine the character encoding. All other heuristics and sources of information are solely for error recovery.

These rules apply only in the absence of protocol-level documentation; in particular, when the MIME types text/xml and application/xml are defined, the recommendations of the relevant RFC will supersede these rules.

G. W3C XML Working Group (Non-Normative)

This specification was prepared and approved for publication by the W3C XML Working Group (WG). WG approval of this specification does not necessarily imply that all WG members voted for its approval. The current and former members of the XML WG are:

Jon Bosak, Sun (Chair); James Clark (Technical Lead); Tim Bray, Textuality and Netscape (XML Co-editor); Jean Paoli, Microsoft (XML Co-editor); C. M. Sperberg-McQueen, U. of Ill. (XML Co-editor); Dan Connolly, W3C (W3C Liaison); Paula Angerstein, Texcel; Steve DeRose, INSO; Dave Hollander, HP; Eliot Kimber, ISOGEN; Eve Maler, ArborText; Tom Magliery, NCSA; Murray Maloney, Muzmo and Grif; Makoto Murata, Fuji Xerox Information Systems; Joel Nava, Adobe; Conleth O'Connell, Vignette; Peter Sharpe, SoftQuad; John Tigue, DataChannel

Glossary

action—The portion of a construction rule that describes how the document element (pattern) should be formatted.

Active Channel—A Microsoft technology that uses the Channel Definition Language (an XML vocabulary) to create channels of regularly updated information that users can subscribe to within Internet Explorer.

ActiveX controls—A stripped-down version of Object Linking and Embedding (OLE) controls with their size and speed optimized for use over the Internet.

APIs (application programming interfaces)—A set of instructions that allow one program to invoke the functions of a second program.

ASCII (American Standard Code for Information Interchange)—A method of coding that translates letters, numbers, and symbols into digital form.

ASP (Active Server Page)—A Web programming technique that enriches commerce and business communications by improving script management. ASPs can execute with a transaction so the transaction is aborted if the script fails.

attribute—Additional items that are added to elements to provide clarity to the element.

attribute list declaration—A listing in the Document Type Definition (DTD) of all the attributes that can be used with a given element. This listing includes the attributes, their values and defaults (if the values are fixed), and whether the attribute is required or optional.

attribute name—The name used to identify the attribute in the Document Type Definition (DTD) and reference it in a document.

attribute specification—An individual listing for a single attribute within the attribute list declaration.

attribute type—The value that identifies the attribute as a string, tokenized, or enumerated attribute.

attribute value—A list in the specification of all the possible values an attribute can take. In a document, this is the specific value assigned to the attribute by the document developer.

AVI (Audio Video Interleave)—One of several file formats used to encode digital video files.

bidirectional links—A hyperlink that can be traversed in more than one direction. Bidirectional links are an XLink convention.

binary entity—Anything that's not an XML-encoded resource. For example, audio and video files are binary entities.

box properties—A group of Cascading Style Sheet (CSS) properties and values that govern the margins, padding, height, width, and border aspects of any element.

BSML (Bioinformatic Sequence Markup Language)—A developing XML vocabulary intended to provide a standard method for encoding and displaying DNA, RNA, and protein sequence information between programs and over the Internet.

CDF (Channel Definition Format)—Developed by Microsoft, an XML vocabulary that lets a developer use a variety of delivery mechanisms to publish collections of information called channels from any Web server to any Internet-compatible appliance.

CGI (Common Gateway Interface)—Scripts that execute programs on a Web server.

channel—A server-push mechanism defined using Channel Definition Format (CDF) that allows developers to send collections of Web data to users at one time. Channel content is delivered to users who have subscribed to receive it.

channel manager—A component of Microsoft Internet Explorer 4 that works in conjunction with the browser display area to allow users to sort through and view information downloaded from a subscribed channel.

character data—The text (other than markup) included within document elements. Not all elements must necessarily allow character data as content. As with element content, character data content must be defined by the Document Type Definition (DTD) as part of an element's content.

character references—All the text used in the document to create declarations, markup, and text inside XML elements.

child element—An element that is contained (nested) within another element. A child element may also be a parent of other, lower-level elements.

CKML (Conceptual Knowledge Markup Language)—An XML vocabulary used to represent knowledge and data analysis, which serves to create models for rational thinking, judgement, and decision-making.

classification properties—A group of Cascading Style Sheet (CSS) properties and values that govern the way white space and lists are displayed.

CML (Chemical Markup Language)—A content- and presentation-based XML vocabulary that is used to describe and process chemical compound data.

comments—Notes in an XML document that are ignored by an XML processor.

Competence Gap Analysis Tool—An elaborate system created by RivCom, a consulting firm in England (**www.rivcom.com**), for Shell Services International. This system was designed to be an interactive tool to help people define the skill levels needed for certain jobs within the organization and how those skills rated in the overall job requirements.

construction rule—The cornerstone of an Extensible Style Language (XSL) style sheet; contains the formatting instructions for any given document element.

content—Anything found between the start- and end-tags of an element. Content can include element content, character data, or mixed content.

content model—The definition in a Document Type Definition (DTD) of what content is allowed within any given element.

content-based markup—Markup that is robust enough to describe information so it can be processed by one or more applications or delivered in ways other than traditional visual presentation (such as aurally or in Braille).

CSS (Cascading Style Sheets)—A set of style rules that governs how HTML and XML elements and tags are shown by a browser or other display mechanism.

declaration—Markup that gives the XML processor special instructions on how to process a document.

default rule—In an Extensible Style Language (XSL) style sheet, the construction rule that describes how all rules not governed by other construction rules should be formatted.

digital signature—A security method that attaches the electronic equivalent of a handwritten signature to a message, so it can be verified by the receiver as originating from the destination listed in the message header.

document element—*See* **element**.

document type declaration—Used to associate the XML document with its corresponding Document Type Definition (DTD). Also called the **DOCTYPE** declaration.

DOM (Document Object Model)—A way to describe an XML document to another application or programming language as a series of objects in a hierarchical tree to make it easier to access and manipulate the elements in the document.

DRP (Distribution and Replication Protocol)—A new protocol that has been proposed by Marimba Corporation. DRP is intended to optimize and speed up delivery of information over the Internet.

DSO (Data Source Object)—*See* **XML DSO**.

DSSSL (Document Style Semantics and Specification Language)—The original Standard Generalized Markup Language (SGML) style sheet language. It is an ISO standard and an established mechanism for directing the display of documents that are described by advanced markup languages.

DTD (Document Type Definition)—A Standard Generalized Markup Language (SGML) or XML specification for a document that organizes structural elements and markup definitions so they can be used to create documents.

Dynamic HTML—HTML that is combined with style sheets and scripts to create Web pages that change in response to user interactions.

EAD (Encoded Archival Description)—An XML vocabulary used to develop a nonproprietary encoding standard for library documents, including indexes, archives, and any other type of holdings that may be found in libraries and museums.

element—A component of a document. An element consists of markup and the text contained within the markup. The combination of elements, as defined by the document's related Document Type Definition (DTD), makes up the main part of an XML document.

element content—Other elements (tag pairs) that can be included within an element. The elements that can be nested within a tag (and the order in which they must appear) are defined for each element within the Document Type Definition (DTD).

empty element—An element that has no content of any kind.

entity—Essentially, a unit of storage in which the contents of the storage unit are associated with a name. Whenever the name is invoked in an XML document, the unit's contents are inserted in place of the name, just as a less-than sign (<) is displayed in place of the entity **<**.

extended link—In XLink, a link that is stored in an external file and allows you to express relationships between more than two resources.

extended link groups—In XLink, special types of extended links that are used to store a list of links to other documents.

Extended Pointers—*See* **XPointer**.

Extensible Linking Language—*See* **XLink**.

external DTD—The portion of a document's Document Type Definition (DTD) stored in an external file.

external entity—An entity that describes information stored in a file that is external to the document that calls the entity.

flow object—In Extensible Style Language (XSL), structures used to describe how the content of a document should be formatted. Flow objects are linked to elements with construction rules.

font properties—A group of Cascading Style Sheet (CSS) properties and values that provide font specifics for document elements.

formatting process—In Document Style Semantics and Specification Language (DSSSL) terms, a standard way to supply formatting information for XML documents. It's controlled by the style specification.

GedML (Genealogical Data in XML)—An XML vocabulary created to provide a standard method for presenting, exchanging, and manipulating genealogical data across a network and with other users.

general entity—An entity that is widely used in HTML for coding specific characters, such as the ampersand (&), accent marks, angle brackets (which are used to define tags), or any nonbasic ASCII characters.

graphs—Used in the Resource Description Framework (RDF) world (and in the larger world of computer science) as a physical map of data.

HTTP (Hypertext Transfer Protocol)—The protocol for communication between a Web server and a Web browser (uses HTML).

hybrid channel—A mix between news, immersion, and notification channels.

HyTyme—A standard used within the Standard Generalized Markup Language (SGML) specification that defines the inline and out-of-line link structures and some semantic features, including traversal control and presentation of objects.

ICE (Information and Content Exchange)—An XML vocabulary intended to provide automatic, controlled exchange and management of online assets between business partners. ICE gives businesses a standard way to set up online relationships with other businesses and to transfer and share information.

ID—A unique identifier for an element within a document.

ID Pointers—In XLink, cross-references for those elements with the IDs quoted within the document.

IIS (Internet Information Server)—Web server software by Microsoft that is included and implemented with Windows NT Server.

IMS Metadata Specification—A specification that uses XML to offer effective delivery of high-quality training materials over the Internet. It also supports the management of materials and types of data relating to Web sites.

inline link—An XLink term that describes a link that serves as one of its own resources. More specifically, an inline link is one where the content of the linking element acts as a resource. An example of such a link is the HTML **<A>** element.

interface elements—XML elements that don't fall into the category of either a content or presentation element. The **<MATH>** element, found in the MathML vocabulary, is an example of an interface element.

internal DTD subset—The portion of a document's Document Type Definition (DTD) that is included within the document.

internal entity—An entity whose contents are included directly within the entity's declaration in the Document Type Definition (DTD). Internal entities are self-contained and do not reference any content outside of the DTD.

intranet—An internal, private network that uses the same standards and protocols as the Internet.

ISO 10646—The International Organization for Standards's official name for the Universal Character Set (UCS), which is equivalent to Unicode.

Java—An objected-oriented programming language developed by Sun Microsystems that is used for Web application development.

Java class files—The file or set of files behind a Java applet that contains the actual instructions that drive the applet.

JavaScript—A scripting language, supported by Netscape 2 and higher, and Internet Explorer 4 and higher, that is used to script Web pages.

JSML (Java Speech Markup Language)—An XML vocabulary intended to allow developers to create applications that annotate text for playback through speech synthesizers via the Java Speech API. This data format provides detailed information on how the text should be spoken through the synthesizer.

JVM (Java Virtual Machine)—A utility that interprets and displays the results of Java code. JVMs are usually built into Web browsers.

language processor—*See* **parser**.

link—An XLink term that describes a connection or relationship between two or more data objects or portions of data objects.

linking element—An XLink term that describes an element that specifies the existence of a link and describes its characteristics.

local resource—An XLink term that describes the content of an inline linking element. It specifies the content-role and content-title of the link.

location term—The key ingredient and basic addressing information unit in an XPointer that describes the exact spot within a resource that is linked to.

locator—An XLink term that describes a piece of data (provided as part of a link) that identifies a resource and can be used to locate it.

MathML (Mathematical Markup Language)—A content- and presentation-based XML vocabulary that is used to describe and process mathematical data.

MCF (Meta Content Framework)—A content-based XML vocabulary that is used to describe collections of documents residing on a network in a standard metadata format.

metadata—Data that provides information about other resources.

metalanguage—A language used to describe metadata.

mixed content—A combination of element and character data that can be included as content for any given element.

multidirectional link—An XLink term that describes a link that can be traversed from more than one of its resources. It's more than just a link that provides a mechanism to go back to a previously visited resource or link. Instead, a multidirectional link gives the user the ability to move up, down, left, right, or backward—in other words, in just about any direction.

namespaces—An advanced XML technology that uses processing instructions (PIs) to assign unique names in a document to Uniform Resource Identifiers.

nesting—A description of how elements are contained within one another.

nodes—Instances of data on a graph.

non-validating parser—Software programs that check XML documents for well-formedness but not validity. This type of parser ignores information provided in an accompanying Document Type Definition (DTD). If the document is missing a DTD, it will not report errors.

notations—An XML declaration that associates a type of binary entity, such as a GIF or JPEG file, with a processing application, such as LView or Paint Shop Pro.

ObjectStore—An object database management system that provides native storage for structured data, such as XML, C++ objects, or Java objects.

ODBC (Open Database Connectivity)—A Microsoft standard API that allows database files of various formats to communicate effectively.

OFX (Open Financial Exchange)—An XML vocabulary that is a spin-off of the Standard Generalized Markup Language (SGML) applications that work behind the scenes in Microsoft's Money and Intuit's Quicken packages.

OML (Ontology Markup Language)—An XML vocabulary that allows Web-page authors to annotate their Web pages so the pages can be read by machines and processed with intelligent agent software.

OpenTag—An XML vocabulary designed to create a standardized way to code diverse file types through the use of a common markup method.

OSD (Open Software Description)—An XML vocabulary used to describe software components, software versions, and the underlying structure of software packages and their components for delivery over a network. OSD can work in conjunction with Channel Definition Format (CDF) to update software over the Internet or over an intranet.

OTP (Open Trading Protocol)—An XML vocabulary proposed by MasterCard International, along with AT&T, Hewlett-Packard, and Wells Fargo, and used for the exchange of financial information. It can help financial companies transfer information about their clients through disparate financial systems without the need to replace their existing systems.

out-of-line link—An XLink term that describes a link whose content does not serve as one of the original link's resources. Out-of-line links don't even have to occur in the same document. They are used within multidirectional links and when read-only resources have outgoing links.

parameter entity—An entity used strictly within a Document Type Definition (DTD) to create an alias for a group of elements (usually attributes or element content) that is used frequently within the DTD.

parent element—An element that has one or more elements as content. A parent element of a child element, or elements, may also be the child of another, higher-level element.

parser—A software program that breaks down the XML document into its element tree and checks its syntax.

participating resource—An XLink term that describes a resource that belongs to a link.

pattern—The portion of a construction rule that identifies the document element to receive the formatting (action).

PCDATA (parsed character data)—Element content made up of only plain text.

PGML (Precision Graphics Markup Language)—An XML vocabulary that provides a 2D scalable graphics language designed to offer vector graphics and precision graphic specifications to artists.

PostScript format—An Adobe page description language used to create print images for output on suitably equipped print engines.

presentation-based markup—Markup whose primary function is to describe text that will be rendered visually by a browser. HTML is a presentation-based markup language.

priority-expression—In Extensible Style Language (XSL), an optional expression that assigns priorities to elements in the second Document Type Definition (DTD) for matching to elements in the first DTD. If two elements in the second DTD potentially match a single element in the first DTD, the one with the higher priority is used in the transformation.

processing instructions (PIs)—Instructions from the XML document that are passed through the parser to the display software to tell the software how to process all or part of the document. A PI can be included anywhere inside an XML document.

Glossary

processor declaration—An XML declaration that tells the processor what standards to use, what type of document is being processed, and where the Document Type Definition (DTD) that actually constructs the document is stored.

production rule—Information in the XML specification that is necessary for creating well-formed or valid XML code.

query-expression—In Extensible Style Language (XSL), an expression used to create a list of the elements in one Document Type Definition (DTD) that can possibly be transformed into a specific element in the second DTD.

RDF (Resource Description Framework)—A content-based XML vocabulary that is used to describe Internet resources in a standard metadata format that is usable by a wide variety of clients and servers.

RELML (Real Estate Listing Markup Language)—An XML-based vocabulary under development by OpenMLS. RELML will use OpenMLS software to create a system that will work with existing MLS systems to generate XML data that can be used to search the MLS database.

remote resource—An XLink term that describes any participating resource of a link to which a locator points. It specifies the role, title, show, actuate, and behavior attributes of the link.

resource—An XLink term that describes a service or group of information (an object) that is specified in a link. A resource could be a file, an image, documents, programs, database query results, or a sound file. More specifically, a resource can be anything that can be accessed via a URL.

RMD (Required Markup Declaration)—A declaration within an XML document that provides the processing application with the version of XML used to build the document. The RMD also tells the processing application whether an associated Document Type Definition (DTD) should be processed along with the document.

root rule—In Extensible Style Language (XSL), the construction rule that describes how a document's document element should be formatted.

SAX (Simple API for XML)—An event-based interface created specifically for XML parsers that are written in object-oriented applications, such as Java.

scripting language—One of several interpreted programming languages used to control the behavior of Web pages in response to user activities.

SDQL (Standard Document Query Language)—A component of both the Document Style Semantics and Specification Language (DSSSL) transformation language and the DSSSL style language. It is used to locate a specific part of a document's content to process it.

selector—In a Cascading Style Sheet (CSS), one of the two parts of a style rule. It defines the markup element to which the style rule is applied.

SGML (Standard Generalized Markup Language)—A generic text-based markup language used to describe the content and structure of documents.

simple link—An XML link that uses the **HREF** attribute to point to only one resource. All HTML links are simple links.

SMIL (Synchronized Multimedia Integration Language)—An XML vocabulary that assists developers in integrating multimedia into their sites. SMIL provides a standardized way to describe multimedia and the various components needed to use, display, and manipulate it on the Internet.

sosofo (Specification of a Sequence of Flow Objects)—In Extensible Style Language (XSL), the specification for a flow object.

string attributes—XML attributes that allow the user to define any value for the attribute.

style sheet—A document that uses markup to provide information about the structure and content of another document or set of documents. A style sheet also provides information about the document's style and presentation to the software package used to parse and process the document.

subresource—An XLink term that describes a portion of a resource that specifies another resource (such as an entire document that is specified for retrieval and display).

TecML (Technical Markup Language)—An application-independent XML vocabulary used to describe technical information.

TEIP3 (Text Encoding Initiative Guidelines)—The guidelines on which the entire XLink language is based. These guidelines provide structures for creating links, aggregate objects, and link collections.

text entity—Character data assigned as content to an entity name.

text properties—A set of Cascading Style Sheet (CSS) properties and values that provides text specifics for document elements.

TIM (Telecommunication Interchange Markup)—An XML vocabulary used to provide a standard mechanism for offering industry standards associated with the provision, procurement, and use of telecommunications equipment, products, and services.

Glossary

TML (Tutorial Markup Language)—An XML vocabulary designed specifically for creating and working with educational applications.

TMX (Translation Memory eXchange)—An XML vocabulary designed to allow easier exchange of translation memory data between tools and/or translation vendors with little or no loss of critical data during the process.

tokenized attribute—A name for seven different types of predefined attributes that play a specific role in XML documents and that must have a particular kind of value.

transform-expression—In Extensible Style Language (XSL), an expression used to evaluate the elements in the list generated by the query-expression and, if they meet the transformation specification requirements, transform them into the elements designated by the second Document Type Definition (DTD).

traversal—An XLink term that describes the action of using a link to access a resource. Traversals are usually initiated by a user action or by some sort of program control.

UML eXchange Format—An XML vocabulary created for software developers as a mechanism for transferring Unified Modeling Language (UML) models. The application format is powerful enough to allow developers to express, publish, and exchange UML models universally.

Unicode—The ISO 10646 character set that uses 16-bit patterns to represent characters.

valid XML document—A document that adheres to its Document Type Definition (DTD).

validating parser—Software programs that check XML documents for validity, which means they check for the presence of the document's Document Type Definition (DTD) and whether the document conforms to it.

WebDAV (Distributed Authoring and Versioning on the World Wide Web)—An XML vocabulary intended to define Hypertext Transfer Protocol (HTTP) methods and semantics for creating, removing, querying, and editing Web pages remotely.

well-formed documents—Documents that have to conform to only the XML standard instead of to the XML specification and their Document Type Definition (DTD).

Glossary

WIDL (Web Interface Definition Language)—A content-based XML vocabulary that is used to describe Web APIs.

wildcards—In Extensible Style Language (XSL), a convention used within patterns to make element-matching easier.

Wireless Application Protocol—An XML vocabulary that offers standards for wireless network transmissions and scaling across various transport options and device types.

XLink—XML's linking language (previously known as the Extensible Link Language or XML-Link), which allows users to create powerful links in XML documents.

XML application—A specific implementation of XML that is a Document Type Definition (DTD) or set of DTDs designed to serve a specific purpose. Also known as an XML vocabulary.

XML declaration—A declaration that tells the processor to use a specific version of the XML specification to process the document as an XML document.

XML DSO (XML Data Source Object)—A Microsoft proprietary technology that uses the data-binding facility found in Dynamic HTML to bind structured XML data to HTML.

XML OM (Object Model)—A model that enables developers to interact with XML data within the browser by exposing HTML as objects based on the Document Object Model (DOM).

XML processor—A software module that is used to read XML documents and provide access to their structure and content.

XML specification—A technical description that outlines exactly how elements must be declared and how XML must be constructed for XML processors (which interpret XML code) to process the XML information properly and send it on to the Web browser for display.

XPointer—A companion to XLink, the mechanism that provides developers with a way to designate various resources by using terms that specify locations in documents or resources. Sometimes referred to as the XML Pointer Language.

XSL (Extensible Style Language)—A style sheet mechanism that is customized for XML.

Glossary

Index

Symbols

& (ampersand)
    displaying in document text, 60
    in element declarations, 205
    in entity references, 14, 60, 61
    escape character string, 134
    Unicode assignment, 134
    XML predefined entity, 306
< > (angle brackets)
    in comment delimiters, 30, 136
    escape character strings, 134
    tag delimiters, 14
    Unicode assignments, 134
    in well-formed documents, 26
' (apostrophe, XML predefined entity), 306
* (asterisk)
    in element content notation system, 248
    in element declarations, 164, 203, 205
    in production rules, 54
    in XPointer location terms, 297
^ (caret symbol, in production rules), 55
: (colon)
    in CSS declarations, 382
    in CSS style rules, 375
, (comma)
    in element content notation system, 248
    in element declarations, 164, 205
!--, -- (comment delimiters), 16, 136
/* (comment delimiters, in production rules), 54
-- (dashes or hyphens, in comment delimiter),
    30, 136, 175
! (exclamation point, in comment delimiter), 30
/ (forward slash)
    in closing tags, 10
    in empty tags, 25
// (forward slashes, in DTD declarations), 129
< (left angle bracket)
    escape character string, 134
    Unicode assignment, 134
    XML predefined entity, 306
{ (left curly brace, in CSS declarations), 382
- (minus sign, in DTD declarations), 129
( ) (parentheses)
    in element content notation system, 248

    in element declarations, 205
    in production rules, 54
% (percent sign)
    declaring parameter entities, 304, 331
    parameter entities in content models, 249–250
    parsing nested entities, 155
. (period)
    in CSS declarations, 382
    in XPointer location terms, 297
| (pipe character or vertical bar)
    in element content notation system, 248
    in element declarations, 203, 205, 212
    in production rules, 54
    specifying XPointers, 294–295, 295
+ (plus sign)
    in DTD declarations, 129
    in element content notation system, 248
    in element declarations, 164, 204, 205, 211
    in production rules, 55
(pound sign, specifying XPointers), 294–295
<?, ?> (processing instruction delimiters), 176
? (question mark)
    in element content notation system, 248
    in element declarations, 204, 205, 211
"(quotation mark, XML predefined entity), 306
" " (quotation marks)
    enclosing attribute values, 11, 76, 218, 596, 603, 607
    enclosing entity content, 311
    in entity declarations, 13
    in production rules, 55
> (right angle bracket)
    escape character string, 134
    Unicode assignment, 134
    XML predefined entity, 306
} (right curly brace, in CSS declarations), 382
; (semicolon)
    in CSS declarations, 382
    in entity references, 14, 60, 61
    parameter entities in content models, 249–250
    referencing parameter entities, 331
[ ] (square brackets)
    internal DTDs, 128
    in production rules, 54

A

C

R

S

Learn More Faster

ISBN: 1-57610-281-5
$49.99 U.S. • $69.99 Canada
Available Now

ISBN: 1-57610-283-1
$49.99 U.S. • $69.99 Canada
Available Now

ISBN: 1-57610-282-3
$49.99 U.S. • $69.99 Canada
Available Now

Regardless of your experience, you'll reach for our books time and time again.

CORIOLIS
Technology Press™

Blue, Black, and Gold books. Novice, intermediate, advanced. Easy-to-identify classifications for an innovative new concept in technology publishing.

A completely new series. Each title written to address the specific needs of the system developer, user, or engineer—at the level of his or her concern.

ACQUIRE MORE KNOWLEDGE

When you are learning a new technology, Blue Books are the complete, hands-on tutorials you'll want to reach for first. Their highly interactive, project-based, "learn-by-doing" approach helps ensure that you will learn more at a much faster rate than you can with other tutorials.

USE YOUR KNOWLEDGE

Black Books are indispensable problem-solving guides. Their unique format, which provides very thorough, in-depth, highly technical overviews followed by highly practical "immediate solutions," will help you quickly complete any task: large or small, simple or complex.

EXPAND YOUR KNOWLEDGE

Gold Books are the professional-level guides you'll turn to when you want to expand your horizons. Their highly conceptual but practical approach will teach you how to think in new ways and push your skills to a new level.

Blue, Black, and Gold. They're comprehensive, illustrated, and easy to understand. Experience the difference. Look for these and other soon-to-be-released titles from Coriolis. Of course!

Available at Bookstores and Computer Stores Nationwide

Telephone 800.410.0192 • International callers 602.483.0192
www.coriolis.com

Prices are subject to change without notice. ©1998 The Coriolis Group, Inc. All rights reserved. 8/98

What's On The CD-ROM

The contents of the companion CD-ROM will help you start creating XML documents right away. The CD-ROM features the following:

- *Shareware and demonstration software packages*—Try out several of the most popular XML parsers, browsers, and development systems to find the ones that fit your specific needs.
- *HTML files that link to all the URLs mentioned in the book*—The book's Web site provides you with quick access to all of the URLs listed in the book and includes contact information for both *XML Black Book* authors.
- *Code files*—Code samples from the book allow you to easily edit and change existing XML files in your favorite text or XML editor.

See the readme files in each folder for acknowledgments, descriptions, copyrights, installation instructions, limitations, and other important information.

Requirements:

- A PC with a 486 or better processor or a Macintosh computer with a Power PC or better processor
- 16MB of RAM minimum, 32MB recommended
- Windows 95/98 or NT or Macintosh operating system 7.5 or later
- A Web browser capable of displaying Java, Internet Explorer 4 recommended